D0941223

A D D I S O N - W E S L E Y MATHEMATICS 11
BRITISH COLUMBIA EDITION

Brendan Kelly
Professor of Mathematics
Faculty of Education
University of Toronto
Ontario

Bob Alexander
Assistant Co-ordinator
  of Mathematics
Toronto Board of Education
Toronto, Ontario

Paul Atkinson
Principal
Glenview Park
Secondary School
Cambridge, Ontario

Contributing Author
Jim Swift
District Resource Teacher
Nanaimo School Board
Nanaimo, British Columbia

Addison-Wesley Publishers Limited

Don Mills, Ontario
Reading, Massachusetts
Menlo Park, California
New York
Wokingham, England
Amsterdam • Bonn
Sydney • Singapore
Tokyo • Madrid
Bogatá • Santiago
San Juan

Design
John Zehethofer
Assembly and Technical Art
Frank Zsigo
Art in Answers
Pronk & Associates
Editorial
Lesley Haynes
Typesetting
Q Composition
Printer
Ronalds Printing, Vancouver

Photographic Credits
The publisher wishes to thank the following sources for photographs and other illustrative materials used in this book. We will gladly receive information enabling us to rectify any errors or references in credits.
Cover, Richard Simpson; 7, CP Rail; 24, NASA, Daily Telegraph/Masterfile; 25, NASA; 39, Erich Hoyt; 40, Toronto General Hospital, Manitoba Department of Tourism and Recreation; 44, Addison-Wesley photo library; 58, The Toronto Star; 65, NASA; 105, Jandec Inc.; 106, Mexican Government Tourist Office; 136, John P. Kelly; 141, Pioneer Racing; 142, Four by Five Photography Inc., T. Gregg Eligh/Miller Comstock Inc.; 150, Addison-Wesley photo library, Metropolitan Toronto Police College; 157, Toronto General Hospital; 176, Augustin Estrada; 179, Prince Edward Island Tourist Office; 180, Ontario Department of Transportation and Communications; 193, Mel DiGiacomo/Image Bank; 233, Metropolitan Toronto Police College; 283, Ian Crysler; 327, Roberts/Miller Comstock Inc.; 369, Swiss National Tourist Office

Written, printed, and bound in Canada

ISBN   0-201-50776-5

A   B   C   D   E   F   – RF –   94   93   92   91   90   89

Features of Mathematics 11

CONCEPT DEVELOPMENT

Mathematics 11 is carefully sequenced to develop concepts in mathematics. Concepts are explained with several examples, each of which has a detailed solution.

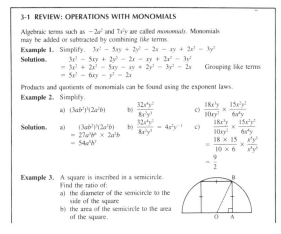

REINFORCEMENT

An abundance of exercises is provided to reinforce skills and concepts. These exercises are graded by difficulty with an appropriate balance of A, B, and C exercises. The A exercises may sometimes be completed mentally and the answers given orally or the questions may be used as additional examples when teaching the lesson. The B exercises are intended for the students to consolidate their learning of the concepts that were taught. The C exercises present a challenge and usually involve extensions of the concepts taught in that section.

Review Exercises and *Cumulative Reviews* provide additional practice. Answers to all questions are included in the text.

TECHNOLOGY

A contemporary mathematics program must reflect the impact of calculators and computers on society.

Mathematics 11 assumes that students will use scientific calculators where appropriate. It is up to the students to familiarize themselves with their calculators.

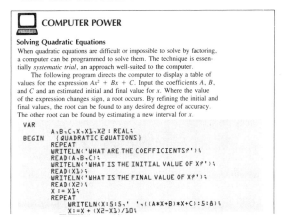

COMPUTER POWER features provide opportunities for students to explore mathematical problems using a computer. It is assumed that students know how to enter a program in PASCAL, but is not necessary for them to understand the program.

APPLICATIONS OF MATHEMATICS

Students can better understand mathematical principles when they are related to their applications. For this reason, applications are integrated throughout *Mathematics 11*.

Every chapter begins with an applied problem that is solved as an example in the chapter.

5 Functions

In a drag race, cars accelerate from a standing start towards a finish line a fixed distance away. How would you calculate the speed of the car at any moment during the race? (See Section 5-7 *Example 1*.)

Many sections begin with an application which illustrates the necessity for the mathematics that follows.

5-6 INVERSE VARIATION

Police often identify speeders on a highway by measuring, from the air, the time it takes a car to cover a marked portion of the road. The table shows how the speed of a car is related to the time it takes to travel 0.5 km.

Time t (s)	Speed v (km/h)
20	90
40	45
60	30
80	22.5
100	18

Applications are also included throughout the exercises.

8. In a system of two pulleys turned by a single belt, the number of revolutions per minute of each pulley varies inversely as its radius. If one pulley has a radius of 50 cm, and rotates at 120 r/min, what is the rotational speed of the other pulley if its radius is 80 cm?

9. The time required to fly from Quebec City to Vancouver varies inversely as the average speed. When the average speed is 700 km/h, the flying time is 5.5 h.
   a) How long would the trip take at an average speed of 550 km/h?
   b) What is the average speed if the time taken is 4.25 h?

10. Boyle's Law states that if the temperature is kept constant, the volume of a gas varies inversely as the pressure. A tank contains 10 L of hydrogen at a pressure of 550 kPa. If the hydrogen is released into the atmosphere where the pressure is 100 kPa, what volume would it occupy?

11. If the temperature of a gas is kept constant, what happens to the volume when the pressure is: a) doubled b) tripled c) divided by 2?

PROBLEM SOLVING

Problem solving is integrated throughout the program, with many of the exercises providing challenging problems for the students to solve. In addition, a variety of special features are included which promote the development of problem-solving skills.

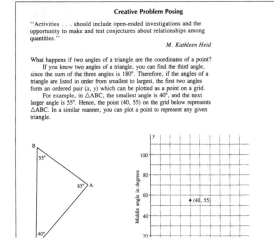

PROBLEM SOLVING

Creative Problem Posing

"Activities . . . should include open-ended investigations and the opportunity to make and test conjectures about relationships among quantities."

M. Kathleen Heid

What happens if two angles of a triangle are the coordinates of a point?

If you know two angles of a triangle, you can find the third angle, since the sum of the three angles is 180°. Therefore, if the angles of a triangle are listed in order from smallest to largest, the first two angles form an ordered pair (x, y) which can be plotted as a point on a grid.

For example, in △ABC, the smallest angle is 40°, and the next larger angle is 55°. Hence, the point (40, 55) on the grid below represents △ABC. In a similar manner, you can plot a point to represent any given triangle.

Understand the problem
● If you know the angles of a triangle, how do you determine the ordered pair (x, y)? Can you do this for any triangle?
● Try drawing a few triangles and plotting the points to represent them.

Think of a strategy and carry it out
● Draw several right triangles, and plot the points to represent them.

Look back
● Do the points lie on a line segment? What are the endpoints of this segment? What is the equation of the segment?
● Is y a function of x? What are the domain and the range of the function?
● Where are the points which represent equilateral triangles? isosceles triangles? acute triangles? obtuse triangles?
● Write a report of your discoveries.

Up to now in your study of mathematics, most or all of the problems you solved have probably been in your textbook or provided by your teacher. In other words, somebody else created the problem for you. But mathematicians do not always solve problems that have been created by others. They also create their own problems.

How does a mathematician create problems? One way has been suggested in the *Look back* sections of the *PROBLEM SOLVING* pages in this book. In these sections, problems related to the problem on the page are often suggested. Perhaps you did this after solving other problems. Did you ever "look back" and think of another related problem? If you did, you created a problem.

Another way of creating problems is suggested by the problem on the facing page. How did the person who created the problem happen to think of it? This problem involves two different topics in mathematics — angles of a triangle and the coordinates of a point. Suppose we

The *PROBLEM SOLVING* feature is a two-page spread in every chapter which extends the strategies that were developed in earlier grades. The problems are graded by difficulty into B, C, and D problems. The B problems may require some ingenuity to solve. The C problems are challenging, and are similar to the problems that are found in mathematics contests. Some of the D problems are extremely difficult, and may approach the level of difficulty of the problems that occur in olympiad competitions. It is not expected that many students will solve the D problems.

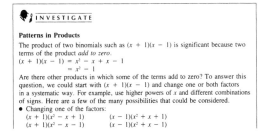

INVESTIGATE

Patterns in Products

The product of two binomials such as $(x + 1)(x - 1)$ is significant because two terms of the product *add to zero*.

$$(x + 1)(x - 1) = x^2 - x + x - 1$$
$$= x^2 - 1$$

Are there other products in which some of the terms add to zero? To answer this question, we could start with $(x + 1)(x - 1)$ and change one or both factors in a systematic way. For example, use higher powers of x and different combinations of signs. Here are a few of the many possibilities that could be considered.

● Changing one of the factors:

$(x + 1)(x^2 - x + 1)$ $(x - 1)(x^2 + x + 1)$
$(x + 1)(x^2 - x - 1)$ $(x - 1)(x^2 + x - 1)$

Frequent *INVESTIGATE* features are starting points for mathematical investigations to help the student develop analytic skills. These features always relate to the concepts that are developed in the sections in which they occur.

The *MATHEMATICS AROUND US* features outline applications of mathematics in the sciences, the arts, business, and industry.

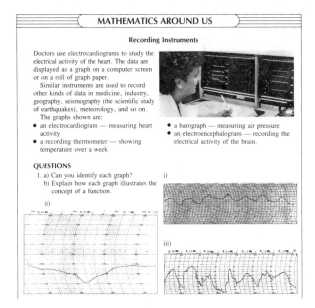

MATHEMATICS AROUND US

Recording Instruments

Doctors use electrocardiograms to study the electrical activity of the heart. The data are displayed as a graph on a computer screen or on a roll of graph paper.

Similar instruments are used to record other kinds of data in medicine, industry, geography, seismography (the scientific study of earthquakes), meteorology, and so on.

The graphs shown are:
- an electrocardiogram — measuring heart activity
- a recording thermometer — showing temperature over a week
- a barograph — measuring air pressure
- an electroencephalogram — recording the electrical activity of the brain.

QUESTIONS
1. a) Can you identify each graph?
   b) Explain how each graph illustrates the concept of a function.

i)

ii)

iii)

THE MATHEMATICAL MIND features offer insights into the work of mathematicians and the historical development of mathematics. Anecdotes of human interest that are part of history are included. In this feature, problems related to the topic are presented for the student to solve.

THE MATHEMATICAL MIND

The Origin of the Function Concept

The concept of a function originated in the seventeenth century, when scientists and mathematicians became interested in the study of motion.
- Galileo showed that the path of a projectile fired into the air is a parabola.

- The moon's motion was studied because knowledge of its position was used to determine longitude at sea.

Since moving objects follow a single line or a curve, mathematicians thought that a function was defined by a single equation. For example, this definition was given by James Gregory in 1667.

Leonhard Euler 1707–1783

As late as 1734, Leonhard Euler defined a function as any expression formed in any manner from a variable quantity and constants. He also introduced the $f(x)$ notation.

By 1750, scientists studying vibrating strings had encountered an example of a function that could not be defined by a single equation. This caused a controversy over the question of what a function was. Euler extended the definition to include cases where there were different expressions in different intervals of the domain. For example, Euler would have considered the following expression to be a single function.

$$f(x) = \begin{cases} x + 6, & \text{if } x \leq -2 \\ x^2, & \text{if } -2 \leq x \leq 2 \\ x + 2, & \text{if } x \geq 2 \end{cases}$$

Contents

1 The Real Numbers

Modern communications systems depend on
geosynchronous satellites which are placed in orbit above
the equator. Such a satellite is synchronized with the
Earth's rotation, and appears to be stationary. Its height
and speed are adjusted so that it travels once around
the Earth in exactly 24 h. How high should a
communications satellite be placed? (See Section 1-8
Example 3.)

1-1 THE NATURAL NUMBERS

Over 5000 years ago the Egyptians used symbols to describe quantities up to and beyond one million. Today we use the Hindu-Arabic numerals and place value to represent such numbers.

1, 2, 3, . . . 98, 99, 100, . . . 998, 999, 1000, . . .

Mathematicians refer to these counting numbers as the set of *positive integers*, or *natural numbers*.

From about 550 B.C. to 250 B.C. mathematics flourished in ancient Greece. Since the Greeks were mainly interested in geometry, they classified numbers according to the shapes they could represent. For example, numbers which correspond to a triangular array of dots are called *triangular numbers*.

Example 1. Find the eighth triangular number.

Solution. A pattern in the sequence of triangular numbers can be found by subtracting consecutive terms.

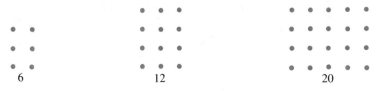

According to the pattern, the next three differences in the sequence are 6, 7, 8. The eighth triangular number is 15 + 6 + 7 + 8, or 36.

Since a *composite number* is a product of at least two factors (greater than 1), any composite number can be represented by a rectangular array of dots. A *prime number*, having no factor greater than 1 (except itself), cannot be represented in this way.

Every composite number can be written as a product of prime factors in only one way (except for the order of the factors). Our method of finding this product, or *prime factorization*, is the same as that used by the Greeks over 2000 years ago, except that we have the assistance of calculators.

Example 2. Express as a product of prime factors. a) 1683 b) 659

Solution. a) By calculator, $\sqrt{1683} \doteq 41$. If 1683 has prime factors, at least one of them must be less than 41 otherwise their product would be greater than 1683. The prime numbers less than 41 are:
2, 3, 5, 7, 11, 13, 17, 19, 23, 29, 31, 37
2 is *not* a factor of 1683.
3 *is* a factor of 1683: $1683 \div 3 = 561$
3 *is* a factor of 561: $561 \div 3 = 187$
3, 5, and 7 are *not* factors of 187.
11 is a factor of 187: $187 \div 11 = 17$
Since 17 is also prime, the prime factorization of 1683 is:
$3 \times 3 \times 11 \times 17$
Therefore, $1683 = 3^2 \times 11 \times 17$

b) By calculator, $\sqrt{659} \doteq 26$. The possible prime factors of 659 are: 2, 3, 5, 7, 11, 13, 17, 19, 23. Using a calculator, it is quickly found that none of these primes is a factor of 659. Therefore, 659 is a prime number.

Example 3. Some archaeologists found a bag of coins. They discovered that when the coins were divided into sets of 2, 3, 5 or 7, there was always exactly one coin left over. What was the smallest possible number of coins in the bag?

Solution. Let n represent the number of coins in the bag.
Then, $n - 1$ is divisible by 2, 3, 5, and 7.
The smallest number divisible by 2, 3, 5, and 7 is: $2 \times 3 \times 5 \times 7$, or 210.
That is, $n - 1 = 210$
$n = 211$
The smallest possible number of coins in the bag was 211.

EXERCISES 1-1

(A)

1. Which numbers are prime numbers?
   a) 51 b) 37 c) 67 d) 91 e) 127
   f) 143 g) 159 h) 173 i) 193 j) 231

2. Express as a product of prime factors.
   a) 27 b) 42 c) 68 d) 95 e) 102
   f) 145 g) 180 h) 225 i) 228 j) 387

3. a) Continue this pattern for three more square numbers.

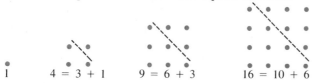

1   4 = 3 + 1   9 = 6 + 3   16 = 10 + 6

   b) What does the pattern in part a) suggest about the sum of any two consecutive triangular numbers?

4. Describe each pattern and find the next three numbers.
   a) 1, 4, 7, 10, . . .   b) 2, 6, 18, 54, . . .   c) 1, 4, 9, 16, . . .
   d) 1, 3, 7, 13, 21, . . .   e) 1, 5, 14, 30, 55, . . .   f) 1, 4, 10, 20, 35, . . .

5. a) Continue this pattern for three more lines.
$$1 = 1^2$$
$$1 + 2 + 1 = 2^2$$
$$1 + 2 + 3 + 2 + 1 = 3^2$$
   b) Draw a series of diagrams to illustrate the patterns in part a).

6. A box of chocolates could be divided equally among 2, 3, 4, 5 or 6 people if it contained one chocolate more. What is the least number of chocolates in the box?

Ⓑ

7. How many 3-digit perfect squares can be formed using the digits 1, 6, and 9? What are they?

8. Give all the 2-digit primes that form primes when their digits are reversed; for example, 17 and 71 are both prime.

9. The following number patterns begin with primes. Continue the patterns for several more numbers. Are all the numbers in each pattern prime?
   a) 41, 47, 53, 59, . . .   b) 5, 17, 29, 41, . . .   c) 11, 13, 17, 23, . . .

10. $259 \times 429 = 111\ 111$ and $1221 \times 91 = 111\ 111$. Use a calculator to find other pairs of numbers with the product 111 111.

11. Show that:
   a) the sum of any two primes greater than 2 is even
   b) the product of any two primes greater than 2 is odd.

12. In 1640, Pierre de Fermat proved that every prime number of the form $4n + 1$ can be expressed as the sum of two squares in exactly one way. For example: $41 = 4(10) + 1$, which is the sum of 25 and 16.
   a) Which primes less than 50 have the form $4n + 1$?
   b) Express each prime in part a) as the sum of two squares.

13. Fermat also stated that no prime of the form $4n + 3$ can be expressed as the sum of two squares. For example: $23 = 4(5) + 3$; no two squares have a sum of 23.
   a) Which primes less than 50 have the form $4n + 3$?
   b) Check that none of the primes in part a) can be expressed as the sum of two squares.

14. Carl Friedrich Gauss was the first to discover that every natural number is either triangular or the sum of two or three triangular numbers. Here are some examples: $13 = 3 + 10$, $23 = 1 + 1 + 21$. Write each number as the sum of two or three triangular numbers.
    a) 11   b) 19   c) 29   d) 30   e) 33   f) 50

15. This question about primes has never been answered: If n is any natural number, is there always at least one prime between n^2 and $(n + 1)^2$? Answer the question for values of n up to 10.

Ⓒ

16. Show that if any two consecutive primes (greater than 2) are added, the sum can be expressed as a product of three prime numbers greater than 1; for example: $23 + 29 = 52$, and $52 = 2 \times 2 \times 13$.

17. Show that, except for 2 and 3, every prime number can be written in the form $6n + 1$ or $6n - 1$, where n is a natural number.

18. a) In the triangle of numbers shown, what numbers are in:
       i) the 10th row
       ii) the nth row?
    b) Describe a method that could be used to determine:
       i) in which row any given number x appears
       ii) the color of the triangle in which any given number x appears.

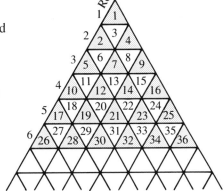

19. a) Show that 1225 is both a triangular and a square number.
    b) Find a 2-digit number that is both triangular and square.

 **INVESTIGATE**

4 and 9 are two squares with a sum and difference both prime.
$9 + 4 = 13$
$9 - 4 = 5$
1. Find other pairs of squares with sum and difference both prime.
2. Find other pairs of squares with sum and difference both composite.
3. Find other pairs of squares with sum and difference prime and composite.
Write a report of your findings.

COMPUTER POWER

The Search for Larger Primes

More than two thousand years ago, Euclid proved that there are infinitely many prime numbers. Since then, mathematicians have tried to find larger and larger primes.

In 1644, the Frenchman, Marin Mersenne, conjectured that the numbers $2^n - 1$ were prime for the following values of n: 2, 3, 5, 7, 13, 17, 19, 31, 67, 127, 257. Although it has since been proved that $2^{67} - 1$ and $2^{257} - 1$ are composite, primes of the form $2^n - 1$ are called *Mersenne primes*.

```
VAR
    I,F : LONGINT;
    N,R : REAL;
BEGIN           { PRIME TESTER}
    REPEAT
    WRITE('WHAT NUMBER DO YOU WANT TO TEST?');
    READ(N);
    IF N <> 1.0 THEN BEGIN
        IF N <> 2.0 THEN BEGIN
            R := SQRT(N);
            F := 0;
            FOR I := 2 TO TRUNC(R) DO BEGIN
                IF((N / I) - INT (N / I)) <= 0.0000001 THEN BEGIN
                    WRITELN(' THE NUMBERS ABOVE ARE TWO FACTORS OF
                    ',TRUNC(N));
                    F := 1;
                    I := TRUNC(R);
                END;
            END;
            IF F = 0 THEN WRITELN(TRUNC(N),' IS A PRIME NUMBER');
        END
        ELSE WRITELN('2 IS A PRIME NUMBER');
    END
    ELSE WRITELN('1 IS NEITHER PRIME NOR COMPOSITE');
    WRITELN('HIT RETURN TO TRY AGAIN');
    UNTIL(READKEY <> CHR(13));
    END.
```

1. Use the program to determine which of these numbers are prime.
   a) 4009   b) 7207   c) 8611   d) 65 537

2. Use the program to find the prime factorization of each number.
   a) 3604   b) 404 629   c) 1 018 161   d) 6 563 647

3. Use the program to test as many Mersenne numbers for primality as you can.

MATHEMATICS AROUND US

The Spiral Tunnels

When British Columbia entered into the Canadian Confederation on July 20, 1871, the federal government agreed to build a railway to link the province with the rest of Canada. The railway was completed in 1885. The track through the mountains was kept to a maximum gradient of 2.2% (a rise of 2.2 m in 100 m of track) with one exception — the section of track between Hector, B.C. and Field, B.C. There, a rise of 297 m in only 6.6 km was necessary. This section became known as Big Hill. Taking trains up and down this hill required additional locomotives, and on the downhill run there was always the danger of runaway trains.

The only way to reduce the gradient of Big Hill to 2.2% was to lengthen the track between the two towns. This was done in 1907–1909 when a pair of spiral tunnels was built into the mountains. These tunnels are the only ones of their kind in North America. As many as 15 trains a day pass through the tunnels in each direction. The long freight trains can be seen coming out of a tunnel before they have finished going in.

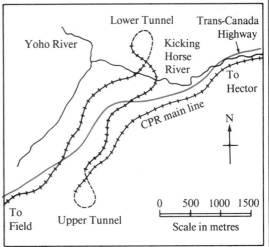

QUESTIONS

1. What was the gradient of the track on Big Hill?

2. By how much did the track have to be lengthened to reduce the gradient to 2.2%?

3. The train in the photograph is passing through Lower Tunnel, which is about 880 m long and curves through 288°. Each car in the train is about 12.2 m long.
   a) How many cars are in the train?
   b) What is the difference in height between the two sections of track shown in the photograph?
   c) If the speed of the train is 40.5 km/h, how long does it take to pass completely through the tunnel?

4. What is the radius of the spiral?

1-2 REVIEW: QUOTIENTS OF NATURAL NUMBERS

When two natural numbers are added or multiplied, the result is a natural number. However, in ancient times when mathematicians attempted to divide a natural number into equal parts, they found that the quotient was not always a natural number. This led to the development of fractions.

About 1650 B.C., the Egyptians had a cumbersome system of writing fractions. They would write a fraction, such as $\frac{7}{8}$, as the sum of unit fractions: $\frac{1}{2} + \frac{1}{4} + \frac{1}{8}$. Since they did not use Hindu-Arabic numerals and had not developed symbols for addition or equality, the expressions they wrote were quite different in appearance from the one above.

A thousand years earlier still, the Babylonians expressed fractions quite differently. Instead of using a fixed numerator, they used denominators that were powers of 60. For the fraction $\frac{7}{8}$ they wrote: $\frac{49}{60} + \frac{210}{3600}$. This seems awkward to us, but our units of time are derived from it. (1 min $= \frac{1}{60}$ h, and 1 s $= \frac{1}{3600}$ h)

Our system of writing fractions as decimals was developed within the last 300 years. It is similar to the Babylonian system, but we use denominators that are powers of 10. To express $\frac{7}{8}$ as a decimal, we divide 7 by 8 and write:

$\frac{7}{8} = 0.875$, which means $\frac{8}{10} + \frac{7}{100} + \frac{5}{1000}$.

Example 1. Express $\frac{5}{27}$ as a decimal.

Solution. By calculator: $5 \div 27 = 0.185\ 185\ 1\ \ldots$
By calculation:

$$
\begin{array}{r}
0.185 \\
27\overline{)5.000} \\
2\ 7 \\
\hline
2\ 30 \\
2\ 16 \\
\hline
140 \\
135 \\
\hline
5
\end{array}
$$

Since 5 is the original numerator, the process repeats.

$\frac{5}{27} = 0.\overline{185}$, the bar shows the part of the decimal that repeats.

The decimal expansion in *Example 1* begins to repeat when a remainder recurs. Since division by 27 can yield only 26 different non-zero remainders (1, 2, 3, . . . , 26), the decimal expansion must repeat after no more than 26 digits. In this case, it repeated after 3 digits.

Any fraction in the form $\dfrac{m}{n}$, where m and n are natural numbers, may be expressed as a terminating decimal or a repeating decimal. In the latter case, the repeating part has no more than $n - 1$ digits.

The next example shows how to find the fraction which corresponds to a repeating decimal.

Example 2. Express $3.1\overline{72}$ in the form $\dfrac{m}{n}$, where $n \neq 0$.

Solution.

Let $x = \quad 3.17272\ldots$ ①   Multiply ① by 10 to isolate the repeating digits.

$10x = \quad 31.7272\ldots$ ②   Multiply ② by 100 since the number of repeating digits is 2.

$1000x = 3172.7272\ldots$ ③   Subtract ② from ③.

$990x = 3141$

$x = \dfrac{3141}{990}$

Therefore, $3.1\overline{72} = \dfrac{3141}{990}$

EXERCISES 1-2

Ⓐ

1. Express in decimal form.

a) $\dfrac{9}{4}$ b) $\dfrac{7}{16}$ c) $\dfrac{5}{12}$ d) $\dfrac{11}{27}$ e) $\dfrac{2}{9}$ f) $\dfrac{11}{7}$ g) $\dfrac{20}{11}$ h) $\dfrac{25}{99}$

2. Express in the form $\dfrac{m}{n}$.

a) $2.\overline{54}$ b) $0.\overline{415}$ c) $1.6\overline{35}$ d) $4.29\overline{3}$ e) $3.\overline{125}$ f) $6.2\overline{8}$

3. Use a calculator to verify each equation.

a) $\dfrac{9}{10} = \dfrac{1}{2} + \dfrac{1}{4} + \dfrac{1}{10} + \dfrac{1}{20}$

b) $\dfrac{4}{9} = \dfrac{26}{60} + \dfrac{40}{3600}$

c) $\dfrac{13}{15} = \dfrac{1}{3} + \dfrac{1}{4} + \dfrac{1}{5} + \dfrac{1}{12}$

d) $\dfrac{5}{6} = \dfrac{47}{60} + \dfrac{180}{3600}$

e) $\dfrac{29}{20} = \dfrac{1}{2} + \dfrac{1}{3} + \dfrac{1}{4} + \dfrac{1}{5} + \dfrac{1}{6}$

f) $\dfrac{5}{9} = \dfrac{33}{60} + \dfrac{20}{3600}$

Ⓑ

4. The Rhind papyrus, an Egyptian scroll dating from about 1650 B.C., is a collection of 85 problems in arithmetic and geometry. Problem 6 shows that to divide 9 loaves among 10 people, each person should be given $\frac{2}{3}$, then $\frac{1}{5}$, and then $\frac{1}{30}$ of a loaf. Verify that this is correct.

5. In the Rhind papyrus, the expression for:
   a) $\frac{2}{7}$ was $\frac{1}{4} + \frac{1}{28}$
   b) $\frac{2}{99}$ was $\frac{1}{66} + \frac{1}{198}$
   c) $\frac{2}{61}$ was $\frac{1}{40} + \frac{1}{244} + \frac{1}{488} + \frac{1}{610}$.

   Use a calculator to verify that the expressions are correct.

6. Express as a common fraction.
   a) $1.4\overline{65}$
   b) $3.0\overline{27}$
   c) $5.\overline{41}$
   d) $0.73\overline{6}$
   e) $1.4\overline{142}$
   f) $0.7\overline{259}$

7. a) Express $0.\overline{9}$ as the quotient of two integers.
   b) Verify the result of part a) by multiplying both sides of the equation $\frac{1}{3} = 0.3333\ldots$ by 3.

8. Express as a repeating decimal.
   a) $0.\overline{7} - 0.\overline{3}$
   b) $0.\overline{26} + 0.\overline{31}$
   c) $0.\overline{42} - 0.\overline{1}$
   d) $0.\overline{6} \times 0.5$
   e) $0.\overline{3} \times 0.\overline{2}$
   f) $0.\overline{36} \times 0.41\overline{6}$

9. a) Continue the pattern for 5 more rows.
   $$\frac{1}{2} + \frac{1}{2 \times 1} = 1$$
   $$\frac{1}{3} + \frac{1}{3 \times 2} = \frac{1}{2}$$
   $$\frac{1}{4} + \frac{1}{4 \times 3} = \frac{1}{3}$$

   b) Assuming that the pattern in part a) continues, write each fraction as the sum of unit fractions.
   i) $\frac{1}{9}$
   ii) $\frac{1}{12}$
   iii) $\frac{1}{20}$

10. a) Continue each pattern for 5 more rows.

i)
$$\frac{1}{2 \times 1} = \frac{1}{2}$$

$$\frac{1}{2 \times 1} + \frac{1}{3 \times 2} = \frac{2}{3}$$

$$\frac{1}{2 \times 1} + \frac{1}{3 \times 2} + \frac{1}{4 \times 3} = \frac{3}{4}$$

ii)
$$\frac{1}{3 \times 1} = \frac{1}{3}$$

$$\frac{1}{3 \times 1} + \frac{1}{5 \times 3} = \frac{2}{5}$$

$$\frac{1}{3 \times 1} + \frac{1}{5 \times 3} + \frac{1}{7 \times 5} = \frac{3}{7}$$

b) Use the patterns in part a) to write each fraction as a sum of unit fractions.

i) $\dfrac{8}{9}$

ii) $\dfrac{8}{17}$

11. Use the table to express each decimal
as a sum of unit fractions.
a) 0.45   b) 0.55   c) 0.65

$$\frac{4}{10} = \frac{1}{3} + \frac{1}{15}$$

$$\frac{5}{10} = \frac{1}{2}$$

$$\frac{6}{10} = \frac{1}{2} + \frac{1}{10}$$

12. A vessel holds a quantity of water; another vessel holds an equal quantity of wine. A glass of water is taken from the first vessel, poured into the wine, and the contents stirred. A glass of the mix is then taken and poured into the water. Is there more water in the wine or more wine in the water?

♟ INVESTIGATE

Interesting Numbers

The number 252 is interesting.
The sum of the first two digits: 2 + 5 = 7
The sum of the last two digits: 5 + 2 = 7
The number 252 is divisible by 7: 252 ÷ 7 = 36
The number 343 has the same characteristics.
3 + 4 = 7   4 + 3 = 7   343 ÷ 7 = 49

1. Find other three-digit numbers with the same characteristics.

2. Numbers like 252 have the form $100a + 10b + a$.
Show that numbers of this form, where $a + b = 7$, are divisible by 7.

3. Consider the number 494.
4 + 9 = 13   9 + 4 = 13   494 ÷ 13 = 38
Find other three-digit numbers with these characteristics.

4. Show that a number of the form $100a + 10b + a$, where $a + b = 13$, is divisible by 13.

COMPUTER POWER

An Unsolved Arithmetic Problem

Start with any positive integer.
If it is even, divide it by 2; if it is odd, multiply it by 3 and add 1.
Repeat this procedure until the number 1 occurs.

For example, starting with 35, the result is:
35   106   53   160   80   40   20   10   5   16   8   4   2   1.
There are 14 numbers, and the greatest is 160.

If other starting numbers are used, is the final number always 1?

No one knows the answer to this question, but it has been checked on a computer by Nabuo Yoneda of the University of Tokyo for every starting number up to 2^{40}, or 1 099 511 627 776. In every case the number 1 eventually occurred.

The following program can be used to generate the string of numbers for any starting number. The computer also gives the number of terms and the greatest term.

```
VAR
        A,B,N,MAX : INTEGER;
BEGIN   {AN UNSOLVED ARITHMETIC PROBLEM}
        REPEAT
            WRITE('WHAT IS THE STARTING NUMBER?');
            READ(A); N := 1; MAX := A;
            REPEAT
                B :=(A DIV 2) * 2;
                IF(A = B) THEN A := A DIV 2
                ELSE A := 3 * A + 1;
                WRITE(A,' '); N := SUCC(N);
                IF(A > MAX) THEN MAX := A;
            UNTIL(A <= 1);
            WRITELN; WRITELN('NUMBER OF TERMS:',N);
            WRITELN('GREATEST TERM:',MAX);
            WRITELN('PRESS RETURN TO REPEAT');
        UNTIL(READKEY <> CHR(13));
END.
```

1. Use the program to obtain the strings of numbers for different starting numbers, including 27 and 255.

2. Can you explain why the greatest term is always even?

3. Find some results in which the starting number itself is the greatest term.

4. a) Find a starting number less than 25 which gives a string of 11 numbers.
   b) Find two consecutive starting numbers less than 25 which give strings of 10 numbers.

1-3 REVIEW: THE INTEGERS AND RATIONAL NUMBERS

The natural numbers and fractions have been in use for thousands of years. The negative numbers and zero first appeared in the seventh century A.D. Even then the negative numbers were not generally accepted for another thousand years, for the great mathematicians thought it absurd to have numbers less than zero. Integers and their quotients, called rational numbers, have been a part of mathematics for only the last 200 years.

> These numbers are *integers* . . . , $-3, -2, -1, 0, 1, 2, 3, . . .$

> Any number that can be written in the form $\dfrac{m}{n}$, where m and n are integers and $n \neq 0$, is called a *rational number*.

Example 1. Simplify.

   a) $7[(+6)(-3) - (-8)(-4)]$ b) $\dfrac{+3}{(+2)(-4)} - \dfrac{(-5)}{(+2)}$

Solution.   a) $7[(+6)(-3) - (-8)(-4)] = 7[(-18) - (+32)]$
$$= 7[-50]$$
$$= -350$$

   b) $\dfrac{+3}{(+2)(-4)} - \dfrac{(-5)}{(+2)} = \dfrac{3}{-8} + \dfrac{5}{2}$
$$= -\dfrac{3}{8} + \dfrac{20}{8}$$
$$= \dfrac{17}{8}, \text{ or } 2.125$$

Example 2. Find the value of the expression $x^2 - \dfrac{3x}{y}$ if:

   a) $x = -3, y = 4$ b) $x = -\dfrac{1}{2}, y = -\dfrac{5}{4}.$

Solution.   a) $x^2 - \dfrac{3x}{y} = (-3)^2 - \dfrac{3(-3)}{4}$ b) $x^2 - \dfrac{3x}{y} = \left(-\dfrac{1}{2}\right)^2 - \dfrac{3\left(-\dfrac{1}{2}\right)}{-\dfrac{5}{4}}$

$$= 9 + \dfrac{9}{4}$$
$$= \dfrac{45}{4}, \text{ or } 11.25$$

$$= \dfrac{1}{4} - 3\left(-\dfrac{1}{2}\right)\left(-\dfrac{4}{5}\right)$$
$$= \dfrac{1}{4} - \dfrac{6}{5}$$
$$= -\dfrac{19}{20}, \text{ or } -0.95$$

The impetus for the extension of the concept of number to include integers and rational numbers grew out of attempts to interpret roots of equations. Originally, equations with negative roots, such as those in the following example, were rejected as not solvable.

Example 3. Solve.

$$\text{a) } 3 - 2(5 + x) = 2x - (1 - x) \quad \text{b) } \frac{1 - 2x}{2} - 1 = \frac{2x + 1}{3}$$

Solution.

a) $3 - 2(5 + x) = 2x - (1 - x)$
$3 - 10 - 2x = 2x - 1 + x$
$-7 - 2x = 3x - 1$
$-2x - 3x = -1 + 7$
$-5x = 6$
$$x = -\frac{6}{5}$$

b) $\dfrac{1 - 2x}{2} - 1 = \dfrac{2x + 1}{3}$

Multiply each side by 6.
$3(1 - 2x) - 6 = 2(2x + 1)$
$3 - 6x - 6 = 4x + 2$
$-5 = 10x$
$$x = -\frac{1}{2}$$

EXERCISES 1-3

Ⓐ

1. Simplify.
   a) $(-27) - 11 - (-9)$
   b) $36 \div (-3) \div 4$
   c) $(-3)(-4)(-2)(-5)$
   d) $(-8)(3) + (-12) - 14$

2. Simplify.
   a) $12 \div (-4) + (5)(-3)$
   b) $52 - 7(-3) + (-20)$
   c) $3[6 + 14 \div (-5) - 5 \times 2]$
   d) $[8 - (6 \div 3 \times 10)][3 - 8]$
   e) $[-7 - 10 \times 2] - 6(-4)$
   f) $6[4 + 8 - 3(9 - 7) - 13]$

3. If $x = -3, y = 2,$ and $z = -1$, evaluate:
   a) $2x^2yz$
   b) $5x - 3y + 4z$
   c) $xy^2 - xz^2 - xyz$
   d) $2y^2z - 3x^2y + xz$
   e) $\dfrac{3x + 2y}{xz} + \dfrac{xy}{z}$.

4. Simplify.
   a) $\dfrac{13}{6} \times (-9)$
   b) $-\dfrac{21}{8} \times \left(-\dfrac{11}{3}\right)$
   c) $\dfrac{3}{4} \times \dfrac{-3}{-10}$
   d) $\dfrac{3}{-8} \times \dfrac{-2}{15}$
   e) $\dfrac{3}{8} \div \left(-\dfrac{9}{16}\right)$
   f) $-\dfrac{11}{3} \div \dfrac{5}{-3}$

5. Simplify.
   a) $\dfrac{-3}{8} - \dfrac{-3}{4}$
   b) $\dfrac{-5}{9} + \dfrac{11}{24}$
   c) $\dfrac{-4}{-3} - \dfrac{3}{-2}$
   d) $\dfrac{13}{4} + \left(-\dfrac{13}{3}\right)$
   e) $-\dfrac{13}{4} - \dfrac{13}{3}$
   f) $\dfrac{17}{15} - \dfrac{19}{6}$

6. Simplify.

   a) $-\dfrac{3}{5} + \dfrac{8}{-2} \times \left(\dfrac{-6}{5}\right)$

   b) $\left(\dfrac{-3}{4} - \dfrac{3}{-4}\right) \div 3$

   c) $-8\left(\dfrac{3}{5} - \dfrac{1}{2}\right)$

   d) $\dfrac{2}{5}\left(-\dfrac{1}{3}\right)\left(-\dfrac{6}{2}\right) + \dfrac{3}{5}$

   e) $\dfrac{9}{8} \times \dfrac{1}{3} - \dfrac{1}{4}\left(\dfrac{-5}{6}\right) + \dfrac{2}{3}\left(-\dfrac{1}{4}\right)$

   f) $\left[\left(-\dfrac{4}{5}\right) \div \dfrac{5}{2}\right] - \left[\dfrac{3}{-4} \times \left(-\dfrac{7}{5}\right)\right]$

7. If $x = -\dfrac{1}{4}$ and $y = -\dfrac{2}{3}$, evaluate:

   a) $xy - 3y^2$

   b) $3x^2y + y^2$

   c) $2x^2y - \dfrac{3}{2}xy$.

8. Solve.

   a) $9x - 4 = 23$

   b) $5y + 3 = -32$

   c) $3x - (5x - 11) = -13$

   d) $x + 5 = 4(5 + x)$

   e) $\dfrac{3x - 2}{6} = \dfrac{5}{3}$

   f) $\dfrac{x}{3} + \dfrac{x}{5} = \dfrac{1}{3} - \dfrac{2x}{5}$

Ⓑ

9. If $a = \dfrac{3}{-4}$ and $b = \dfrac{-1}{3}$, evaluate:

   a) $\dfrac{2a^2 + 4b}{14b^2}$

   b) $\dfrac{12ab + 4b}{5b}$

   c) $\dfrac{2a + 7b - ab}{7a^2}$.

10. The cost C dollars per hour of operating a certain type of aircraft is given by the formula $C = 1150 + \dfrac{m}{250} + \dfrac{20\,000\,000}{m}$, where m is the cruising altitude in metres. Find the hourly cost of operating the aircraft at: a) 7500 m   b) 10 000 m.

11. Solve.

   a) $2(3x + 17) + 2x = 4(x - 9) + 52$

   b) $\dfrac{6(x - 2)}{5} = \dfrac{5(x - 2)}{4}$

   c) $4(2x - 7) + 34 = 4(3x + 1) - 6(x - 3)$

   d) $\dfrac{x - 7}{2x + 1} = 3$

Ⓒ

12. The coin box of a vending machine contains twice as many dimes as quarters. If the total value of the coins is $22.50, how many quarters are there?

13. If $x = 5$ is the solution of each equation, find each value of k.

   a) $2x - k = 3 - x$

   b) $2 + 3x = 8 - (x - k)$

   c) $2x + k = kx - 6$

   d) $k - x - 1 = 2(x - 3) + k(1 + 2x)$

14. Solve, if possible.

   a) $5(n + 2) = 6(n - 3) + n$

   b) $y + (1 + y) = 2(y + 1)$

   c) $80 - 4x = 3(20 - x)$

   d) $3(q + 3) = 4(q - 1) - q$

1-4 REVIEW: FROM RATIONALS TO IRRATIONALS

The followers of the Greek mathematician Pythagoras made a considerable study of numbers. These Pythagoreans were a secret society who combined mathematical investigation with numerology and mysticism. To them is attributed the discovery of many geometrical theorems, as well as the analysis of triangular, square, and other numbers discussed earlier.

   The Pythagoreans found points on the number line which do not correspond to any rational numbers. New numbers had to be defined to represent such points. Since they are not rational numbers, they are called irrational numbers.

An *irrational number* is one that cannot be represented in the form $\dfrac{m}{n}$, where m and n are integers and $n \neq 0$. The decimal expansion of an irrational number neither terminates nor repeats.

   The Greeks found several examples of irrational numbers, and it was eventually proved that any number of the form $\sqrt{n}$, where n is not a perfect square, is irrational. An irrational number in this form is called a *radical*.

Example 1.   Which of these numbers are irrational?

   a) $\sqrt{7}$ b) $\sqrt{144}$ c) $\sqrt{p}$, where p is prime   d) $\sqrt{11} - 1$

Solution.   a) Since 7 is not a perfect square, $\sqrt{7}$ is irrational.

   b) Since $144 = 12^2$, $\sqrt{144} = 12$, which is rational.

   c) Primes are not perfect squares, therefore $\sqrt{p}$ is irrational.

   d) Since 11 is not a perfect square, $\sqrt{11}$ is irrational. Subtracting 1 does not affect the decimal portion of the expansion of $\sqrt{11}$, therefore $\sqrt{11} - 1$ is irrational.

   Example 1 suggests that the result of adding a rational number to, or subtracting it from an irrational number is an irrational number.

Example 2.   Show that $\sqrt{2} \times \sqrt{5} = \sqrt{2 \times 5}$

Solution. $(\sqrt{2} \times \sqrt{5})^2 = \sqrt{2} \times \sqrt{5} \times \sqrt{2} \times \sqrt{5}$

$= (\sqrt{2})^2 \times (\sqrt{5})^2$

$= 2 \times 5$

Take the square root of each side.

$\sqrt{2} \times \sqrt{5} = \sqrt{2 \times 5}$

The above result suggests the following property for radicals.

$$\sqrt{a} \times \sqrt{b} = \sqrt{a \times b} \qquad a, b \geqslant 0$$

The next example applies this property, and shows that the product of two or more irrational numbers is not necessarily irrational.

Example 3. Simplify.

a) $3\sqrt{2} \times 2\sqrt{7}$ b) $5\sqrt{6} \times \sqrt{10} \times 2\sqrt{15}$

Solution. a) $3\sqrt{2} \times 2\sqrt{7} = 3 \times 2 \times \sqrt{2 \times 7}$
$$= 6\sqrt{14}$$
b) $5\sqrt{6} \times \sqrt{10} \times 2\sqrt{15} = 2 \times 5 \times \sqrt{6 \times 10 \times 15}$
$$= 10\sqrt{900}$$
$$= 10 \times 30$$
$$= 300$$

The same property can be used to express radicals in simplest form.

Example 4. Simplify.

a) $\sqrt{44}$ b) $\sqrt{72}$

Solution. a) $\sqrt{44} = \sqrt{4 \times 11}$ b) $\sqrt{72} = \sqrt{36} \times \sqrt{2}$
$$\phantom{\sqrt{44}} = \sqrt{4} \times \sqrt{11} \qquad\qquad = 6\sqrt{2}$$
$$\phantom{\sqrt{44}} = 2\sqrt{11}$$

Many irrational numbers are not radicals. The best known of the non-radical irrational numbers is the number we denote by π. In 1761, the German mathematician Lambert proved that π was irrational. In 1986, a computer generated a 29 360 129-digit decimal expansion of π and, as expected, it never repeats.

Radicals like $\sqrt{44}$ and $\sqrt{72}$ are known as *entire radicals*, while radicals like $2\sqrt{11}$ and $6\sqrt{2}$ are called *mixed radicals*. It is often necessary to change from one form to the other.

Example 5. Identify each number as a mixed radical or an entire radical, then change it to the other form.

a) $4\sqrt{3}$ b) $\sqrt{18}$ c) $\sqrt{75}$

d) $2\sqrt{5}$ e) $\sqrt{80}$ f) $12\sqrt{3}$

Solution. a) $4\sqrt{3}$ is a mixed radical. b) $\sqrt{18}$ is an entire radical.
$$\quad 4\sqrt{3} = \sqrt{4} \times \sqrt{4} \times \sqrt{3} \qquad \sqrt{18} = \sqrt{9} \times \sqrt{2}$$
$$\quad\quad = \sqrt{48} \qquad\qquad\qquad\quad = 3\sqrt{2}$$

c) $\sqrt{75}$ is an entire radical. d) $2\sqrt{5}$ is a mixed radical.
$$\quad \sqrt{75} = \sqrt{25} \times \sqrt{3} \qquad 2\sqrt{5} = \sqrt{2} \times \sqrt{2} \times \sqrt{5}$$
$$\quad\quad = 5\sqrt{3} \qquad\qquad\qquad = \sqrt{20}$$

e) $\sqrt{80}$ is an entire radical. f) $12\sqrt{3}$ is a mixed radical.
$$\quad \sqrt{80} = \sqrt{16} \times \sqrt{5} \qquad 12\sqrt{3} = \sqrt{12} \times \sqrt{12} \times \sqrt{3}$$
$$\quad\quad = 4\sqrt{5} \qquad\qquad\qquad = \sqrt{432}$$

EXERCISES 1-4

(A)

1. Which of these numbers are irrational?
   a) $\sqrt{17}$ b) $\sqrt{196}$ c) $\sqrt{21} + 1$ d) $\sqrt{7} + \sqrt{9}$ e) $\sqrt{51} \times \sqrt{51}$

2. Simplify.
   a) $\sqrt{36 + 64}$ b) $\sqrt{2.56}$ c) $\sqrt{0.09}$ d) $\sqrt{\dfrac{49}{81}}$ e) $\sqrt{\dfrac{121}{36}}$

3. Simplify.
   a) $\sqrt{6} \times \sqrt{5}$ b) $\sqrt{7} \times \sqrt{3}$ c) $(8\sqrt{3})(7\sqrt{2})$
   d) $(-5\sqrt{6})(-3\sqrt{7})$ e) $(12\sqrt{7})(-8\sqrt{11})$ f) $(-15\sqrt{7})(-5\sqrt{10})$

4. Simplify.
   a) $\sqrt{18}$ b) $\sqrt{12}$ c) $\sqrt{50}$ d) $\sqrt{80}$ e) $\sqrt{112}$ f) $\sqrt{132}$

5. Simplify.
   a) $2\sqrt{6} \times 5\sqrt{3}$ b) $4\sqrt{5} \times 7\sqrt{10}$ c) $8\sqrt{10} \times 3\sqrt{6}$
   d) $(9\sqrt{15})(-4\sqrt{6})$ e) $(-6\sqrt{6})(5\sqrt{12})$ f) $(-5\sqrt{10})(-7\sqrt{8})$

6. Identify each number as a mixed radical or an entire radical, then change it to its other form.
   a) $\sqrt{32}$ b) $2\sqrt{6}$ c) $\sqrt{98}$ d) $3\sqrt{5}$ e) $\sqrt{320}$ f) $9\sqrt{5}$

(B)

7. Simplify.
   a) $2\sqrt{3} \times 5\sqrt{6} \times 3\sqrt{2}$ b) $4\sqrt{10} \times 6\sqrt{6} \times 3\sqrt{5}$
   c) $3\sqrt{6} \times 2\sqrt{18} \times \sqrt{15}$ d) $(5\sqrt{8})(-3\sqrt{6})(2\sqrt{15})$

8. Estimate.
   a) $\sqrt{30}$ b) $\sqrt{200}$ c) $\sqrt{125}$ d) $\sqrt{0.9}$ e) $\sqrt{150}$ f) $\sqrt{2.52}$

9. Use a calculator to arrange each set in order from least to greatest.
   a) $5\sqrt{2}, 4\sqrt{3}, 3\sqrt{6}, 2\sqrt{14}, 2\sqrt{10}$
   b) $-6\sqrt{2}, -4\sqrt{5}, -2\sqrt{17}, -5\sqrt{3}, -4\sqrt{6}$
   c) $4\sqrt{7}, 5\sqrt{5}, 6\sqrt{3}, 8\sqrt{2}, 3\sqrt{14}$

10. Use the diagram to show that
    $\sqrt{20} = 2\sqrt{5}$ and $\sqrt{45} = 3\sqrt{5}$.

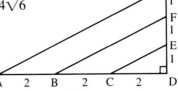

11. P, Q, R, and S are the midpoints of the sides of a square ABCD. If AB $= 4\sqrt{2}$ cm, find the area of PQRS.

(C)

12. Which number of each pair is the greater? (Do not use a calculator.)
    a) $5\sqrt{3}, 6\sqrt{2}$ b) $7\sqrt{2}, 4\sqrt{6}$ c) $3\sqrt{5}, 4\sqrt{3}$
    d) $-8\sqrt{3}, -10\sqrt{2}$ e) $2\sqrt[3]{7}, 3\sqrt[3]{2}$ f) $\dfrac{3}{4}\sqrt{12}, \dfrac{2}{3}\sqrt{14}$

THE MATHEMATICAL MIND

The Dilemma of the Pythagoreans

The Pythagoreans knew how to represent points on a number line by rational numbers. They believed intuitively that since a rational number can be written as a ratio of any two natural numbers, all points on the line can be represented in this way.

However, by the end of the fifth century B.C., the Pythagoreans found a point on the number line that does not correspond to a rational number. They proved that the length of the diagonal of a unit square cannot be written in the form $\frac{m}{n}$. This means there is no rational number for the point P on the number line shown.

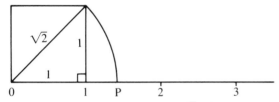

The Pythagoreans proved that $\sqrt{2}$ is not a rational number by the technique known as "indirect proof", or "proof by contradiction". If $\sqrt{2}$ is a rational number, then there are natural numbers m and n such that $\sqrt{2} = \frac{m}{n}$.

Square both sides.

$$(\sqrt{2})^2 = \left(\frac{m}{n}\right)^2$$

$$2 = \frac{m^2}{n^2}$$

$$2n^2 = m^2$$

Since a perfect square has an even number of prime factors, then m^2 has an even number of prime factors and $2n^2$ has an odd number. This is impossible. Therefore, $\sqrt{2}$ cannot be a rational number.

This, then, was the dilemma of the Pythagoreans. The number $\sqrt{2}$ existed because it was the length of the diagonal of a unit square. Yet, they did not see how it could exist since it was not a rational number.

QUESTIONS

1. Prove that $\sqrt{3}$ is irrational by indirect proof.

2. Use the fact that $\sqrt{2}$ is irrational to prove that $\sqrt{2} + 5$ is irrational.

3. Can the length, width, and diagonal of a rectangle all be rational numbers? Explain your answer.

1-5 REVIEW: RADICAL ARITHMETIC

Although the ancient Greeks discovered irrational numbers, they never developed the symbols needed to use radicals. It wasn't until 1525 that the square root symbol appeared, possibly derived from the written letter "r" (for *root*).

To add or subtract radicals, first simplify each radical by extracting all perfect-square factors. Then combine like radicals.

Example 1.   Simplify.   a) $\sqrt{12} + \sqrt{27}$ b) $3\sqrt{8} + 2\sqrt{3} - 2\sqrt{75} + 4\sqrt{50}$

Solution.   a) $\sqrt{12} + \sqrt{27} = \sqrt{4 \times 3} + \sqrt{9 \times 3}$
$$= 2\sqrt{3} + 3\sqrt{3}$$
$$= 5\sqrt{3}$$

b) $3\sqrt{8} + 2\sqrt{3} - 2\sqrt{75} + 4\sqrt{50}$
$$= 3 \times 2\sqrt{2} + 2\sqrt{3} - 2 \times 5\sqrt{3} + 4 \times 5\sqrt{2}$$
$$= 6\sqrt{2} + 20\sqrt{2} + 2\sqrt{3} - 10\sqrt{3}$$
$$= 26\sqrt{2} - 8\sqrt{3}$$

Products involving radicals can be expanded using the distributive law.

Example 2.   Expand and simplify.
   a) $5\sqrt{2}(2\sqrt{3} - \sqrt{8})$ b) $(5\sqrt{7} - 2\sqrt{3})(\sqrt{7} + 4\sqrt{3})$
   c) $(\sqrt{x} - 2)^2$ d) $(3 - 2\sqrt{5})(3 + 2\sqrt{5})$

Solution.   a) $5\sqrt{2}(2\sqrt{3} - \sqrt{8}) = 10\sqrt{6} - 5\sqrt{16}$
$$= 10\sqrt{6} - 20$$

b) $(5\sqrt{7} - 2\sqrt{3})(\sqrt{7} + 4\sqrt{3}) = 5(\sqrt{7})^2 + 20\sqrt{21} - 2\sqrt{21} - 8(\sqrt{3})^2$
$$= 35 + 18\sqrt{21} - 24$$
$$= 11 + 18\sqrt{21}$$

c) $(\sqrt{x} - 2)^2 = (\sqrt{x} - 2)(\sqrt{x} - 2)$
$$= (\sqrt{x})^2 - 2\sqrt{x} - 2\sqrt{x} + 4$$
$$= x - 4\sqrt{x} + 4$$

d) $(3 - 2\sqrt{5})(3 + 2\sqrt{5}) = 3^2 - (2\sqrt{5})^2$
$$= 9 - 20$$
$$= -11$$

Example 2d shows that the product of expressions involving radicals can be a rational number.

Division is the inverse of multiplication.

$54 \div 6 = 9$ since $9 \times 6 = 54$

Likewise, $\sqrt{21} \div \sqrt{3} = \sqrt{7}$ since $\sqrt{7} \times \sqrt{3} = \sqrt{21}$

Example 3. Simplify.

a) $\dfrac{\sqrt{76}}{\sqrt{2}}$ b) $\dfrac{12\sqrt{42}}{4\sqrt{6}}$ c) $\dfrac{4\sqrt{90}}{3\sqrt{72}}$

Solution. a) $\dfrac{\sqrt{76}}{\sqrt{2}} = \sqrt{38}$

b) $\dfrac{12\sqrt{42}}{4\sqrt{6}} = \dfrac{12}{4} \times \sqrt{\dfrac{42}{6}}$

$= 3\sqrt{7}$

c) It is often best to express radicals in simplest form before dividing.

$\dfrac{4\sqrt{90}}{3\sqrt{72}} = \dfrac{4 \times 3\sqrt{10}}{3 \times 6\sqrt{2}}$

$= \dfrac{2\sqrt{10}}{3\sqrt{2}}$

$= \dfrac{2\sqrt{5}}{3}$

Example 4. The time it takes for a pendulum to swing back and forth once depends only on the length of the pendulum. This period T seconds is given by the formula $T = 2\pi\sqrt{\dfrac{l}{9.8}}$, where l is the length of the pendulum in metres. By what factor is the period increased when the pendulum length is tripled?

Solution. For pendulum length l: $T_1 = 2\pi\sqrt{\dfrac{l}{9.8}}$

$\doteq 2\sqrt{l}$

For pendulum length $3l$: $T_2 = 2\pi\sqrt{\dfrac{3l}{9.8}}$

$\doteq 2\sqrt{3l}$

$\dfrac{T_2}{T_1} = \dfrac{2\sqrt{3l}}{2\sqrt{l}}$

$= \sqrt{3}$

The period is increased by a factor of $\sqrt{3}$ when the length of the pendulum is tripled.

EXERCISES 1-5

(A)

1. Simplify.
   a) $\sqrt{20} + \sqrt{5}$
   b) $\sqrt{12} + \sqrt{3}$
   c) $2\sqrt{18} - \sqrt{2}$
   d) $3\sqrt{7} + 5\sqrt{28}$
   e) $3\sqrt{40} + 2\sqrt{10}$
   f) $5\sqrt{48} - 11\sqrt{3}$

2. Simplify.
   a) $\sqrt{50} - \sqrt{18}$
   b) $\sqrt{12} + \sqrt{75}$
   c) $\sqrt{24} + \sqrt{54}$
   d) $\sqrt{8} - \sqrt{32}$
   e) $\sqrt{175} + \sqrt{63}$
   f) $\sqrt{80} - \sqrt{45}$

3. Simplify.
   a) $5\sqrt{12} - 2\sqrt{48}$
   b) $7\sqrt{24} + 3\sqrt{96}$
   c) $8\sqrt{63} - 3\sqrt{175}$
   d) $9\sqrt{32} - 12\sqrt{18}$
   e) $11\sqrt{54} + 6\sqrt{150}$
   f) $7\sqrt{20} - 6\sqrt{45}$

4. Simplify.
   a) $\sqrt{3}(\sqrt{5} + \sqrt{7})$
   b) $4\sqrt{3}(7\sqrt{2} - 3\sqrt{5})$
   c) $5\sqrt{6}(2\sqrt{a} + 4\sqrt{b})$
   d) $9\sqrt{5}(2\sqrt{15} - 7\sqrt{3})$
   e) $2\sqrt{y}(4\sqrt{2} - 3\sqrt{y})$
   f) $7\sqrt{2}(3\sqrt{18} + 2\sqrt{2})$

5. Simplify.
   a) $(\sqrt{3} + \sqrt{5})(2\sqrt{3} - \sqrt{5})$
   b) $(2\sqrt{5} - 3\sqrt{7})(\sqrt{5} + 2\sqrt{7})$
   c) $(3\sqrt{x} - 2\sqrt{y})(5\sqrt{x} + 3\sqrt{y})$
   d) $(2\sqrt{3} - 3\sqrt{2})(4\sqrt{3} - \sqrt{2})$
   e) $(4\sqrt{6} + 2\sqrt{3})(7\sqrt{6} + 4\sqrt{3})$
   f) $(8\sqrt{m} - 3\sqrt{n})(2\sqrt{m} - 5\sqrt{n})$

6. Simplify.
   a) $\dfrac{24\sqrt{14}}{8\sqrt{2}}$
   b) $\dfrac{-15\sqrt{30}}{45\sqrt{6}}$
   c) $\dfrac{18\sqrt{39}}{-6\sqrt{3}}$
   d) $\dfrac{54\sqrt{70}}{9\sqrt{5}}$
   e) $\dfrac{36\sqrt{22}}{-90\sqrt{2}}$
   f) $\dfrac{60\sqrt{51}}{-4\sqrt{3}}$
   g) $\dfrac{32\sqrt{35}}{4\sqrt{7}}$
   h) $\dfrac{28\sqrt{55}}{42\sqrt{11}}$

(B)

7. Simplify.
   a) $4\sqrt{45} + 3\sqrt{80} - 11\sqrt{20}$
   b) $3\sqrt{50} + 6\sqrt{32} - 4\sqrt{18}$
   c) $2\sqrt{150} - 5\sqrt{54} - 3\sqrt{24}$
   d) $5\sqrt{18} + 6\sqrt{8} - 2\sqrt{32}$
   e) $3\sqrt{40} - 5\sqrt{90} - 2\sqrt{160}$
   f) $9\sqrt{45} + 5\sqrt{125} - 6\sqrt{245}$

8. Simplify.
   a) $3\sqrt{2}(4\sqrt{7} - 5\sqrt{2})$
   b) $6\sqrt{3}(3\sqrt{12} - 2\sqrt{75})$
   c) $-5\sqrt{6}(2\sqrt{3} - 3\sqrt{2})$
   d) $4\sqrt{3}(3\sqrt{6} + 2\sqrt{7} - 5\sqrt{3})$
   e) $5\sqrt{a}(\sqrt{18} + 7\sqrt{a} - 5\sqrt{8})$
   f) $8\sqrt{b}(4\sqrt{2} - 2\sqrt{3} - 3\sqrt{b})$

9. Simplify.
   a) $(\sqrt{5} + \sqrt{2})(\sqrt{5} - \sqrt{2})$
   b) $(3\sqrt{m} - 2\sqrt{n})(3\sqrt{m} + 2\sqrt{n})$
   c) $(4\sqrt{6} + 8\sqrt{2})(4\sqrt{6} - 8\sqrt{2})$
   d) $(5\sqrt{2} - 3\sqrt{6})^2$
   e) $(7\sqrt{x} + 4\sqrt{y})^2$
   f) $2\sqrt{2}(3\sqrt{3} + 5\sqrt{7})^2$

10. Simplify.

a) $\dfrac{12\sqrt{20}}{3\sqrt{5}}$

b) $\dfrac{18\sqrt{24}}{-3\sqrt{8}}$

c) $\dfrac{-24\sqrt{45}}{72\sqrt{20}}$

d) $\dfrac{-30\sqrt{40}}{-5\sqrt{18}}$

e) $\dfrac{45\sqrt{54}}{18\sqrt{12}}$

f) $\dfrac{-60\sqrt{96}}{12\sqrt{27}}$

g) $\dfrac{12\sqrt{40}}{8\sqrt{45}}$

h) $\dfrac{15\sqrt{84}}{10\sqrt{63}}$

11. From a height of h metres, the distance d kilometres to the horizon is given by the formula $d \doteq 3.6\sqrt{h}$.
    a) By what factor is the distance to the horizon increased when:
       i) the height is doubled   ii) the height is tripled?
    b) By what factor must the height be increased so that the distance to the horizon is doubled?

12. The period of a pendulum T seconds is given by the formula $T = 2\pi\sqrt{\dfrac{l}{9.8}}$, where l is the length of the pendulum in metres.
    a) By what factor is the period increased when the length is:
       i) quadrupled   ii) increased fivefold?
    b) By what factor must the length be increased for the period:
       i) to triple   ii) to increase by a factor of $2\sqrt{2}$?

ⓒ

13. When at rest, a meson decays radioactively in t_0 μs (microsecond). At a speed v, the time for decay is increased to t μs where $t = \dfrac{t_0}{\sqrt{1 - \left(\dfrac{v}{c}\right)^2}}$, c being the speed of light. By what factor is the decay time increased when the meson is travelling at half the speed of light?

14. a) By substituting convenient values for a and b, show that, in general, $\sqrt{a} + \sqrt{b} \neq \sqrt{a + b}$.
    b) Are there any values of a and b such that $\sqrt{a} + \sqrt{b} = \sqrt{a + b}$?

 INVESTIGATE

If n is a perfect square, what is the next perfect square?

PROBLEM SOLVING

A Short History of Problem Solving

Mathematics, a product of the human mind, has been used to solve significant problems of the past and present.

Is the Earth or the sun the centre of the solar system?
Before the sixteenth century, people believed that the heavenly bodies moved around the Earth. In 1543, Nicolas Copernicus suggested instead that the Earth and other planets revolved around the sun. The discovery that the Earth was not the centre of the solar system had a profound effect on civilization and raised many new mathematical problems.

How high should a communications satellite be?
A communications satellite, high in orbit above the Earth, can relay a signal to a receiver many thousands of kilometres away. Because it must always be above the same point on the Earth, its orbit must be synchronized with the Earth's rotation. Mathematical formulas have been developed to determine the altitude of the satellite and its velocity.

Most significant mathematical problems that have been studied in the past have turned out to have important applications. Here is an example.

What is the largest known prime number?
In 1876 the largest known prime number had 39 digits. Until recently, only mathematicians were interested in prime numbers. Who would have thought in 1876 that prime numbers would turn out to have important applications in cryptography? Who would have thought that prime numbers would be used to test computers? As of 1988, the largest known prime had 65 050 digits! It was found by coincidence in 1985 while running a program to test a new super computer.

Problem solving strategies
In earlier grades, you may have learned certain strategies that are useful for solving problems. These strategies include:

- Identify a pattern
- Solve a simpler related problem
- Work backwards
- Use a diagram or a graph
- Make a table
- Look for a counterexample
- Use indirect proof
- Consider all possibilities
- Check for hidden assumptions
- Use systematic trial
- Make an organized list
- Make a reasonable assumption

To solve the problems in the *PROBLEM SOLVING* pages of this book, you may need to use mathematical concepts from the entire curriculum. The strategies listed above, or other strategies, may be helpful. Many problems are not particularly difficult, although some ingenuity will be needed to solve some of them. Be persistent — try a problem, set it aside, try it again later, or try another strategy. Some problems are extremely difficult. Do not be disappointed if you never solve them.

 PROBLEM SOLVING

Don't Make the Problem Harder

". . . there is no right way to approach solving a math problem."
Marilyn Burns

Two numbers have a sum of $\sqrt{7}$ and a difference of $\sqrt{3}$.
What is the product of the two numbers?

Understand the problem
- What are we asked to find?
- Are we asked to find the two numbers?

Think of a strategy
- We could let the numbers be x and y and write two equations.
  $$x + y = \sqrt{7}$$
  $$x - y = \sqrt{3}$$
- We could solve for x and y, and then multiply the results together.
- This is correct, but it involves unnecessary calculations with square roots.
- Since we do not need to know the values of x and y, a more elegant method might lead directly to the product xy.
- Recall that the sum, difference, and product of two numbers are contained in the formulas for the square of a binomial.
  $$(x + y)^2 = x^2 + 2xy + y^2 \text{ and } (x - y)^2 = x^2 - 2xy + y^2$$
- Do you see how to combine $(x + y)^2$ and $(x - y)^2$ to obtain an expression involving xy?

Carry out the strategy
- Simplify $(x + y)^2 - (x - y)^2$.
- Since we know the values of $x + y$ and $x - y$, we can substitute these in the above expression, and use the result to find the value of xy.

Look back
- Did you get 1 for the product of the two numbers?
- Check that this method is easier than the method of solving the equations.
- Discuss how this problem illustrates the quotation by Marilyn Burns at the top of the page.

PROBLEMS

1. A farmer offered to cut a log into three pieces for $5.00. How much should he charge to cut the log into six pieces?

2. Find three natural numbers x, y, and z such that $x^1 + y^2 = z^3$.

3. Two numbers have a sum of 5 and a product of 10. Find the sum of their reciprocals.

4. In square ABCD (below left), M and N are the midpoints of AD and BC respectively. If the sides have length x centimetres, find the area of the shaded rhombus.

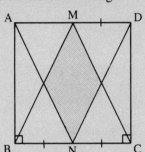
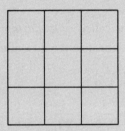

5. Copy the diagram (above right). Write the digits from 1 to 9 in the spaces such that the 3-digit number in the second row is double the 3-digit number in the first row, and the 3-digit number in the third row is triple the 3-digit number in the first row.

6. Solve this system. $\quad 29x + 19y = 260$
$\qquad\qquad\qquad 19x + 29y = 220$

7. Two sides of a triangle have length 6 and 8. The length of the third side is an integer.
   a) How many triangles are there satisfying these conditions?
   b) How many of the triangles are isosceles? acute? obtuse?

8. Prove that two unequal numbers, each of which is the square of the other, have a product of 1.

9. Solve this equation. $(x^2 + 3x - 2)(x^2 + 3x - 6) = 32$

10. Solve this equation. $\dfrac{x - a}{b + c + d} + \dfrac{x - b}{a + c + d} + \dfrac{x - c}{a + b + d} + \dfrac{x - d}{a + b + d} = 4$

11. Prove that for all natural numbers m and n, the expression $\dfrac{(m + 1)n + m}{mn + (m - 1)}$ is in lowest terms.

1-6 RATIONALIZING THE DENOMINATOR

When radicals were first used, mathematicians quickly discovered that not all expressions with radicals in the denominator, such as $\dfrac{5}{\sqrt{2}}$, could be simplified by division. The division operation was impossible to perform because the divisor was an infinite non-repeating decimal. So, they rewrote the expression, multiplying numerator and denominator by the radical in the denominator. This makes the denominator a rational number.

$$\frac{5}{\sqrt{2}} = \frac{5}{\sqrt{2}} \times \frac{\sqrt{2}}{\sqrt{2}} \qquad \text{Equivalent to}$$
$$\text{multiplying by 1.}$$
$$= \frac{5\sqrt{2}}{2}$$

This procedure is called *rationalizing the denominator*.

Example 1.   Rationalize the denominator.

a) $\dfrac{3}{\sqrt{6}}$ 　　　　 b) $\dfrac{2}{\sqrt{18}}$ 　　　　 c) $\dfrac{3\sqrt{2} - 5}{\sqrt{2}}$

Solution.　a) $\dfrac{3}{\sqrt{6}} = \dfrac{3}{\sqrt{6}} \times \dfrac{\sqrt{6}}{\sqrt{6}}$ 　　　　 b) $\dfrac{2}{\sqrt{18}} = \dfrac{2}{3\sqrt{2}}$

$$\qquad\qquad = 3\frac{\sqrt{6}}{6} \qquad\qquad\qquad\qquad = \frac{2}{3\sqrt{2}} \times \frac{\sqrt{2}}{\sqrt{2}}$$

$$\qquad\qquad = \frac{\sqrt{6}}{2} \qquad\qquad\qquad\qquad = \frac{2\sqrt{2}}{6}$$

$$\qquad\qquad\qquad\qquad\qquad\qquad\qquad\qquad = \frac{\sqrt{2}}{3}$$

c) $\dfrac{3\sqrt{2} - 5}{\sqrt{2}} = \dfrac{3\sqrt{2} - 5}{\sqrt{2}} \times \dfrac{\sqrt{2}}{\sqrt{2}}$

$$= \frac{6 - 5\sqrt{2}}{2}$$

$$= 3 - \frac{5}{2}\sqrt{2}$$

In *Example 2d)* of the previous section, we found that the result of simplifying $(3 - 2\sqrt{5})(3 + 2\sqrt{5})$ was -11, a rational number. $(3 - 2\sqrt{5})$ and $(3 + 2\sqrt{5})$ are called *conjugates*, and the fact that the product of conjugates is a rational number can be used to simplify expressions having binomial denominators with radical terms.

Example 2.   Simplify.

a) $\dfrac{14}{3 + \sqrt{2}}$ 　　　　　 b) $\dfrac{3\sqrt{2} - 2\sqrt{5}}{2\sqrt{2} - \sqrt{5}}$

Solution.   a) The conjugate of $3 + \sqrt{2}$ is $3 - \sqrt{2}$. Multiply the numerator and the denominator by $3 - \sqrt{2}$.

$$\frac{14}{3 + \sqrt{2}} = \frac{14}{3 + \sqrt{2}} \times \frac{3 - \sqrt{2}}{3 - \sqrt{2}}$$

$$= \frac{14(3 - \sqrt{2})}{9 - 2}$$

$$= 2(3 - \sqrt{2})$$

$$= 6 - 2\sqrt{2}$$

b) Multiply the numerator and the denominator by $2\sqrt{2} + \sqrt{5}$.

$$\frac{3\sqrt{2} - 2\sqrt{5}}{2\sqrt{2} - \sqrt{5}} = \frac{3\sqrt{2} - 2\sqrt{5}}{2\sqrt{2} - \sqrt{5}} \times \frac{2\sqrt{2} + \sqrt{5}}{2\sqrt{2} + \sqrt{5}}$$

$$= \frac{12 + 3\sqrt{10} - 4\sqrt{10} - 10}{8 - 5}$$

$$= \frac{2 - \sqrt{10}}{3}$$

When the denominator contains algebraic expressions involving radicals, the same methods can be used to write an equivalent expression with no radicals in the denominator. The resulting denominator is not necessarily a rational number.

Example 3.   Write an equivalent expression with no radicals in the denominator.

a) $\dfrac{3}{\sqrt{x}}, \ x \neq 0$ \qquad\qquad\qquad b) $\dfrac{2x}{\sqrt{x} - y}, \ \sqrt{x} \neq y$

Solution.   a) $\dfrac{3}{\sqrt{x}} = \dfrac{3}{\sqrt{x}} \times \dfrac{\sqrt{x}}{\sqrt{x}}$ \qquad b) $\dfrac{2x}{\sqrt{x} - y} = \dfrac{2x}{\sqrt{x} - y} \times \dfrac{\sqrt{x} + y}{\sqrt{x} + y}$

$$= \frac{3\sqrt{x}}{x} \qquad\qquad\qquad = \frac{2x(\sqrt{x} + y)}{x - y^2}$$

EXERCISES 1-6

Ⓐ

1. Rationalize the denominator.

a) $\dfrac{2}{\sqrt{5}}$ \qquad b) $\dfrac{7}{\sqrt{11}}$ \qquad c) $\dfrac{-4}{\sqrt{3}}$ \qquad d) $\dfrac{5\sqrt{2}}{\sqrt{7}}$

e) $\dfrac{6\sqrt{10}}{-\sqrt{3}}$ \qquad f) $\dfrac{12\sqrt{7}}{7\sqrt{5}}$ \qquad g) $\dfrac{18\sqrt{5}}{3\sqrt{2}}$ \qquad h) $\dfrac{20\sqrt{7}}{-4\sqrt{3}}$

2. Express in simplest form.

a) $\dfrac{3\sqrt{6}}{\sqrt{20}}$ \qquad b) $\dfrac{4\sqrt{5}}{\sqrt{8}}$ \qquad c) $\dfrac{-9\sqrt{12}}{\sqrt{18}}$ \qquad d) $\dfrac{15\sqrt{3}}{3\sqrt{8}}$

e) $\dfrac{-24\sqrt{7}}{-3\sqrt{12}}$ \qquad f) $\dfrac{14\sqrt{3}}{2\sqrt{28}}$ \qquad g) $\dfrac{20\sqrt{24}}{3\sqrt{20}}$ \qquad h) $\dfrac{36\sqrt{18}}{8\sqrt{8}}$

(B)

3. Simplify.

a) $\dfrac{2\sqrt{3} + 4}{\sqrt{3}}$
b) $\dfrac{5\sqrt{7} - 3}{\sqrt{7}}$
c) $\dfrac{4\sqrt{5} - 2}{\sqrt{5}}$
d) $\dfrac{6\sqrt{2} - \sqrt{3}}{\sqrt{3}}$

e) $\dfrac{8\sqrt{6} + \sqrt{5}}{\sqrt{5}}$
f) $\dfrac{3\sqrt{10} - \sqrt{2}}{\sqrt{2}}$
g) $\dfrac{5\sqrt{8} + 2\sqrt{3}}{\sqrt{6}}$
h) $\dfrac{3\sqrt{12} - 4\sqrt{3}}{2\sqrt{2}}$

4. Rationalize the denominator.

a) $\dfrac{\sqrt{3}}{\sqrt{5} - \sqrt{2}}$
b) $\dfrac{\sqrt{5}}{\sqrt{7} + \sqrt{3}}$
c) $\dfrac{\sqrt{11}}{8 - \sqrt{5}}$
d) $\dfrac{2\sqrt{5}}{\sqrt{6} + \sqrt{3}}$

e) $\dfrac{5\sqrt{6}}{\sqrt{12} - 5}$
f) $\dfrac{4\sqrt{7}}{\sqrt{15} - \sqrt{10}}$
g) $\dfrac{6\sqrt{3}}{5 + \sqrt{2}}$
h) $\dfrac{9\sqrt{5}}{\sqrt{11} - \sqrt{5}}$

5. Simplify.

a) $\dfrac{3\sqrt{2} + \sqrt{3}}{2\sqrt{3} + \sqrt{2}}$
b) $\dfrac{5\sqrt{3} + \sqrt{2}}{2\sqrt{3} - \sqrt{2}}$
c) $\dfrac{5\sqrt{3} - 3\sqrt{5}}{\sqrt{5} - \sqrt{3}}$

d) $\dfrac{3 + 2\sqrt{5}}{3\sqrt{5} - 4}$
e) $\dfrac{2\sqrt{7} - 4\sqrt{3}}{3\sqrt{7} + \sqrt{3}}$
f) $\dfrac{\sqrt{7} + 3\sqrt{2}}{9 + 2\sqrt{14}}$

6. Find an equivalent expression with no radicals in the denominator.

a) $\dfrac{5x}{\sqrt{y}}$
b) $\dfrac{3\sqrt{m}}{\sqrt{m - n}}$
c) $\dfrac{3}{\sqrt{2a + b}}$
d) $\dfrac{x}{\sqrt{x} + 1}$

e) $\dfrac{2\sqrt{3}}{\sqrt{2x} - 1}$
f) $\dfrac{-1}{3 - \sqrt{x}}$
g) $\dfrac{2a}{\sqrt{5} - \sqrt{a}}$
h) $\dfrac{5x}{\sqrt{x} + \sqrt{3}}$

(C)

7. Rationalize the denominator of the reciprocal.

a) $\sqrt{2}$
b) $\sqrt{12}$
c) $\sqrt{50}$
d) $\sqrt{2} - 1$

e) $\sqrt{3} + \sqrt{2}$
f) $2\sqrt{5} - 3\sqrt{2}$

8. Simplify.

a) $\dfrac{1}{2 + \sqrt{3}} + \dfrac{1}{2 - \sqrt{3}}$
b) $\dfrac{3}{\sqrt{5} - \sqrt{2}} - \dfrac{1}{\sqrt{5} + \sqrt{2}}$

c) $\dfrac{6}{\sqrt{2}} + \dfrac{2}{\sqrt{2} + 1}$
d) $\dfrac{1}{\sqrt{x} - \sqrt{y}} + \dfrac{1}{\sqrt{x} + \sqrt{y}}$

e) $\dfrac{m}{\sqrt{m} - \sqrt{n}} - \dfrac{m}{\sqrt{m} + \sqrt{n}}$
f) $\dfrac{4a}{\sqrt{2a} - b} - \dfrac{a}{\sqrt{2a} + b}$

9. Rationalize the numerator.

a) $\dfrac{\sqrt{2}}{4}$
b) $\dfrac{\sqrt{5}}{3}$
c) $\dfrac{\sqrt{x}}{xy}$
d) $\dfrac{\sqrt{x} + 1}{x}$

e) $\dfrac{\sqrt{a} + 2\sqrt{b}}{\sqrt{a}}$
f) $\dfrac{-\sqrt{m} + 2n}{\sqrt{m} - \sqrt{n}}$
g) $\dfrac{\sqrt{x} - \sqrt{y}}{\sqrt{x} + \sqrt{y}}$
h) $\dfrac{2\sqrt{a} - 3\sqrt{b}}{2\sqrt{a} + 3\sqrt{b}}$

1-7 REVIEW: THE REAL NUMBERS

In the fifth century B.C., the Pythagoreans found points on the number line that did not correspond to rational numbers. In the nineteenth century A.D., mathematicians wondered if there were points on the number line with no corresponding decimals. It wasn't until 1876 that the German mathematician Richard Dedekind proved that every point on the number line has a corresponding decimal, and conversely, every decimal corresponds to a point on the number line.

> All numbers that can be represented by decimals are real numbers. These numbers correspond to every point on the number line.

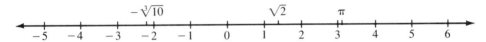

This diagram shows how the various types of numbers are related.

The Real Numbers

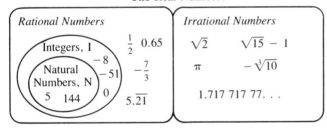

Example. Classify each number as rational or irrational.

a) $7.3\overline{756}$ b) $0.010\ 010\ 001\ 000\ 010\ \ldots$ c) $\dfrac{\sqrt{3}}{\sqrt{48}}$ d) 7π

Solution. a) $7.3\overline{756}$ is a repeating decimal and therefore a rational number.

b) The digits follow a pattern, but a non-repeating pattern.
$0.010\ 010\ 001\ 000\ 010\ \ldots$ is irrational.

c) $\dfrac{\sqrt{3}}{\sqrt{48}} = \sqrt{\dfrac{1}{16}}$

$\qquad = \dfrac{1}{4}$, which is rational

d) If 7π were rational, we could write $7\pi = \dfrac{a}{b}$, where a and b are natural numbers.
It would follow that $\pi = \dfrac{a}{7b}$, which is rational. But π is irrational.

Therefore, 7π cannot be rational; it is irrational.

EXERCISES 1-7

(A)

1. Which numbers appear to be irrational?
   a) 2.363 663 666 3 . . .   b) −0.123 456 78 . . .
   c) 1.407 240 724 . . .   d) 5.312 312 231 . . .
   e) −17.717 171 71 . . .   f) 4.925 925 92 . . .
   g) 8.069 069 069 . . .   h) −24.734 659 28 . . .

2. Which numbers are irrational?
   a) $\sqrt{34}$ b) $\sqrt{256}$ c) $\sqrt{36 + 49}$
   d) $2\sqrt{18} - \sqrt{3}$ e) $\sqrt{25 + 56}$ f) $\sqrt{6.25}$

   g) $\sqrt{16} - \sqrt{12}$ h) $\sqrt{\dfrac{65}{9}}$ i) $7 - \sqrt{169}$

3. Which numbers are rational and which are irrational?
   a) 0.010 120 230 123 4 . . .   b) 3.131 313 131 313 . . .
   c) −1.357 957 957 957 . . .   d) 0.707 007 000 700 . . .
   e) 2.179 652 389 57 . . .   f) −5.246 810 121 4 . . .

(B)

4. To which of the sets of numbers listed
   does each number belong?
   a) $\sqrt{37}$ b) $-5.1\overline{62}$
   c) $\sqrt{169}$ d) −2.357 911 13 . . .
   e) $-\dfrac{29}{5}$ f) $\sqrt{2}$
   g) $\sqrt{49 + 16}$ h) $\sqrt{48} - \sqrt{18}$

   > Natural numbers, N
   > Integers, I
   > Rational numbers, Q
   > Irrational numbers, Q′
   > Real numbers, R

5. Using the $\boxed{\sqrt{}}$ key on a calculator, $\sqrt{5} = 2.236\ 067\ 9$. This is a rational number, but $\sqrt{5}$ is irrational. Can a number be both rational and irrational? Explain.

6. Find a rational number and an irrational number between each pair of numbers.
   a) $2.\overline{5791}$ and $2.\overline{5792}$
   b) $-6.\overline{327}$ and −6.327 332 733 2 . . .
   c) 4.190 119 011 190 . . . and 4.190 219 021 190 . . .

(C)

7. Using the $\boxed{\sqrt{}}$ key on a calculator, $\sqrt{0.444\ 444\ 4} = 0.666\ 666\ 6$

   a) Write fractions in the form $\dfrac{m}{n}$ for 0.444 444 4 and 0.666 666 6, and use them to explain the calculator result.

   b) Find another number which gives a similar result.

8. The solution of $3x + 12 = 3$ is real, rational, and an integer. Describe the solution(s) of each equation.
   a) $3x + 5 = 17$ b) $19 + 6x = 7$ c) $5 + 4x = 11$
   d) $x^2 + 3 = 12$ e) $x^2 + 1 = 4$ f) $x^2 + 4 = 1$

1-8 SOLVING RADICAL EQUATIONS

The design of a domed stadium calls for a roof which is part of a sphere. If the diameter of the base of the stadium is 200 m, and the roof is 75 m above the centre of the playing field, what is the radius of the sphere?

 This problem can be answered by solving the following equation for r, where h is the height of the roof, and c is the diameter of the base.

$$\sqrt{4h(2r - h)} = c$$

Substitute 200 for c and 75 for h.

$$\sqrt{300(2r - 75)} = 200$$

 In this equation, the variable occurs under a radical sign. For this reason the equation is called a *radical equation*. The equation can be solved by squaring both sides.

$$(\sqrt{300(2r - 75)})^2 = 200^2$$
$$300(2r - 75) = 40\ 000$$
$$6r - 225 = 400$$
$$6r = 625$$
$$r \doteq 104.2$$

The radius of the sphere is approximately 104 m.

 The steps used in solving the above equation are used to solve other radical equations.

Example 1. Solve.

  a) $\sqrt{x - 3} - 3 = 0$ b) $\sqrt{x - 3} + 3 = 0$

Solution.   a) $\sqrt{x - 3} - 3 = 0$ b) $\sqrt{x - 3} + 3 = 0$

     Isolate the radical.   Isolate the radical.
$$\sqrt{x - 3} = 3 \qquad\qquad \sqrt{x - 3} = -3$$
     Square both sides.   Square both sides.
$$(\sqrt{x - 3})^2 = 3^2 \qquad\qquad (\sqrt{x - 3})^2 = (-3)^2$$
$$x - 3 = 9 \qquad\qquad\qquad x - 3 = 9$$
$$x = 12 \qquad\qquad\qquad\quad x = 12$$

Check.   When $x = 12$,   When $x = 12$,
$$\text{L.S.} = \sqrt{x - 3} - 3 \qquad\quad \text{L.S.} = \sqrt{x - 3} + 3$$
$$= \sqrt{9} - 3 \qquad\qquad\qquad = \sqrt{9} + 3$$
$$= 0 \qquad\qquad\qquad\qquad = 6$$
$$\text{R.S.} = 0 \qquad\qquad\qquad\quad \text{R.S.} = 0$$

     The solution is correct.   The solution is not correct.
     That is, 12 is the only root of   That is, 12 is not a root of the
     the equation   equation $\sqrt{x - 3} + 3 = 0$. This
     $\sqrt{x - 3} - 3 = 0$.   equation has no real roots.

In *Example 1b* we could have predicted that the equation has no real roots. Since the radical sign always denotes the positive square root, it is impossible for the left side of the equation, $\sqrt{x-3}+3$, to be equal to 0. This example shows that the operation of squaring both sides of an equation may lead to numbers that do not satisfy the original equation. These are called *extraneous roots*. They are roots of the equation that was obtained after squaring, but they are not roots of the original equation.

Extraneous roots are often introduced when you square both sides of an equation. For this reason, you must identify extraneous roots.

> To solve a radical equation, follow these steps.
> *Step 1.* Isolate the radical on one side of the equation.
> *Step 2.* Square both sides of the equation.
> *Step 3.* Identify extraneous roots and reject them.

Example 2. Solve.   a) $4 - \sqrt{4 + x^2} = x$ b) $4 + \sqrt{4 + x^2} = x$

Solution.   a) $4 - \sqrt{4 + x^2} = x$

Isolate the radical.
$$-\sqrt{4 + x^2} = x - 4$$
Square both sides.
$$(-\sqrt{4 + x^2})^2 = (x - 4)^2$$
$$4 + x^2 = x^2 - 8x + 16$$
$$8x = 12$$
$$x = 1.5$$

Check.   When $x = 1.5$
$$\text{Left Side} = 4 - \sqrt{4 + 1.5^2}$$
$$= 4 - 2.5$$
$$= 1.5$$
$$\text{Right Side} = 1.5$$
1.5 is a root of the equation.

b) $4 + \sqrt{4 + x^2} = x$

Isolate the radical.
$$\sqrt{4 + x^2} = x - 4$$
Square both sides.
$$(\sqrt{4 + x^2})^2 = (x - 4)^2$$
$$4 + x^2 = x^2 - 8x + 16$$
$$8x = 12$$
$$x = 1.5$$

Check.   When $x = 1.5$
Left Side $= 4 + \sqrt{4 + 1.5^2}$
$= 4 + 2.5$
$= 6.5$
Right Side $= 1.5$
1.5 is an extraneous root. The equation has no real root.

In *Example 2*, the extraneous roots were identified by checking the possible roots obtained. Another method is to identify the possible values of x after the radical has been isolated. For example, this equation was obtained in *Example 2a*, $-\sqrt{4 + x^2} = x - 4$. Since the left side of the equation is always negative, the right side must also be negative. This introduces a restriction on x, namely, $x - 4 < 0$, or $x < 4$. From this point on, the solution is valid only if $x < 4$. Since $1.5 < 4$, 1.5 can be a solution of the given equation.

Using a similar method, an equation such as $\sqrt[3]{3x - 2} - 2 = 1$ could be solved by isolating the cube root, and cubing both sides.

Example 3.   When a satellite is h kilometres above the Earth the period, or time for one complete orbit, T minutes is given by this formula.
$T = 1.66 \times 10^{-4} \sqrt{(6370 + h)^3}$.
How high should a satellite be placed above the equator so that it always appears to be above the same point on the ground? Give your answer to the nearest hundred kilometres.

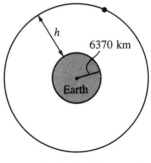

Solution.   The period of the satellite has to equal the period of the Earth's rotation, which is 24 h, or 1440 min.
Substitute 1440 for T in the formula.
$$1440 = 1.66 \times 10^{-4} \sqrt{(6370 + h)^3}$$
Isolate the radical.
$$\frac{1440}{1.66 \times 10^{-4}} = \sqrt{(6370 + h)^3}$$
Since the left side is positive, there are no restrictions on h.
Therefore, there are no extraneous roots.
Square both sides.
$7.525\,039\,9 \times 10^{13} = (6370 + h)^3$
Solve by taking the cube root of both sides.
$42\,219 = 6370 + h$
$35\,849 = h$
To the nearest hundred kilometres, the satellite should be placed 35 800 km above the ground.

EXERCISES 1-8

Ⓐ

1. Solve.
   a) $\sqrt{3x + 1} = 7$
   b) $\sqrt{2x + 7} = 5$
   c) $2\sqrt{x} = 8$
   d) $12\sqrt{x} = 30$
   e) $\sqrt{x} + 3 = 4$
   f) $\sqrt{x} - 6 = -3$

2. Solve.
   a) $\sqrt{x + 2} - 5 = 0$
   b) $\sqrt{x - 4} - 7 = 0$
   c) $\sqrt{2x + 7} - 9 = 0$
   d) $\sqrt{2x + 1} + 5 = 8$
   e) $\sqrt{7x - 3} - 2 = 3$
   f) $\sqrt{3x - 1} + 7 = 10$

3. Solve.
   a) $2 = 3\sqrt{2x - 5}$
   b) $\sqrt{5x + 2} - 3 = 1$
   c) $-2\sqrt{6x + 1} = 14$
   d) $5 + \sqrt{4x - 3} = 9$
   e) $-7 + 5\sqrt{2x + 3} = 8$
   f) $-3\sqrt{2x + 1} + 5 = -4$

4. Determine, by inspection, which of the following equations have extraneous roots.
   a) $\sqrt{x + 3} + 5 = 0$
   b) $\sqrt{3x - 2} - 2 = 3$
   c) $4 + \sqrt{2x - 7} = 0$
   d) $-4 + \sqrt{3x + 1} = 0$
   e) $7 + 5\sqrt{2x + 3} = 4$
   f) $3\sqrt{x + 1} + 2 = 8$

Ⓑ

5. The formula for the length d of the diagonal of a rectangle with sides of length a and b is $d = \sqrt{a^2 + b^2}$. Solve the formula for a.

6. Solve.
   a) $4\sqrt{2x + 7} - 5 = 7$
   b) $4 + 2\sqrt{5x - 3} = 12$
   c) $3 + 4\sqrt{8x - 3} = 15$
   d) $-5\sqrt{8x - 4} + 3 = 18$
   e) $7\sqrt{9x + 12} - 5 = 16$
   f) $-20 + 6\sqrt{2x + 17} = -2$

7. Solve.
   a) $6 - \sqrt{x^2 - 12} = x$
   b) $\sqrt{x^2 - 16} - x = -8$
   c) $x + \sqrt{x^2 - 5} = 7$
   d) $x - \sqrt{x^2 - 5} = 7$
   e) $\sqrt{x^2 + 7} + 5 = x$
   f) $\sqrt{x^2 + 3} = x + 1$

8. Solve.
   a) $x + \sqrt{3 + x^2} = 3$
   b) $1 + \sqrt{6 + x^2} = x + 2$
   c) $\sqrt{4x^2 + 9} + 9 = 2x$
   d) $\sqrt{4x^2 + 9} - 9 = 2x$
   e) $2x - \sqrt{4x^2 + 1} = -7$
   f) $2x - 2\sqrt{x^2 - 2} = 4$

9. Solve.
   a) $\sqrt[3]{x} = 2$
   b) $\sqrt[3]{2x} + 1 = 5$
   c) $\sqrt[3]{3x - 2} - 2 = 1$
   d) $4 - \sqrt[3]{5x + 1} = 8$
   e) $2 + \sqrt[3]{4 - 2x} = -4$
   f) $2\sqrt[3]{3x + 2} + 7 = 3$

10. At the scene of an accident, police can estimate the speed a car had been travelling by the length of the skid marks. One formula used for this purpose is $v = -7 + 8.2\sqrt{d}$, where v is the speed in kilometres per hour and d is the length of the skid marks in metres.
    a) Solve the formula for d.
    b) How long would be the skid marks of a car braking from:
        i)   60 km/h   ii)   90 km/h   iii)   120 km/h?
    c) What was the speed of the car if the length of its skid marks were:
        i)   50 m   ii)   100 m   iii)   150 m?

11. Solve for the variable indicated.

    a) $T = 2\pi\sqrt{\dfrac{l}{g}}, \quad l$

    b) $u = \sqrt{v^2 - 2as}, \quad a$

    c) $V = \sqrt{\dfrac{2gE}{W}}, \quad W$

    d) $m = \dfrac{M}{\sqrt{1 - \dfrac{v^2}{c^2}}}, \quad c$

    e) $v = \sqrt{\dfrac{F}{mk} - u^2}, \quad k$

    f) $e = \sqrt{\dfrac{h^2 - 2ma^2E}{2ma}}, \quad E$

12. The total surface area A of a cone with base radius r and height h is given by the formula $A = \pi r(r + \sqrt{r^2 + h^2})$. Solve this formula for h.

13. In $\triangle ABC$, $\angle B = 90°$, and AB is 1 cm longer than BC. If the perimeter of the triangle is 70 cm, find the lengths of the three sides.

Ⓒ

14. Solve the equation $x - 7\sqrt{x} + 12 = 0$ in two different ways.
    a) As a radical equation
    b) As a quadratic equation in $\sqrt{x}$

15. The diagram shows a sector of a circle with radius r. If h is as defined on the diagram, then the chord length c is given by this formula.
    $c = \sqrt{4h(2r - h)}$
    Solve the formula for h.

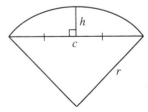

16. Check the results of *Exercise 15* as follows.
    a) Substitute the value of c which would result if the sector were a semicircle.
    b) Determine a condition that must be satisfied by r and c.

17. Without solving, determine which radical equations have no real roots.
    a) $\sqrt{x - 5} = 8 - x$
    b) $\sqrt{2x + 10} = -2 - x$
    c) $2x - 12 = \sqrt{17 - 3x}$
    d) $\sqrt{-7 - 3x} = 5x + 4$
    e) $4 + \sqrt{6 - 20x} = 10x$
    f) $-100x = \sqrt{15x - 1.5} - 11$

18. Explain the difference between an equation having extraneous roots and one having no real roots. Illustrate your answer with specific examples.

Review Exercises

1. Express each number as a product of prime factors.
   a) 1470
   b) 1365
   c) 5236

2. Express each decimal as a common fraction.
   a) $1.7\overline{36}$
   b) $1.5\overline{85}$
   c) $2.\overline{123}$
   d) $3.1\overline{4}$

3. Write each expression as a repeating decimal.
   a) $0.\overline{4} - 0.\overline{1}$
   b) $0.\overline{83} + 0.\overline{07}$
   c) $4.\overline{14} - 3.\overline{9}$
   d) $0.\overline{7} \times 0.\overline{6}$

4. If $x = -\dfrac{2}{3}$ and $w = \dfrac{1}{-4}$, evaluate:

   a) $\dfrac{3x^2 - 2w}{3w^2}$
   b) $\dfrac{7xw + 3w}{5w}$
   c) $\dfrac{3x + 2w - 2xw}{4x^2}$.

5. Solve.
   a) $2(3x - 7) + 7 = 5(x - 9) - 17$
   b) $19(2x - 1) + 11 = 15x - 5(2 - 3x)$
   c) $\dfrac{7(x - 3)}{8} = \dfrac{8(x + 2)}{3}$
   d) $6(3x - 5) + 27 = 5(2x + 3) - 7(x + 3)$

6. a) Change to mixed radicals.
   i) $\sqrt{24}$
   ii) $\sqrt{45}$
   iii) $\sqrt{112}$
   iv) $\sqrt{605}$
   b) Change to entire radicals.
   i) $3\sqrt{7}$
   ii) $5\sqrt{2}$
   iii) $4\sqrt{5}$
   iv) $7\sqrt{6}$

7. Simplify.
   a) $2\sqrt{5} \times 3\sqrt{2} \times \sqrt{10}$
   b) $5\sqrt{3} \times 2\sqrt{2} \times 2\sqrt{6}$
   c) $5\sqrt{5} \times 8\sqrt{3} \times 2\sqrt{15}$
   d) $(-4\sqrt{3})(-3\sqrt{2})(-5\sqrt{7})$

8. Simplify.
   a) $3\sqrt{30} + 2\sqrt{64} - 5\sqrt{12}$
   b) $4\sqrt{40} + 8\sqrt{24} - 3\sqrt{48}$
   c) $7\sqrt{120} - 3\sqrt{52} - 2\sqrt{28}$
   d) $8\sqrt{24} + 3\sqrt{6} - 4\sqrt{54}$

9. Simplify.
   a) $3\sqrt{x} - 7\sqrt{x} + \sqrt{x}$
   b) $\sqrt{8x} + \sqrt{12y} + \sqrt{18x} - \sqrt{75y}$
   c) $(2\sqrt{x} - 5)(\sqrt{x} + 3)$
   d) $3\sqrt{2}(\sqrt{2x} + 1)^2$

10. Simplify.
   a) $2\sqrt{3}(3\sqrt{8} - 4\sqrt{2})$
   b) $7\sqrt{3}(4\sqrt{24} - 3\sqrt{50})$
   c) $(5\sqrt{5} + 2\sqrt{3})(5\sqrt{5} - 2\sqrt{3})$
   d) $(6\sqrt{3} - 2\sqrt{6})^2$

11. Simplify.
   a) $\dfrac{12\sqrt{12}}{4\sqrt{2}}$
   b) $\dfrac{16\sqrt{50}}{-5\sqrt{10}}$
   c) $\dfrac{-40\sqrt{50}}{-8\sqrt{125}}$
   d) $\dfrac{3\sqrt{5} + 5}{\sqrt{5}}$
   e) $\dfrac{6\sqrt{7} - 4}{\sqrt{7} - \sqrt{2}}$
   f) $\dfrac{4\sqrt{18} - 3\sqrt{2}}{\sqrt{5} + \sqrt{3}}$

12. Solve.
   a) $3 - \sqrt{5 + x^2} = x$
   b) $\sqrt{x^2 - 2} + 4 = x$
   c) $\sqrt{9x^2 + 4} - 8 = 3x$
   d) $\sqrt[3]{2x + 1} - 5 = -3$

2 Powers

Canada's most massive tree is a Douglas fir on Vancouver Island. How can its height be estimated from the diameter of its base? (See Section 2-4 *Example 4*.)

2-1 REVIEW: POWERS AND EXPONENTS

A flu virus is about 10^{-5} mm in diameter.

10^{63} grains of sand would fill the observable universe.

Exponential notation was introduced into mathematics in 1637 by the French mathematician René Descartes. This notation allows scientists such as biologists, astronomers, and statisticians to express both very large and very small numbers more compactly. Not only is it a convenient symbolism for representing powers, it has also been possible to develop techniques for operating with them.

Example 1. a) Write as a power.
      i) $7 \times 7 \times 7$ ii) $w \times w \times w \times w \times w$
     b) Simplify. $2(-2)^3 + 4(3)^2$

Solution. a) i) $7 \times 7 \times 7 = 7^3$ ii) $w \times w \times w \times w \times w = w^5$
     b) $2(-2)^3 + 4(3)^2 = 2(-8) + 4(9)$
$$= -16 + 36$$
$$= 20$$

Example 2. The number of insects in a colony doubles every month. There are currently about 1000 insects in the colony.
    a) How many insects will there be after one year?
    b) Write an expression to represent the number of insects after n months.

Solution. a) Number of insects after
    month 1: $1000 \times 2 = 2000$
    month 2: $1000 \times 2 \times 2 = 1000 \times 2^2$, or 4000
    month 3: $1000 \times 2 \times 2 \times 2 = 100 \times 2^3$, or 8000
    .
    .
    .
    month 12: $1000 \times 2^{12} = 1000 \times 4096$, or 4 096 000
    There would be about four million insects.
   b) After n months, the number of insects would be 1000×2^n.

Compound Interest

Each November the federal government offers a new issue of Canada Savings Bonds for sale to the public. When you buy one of these bonds, you are actually loaning your money to the government. In return, the government pays you interest for the use of your money. With a Compound Interest Bond, the interest earned each year is added to the value of the bond. Then, in the following year this interest also earns interest. That is, the bond earns "interest on the interest". Interest calculated in this manner is called *compound interest*.

Suppose you buy a $500 Compound Interest Bond which has an interest rate of 9%. You can calculate its value each year as follows:

1st year: Interest earned: $500.00 × 0.09 = $45.00
Value of bond after 1st year: $500.00 + $45.00 = $545.00
2nd year: Interest earned: $545.00 × 0.09 = $49.05
Value of bond after 2nd year: $545.00 + $49.05 = $594.05
3rd year: Interest earned: $594.05 × 0.09 = $53.46
Value of bond after 3rd year: $594.05 + $53.46 = $647.51

If the value at the beginning of any year is P, then:
- the interest earned during the year is $0.09P$
- the value of the bond at the end of the year is $P + 0.09P$, or $1.09P$.

$$\frac{\text{Value of bond at the}}{\text{end of any year}} = \frac{\text{Value at the beginning}}{\text{of the year}} \times 1.09$$

Using this principle, we can obtain a formula for the value of the bond after n years.

Value, in dollars, at the end of:

year 1: $500(1.09)$
year 2: $500(1.09)(1.09) = 500(1.09)^2$, or 594.05
year 3: $500(1.09)(1.09)(1.09) = 500(1.09)^3$, or 647.51

. .
. .
. .

year n: $500(1.09)^n$

In the above calculations, we assumed that interest is credited once each year. We say that the interest is *compounded annually*. The same pattern occurs when any amount of money is invested at a given interest rate, compounded annually, for a given number of years.

When an amount of money P (the principal) is invested at an interest rate i, compounded annually, the accumulated amount A after n years is given by the formula:
$A = P(1 + i)^n$

Example 3. Find the accumulated amount of $2000 invested at 10.5% compounded annually for 10 years.

Solution. Use the formula $A = P(1 + i)^n$ $P = 2000$

$$A = 2000(1.105)^{10}$$ $i = 0.105$

$$\doteq 2000(2.714\ 080\ 8)$$ $n = 10$

$$\doteq 5428.16$$

The accumulated amount is $5428.16.

EXERCISES 2-1

Ⓐ

1. Write as a power.
   a) $2 \times 2 \times 2 \times 2 \times 2 \times 2 \times 2$ b) $a \times a \times a \times a \times a \times a \times a \times a$
   c) $\left(-\dfrac{3}{4}\right)\left(-\dfrac{3}{4}\right)\left(-\dfrac{3}{4}\right)\left(-\dfrac{3}{4}\right)\left(-\dfrac{3}{4}\right)$ d) $(3x)(3x)(3x)(3x)$

2. Simplify.
   a) $6^2 + 8^2$ b) $(6 + 8)^2$ c) $(-3)^3 - 5^2$
   d) $(-1)^5 + (-2)^3$ e) $2(-1)^4 + 5(-3)^2$ f) $3(2)^3 - 2(3)^2$

3. Find, using a calculator.
   a) 3^7 b) 5^6 c) $(1.2)^4$ d) π^3 e) 7^{12} f) 2^{30}

4. Evaluate for: i) $n = 3$ ii) $n = 6$.
   a) 100×2^n b) 100×3^n c) $100 \times (0.5)^n$
   d) $5000 \times (0.8)^n$ e) $25 \times (0.75)^n$ f) $1.8 \times (1.15)^n$

5. A hive contains 100 bees. If the population doubles every month:
   a) which expression represents the number of bees after 5 months?
      i) 100×5^2 ii) 100×2^5 iii) $(100 \times 2)^5$ iv) $(100 \times 5)^2$
   b) how many bees are there after: i) 3 months   ii) 7 months?

Ⓑ

6. Express the first number as a power of the second.
   a) 27, 3   b) 125, 5   c) $-32, -2$ d) $81, -3$ e) 2.0736, 1.2

7. Which is the greater number?
   a) 2^7 or 5^3 b) 3^4 or 4^3 c) 3^6 or 9^3 d) 2^{10} or 10^3

8. Arrange from greatest to least.
   a) $3^3, 2^3, 4^2, 7^2, 3^2$ b) $(-3)^4, 2^7, (-5)^3, (-2)^8, (-2)^9$

9. Find each accumulated amount, compounded annually.
   a) $1000 for 6 years at 7%   b) $500 for 20 years at 9%
   c) $215 for 3 years at 10%   d) $720 for 8 years at 7.5%

10. Find the value of a $1000 Canada Savings Compound Interest Bond at 10.25% after: a) 3 years   b) 5 years   c) 8 years.

11. A person 20 years old deposits $1000 in an account that accumulates at 12% compounded annually. Find the accumulated amount when the person is 65 years old.

12. A donor gave $75 000 to a town council stipulating that it was to be invested for 10 years and the accumulated amount used to enlarge the public library. If the money earned 8% interest compounded annually, how much was available to spend on the library?

13. If a cottage, originally bought for $30 000, appreciates at the rate of 7% per year, what is it worth after:
    a) 5 years   b) 12 years   c) *n* years?

14. If the rate of inflation is 8% per year, how much would you expect to pay for a loaf of bread now priced at 89¢ in:
    a) 3 years   b) 5 years   c) 10 years?

15. The table shows the population of some of the world's largest cities and their approximate annual growth rate. Assuming that these growth rates are maintained, estimate the population of each city in the year:
    a) 2000   b) 2025.

City	Population in millions (1985)	Annual growth rate
Mexico City	16	4.0%
Lagos	5	4.1%
New York	15	0.5%
Tokyo	17	0.1%
Delhi	7	3.2%
Calcutta	11	3.0%

16. Radium-226 is a radioactive substance with a halflife of 1600 years. This means that over this period half the atoms in a sample will have decayed to form other substances.
    a) What percent of radium-226 remains after: i) 3200 years   ii) 6400 years?
    b) Write an expression for the percent of radium-226 remaining after *n* years.

17. A pump removes 10% of the air in a tank each minute.
    a) What percent of the air is left after: i) 1 min   ii) 2 min   iii) 20 min?
    b) How long would it take to reduce the air to: i) 50%   ii) 10%?
    c) Write an expression to represent the percent of air remaining after *n* minutes.

18. If a ball is dropped from a height of 2.5 m and allowed to bounce freely, the height *h* metres to which it bounces is given by the formula $h = 2.5(0.8)^n$, where *n* is the number of bounces.
    a) What height does the ball reach after:
       i) the third bounce   ii) the tenth bounce?
    b) After what bounce does the ball reach a height of approximately 0.5 m?

19. Each year, the value of a car depreciates to 70% of its value the previous year. If a car was bought new for $10 000:
    a) find its value after 5 years to the nearest $100
    b) write an expression to represent its value after *n* years.

2-2 REVIEW: EXPONENT LAWS FOR POSITIVE INTEGRAL EXPONENTS

Is there life anywhere else in the universe, or are we alone? That life does exist elsewhere in our galaxy is not beyond the bounds of possibility. Frank Drake of Cornell University has even developed an equation to estimate the number of extraterrestrial technological civilizations (ETCs) that exist at any moment. His equation is:

$$\begin{array}{c}\text{Number of ETCs}\\\text{at any moment}\end{array} = \begin{array}{c}\text{Number of ETCs}\\\text{that ever existed}\end{array} \times \frac{\text{Average lifetime of such a civilization}}{\text{Age of the galaxy}}$$

For our galaxy, we have

$$\text{number of ETCs at any moment} = 10^7 \times \frac{10^6}{10^{10}}$$
$$= 10^3$$
$$= 1000$$

There is a possibility of 1000 planets possessing intelligent life. We are presently trying to communicate with them.

This illustration involves two of the laws for operating with exponents. In this section, more of these laws will be reviewed and applied.

Example 1. Simplify.

  a) $x^5 \times x^2$ b) $m^7 \div m^3$ c) $(a^2)^3$ d) $(ab)^4$ e) $\left(\dfrac{x}{y}\right)^2$

Solution. In each case, the definition of an exponent, as indicating repeating factors, is used.

a) $x^5 \times x^2 = (x \times x \times x \times x \times x)(x \times x)$
$\qquad\qquad = x^7$

b) $m^7 \div m^3 = \dfrac{m \times m \times m \times m \times m \times m \times m}{m \times m \times m}$
$\qquad\qquad = m^4$

c) $(a^2)^3 = a^2 \times a^2 \times a^2$
$\qquad\quad = (a \times a)(a \times a)(a \times a)$
$\qquad\quad = a^6$

d) $(ab)^4 = ab \times ab \times ab \times ab$
$\qquad\quad = (a \times a \times a \times a)(b \times b \times b \times b)$
$\qquad\quad = a^4b^4$

e) $\left(\dfrac{x}{y}\right)^2 = \left(\dfrac{x}{y}\right)\left(\dfrac{x}{y}\right)$
$\qquad\quad = \dfrac{x^2}{y^2}$

The results of *Example 1* illustrate the following exponent laws, where m and n are positive integers.

Law 1. $x^m \times x^n = x^{m+n}$

Law 2. $x^m \div x^n = x^{m-n}$ $(m > n, x \neq 0)$

Law 3. $(x^m)^n = x^{mn}$

Law 4. $(xy)^n = x^n y^n$

Law 5. $\left(\dfrac{x}{y}\right)^n = \dfrac{x^n}{y^n}$ $(y \neq 0)$

The restrictions that m and n are positive integers and $m > n$ in the second law will be dropped in the next two sections.

The exponent laws may be used to simplify products and quotients involving powers.

Example 2. Simplify.

a) $\dfrac{(x^2)^3}{(2x)^2}$

b) $(a^m b^3)^n (ab^n)^2$

Solution. a) $\dfrac{(x^2)^3}{(2x)^2} = \dfrac{x^6}{4x^2}$

$= \dfrac{x^{6-2}}{4}$

$= \dfrac{1}{4}x^4$

b) $(a^m b^3)^n (ab^n)^2 = a^{mn} b^{3n} \times a^2 b^{2n}$

$= a^{mn+2} b^{3n+2n}$

$= a^{mn+2} b^{5n}$

Example 3. If $x = m^3$ and $y = 2n^2$, write each expression in terms of m and n.

a) $2x^2 y^4$

b) $\left(\dfrac{3x^3 y^2}{2xy}\right)^3$

Solution. a) $2x^2 y^4 = 2(m^3)^2 (2n^2)^4$

$= 2m^6 \times 16n^8$

$= 32m^6 n^8$

b) Simplify the expression.

$\left(\dfrac{3x^3 y^2}{2xy}\right)^3 = \left(\dfrac{3}{2}x^2 y\right)^3$

$= \dfrac{27}{8}x^6 y^3$

Substitute.

$= \dfrac{27}{8}(m^3)^6 (2n^2)^3$

$= \dfrac{27}{8}m^{18} \times 8n^6$

$= 27m^{18} n^6$

EXERCISES 2-2

Ⓐ

1. Simplify.
   a) $x^9 \times x^{23}$
   b) $m^{17} \div m^7$
   c) $y^4 \times y^{11}$
   d) $a^{12} \div a^3$
   e) $c^8 \times c^{15} \times c^4$
   f) $x^{32} \div x^8 \div x^4$

2. Simplify.
   a) $9x^5 \times 7x^{12}$
   b) $75m^{18} \div 15m^6$
   c) $(-2n^3)^2$
   d) $-24a^{20} \div 6a^{10}$
   e) $12y^9 \times 8y^{12}$
   f) $(-3c^4)^5$

3. Simplify.
   a) $a^7b^4 \times a^9b^3$
   b) $m^{11}n^8 \div m^5n^4$
   c) $-7c^{12}d^5 \times 6c^8d^6$
   d) $(xy^2)^3$
   e) $36a^{15}b^{12} \div 9a^5b^4$
   f) $(x^2y^3)^2(x^2y)^4$

Ⓑ

4. Simplify.
   a) $(x^3)^2(3x)^2$
   b) $(2a^3)^4(5a^2)^3$
   c) $(4m^3n^5)^3(-3m^2n^6)^3$
   d) $\left(\dfrac{12x^3y^2}{9xy}\right)\left(\dfrac{18x^5y^3}{4x^2y^2}\right)$
   e) $\dfrac{(a^2b^3)^4}{(ab^2)^3}$
   f) $\left(\dfrac{24c^8d^5}{-8c^2d}\right)\left(\dfrac{15c^3d^9}{18cd^5}\right)$

5. Evaluate for $x = 2$ and $y = -1$.
   a) $(x^3y^2)(x^2y^4)$
   b) $x^8y^{12} \div x^4y^4$
   c) $(3x^4y)(5x^2y^6)$
   d) $\dfrac{(-6x^5y^2)(8x^3y)}{(4x^2)^2}$
   e) $\dfrac{9x^3y^5 \times 8x^4y^3}{18x^5y^7}$
   f) $\dfrac{(4x^3y^2)^2(3x^5y^9)^3}{(6x^7y^2)^2}$

6. Simplify.
   a) $(x^a)^3(x^{a+1})^2$
   b) $(3^m)^2(3^{m+4})$
   c) $(c^{2a})^3(c^{a+2})^4$
   d) $\dfrac{(2a^{3x})(3a^{2x-1})^4}{(6a^x)^2}$
   e) $\dfrac{(r^{5x})^{2y}}{(r^{xy})^4}$
   f) $\dfrac{(x^{2m}y^{n+1})^3}{x^{3m+1}y^n}$

7. Express as a power of 2.
   a) $2^n \times 4^n$
   b) $16^n \div 2^n$
   c) $(2^n)(4^{n+1})(8^{n+2})$
   d) $8^{3n} \div 4^{2n}$
   e) $\dfrac{(4^n)(2^{n+3})}{8^{n+1}}$
   f) $(4^{3n+1})(2^{n+5}) \div 16^{n+1}$

8. a) Find, using a calculator.   i) 2^{10} ii) 5^{10} iii) 6^9
   b) Use the results of part a) to estimate the value of each power.
      i) 2^{13} ii) 2^{50} iii) 5^{20} iv) 5^{12} v) 6^{27} vi) 6^{11}

9. If $x = 3m^2$ and $y = m^3$, write each expression in terms of m.
   a) $2x^2y$
   b) $(x^3y^2)^2$
   c) $5x^3y^4 \div (3xy)^2$
   d) $\left(\dfrac{5x^3y^2}{2xy}\right)^2$

10. If $x = a^2$ and $y = 2b^3$, write each expression in terms of a and b.
    a) $3x^3y^2$
    b) $(2x^2y^3)^2$
    c) $\dfrac{5x^4y^3}{2x^2y}$
    d) $\left(\dfrac{3x^7y^4}{6x^4y^2}\right)^2$

11. If $m = x^a$, write each expression in terms of x and a.

    a) m^2 b) m^a c) $(mx)^2 \left(\dfrac{m}{x} \right)^3$

12. Some bacteria reproduce by splitting into two new cells about every half hour.

    a) If a single bacterium began reproducing at noon, about how many bacteria would be present at:

        i) 3 P.M.   ii) 6 P.M.   iii) midnight   iv) noon the next day?

    b) Write an expression which represents the number of bacteria present after n hours.

    c) Give reasons why the growth of bacteria must ultimately slow down.

Ⓒ

13. Given $b = a^3$ and $c = a^5$

    a) Write each expression as a power of a.   i) b^2c ii) b^3c

    b) Write each expression as a product of powers of b and c.   i) a^{13} ii) a^{16}

    c) Show that if x is any integer greater than 7, a^x can be expressed in one of the forms b^m, c^n, or b^mc^n, where m and n are natural numbers.

14. Simplify, without using a calculator.

    a) $\dfrac{5 \times 2^{12} - 2^{10}}{2^6}$ b) $\dfrac{2^{12} + 2^{15}}{2^{12} + 2^{14}}$

15. Show that each equation is true.

    a) $2^x + 2^{x+1} = 3 \times 2^x$ b) $2^x + 2^{x+1} + 2^{x+2} = 7 \times 2^x$

16. Find the exact value of each power.

    a) 2^{30} b) 5^{12} c) 3^{20}

 INVESTIGATE

To find how accurately a calculator or computer performs successive calculations:

1. Enter the number 1.000 000 1 in a calculator and press the $\boxed{x^2}$ key 27 times. Compare your result with those of students using different calculators.

2. Use a computer to square 1.000 000 1 twenty-seven times and compare the result with those above.

3. The correct result, to 8 significant digits, is 674 530.47. Which calculator or computer gave:

    i)   the most accurate result   ii)   the least accurate result?

4. The procedure of squaring 1.000 000 1 twenty-seven times is equivalent to evaluating $(1.000\ 000\ 1)^n$ for a certain value of n. What is the value of n?

2-3 REVIEW: EXTENDING THE EXPONENT LAWS: INTEGRAL EXPONENTS

Powers such as 5^0 and 2^{-3} cannot be defined in terms of repeated factors because the exponents are not positive integers. If the exponent law $x^m \div x^n$ $(m > n)$, is extended to the cases where $m = n$ and $m < n$, we can give meaning to expressions such as 5^0 and 2^{-3}. By extending the law:

$$\frac{5^2}{5^2} = 5^{2-2}$$

$$= 5^0$$

Since $\dfrac{5^2}{5^2} = 1$

then $5^0 = 1$

$$\frac{2^4}{2^7} = 2^{4-7}$$

$$= 2^{-3}$$

Since $\dfrac{2^4}{2^7} = \dfrac{\cancel{2} \times \cancel{2} \times \cancel{2} \times \cancel{2}}{\cancel{2} \times \cancel{2} \times \cancel{2} \times \cancel{2} \times 2 \times 2 \times 2}$

$$= \frac{1}{2^3}$$

then $2^{-3} = \dfrac{1}{2^3}$

These examples suggest that x^0 should be defined to equal 1, and that x^{-n} should be defined as the reciprocal of x^n.

$$x^0 = 1 \quad (x \neq 0) \qquad x^{-n} = \frac{1}{x^n} \quad (n \in I, x \neq 0)$$

ϵ means "is a member of".

Example 1. Find.

    a) 3^{-4} b) $(0.1)^{-3}$ c) $\left(\dfrac{2}{3}\right)^{-2}$ d) $x^{-1} + y^{-1}$

Solution.   a) $3^{-4} = \dfrac{1}{3^4}$

$$= \frac{1}{81}$$

b) $(0.1)^{-3} = \left(\dfrac{1}{10}\right)^{-3}$

$$= \frac{1}{\left(\dfrac{1}{10}\right)^3}$$

$$= \frac{1}{\dfrac{1}{1000}}$$

$$= 1000$$

c) $\left(\dfrac{2}{3}\right)^{-2} = \dfrac{1}{\left(\dfrac{2}{3}\right)^2}$

$$= \frac{1}{\dfrac{4}{9}}$$

$$= \frac{9}{4}$$

d) $x^{-1} + y^{-1} = \dfrac{1}{x} + \dfrac{1}{y}$

$$= \frac{y + x}{xy}$$

Many problems and formulas concerning growth or decay may involve negative exponents.

Example 2. The number of insects in a colony doubles every month. If there are now 1000 insects in the colony, about how many were in the colony three months ago?

Solution. Let x be the number of insects 3 months ago. Then, after 3 successive doublings the colony grows to 1000 insects.

$$x \times 2^3 = 1000$$
$$x = \frac{1000}{2^3}$$
$$= 125$$

There were about 125 insects in the colony 3 months ago.

The solution to *Example 2* can be calculated a different way.
From *Example 2* in Section 2-1, the number of insects after n months is

1000×2^n. Substitute -3 for n to obtain $1000 \times 2^{-3} = 1000 \times \dfrac{1}{2^3}$

$$= \frac{1000}{8}$$
$$= 125$$

EXERCISES 2-3

(A)

1. Find.
   a) 9^0 b) 3^{-2} c) 2^{-3} .   d) $(-7)^0$ e) $(-2)^{-3}$ f) $(-3)^{-2}$

2. Find.
   a) $\left(\dfrac{3}{4}\right)^0$ b) $\left(\dfrac{1}{5}\right)^{-2}$ c) $\left(\dfrac{2}{3}\right)^{-2}$ d) $\left(\dfrac{7}{4}\right)^2$ e) $\left(-\dfrac{1}{2}\right)^{-3}$ f) $\left(-\dfrac{3}{2}\right)^{-1}$

3. Find, using a calculator. Give the results to 4 decimal places.
   a) 2^{-3} b) $(1.7)^{-4}$ c) $(2.3)^{-3}$ d) $(1.01)^{-12}$ e) $(0.4)^{-5}$ f) $(1.25)^{-7}$

4. Simplify, using a calculator.
   a) $100(1.05)^8$ b) $100(1.02)^{-10}$ c) $450(1.15)^7$ d) $750(1.09)^{-5}$

5. Evaluate to 3 decimal places for: i) $n = -2$ ii) $n = -5$.
   a) 3^n b) 10^n c) $(1.5)^n$ d) $(1.06)^n$ e) $(1.18)^n$ f) $(0.92)^n$

6. A colony of 10 000 bees doubles in number every month.
   a) Which expression represents the number of bees 3 months ago?
      i) $10\,000 \times 2^3$ ii) $10\,000 \times 3^{-2}$ iii) $10\,000 \times 2^{-3}$
   b) How many bees were there: i) 2 months ago   ii) 5 months ago?

Ⓑ

7. Simplify.

a) $3^2 - 3^{-2}$ b) $(-2)^{-3} + 3^{-2}$ c) $\dfrac{3^{-1} - 3^{-2}}{(3^{-1})(3^{-2})}$ d) $\dfrac{7^0}{(4^{-2} - 2^{-3})^{-1}}$

8. Evaluate for $x = 2$ and $y = -3$.

a) x^{-3} b) y^{-2} c) $(xy)^{-2}$ d) 5^x e) 7^{-x} f) $(x^y)(y^x)$

9. Evaluate for $x = -2$ and $y = 5$.

a) $2^x + y^{-1}$ b) $3^{-x} - y$ c) $2x^{-1} + 5y^{-1}$ d) $(3x^{-1} - y^{-1})^{-2}$

10. Which number of each pair is the greater?

a) $7^{-1}, 7^{-2}$ b) $\left(\dfrac{5}{3}\right)^{-2}, \left(\dfrac{3}{5}\right)^{-2}$ c) $\left(-\dfrac{1}{3}\right)^{-5}, \left(-\dfrac{1}{5}\right)^{-3}$ d) $10^{-1}, (0.1)^2$

11. In how many different ways can you simplify 2×5^{-3} using a calculator?

12. Simplify.

a) $x^7 \times x^{-12}$ b) $m^4 \div m^6$ c) $-24c^5d^3 \div 4c^8d^{-3}$ d) $\dfrac{12m^5n^{-2} \times 5m^{-11}n^6}{15m^3n^{-4}}$

13. Simplify, and check with a calculator.

a) $12^{-11} \times 12^9 \div 12^{-4}$ b) $(7^8)^{-2} \div 7^4 \times 7^{11}$ c) $2^5 \times 3^4 \times 3^{-5} \times 2^{-4}$

14. Evaluate for $a = 4$ and $b = -3$.

a) $a^3 \times a^{-2}$ b) $a^7b^2 \div a^5b^4$ c) $2a^{-3}b^2 \times 7a^2b^{-1}$

d) $45a^{-2}b^5 \div 9a^{-4}b^3$ e) a^{b+1} f) $(3b^a)^0 - \left(\dfrac{a}{b}\right)^{-1}$

15. A radioactive element has a halflife of one week. How much of a 1000 g sample of the element:
   a) will there be in i) 3 weeks   ii) 7 weeks?
   b) was there i) 4 weeks ago   ii) 9 weeks ago?

16. What amount of money invested at 12% compounded annually will grow to $2500 in 4 years?

Ⓒ

17. Given $b = a^3$ and $c = a^7$
   a) Write each expression as a power of a.   i) b^3c^{-1} ii) $b^{-2}c$
   b) Write each expression in the form b^mc^n, where m and n are integers.
      i) a^{11} ii) a^0 iii) a^{-1}
   c) Show that if x is any integer, a^x can always be expressed in the form b^mc^n, where m and n are integers.

18. Find the exact value of each power.   a) 2^{-8} b) 2^{-10} c) 25^{-4}

2-4 EXTENDING THE EXPONENT LAWS: RATIONAL EXPONENTS

The exponent laws were first established for positive integral exponents. They were later extended to all integral exponents using this definition of a negative exponent:

$$x^{-n} = \frac{1}{x^n}.$$

Finally, in 1655, John Wallis completed the extension of the exponent laws to all fractional and therefore all rational exponents.

To give meanings to such expressions as $3^{\frac{1}{2}}$ and $5^{-\frac{1}{3}}$, the exponent law $x^m \times x^n = x^{m+n}$ is extended to cases where m and n are rational numbers. By extending the law:

$$3^{\frac{1}{2}} \times 3^{\frac{1}{2}} = 3^{\frac{1}{2}+\frac{1}{2}} \qquad\qquad 5^{-\frac{1}{3}} \times 5^{-\frac{1}{3}} \times 5^{-\frac{1}{3}} = 5^{-\frac{1}{3}-\frac{1}{3}-\frac{1}{3}}$$
$$= 3 \qquad\qquad\qquad\qquad\qquad = 5^{-1}$$

Since $\sqrt{3} \times \sqrt{3} = 3$ $\qquad\qquad\qquad\qquad\qquad\qquad = \dfrac{1}{5}$

then $\qquad\quad 3^{\frac{1}{2}} = \sqrt{3}$

Since $\qquad \sqrt[3]{\dfrac{1}{5}} \times \sqrt[3]{\dfrac{1}{5}} \times \sqrt[3]{\dfrac{1}{5}} = \dfrac{1}{5}$

then $\qquad\qquad\qquad\qquad 5^{-\frac{1}{3}} = \sqrt[3]{\dfrac{1}{5}}$

$$= \frac{1}{\sqrt[3]{5}}$$

These examples suggest that $x^{\frac{1}{n}}$ should be defined as the nth root of x, and $x^{-\frac{1}{n}}$ as its reciprocal.

$$x^{\frac{1}{n}} = \sqrt[n]{x} \qquad n \in N \qquad x \geq 0 \text{ if } n \text{ is even.}$$

$$x^{-\frac{1}{n}} = \frac{1}{\sqrt[n]{x}} \qquad n \in N, x \neq 0 \qquad x > 0 \text{ if } n \text{ is even.}$$

Example 1. Find.

a) $49^{\frac{1}{2}}$ b) $(-8)^{\frac{1}{3}}$ c) $16^{-\frac{1}{4}}$ d) $(-64)^{-\frac{1}{3}}$

Solution.   a) $49^{\frac{1}{2}} = \sqrt{49}$ b) $(-8)^{\frac{1}{3}} = \sqrt[3]{-8}$
$$= 7 \qquad\qquad\qquad\qquad\qquad\qquad = -2$$

c) $16^{-\frac{1}{4}} = \dfrac{1}{16^{\frac{1}{4}}}$ d) $(-64)^{-\frac{1}{3}} = \dfrac{1}{(-64)^{\frac{1}{3}}}$

$$= \frac{1}{\sqrt[4]{16}} \qquad\qquad\qquad\qquad\qquad = \frac{1}{\sqrt[3]{-64}}$$

$$= \frac{1}{2} \qquad\qquad\qquad\qquad\qquad\qquad = -\frac{1}{4}$$

Example 2. Express each root as a power.

a) $\sqrt{2}$ b) $\sqrt[3]{36}$ c) $\dfrac{1}{\sqrt[3]{5}}$ d) $\dfrac{1}{\sqrt[4]{11}}$

Solution. a) $\sqrt{2} = 2^{\frac{1}{2}}$ b) $\sqrt[3]{36} = 36^{\frac{1}{3}}$ c) $\dfrac{1}{\sqrt[3]{5}} = 5^{-\frac{1}{3}}$ d) $\dfrac{1}{\sqrt[4]{11}} = 11^{-\frac{1}{4}}$

Since $36 = 6^2$, the expression in *Example 2b)* may be written in other ways.

$$\sqrt[3]{36} = \sqrt[3]{6^2} \qquad \text{or} \qquad \sqrt[3]{36} = \sqrt[3]{6} \times \sqrt[3]{6}$$
$$= (6^2)^{\frac{1}{3}} \qquad\qquad\qquad\qquad = 6^{\frac{1}{3}} \times 6^{\frac{1}{3}}$$
$$\qquad\qquad\qquad\qquad\qquad\qquad = (6^{\frac{1}{3}})^2$$

Since we have extended the exponent laws to hold for rational numbers, we may write each of the above results as $6^{\frac{2}{3}}$. This suggests the following definition for $x^{\frac{m}{n}}$, where n is a positive integer.

$$x^{\frac{m}{n}} = \sqrt[n]{x^m} = \left(\sqrt[n]{x}\right)^m \qquad x \geq 0 \text{ if } n \text{ is even.}$$

Example 3. Find.

a) $25^{\frac{3}{2}}$ b) $(-8)^{\frac{2}{3}}$ c) $81^{0.75}$ d) $\left(-\dfrac{1}{8}\right)^{-\frac{2}{3}}$

Solution.

a) $25^{\frac{3}{2}} = (\sqrt{25})^3$ b) $(-8)^{\frac{2}{3}} = (\sqrt[3]{-8})^2$
$\qquad\quad = 5^3 \qquad\qquad\qquad\qquad\quad = (-2)^2$
$\qquad\quad = 125 \qquad\qquad\qquad\qquad\quad = 4$

c) $81^{0.75} = 81^{\frac{3}{4}}$ d) $\left(-\dfrac{1}{8}\right)^{-\frac{2}{3}} = \dfrac{1}{\left(-\dfrac{1}{8}\right)^{\frac{2}{3}}}$
$\qquad\quad = (\sqrt[4]{81})^3$
$\qquad\quad = 3^3 \qquad\qquad\qquad\qquad\qquad = \dfrac{1}{\left(\sqrt[3]{-\dfrac{1}{8}}\right)^2}$
$\qquad\quad = 27$
$\qquad\qquad\qquad\qquad\qquad\qquad\qquad = \dfrac{1}{\dfrac{1}{4}}$
$\qquad\qquad\qquad\qquad\qquad\qquad\qquad = 4$

Problems and formulas may involve fractional exponents.

Example 4. The height h metres of a Douglas fir tree can be estimated from the formula $h = 34.1 \times d^{0.67}$, where d metres is the diameter at its base. Estimate the height of Canada's largest tree, which has a base diameter of 4.35 m.

Solution. Substitute 4.35 for d in the formula.

$h = 34.1 \times (4.35)^{0.67}$
$\quad \doteq 91.3$

Canada's largest tree has a height of about 91 m.

EXERCISES 2-4

Ⓐ

1. Find.
   a) $64^{\frac{1}{2}}$ b) $36^{\frac{1}{2}}$ c) $8^{\frac{1}{3}}$ d) $32^{\frac{1}{5}}$ e) $400^{0.5}$ f) $-125^{\frac{1}{3}}$

2. Express as a power.
   a) $\sqrt{7}$ b) $\sqrt{135}$ c) $\sqrt[3]{12}$ d) $\sqrt[4]{21}$ e) $\sqrt{29}$ f) $\sqrt[5]{19}$

3. Find.
   a) $8^{\frac{2}{3}}$ b) $16^{\frac{3}{2}}$ c) $36^{\frac{3}{2}}$ d) $27^{\frac{2}{3}}$ e) $100^{0.5}$ f) $16^{0.75}$

4. Find.
   a) $4^{2.5}$ b) $(-8)^{\frac{5}{3}}$ c) $81^{1.5}$ d) $32^{0.6}$ e) $(0.16)^{1.5}$ f) $(-27)^{\frac{4}{3}}$

5. Find.
   a) $9^{-\frac{1}{2}}$ b) $8^{-\frac{1}{3}}$ c) $25^{-\frac{1}{2}}$ d) $16^{-\frac{1}{4}}$ e) $81^{-0.5}$ f) $81^{-0.25}$

6. Find.
   a) $27^{-\frac{2}{3}}$ b) $16^{-1.5}$ c) $81^{\frac{3}{4}}$ d) $32^{-0.4}$ e) $8^{\frac{4}{3}}$ f) $16^{-\frac{3}{4}}$

7. Find.
   a) $\left(\dfrac{9}{16}\right)^{\frac{1}{2}}$ b) $\left(\dfrac{1}{9}\right)^{-\frac{3}{2}}$ c) $\left(-\dfrac{1}{32}\right)^{0.8}$ d) $\left(\dfrac{16}{54}\right)^{-\frac{2}{3}}$ e) $\left(\dfrac{81}{16}\right)^{-0.75}$ f) $\left(\dfrac{49}{25}\right)^{\frac{3}{2}}$

8. Find with a calculator, giving the results to 4 decimal places.
   a) $10^{\frac{1}{4}}$ b) $30^{0.7}$ c) $7^{\frac{2}{3}}$ d) $15^{1.4}$ e) $\sqrt[8]{2.17}$ f) $\sqrt[1.5]{6.4}$

9. The number of trout in a stocked lake is given by the expression $1800(1.12)^n$, where n is the number of months since the start of the trout season.
   a) How many trout will there be in:
      i) 1.25 months   ii) 3.4 months?
   b) How many trout were there:
      i) 0.5 month before the season opened   ii) 2.8 months before the season opened?

Ⓑ

10. Express as a power.
    a) $(\sqrt[3]{10})^2$ b) $(\sqrt[4]{12})^5$ c) $(\sqrt[7]{36})^3$ d) $(\sqrt[5]{94})^{17}$ e) $\dfrac{1}{(\sqrt[3]{25})^4}$ f) $\dfrac{1}{(\sqrt{52})^7}$

11. Express the first number as a power of the second.

    a) $(\sqrt[3]{2})^7, 2$ b) $\sqrt[4]{6^3}, 6$ c) $\sqrt{8^3}, 2$ d) $(\sqrt[5]{25})^4, 5$ e) $\sqrt[7]{49^5}, 7$ f) $(\sqrt{81})^4, 3$

12. A cube has a volume of V cubic centimetres. Write each measurement as a power of V.

    a) the length of an edge   b) the area of a face

13. Simplify.

    a) $8^{\frac{1}{3}} \times 9^{\frac{1}{2}}$ b) $25^{\frac{3}{2}} \times 8^{\frac{2}{3}}$ c) $81^{\frac{1}{4}} \times 27^{\frac{2}{3}}$ d) $32^{\frac{2}{5}} \times 243^{\frac{2}{5}}$ e) $64^{\frac{2}{3}} \times 125^{\frac{1}{3}}$

14. Simplify.

    a) $(\sqrt[4]{9})^2$ b) $25^{\frac{1}{2}} - 8^{\frac{4}{3}}$ c) $\sqrt[3]{2^{-6}}$ d) $9^{\frac{1}{2}} - \left(\frac{1}{8}\right)^{-\frac{2}{3}}$

    e) $(8^{\frac{1}{3}} + 27^{\frac{1}{3}} + 64^{\frac{1}{3}})^{\frac{1}{2}}$ f) $\left(\sqrt[3]{125^{\frac{1}{3}} + 32^{\frac{4}{5}} + 36^{\frac{1}{2}}}\right)^2$

15. If $10^{0.3} \doteq 1.995$, evaluate each power without using a calculator.

    a) $10^{1.3}$ b) $10^{2.3}$ c) $10^{-0.7}$ d) $10^{-1.7}$

16. Evaluate for $x = 64$.

    a) $(x^{\frac{1}{2}})(x^{\frac{1}{3}})$ b) $x^{\frac{1}{2}} \div x^{\frac{1}{3}}$ c) $(x^{-\frac{2}{3}})(x^{\frac{3}{2}})$ d) $(x^{-\frac{1}{2}})^3$ e) $(x^{-\frac{4}{3}})^{-\frac{1}{2}}$

17. The population of a colony of birds triples every 10 years. At the present time there are about 250 birds in the colony.

    a) Which number represents the number of birds in the colony after n years?
       i) 250×3^{10n} ii) $250 \times n^{30}$ iii) $250 \times 3^{\frac{n}{10}}$ iv) $250 \times 3^{\frac{10}{n}}$

    b) About how many birds will be in the colony:
       i) 1 year from now   ii) 3 years from now   iii) 5 years from now?

    c) About how many birds were in the colony:
       i) 1 year ago   ii) 3 years ago   iii) 5 years ago?

18. There are approximately 500 wolves in Algonquin Provincial Park. Under ideal conditions this population would double every 35 years.

    a) What is the possible wolf population of the Park in:
       i) 10 years   ii) 25 years   iii) 50 years?

    b) How many wolves were in the Park: i) 10 years ago   ii) 20 years ago?

    c) Do you think that the wolves in Algonquin Park live under ''ideal'' conditions?

19. The skin area A square metres of a person's body can be estimated from the formula $A = 0.025h^{0.42}w^{0.5}$, where h is the person's height in centimetres and w the mass in kilograms.

    a) Estimate the skin area of a person 170 cm tall who has a mass of 80 kg.

    b) Estimate the area of your skin.

Ⓒ

20. When a satellite is h kilometres above the Earth, the period T minutes, or the time for one complete revolution is given by the formula
    $T = 1.66 \times 10^{-4}(6370 + h)^{1.5}$.

    a) Calculate the period of a satellite at an altitude of: i) 200 km   ii) 600 km.

b) If the satellite has the same angular velocity as the Earth, it appears to be stationary.
   i) What is the period of such a satellite?
   ii) What is the altitude of a "stationary" satellite?

21. A filter 1 cm thick transmits 90% of the light falling on it.
    a) What percent of the light will be transmitted by a filter of the same material of thickness: i) 2 cm   ii) 3 cm   iii) n centimetres?
    b) Show that the percent of light transmitted by a filter 0.5 cm thick is $100(0.9)^{0.5}$.
    c) What percent of the light will pass through a filter of thickness:
       i) 0.7 cm   ii) 1.3 cm?
    d) What thickness of filter transmits: i) 75% of the light   ii) 50% of the light?

22. a) Three students discussed the meaning of the statement $(2.3)^{4.7} \doteq 50.13$. Their discussion went as follows:
    Andy: "It means 2.3 multiplied by itself 4.7 times is equal to about 50.13."
    Jack: "In an expression like 2^4, 2 is multiplied by itself three times, not four. Therefore the statement means 2.3 multiplied by itself 3.7 times equals about 50.13."
    Renée: "No! You can't multiply a number by itself a fractional number of times. $(2.3)^{4.7}$ may be written $(2.3)^{\frac{47}{10}}$. That is, 47 factors each equal to the tenth root of 2.3 multiplied together is about 50.13."
    Which student is correct?
    b) Evaluate each expression and give its meaning.   i) $(3.8)^{2.6}$ ii) $\sqrt[3.2]{22.5}$

 INVESTIGATE

A number of interesting investigations are associated with the use of rational exponents.

1. a) Find.   i) 3^7 ii) $(-3)^7$ iii) $(-4)^{\frac{1}{2}}$ iv) $(-243)^{\frac{1}{5}}$
   b) Use a calculator or computer to evaluate the expressions in part a) and compare the results.

2. Most scientific calculators can obtain square roots in two ways.
   • by using the $\boxed{\sqrt{}}$ key
   • by using the sequence of keys $\boxed{y^x}$ 0.5 $\boxed{=}$
   Find the square roots of different numbers by both methods and compare the results. Is there any difference in the time it takes to do the calculations?

3. The definition of a power with a rational exponent, $x^{\frac{m}{n}}$, gives two expressions: $\left(\sqrt[n]{x}\right)^m$ and $\sqrt[n]{x^m}$. Evaluate each expression in these two ways and compare the results.
   i) $(-64)^{\frac{2}{3}}$ ii) $(-64)^{\frac{4}{6}}$

4. Write a report of your findings.

PROBLEM SOLVING

The Lunes of Hippocrates

"The scope of problem-solving activities is as wide as one wishes to make it."

Christine Taylor

In ancient Greece, about 440 B.C., Hippocrates of Chios made a famous discovery. He found a way to calculate the areas of certain regions enclosed by circular arcs. These regions are called *lunes*. The problem below is similar to the problems he solved.

In the diagram, the quarter-circular region AOB is called a *quadrant*. On AB as a diameter, a semicircle is constructed. If r represents the radius OA, determine an expression for the area of the shaded lune.

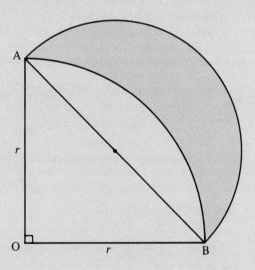

Understand the problem
- What is   a) lune?   b) a quadrant?

Think of a strategy
- Write expressions for the areas of the various regions on the diagram.

Carry out the strategy
- Since there is a right triangle, the Pythagorean Theorem may be needed.
- Form expressions in r for the areas of △AOB, the quadrant AOB, and the semicircle.
- Can you find a way to combine the regions to form the lune? If so, you can do the same thing with the expressions to find its area!

Look back
- Does the area of the lune equal the area of the triangle?
- The region between AB and the lune is called a *segment* of the circle. What is an expression for the area of the segment?

PROBLEMS

Ⓑ

1. Ann guessed that a jar in a store window contained 475 jelly beans. Bill guessed 455 beans, and Cory guessed 510. One guess was wrong by 20, another by 15, another by 40. How many jelly beans were in the jar?

2. A horse salesman sold horses to two customers. To his first customer he sold half his horses plus half a horse. To his second customer he sold half of his remaining horses plus half a horse. Both customers received whole horses, not half horses, and he had no horses left. How many horses did he start with?

3. How many non-congruent triangles can be drawn to join three vertices of a cube? Identify each triangle.

4. On side AC of an equilateral △ABC, two circular arcs are constructed, with centres B and the midpoint of AC. If the triangle has sides of length r, find an expression for the area of the shaded lune.

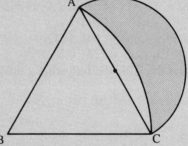

Ⓒ

5. a) Theresa programmed a computer to print out the exact answer to this multiplication problem: $1 \times 2 \times 3 \times \ldots \times 50$. How many zeros were at the end of the product?

   b) If n is any natural number, how could you find the number of zeros at the end of the product $1 \times 2 \times 3 \times \ldots \times n$?

6. C is any point on a circle with diameter AB. On sides AC and BC of △ABC, semicircles are drawn exterior to the triangle. Prove that the total area of the two shaded lunes is equal to the area of △ABC.

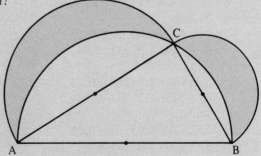

Ⓓ

7. The number 1210 has an unusual property. The first digit is the number of 0s in the number, the second digit is the number of 1s, the third digit the number of 2s, and the fourth digit the number of 3s.

   a) Find another 4-digit number with this property.

   b) Find other numbers with a similar property.

MATHEMATICS AROUND US

Measuring Air Pollution

The pollution generated by automobiles and industry in heavily populated areas occasionally becomes a danger to health. It is therefore important to have a measure of the amount of air pollution so that appropriate action can be taken before serious health problems develop.

In Ontario, an Air Pollution Index (API) is determined for certain areas of the province. This index depends on two quantities which are constantly being monitored:

CoH — the coefficient of haze, a measure of the suspended particles in the air;

SO_2 — the concentration of sulphur dioxide in parts per million.

Here is how the API is measured for three areas of Ontario.

Toronto: $0.2[30.5 \text{ CoH} + 126.0 \text{ SO}_2]^{1.35}$

Hamilton: $2.5[13.9 \text{ CoH} + 104.5 \text{ SO}_2]^{0.8}$

Sudbury: $1.84[11.0 \text{ CoH} + 161.0 \text{ SO}_2]^{0.87}$

To interpret the API, the following guide is used.

			Sources of pollution may be ordered to curtail operations.	Sources of pollution will be ordered to curtail operations.
Acceptable range	Warning range			

```
0                 32      50                        100
```

QUESTIONS

1. Calculate the API for each town.
   a) Toronto:
      i)   CoH 0.42, SO_2 0.13
      ii) CoH 1.3, SO_2 0.24
   b) Hamilton:
      i)   CoH 1.84, SO_2 0.24
      ii) CoH 2.2, SO_2 0.18
   c) Sudbury:
      i)   CoH 0.92, SO_2 0.36
      ii) CoH 1.6, SO_2 0.40

2. In Toronto, the highest API occurred at about the time of the Grey Cup game in 1962. Visibility on the playing field was so poor that it was necessary to complete the game on the following day. At the time, the values of CoH and SO_2 were about 2.7 and 0.44 respectively. Calculate the API for these values.

3. Suggest why there is a different formula for calculating the API for each city.

2-5 SIMPLIFYING EXPRESSIONS USING EXPONENT LAWS

The exponent laws may be used to simplify products, quotients, and roots involving powers with integral or rational exponents.

Example 1. Simplify.

a) $3^{\frac{1}{2}} \times 3^{\frac{5}{2}}$ b) $(-2^{\frac{2}{3}} \times 5^{-\frac{1}{2}})^6$ c) $(\sqrt[3]{2^8})^{-\frac{1}{2}}$

Solution.

a) $3^{\frac{1}{2}} \times 3^{\frac{5}{2}} = 3^{\frac{1}{2}+\frac{5}{2}}$
$= 3^3$
$= 27$

b) $(-2^{\frac{2}{3}} \times 5^{-\frac{1}{2}})^6$
$= (-2^{\frac{2}{3}})^6(5^{-\frac{1}{2}})^6$
$= (-2)^4(5^{-3})$
$= \dfrac{16}{125}$

c) $(\sqrt[3]{2^8})^{-\frac{1}{2}} = (2^{\frac{8}{3}})^{-\frac{1}{2}}$
$= 2^{-\frac{4}{3}}$
$= \dfrac{1}{2^{\frac{4}{3}}}$
$= \dfrac{1}{(\sqrt[3]{2})^4}$

Example 2. Simplify.

a) $\dfrac{x^2 y^{\frac{1}{2}}}{x^{-3} y}$ b) $(xy^{\frac{1}{2}})^{-3}(x^{-2}y)^{\frac{1}{2}}$ c) $\sqrt{(12x^5 y^{-3})(3xy^0)}$

Solution.

a) $\dfrac{x^2 y^{\frac{1}{2}}}{x^{-3} y}$
$= x^{2-(-3)} y^{\frac{1}{2}-1}$
$= x^5 y^{-\frac{1}{2}}$
$= \dfrac{x^5}{y^{\frac{1}{2}}}$

b) $(xy^{\frac{1}{2}})^{-3}(x^{-2}y)^{\frac{1}{2}}$
$= (x^{-3}y^{-\frac{3}{2}})(x^{-1}y^{\frac{1}{2}})$
$= x^{-4}y^{-1}$
$= \dfrac{1}{x^4 y}$

c) $\sqrt{(12x^5 y^{-3})(3xy^0)}$
$= (36x^6 y^{-3})^{\frac{1}{2}}$
$= 6x^3 y^{-\frac{3}{2}}$
$= \dfrac{6x^3}{y^{\frac{3}{2}}}$

Example 3. Expand and simplify.

a) $(2^{\frac{1}{2}} + 3^{\frac{1}{2}})(2^{\frac{1}{2}} - 3^{\frac{1}{2}})$ b) $(\sqrt[3]{a} + \sqrt[3]{a^{-1}})(\sqrt[3]{a} - \sqrt[3]{a^{-1}})$

Solution.

a) $(2^{\frac{1}{2}} + 3^{\frac{1}{2}})(2^{\frac{1}{2}} - 3^{\frac{1}{2}}) = 2^{\frac{1}{2}+\frac{1}{2}} - 2^{\frac{1}{2}} \times 3^{\frac{1}{2}} + 3^{\frac{1}{2}} \times 2^{\frac{1}{2}} - 3^{\frac{1}{2}+\frac{1}{2}}$
$= 2 - 6^{\frac{1}{2}} + 6^{\frac{1}{2}} - 3$
$= 2 - 3$
$= -1$

b) $(\sqrt[3]{a} + \sqrt[3]{a^{-1}})(\sqrt[3]{a} - \sqrt[3]{a^{-1}}) = (a^{\frac{1}{3}} + a^{-\frac{1}{3}})(a^{\frac{1}{3}} - a^{-\frac{1}{3}})$
$= a^{\frac{2}{3}} - a^{-\frac{2}{3}}$

EXERCISES 2-5

1. Simplify.

   a) $2^2 \times 2^{-3}$ b) $3^2 \div 3^{-2}$ c) $2^3 \div 2^7$ d) $5^4 \times 5^{-6}$

2. Simplify.

   a) $6^{\frac{2}{3}} \times 6^{\frac{4}{3}}$ b) $2^{\frac{5}{2}} \div 2^{\frac{3}{2}}$ c) $5^{-\frac{4}{3}} \div 5^{\frac{2}{3}}$ d) $10^{\frac{3}{5}} \times 10^{-\frac{8}{5}}$

3. Simplify.

   a) $(3^{\frac{1}{3}} \times 5^{-\frac{1}{2}})^6$ b) $(5^{\frac{9}{4}} \div 5^{-\frac{3}{4}})^{-\frac{1}{2}}$ c) $(\sqrt[3]{27^2})^{\frac{1}{2}}$ d) $(\sqrt{16^3})^{-\frac{1}{6}}$

4. Simplify.
   a) $x^2 \div x^5$ b) $m^{\frac{2}{3}} \times m^{\frac{4}{3}}$ c) $(n^{\frac{1}{2}})^{-6}$ d) $x^{-\frac{3}{2}} \div x^{-\frac{1}{4}}$

5. Simplify.
   a) $m^2n^5 \times m^3n^{-7}$ b) $a^{\frac{2}{3}}b^{\frac{2}{5}} \times a^{\frac{4}{3}}b^{-\frac{12}{5}}$ c) $(xy^{\frac{2}{3}})^6 \div (x^{\frac{1}{2}}y^{\frac{1}{4}})^8$
   d) $(9a^4b^{-2} \times 4a^2b^{-6})^{\frac{1}{2}}$ e) $12x^{-\frac{3}{4}}y^{-2} \div 4x^{\frac{3}{4}}y^{-2}$ f) $8m^{\frac{1}{3}}n^{-\frac{5}{3}}(-2m^{-\frac{2}{3}}n^{\frac{1}{3}})^{-4}$

Ⓑ

6. Simplify.
   a) $2^5 \times 8^{-2}$ b) $27^{\frac{2}{3}} \div 9^{\frac{1}{2}}$ c) $16^{\frac{3}{4}} \times 4^{\frac{3}{2}}$ d) $9^{\frac{5}{2}} \div 81^{\frac{7}{4}}$

7. Simplify.
   a) $5^{\frac{3}{2}} \times 125^{\frac{1}{2}}$ b) $6^{\frac{3}{4}} \div 36^{-\frac{1}{3}}$ c) $8^{\frac{2}{5}} \times 16^{-\frac{2}{5}}$ d) $125^{-\frac{2}{3}} \div (\sqrt{5})^{-3}$

8. Simplify.
   a) $\dfrac{2a^{\frac{1}{2}} \times a^{\frac{2}{3}}}{9a^{-\frac{5}{3}}}$ b) $(27x^2)^{\frac{1}{3}}(16x^{-2})^{\frac{1}{4}}$ c) $\sqrt{\dfrac{50x^2y^4}{5x^4y^7}}$ d) $\dfrac{(x^2y)^{-\frac{5}{2}}}{(x^3y^{-3})^{\frac{1}{6}}}$

9. Simplify.
   a) $\left(\dfrac{a^{-2}b^3}{c^4}\right)^3$ b) $\dfrac{36x^{-2}y^3z^{-4}}{12xy^{-2}z^{-2}}$ c) $\sqrt{\dfrac{32x^{-5}y^2 \times 18x^2y}{4xy^{-3}}}$

Ⓒ

10. Simplify.
   a) $\dfrac{x^a \times x^{3a}}{x^{-2a}}$ b) $\dfrac{m^{2n} \times m^{-3n} \times m^n}{m^{3-n}}$ c) $\dfrac{(m^{x-1})(m^{2x+5})}{m^{3x-1}}$ d) $\dfrac{(c^{a+b})(c^{a-b})}{c^2}$

11. Simplify.
   a) $3^{2x} \times 27^x$ b) $\dfrac{2^n \times 4^{n-1}}{8^{n-2}}$ c) $\dfrac{25^{3a+1} \times 5^{a-3}}{125^a}$
   d) $\dfrac{81^{1-2x} \times 4^{2x+3}}{16^{2-3x}}$ e) $\dfrac{36^{a-2b} \times 6^{a+6}}{216^{2a-3b}}$ f) $\dfrac{16^{2m-n} \times 9^{m+3n}}{27^{m+n} \times 8^{m-n}}$

12. If $x = a^{-2}$ and $y = a^{\frac{2}{3}}$, write each expression in terms of a.
   a) $x^{-3}y^3$ b) $\dfrac{x^2}{y}$ c) $(x^{\frac{1}{2}}y^{\frac{2}{3}})^2$ d) $x^{\frac{2}{3}}y^2$ e) $x^{\frac{3}{5}}y^{\frac{1}{2}}$ f) $(x^{\frac{3}{4}} \div y^{-\frac{1}{2}})^3$

13. Expand and simplify.
   a) $a^{\frac{1}{2}}(2a^{\frac{1}{2}} + a^{-\frac{3}{2}})$ b) $x^{\frac{2}{3}}(5x^{\frac{4}{3}} - 3x^{\frac{1}{3}})$ c) $3m^{\frac{3}{2}}(2m^{-\frac{1}{2}} - m^{\frac{1}{2}})$
   d) $5^{\frac{1}{4}}(5^{\frac{3}{4}} + 5^{-\frac{5}{4}})$ e) $4x^{\frac{2}{3}}(7x^6 + 3x^{\frac{4}{3}})$ f) $9^{\frac{2}{3}}(9^{-\frac{1}{6}} - 9^{-\frac{7}{6}})$

14. Expand and simplify.
   a) $(5^{\frac{1}{2}} + 2^{\frac{1}{2}})(5^{\frac{1}{2}} - 2^{\frac{1}{2}})$ b) $(x^{\frac{3}{2}} - x^{\frac{7}{2}})(x^{\frac{3}{2}} + x^{\frac{7}{2}})$
   c) $(2a^{\frac{5}{2}} - 7a^{\frac{1}{2}})(3a^{\frac{3}{2}} - a^{\frac{1}{2}})$ d) $(4x^{\frac{4}{3}} + 9x^{\frac{1}{3}})(3x^{\frac{4}{3}} - 2x^{\frac{2}{3}})$

15. Simplify.
   a) $\left(\sqrt{49y^{\frac{2}{m}}}\right)^{-\frac{1}{n}}$ b) $\sqrt{8x^ay^{\frac{3}{a}}}$ c) $\dfrac{\sqrt[3]{a} \times b^{-\frac{1}{4}}}{\sqrt[4]{b} \times a^{-\frac{1}{3}}} \div \left(\dfrac{a^{\frac{1}{3}}}{\sqrt{b}}\right)^{-1}$

2-6 SOLVING EQUATIONS INVOLVING EXPONENTS

The exponent laws may be used to solve equations involving exponents.

Example 1. Solve. a) $x^{\frac{3}{4}} = 8$ b) $2y^{\frac{2}{3}} = 18$

Solution.   a) $x^{\frac{3}{4}} = 8$

To simplify the left side of the equation, raise it to the power $\frac{4}{3}$.
Do the same to the right side.

$$(x^{\frac{3}{4}})^{\frac{4}{3}} = 8^{\frac{4}{3}}$$
$$x = (\sqrt[3]{8})^4$$
$$= 16$$

b) $2y^{\frac{2}{3}} = 18$

Divide both sides by 2.

$$y^{\frac{2}{3}} = 9$$

Raise both sides to the power $\frac{3}{2}$.

$$(y^{\frac{2}{3}})^{\frac{3}{2}} = 9^{\frac{3}{2}}$$
$$y = (\sqrt[2]{9})^3$$
$$= 27$$

Often, the variable may appear as the exponent in an equation.
For example, in a ladies-singles tennis tournament there are 64 entries.
If each competitor plays until she loses, the number of rounds, n,
required is found by solving the equation $2^n = 64$.
To solve the equation, express 64 as a power of 2.
$$2^n = 2^6$$
Since the bases are the same, the exponents are equal.
$$n = 6$$
Six rounds of tennis must be played in the competition.

An equation such as $2^n = 64$ is called an *exponential equation*,
since the unknown is the exponent or in the exponent. Other exponential
equations are:
$$5^x = 625 \qquad 16^{3n-2} = 2.$$
Such equations can be solved by expressing both sides as powers of the
same base.

Example 2. Solve. $3^x = 81$

Solution.   Write 81 as a power of 3. $3^x = 3^4$
When the powers are equal and the bases are the same, the exponents
are equal.
Therefore, $x = 4$

Example 3.   Solve.

a) $2^{x+3} = 16$ b) $9^{x-1} = 27$

Solution.   a) Write 16 as a power of 2. $2^{x+3} = 2^4$
Since the bases are the same, the exponents are equal.
$$x + 3 = 4$$
$$x = 1$$
b) Write both sides as powers of 3.
L.S. $= 9^{x-1}$ R.S. $= 3^3$
   $= (3^2)^{x-1}$
   $= 3^{2x-2}$
The equation becomes $3^{2x-2} = 3^3$
Since the bases are the same, the exponents are equal.
$$2x - 2 = 3$$
$$2x = 5$$
$$x = 2.5$$

Example 4.   The number of insects in a colony doubles every month. If there are now 250 insects, about how long will it take for the colony to grow to 8000?

Solution.   Let n be the required number of months.
Then, $250 \times 2^n = 8000$
$$2^n = \frac{8000}{250}$$
$$= 32$$
$$n = 5$$
In 5 months, the colony will number 8000 insects.

Example 5.   How long does it take money invested at 12% compounded annually to double in value?

Solution.   Let n denote the number of years for a sum of money to double.
The value of $1 after n years is $1(1.12)^n$.
The condition that the money doubles in n years is $(1.12)^n = 2$
We solve the equation by systematic trial, trying various values of n.

n	5	6	7
$(1.12)^n$	1.762	1.974	2.211

Since $1.974 \doteq 2$, then $(1.12)^6 \doteq 2$, and $n \doteq 6$
Money invested at 12% compounded annually doubles in value in approximately 6 years.

EXERCISES 2-6

(A)

1. Solve.

a) $x^{\frac{1}{2}} = 7$ b) $x^{\frac{1}{3}} = 4$ c) $x^{\frac{1}{4}} = 2$ d) $x^{\frac{2}{3}} = 4$

e) $x^{\frac{3}{4}} = 27$ f) $x^{\frac{3}{2}} = 125$ g) $x^{\frac{5}{3}} = 32$ h) $2x^{\frac{4}{5}} = 162$

2. Solve.
   a) $2^x = 32$
   b) $10^x = 100\ 000$
   c) $3^x = 81$
   d) $5^x = 625$
   e) $(-2)^x = -128$
   f) $4^x = 64$
   g) $9^x = 729$
   h) $20^x = 8000$
   i) $7^x = 2401$

3. Solve.
   a) $2^{x+1} = 4$
   b) $2^{x-1} = 8$
   c) $3^{x-5} = 9$
   d) $5^{x+3} = 25$
   e) $10^{x+1} = 1000$
   f) $4^{x+2} = 16$

4. Solve.
   a) $7^x = 1$
   b) $6^x = \dfrac{1}{36}$
   c) $5^x = 5$
   d) $10^x = 0.01$

5. How long does it take money invested at 9% compounded annually to double in value?

6. How long will it take $1000 to triple if it is invested at 12% compounded annually?

Ⓑ

7. Solve.
   a) $2^{2x+1} = 8$
   b) $3^{2-x} = 9$
   c) $5^{3x-2} = 25$
   d) $9^{x+1} = 1$
   e) $4^x = 32$
   f) $9^x = 27$
   g) $8^{x+2} = 16$
   h) $9^{1-2x} = 81$
   i) $16^{x-1} = 64$

8. Solve.
   a) $3 \times 2^x = 12$
   b) $5 \times 2^x = 40$
   c) $10 \times 3^x = 270$
   d) $10 \times 2^x = 640$
   e) $6 \times 3^x = 162$
   f) $4 \times 5^x = 500$
   g) $3 \times 6^x = 108$
   h) $4 \times 7^x = 4$
   i) $2 \times 4^x = 1$

9. The number of ants in a nest doubles every month. If there are now 600 ants, about how long will it take for their number to grow to 9600?

10. If the salt content of Lake Ontario continues to increase at the rate given in the news item:
    a) write an expression for the salt concentration after n years
    b) in about how many years will the lake have the same salt concentration as the Dead Sea?

SALT HARMS ENVIRONMENT

TORONTO. Salt spread on roads in winter is finding its way into Lake Ontario and causing the lake's salt content to double every five years. The present level is about 25 parts per million. There is, however, no immediate danger of the lake becoming another Dead Sea which has a salt content of 10 000 parts per million.

Ⓒ

11. Solve and check.
    a) $4^x + 4^{x+1} = 40$
    b) $3^x - 3^{x-1} = \dfrac{2}{27}$
    c) $5 \times 2^x - 3 \times 2^{x-1} = 224$

12. Solve by systematic trial. Give the answers to 2 decimal places.
    a) $x^x = 2$
    b) $2^x + x = 10$
    c) $2^x + x^2 = 12$

Review Exercises

1. Express the first number as a power of the second.
   a) 81, 3 b) 1296, 6 c) $-16\,807$, -7 d) -3.375, -1.5

2. If a cottage, originally bought for $25 000, appreciates at the rate of 6% per year, what is it worth after: a) 3 years b) 7 years c) n years?

3. If a ball is dropped from a height of 3.0 m and allowed to bounce freely, the height h metres to which it bounces is given by the formula $h = 3.0(0.9)^n$, where n is the number of bounces.
   a) What height does the ball reach after:
      i) the fourth bounce   ii) the seventh bounce?
   b) After what bounce does the ball reach a height of less than 1 m?

4. Simplify.
   a) $(x^a)^4(x^{2a+1})^3$ b) $(2^b)^4(2^{b+2})^2$ c) $\dfrac{(w^{4x})^{3z}}{(w^{xz})^3}$ d) $\dfrac{(w^{3m}x^{b+2})^2}{w^{2m+1}x^b}$

5. If $x = a^3$ and $y = 3b^2$, write each expression in terms of a and b.
   a) $4x^2y^3$ b) $(3x^3y^4)^3$ c) $\dfrac{4x^5y^3}{3x^3y^2}$ d) $\left(\dfrac{5x^6y^5}{10x^5y^3}\right)^3$

6. Simplify.
   a) $x^8 \times x^{-13}$ b) $w^5 \div w^7$ c) $4b^{-4} \times 9b^{-6}$ d) $-21c^4d^4 \div 7c^5d^{-6}$

7. Express each root as a power.
   a) $\sqrt[3]{19^2}$ b) $\sqrt{28^5}$ c) $\sqrt[5]{13^2}$ d) $\sqrt{33^3}$ e) $\sqrt[3]{(-7)^{11}}$ f) $\sqrt[10]{43^3}$

8. Simplify.
   a) $100(1.05)^{2.7}$ b) $400(1.12)^{3.4}$ c) $1250(1.08)^{-4.2}$ d) $265(0.85)^{-3.7}$

9. The number of insects in a colony doubles every month. If there are now 1000 insects in the colony, about how many insects will there be 2 weeks from now?

10. Simplify.
    a) $3^{\frac{3}{2}} \times 243^{\frac{1}{2}}$ b) $5^{\frac{3}{4}} \times 25^{-\frac{1}{3}}$ c) $343^{-\frac{2}{3}} \div (\sqrt{7})^3$ d) $(-216)^{\frac{3}{5}} \div (-6)^{\frac{3}{4}}$

11. Simplify.
    a) $2^{3x} \times 8^x$ b) $\dfrac{3^{n+1} \times 9^{n-1}}{27^{n-3}}$ c) $\dfrac{4^{4a-1} \times 64^{2a+2}}{256^{2a}}$

12. Solve.
    a) $2^x = 16$ b) $10^x = 1000$ c) $10^x = 0.1$ d) $3^x = 1$ e) $4^x = 2$

13. Solve.
    a) $2^{x+1} = 8$ b) $3^{x-1} = 81$ c) $2^{3x+1} = 32$ d) $6^{2x-1} = 1$

14. Solve.
    a) $3 \times 5^x = 75$ b) $10 \times 2^x = 160$ c) $4 \times 3^x = 324$

15. How long will it take $1000 to grow to $1500 when it is invested at 8% compounded annually?

3 Polynomials and Rational Expressions

Research scientists believe that by the year A.D. 2000 space colonies will be technically possible. One proposal is for a wheel-like colony 2000 m in diameter with an interior diameter of 200 m. How may the volume of the space colony be found? (See Section 3-4 *Example 5*.)

3-1 REVIEW: OPERATIONS WITH MONOMIALS

Algebraic terms such as $-2a^2$ and $7x^2y$ are called *monomials*. Monomials may be added or subtracted by combining *like* terms.

Example 1. Simplify. $3x^2 - 5xy + 2y^2 - 2x - xy + 2x^2 - 3y^2$

Solution.
$$3x^2 - 5xy + 2y^2 - 2x - xy + 2x^2 - 3y^2$$
$$= 3x^2 + 2x^2 - 5xy - xy + 2y^2 - 3y^2 - 2x \qquad \text{Grouping like terms}$$
$$= 5x^2 - 6xy - y^2 - 2x$$

Products and quotients of monomials can be found using the exponent laws.

Example 2. Simplify.

a) $(3ab^2)^3(2a^2b)$ 　　b) $\dfrac{32x^4y^2}{8x^2y^3}$ 　　c) $\dfrac{18x^3y}{10xy^2} \times \dfrac{15x^2y^2}{6x^4y}$

Solution.
a) $(3ab^2)^3(2a^2b)$
$= 27a^3b^6 \times 2a^2b$
$= 54a^5b^7$

b) $\dfrac{32x^4y^2}{8x^2y^3} = 4x^2y^{-1}$

c) $\dfrac{18x^3y}{10xy^2} \times \dfrac{15x^2y^2}{6x^4y}$

$= \dfrac{18 \times 15}{10 \times 6} \times \dfrac{x^5y^3}{x^5y^3}$

$= \dfrac{9}{2}$

Example 3. A square is inscribed in a semicircle. Find the ratio of:
a) the diameter of the semicircle to the side of the square
b) the area of the semicircle to the area of the square.

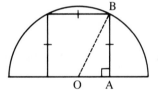

Solution.
a) Let the side of the square be $2x$ and the radius of the semicircle r. Then, in right $\triangle OAB$, 　$r^2 = x^2 + (2x)^2$
$$= 5x^2$$
$$r = \sqrt{5}x$$

$\dfrac{\text{Diameter of semicircle}}{\text{Side of square}}$ is $\dfrac{2r}{2x} = \dfrac{2\sqrt{5}x}{2x}$

$$= \dfrac{\sqrt{5}}{1}$$

b) Area of semicircle $= \dfrac{1}{2}\pi r^2$ 　　　Area of square $= (2x)^2$

$\qquad\qquad\qquad = \dfrac{1}{2}\pi(\sqrt{5}x)^2$ 　　　　　　$= 4x^2$

$\qquad\qquad\qquad = \dfrac{5}{2}\pi x^2$

$\dfrac{\text{Area of semicircle}}{\text{Area of square}}$ is $\dfrac{\frac{5}{2}\pi x^2}{4x^2} = \dfrac{5\pi}{8}$

EXERCISES 3-1

(A)

1. Simplify.
   a) $3x + 7 + 5x - 2$
   b) $2m - 11 - 9m + 4$
   c) $8a - 3b - 12a + 7b$
   d) $4x + 7y - 13x + 6y$
   e) $6a + 2b + 17a - 9b + 7a$
   f) $3x - 5y - 8y + 9x - 17x + 2y$

2. Simplify.
   a) $5a^2 - 3a + 2 - a^2 + 7a - 9$
   b) $12m^2 + 9m - 3 - 7m^2 - 4m + 6$
   c) $3x^2 - 7x - 4 + 5x^2 + 2x - 9$
   d) $11s^2 - 8 - 3s - 6s^2 + 17s - 4$
   e) $8x^2 - 12x - 15x^2 + 4 - 7x - 10$
   f) $a^2 - 6a + 4 - 7a^2 - 5a - 19$

3. Simplify.
   a) $4x^2 - 2xy + 5y^2 - 3x^2 + 7xy - 2y^2$
   b) $2a^2 + 7ab - 12b^2 - 8a^2 + 5b^2 - 10ab$
   c) $6x^2 - 4xy - 3y^2 - 19xy + 12y^2 + 11x^2$
   d) $18x^2 - 7xy + 5y^2 - 11x^2 + 15yx - 23y^2 + 2x^2$
   e) $16s^2t + 9 - 35st^2 - 12s^2t + 26t^2s - 41s^2t + 19 - 5t^2s$
   f) $15x^2y - 4xy^2 - 37yx^2 + 11 + 22xy^2 - 19xy^2 + 5y^2x - 18$

4. Simplify.
   a) $(7a^2b)(4a^2b^3)$
   b) $(4x^3y^2)(5x^2y^7)$
   c) $(-8m^5n^2)(3m^2n^6)$
   d) $(-9x^2y^3)(-6x^3y^7)$
   e) $(-12mn^3)(3m^5n^3)$
   f) $(6a^2b^4)(7a^2b^3)$

5. Simplify.
   a) $(3a^2b)^2(5a^2b^3)$
   b) $(2x^3y^2)^3(-7x^4y)$
   c) $(5mn^2)^2(-3m^3n)^2$
   d) $(-2x^2y)^3(3x^3y^5)^2$
   e) $(4a^5b^3)^3(3a^4b^2)^2$
   f) $(3xy^3)^2(-2x^4y^3)^5$

6. The formulas for the volumes of a sphere and a cone, and the surface area of a cylinder are given in the diagrams. Express V and A in terms of the diameter d instead of the radius r.

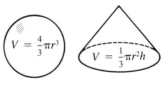

$$V = \frac{4}{3}\pi r^3$$

$$V = \frac{1}{3}\pi r^2 h$$

$$A = 2\pi r^2 + 2\pi rh$$

7. Simplify.
   a) $\dfrac{24x^3y^8}{-6x^2y^2}$
   b) $\dfrac{48m^6n^9}{3m^2n^3}$
   c) $\dfrac{-51a^5b^3}{3a^2b^8}$
   d) $\dfrac{-36x^{10}y^4}{9x^4y^3}$
   e) $\dfrac{85a^6b^3}{5a^2b^3}$
   f) $\dfrac{87x^4y^6}{-3x^4y^4}$

8. The length of a rectangle is $12x^2y$ centimetres. Find the width if:
   a) the area is   i) $24x^3y^2$ square centimetres   ii) $4xy^3$ square centimetres
   b) the perimeter is $30x^2y$ centimetres.

B

9. Simplify.

a) $\dfrac{10x^4y}{27x^2y^3} \times \dfrac{18x^3y^2}{25xy^4}$

b) $\dfrac{4x^3y^2}{7xy^5} \times \dfrac{28x^3y^4}{36x^2y^3}$

c) $\dfrac{-12m^4n^2}{35m^3n^5} \times \dfrac{-15m^2n^6}{-48m^2n^2}$

d) $\dfrac{(2x^2y)^3}{15x^3y^2} \times \dfrac{40x^3y^2}{6x^2y^7}$

e) $\dfrac{14a^2b^5c^3}{45a^3b^2c} \times \dfrac{-18a^5b^2c}{21a^2b^2c^4}$

f) $\dfrac{-16x^2yz^3}{9x^4yz^5} \times \dfrac{12x^3yz^2}{-40x^2y^2z} \times \dfrac{15xy^6z^3}{-8x^2y^4z^6}$

10. A square is inscribed in a circle. Find the ratio of:
    a) their areas
    b) their perimeters.

11. A rectangle, twice as long as it is wide, is inscribed in a circle. Find the ratio of the area of the circle to the area of the rectangle.

12. A cone has the same height as a cylinder but twice the diameter. Find the ratio of their volumes.

13. A closed cylinder, with a height equal to its diameter, has the same diameter as a sphere. Find the ratio of:
    a) their volumes
    b) their surface areas.

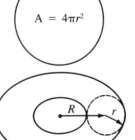

$A = 4\pi r^2$

14. The formula for the volume V of a torus is $V = 2\pi^2 Rr^2$. Find the volume if:
    a) $R = 2r$
    b) $R = 6x^2y$ and $r = 2xy^2$.

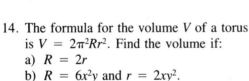

C

15. A cylinder, with a height equal to its diameter, is inscribed in a sphere. Find the ratio of the volume of the cylinder to the volume of the sphere.

3-2 REVIEW: OPERATIONS WITH POLYNOMIALS

Expressions formed by adding or subtracting monomials are called *polynomials*. Examples are:

$2m + 3n$ $x^2 - 6xy + 9y^2$.

Polynomials are added or subtracted by combining like terms. To multiply a polynomial by a monomial, apply the distributive law.

Example 1. Simplify.

a) $(3m^2 - 8m + 9) - (5m^2 + 6m - 2)$
b) $5a(a^2 - 2ab - b^2) - 3b[a^2 + 2b(a - 4b)]$

Solution.

a) $\quad (3m^2 - 8m + 9) - (5m^2 + 6m - 2)$
$= 3m^2 - 8m + 9 - 5m^2 - 6m + 2$
$= -2m^2 - 14m + 11$

b) $\quad 5a(a^2 - 2ab - b^2) - 3b[a^2 + 2b(a - 4b)]$
$= 5a^3 - 10a^2b - 5ab^2 - 3b[a^2 + 2ab - 8b^2]$
$= 5a^3 - 10a^2b - 5ab^2 - 3a^2b - 6ab^2 + 24b^3$
$= 5a^3 - 13a^2b - 11ab^2 + 24b^3$

To find the product of two polynomials, multiply each term of one polynomial by each term of the other polynomial.

Example 2. Simplify.

a) $(2x + y)(x - 3y)$
b) $(2x + y - 3)(x + y - 2)$
c) $3(2m - 5n)(m + 4n) - (3m - 2n)^2$

Solution.

a) $(2x + y)(x - 3y) = 2x(x - 3y) + y(x - 3y)$
$\qquad\qquad\qquad\quad = 2x^2 - 6xy + xy - 3y^2$
$\qquad\qquad\qquad\quad = 2x^2 - 5xy - 3y^2$

b) $\quad (2x + y - 3)(x + y - 2)$
$= 2x(x + y - 2) + y(x + y - 2) - 3(x + y - 2)$
$= 2x^2 + 2xy - 4x + xy + y^2 - 2y - 3x - 3y + 6$
$= 2x^2 + 3xy + y^2 - 7x - 5y + 6$

c) $\quad 3(2m - 5n)(m + 4n) - (3m - 2n)^2$
$= 3(2m^2 + 3mn - 20n^2) - (9m^2 - 12mn + 4n^2)$
$= 6m^2 + 9mn - 60n^2 - 9m^2 + 12mn - 4n^2$
$= -3m^2 + 21mn - 64n^2$

Example 3. If the radius r of a circle is increased by x, find the increase in:

a) the circumference   b) the area.

Solution.

a) Circumference of original circle is $2\pi r$.
Circumference of enlarged circle is $2\pi(r + x)$.
Increase in circumference is
$2\pi(r + x) - 2\pi r$
$= 2\pi r + 2\pi x - 2\pi r$
$= 2\pi x$

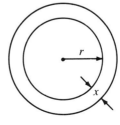

b) Area of original circle is πr^2.
   Area of enlarged circle is $\pi(r + x)^2$.
   Increase in area is
   $$\pi(r + x)^2 - \pi r^2$$
   $$= \pi(r^2 + 2rx + x^2) - \pi r^2$$
   $$= \pi r^2 + 2\pi rx + \pi x^2 - \pi r^2$$
   $$= 2\pi rx + \pi x^2$$
   The increase in area is $2\pi rx + \pi x^2$.

EXERCISES 3-2

1. Simplify.
   a) $(8a - 13b) - (12a + 4b)$
   b) $(5x^2 - 3y^2) - (7x^2 + y^2) + (3x^2 - 2y^2)$
   c) $(3m^2 - 8m + 9) - (5m^2 + 6m - 2)$
   d) $(5a^2 + 9ab - 3b^2) + (7a^2 - 16ab + 14b^2)$
   e) $(3ab + 7bc - 19ac) + (-11ab + 7ac - 32bc)$
   f) $(5m^2 + 3m - 9) + (8m^2 - 14m + 16) - (6m^2 - 11m + 4)$

2. Simplify.
   a) $4(2x + 7y) - 3(5x - 2y)$
   b) $7a(3a - 8) + 5a(6a + 4)$
   c) $14mn(3m - 2n) - 5mn(6m + 4n)$
   d) $2x(5x - 7y + 3) - 8x(2x + 3y - 1)$
   e) $7a(3a + 5b - 2) + 2a(5a - 11b + 17)$
   f) $5xy(2x - 3y - 7) + 2xy(8x - 13y + 21)$

3. Simplify.
   a) $3[5a - (2 - 4b)] + 5[2a - (7 + 3b)]$
   b) $4[2x - (6y + 3)] - 7[4x - (5y - 9)]$
   c) $2x[5x - (4 + 7y)] - 6x[3x - (2y - 5)]$
   d) $5a[2a + 3(4a - 9)] + 3a[a - 7(2a + 6)]$
   e) $3m[m - 4m(n - 5)] - 2m^2(3m - 2n + 7)$
   f) $8x[2x - 3y(x + 2)] - 5x[4x - 7y(2x - 9)]$

4. Simplify.
   a) $(3x + 7)(5x - 2)$ b) $(2m + 9)(4m + 5)$ c) $(7x - 3y)^2$
   d) $(8a - 5b)(7a - 11b)$ e) $(4x + 3y)(4x - 3y)$ f) $2(5x - 9y)(8x - 3y)$

5. A square has sides of length x. If each side is increased by an amount h, find the increase in area.

6. Simplify.
   a) $(3x + 7y)(2x + 5y) + (4x - 3y)(5x + 6y)$
   b) $(6a - 5b)(3a + 2b) - 2(2a + 7b)(4a - 3b)$
   c) $3(4m - 7n)(3m - 2n) - (7m - 5n)(7m + 5n)$
   d) $(6x - 2y)(4x + 7y) + (3x - 5y)^2$
   e) $(5x - 2y)^2 - (5x + 2y)^2$
   f) $(3a^2 + 8b)(2a^2 - 5b) - 3(4a^2 - 2b)^2$

7. Simplify.
   a) $3(2x - y)^2 - 2(x - 3y)^2$
   b) $4(2x - 3)^2 - 3(3x - 2)^2$
   c) $2(a - 3)^2 + 1$
   d) $5(2m + 7)^2 - 7(m - 3)(2m + 4)$
   e) $3(2x - 5)^2 - 14$
   f) $6(3a^2 + 2b)^2 + 3a^2(2a - 5b)^2$

8. Simplify.
   a) $(2m + 3)(5m^2 - 3m + 8)$
   b) $(3x - 7y)(2x - 4y - 5)$
   c) $(2a - 5b)(3a^2 + 2ab - b^2)$
   d) $3(x + 2y)(5x^2 - 2xy + 3y^2)$
   e) $(x^2 + 2x + 3)(2x^2 - 5x - 1)$
   f) $4a(2a^2 - 3ab + b^2)(3a^2 + ab - 2b^2)$

9. Simplify.
   a) $(x + 5)(x - 3)(x + 1)$
   b) $(2a - 1)(a + 5)(2a + 1)$
   c) $2(x - 3)^2(x - 1)$
   d) $(4m + 7n)(2m + 3n)(m - 5n)$
   e) $3(2a - 5b)(3a + 2b)(3a - 2b)$
   f) $5(2x - 7y)(4x + 3y)^2$

B

10. A cube has edges of length x. If each edge is increased by an amount h, find the increase in:
    a) surface area
    b) volume.

11. Simplify.
    a) $2(3x - 4)(2x - 5) - 3(x + 3)(5x + 2) - (4x - 7)(2x + 5)$
    b) $3(2a + b)(5a - 2b) - 6(3a - 4b)^2 - (5a + 3b)(5a - 3b)$
    c) $(2m + 3)(3m^2 + 4m - 5) - (m - 2)(2m^2 + 3m - 8)$
    d) $(2x + 4y)(x - 2y + 1) - (3x - y)(5x + 3y - 4)$
    e) $(3a - 2b)(2a + 7b)^2 - (4a + 3b)^2(2a - 5b)$
    f) $3(4x - 2)(2x^2 + x + 6) - (2x - 3)(3x - 2)^2$

12. A shipping crate measures $(3x + 5)$ metres by $(2x - 3)$ metres by $(2x + 4)$ metres.
    a) Find expressions for its volume and surface area.
    b) Evaluate the expressions in part a) for $x = 2.5$.

13. A cylinder has a radius of $(3x - 2)$ centimetres and a height of $(2x + 5)$ centimetres. Find expressions for its volume and surface area.

14. The stopping distance d metres for a car travelling at v kilometres per hour is given by the formula $d = 0.20v + 0.15v^2$. Find the increase in stopping distance when v is increased by x kilometres per hour.

15. When an object of mass m is travelling at a speed v, its kinetic energy E is given by the formula $E = \frac{1}{2}mv^2$. If the speed is increased by an amount x, find an expression to represent the change in kinetic energy.

16. A car brakes and decelerates uniformly. After t seconds, it has travelled a distance of d metres where d is related to t by the formula $d = 40t - 2t^2$, $t \leq 10$. How far does the car travel in the next second?

17. Find the volume of the unshaded portion of the rectangular prism (below left).

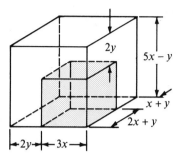
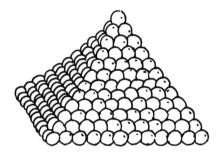

Ⓒ

18. When there are n coconuts in the bottom row of a square pyramid of coconuts (above right), the total number of coconuts N is given by the formula

$N = \frac{1}{3}n^3 + \frac{1}{2}n^2 + \frac{1}{6}n$. How many additional coconuts would be needed to make a

pyramid with one more layer?

INVESTIGATE

Patterns in Products

The product of two binomials such as $(x + 1)(x - 1)$ is significant because two terms of the product *add to zero*.
$$(x + 1)(x - 1) = x^2 - x + x - 1$$
$$= x^2 - 1$$
Are there other products in which some of the terms add to zero? To answer this question, we could start with $(x + 1)(x - 1)$ and change one or both factors in a systematic way. For example, use higher powers of x and different combinations of signs. Here are a few of the many possibilities that could be considered.

- Changing one of the factors:

$(x + 1)(x^2 - x + 1)$ $(x - 1)(x^2 + x + 1)$

$(x + 1)(x^2 - x - 1)$ $(x - 1)(x^2 + x - 1)$

$(x + 1)(x^3 + x^2 - x - 1)$ $(x - 1)(x^3 + x^2 + x + 1)$

$(x + 1)(x^3 - x^2 + x - 1)$ $(x - 1)(x^3 + x^2 - x - 1)$

- Changing both factors:

$(x^2 + x + 1)(x^2 + x - 1)$ $(x^3 + x^2 + x + 1)(x^2 - x + 1)$

1. Using examples such as those above, try to arrange the powers and signs so that some of the terms of the product add to zero. Write the results in a systematic way that shows the underlying patterns.

2. Use the patterns in the results of *Question 1* to factor these expressions.

  a) $x^3 + 1$ b) $8a^3 - 1$ c) $x^5 - 1$

  d) $x^3 + y^3$ e) $x^4 + x^2 + 1$ f) $x^6 + x^4 - x^2 - 1$

3-3 REVIEW: FACTORING TRINOMIALS

A method of factoring a trinomial of the form $ax^2 + bx + c$ is suggested
by the way the product of two binomials is obtained.

$$(2x + 7)(x - 5) = 2x(x - 5) + 7(x - 5)$$
$$= 2x^2 - 10x + 7x - 35$$

The integers -10 and 7 have a sum -3
and a product -70, the same as
the product of 2 and -35.

$$= 2x^2 - 3x - 35$$

This indicates that a trinomial of the form $ax^2 + bx + c$ can be factored
if two integers can be found with a sum b and a product ac.

Example 1.   Factor. $2x^2 + 7x + 5$

Solution.

$$2x^2 + 7x + 5$$ What two integers have a sum 7
and a product 10?

The integers are 5 and 2. The trinomial can be factored by writing the
second term as $5x + 2x$ and then grouping the terms to find a common
factor.

$$2x^2 + 7x + 5 = 2x^2 + 5x + 2x + 5$$
$$= x(2x + 5) + 1(2x + 5)$$
$$= (2x + 5)(x + 1)$$

Example 2.   Factor. a) $6x^2 - 11xy + 3y^2$ b) $12a^3 - 94a^2 - 16a$

Solution.   a) $6x^2 - 11xy + 3y^2 = 6x^2 - 9xy - 2xy + 3y^2$
$$= 3x(2x - 3y) - y(2x - 3y)$$
$$= (2x - 3y)(3x - y)$$

b) $12a^3 - 94a^2 - 16a = 2a(6a^2 - 47a - 8)$ Extract the
$$= 2a(6a^2 + a - 48a - 8)$$ common factor
$$= 2a[a(6a + 1) - 8(6a + 1)]$$ first.
$$= 2a(6a + 1)(a - 8)$$

EXERCISES 3-3

Ⓐ

1. Factor.
   a) $x^2 + 5x + 6$ b) $m^2 - 9m + 20$ c) $a^2 + 5a - 14$
   d) $m^2 - 5m - 24$ e) $x^2 - 15x + 54$ f) $x^2 + 5x - 84$

2. Factor.
   a) $2m^2 + 7m + 3$ b) $5x^2 - 7x + 2$ c) $3a^2 - 10a + 3$
   d) $4x^2 + x - 3$ e) $3s^2 - s - 2$ f) $2m^2 + 5m - 7$

3. Factor.
   a) $3x^2 + 7xy + 2y^2$
   b) $2m^2 - 5mn + 3n^2$
   c) $3a^2 + 5ab - 2b^2$
   d) $5m^2 - 3mn - 2n^2$
   e) $21x^2 - 10xy + y^2$
   f) $3x^2 - 16xy + 5y^2$

4. Factor.
   a) $6s^2 + 11s + 5$
   b) $6m^2 - m - 2$
   c) $2a^2 - 11a + 12$
   d) $3x^2 - 17x - 6$
   e) $4m^2 + 8m + 3$
   f) $6m^2 - 17m + 12$

5. Factor.
   a) $2x^2 + 9xy + 4y^2$
   b) $3a^2 - 8ab + 5b^2$
   c) $6m^2 - 7mn + 2n^2$
   d) $4x^2 + 11xy + 6y^2$
   e) $2p^2 - pq - 10q^2$
   f) $6s^2 - st - 15t^2$

Ⓑ

6. Factor.
   a) $6s^2 + 11s - 10$
   b) $6m^2 - m - 40$
   c) $10a^2 + 51a + 27$
   d) $8x^2 + 38x + 45$
   e) $24m^2 - 38m + 15$
   f) $21x^2 + 10x - 16$

7. Factor.
   a) $36x^2 - 48x - 20$
   b) $14x^2 + 49x + 42$
   c) $48x^2 - 200x + 200$
   d) $24m^3 + 68m^2 + 48m$
   e) $10a^3b - 55a^2b + 60ab$
   f) $24m^3n - 66m^2n + 45mn$

8. Factor.
   a) $m^4 + 6m^2 - 16$
   b) $3x^4 - 16x^2y^2 + 5y^4$
   c) $2a^4 - a^2 - 15$
   d) $12x^4 - 5x^2y^2 - 2y^4$
   e) $2x^5 + 14x^3 + 20x$
   f) $16s^5 - 64s^3t^2 + 60st^4$

9. Factor.
   a) $5p^2 + pq - 18q^2$
   b) $8m^2 - 2mn - 21n^2$
   c) $15x^2 - 34xy + 15y^2$
   d) $32s^2 - 92st + 45t^2$
   e) $24p^2 + 2pq - 15q^2$
   f) $-6x^2 - 17xy + 14y^2$

Ⓒ

10. Factor.
    a) $(3x)^2 + 2(3x) + 1$
    b) $(5x)^2 - 3(5x) + 2$
    c) $(6m)^2 + 8(6m) + 7$
    d) $(2a)^2 + 8(2a) + 15$
    e) $(4p)^2 + 2(4p) - 15$
    f) $(3x)^2 - 2(3x) - 8$

11. Factor.
    a) $(a + b)^2 + 7(a + b) + 12$
    b) $(p - q)^2 - 5(p - q) + 6$
    c) $(2m + n)^2 + 3(2m + n) - 10$
    d) $(4x + y)^2 - 8(4x + y) + 15$
    e) $(x - 2y)^2 - 10(x - 2y) + 21$
    f) $(3x + 5y)^2 - 3(3x + 5y) - 18$

12. Factor.
    a) $2(5x)^2 + 7(5x) + 3$
    b) $3(2m)^2 + 8(2m) - 3$
    c) $4(3a - b)^2 + 21(3a - b) + 5$
    d) $6(x + 5y)^2 - 7(x + 5y) + 2$
    e) $8(2p + q)^2 - 10(2p + q) + 3$
    f) $10(3x^2 + 2y)^2 - 29(3x^2 + 2y) - 21$

13. In how many ways can each trinomial be factored?
    a) $5x^2 + 20x + 20$
    b) $5x^2 + 5x - 10$
    c) $4x^2 + 16x + 16$
    d) $4x^2 + 4x - 8$
    e) $6x^2 + 24x + 24$
    f) $6x^2 + 6x - 12$

COMPUTER POWER

Factoring Trinomials

Factoring trinomials in which the coefficients are very large numbers can be tedious and time-consuming. In such cases a computer can be of assistance. The sequence of steps in factoring a trinomial of the form $Ax^2 + Bx + C$ has been written into the program below.

```
LABEL 160, 180, 190, 220, 230;
VAR
        CH: CHAR;
        A,B,C,Q,P,R,T : REAL;
        X,M : INTEGER;
BEGIN     {FACTORING TRINOMIALS}
        WRITELN('WHAT ARE THE COEFFICIENTS?');
        READ(A,B,C); WRITELN;

        M : = TRUNC(SQRT(ABS( A * C)));
        X : = -M;

        FOR X : =-M TO M DO BEGIN
        IF(X =0) THEN GOTO 160;
        IF((X+A*C/X)=B) THEN GOTO 180;
160:    END;
        WRITELN('THERE ARE NO LINEAR FACTORS');
        GOTO 230;
180:    P : = ABS(A); Q : = ABS(X);
190:    R : = P-TRUNC(P/Q) * Q;
        IF(R = 0) THEN GOTO 220;
        P : = Q; Q : = R; GOTO 190;
220:    WRITELN('FACTORS: (',(A/Q):5:3,' ',(X/Q):5:3,')'
        (',Q:5:3,' ',(C*Q/X):5:3,')')');
230:    CH : = READKEY;
END.
```

When the program was used to factor the trinomial $40x^2 - 114x + 54$, the following output was obtained.

```
WHAT ARE THE COEFFICIENTS?  40, -114, 54
FACTORS:  (5  -3)(8   -18)
```

This shows that $40x^2 - 114x + 54 = (5x - 3)(8x - 18)$.

1. Factor completely.
   a) $10x^2 + 21x + 8$ b) $8a^2 - 42a + 27$ c) $12x^2 - 25xy - 75y^2$
   d) $24 + 26t - 15t^2$ e) $12x^2 + 78x + 90$ f) $50x^2 - 155xy - 70y^2$
   g) $162a^2 - 567ab + 360b^2$ h) $128 - 448m + 392m^2$

2. Investigate how the program can give a complete factorization of each polynomial.
   a) $884x^2 + 1003x - 306$ b) $2024x^2 + 3657x + 1495$

PROBLEM SOLVING

The Most Famous Problem in Mathematics

"I have discovered a truly marvelous demonstration of this proposition which this margin is too narrow to contain."

Pierre de Fermat

Pierre de Fermat was one of the great mathematicians of the seventeenth century. He had the habit of writing his results, often without the proofs, in the margins of his books. Therefore, his successors had to discover the proofs for themselves. But there is one result that no one has been able to prove, and because of the above quotation in which Fermat claimed to have a proof, this problem has become perhaps the most famous problem in mathematics. It is called Fermat's Last Theorem.

Fermat's Last Theorem

If x, y, z, and n are natural numbers, the equation $x^n + y^n = z^n$ has no solution if $n > 2$.

Since Fermat's time, many great mathematicians have spent years trying to prove this theorem. A few even claimed to have proofs, which turned out to contain errors! We know now that if the equation $x^n + y^n = z^n$ has any integral solutions, then n must be greater than 125 000. Although Fermat's Last Theorem is so difficult that it has never been proved, several related problems are much easier to solve.

Prove that if Fermat's Last Theorem can be proved for any exponent k, then it is true for all multiples of k.

Think of a strategy and carry it out

- Suppose there is a natural number k such that $x^k + y^k = z^k$.
- Let m be a multiple of k; that is, $m = dk$. Can you prove that $x^m + y^m = z^m$?

Look back

- By 1825, various mathematicians had found elaborate proofs of the theorem for $n = 3, 4, 5$, and 7. This meant that the theorem was true for many other values of n. What values of n were they?
- To prove Fermat's Last Theorem, it is only necessary to consider the cases where n is a prime number.
- Is it correct to call Fermat's Last Theorem a "theorem"? Explain.

PROBLEMS

Ⓑ

1. Give examples of natural numbers that satisfy each equation.
   a) $x^2 + y^2 + z^2 = w^2$ b) $x^3 + y^3 + z^3 = w^3$
   c) $x^2 + y^2 = z^2 + w^2$ d) $x^3 + y^3 = z^3 + w^3$

2. Two numbers have a sum of 9 and a product of 12. Find their difference.

3. If $x = y$, prove that $4xy = (x + y)^2$.

4. The diagram shows a cross section through a torus. The dimensions of the torus are as follows: d, inside diameter; D, outside diameter; r, radius of circular cross section; R, radius from centre of torus to centre of cross section.
   a) Express in terms of R and r.
      i) D ii) d
   b) Express in terms of D and d.
      i) R ii) r
   c) The formulas for the surface area A and volume V of a torus are $A = 4\pi^2 Rr$ and $V = 2\pi^2 Rr^2$. Express these formulas in terms of D and d.
   d) Substitute the results of part a) into the formulas obtained in part c), and simplify the results.

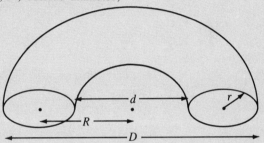

5. The ancient oriental Yin-Yang symbol consists of a circular region bisected by a curve passing through the centre, formed by two semicircles. Show how to draw a curve which bisects both regions.

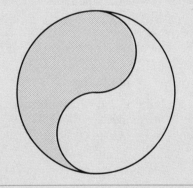

Ⓒ

6. Find values of A and B such that $\dfrac{7x - 11}{(x + 2)(x - 3)} = \dfrac{A}{x + 2} + \dfrac{B}{x - 3}$ $x \neq -2, 3$.

7. Prove that $\dfrac{1}{2} \times \dfrac{3}{4} \times \dfrac{5}{6} \times \ldots \times \dfrac{35}{36} < \dfrac{1}{6}$.

8. In *Problem 5*, show how to draw a straight line which bisects both regions.

Ⓓ

9. Observe that both $x^2 + 5x + 6$ and $x^2 + 6x + 5$ can be factored. Are there other trinomials of the form $x^2 + bx + c$ and $x^2 + cx + b$ which can be factored? Either obtain an algorithm to generate all of them, or prove that there are no others.

3-4 REVIEW: FACTORING A DIFFERENCE OF SQUARES AND A TRINOMIAL SQUARE

A polynomial in the form $x^2 - y^2$ is called a *difference of squares*, and is factored:

$x^2 - y^2 = (x - y)(x + y)$.

Using the above identity, we can express any difference of squares as a product. As always, look for a common factor first.

Example 1. Factor.

a) $81x^2 - 64y^2$ b) $12a^3 - 27a$

Solution.   a) $81x^2 - 64y^2 = (9x - 8y)(9x + 8y)$

b) $12a^3 - 27a = 3a(4a^2 - 9)$
$$= 3a(2a - 3)(2a + 3)$$

Example 2. Factor.

a) $m^4 - 16$ b) $(2x - 3)^2 - (y + 2)^2$

Solution.   a) $m^4 - 16 = (m^2 - 4)(m^2 + 4)$
$$= (m - 2)(m + 2)(m^2 + 4)$$

b) $(2x - 3)^2 - (y + 2)^2$
$$= [(2x - 3) - (y + 2)][(2x - 3) + (y + 2)]$$
$$= (2x - y - 5)(2x + y - 1)$$

When a binomial is squared, the result is called a *trinomial square*.

$(x + y)^2 = x^2 + 2xy + y^2$

$(x - y)^2 = x^2 - 2xy + y^2$

These identities can be used to recognize and factor trinomial squares.

Example 3. Factor.

a) $x^2 - 14x + 49$ b) $-2z^2 + 20z - 50$

Solution.   a) Since x^2 and 49 are the squares of x and -7, and since $-14x$ is double the product of x and -7, $x^2 - 14x + 49$ is a trinomial square.
$$x^2 - 14x + 49 = (x - 7)^2$$

b) $-2z^2 + 20z - 50 = -2(z^2 - 10z + 25)$
$$= -2(z - 5)^2$$

Example 4. Factor.

a) $x^2 - 8x + 16 - y^2$ b) $4a^2 - 9b^2 - c^2 + 6bc$

Solution.   a) $x^2 - 8x + 16 - y^2 = (x^2 - 8x + 16) - y^2$
$$= (x - 4)^2 - y^2$$
$$= [(x - 4) - y][(x - 4) + y]$$
$$= (x - 4 - y)(x - 4 + y)$$

b) $4a^2 - 9b^2 - c^2 + 6bc = 4a^2 - (9b^2 - 6bc + c^2)$
$$= 4a^2 - (3b - c)^2$$
$$= [2a - (3b - c)][2a + (3b - c)]$$
$$= (2a - 3b + c)(2a + 3b - c)$$

Example 5. Research scientists believe that by the year A.D. 2000 space colonies will be technically possible. One proposal is for a wheel-like colony 2000 m in diameter with an interior diameter of 200 m. The volume of the interior V is given by $V = \frac{1}{4}\pi^2(a^3 - a^2b - ab^2 + b^3)$, where a and b are the external and internal radii.

a) Express V as a product of algebraic factors.
b) What is the volume of the space colony?

Solution.   a) $V = \frac{1}{4}\pi^2(a^3 - a^2b - ab^2 + b^3)$

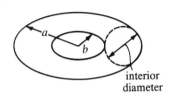

interior diameter

$$= \frac{1}{4}\pi^2[a^2(a - b) - b^2(a - b)]$$

$$= \frac{1}{4}\pi^2(a^2 - b^2)(a - b)$$

$$= \frac{1}{4}\pi^2(a - b)^2(a + b)$$

b) From the data, $a = 1000$ and $b = 800$
Substitute these values in the formula.

$$V = \frac{1}{4}\pi^2(1000 - 800)^2(1000 + 800)$$

$$= \frac{1}{4}\pi^2(40\ 000)(1800)$$

$$= 18\ 000\ 000\pi^2$$

$$\doteq 178\ 000\ 000$$

The volume of the space colony is about 178 000 000 m³.

EXERCISES 3-4

Ⓐ

1. Factor.
   a) $4x^2 - 25$
   b) $16m^2 - 81n^2$
   c) $36a^2 - 121$
   d) $9s^2 - 49t^2$
   e) $64x^2 - 169y^2$
   f) $400a^2 - 81b^2$

2. Factor.
   a) $48a^2 - 147b^2$
   b) $50m^3 - 18m$
   c) $20x^3 - 405xy^2$
   d) $63a^3 - 112ab^2$
   e) $100x^3y^2 - 324xy^4$
   f) $54y - 384x^2y$

3. Factor.
   a) $x^4 - 81$
   b) $12m^4 - 75n^4$
   c) $32a^4 - 1250b^4$
   d) $9s^4t - \frac{1}{4}t^3$
   e) $\frac{16}{25}x^2y^2 - \frac{36}{49}y^4$
   f) $256x^8 - y^8$

4. Factor.
   a) $(5x - 2)^2 - 49$
   b) $4m^2 - (6m - 7)^2$
   c) $16(3x - y)^2 - 81y^2$
   d) $(2x - 7y)^2 - (3x + 2y)^2$
   e) $(5m + 2)^2 - (3m - 8)^2$
   f) $9(2a + 5b)^2 - 4(7a - 3b)^2$

5. Factor.
   a) $(a^2 + 2a)^2 - 64$ b) $(2x^2 - 6x)^2 - 1296$
   c) $(2x^2 + 3xy)^2 - 4y^4$ d) $36n^4 - (3m^2 + 7mn)^2$
   e) $(a^2 - 13a)^2 - 900$ f) $2(x^2 - 10xy)^2 - 1152y^4$

6. Factor.
   a) $x^2 + 10x + 25$ b) $m^2 - 14m + 49$ c) $4a^2 + 12a + 9$
   d) $x^2 - 18xy + 81y^2$ e) $36x^2 + 132xy + 121y^2$ f) $9x^2 - 42xy + 49y^2$

(B)

7. Factor.
   a) $49m^2 + 70m + 25$ b) $12a^2 - 108a + 243$
   c) $16s^2 + 88s + 121$ d) $-32x^2 + 48xy - 18y^2$
   e) $9m^2 - 60mn + 100n^2$ f) $45x^2 - 210xy + 245y^2$

8. Factor.
   a) $m^2 + 6m + 9 - n^2$ b) $4x^2 - 20x + 25 - 16y^2$
   c) $9a^2 - 12a + 4 - 49b^2$ d) $x^2 + 8xy + 16y^2 - 81$
   e) $4s^2 - 20st + 25t^2 - 9$ f) $25x^2 - 80x + 64 - 64y^2$

9. Factor.
   a) $a^2 - b^2 + 8bc - 16c^2$ b) $x^2 - y^2 - 14yz - 49z^2$
   c) $25 - m^2 - 12mn - 36n^2$ d) $4s^2 - 9t^2 - 12t - 4$
   e) $x^2 - a^2 - y^2 - 2ay$ f) $a^2 - 2a + 1 - b^2 + 2bc - c^2$

10. Factor.
    a) $x^2 + 9y^2 - 25z^2 - 6xy$ b) $9m^2 - 49p^2 - 4n^2 - 28np$
    c) $x^3 + x^2 - x - 1$ d) $a^2 + 2a + 1 - b^2 + 6b - 9$
    e) $a^{2n} - b^{2n}$ f) $2x^4 - 20x^2 + 18$

11. A cylinder of height h has outside radius R and inside radius r (below left). Find an expression for the total surface area of the cylinder and write it as a product of algebraic factors.

 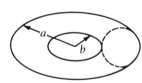

12. The surface of a torus-shaped subway tunnel of external radius a units and internal radius b units is to be lined with a strengthening material (above right). The surface area A of the tunnel is given by $A = \pi^2 a^2 - \pi^2 b^2$.
    a) Express A as a product of algebraic factors.
    b) If the diameter of the tunnel is 10 m and the external diameter of the subway is 15 km, what is the surface area in square metres?

(C)

13. Astronomers calculate the temperature T of a star from the equation $E = kT^4$, where k is a constant and E is the energy radiated by the star. If the temperature increases by an amount x, find an expression to represent the increase in energy radiated by the star, and write it as a product of factors.

3-5 FACTORING THE SUM AND DIFFERENCE OF CUBES

Only a *difference* of squares, not the sum, can be expressed as the product
of two factors. However, both the sum *and* difference of two cubes
can be factored, using the following identities. They may be easily verified
by expansion.

$x^3 - y^3 = (x - y)(x^2 + xy + y^2)$
$x^3 + y^3 = (x + y)(x^2 - xy + y^2)$

Example.   Factor.

a) $x^3 - 64$ b) $8y^3 + 27$ c) $27x^3 - 8y^3$

Solution. a) $x^3 - 64 = x^3 - 4^3$
$= (x - 4)(x^2 + 4x + 16)$
b) $8y^3 + 27 = (2y)^3 + 3^3$
$= (2y + 3)[(2y)^2 - 6y + 9]$
$= (2y + 3)(4y^2 - 6y + 9)$
c) $27x^3 - 8y^3 = (3x)^3 - (2y)^3$
$= (3x - 2y)(9x^2 + 6xy + 4y^2)$

EXERCISES 3-5

(A)

1. Factor.
   a) $z^3 - 27$ b) $y^3 + 1$ c) $8x^3 - 64$
   d) $a^3 - 8b^3$ e) $8x^3 + 27y^3$ f) $64x^3 + 1$

(B)

2. Express as a product and simplify all factors.
   a) $(x + 1)^3 - 1$ b) $(2x)^3 + 1$ c) $(x + 2)^3 - x^3$
   d) $(2x + 1)^3 + (2y)^3$ e) $(a + 2b)^3 - (a - 2b)^3$ f) $(x + y)^3 + (x - y)^3$
   g) $(x + 3)^3 + (x - 3)^3$ h) $(4 - 3a)^3 - (4 + 3a)^3$ i) $(m - 2n)^3 + (m + 2n)^3$

3. Factor.
   a) $x^6 - y^6$ b) $x^6 + y^6$ c) $64a^6 - 1$
   d) $1 + 64y^6$ e) $(x + y)^6 - (x - y)^6$ f) $(x + y)^6 + (x - y)^6$

(C)

4. The volume V of the frustum of a right
   circular cone of radii a and b and height
   h is given by
   $$V = \frac{1}{3}\pi h \left(\frac{b^3 - a^3}{b - a} \right).$$

   a) Express V as a polynomial in a
      and b.
   b) Show that when $a = b$ the formula
      becomes $V = \pi a^2 h$.

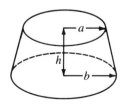

3-6 FACTORING BY GROUPING

To factor a polynomial means to express it as a product. This can be done when all the terms share a common factor.

Example 1. Factor.

    a) $4a^3b^2 - 8a^2b^2 + 12ab$ b) $-6x^4y + 15x^3y - 3x^2y$

Solution. a) The greatest common factor is $4ab$.

         $4a^3b^2 - 8a^2b^2 + 12ab = 4ab(a^2b - 2ab + 3)$

         b) The greatest common factor is $3x^2y$.

         $-6x^4y + 15x^3y - 3x^2y = 3x^2y(-2x^2 + 5x - 1)$

Some expressions have binomials or trinomials as common factors.

Example 2. Factor.

    a) $2x(3x - 4y) + 5y(3x - 4y)$

    b) $(a^2 + 3a + 1)a - 2(a^2 + 3a + 1)$

    c) $x^2(2m + 5) - 3x(2m + 5) - 10(2m + 5)$

Solution. a) $2x(3x - 4y) + 5y(3x - 4y) = (3x - 4y)(2x + 5y)$

         b) $(a^2 + 3a + 1)a - 2(a^2 + 3a + 1) = (a^2 + 3a + 1)(a - 2)$

         c) $x^2(2m + 5) - 3x(2m + 5) - 10(2m + 5)$

            $= (2m + 5)(x^2 - 3x - 10)$ Factor.

            $= (2m + 5)(x - 5)(x + 2)$

A factor may be common to only some of the terms of a polynomial, but sometimes these terms can be *grouped* so that the polynomial can be factored.

Example 3. Factor.

    a) $ax + ay + bx + by$

    b) $6x^2 + 2xy - 15x - 5y$

    c) $6m^2n - 12mn^2 + 20n^2 - 10mn$

    d) $60x^4y + 36x^3y^2 - 15x^2y^3 - 9xy^4$

Solution. a) The common factor of the first two terms is a; that of the last two terms is b.

         $ax + ay + bx + by = a(x + y) + b(x + y)$

                          $= (x + y)(a + b)$

         b) $6x^2 + 2xy - 15x - 5y = 2x(3x + y) - 5(3x + y)$

                                 $= (3x + y)(2x - 5)$

         Or, the order of the terms may be changed before grouping.

         $6x^2 + 2xy - 15x - 5y = 6x^2 - 15x + 2xy - 5y$

                                 $= 3x(2x - 5) + y(2x - 5)$

                                 $= (2x - 5)(3x + y)$

         c) $6m^2n - 12mn^2 + 20n^2 - 10mn$

         $= 2n(3m^2 - 6mn + 10n - 5m)$

         $= 2n[3m(m - 2n) + 5(2n - m)]$

         $= 2n[3m(m - 2n) - 5(m - 2n)]$ $5(2n - m) = -5(m - 2n)$

         $= 2n(m - 2n)(3m - 5)$

d) $\quad 60x^4y + 36x^3y^2 - 15x^2y^3 - 9xy^4$
$= 3xy(20x^3 + 12x^2y - 5xy^2 - 3y^3)$
$= 3xy[4x^2(5x + 3y) - y^2(5x + 3y)]$
$= 3xy[(5x + 3y)(4x^2 - y^2)]$
$= 3xy(5x + 3y)(2x + y)(2x - y)$

EXERCISES 3-6

(A)

1. Factor.
   a) $6x^2y + 15xy^2 - 27xy$
   b) $35m^3n^3 - 21m^2n^2 + 56m^2n$
   c) $12a^3b^2 + 28a^2b^3 - 44ab^4$
   d) $36s^4t^2 - 45s^2t^3 - 18st^4$
   e) $20x^3y^3 + 45x^2y^4 - 35xy^5$
   f) $42a^2b^3 - 18a^3b + 48ab^2$

2. Factor.
   a) $12x^3y^2 - 18x^2y^3 + 24x^2y^2$
   b) $28a^3b^2 - 12a^2b^3 - 48ab^4$
   c) $45m^4n + 30m^3n^2 - 75m^2n^3$
   d) $39x^3y^5 - 65x^3y^4 - 26x^5y^3$

3. Factor.
   a) $3x(2a - 7) + 5y(2a - 7)$
   b) $9x^2(4x + 3y) - y^2(4x + 3y)$
   c) $4a^2(2a - 5b) - 7b^2(5b - 2a)$
   d) $5m^2(3m - 7n + 2) + 9n^2(3m - 7n + 2)$
   e) $12x^2(4x^2 - 7x + 9) - x(4x^2 - 7x + 9) - (4x^2 - 7x + 9)$
   f) $4x^2(7x - 2y) - 5xy(7x - 2y) + (7x - 2y) + 11y^2 (2y - 7x)$

4. Factor.
   a) $5x^2y(3x^2 - 11y^2) + 4(3x^2 - 11y^2)$
   b) $2m^2(5m^2 + 3) - 7n^2(5m^2 + 3)$
   c) $6x^2(4x - 7y) - 2y^2(7y - 4x)$
   d) $16x^2(4x^2 + 5xy - 3y^2) - 25y^2(4x^2 + 5xy - 3y^2)$
   e) $3a^2(2a^2 + 9ab - 5b^2) + 4ab(2a^2 + 9ab - 5b^2) - 2b^2(2a^2 + 9ab - 5b^2)$
   f) $2m(5m^2 - 2mn + 3n) + 7mn(5m^2 - 2mn + 3n) - 13n(5m^2 - 2mn + 3n)$

5. Factor.
   a) $xm - xn + ym - yn$
   b) $10ax + 4ay - 15x - 6y$
   c) $9am + 3bm + 6an + 2bn$
   d) $14ax - 63x - 10ay + 45y$
   e) $28x^2 - 16xy + 21x - 12y$
   f) $48x^2 - 56x - 30xy + 35y$

6. Factor.
   a) $x^2 - xz - xy + yz$
   b) $x^3 + x^2 - x - 1$
   c) $21x^3 + 2y - 6x^2y - 7x$
   d) $1 + ab + a + b$
   e) $2x^3 - 3x^2 + 3 - 2x$
   f) $(x + y)^2 - x - y$

7. Factor.
   a) $x^3 + x^2 + 2x + 2$
   b) $2ac + 3ad - 2bc - 3bd$
   c) $a^3 - 4a + 4 - a^2$
   d) $(x + y)^2 + 4x + 4y$
   e) $a + ab - ac - abc$
   f) $a(a - b)^2 - a + b$

Ⓑ

8. Factor.
   a) $2(3m + 1)^2 - 7(3m + 1) - 15(3m + 1)$ b) $6(2x + y)^2 - 26x - 13y + 6$
   c) $4(3x + 1)^2 - 25(2x + y)^2$ d) $2m^3 - 128mn^2 - m^2 + 64n^2$
   e) $8a^3(3a - 2) - 3a + 2$ f) $36x^2(5x - 7y) + 49y^2(7y - 5x)$

9. Factor.
   a) $10(3m - 2)^2 + 7(3m - 2) - 12$
   b) $100m^2(9m^2 - 12m + 4) - 25(9m^2 - 12m + 4)$
   c) $4(x + 3y)^2 - 4x - 12y - 3$
   d) $10x^3 - 14x^2 - 15xy^2 + 21y^2$
   e) $4x^2(2x + 5y) - 13xy(2x + 5y) + 3y^2(2x + 5y)$

10. A rectangle has a perimeter P and a length x. Find expressions in terms of P and x for the width and the area.

11. Find the surface area of the top of the washer (below left).

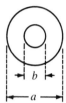
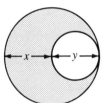

12. In the diagram (above right), find:
    a) the circumference of the larger circle   b) the area of the shaded region.

13. A circular cylinder has a radius r and a height h.
    a) If the radius is increased by x, the height staying the same, find the increase
       in: i) surface area   ii) volume.
    b) If the height is increased by y, the radius staying the same, find the increase
       in: i) surface area   ii) volume.

14. Factor.
    a) $a^4 - 2a^3 - a^3b + 2a^2b$ b) $x^3y + x^2y^2 - 3x^2y - 3xy^2$
    c) $3m^3 + 12m^2 + 12mn + 3m^2n$ d) $6a^3b^2 - 6a^2b^3 + 4a^2b^2 - 4ab^3$
    e) $10m^4 - 10m^3n - 15m^3 + 15m^2n$ f) $24x^4y - 8x^3y^2 - 36x^3y + 12x^2y^2$

Ⓒ

15. Prove that the difference between a 3-digit number and the number formed by reversing its digits is divisible by 99.

16. Prove that a 3-digit number is divisible by 9 if, and only if, the sum of its digits is divisible by 9.

17. A rectangle of length l and width w is inscribed in a circle. Semicircles are drawn on each side, as shown. Prove that the total shaded area is equal to the area of the rectangle.

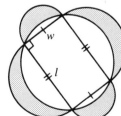

3-7 SIMPLIFYING RATIONAL EXPRESSIONS

The development of rational numbers arose naturally from the concept
of the quotient of two integers. Similarly, the concept of the quotient of
two polynomials led to the development of rational expressions.

> Any algebraic expression that can be written as the quotient of
> two polynomials is called a *rational expression*.

These are rational expressions.

$$\frac{x - 1}{2x + 3} \qquad \frac{2x^2 - 9xy + 7y^2}{5xy} \qquad 17x^2 - 6$$

These are not rational expressions.

$$\frac{1 + \sqrt{a}}{\sqrt{a^2 + 1}} \qquad \frac{x^2 + 6}{\sqrt{x}} \qquad \sqrt{x} + 3$$

Rational expressions, like rational numbers in the $\frac{m}{n}$ form, can be
reduced to lower terms by dividing numerator and denominator by any
non-zero factor common to both.

Example 1. Reduce to lowest terms.

a) $\dfrac{15x^2y}{6xy^2}$ 　　　　 b) $\dfrac{x^2 - 9x + 20}{2x - 10}$ 　　　 c) $\dfrac{m^3 - mn^2}{mn - m^2}$

Solution. 　　a) $\dfrac{15x^2y}{6xy^2} = \dfrac{(3xy)(5x)}{(3xy)(2y)}$

$$= \frac{5x}{2y}$$

b) $\dfrac{x^2 - 9x + 20}{2x - 10} = \dfrac{(x - 5)(x - 4)}{2(x - 5)}$

$$= \frac{x - 4}{2}$$

c) $\dfrac{m^3 - mn^2}{mn - m^2} = \dfrac{m(m^2 - n^2)}{m(n - m)}$

$$= \frac{(m - n)(m + n)}{n - m} \qquad m - n \text{ is the opposite of } n - m.$$

$$= \frac{(m - n)(m + n)}{-(m - n)} \qquad \text{Writing } n - m \text{ as } -(m - n)$$

$$= \frac{m + n}{-1}$$

$$= -m - n$$

When a rational expression is reduced to lowest terms, the result can be checked by substituting a convenient value for the variable. For example, in *Example 1b)* we showed that:

$$\frac{x^2 - 9x + 20}{2x - 10} = \frac{x - 4}{2}.$$

To check this, substitute 3 for x:

$$\text{L.S.} = \frac{3^2 - 9(3) + 20}{2(3) - 10} \qquad \text{R.S.} = \frac{3 - 4}{2}$$

$$= \frac{2}{-4} \qquad\qquad\quad = -\frac{1}{2}$$

$$= -\frac{1}{2}$$

The result is correct.
But, if 5 is substituted for x:

$$\text{L.S.} = \frac{5^2 - 9(5) + 20}{2(5) - 10} \qquad \text{This reduces to } \frac{0}{0}, \text{ which is not defined.}$$

$$\text{R.S.} = \frac{5 - 4}{2}$$

$$= \frac{1}{2}$$

The fact that the left side does not equal the right side shows that $\frac{x^2 - 9x + 20}{2x - 10} = \frac{x - 4}{2}$ is *not* true when $x = 5$. The reason is that 5 is a value of x for which the denominator of the given rational expression equals 0. Since division by 0 is not defined, the rational expression is not defined when $x = 5$.

> A rational expression is not defined when its denominator is equal to 0.

Example 2. For what value(s) of the variable is each expression undefined?

a) $\dfrac{2x^2 + 10x}{2x - 6}$ \qquad b) $\dfrac{-7y}{y^2 + y}$ \qquad c) $\dfrac{z^2 + 4z + 3}{z^2 + 5z + 6}$

Solution.   In each case, let the denominator equal zero.

a) Let $2x - 6 = 0$

$$x = 3$$

The expression $\dfrac{2x^2 + 10x}{2x - 6}$ is undefined when $x = 3$.

b) Let $y^2 + y = 0$

$$y(y + 1) = 0$$

$$y = 0 \text{ or } y = -1$$

The expression $\dfrac{-7y}{y^2 + y}$ is undefined when $y = 0$ or $y = -1$.

c) Let $z^2 + 5z + 6 = 0$

$(z + 2)(z + 3) = 0$

$z = -2$ or $z = -3$

The given expression is undefined when $z = -2$ or $z = -3$.

When a rational expression is simplified, the result is true only for values of the variable for which the expression is defined.

Example 3. Given   a) $\dfrac{x^2 - 5x + 4}{12 - 3x}$ b) $\dfrac{x + 5}{x^2 - 25}$

    i) Simplify each expression.

    ii) For what values of x is each result true?

Solution.   a) i) $\dfrac{x^2 - 5x + 4}{12 - 3x} = \dfrac{(x - 4)(x - 1)}{3(4 - x)}$

$$= \dfrac{x - 1}{-3}$$

$$= \dfrac{1 - x}{3}$$

    ii) $\dfrac{x^2 - 5x + 4}{12 - 3x}$ is undefined when $12 - 3x = 0$, or $x = 4$. This

        means that $\dfrac{x^2 - 5x + 4}{12 - 3x} = \dfrac{1 - x}{3}$ is true for all real values of

        x except 4.

    b) i) $\dfrac{x + 5}{x^2 - 25} = \dfrac{x + 5}{(x + 5)(x - 5)}$

$$= \dfrac{1}{x - 5}$$

    ii) $\dfrac{x + 5}{x^2 - 25}$ is undefined when $x^2 - 25 = 0$

$$(x + 5)(x - 5) = 0$$

$$x = -5 \text{ or } x = 5$$

        This means that $\dfrac{x + 5}{x^2 - 25} = \dfrac{1}{x - 5}$ is true for all real values of x

        except -5 and 5.

When working with rational expressions, it is usually inconvenient to write the restrictions on the variable for every expression. Therefore, when no restriction is stated, it is assumed that the expression is defined for all values of the variable for which the denominator is *not* zero.

EXERCISES 3-7

Ⓐ

1. Reduce to lowest terms.

a) $\dfrac{24m^2n}{15mn^2}$ b) $\dfrac{-25a^2b^3c}{40a^3bc^2}$ c) $\dfrac{18st^3}{54s^2t}$ d) $\dfrac{45x^2y^2}{-72xy^3}$ e) $\dfrac{-85m^6n^2}{-34mn^5}$

2. Reduce to lowest terms.

a) $\dfrac{6x^2 - 15xy}{9x^2 + 12x}$ b) $\dfrac{20m^2n - 24mn}{8m^2 + 12m}$ c) $\dfrac{7a^3 - 14a^2b}{14a^3 - 7a^2b}$

d) $\dfrac{6x^2 - 4xy}{-2x^2 + 2xy}$ e) $\dfrac{12m^2n^2 - 9n^4}{15mn^2 + 6n^3}$ f) $\dfrac{4x^2y - 6xy + 14y}{16y - 6xy}$

Ⓑ

3. Simplify.

a) $\dfrac{m^2 + mn - 2n^2}{3mn - 3m^2}$ b) $\dfrac{x^2 - xy - 6y^2}{2x^2y + 4xy^2}$ c) $\dfrac{2a^2 + 11ab + 15b^2}{-4a^2 - 12ab}$

d) $\dfrac{10s^3t + 15s^2t^2}{4s^2 + 12st + 9t^2}$ e) $\dfrac{6x^2 - 23xy + 20y^2}{35xy^2 - 14x^2y}$ f) $\dfrac{9mn^2 - 12m^2n}{8m^2 - 26mn + 15n^2}$

4. Simplify.

a) $\dfrac{x^2 + 5xy + 6y^2}{x^2 - 4y^2}$ b) $\dfrac{-2m^2 + 9mn - 10n^2}{m^2 - 5mn + 6n^2}$ c) $\dfrac{6a^2 + 7ab - 3b^2}{4a^2 + 16ab + 15b^2}$

d) $\dfrac{y^2 - 16x^2}{8x^2 + 14xy + 3y^2}$ e) $\dfrac{15m^2 - 26mn - 21n^2}{6m^2 - 5mn - 21n^2}$ f) $\dfrac{15x^2 - 46xy + 16y^2}{4y^2 - 25x^2}$

5. For what value(s) of the variable is each expression undefined?

a) $\dfrac{9x^3y}{15x}$ b) $\dfrac{8y}{y^2 - 2y}$ c) $\dfrac{3x^2 + 5x - 2}{5x - 20}$

d) $\dfrac{x^2 + 6x + 9}{x^2 + 7x - 8}$ e) $\dfrac{x^2 + 7x + 6}{x^2 - 6x - 7}$ f) $\dfrac{y^2 - 16}{y^2 - 8y + 16}$

6. Simplify, and state the value(s) of the variable for which each result is true.

a) $\dfrac{28x^2}{10x}$ b) $\dfrac{2x^2 + 5x - 3}{3 - 6x}$ c) $\dfrac{m^2 + 7m + 10}{m^2 + 10m + 25}$

d) $\dfrac{24ab - 8a^2b}{a^2 - 9}$ e) $\dfrac{x^3 - x^2}{x^3 + x^2}$ f) $\dfrac{6x^3 + 4x^2}{2x^2 + 14}$

Ⓒ

7. Simplify.

a) $\dfrac{10x^2 + 25xy - 15y^2}{2x^2 + 12xy + 18y^2}$ b) $\dfrac{-12m^3 + 44m^2n - 24mn^2}{14m^2n - 63mn^2 + 63n^3}$

c) $\dfrac{6x^2y + xy - y}{4x^2 + 8x + 3}$ d) $\dfrac{2x^3 - 22x^2 + 56x}{64 - 4x^2}$

e) $\dfrac{80y^2 - 5x^4y^2}{3x^3 - 6x^2 + 12x - 24}$ f) $\dfrac{18a^2b^2 + 48ab^3 + 32b^4}{45a^2b - 80b^3}$

3-8 MULTIPLYING AND DIVIDING RATIONAL EXPRESSIONS

The same procedures are used to multiply and divide rational expressions as are used to multiply and divide rational numbers.

Example 1. Simplify.

a) $\dfrac{12a^2b}{15} \times \dfrac{5ab}{8b^2}$

b) $\dfrac{6(x - 5y)}{xy^2} \div \dfrac{9(x - 5y)}{y(x + 3y)}$

Solution.

a) $\dfrac{12a^2b}{15} \times \dfrac{5ab}{8b^2} = \dfrac{\cancel{12}a^2b}{\cancel{15}} \times \dfrac{\cancel{5}ab}{\cancel{8}b^2}$

$= \dfrac{a^3}{2}$

b) $\dfrac{6(x - 5y)}{xy^2} \div \dfrac{9(x - 5y)}{y(x + 3y)} = \dfrac{\overset{2}{\cancel{6}}(x - 5y)}{xy^2} \times \dfrac{y(x + 3y)}{\underset{3}{\cancel{9}}(x - 5y)}$ Multiplying by the reciprocal

$= \dfrac{2(x + 3y)}{3xy}$

Sometimes, the numerator or denominator must be factored before the expression can be simplified.

Example 2. Simplify.

a) $\dfrac{2x + 6}{x^2 + 7x + 10} \times \dfrac{x^2 + 3x - 10}{x^2 - 4}$

b) $\dfrac{a^2 + 5a - 14}{a^2 + 8a + 7} \div \dfrac{a^2 - 4a + 4}{3a^2 - 6a}$

Solution.

a) $\dfrac{2x + 6}{x^2 + 7x + 10} \times \dfrac{x^2 + 3x - 10}{x^2 - 4} = \dfrac{2(x + 3)}{(x + 2)(x + 5)} \times \dfrac{(x + 5)(x - 2)}{(x + 2)(x - 2)}$

$= \dfrac{2(x + 3)}{(x + 2)^2}$

b) $\dfrac{a^2 + 5a - 14}{a^2 + 8a + 7} \div \dfrac{a^2 - 4a + 4}{3a^2 - 6a} = \dfrac{a^2 + 5a - 14}{a^2 + 8a + 7} \times \dfrac{3a^2 - 6a}{a^2 - 4a + 4}$

$= \dfrac{(a + 7)(a - 2)}{(a + 7)(a + 1)} \times \dfrac{3a(a - 2)}{(a - 2)(a - 2)}$

$= \dfrac{3a}{a + 1}$

Example 3.   The kinetic energy E of an object is given by the formula $E = \frac{1}{2}mv^2$, where m is its mass and v its speed. Find the ratio of the kinetic energies of two racing cars if the ratio of their masses is 2 : 3 and the ratio of their speeds is 5 : 4.

Solution.   Let the mass of car 1 be $2x$.
Then the mass of car 2 is $3x$.
Let the speed of car 1 be $5y$.
Then the speed of car 2 is $4y$.

$$\frac{\text{Kinetic energy of car 1}}{\text{Kinetic energy of car 2}} = \frac{\frac{1}{2}(2x)(5y)^2}{\frac{1}{2}(3x)(4y)^2}$$

$$= \frac{25}{24}$$

The ratio of their kinetic energies is 25 : 24.

In arithmetic a fraction such as $\dfrac{2 + \frac{3}{4}}{5 - \frac{1}{3}}$, which has other fractions in its numerator and/or denominator, is called a *complex fraction*. To simplify a complex fraction, we multiply the numerator and the denominator by the common denominator of the individual fractions.

$$\frac{2 + \frac{3}{4}}{5 - \frac{1}{3}} = \frac{\left(2 + \frac{3}{4}\right)}{\left(5 - \frac{1}{3}\right)} \times \frac{12}{12}$$

$$= \frac{24 + 9}{60 - 4}$$

$$= \frac{33}{56}$$

Sometimes, the numerator and denominator of a rational expression contain rational expressions.

Example 4. Simplify.

a) $\dfrac{y + \dfrac{3y}{2}}{2y - \dfrac{4y}{3}}$

b) $\dfrac{a + 1 - \dfrac{a^2 + 2}{a - 3}}{3 + \dfrac{a^2 - a}{a - 3}}$

Solution.

a) $\dfrac{y + \dfrac{3y}{2}}{2y - \dfrac{4y}{3}}$ The common denominator is 2.

The common denominator is 3.

Multiply the numerator and the denominator by their common denominator 2(3), or 6.

$$\dfrac{y + \dfrac{3y}{2}}{2y - \dfrac{4y}{3}} = \dfrac{\left(y + \dfrac{3y}{2}\right)}{\left(2y - \dfrac{4y}{3}\right)} \times \dfrac{6}{6}$$

$$= \dfrac{6y + 9y}{12y - 8y}$$

$$= \dfrac{15y}{4y}$$

$$= \dfrac{15}{4}, y \neq 0$$

b) $\dfrac{a + 1 - \dfrac{a^2 + 2}{a - 3}}{3 + \dfrac{a^2 - a}{a - 3}}$ The common denominator is $a - 3$.

$$\dfrac{a + 1 - \dfrac{a^2 + 2}{a - 3}}{3 + \dfrac{a^2 - a}{a - 3}} = \dfrac{\left(a + 1 - \dfrac{a^2 + 2}{a - 3}\right)}{\left(3 + \dfrac{a^2 - a}{a - 3}\right)} \times \dfrac{(a - 3)}{(a - 3)}$$

$$= \dfrac{(a + 1)(a - 3) - (a^2 + 2)}{3(a - 3) + a^2 - a}$$

$$= \dfrac{a^2 - 2a - 3 - a^2 - 2}{3a - 9 + a^2 - a}$$

$$= \dfrac{-2a - 5}{a^2 + 2a - 9}$$

EXERCISES 3-8

Ⓐ

1. Simplify.

a) $\dfrac{8m^2}{3mn} \times \dfrac{6mn^2}{4m}$

b) $\dfrac{15a^2b}{28a^3} \times \dfrac{-21b^2}{10ab}$

c) $\dfrac{12xy^3}{25x^2y^2} \div \dfrac{18x^2y}{15xy^2}$

d) $\dfrac{35st}{-24s^2t^3} \times \dfrac{-42st^2}{56s^3t}$

e) $\dfrac{-52xy^2}{32xy} \div \dfrac{-39x^3y}{-48y^2}$

f) $\dfrac{63a^3bc^2}{40ab^2} \div \dfrac{27a^2bc^4}{-15ab^3c}$

2. If $x = 2k$ and $y = 3k$, write each expression in terms of k.

a) $3x^2y$

b) $\dfrac{9x^3}{10y^2}$

c) $\dfrac{(4x^2y)^2}{3xy}$

d) $(5x^3y^2)(2xy^3)$

3. If $x = 5a$ and $y = \dfrac{1}{2b}$, write each expression in terms of a and b.

a) $4xy^2$

b) $(3x^2y)(2xy)$

c) $\dfrac{12x^2y}{25y^2}$

d) $\dfrac{(2xy^2)^2}{5xy}$

4. Simplify.

a) $\dfrac{x + \dfrac{2x}{3}}{6}$

b) $\dfrac{4a + \dfrac{a}{2}}{3a}$

c) $\dfrac{6x - \dfrac{3x}{5}}{3x}$

d) $\dfrac{3m - \dfrac{2m}{5}}{2m + \dfrac{3m}{5}}$

e) $\dfrac{5s - \dfrac{3s}{4}}{s - \dfrac{5s}{4}}$

f) $\dfrac{\dfrac{5x}{6} - 2x}{5x - \dfrac{x}{3}}$

Ⓑ

5. Simplify.

a) $\dfrac{5(2x - y)}{-3xy^2} \times \dfrac{6x^3y}{x(2x - y)}$

b) $\dfrac{4m(m - 2n)}{7(m + 3n)} \times \dfrac{3(m + 3n)}{6m^2(n - 2m)}$

c) $\dfrac{8a(2a + 5b)}{-6ab^2} \div \dfrac{-2(2a + 5b)}{a^2b(a - 3b)}$

d) $\dfrac{4(3y - x^2)}{25x(x + 2y)} \times \dfrac{15y(x + 2y)}{12(x^2 - 3y)}$

e) $\dfrac{6s(3s + 7)}{35(2s - t)} \div \dfrac{15s^2(3s + 7)}{-42(2s + t)}$

f) $\dfrac{4xy^2(8x - 3y)}{25x^3(5x^2 + 3y)} \times \dfrac{10x(5x^2 + 3y)}{2y(3y - 8x)}$

6. Simplify.

a) $\dfrac{4x^2 - 10}{x + 3y} \times \dfrac{18y^2 - 2x^2}{6x^2 - 15}$

b) $\dfrac{9a^2 - 16b^2}{4a^2 + 12ab} \div \dfrac{12ab - 9a^2}{8a + 24b}$

c) $\dfrac{6mn^2}{6m - 9} \times \dfrac{2m - 3}{-18m^2n}$

d) $\dfrac{3x^2 - 6xy}{4x + 20y} \div \dfrac{18xy - 9x^2}{3xy + 15y^2}$

e) $\dfrac{8mn}{4n^2 - m^2} \div \dfrac{4n^2}{3(m - 2n)^2}$

f) $\dfrac{20ab - 4a^2}{3ab} \times \dfrac{6ab + 6a^2}{5ab - 25b^2}$

7. Simplify.

a) $\dfrac{x + 3 - \dfrac{5x}{4}}{x - 1 + \dfrac{3x}{4}}$

b) $\dfrac{m - 2 + \dfrac{3m}{8}}{2m - 1 - \dfrac{3m}{4}}$

c) $\dfrac{3x + 1 - \dfrac{4x}{5}}{2x - 1 - \dfrac{3x}{5}}$

d) $\dfrac{2x + 5 + \dfrac{3x}{7}}{x - 3 - \dfrac{5x}{14}}$

e) $\dfrac{8a + 5 - \dfrac{3a}{2}}{3a - 7 + \dfrac{5a}{2}}$

f) $\dfrac{4x - 12 + \dfrac{3x}{8}}{8x - 24 + \dfrac{3x}{4}}$

8. Simplify.

a) $\dfrac{x - \dfrac{2}{x + 2}}{x + \dfrac{3}{x + 2}}$

b) $\dfrac{2m + \dfrac{5}{m - 3}}{5m - \dfrac{2}{m - 3}}$

c) $\dfrac{3a - \dfrac{4a}{2a + 5}}{5a - \dfrac{3a}{2a + 5}}$

d) $\dfrac{8x + \dfrac{4x}{5 - 2x}}{4x + \dfrac{2x}{5 - 2x}}$

e) $\dfrac{3m + \dfrac{2m + 1}{5m - 2}}{m - \dfrac{3m + 2}{5m - 2}}$

f) $\dfrac{5x - \dfrac{2x + 3}{3x - 4}}{2x - \dfrac{3x - 5}{3x - 4}}$

9. Simplify.

a) $\dfrac{x - 3 - \dfrac{2}{x + 2}}{x + \dfrac{3}{x + 2}}$

b) $\dfrac{2x - 1 + \dfrac{3x}{x + 1}}{3x - \dfrac{x}{x + 1}}$

c) $\dfrac{m - 2 - \dfrac{m^2 + m}{m - 1}}{m + \dfrac{2m}{m - 1}}$

d) $\dfrac{2a + \dfrac{5a^2 - 3}{2a - 1}}{3a - \dfrac{2a}{2a - 1}}$

e) $\dfrac{x - 3 - \dfrac{x^2 - 5x}{x - 2}}{x + \dfrac{2x}{x - 2}}$

f) $\dfrac{2s - 5 - \dfrac{2s^2 - 3s}{s + 1}}{3s - 1 - \dfrac{2s + 1}{s + 1}}$

10. Simplify.

a) $\dfrac{a^2 + 4a - 21}{-a^2 + 8a - 15} \div \dfrac{a^2 + 6a - 7}{a^2 - 4a - 5}$

b) $\dfrac{x^2 + 11xy + 28y^2}{x^2 + 12xy + 32y^2} \div \dfrac{x^2 + 9xy + 14y^2}{x^2 + 6xy - 16y^2}$

c) $\dfrac{x^2 - 16y^2}{x^2 - 2xy} \times \dfrac{x^2 - 4xy}{x^2 - 6xy + 8y^2} \div \dfrac{x^2 + 4xy}{x - 2y}$

d) $\dfrac{3m^2 - 30mn + 48n^2}{m^2 + 3mn - 10n^2} \times \dfrac{m^2 + 8mn + 15n^2}{128n^2 - 2m^2}$

e) $\dfrac{6s^3 - 13s^2t - 5st^2}{6s^2 - st - t^2} \times \dfrac{6s^2 + 5st - 4t^2}{8s^2 - 50t^2}$

11. The resistance R of a wire to an electric current is given by the formula $R = \dfrac{kl}{A}$, where k is a constant, l is the length, and A is the cross-sectional area of the wire. Find the ratio of the resistances of two wires of the same material having lengths in the ratio 3 : 8 and cross-sectional areas in the ratio 1 : 4.

12. Two cylinders have radii in the ratio 6 : 5 and heights in the ratio 7 : 9. Find the ratio of:
    a) their volumes
    b) their surface areas.

13. In house construction, the safe load m kilograms on a floor joist l metres long is given by the formula $m = \dfrac{4th^2}{l}$, where t is the thickness and h the height of the joist in centimetres. By what factor is each joist stronger than a 5 cm by 10 cm joist?
    a) 5 cm by 15 cm
    b) 5 cm by 20 cm

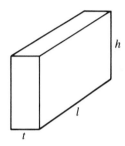

Ⓒ

14. For any triangle of side lengths a, b, and c, the radii of the inscribed circle and the circumcircle, r and R respectively, are given by these formulas.

$$r^2 = \frac{(-a + b + c)(a - b + c)(a + b - c)}{4(a + b + c)}$$

$$R^2 = \frac{a^2b^2c^2}{(a + b + c)(-a + b + c)(a - b + c)(a + b - c)}$$

    a) Find the product R^2r^2, and use the result to express R in terms of r.
    b) Find expressions for R and r if $\angle B$ is 90°.

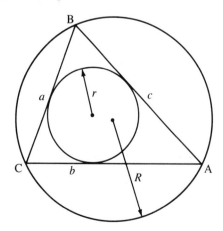

3-9 ADDING AND SUBTRACTING RATIONAL EXPRESSIONS

To add or subtract rational expressions it is necessary, as with rational numbers, to raise them to higher terms to obtain the lowest common denominator (l.c.d.).

Example 1. Simplify.

a) $\dfrac{1}{x^2} + \dfrac{5}{xy}$ b) $\dfrac{2}{5mn} - \dfrac{3n + 3m^2}{2m^2} + 3$ c) $\dfrac{x + 5}{x - 3} - \dfrac{x - 2}{x + 1}$

Solution.   a) The l.c.d. is x^2y.

$$\frac{1}{x^2} + \frac{5}{xy} = \frac{1}{x^2} \times \frac{y}{y} + \frac{5}{xy} \times \frac{x}{x}$$

$$= \frac{y}{x^2y} + \frac{5x}{x^2y}$$

$$= \frac{y + 5x}{x^2y}$$

b) The l.c.d. is $10m^2n$.

$$\frac{2}{5mn} - \frac{3n + m^2}{2m^2} + 3$$

$$= \frac{2}{5mn} \times \frac{2m}{2m} - \left(\frac{3n + m^2}{2m^2}\right) \times \frac{5n}{5n} + 3 \times \frac{10m^2n}{10m^2n}$$

$$= \frac{4m}{10m^2n} - \frac{(15n^2 + 5m^2n)}{10m^2n} + \frac{30m^2n}{10m^2n}$$

$$= \frac{4m - 15n^2 - 5m^2n + 30m^2n}{10m^2n}$$

$$= \frac{4m - 15n^2 + 25m^2n}{10m^2n}$$

c) The l.c.d. is $(x - 3)(x + 1)$.

$$\frac{x + 5}{x - 3} - \frac{x - 2}{x + 1} = \frac{x + 5}{x - 3} \times \frac{x + 1}{x + 1} - \frac{x - 2}{x + 1} \times \frac{x - 3}{x - 3}$$

$$= \frac{(x^2 + 6x + 5) - (x^2 - 5x + 6)}{(x - 3)(x + 1)}$$

$$= \frac{11x - 1}{(x - 3)(x + 1)}$$

Frequently, the denominators of rational expressions must be factored to determine the l.c.d.

Example 2. Simplify.

a) $\dfrac{1}{2x - 6} - \dfrac{x}{x^2 - 9}$ b) $\dfrac{x + 5}{x^2 - 2x - 15} + \dfrac{5x - 2}{5x - x^2}$

Solution. a) $\dfrac{1}{2x - 6} - \dfrac{x}{x^2 - 9} = \dfrac{1}{2(x - 3)} - \dfrac{x}{(x - 3)(x + 3)}$

$$= \dfrac{1}{2(x - 3)} \times \dfrac{x + 3}{x + 3} - \dfrac{x}{(x - 3)(x + 3)} \times \dfrac{2}{2}$$

$$= \dfrac{x + 3 - 2x}{2(x - 3)(x + 3)}$$

$$= \dfrac{3 - x}{2(x - 3)(x + 3)}$$

$$= \dfrac{-1}{2(x + 3)}$$

b) $\dfrac{x + 5}{x^2 - 2x - 15} + \dfrac{5x - 2}{5x - x^2}$

$= \dfrac{x + 5}{(x - 5)(x + 3)} + \dfrac{5x - 2}{x(5 - x)}$ Write $5 - x$ as $-(x - 5)$.

$= \dfrac{x + 5}{(x - 5)(x + 3)} \times \dfrac{x}{x} - \dfrac{5x - 2}{x(x - 5)} \times \dfrac{x + 3}{x + 3}$

$= \dfrac{x^2 + 5x - (5x^2 + 13x - 6)}{x(x - 5)(x + 3)}$

$= \dfrac{-4x^2 - 8x + 6}{x(x - 5)(x + 3)}$

Real-world problems often involve the addition or subtraction of rational expressions.

Example 3. Water has an unusual property; at temperatures below 4°C, it expands as it cools. At 4°C, the density of water is 1 kg/L. If 1 kg of water, cooling from 4°C, increases in volume by x litres, by how much does its density decrease?

Solution. Density $= \dfrac{\text{mass}}{\text{volume}}$

At 4°C, volume of 1 kg of water is 1 L

density of 1 kg of water is 1 kg/L

At a lower temperature, volume of 1 kg of water is $(1 + x)$ litres

density of 1 kg of water is $\dfrac{1}{(1 + x)}$ kilograms/L

Decrease in density $= 1 - \dfrac{1}{1 + x}$

$$= \dfrac{1 + x}{1 + x} - \dfrac{1}{1 + x}$$

$$= \dfrac{x}{1 + x}$$

The decrease in density of 1 kg of water which increases in volume by x litres is $\dfrac{x}{1 + x}$ kilograms per litre.

EXERCISES 3-9

Ⓐ

1. Simplify.

   a) $\dfrac{2}{x} + \dfrac{3}{y}$

   b) $\dfrac{8}{x} - \dfrac{5}{x^2}$

   c) $\dfrac{4}{x^2} + \dfrac{11}{xy}$

   d) $\dfrac{7}{xy^2} - \dfrac{15}{x^2y}$

   e) $\dfrac{12}{xy} - \dfrac{9}{yz}$

   f) $\dfrac{6}{x^2} + \dfrac{19}{y^2}$

2. Simplify.

   a) $\dfrac{5m}{n} - \dfrac{3n}{m}$

   b) $\dfrac{17a}{bc} + \dfrac{5b}{ac}$

   c) $\dfrac{8y}{x} + \dfrac{13x}{y^2}$

   d) $\dfrac{2s}{t^2} - \dfrac{11s}{t}$

   e) $\dfrac{15n^2}{m} + \dfrac{11n}{m^2}$

   f) $\dfrac{23x}{y^2} - \dfrac{16y}{x}$

3. Simplify.

   a) $\dfrac{3x}{y^2} + \dfrac{2x - 5y}{xy}$

   b) $\dfrac{2a}{b^2} - \dfrac{6a + 11}{ab}$

   c) $\dfrac{7x - 2y}{xy^2} - \dfrac{12x - 5y}{x^2y}$

   d) $\dfrac{4a}{3b} + \dfrac{2a - 9b}{4a}$

   e) $\dfrac{9s - 5t}{4t} + \dfrac{3t}{5s}$

   f) $\dfrac{8x - 3y}{7x} - \dfrac{2x + 5y}{4y}$

4. Simplify.

   a) $\dfrac{3x}{10y} + \dfrac{8x - 7}{4x}$

   b) $\dfrac{5m + 9}{8m} - \dfrac{5m}{6n}$

   c) $\dfrac{2a - 5}{4a} - \dfrac{7a + 2}{6b}$

   d) $\dfrac{6x - 11y}{9x} + \dfrac{3x - 16y}{6y}$

   e) $\dfrac{12m - 5n}{6m} - \dfrac{4m + 9n}{10n}$

5. Simplify.

   a) $\dfrac{2}{3xy} + \dfrac{7x^2 - 4y}{5x^2} + 1$

   b) $\dfrac{3a + b^2}{4b^2} - \dfrac{7}{5ab} - 2$

   c) $\dfrac{9m}{7n^2} + \dfrac{3m^2 - 8n}{4mn^2} + \dfrac{5}{n}$

   d) $\dfrac{2x + 3y^2}{8xy} - 3 - \dfrac{5x^2 - 2y}{6x^2}$

6. Simplify.

   a) $\dfrac{5}{m + 3} + \dfrac{7}{m + 4}$

   b) $\dfrac{2a}{3a - 4} + \dfrac{7a}{5a - 2}$

   c) $\dfrac{9m}{3m - 7} - \dfrac{2m}{5m - 3}$

   d) $\dfrac{x + 3}{x + 5} + \dfrac{x - 2}{x + 4}$

   e) $\dfrac{5x + 2}{3x - 2} - \dfrac{3x - 7}{2x + 5}$

   f) $\dfrac{2m + 9}{5m - 4} - \dfrac{3m + 1}{2m - 3}$

7. Simplify.

a) $\dfrac{7a}{2a - 10} + \dfrac{4a}{3a - 15}$

b) $\dfrac{9x}{4 - x^2} - \dfrac{3}{x + 2}$

c) $\dfrac{3x}{4x^2 - 10x} - \dfrac{x}{35 - 14x}$

d) $\dfrac{7m}{6m^2 - 15m} + \dfrac{12m}{25 - 4m^2}$

e) $\dfrac{2a}{a^2 - 6a + 8} + \dfrac{7a}{a^2 - a - 12}$

f) $\dfrac{7x}{x^2 - x - 12} - \dfrac{4x}{x^2 + 2x - 3}$

(B)

8. Simplify.

a) $\dfrac{x - 3}{x^2 - 9x + 20} + \dfrac{2x - 1}{x^2 - 7x + 12}$

b) $\dfrac{3x + 2}{36 - x^2} - \dfrac{x - 4}{x^2 - 8x + 12}$

c) $\dfrac{a - 2}{32 + 4a - a^2} - \dfrac{a - 1}{a^2 - 2a - 48}$

d) $\dfrac{2m + 5}{m^2 - 6m + 5} + \dfrac{4m - 3}{m^2 - 5m + 4}$

e) $\dfrac{x - 6}{x^2 - 11x + 28} - \dfrac{x - 5}{x^2 - 8x + 7}$

f) $\dfrac{3a + 2}{a^2 + 10a + 21} + \dfrac{5a - 4}{15 + 2a - a^2}$

9. The time t to travel a distance d at a constant speed v can be obtained from the formula $d = vt$. If the speed is increased by x, find an expression to represent the decrease in time to travel the same distance.

10. The volume v litres of a sample of hydrogen chloride gas is given by the formula $pv = 280$, where p is the pressure in kilopascals. If p is increased by x kilopascals, what is the corresponding decrease in volume?

11. The intensity of light I reaching a screen from a light source r metres away is given by the formula $I = \dfrac{k}{r^2}$, where k is a constant. Find an expression for the change in I when the light source is moved x metres farther from the screen.

12. It is 160 km from Camden to Newport. How much time is saved on the trip by increasing an average speed of 80 km/h by x kilometres per hour?

(C)

13. What value of k makes each equation a true statement?

a) $\dfrac{5}{8m} - \dfrac{7m}{6} = \dfrac{k}{24m}$

b) $\dfrac{3}{x - 5} - \dfrac{k}{x + 2} = \dfrac{46 - 5x}{(x - 5)(x + 2)}$

c) $\dfrac{k}{8a} - \dfrac{5}{12a} = \dfrac{53}{24a}$

d) $\dfrac{2a + 4}{2a - 1} - \dfrac{k}{a + 5} = \dfrac{21a + 17}{(2a - 1)(a + 5)}$

3-10 APPLICATIONS OF RATIONAL EXPRESSIONS

Many problems in engineering and science involve rational expressions. The expressions are almost always simpler than those worked with earlier in the chapter.

Example 1. A rectangular poster is to have an area of 6000 cm². If w, l, and P represent its width, length, and perimeter respectively, write an expression in terms of w for:

   a) the length   b) the perimeter

   c) the change in length when the width is increased by 1 cm.

Solution.   a) $wl = 6000$

$$l = \frac{6000}{w}$$

b) $P = 2(l + w)$

$$= 2\left(\frac{6000}{w} + w\right)$$

$$= 2\left(\frac{6000 + w^2}{w}\right)$$

c) When w increases to $w + 1$, l decreases to $\dfrac{6000}{(w + 1)}$.

$$\text{Change in length} = \frac{6000}{w} - \frac{6000}{w + 1}$$

$$= \frac{6000w + 6000 - 6000w}{w(w + 1)}$$

$$= \frac{6000}{w(w + 1)}$$

Example 2. Car A leaves town travelling east at 80 km/h. Car B leaves 10 min later travelling at v kilometres per hour and overtakes car A after t hours.

   a) Find the distance, in terms of v and t, that each car travels until B overtakes A.

   b) Express t in terms of v, and draw a graph.

   c) How fast would car B have to travel to overtake car A in 30 min?

Solution.   a) At the moment of overtaking:

car B has travelled for t hours, and covered a distance of vt kilometres

car A has travelled for t hours + 10 min, and covered a distance of

$$80\left(t + \frac{10}{60}\right), \text{ or } \left(80t + \frac{40}{3}\right) \text{ kilometres}$$

b) Since both cars have covered the same distance: $vt = 80t + \dfrac{40}{3}$

To solve for t we write: $vt - 80t = \dfrac{40}{3}$

$$t(v - 80) = \frac{40}{3}$$

$$t = \frac{40}{3(v - 80)}$$

Substitute values of *v*.

v	*t*
85	2.67
90	1.33
95	0.89
100	0.67
105	0.53
110	0.44
115	0.38
120	0.33

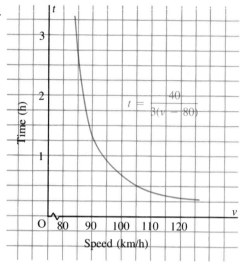

c) From the graph, $v \doteq 105$ km/h when $t = 30$ min.

For a more accurate value, substitute $\frac{1}{2}$ for *t* in the equation above.

$$\frac{1}{2} = \frac{40}{3(v - 80)}$$
$$3v - 240 = 80$$
$$3v = 320$$
$$v = \frac{320}{3}$$
$$\doteq 107$$

Car B would have to travel at approximately 107 km/h to overtake car A in 30 min.

EXERCISES 3-10

1. In *Example 1*, express the change in the perimeter of the poster in terms of the width if the width is increased by 1 cm.

2. A rectangular board has an area of 6000 cm² and a width of *w* centimetres.
   a) Write an expression for the length of the board.
   b) If the width is increased by *x* centimetres, write an expression for:
      i) the decrease in length   ii) the change in perimeter.

3. In *Example 2*, assume that car B's speed is 100 km/h.
   a) How long will it take car B to overtake car A?
   b) By how much is the time to overtake lessened if car B's speed is increased by *x* kilometres per hour?
   c) Graph the relation formed in part b).
   d) Interpret the above results if $x < 0$.

4. Gordana starts out on a snowmobile trail and travels at 30 km/h. Heidi leaves 5 min later travelling at v kilometres per hour and overtakes Gordana after t hours.
   a) Express t in terms of v, and draw the graph.
   b) How fast would Heidi have to travel to overtake Gordana in 20 min?

(B)

5. In *Example 2*, by how many minutes would the time for car B to overtake car A be shortened if car B's speed is increased by x kilometres per hour?

6. A rectangular lot with an area of 2000 m² is to be fenced on three sides, the fourth side being a stream. The sections of fence opposite each other are x metres long.
   a) Express the total length of fencing L in terms of x, and draw the graph.
   b) Use the graph to estimate the dimensions of the lot requiring the least amount of fencing.

7. An open cardboard box with a square base with a side of x centimetres has a volume of 100 cm³.
   a) Express in terms of x.
      i) the height h of the box
      ii) the area A of cardboard
   b) From a graph of A against x, estimate the dimensions of the box that has the least amount of cardboard.

8. A poster is to have 400 cm² of printed matter with margins of 10 cm at the top and bottom and 5 cm at each side. The width, height, and area of the poster are w, h, and A respectively.
   a) Express h in terms of w.
   b) Express A in terms of w, and draw the graph.

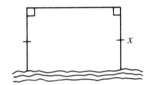

9. When two resistances r and s are connected in parallel, their combined resistance R can be obtained from the formula $\frac{1}{R} = \frac{1}{r} + \frac{1}{s}$. If r is increased by x ohms and s decreased by x ohms, what is the change in the combined resistance?

(C)

10. A sailor falls overboard from a ship in a convoy travelling at 10 km/h. Two minutes later a ship travels back from the convoy at 20 km/h for the rescue. It takes 1 min to pick the sailor up and then the rescue ship returns at 20 km/h to the convoy which has continued on its way at a steady 10 km/h.
    a) How much time elapses from the sailor falling overboard to the ship rejoining the convoy?
    b) If the speed of the rescue ship is v kilometres per hour, express the rescue time t minutes in terms of v, and draw a graph for reasonable values of v.
    c) From the graph, find t when v is: i) 12 km/h   ii) 15 km/h.

Review Exercises

1. Simplify.
   a) $9m^2 + 3mn - 4n^2 - 5m^2 - 14mn - 11n^2$
   b) $-5s^2 - 3st + 16t^2 + 9st - 3s^2 - 8t^2$
   c) $a^2 - 5b^2 + 3ab - 7b^2 - 8ab - 4a^2$
   d) $29m^2n^3 + 19m^2n^2 - 41mn^3 - 13n^2m^2 + 17mn^3 - 15m^2n^3$

2. Simplify.
   a) $(8ab)(7a^2b^3)$ b) $(-9a^3b)(7ab^3)$ c) $(-13x^5y)(-12x^5y^4)$
   d) $(14m^3n^3)(-13nm^2)$ e) $(3x^2y)(8x^3y)$ f) $(17s^6t^3)(-6s^5t^4)$

3. Simplify.
   a) $\dfrac{14x^3y^2}{35xy} \times \dfrac{39x^4y^3}{2x^3y^4}$ b) $\dfrac{-15ab^2}{75a^2b} \times \dfrac{50a^3b}{ab^4}$
   c) $\dfrac{(3x^2y)^2}{27x^3y} \times \dfrac{63xy^2}{(4xy)^3}$ d) $\dfrac{7abc}{63a^2bc} \times \dfrac{27a^3b^2c^3}{3ab^2c^2}$

4. Simplify.
   a) $(x + 2y)(x + 3y) + (2x + y)(3x + y)$
   b) $(a - 2b)(a + 3b) - (2a - b)(3a + b)$
   c) $(3m + 2n)^2 - 2(2m - n)^2$
   d) $(11x - 2y)(11x + 2y) + (2x - 11y)(11y + 2x)$

5. Factor.
   a) $4x^2 - 16x + 15$ b) $3w^2 - 14w + 15$
   c) $9x^2 + 12x + 4$ d) $6m^2 - m - 15$

6. Factor.
   a) $6m^2 - 7mn + 2n^2$ b) $4a^2 - ab - 3b^2$
   c) $3a^2 - 10ab - 8b^2$ d) $-2x^2 + 13x - 15$

7. Factor.
   a) $(3x + 4)^2 - (2x - 3)^2$ b) $81m^2 - (9m + 3)^2$
   c) $4x^2 + 20x + 25$ d) $9x^2 - 24x + 16$
   e) $a^2 - 2ab + b^2 + a - b$ f) $9x^2 - 25y^2 + 10y - 1$

8. Factor.
   a) $2ax - ay + 4bx - 2by$ b) $6sm + 9tm - 4sn - 6tn$
   c) $18ax + 24x - 3ay - 4y$ d) $35x^2 - 20xy - 42x + 24y$

9. Factor.   a) $125x^3 - 27y^3$ b) $(a - 1)^3 + (a + 1)^3$

10. For what value(s) of the variable is each expression undefined?
    a) $\dfrac{x^2 + 10x + 11}{x^2 - 121}$ b) $\dfrac{m^2 + 8m + 12}{m^2 + 12m + 36}$
    c) $\dfrac{4s^2 + st + t^2}{10st + 15t}$ d) $\dfrac{2a^2 + 5ab - 3b^2}{9a^2 - 25b^2}$
    e) $\dfrac{3cd^2}{6c^2 - cd - 12d^2}$ f) $\dfrac{r^2s + 3rs^2 + 2s^3}{12r^3 - 7r^2s - 12rs^2}$

11. Simplify.

a) $\dfrac{x^2 - 25}{6x - 2x^2} \times \dfrac{x^2 - 7x + 12}{x^2 + x - 20}$

b) $\dfrac{6m^2 - 18mn}{m^2 - 5mn + 6n^2} \times \dfrac{m^2 + 2mn - 8n^2}{8m^2 + 32mn}$

c) $\dfrac{2a^2 + 7ab + 3b^2}{3a^2 + 13ab + 12b^2} \div \dfrac{4a^2 + 4ab + b^2}{3a^2 - 2ab - 8b^2}$

d) $\dfrac{x^4y^2 - x^2y^4}{x^2 + 2xy + y^2} \div \dfrac{(x - y)^2}{3x^2 + 3xy}$

12. Simplify.

a) $\dfrac{8m - 5}{m^2} + \dfrac{7}{mn}$

b) $\dfrac{9x^2 + 4x}{xy^2} - \dfrac{3}{xy}$

c) $\dfrac{5s^2}{t^2} - \dfrac{2s - 9}{s^2t}$

d) $\dfrac{6m - 2}{5m} - \dfrac{3m}{2n}$

e) $\dfrac{5x}{3y} - \dfrac{8x + 2y}{7x}$

f) $\dfrac{2m + 11n}{5m} - \dfrac{6m - 9n}{3n}$

13. Simplify.

a) $\dfrac{3}{y - x} - \dfrac{2x}{x^2 - y^2}$

b) $\dfrac{x^2 + 3x + 2}{x^2 - 1} - \dfrac{2x}{x + 1}$

c) $\dfrac{5x^2 - 10x}{4 - x^2} - \dfrac{x^2 + 4x + 4}{(x + 2)(x - 3)}$

d) $\dfrac{x^2 + 4x + 3}{x^2 + 5x + 4} - \dfrac{x^2 - 9}{x^2 - 6x + 9}$

e) $\dfrac{x^2 - 49}{x^2 - 8x + 7} - \dfrac{2 - 2x}{x^2 - 1}$

f) $\dfrac{2a + 4}{a^2 - 4} - \dfrac{3a - 2}{2 - a}$

14. Simplify.

a) $\dfrac{x + 2 - \dfrac{3}{x + 4}}{x + \dfrac{2}{x + 4}}$

b) $\dfrac{m + 3 - \dfrac{4m}{m - 2}}{m - 1 + \dfrac{3m}{m - 2}}$

c) $\dfrac{a + 2 - \dfrac{5a^2 + 7}{3a - 2}}{a - 4 - \dfrac{2a^2}{3a - 2}}$

d) $\dfrac{2x - 5 - \dfrac{3x^2 + 7}{x + 1}}{3x + 2 - \dfrac{x^2 + 3x}{x + 1}}$

15. When two thin lenses with focal lengths a and b are in contact, the focal length F of the combination can be obtained from the formula $\dfrac{1}{F} = \dfrac{1}{a} + \dfrac{1}{b}$. The focal length of a combination of two identical lenses is 50 mm. If one lens is replaced by another having a focal length x millimetres less than the one it replaces, by how much does the focal length of the combination change?

16. A garbage disposal bin with a volume of 80 m³ has a square base, w metres by w metres. Write an expression in terms of w for:
   a) the height h of the bin
   b) the change in height when each side of the base is decreased by 1 m.

Cumulative Review, Chapters 1-3

1. Simplify.
   a) $3\sqrt{12} + 4\sqrt{27} - \sqrt{75}$
   b) $\sqrt{32} - 2\sqrt{24} - 4\sqrt{18}$
   c) $2\sqrt{5}(3\sqrt{7} + 8\sqrt{12})$
   d) $(4\sqrt{3} - 2\sqrt{5})(4\sqrt{3} + 2\sqrt{5})$

2. Simplify.
   a) $\dfrac{33\sqrt{6}}{3\sqrt{24}}$
   b) $\dfrac{12}{5\sqrt{7}}$
   c) $\dfrac{8\sqrt{2} - 6}{\sqrt{2}}$
   d) $\dfrac{6\sqrt{5} + \sqrt{8}}{\sqrt{5}}$

3. Solve.   a) $\sqrt{5x + 4} = 7$ b) $\sqrt{2x - 3} + 3 = x$ c) $2x + 2\sqrt{x} = 5$

4. Simplify.   a) $4(3)^2 - 3(2)^4$ b) $(-4)^2 + (-3)^4$ c) $-5^4 + 6^3$

5. Simplify.
   a) $2a^4b \times 4a^3b^5$
   b) $8c^5b^{-2} \times 3c^{-1}b^{-6}$
   c) $18y^4h^5 \div 9yh^3$
   d) $24x^{-2}y^7 \div 8x^3y^{-4}$
   e) $(4m^8n^{-2})^3$
   f) $\dfrac{(x^{a+1})^2(x^{a-3})^3}{(x^3)^a}$

6. What amount of money invested at 9% compounded annually will grow to $7000 in 4 years?

7. Express as a power.   a) $\sqrt[3]{17^4}$ b) $(\sqrt{19})^7$ c) $\dfrac{1}{\sqrt[5]{73}}$

8. Simplify.   a) $4^{\frac{5}{2}}$ b) $\left(\dfrac{16}{625}\right)^{0.25}$ c) $81^{-\frac{3}{4}}$ d) $49^{\frac{1}{2}} - 64^{\frac{5}{6}}$

9. Solve.
   a) $5^x = 3125$
   b) $\left(\dfrac{4}{5}\right)^x = \dfrac{64}{125}$
   c) $7^x = \dfrac{1}{343}$
   d) $3^x + 4 = 85$

10. The number of chinch bugs in a lawn doubles every month. If there are about 300 bugs now, how long will it take for their number to grow to 19 000?

11. Simplify.
    a) $4m^2n - 3mn^2 + m^2n - 5mn^2$
    b) $(2ab)(-4a^2b^3)$
    c) $(x^4y^3)^5(xy^2)^3$

12. Factor completely.
    a) $4x^2y^3 + 12x^3y^2 - 20x^3y^3$
    b) $a^2x + b^2y + b^2x + a^2y$
    c) $15x^3y^3 - 12x^3y^2 - 10x^2y^3 + 8x^2y^2$
    d) $8a^2 + 22a + 5$
    e) $24b^2 - 26bc + 5c^2$
    f) $4a^2 - 28a + 49$
    g) $9z^2 - 144r^2$
    h) $y^2 - m^2 + 10mc - 25c^2$
    i) $y^3 - 125$
    j) $27a^3 + 8d^3$

13. Simplify.
    a) $\dfrac{a^2 - 4a}{a^2 + 12a + 36} \times \dfrac{a^2 - 36}{a^2 - 10a + 24}$
    b) $\dfrac{x^4 - y^4}{x^2 + xy - 2y^2} \div \dfrac{x^2 + 2xy + y^2}{x^2 + 10xy + 16y^2}$
    c) $\dfrac{5}{2y} + \dfrac{y - 6}{y - 3}$
    d) $\dfrac{9}{x^2 - 2x - 3} - \dfrac{7}{x^2 - 10x + 21}$

4 Quadratic Equations

In the 1984 Summer Olympics, the Canadian diver,
Sylvie Bernier, won a gold medal in springboard diving.
After she leaves the board, how long does it take her
to reach the water? (See Section 4-5 *Example 3*.)

4-1 QUADRATIC EQUATIONS

Daring divers in Acapulco, Mexico, dive into the sea from high on the cliffs. The time t it takes them to reach the water is given by an equation such as:
$4.9t^2 - t - 35 = 0$.
This is an example of a quadratic equation.

> An equation that can be written in the form
> $ax^2 + bx + c = 0$, where $a \neq 0$,
> is called a *quadratic equation*.

These are quadratic equations because they can be written in the form $ax^2 + bx + c = 0$, $a \neq 0$.

$(x - 5)(x + 2) = 0$ $9y - 0.6y^2 = 0$
$1 + \sqrt{3}x - x^2 = 0$ $5x^2 - 4 = 41$

These are *not* quadratic equations because they cannot be written in the form $ax^2 + bx + c = 0$, $a \neq 0$.

$2x - 3 = 6x + 9$
$x^3 + 2x^2 - 3x - 6 = 0$
$(x + 1)(x - 4)(x + 2) = 0$

The terms of a quadratic equation are named as follows:

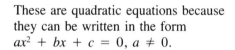

$$ax^2 + bx + c = 0$$

quadratic   linear   constant
term   term   term

     In the equation $5x^2 - 4 = 41$, there is no linear term. Such an equation is solved by reducing it to the form $x^2 = c$, then taking the square root of each side. Two solutions are obtained:
$x = \sqrt{c}$ and $x = -\sqrt{c}, \quad c > 0$.

Example 1.   Solve.

     a) $5x^2 - 4 = 41$ b) $19 - 3x^2 = 4$
     c) $x^2 + 12 = 3$ d) $ax^2 + b = c$ $(a \neq 0)$

Solution.   a) $5x^2 - 4 = 41$ b) $19 - 3x^2 = 4$
           $5x^2 = 45$ $15 = 3x^2$
            $x^2 = 9$ $5 = x^2$
            $x = \pm 3$ $x = \pm\sqrt{5}$

     c) $x^2 + 12 = 3$ d) $ax^2 + b = c$
          $x^2 = -9$ $ax^2 = c - b$

     There is no solution in the set of real numbers.

$$x^2 = \frac{c - b}{a}$$

$$x = \pm\sqrt{\frac{c - b}{a}}, \quad \frac{c - b}{a} \geq 0$$

The solutions of many problems involve quadratic equations without linear terms.

Example 2. The distance d metres that an object falls from rest in t seconds is given by the formula $d = 4.9t^2$.

a) How far does an object fall from rest in 3 s?

b) How long does it take an object to fall 200 m?

Solution. a) Substitute 3 for t in the formula. $\quad d = 4.9 \times 3^2$

$$= 44.1$$

In 3 s, an object will fall about 44 m.

b) Substitute 200 for d in the formula. $\quad 200 = 4.9t^2$

$$t = \pm\sqrt{\frac{200}{4.9}}$$

$$\doteq \pm 6.4$$

Since $t > 0$, the negative root is rejected. It takes about 6.4 s to fall 200 m.

EXERCISES 4-1

(A)

1. Solve.

   a) $m^2 - 5 = 11$
   b) $4x^2 - 9 = 0$
   c) $2a^2 + 1 = 51$
   d) $3s^2 + 29 = 2$
   e) $(x - 4)^2 = 18$
   f) $4(m + 3)^2 = 32$

2. Find the length of the side of a square if its area is:

   a) 12 cm²
   b) 32 m²
   c) 1.5 km²

3. Use the formula in *Example 2* to determine:

   a) how far an object falls in 5.2 s
   b) how long it takes an object to fall 500 m.

(B)

4. Solve and check.

   a) $2x^2 + 3 = 7$
   b) $5a^2 - 8 = 42$
   c) $3(5 - s)^2 = 30$
   d) $15(m^2 - 4) = 4(m^2 + 7)$
   e) $4(x^2 + 3) - 28 = 2(x^2 - 5)$
   f) $7(2a^2 - 9) = 3(a^2 + 5) - 1$

5. Solve.

   a) $(x + 1)(2x + 4) = (x + 2)(x + 4)$
   b) $(x + 4)(2x + 1) = (x + 5)(x + 4)$
   c) $(x + 2)(4x + 1) = (x + 3)(2x + 3)$
   d) $(2x - 3)(x - 5) = (x - 6)(x - 7)$
   e) $(2x + 1)(x + 7) = (x + 7)(x + 8)$
   f) $(2x + 7)(2x - 5) = (2x - 8)(x + 6)$

6. The maximum distance d kilometres that a lighthouse beam can be seen is given by the formula $d^2 = 13h$, where h metres is the height of the light above water level.
   a) Calculate the maximum distance of visibility for a height of:
      i) 50 m
      ii) 100 m.
   b) Calculate the height required for a maximum distance of visibility of:
      i) 30 km
      ii) 60 km.

7. Solve for the variable(s) indicated.
   a) $a^2 + b^2 = c^2$ a, b, c
   b) $v^2 = u^2 + 2as$ v, u
   c) $A = \pi r^2$ r
   d) $V = \pi r^2 h$ r

8. Calculate the radius of a circle that has an area of:
   a) 100 cm²   b) 1.5 m²   c) 9π km².

9. The surface area A of a ball of radius r is given by the formula $A = 4\pi r^2$.
   a) Find the surface area of a ball of radius:
      i) 4 cm
      ii) 12.5 cm.
   b) Find the radius of a ball that has a surface area of:
      i) 296 cm²
      ii) 1348 cm².

10. The volume V of a cone is given by the
    formula $V = \dfrac{1}{3}\pi r^2 h$.

    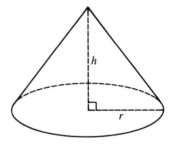

    a) Find the volume of a cone with radius 15 m and height 12 m.
    b) Solve the formula for r.
    c) What is the radius of a conical pile of sand with volume 425 000 m³ and height:
       i) 45 m
       ii) 60 m?

11. Mario, the manager of Paisano Pizza, determines the approximate selling price C dollars of a basic pizza by the formula $C = \dfrac{d^2 + 337.5}{275}$, where d is the diameter in centimetres.
    a) Solve the formula for d.
    b) What is the diameter of a pizza that costs:
       i) $3.50
       ii) $4.50?
    c) How much should Mario charge for a pizza 40 cm in diameter?

12. The kinetic energy E joules of a mass m kilograms moving with a speed of v metres per second is given by the formula $E = \frac{1}{2}mv^2$.
    a) Calculate the kinetic energy of a 2000 kg car travelling at:
       i) 50 km/h   ii) 100 km/h.
    b) Calculate the velocity of a 2000 kg car when its kinetic energy is:
       i) 10^2 kJ   ii) 10^3 kJ.

13. A square rug placed in a square room leaves 2.85 m² of hardwood floor showing. Find the dimensions of the rug if the room is 3.1 m square.

14. A circular walkway of outside radius 3.4 m is to be made of interlocking paving stones. If 16.7 m² of paving stones are used, what is the inside radius of the walkway?

15. A solid steel cylinder of height 1.4 m is placed inside a cylindrical tube with the same height. If 1.25 kL of oil can then be added to the tube, find:
    a) the diameter of the tube if the radius of the cylinder is 0.6 m;
    b) the diameter of the cylinder if the diameter of the tube is 2.0 m.

©

16. A 5 kg mass, suspended by a string, is pulled to one side and released. If pulling it to one side gives it 12 J of potential energy, and there is no loss when potential energy is changed into kinetic energy, what will be the speed of the mass at its lowest point?

17. The diagram shows a storage shed being constructed from equilateral triangles. The area A of an equilateral triangle with sides of length x is given by the formula $A = \frac{\sqrt{3}}{4}x^2$.

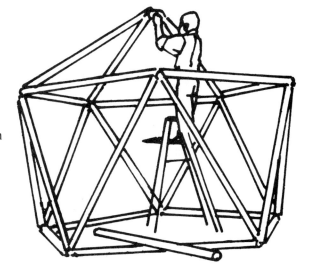

    a) How many equilateral triangles will there be in the finished shed?
    b) If the sides of each triangle are 2.5 m long, find the total outside area of the shed.
    c) How long should the sides of each triangle be for the shed to have an outside area of 100 m²?

4-2 SOLVING QUADRATIC EQUATIONS BY GRAPHING

Quadratic equations with a linear term, such as $4x^2 - 12x - 7 = 0$, first appeared in problems which were studied by the ancient Babylonians and Egyptians about 2000 B.C. Since then, various techniques have been developed to solve such equations.

About 350 years ago, the French mathematician, René Descartes, introduced the idea of plotting points on a grid. When a quadratic expression is plotted on a grid, the expression equals zero where its graph crosses the x-axis. Solving a quadratic equation is finding those values of x.

Example 1.   Solve by graphing and check the result. $4x^2 - 12x - 7 = 0$

Solution.   Let $y = 4x^2 - 12x - 7$. Make a table of values for various values of x, plot the ordered pairs (x, y) on a grid, and draw a smooth curve through them.

x	y
-2	33
-1	9
0	-7
1	-15
2	-15
3	-7
4	9
5	33

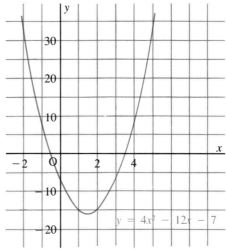

The expression is equal to 0 where the graph crosses the x-axis. The roots of the equation $4x^2 - 12x - 7 = 0$ are about -0.5 and 3.5.

Check.   When $x = -0.5$,
L.S. $= 4(-0.5)^2 - 12(-0.5) - 7$ R.S. $= 0$
   $= 1 + 6 - 7$
   $= 0$
When $x = 3.5$,
L.S. $= 4(3.5)^2 - 12(3.5) - 7$ R.S. $= 0$
   $= 49 - 42 - 7$
   $= 0$
The roots -0.5 and 3.5 are correct.

The curve in *Example 1* is called a *parabola*. Parabolas occur when a ball is thrown, bounced, or hit, and have properties used in the design of telescopes, antennas, and solar furnaces.

The equation in *Example 1* has two different roots. But not all quadratic equations have two different roots.

Example 2. Solve graphically.

a) $4x^2 - 12x + 9 = 0$ b) $4x^2 - 12x + 25 = 0$

Solution. The table of values and graph for each equation are shown below.

a)

x	y
-2	49
-1	25
0	9
1	1
2	1
3	9
4	25
5	49

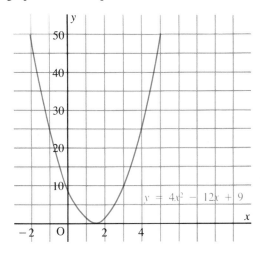

$4x^2 - 12x + 9 = 0$ has two equal roots, 1.5.

b)

x	y
-1	41
0	25
1	17
2	17
3	25
4	41

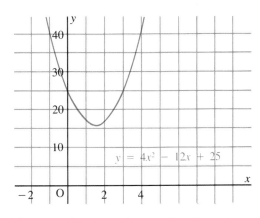

$4x^2 - 12x + 25 = 0$ has no solution in the set of real numbers.

The exact values of roots of quadratic equations can seldom be read from a graph, though they can be estimated. The two preceding examples suggest that a quadratic equation may have two different roots, two equal roots, or, in the set of real numbers, no roots.

EXERCISES 4-2

(A)

1. For each graph, state the quadratic equation it represents and estimate the roots of the equation.

a)
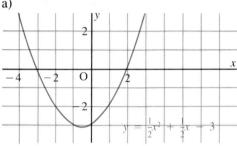

b)
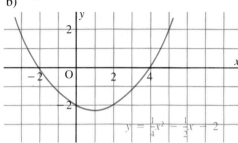

c)
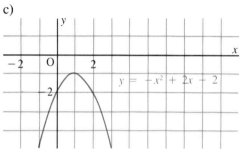

d)
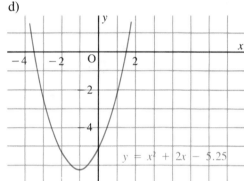

2. Solve graphically.
   a) $2x^2 - 13x + 20 = 0$ b) $4x^2 + 16x - 9 = 0$
   c) $4x^2 + 8x + 3 = 0$ d) $6x^2 + x - 15 = 0$
   e) $4x^2 - 20x + 25 = 0$ f) $6x^2 - 5x + 2 = 0$

(B)

3. Solve graphically.
   a) $6x^2 - 5x - 6 = 0$ b) $6x^2 + 5x - 21 = 0$ c) $4x^2 + 8x - 45 = 0$
   d) $x^2 + 4x - 3 = 0$ e) $8x^2 + 22x + 9 = 0$ f) $x^2 - 8x + 13 = 0$

4. Solve graphically and check.
   a) $2x^2 - 7x + 3 = 0$ b) $4x^2 + 4x - 15 = 0$ c) $3x^2 - 2x + 2 = 0$
   d) $2x^2 + 15x + 28 = 0$ e) $4x^2 + 28x + 49 = 0$ f) $4x^2 - 4x - 3 = 0$

5. If $4x^2 - 20x + 25 = 0$ has two equal roots, which of these equations has:
   i) two different roots   ii) no roots?
       a) $4x^2 - 20x + 30 = 0$ b) $4x^2 - 20x + 20 = 0$

(C)

6. x_1 and x_2 are the roots of $x^2 - 8x + 13 = 0$, and x_3 and x_4 are the roots of $x^2 - 8x + 10 = 0$. If $x_1 < x_2$ and $x_3 < x_4$, which of these statements is true?
   a) $x_1 < x_2 < x_3 < x_4$ b) $x_1 < x_3 < x_2 < x_4$
   c) $x_3 < x_1 < x_2 < x_4$ d) $x_1 < x_3 < x_4 < x_2$

7. If $x^2 - 8x + 13 = 0$ has roots x_1 and x_2, and $x_1 < x_2$, for what range of values of k will $x^2 - 8x + k = 0$ have roots x_3 and x_4, $x_3 < x_4$, such that:
   a) $x_3 < x_1 < x_2 < x_4$ b) $x_1 < x_3 < x_4 < x_2$?

 INVESTIGATE

Solving Quadratic Equations With Calculators

Quadratic equations can be solved in many different ways. The methods suggested here are simple in concept but involve a considerable amount of arithmetic. They are therefore appropriate for calculators. Consider the equation $x^2 + 3x - 15 = 0$.

Solving by Systematic Trial

$x^2 + 3x - 15 = 0$ can be written $x(x + 3) = 15$. Find a value of x that, when substituted in $x(x + 3)$, gives a result as close to 15 as possible. Since $2(2 + 3) = 10$, and $3(3 + 3) = 18$, there must be a root between 2 and 3.
Try 2.6: $(2.6)(2.6 + 3) = 14.56$ 2.6 is too small.
Try 2.7: $(2.7)(2.7 + 3) = 15.39$ 2.7 is too great.
Therefore, the root is between 2.6 and 2.7. By trying numbers between 2.6 and 2.7, we can find the root to as many decimal places as desired.

Solving by Using an Expression for x
$x^2 + 3x - 15 = 0$ can be written $x(x + 3) = 15$
$$x = \frac{15}{x + 3}$$
Now, by systematic trial, try to find a value of x such that both sides of this equation are equal.
Try 2.6: $\dfrac{15}{2.6 + 3} \doteq 2.679$ 2.6 is too small.

Try 2.7: $\dfrac{15}{2.7 + 3} \doteq 2.632$ 2.7 is too great.
This shows that the root is between 2.6 and 2.7, and we can find the root as accurately as desired by continuing the process.

1. Find the other root of $x^2 + 3x - 15 = 0$ to 3 decimal places by either of the above methods.

2. Find another way of rearranging $x^2 + 3x - 15 = 0$ so that x is equal to an expression containing x. Then find the roots to 3 decimal places, as before.

3. Write a report outlining the advantages and disadvantages of these methods for solving quadratic equations.

4-3 SOLVING QUADRATIC EQUATIONS BY FACTORING

Solving quadratic equations by graphing is time-consuming and does not always give exact roots. It is therefore important to develop algebraic methods of solving them.

Some quadratic equations can be solved by factoring. This method depends on the following important property of real numbers.

> If $AB = 0$, then $A = 0$, or $B = 0$, or both.

Example 1. Solve and check.

a) $x^2 - 3x + 2 = 0$ b) $4y^2 + 12y + 9 = 0$

Solution.

a) $\quad x^2 - 3x + 2 = 0$
$(x - 1)(x - 2) = 0$
Either $x - 1 = 0$
$x = 1$
or $x - 2 = 0$
$x = 2$

b) $\quad 4y^2 + 12y + 9 = 0$
$(2y + 3)(2y + 3) = 0$
That is, $2y + 3 = 0$
$y = -\dfrac{3}{2}$

Check.

a) If $x = 1$,
$x^2 - 3x + 2 = 1 - 3 + 2$
$= 0$
If $x = 2$,
$x^2 - 3x + 2 = 4 - 6 + 2$
$= 0$
Both solutions are correct.

b) If $y = -\dfrac{3}{2}$,
$4y^2 + 12y + 9$
$= 4\left(\dfrac{9}{4}\right) + 12\left(-\dfrac{3}{2}\right) + 9$
$= 9 - 18 + 9$
$= 0$
The solution is correct.

When a quadratic expression has two equal factors, as in *Example 1b)*, it is customary to say that the corresponding quadratic equation has *two equal roots*.

Example 2. Solve.

a) $3x(x - 4) = 2(x + 1) + 3$ b) $2a + \dfrac{5}{2} = \dfrac{3}{a}$

Solution.

a) $3x(x - 4) = 2(x + 1) + 3$
$3x^2 - 12x = 2x + 5$
$3x^2 - 14x - 5 = 0$
$(3x + 1)(x - 5) = 0$
Either $3x + 1 = 0$ $\quad$ or $\quad$ $x - 5 = 0$
$x = -\dfrac{1}{3}$ $\qquad\qquad$ $x = 5$

The roots of the equation are $-\dfrac{1}{3}$ and 5.

b) $2a + \dfrac{5}{2} = \dfrac{3}{a}$

Multiply both sides by $2a$, $a \neq 0$.

$4a^2 + 5a = 6$

$4a^2 + 5a - 6 = 0$

$(4a - 3)(a + 2) = 0$

Either $4a - 3 = 0$ or $a + 2 = 0$

$a = \dfrac{3}{4}$ $a = -2$

The roots of the equation are $\dfrac{3}{4}$ and -2.

Equations with higher powers can sometimes be solved using similar techniques.

Example 3.   Solve. $2x^4 - 3x^2 - 5 = 0$

Solution. $2x^4 - 3x^2 - 5 = 0$

$(2x^2 - 5)(x^2 + 1) = 0$

Either $2x^2 - 5 = 0$ or $x^2 + 1 = 0$

$x^2 = \dfrac{5}{2}$ $x^2 = -1$

            This has no real solution.

$x = \pm \sqrt{\dfrac{5}{2}}$

Example 4.   A rectangle, 3 cm longer than it is wide, has a diagonal 15 cm long. Find the dimensions of the rectangle.

Solution.   Let the width of the rectangle be x and its length $x + 3$.

By the Pythagorean Theorem

$(x + 3)^2 + x^2 = 15^2$

$x^2 + 6x + 9 + x^2 = 225$

$2x^2 + 6x - 216 = 0$

$x^2 + 3x - 108 = 0$

$(x + 12)(x - 9) = 0$

Either $x + 12 = 0$ or $x - 9 = 0$

$x = -12$ $x = 9$

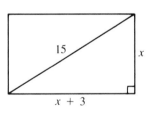

Since the dimensions cannot be negative, the only admissible solution is $x = 9$. The dimensions of the rectangle are 9 cm by $(9 + 3)$ cm, or 12 cm.

EXERCISES 4-3

Ⓐ

1. Solve.
   a) $x^2 - 4x + 3 = 0$ b) $y^2 + 8y + 15 = 0$ c) $m^2 - m - 56 = 0$
   d) $2a^2 + a - 15 = 0$ e) $x^2 - 64 = 0$ f) $9m^2 - 12m + 4 = 0$

2. Solve and check.
   a) $x^2 + 3x - 10 = 0$ b) $m^2 - 12m + 35 = 0$ c) $a^2 - 5a - 6 = 0$
   d) $y^2 - 11y = 0$ e) $4c^2 - 49 = 0$ f) $2x^2 - 7x - 15 = 0$

3. Solve.
   a) $y^2 - 10y = 2y - 36$ b) $m^2 + 8m = 3m + 24$
   c) $x(x - 6) = 2(x - 8)$ d) $a(a - 9) = 2(a - 14)$
   e) $3c(c - 3) = c(c - 2) + 15$ f) $6x(x + 3) + 5 = 2(x^2 - x - 10)$

Ⓑ

4. Solve.
   a) $5x^2 - x - 18 = 0$ b) $6z^2 - 5z - 4 = 0$
   c) $3y^2 + 15y - 18 = 0$ d) $6x^2 + 17x - 14 = 0$
   e) $2t^2 - 24t + 72 = 0$ f) $25m^2 - 36 = 0$

5. Solve.
   a) $2m(m + 3) = 5(3 + m)$
   b) $3v(v + 2) = 2(v^2 - 4)$
   c) $x(x + 3) = -2(3x + 10)$
   d) $3a(a - 4) - 5 = 2(a - 3) - 7$
   e) $(2x - 1)(x - 3) = (x + 1)(x - 2)$
   f) $3(x - 2)(x + 2) + 5x = 2x(x + 4) + 16$

6. Solve.
   a) $6x(x - 2) - 3 = 2(x - 2)(x + 2) - 4$
   b) $3(c - 1)^2 - 2 = (c - 4)(c + 1) + 7$
   c) $(2y + 1)(2y - 3) + 5 = (y + 8)(y - 5) + 48$
   d) $(2p - 1)^2 - 3 = (p - 2)(p - 1)$
   e) $2(x - 1)(x - 2) = (x - 5)(x + 4) + 5x$
   f) $(2x - 1)(x - 3) = (x + 2)(x + 3) - x(2x - 1) + 7$

7. Solve.
   a) $x^4 - 13x^2 + 36 = 0$ b) $p^4 + 5p^2 - 6 = 0$ c) $2x^4 - 5x^2 + 3 = 0$
   d) $4a^4 - 13a^2 + 9 = 0$ e) $3p^4 - 14p^2 - 5 = 0$ f) $4m^4 + 12m^2 + 9 = 0$

8. Solve and check for extraneous roots.
   a) $x = \sqrt{3x - 2}$ b) $x = \sqrt{14 - 5x}$ c) $x = \sqrt{3x + 4}$
   d) $x = \sqrt{2x + 15}$ e) $x = \sqrt{5x - 6}$ f) $x = \sqrt{-3x - 2}$

9. Find two consecutive integers with a product of: a) 56   b) 156.

10. What number and its square differ by: a) 20   b) 30?

11. The sum of the squares of two consecutive integers is 145. Find the integers.

12. The sum of the squares of three consecutive integers is 149. Find the integers.

13. The hypotenuse of a right triangle is 29 cm. If the other two sides differ by 1 cm, what are their lengths?

14. Show that, if k is any real number, the equation $x^2 + (k + 1)x + k = 0$ always has real roots. For what value of k are the roots equal?

15. Solve.

a) $x - \dfrac{7}{2} = \dfrac{2}{x}$

b) $3a - \dfrac{17}{5} = -\dfrac{4}{5a}$

c) $y + \dfrac{12}{5} = \dfrac{32}{5y}$

d) $m + \dfrac{7}{3} = \dfrac{2}{m}$

e) $2s - \dfrac{14}{3s} = -\dfrac{17}{3}$

f) $2x + \dfrac{27}{4x} = \dfrac{15}{2}$

16. Solve.

a) $x + \dfrac{8}{x + 5} = 4$

b) $x + \dfrac{30}{x + 8} = 3$

c) $x - \dfrac{1}{x - 2} = 2$

d) $x + \dfrac{6}{x + 4} = 3$

e) $x + \dfrac{8}{x + 6} = 3$

f) $x - \dfrac{1}{x + 4} = -4$

Ⓒ

17. Find the ratio $x : y$.
a) $x^2 - 5xy + 6y^2 = 0$
b) $x^2 + 7xy + 12y^2 = 0$
c) $2x^2 + 9xy - 5y^2 = 0$
d) $6x^2 + 11xy - 10y^2 = 0$
e) $6x^2 - xy - 15y^2 = 0$
f) $8x^2 - 38xy + 35y^2 = 0$

18. If one root is 5, find the value of k and the other root.
a) $x^2 - 3x + k = 0$
b) $x^2 + kx + 40 = 0$
c) $x^2 + kx + 25 = 0$
d) $2x^2 - 13x + k = 0$

19. Solve for x.
a) $x^2 + a = 0$
b) $x^2 - ax = 0$
c) $ax^2 - b = 0$
d) $\dfrac{a}{x} + bx = 0$
e) $x^2 - (a + b)x + ab = 0$

20. The product of the squares of two consecutive integers is 17 424. Find the integers.

21. Solve for x.
a) $x^2 + ax = ab + bx$
b) $2x^2 - 4bx = ax - 2ab$
c) $x^2 - 2pq = p^2 + q^2$
d) $x^2 - 3ax + 2a^2 = ab + b^2$

COMPUTER POWER

Solving Quadratic Equations

When quadratic equations are difficult or impossible to solve by factoring, a computer can be programmed to solve them. The technique is essentially *systematic trial*, an approach well-suited to the computer.

The following program directs the computer to display a table of values for the expression $Ax^2 + Bx + C$. Input the coefficients A, B, and C and an estimated initial and final value for x. Where the value of the expression changes sign, a root occurs. By refining the initial and final values, the root can be found to any desired degree of accuracy. The other root can be found by estimating a new interval for x.

```
VAR
        A,B,C,X,X1,X2 : REAL;
BEGIN   { QUADRATIC EQUATIONS }
        REPEAT
        WRITELN('WHAT ARE THE COEFFICIENTS?');
        READ(A,B,C);
        WRITELN('WHAT IS THE INITIAL VALUE OF X?');
        READ(X1);
        WRITELN('WHAT IS THE FINAL VALUE OF X?');
        READ(X2);
        X := X1;
        REPEAT
            WRITELN(X:5:5,'  ',((A*X+B)*X+C):5:8);
            X:=X + (X2-X1)/10;
        UNTIL(X >=X2);
        WRITELN;
        WRITELN('PRESS RETURN TO REPEAT');
        UNTIL(READKEY <> CHR(13));
END.
```

When the program was used to solve $2x^2 - 7x - 6 = 0$, this was part of the display.

X	EXPRESSION
4	-2
4·2	-·12000007
4·4	1·91999999
4·6	4·11999998

$\left.\begin{array}{c} \\ \\ \end{array}\right\}$ The value changes sign.

For greater accuracy, the values for x_1 and x_2 could be changed to 4.2 and 4.22. Use the program to find another root between -2 and 0.

1. Solve.
   a) $10x^2 + 11x - 153 = 0$ b) $2x^2 - 9x + 3 = 0$
   c) $32x^2 - 60x - 27 = 0$ d) $x^2 - x - 1 = 0$

2. The sum of two numbers is 10. The square of one number is double the square of the other. Find the numbers.

4-4 SOLVING QUADRATIC EQUATIONS BY COMPLETING THE SQUARE

During the period A.D. 700 to A.D. 1100, Arab and Hindu mathematicians gradually developed formal rules for solving quadratic equations. These rules were often taught orally and in verse. The methods used were equivalent to the method developed in this section. It can be used to solve any quadratic equation, including those that cannot be solved by factoring. It depends on recognizing the form of a trinomial which is a perfect square.

Example 1.   Which of these trinomials is a perfect square?

    a) $x^2 + 10x + 25$ b) $x^2 - 8x + 9$

Solution.   a) $x^2 + 10x + 25$

                This trinomial is a perfect square, since $x^2 + 10x + 25 = (x + 5)^2$

                The constant term 25 is the square of $\frac{1}{2}(10)$.

          b) $x^2 - 8x + 9$

                This trinomial is not a perfect square since the constant term 9 is not

                the square of $\frac{1}{2}(-8)$.

      As *Example 1* suggests, the constant term of a perfect-square trinomial of the form $x^2 + 2ax + a^2$ is the square of half the coefficient of x.

Example 2.   What constant term must be added to each expression to make it a perfect square?

           a) $x^2 - 8x$ b) $x^2 + 14x$ c) $x^2 + 3x$

Solution.   a) $x^2 - 8x$

                The constant term needed is the square of $\frac{1}{2}(-8)$, or 16.

                $x^2 - 8x + 16$ is a perfect square.

          b) $x^2 + 14x$

                The constant term needed is the square of $\frac{1}{2}(14)$, or 49.

                $x^2 + 14x + 49$ is a perfect square.

          c) $x^2 + 3x$

                The constant term needed is the square of $\frac{1}{2}(3)$, or $\frac{9}{4}$.

                $x^2 + 3x + \frac{9}{4}$ is a perfect square.

      The next example shows how to solve any quadratic equation using the method of *completing the square*.

Example 3. Solve.

a) $x^2 + 14x + 40 = 0$ b) $x^2 - 10x + 23 = 0$

Solution. a) $x^2 + 14x + 40 = 0$

Isolate the constant term.

$$x^2 + 14x = -40$$

Add the square of $\frac{1}{2}(14)$ to both sides.

$$x^2 + 14x + 49 = -40 + 49$$
$$(x + 7)^2 = 9$$

Take the square root of both sides.

$$x + 7 = \pm 3$$

$$x = -7 \pm 3$$

$$= -4 \text{ or } -10$$

The roots of the equation are -4 and -10.

b) $x^2 - 10x + 23 = 0$

Isolate the constant term.

$$x^2 - 10x = 23$$

Add the square of $\frac{1}{2}(-10)$ to both sides.

$$x^2 - 10x + 25 = -23 + 25$$
$$(x - 5)^2 = 2$$

Take the square root of both sides.

$$x - 5 = \pm\sqrt{2}$$

$$x = 5 \pm \sqrt{2}$$

The roots of the equation are $5 + \sqrt{2}$ and $5 - \sqrt{2}$.

If the second-degree term has a coefficient other than 1, both sides of the equation should be divided by this coefficient.

Example 4. Find the roots of $2x^2 - 10x + 11 = 0$ to two decimal places.

Solution. $2x^2 - 10x + 11 = 0$

Divide both sides by 2.

$$x^2 - 5x + \frac{11}{2} = 0$$

$$x^2 - 5x = -\frac{11}{2}$$

Add the square of $\frac{1}{2}(-5)$ to both sides.

$$x^2 - 5x + \frac{25}{4} = -\frac{11}{2} + \frac{25}{4}$$

$$\left(x - \frac{5}{2}\right)^2 = \frac{3}{4}$$

Take the square root of both sides.

$$x - \frac{5}{2} = \frac{\pm\sqrt{3}}{2}$$

$$x = \frac{5 \pm \sqrt{3}}{2}$$

$$\doteq 3.37 \text{ and } 1.63$$

The roots are approximately 3.37 and 1.63.

EXERCISES 4-4

(A)

1. Determine if each trinomial is a perfect square.
   a) $x^2 + 6x + 9$　　　　b) $x^2 - 4x + 4$　　　　c) $x^2 + 10x - 25$

   d) $x^2 - 9x + 81$　　　　e) $x^2 - 14x + 49$　　　　f) $x^2 - 3x + \frac{9}{4}$

2. What constant term must be added to make each expression a perfect square?
   a) $x^2 + 6x$　　　　　　b) $x^2 - 2x$　　　　　　c) $x^2 - 20x$
   d) $x^2 + 7x$　　　　　　e) $x^2 - 3x$　　　　　　f) $x^2 + x$
   g) $x^2 - 11x$　　　　　h) $x^2 + 2ax$　　　　　i) $x^2 + bx$

3. Solve by completing the square.
   a) $x^2 + 4x - 12 = 0$　　b) $x^2 + 8x - 33 = 0$　　c) $x^2 - 6x + 7 = 0$
   d) $x^2 - 16x + 50 = 0$　　e) $x^2 - 3x + 1 = 0$　　f) $x^2 + 5x + 3 = 0$

4. Solve.
   a) $x^2 + 12x - 8 = 0$　　b) $x^2 - 18x + 20 = 0$　　c) $x^2 - 3x - 5 = 0$
   d) $x^2 - x - 1 = 0$　　　e) $x^2 + 9x + 16 = 0$　　f) $x^2 + 5x - 3 = 0$

(B)

5. Solve.
   a) $2x^2 + 8x + 5 = 0$　　　　　　b) $3y^2 - 12y + 5 = 0$
   c) $2k^2 - 12k + 3 = 0$　　　　　　d) $3d^2 + 6d + 2 = 0$

6. Solve.
   a) $a^2 - 6a - 9 = 0$　　　　　　b) $2x^2 + x - 5 = 0$
   c) $2r^2 - 7r + 1 = 0$　　　　　　d) $2t^2 - 10t + 3 = 0$
   e) $2x^2 + 3x - 3 = 0$　　　　　　f) $5c^2 - 2c - 6 = 0$

7. Find the roots to 2 decimal places.
   a) $m^2 + 2m - 9 = 0$　　　　　　b) $x^2 + 9x - 12 = 0$
   c) $2s^2 - 3s - 6 = 0$　　　　　　d) $3c^2 + 5c - 11 = 0$
   e) $2y^2 + 7y + 2 = 0$　　　　　　f) $5x^2 - 20x + 3 = 0$

 INVESTIGATE

Show that one root of $x^2 - 12x + 32 = 0$ is double the other. Find other quadratic equations in which one root is double the other. What patterns can you find?

THE MATHEMATICAL MIND

The Algebra of Al-Khowarizmi

You have probably encountered the word *algorithm* in your mathematics studies. It is derived from the name of the ninth century Arab mathematician, Al-Khowarizmi. He was one of the many scholars gathered together by the Caliph of Baghdad, a city on the Tigris river and the capital of present-day Iraq. Little is known of his personal life. It is thought that he lived from about A.D. 780 to A.D. 850. His scientific work, however, is widely known and well documented.

His early work involved the astrolabe and sundial and the measurement of one degree of the Earth's circumference. He also produced a popular work on solving equations, *Al-Kitab Al-jabr wa'l muqa-balah.*

The word, al-jabr, in the title means "restoration", and refers to the fact that equality is restored when the same number is added to or subtracted from both sides of an equation. It is from this word that our word "algebra" is derived.

The word was used in a non-mathematical sense in medieval Europe. There, an "algebrista" was a person who restored broken bones. This was often the barber who, in addition to cutting hair, administered the simpler medical treatments as a sideline. Red and white striped signs, still seen today, indicated that such services were available.

Al-Khowarizmi seemed to write with a deep concern for his readers' difficulties. He often explained several ways to consider a problem. Both his *Al-jabr* and an arithmetic book, written well over 1000 years ago, are still influencing writers of mathematics today.

Al-Khowarizmi gave geometrical rules for solving such equations as $x^2 + 10x = 39$. In the diagram, the unshaded part is $x^2 + 10x$. To complete the square he added 25. Then 25 had to be added to the right side of the equation to restore the equality.

$$x^2 + 10x + 25 = 39 + 25$$
$$(x + 5)^2 = 64$$
$$x + 5 = \pm 8$$
$$x = 3 \text{ and } -13$$

The negative root is not admissible.

QUESTIONS

1. Solve $x^2 + 6x = 91$ by completing the square, and illustrate the solution with a diagram.

2. a) Solve $x^2 + px = q$ by completing the square, and illustrate with a diagram.
   b) Suggest why Al-Khowarizmi would have difficulty solving an equation such as $x^2 - 4x = 45$ by this method. Can you find a geometrical method of illustrating the solution of this equation by completing the square?

4-5 SOLVING QUADRATIC EQUATIONS BY USING A FORMULA

For many centuries, mathematicians considered only equations with numerical coefficients. This meant repeating the whole process of calculation for each equation. Moreover, as they did not recognize negative numbers (they would not, for instance, write $x^2 = 8x + 20$ in the form $x^2 - 8x = 20$) a totally different type of calculation was needed for each type of equation.

About 1550, the French mathematician, François Vieta, introduced the idea of using letters to represent the coefficients of an equation. By that time, negative numbers were becoming accepted. The combination of the two ideas meant that all quadratic equations could be written in the form $ax^2 + bx + c = 0$, and it was possible to develop a single formula that could be used to solve any one of them.

To obtain a formula, we solve the equation, written in the general form, by completing the square.

Consider the general equation.

$$ax^2 + bx + c = 0, \quad a \neq 0$$

Divide both sides by a.

$$x^2 + \frac{b}{a}x + \frac{c}{a} = 0$$

$$x^2 + \frac{b}{a}x = -\frac{c}{a}$$

Add the square of $\frac{1}{2}\left(\frac{b}{a}\right)$ to both sides.

$$x^2 + \frac{b}{a}x + \frac{b^2}{4a^2} = \frac{b^2}{4a^2} - \frac{c}{a}$$

$$\left(x + \frac{b}{2a}\right)^2 = \frac{b^2 - 4ac}{4a^2}$$

Take the square root of each side.

$$x + \frac{b}{2a} = \frac{\pm\sqrt{b^2 - 4ac}}{2a}, \quad b^2 - 4ac \geqslant 0$$

$$x = \frac{-b \pm \sqrt{b^2 - 4ac}}{2a}$$

The roots of the equation $ax^2 + bx + c = 0$, $a \neq 0$, are:

$$\frac{-b + \sqrt{b^2 - 4ac}}{2a} \quad \text{and} \quad \frac{-b - \sqrt{b^2 - 4ac}}{2a}, \text{ where } b^2 - 4ac \geqslant 0.$$

Example 1.   Solve and check.

a) $3x^2 - 5x + 2 = 0$ b) $z^2 - 6z + 7 = 0$

Solution.   a) $x = \dfrac{-b \pm \sqrt{b^2 - 4ac}}{2a}$ $\begin{aligned} a &= 3 \\ b &= -5 \\ c &= 2 \end{aligned}$

$\quad x = \dfrac{-(-5) \pm \sqrt{(-5)^2 - 4(3)(2)}}{2(3)}$

$\quad\quad = \dfrac{5 \pm \sqrt{1}}{6}$

$\quad\quad = 1 \text{ or } \dfrac{2}{3}$

The roots of the equation are 1 and $\dfrac{2}{3}$.

b) $z = \dfrac{-b \pm \sqrt{b^2 - 4ac}}{2a}$ $\begin{aligned} a &= 1 \\ b &= -6 \\ c &= 7 \end{aligned}$

$\quad z = \dfrac{-(-6) \pm \sqrt{(-6)^2 - 4(1)(7)}}{2(1)}$

$\quad\quad = \dfrac{6 \pm \sqrt{36 - 28}}{2}$

$\quad\quad = \dfrac{6 \pm 2\sqrt{2}}{2}$

$\quad\quad = 3 \pm \sqrt{2}$

The roots of the equation are $3 + \sqrt{2}$ and $3 - \sqrt{2}$.

Check.   a) When $x = 1$,   L.S. $= 3(1)^2 - 5(1) + 2$ R.S. $= 0$

$\quad\quad\quad\quad\quad\quad\quad = 3 - 5 + 2$

$\quad\quad\quad\quad\quad\quad\quad = 0$

When $x = \dfrac{2}{3}$,   L.S. $= 3\left(\dfrac{2}{3}\right)^2 - 5\left(\dfrac{2}{3}\right) + 2$ R.S. $= 0$

$\quad\quad\quad\quad\quad\quad\quad = \dfrac{4}{3} - \dfrac{10}{3} + 2$

$\quad\quad\quad\quad\quad\quad\quad = 0$

The solution is correct.

b) When $z = 3 + \sqrt{2}$,   L.S. $= (3 + \sqrt{2})^2 - 6(3 + \sqrt{2}) + 7$

$\quad\quad\quad\quad\quad\quad\quad\quad\quad = 9 + 6\sqrt{2} + 2 - 18 - 6\sqrt{2} + 7$

$\quad\quad\quad\quad\quad\quad\quad\quad\quad = 0$

$\quad\quad\quad\quad\quad\quad\quad\quad\quad = $ R.S.

When $z = 3 - \sqrt{2}$,   L.S. $= (3 - \sqrt{2})^2 - 6(3 - \sqrt{2}) + 7$

$\quad\quad\quad\quad\quad\quad\quad\quad\quad = 9 - 6\sqrt{2} + 2 - 18 + 6\sqrt{2} + 7$

$\quad\quad\quad\quad\quad\quad\quad\quad\quad = 0$

$\quad\quad\quad\quad\quad\quad\quad\quad\quad = $ R.S.

The solution is correct.

Example 2.   Solve. $\dfrac{5x^2}{x^2 - 9} - \dfrac{3}{x - 3} = \dfrac{2x}{x + 3}$

Solution.   Factor the denominators.

$$\frac{5x^2}{(x - 3)(x + 3)} - \frac{3}{x - 3} = \frac{2x}{x + 3}$$

The equation is not defined when

$(x - 3)(x + 3) = 0$ or $x - 3 = 0$ or $x + 3 = 0$

               $x = 3$ and -3 $x = 3$ $x = -3$

Assume that $x \neq 3$ and -3.

Multiply both sides of the equation by $(x + 3)(x - 3)$.

$5x^2 - 3(x + 3) = 2x(x - 3)$

   $5x^2 - 3x - 9 = 2x^2 - 6x$

   $3x^2 + 3x - 9 = 0$

     $x^2 + x - 3 = 0$

$$x = \frac{-b \pm \sqrt{b^2 - 4ac}}{2a} \qquad \begin{array}{l} a = 1 \\ b = 1 \\ c = -3 \end{array}$$

$$= \frac{-1 \pm \sqrt{1 + 12}}{2}$$

The roots are $\dfrac{-1 + \sqrt{13}}{2}$ and $\dfrac{-1 - \sqrt{13}}{2}$.

Example 3.   Sylvie somersaults from a 3 m spring board. Her height h metres above the water t seconds after she leaves the board is given by $h = -4.9t^2 + 8.8t + 3$. How long is it until she reaches the water?

Solution. $h = -4.9t^2 + 8.8t + 3$

Substitute 0 for h.

$0 = -4.9t^2 + 8.8t + 3$

$$t = \frac{-b \pm \sqrt{b^2 - 4ac}}{2a} \qquad \begin{array}{l} a = -4.9 \\ b = 8.8 \\ c = 3 \end{array}$$

$$t = \frac{-8.8 \pm \sqrt{8.8^2 - 4(-4.9)(3)}}{2(-4.9)}$$

$$= \frac{8.8 \pm \sqrt{136.24}}{9.8}$$

$\doteq 2.09$ and -0.29

Since the time is positive, the negative root is rejected. She reaches the water in about 2.1 s.

EXERCISES 4-5

1. Solve.
   a) $x^2 - 6x + 4 = 0$
   b) $x^2 + 3x - 1 = 0$
   c) $x^2 + 7x + 3 = 0$
   d) $x^2 - 5x + 2 = 0$
   e) $x^2 + 4x - 1 = 0$
   f) $x^2 - 8x - 6 = 0$

2. Solve.
   a) $2x^2 - 5x + 2 = 0$
   b) $2x^2 + 7x + 3 = 0$
   c) $3x^2 - 11x - 14 = 0$
   d) $4x^2 - 9x + 5 = 0$
   e) $5x^2 + 7x + 2 = 0$
   f) $6x^2 + 7x - 20 = 0$

3. Solve and check.
   a) $6m^2 - 7m + 2 = 0$
   b) $2c^2 - 25c + 77 = 0$
   c) $6t^2 - t - 1 = 0$
   d) $2p^2 - p - 45 = 0$
   e) $2x^2 - 5x - 12 = 0$
   f) $6x^2 - x - 2 = 0$

4. Find the roots to 2 decimal places.
   a) $2b^2 - 13b + 10 = 0$
   b) $2z^2 - 7z + 4 = 0$
   c) $3x^2 - x - 5 = 0$
   d) $2a^2 - 9a - 1 = 0$
   e) $5t^2 - 3t - 1 = 0$
   f) $2y^2 + 5y + 1 = 0$

5. Find the roots to 2 decimal places.
   a) $5x^2 + 6x - 1 = 0$
   b) $2c(c - 3) = 1$
   c) $3m^2 + 2m - 7 = 0$
   d) $2r(2r + 1) = 3$
   e) $3p^2 - 6p + 1 = 0$
   f) $2a(a - 3) = -1$

6. An Acapulco diver dives into the sea from a height of 35 m. His height h metres t seconds after leaving the cliff is given by $h = -4.9t^2 + t + 35$. How long is it until he reaches the water?

B

7. Solve.
   a) $3x^2 - 4x = 0$
   b) $12m^2 - 192 = 0$
   c) $25c^2 + 70c + 49 = 0$
   d) $\frac{5}{2}y^2 - \frac{3}{2}y - \frac{1}{4} = 0$
   e) $0.2s^2 - s - 3.2 = 0$
   f) $\sqrt{2}x^2 - 5x - \sqrt{8} = 0$

8. Solve and check.
   a) $4m^2 - 17m + 4 = 0$
   b) $6a^2 - 11a + 4 = 0$
   c) $12x^2 - x - 6 = 0$
   d) $3y^2 + 16y - 99 = 0$
   e) $5t^2 - 13t - 6 = 0$
   f) $15s^2 + 7s - 2 = 0$

9. Solve.
   a) $2x^2 + 8x - 5 = 0$
   b) $3x^2 + 10x - 8 = 0$
   c) $x^2 - 7x + 4 = 0$
   d) $(x + 3)(5x + 1) = (2x + 1)(x + 7)$
   e) $(2x - 1)(3x + 5) = (x + 2)(2x - 1)$
   f) $(5x + 1)(x + 2) = 5x - (2x + 1)(2x + 2)$

10. Solve.

a) $\dfrac{x^2 + 6}{3} - \dfrac{7}{2} = \dfrac{x + 10}{2}$

b) $(x + 6)(x - 1) + x^2 = 10x + 9$

c) $\dfrac{4}{x} + \dfrac{x}{4} = \dfrac{5}{2}$

d) $\dfrac{50}{x} - \dfrac{40}{x + 10} = 1$

e) $\dfrac{3}{x + 2} = \dfrac{1}{4} - \dfrac{1}{x - 4}$

f) $(x - 2)(x + 3) = x(5x - 9) - 2$

11. Find the roots to 2 decimal places.

a) $2.4a^2 - 4.6a + 2.1 = 0$

b) $0.4x^2 - 7.5x - 7.9 = 0$

c) $5.75t^2 - 0.02t - 0.01 = 0$

d) $2.7x^2 - 2.4x - 1.6 = 0$

e) $0.32m^2 - 0.5m + 0.17 = 0$

f) $3.0s^2 - 1.7s - 4.5 = 0$

12. Solve.

a) $\dfrac{x}{x - 3} = \dfrac{2x}{x + 2}$

b) $\dfrac{2x - 1}{x + 5} = \dfrac{x + 2}{x + 3}$

c) $\dfrac{3x}{x - 2} + \dfrac{x}{x + 2} = \dfrac{2x - 1}{x + 2}$

d) $\dfrac{5x + 2}{x + 3} = \dfrac{2x}{x + 3} - \dfrac{x}{x - 3}$

e) $\dfrac{3x}{x + 1} - \dfrac{x}{x - 1} = \dfrac{2x + 3}{x + 1}$

f) $\dfrac{2x - 3}{x + 2} - \dfrac{x + 2}{x - 1} = \dfrac{3x}{x - 1}$

13. Solve.

a) $\dfrac{x^2}{x^2 - 4} = \dfrac{2x}{x + 2}$

b) $\dfrac{3x^2}{x^2 - 1} = \dfrac{x}{x + 1} + \dfrac{x}{1 - x}$

c) $\dfrac{3x}{x + 2} + \dfrac{2x^2}{x^2 + 5x + 6} = \dfrac{4}{x + 3}$

d) $\dfrac{2x}{x - 1} - \dfrac{4}{3 - x} = \dfrac{5x^2 - 7}{x^2 - 4x + 3}$

e) $\dfrac{2x^2}{x^2 - 9} - \dfrac{x}{3 - x} = \dfrac{-5}{x + 3}$

f) $\dfrac{3x + 1}{x^2 + x - 2} = \dfrac{2x - 3}{x^2 - x - 6} - \dfrac{5}{x^2 - 4x + 3}$

14. The approximate stopping distance d metres of a car travelling at v kilometres per hour is given by the formula $d = 0.0066v^2 + 0.14v$.
  a) What is the stopping distance for a car travelling at: i) 80 km/h ii) 100 km/h?
  b) Find the highest speed at which a car can be stopped in: i) 35 m   ii) 95 m.

15. The surface area A of a closed cylinder of radius r is given by the formula $A = 6.28r^2 + 47.7r$.
  a) Find the surface area if the radius is: i) 6 cm   ii) 25 cm.
  b) Find the radius if the surface area is: i) 291.28 cm^2 ii) 2128.5 cm^2.

16. A rectangle of unit width is divided into a square and a rectangle. What is the length of the original rectangle if the smaller rectangle has the same length-to-width ratio?

17. What number differs from its reciprocal by: a) 1   b) -1?

18. Solve and check for extraneous roots.

a) $x = \sqrt{55 - 6x}$

b) $x = \sqrt{14x + 51}$

c) $x = \sqrt{\dfrac{11x - 5}{2}}$

d) $3x = \sqrt{6x + 8}$

e) $2x = \sqrt{20x - 21}$

f) $x = \sqrt{\dfrac{-19x - 15}{6}}$

Ⓒ

19. Solve for x.

a) $px^2 + qx + r = 0$

b) $3x^2 + nx - 5 = 0$

c) $\dfrac{k}{x} - x = 3$

d) $x^2 + 4px - p^2 = 0$

e) $\dfrac{3x}{a} + \dfrac{1}{a} = \dfrac{1}{3x}$

f) $x^2 + (3m - 2n)x = 6mn$

20. Square ABCD has sides of length 6 cm. M and N are points on sides BC and DC such that the areas of $\triangle ABM$, $\triangle MCN$, and $\triangle ADN$ are all equal. Find the lengths of BM and DN.

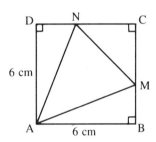

21. a) Solve.

   i) $x^2 - 5x + 7 = 0$

   ii) $-3x^2 + 7x - 11 = 0$

   iii) $2x^2 + 5x + 6 = 0$

   iv) $3x^2 - 7x + 10 = 0$

b) Under what conditions will a quadratic equation have no real roots?

c) Which of these equations have no real roots?

   i) $5x^2 + 4x + 1 = 0$

   ii) $3x^2 - 8x + 7 = 0$

   iii) $6x^2 - 5x - 3 = 0$

   iv) $12x^2 - 19x + 7 = 0$

22. a) Solve.

   i) $x^2 - x - 1 = 0$

   ii) $x^2 - x - 2 = 0$

   iii) $x^2 - x - 3 = 0$

   iv) $x^2 - x - 4 = 0$

b) For what values of n does the equation $x^2 - x - n = 0$ have integral roots?

23. a) Find the sum and product of the roots of each equation.

   i) $x^2 + 4x - 45 = 0$

   ii) $4x^2 + 20x + 21 = 0$

   iii) $6x^2 - 29x + 35 = 0$

   iv) $5x^2 - 6x - 3 = 0$

b) From the results of part a), make a conjecture concerning the sum and product of the roots of $ax^2 + bx + c = 0$.

24. Find the condition that must be satisfied by a, b, and c if the roots of the equation $ax^2 + bx + c$ are in the ratio:

a) $2 : 3$

b) $m : n$.

4-6 THE NATURE OF THE ROOTS OF A QUADRATIC EQUATION

In the previous section we developed the formula $x = \dfrac{-b \pm \sqrt{b^2 - 4ac}}{2a}$

for the roots of the general quadratic equation $ax^2 + bx + c = 0$, $a \neq 0$.
Consider how the formula applies to these three equations:
$x^2 - 6x + 5 = 0$, $x^2 - 6x + 9 = 0$, and $x^2 - 6x + 13 = 0$.

$x^2 - 6x + 5 = 0$

$$x = \frac{6 \pm \sqrt{36 - 20}}{2}$$

$$= \frac{6 \pm \sqrt{16}}{2} \quad \text{Positive}$$

The roots are: $\dfrac{6 + 4}{2} = 5$ ⎫ Two different real roots

and $\dfrac{6 - 4}{2} = 1$ ⎭

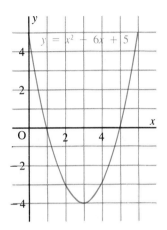

The parabola crosses the
x-axis at two points.

$x^2 - 6x + 9 = 0$

$$x = \frac{6 \pm \sqrt{36 - 36}}{2}$$

$$= \frac{6 \pm \sqrt{0}}{2} \quad \text{Zero}$$

The roots are: $\dfrac{6 + 0}{2} = 3$ ⎫ Two equal real roots

and $\dfrac{6 - 0}{2} = 3$ ⎭

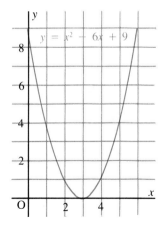

The parabola touches the
x-axis at one point.

$x^2 - 6x + 13 = 0$

$$x = \frac{6 \pm \sqrt{36 - 52}}{2}$$

$$= \frac{6 \pm \sqrt{-16}}{2} \text{ — Negative}$$

The roots are undefined.   No real roots

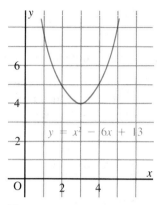

The parabola does not intersect the x-axis.

We can see that the expression under the radical sign plays an important role in the calculation of the roots. This expression enables us to determine the *nature of the roots* without solving the equation. By the nature of the roots we mean:
● whether or not the equation has real roots
● if there are real roots, whether they are different or equal.

The above examples suggest the following conclusions about the nature of the roots of $ax^2 + bx + c = 0$.

If $b^2 - 4ac > 0$, there are two different real roots.
If $b^2 - 4ac = 0$, there are two equal real roots.
If $b^2 - 4ac < 0$, there are no real roots.

The expression $b^2 - 4ac$ is called the *discriminant* of $ax^2 + bx + c = 0$ because it discriminates among the three cases that can occur.

Example 1.   Without solving each equation, determine the nature of its roots.
    a) $4x^2 - 12x + 9 = 0$
    b) $2x^2 + 5x - 1 = 0$
    c) $x^2 - 2x + 3 = 0$

Solution.   The nature of the roots is determined by the value of the discriminant, $b^2 - 4ac$.
    a) $4x^2 - 12x + 9 = 0$ $a = 4, b = -12, c = 9$
        $b^2 - 4ac = (-12)^2 - 4(4)(9)$
                    $= 144 - 144$
                    $= 0$
    There are two equal real roots.
    b) $2x^2 + 5x - 1 = 0$ $a = 2, b = 5, c = -1$
        $b^2 - 4ac = 25 - 4(2)(-1)$
                    $= 33$
    Since $33 > 0$, there are two different real roots.

c) $x^2 - 2x + 3 = 0$ $a = 1, b = -2, c = 3$
$b^2 - 4ac = (-2)^2 - 4(1)(3)$
$\qquad\qquad = -8$
Since $-8 < 0$, the equation has no real roots.

Example 2. Find the values of k for which the equation $x^2 + kx + 9 = 0$ has:
a) equal roots   b) two different real roots.

Solution. $x^2 + kx + 9 = 0$ $a = 1, b = k, c = 9$
$b^2 - 4ac = k^2 - 4(1)(9)$
$\qquad\qquad = k^2 - 36$
a) For equal roots, $k^2 - 36 = 0$
$\qquad\qquad\qquad k^2 = 36$
$\qquad\qquad\qquad k = \pm 6$

The equation has equal roots when $k = 6$ or -6.
b) For two different real roots, $k^2 - 36 > 0$
$\qquad\qquad\qquad\qquad\qquad k^2 > 36$
$\qquad\qquad\qquad\qquad\qquad k > 6$ or $k < -6$
The equation has two different real roots when $k > 6$ or $k < -6$.
This may also be written as $|k| > 6$.

EXERCISES 4-6

(A)

1. Find the value of each discriminant.
   a) $x^2 + 11x + 24 = 0$ b) $x^2 - 4x + 2 = 0$ c) $4x^2 - 20x + 25 = 0$
   d) $2x^2 - 5x + 8 = 0$ e) $3x^2 + 13x - 10 = 0$ f) $7x^2 + 12x + 6 = 0$

2. Which of the equations in *Exercise 1* have:
   a) two different real roots   b) two equal real roots   c) no real roots?

3. Determine the nature of the roots of each equation.
   a) $x^2 - 9x + 7 = 0$ b) $4x^2 + 36x + 81 = 0$
   c) $6x^2 + 22x + 20 = 0$ d) $2x^2 - 7x - 5 = 0$
   e) $5x^2 - 8x + 4 = 0$ f) $49x^2 - 70x + 25 = 0$

(B)

4. a) Solve. i) $x^2 - 2x - 3 = 0$ ii) $x^2 - 2x + 1 = 0$ iii) $x^2 - 2x + 5 = 0$
   b) Graph the expressions in part a) on the same grid, and explain the results of part a) in terms of the graphs.

5. What is the condition that $px^2 + qx + r = 0$ has:
   a) two real roots   b) no real roots?

6. For what values of k does each equation have two different real roots?
   a) $x^2 + kx + 1 = 0$ b) $kx^2 + 4x - 3 = 0$ c) $3x^2 + kx + 2 = 0$

7. For what values of m does each equation have two equal real roots?
   a) $x^2 + mx + 7 = 0$ b) $(2m + 1)x^2 - 8x + 6 = 0$

8. For what values of p does each equation have no real roots?
   a) $x^2 - px - 4 = 0$
   b) $px^2 - 8x + 9 = 0$
   c) $px^2 - 5x + p = 0$

---

9. Which of these equations have real roots for the values of k indicated?
   a) $kx^2 - 2x + 3 = 0, k < \dfrac{1}{3}$
   b) $3x^2 + kx + 2 = 0, |k| < 2\sqrt{6}$
   c) $(2k - 3)x^2 - 7x + 1 = 0, k < 7.5$

10. For what values of k will $x^2 + kx - k + 8 = 0$ have:
    a) equal roots
    b) real roots
    c) no real roots?

11. When a projectile is fired, the vertical component of its initial velocity is such that its height h metres t seconds after firing is given by $h = 250t - 4.9t^2$. Is it possible for the projectile to reach a height of: a) 2.75 km   b) 4.0 km?

12. A small change in the value of the constant term of some quadratic equations has a significant effect on the roots.
    a) Illustrate the truth of this statement by solving each equation.
       i) $x^2 + 50x + 624 = 0$
       ii) $x^2 + 50x + 625 = 0$
       iii) $x^2 + 50x + 626 = 0$
    b) Explain why, in terms of the graphs of the equations.

13. Show that if k is any real number each equation always has real roots.
    a) $kx^2 + (3k + 2)x + (2k + 3) = 0$ b) $(k + 1)x^2 + 2kx + (k - 1) = 0$

14. Show that there are no real numbers x and y such that:
    $$\frac{1}{x + y} = \frac{1}{x} + \frac{1}{y}, \ (x, y \neq 0).$$

15. If the coefficients of $ax^2 + bx + c = 0, (a \neq 0)$, are integers, determine which statements are:
    i) always true
    ii) never true
    iii) sometimes true.
    a) One root is an integer and the other is rational.
    b) One root is rational and the other is irrational.
    c) If the roots are equal, then they are real.
    d) If $ac > 0$, there are no real roots.
    e) If $ac < 0$, the roots are real.

16. Consider the equation $x^2 - 12x + (36 - 4k) = 0$.
    a) If k is an integer, for what values of k will the equation have rational roots?
    b) List some values of k and the roots of the corresponding equations. What patterns can you find? Do the results seem to be related to the coefficients?
    c) If k is a rational number, for what values of k will the equation have rational roots?

17. Show that the product of two consecutive natural numbers can never be a perfect square.

INVESTIGATE

Using the numbers 2, 3, and -8 as coefficients, how many different quadratic equations can be formed?
Is it possible to find three different integers such that for all possible arrangements of the coefficients, the equation will have integral roots?

INVESTIGATE

Show that $x^2 + 4x - 5 = 0$ and $x^2 - 5x + 4 = 0$ have a common real root. What conditions must be satisfied by p and q for the following equations to have a common real root?
$x^2 + px + q = 0$
$x^2 + qx + p = 0$

INVESTIGATE

Other Ways of Solving Quadratic Equations

Three other ways of solving quadratic equations developed by mathematicians in times past are as follows.

- About A.D. 250, the Greek mathematician Diophantus solved quadratic equations of the form $ax^2 + bx + c = 0$ by the method of completing the square. But instead of his first step being the division of both sides by a, he multiplied both sides by a.

- About A.D. 1050, the Hindus developed a way of solving quadratic equations, the first step of which was the multiplication of both sides by a number equal to four times the coefficient of x^2.

- In the 16th century, the French mathematician François Vieta solved quadratic equations by a novel substitution method. To solve an equation such as $x^2 + 6x + 7 = 0$ he substituted $y + k$ for x, where k was a number to be determined. He then rearranged the equation as a quadratic in y and chose a value for k so that the coefficient of the linear term was zero. It was then an easy matter to solve for y, and by adding the chosen value of k, the roots of the original equation were obtained.

1. Solve these equations using the above methods.
   a) $x^2 + 6x + 7 = 0$ b) $3x^2 + x - 2 = 0$
2. Use the above methods to solve $ax^2 + bx + c = 0$ $(a \neq 0)$.

 **PROBLEM SOLVING**

Arithmetic and Geometric Means

"Students are accustomed to encountering mathematics in its finished form. Problem solving is mathematics in the making."

Peggy A. House

For any two positive numbers x and y, we define the arithmetic mean and the geometric mean as follows.

Arithmetic mean: $\dfrac{x + y}{2}$ *Geometric mean:* $\sqrt{xy}$

Prove that the geometric mean is always less than or equal to the arithmetic mean. When are the two means equal?

Understand the problem
- Try some numerical examples. Choose any two positive numbers x and y, and calculate their arithmetic mean and geometric mean.
- Is the geometric mean less than or equal to the arithmetic mean? Under what conditions are they equal?
- Does this prove that the geometric mean will always be less than or equal to the arithmetic mean?

Think of a strategy
- We are required to prove that $\sqrt{xy} \leq \dfrac{x + y}{2}$.
- What formula in algebra involves both the sum of two variables, $x + y$, and their product, xy?

Carry out the strategy
- Start with the formula for the square of a binomial, $(x + y)^2$, and try to rearrange the terms to prove that $\sqrt{xy} \leq \dfrac{x + y}{2}$.
- You will also need the formula for $(x - y)^2$.
- Under what conditions does $\sqrt{xy} = \dfrac{x + y}{2}$?

Look back
- Could we prove that $\sqrt{xy} \leq \dfrac{x + y}{2}$ by squaring both sides and simplifying?
- A rectangle has length x and width y. How long is each side of a square if it has: the same perimeter as the rectangle? the same area as the rectangle?

PROBLEMS

1. Prove that the inequality on the facing page is equivalent to this inequality.

$$\left(\frac{x + y}{2}\right)^2 \leq \frac{x^2 + y^2}{2}$$

2. Sketch some examples of quadrilaterals in which the diagonals bisect each other. What kind of quadrilaterals are they? Prove your prediction.

3. The arithmetic mean and the geometric mean of the roots of a quadratic equation are p and q respectively. Determine the equation.

4. A cube has edges of length n. The faces of the cube are all painted, then it is cut into n^3 smaller cubes.
   a) How many of the smaller cubes have:
      i) no faces painted
      ii) exactly one face painted
      iii) exactly two faces painted
      iv) exactly three faces painted
   b) Use the results of part a) to factor the expression $n^3 - 8$.

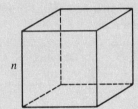

n

5. a) Prove that $x_1y_1 + x_2y_2 \leq \sqrt{x_1^2 + x_2^2}\sqrt{y_1^2 + y_2^2}$.
   b) Under what conditions does the equality hold?

6. If x, y, and z are any three positive numbers, prove that $(x + y)(y + z)(z + x) \geq 8xyz$. Under what conditions does the equality hold?

7. a) Given the three numbers 1, 2, and -3, show that if these three numbers are used as the coefficients of a quadratic equation, in any order, the equation has rational roots.
   b) State a general result suggested by part a) and prove it.

8. If $x + y = 1$, prove that $\left(1 + \dfrac{1}{x}\right)\left(1 + \dfrac{1}{y}\right) \geq 9$.

9. Triangle ABC has sides of length a, b, and c. Prove that $\triangle$ABC is equilateral if, and only if, $(a + b + c)^2 = 3(ab + bc + ac)$.

4-7 SOLVING PROBLEMS USING QUADRATIC EQUATIONS

A variety of problems lead to quadratic equations. The example and the exercises give some idea of this variety.

Example.   Biathlon skiing combines cross-country ski racing with rifle shooting. At Olympic Games and world championships, competitors start singly at one-minute intervals. Frank Ullrich, who is scheduled to start immediately following Anatole Alyabiev, feels that no matter how fast Anatole skis, he can ski 1 km/h faster. What is the average speed of each skier if Frank overtakes Anatole at the first shooting range, which is 4 km from the start?

Solution.   Let x be Anatole's speed in kilometres per hour. The data is organized in this table.

Skier	Distance (km)	Average speed (km/h)	Time (h)
Anatole	4	x	$\dfrac{4}{x}$
Frank	4	$x + 1$	$\dfrac{4}{x + 1}$

Since Frank started 1 min, or $\dfrac{1}{60}$ h, after Anatole:

$$\frac{4}{x} - \frac{4}{x + 1} = \frac{1}{60}$$

$$\frac{4x + 4 - 4x}{x(x + 1)} = \frac{1}{60}$$

$$x(x + 1) = 240$$

$$x^2 + x - 240 = 0$$

$$(x - 15)(x + 16) = 0$$

$$x = 15 \text{ or } -16$$

The equation may be solved using the formula.

The negative solution is rejected because the speed must be positive. Anatole's speed is 15 km/h and Frank's is 16 km/h.

EXERCISES 4-7

Ⓐ

1. Write algebraic equivalents for these verbal expressions.
   a) Two consecutive numbers
   b) Two consecutive odd numbers
   c) Two numbers which differ by 3
   d) The sum of the squares of two numbers which differ by 3
   e) The product of two consecutive even numbers
   f) The sum of the squares of a number and its reciprocal

2. Write algebraic equivalents for these verbal expressions.
   a) The time required to travel 80 km at $(x - 12)$ kilometres per hour
   b) The dimensions of a frame for a picture 40 cm by 60 cm with a border x centimetres wide
   c) The length-to-width ratio of a rectangle with a length 5 units longer than the width
   d) The area of a rectangle with a length 8 units less than three times the width
   e) The profit on each radio when x radios are bought for $15 000 and $x - 2$ are sold for $16 000
   f) The volume of acid in a solution if x litres of a 30% acid solution are added to 20 L of a 25% acid solution

Ⓑ

3. Chris cuts half a rectangular lawn, 40 m by 30 m, by mowing strips of equal width around the perimeter. Jerri cuts the small rectangle left. How wide a strip does Chris cut so that they share the work equally?

4. Students sent flowers costing $20 to a sick classmate. There were four fewer students contributing than was planned, requiring each of the others to give 25¢ more. How many students contributed to the gift?

5. Three pieces of rod measure 20 cm, 41 cm, and 44 cm. If the same amount is cut off each piece, the remaining lengths can be formed into a right triangle. What length is cut off?

6. Dieter makes a journey of 430 km, travelling 160 km by bus and 270 km by car. If the car averages 10 km/h faster than the bus and the whole journey takes 5 h, what is the speed of the car?

7. A storeowner buys a quantity of balls for $600. If they had each cost $0.25 less, she would have had 10 more for the same money. How much did she pay for each ball?

8. The edges of three cubes are consecutive odd integers. If the cubes are stacked as shown the total exposed surface area is 381 cm². Find the lengths of the sides of the cubes.

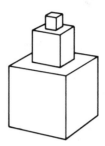

9. When a car reduces its speed by 18 km/h, its wheels, 200 cm in circumference, take 1 s longer to make 50 revolutions. What was the car's original speed?

10. If a bus travelled 10 km/h faster, it would take 2 h less time to make a 315 km trip. What is its speed?

11. Over a distance of 120 km, the average speed of a train is 40 km/h faster than that of a car. If the train covers the distance in 30 min less time, find its average speed.

12. To save fuel on the 240 km trip to their cottage, the Nakamura family reduce their usual average speed by 20 km/h. This lengthens the journey time by 1 h. What is the slower average speed?

13. Antonella bought some calculators for a total of $240. She kept one for herself and sold the rest for $300 making a profit of $5 on each calculator. How many calculators did she buy?

14. Brendan buys a block of shares of Laser Technology for $1875. When the share price increases by $4/share, he sells all but 15 of them for $1740. How many shares did he buy?

15. When a ball is thrown upward, its height, h metres, is given by
    $h = 1.5 + 19.6t - 4.9t^2$, where t seconds is the time after it is thrown.
    For what length of time is the ball higher than 16.2 m?

16. Two taps turned on together can fill a tank in 15 min. By themselves, one takes 16 min longer than the other to fill the tank. Find the time taken to fill the tank by each tap on its own.

17. Car A leaves Toronto for Montreal, 500 km away, at an average speed of 80 km/h. Car B leaves Montreal for Toronto on the same highway 2 h later at 100 km/h. How far are they from Toronto when they pass?

1. Solve.
   a) $(x + 7)(x - 3) = (x + 7)(5 - x)$
   b) $(3x - 9)(x + 2) = (x - 3)(2x + 1)$
   c) $(x + 4)(x - 4) = -9(x + 1)(x - 1)$
   d) $(x + 5)(2x - 3) = (x + 3)(x + 4)$

2. Calculate the radius of a circle that has an area of:
   a) 169 cm²   b) 1772 mm²   c) 16π km².

3. Solve graphically.
   a) $2x^2 + 11x - 6 = 0$ b) $2x^2 - 5x - 12 = 0$
   c) $4x^2 - 25 = 0$ d) $4x^2 + 4x - 15 = 0$

4. Solve.
   a) $x^2 - 5x - 14 = 0$ b) $m^2 + 4m - 32 = 0$
   c) $3v^2 - 2v - 1 = 0$ d) $6t^2 - 11t - 10 = 0$

5. Solve.
   a) $x^2 - 3x - 22 = 4(x - 1)$
   b) $7v(v - 1) = 5(v^2 - 1.2)$
   c) $2(x - 3)(x + 3) + 5x = 0$
   d) $(z - 4)(3z + 2) = (z - 5)(2z + 1) - 1$

6. One side of a right triangle is 2 cm shorter than the hypotenuse and 7 cm longer than the third side. Find the lengths of the sides of the triangle.

7. The height h metres of an infield fly ball t seconds after being hit is given by the formula $h = 30t - 5t^2$. How long is the ball in the air?

8. The length of a rectangular picture is 5 cm greater than the width. Find the dimensions of the picture if its area is:
   a) 150 cm²   b) 300 cm².

9. Solve by completing the square.
   a) $x^2 - 8x - 30 = 0$ b) $x^2 + 6x - 90 = 0$
   c) $x^2 - 5x + 2 = 0$ d) $x^2 + 15x + 25 = 0$

10. Solve by completing the square.
   a) $2x^2 + 9x + 3 = 0$ b) $6x^2 + 2x - 5 = 0$
   c) $7x^2 - 16x + 5 = 0$ d) $10x^2 + 7x - 10 = 0$

11. Solve. Give the answers to 2 decimal places.
   a) $5x^2 + 11x - 12 = 0$ b) $3x^2 + 10x - 32 = 0$
   c) $5x^2 - 15x + 11 = 0$ d) $9x^2 - 6x - 143 = 0$
   e) $12x^2 - 29x + 14 = 0$ f) $20x^2 + x - 12 = 0$

12. The surface area A of a closed cylinder of radius r is given by the formula $A = 6.28r^2 + 92.1r$. Find the radius of the cylinder if the surface area is:
    a) 1138.72 cm²
    b) 1772.98 cm².

13. Solve.
    a) $x^4 - 5x^2 + 4 = 0$
    b) $2x^4 - 13x^2 - 45 = 0$
    c) $6x^4 - 7x^2 - 20 = 0$
    d) $12x^5 - 51x^3 - 54x = 0$

14. Solve.
    a) $\sqrt{3x - 1} + 5 = 7$
    b) $6 - \sqrt{4x + 1} = 1$
    c) $2\sqrt{3x + 5} - 8 = 4$
    d) $4\sqrt{5x - 1} - 9 = 7$
    e) $\dfrac{9x^2}{x^2 - 25} = \dfrac{4x}{x - 5} + \dfrac{x}{x + 5}$
    f) $\dfrac{5x}{x + 4} = \dfrac{3x^2}{x^2 - 16} - \dfrac{2x + 1}{x - 4}$

15. A uniform border on a framed photograph has the same area as the photograph. What are the outside dimensions of the border if the dimensions of the photograph are 25 cm by 20 cm?

16. For what values of m will $x^2 - 2mx + m + 12 = 0$ have:
    a) equal roots
    b) real roots
    c) no real roots?

17. If m is a positive number less than 4, which of these equations has equal roots?
    a) $x^2 + mx + 1 = 0$
    b) $mx^2 + 3x - 5 = 0$
    c) $3x^2 + 2mx + 7 = 0$

18. A grappling iron is thrown vertically to catch on a ledge 7.5 m above the thrower. If its height h metres t seconds after being thrown is given by $h = -4.9t^2 + 11t + 1.5$, will it reach the ledge?

19. A storeowner sold a number of dresses for $75 each. Her percent profit was numerically the same as the cost of each dress. What was the cost of each dress?

20. A rectangular field has a perimeter 500 m and an area 14 400 m². Find the lengths of its sides.

21. C is a point on line segment AB such that $AB \times BC = AC^2$. If AB is 6 cm, find the length of BC to the nearest millimetre.

22. The perimeter of a square exceeds that of another square by 100 m. The area of the larger square exceeds three times that of the smaller by 325 m². Find the lengths of the sides of the squares.

23. Two taps turned on together can fill a tank in 30 min. By themselves, one takes 25 min longer than the other to fill the tank. Find the time taken to fill the tank by each tap on its own.

5 Functions

In a drag race, cars accelerate from a standing start towards a finish line a fixed distance away. How would you calculate the speed of the car at any moment during the race? (See Section 5-7 *Example 1.*)

5-1 RELATIONS

In everyday language we frequently speak of two people or things which are related in some way.

These two are related; they are sisters.

The number of people using the pool is related to the temperature.

The value of a car is related to its age. The ages and values of the cars in a parking lot are displayed in the table and the graph below.

Car	Age (years)	Value ($)
A	1	7000
B	2	5000
C	2	4500
D	4	2500
E	4	3500
F	5	3500
G	7	1200

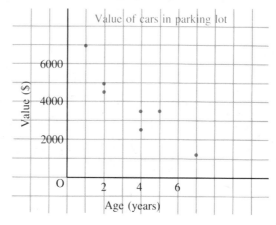

Each point on the graph corresponds to an ordered pair. The first coordinate is the age of the car, and the second is its value. The set of all these ordered pairs R is an example of a relation.

$R = \{(1, 7000), (2, 5000), (2, 4500), (4, 2500), (4, 3500), (5, 3500), (7, 1200)\}$

The set of first coordinates of R is $\{1, 2, 4, 5, 7\}$. This is the set of possible ages of the cars, and is called the domain of R. The set of second coordinates of R is $\{1200, 2500, 3500, 4500, 5000, 7000\}$. This is the set of possible values of the cars, and is called the range of R.

- A *relation R* is a set of ordered pairs.
- The *domain* of *R* is the set of *first* coordinates of the ordered pairs.
- The *range* of *R* is the set of *second* coordinates of the ordered pairs.

A relation can be represented in many different ways.

- A table of values

x	y
0	0
1	1
2	4
3	9
4	16
5	25
6	36

- A graph

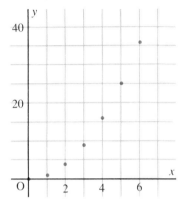

- A set of ordered pairs
  $\{(0, 0), (1, 1), (2, 4), (3, 9), (4, 16), (5, 25), (6, 36)\}$

- An equation
  $y = x^2$
  where $x \in I, 0 \le x \le 6$

In the above relation:
the domain is $\{0, 1, 2, 3, 4, 5, 6\}$
the range is $\{0, 1, 4, 9, 16, 25, 36\}$.

Example 1. A row of trees is planted on the windward side of a section of highway to prevent snow drifting onto it. The trees cause the snow to settle into a drift before it reaches the highway. The distance d metres that the trees need to be from the highway is related to their height h metres by the formula $d = 12 + 5h$. The formula is valid for tree heights from 2 m to 10 m. Graph the relation, and state its domain and range.

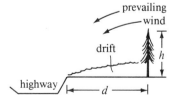

Solution.   Construct a table using values of *h* between 2 and 10.

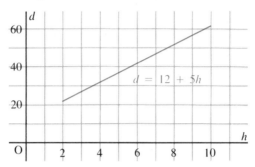

h	d
2	22
4	32
6	42
8	52
10	62

$d = 12 + 5h$

The table shows only the ordered pairs that were used to draw the graph. Joining the points shows that the relation includes more ordered pairs than those used.

The domain, the set of possible first coordinates of the ordered pairs represented by the graph, is the set of tree heights between 2 and 10 inclusive.

The range, the set of possible second coordinates, is the set of distances from the trees to the road between 22 and 62 inclusive.

Given the *graph* of a relation:
The *domain* is the set of *x*-values represented by the graph.

The *range* is the set of *y*-values represented by the graph.

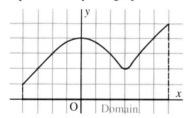

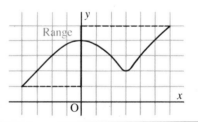

Example 2.   The graph shows the oxygen consumption of the body during and after 5 min of strenuous activity.
  a) What was the greatest rate of oxygen consumption?
  b) When was the oxygen consumption 1000 mL/min?
  c) What are the domain and range of the relation?

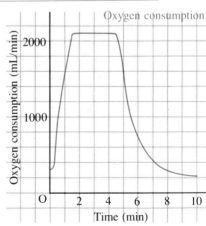

Solution.

a) The greatest rate of consumption was about 2100 mL/min.
b) The rate of consumption was 1000 mL/min after about 0.5 min and 5.5 min.
c) The domain is the set of times represented by the graph. This is the set of positive real numbers up to 10. The range is the set of consumption rates represented by the graph. This is the set of real numbers between 300 and 2100.

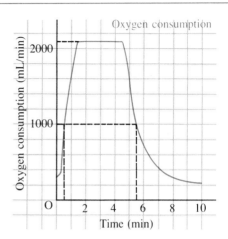

Given the *equation* of a relation:

The *domain* is the set of all values of x for which the equation is defined.

The *range* is the set of all values of y which are defined for the values of x in the domain.

For example, for the relation with equation $y = x^2$: the domain is all real numbers; the range is all non-negative real numbers.

Example 3. Find the domain and range of the relation $y = \sqrt{x - 1}$.

Solution. Since square roots of negative numbers are not real numbers,

then, $x - 1 \geqslant 0$

$x \geqslant 1$

The domain is the set of all real numbers greater than or equal to 1. Since the radical sign indicates a positive square root, the expression $\sqrt{x - 1}$ is never negative. That is, $y \geqslant 0$

The range is the set of all non-negative real numbers.

Ordered pairs need not involve numbers.

Example 4. The four children in the Hayes family are Pat, Sandra, Bill, and Kathy, who were born in that order.
a) Express the relation "is a younger sister of" as a set of ordered pairs.
b) What are the domain and range of the relation?

Solution.

a) The relation is: {(Sandra, Pat), (Kathy, Pat), (Kathy, Sandra), (Kathy, Bill)}.
For the first ordered pair, we say, "Sandra is a younger sister of Pat."
b) The domain is the set of children who are younger sisters; that is, {Sandra, Kathy}. The range is the set of children who have a younger sister; that is, {Pat, Sandra, Bill}.

EXERCISES 5-1

Ⓐ

1. On six consecutive weekends, a hotel made a survey to find out how the temperature affected the number of people using the outdoor pool. The table (below left) shows the results.
   a) List the ordered pairs of the relation.   b) State the domain and range.

Temperature (°C)	Number using pool
15	2
20	10
18	15
23	30
20	25
28	40

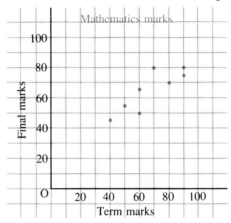

2. The graph (above right) displays the relation between the term marks and final marks of several mathematics students.
   a) List the ordered pairs of the relation.   b) State the domain and range.

3. The Thurs have two sons Craig and Colin and a daughter Gayle.
   a) Express the relation "is a brother of" as a set of ordered pairs.
   b) What are the domain and range of the relation?

4. The world track records, to the nearest second, for races up to 1500 m are given in the table.
   a) Graph the relation between time and distance:
      i) for men   ii) for women.
   b) State the domain and range for each relation in part a).

	World Record	
Distance (m)	Men (s)	Women (s)
100	10	11
200	20	22
400	44	48
800	102	113
1500	211	232

5. The recommended mass corresponding to height for women is given in the table.

Height (cm)	145	150	155	160	165	170	175	180	185
Mass (kg)	46	48	50	53	56	60	63	67	71

   a) Graph the relation.   b) State the domain and range.

6. State the domain and range of each relation.

a)

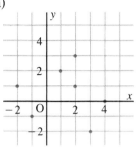

b)

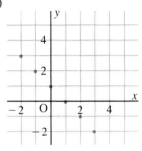

c)

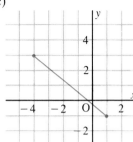

d)

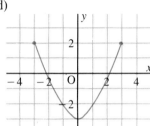

e)

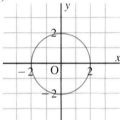

f)

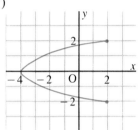

Ⓑ

7. The fuel consumption in the city and on the highway for seven different models of cars is given in the table.
   a) Graph the relation between the highway fuel consumption and city fuel consumption.
   b) What are the domain and range of the relation?

Model	Fuel Consumption (L/100 km)	
	City	**Highway**
Rabbit	6.1	4.2
Civic	8.1	5.3
Omni	10.3	5.5
Corolla	9.7	7.5
Skylark	12.2	7.6
Audi	14.0	9.1
Camaro	18.1	12.7

8. a) Using only the single digit numbers, list the ordered pairs of the relation "is a factor of". For example, (2, 6) indicates that 2 is a factor of 6.
   b) State the domain and range of the relation.

9. The five children of the Lalonde family, in order of birth, are Tobie, Lise, Suzette, Urbain, and Claire.
   a) List the ordered pairs of the relation "is older than".
   b) State the domain and range of the relation.

10. State the domain and range of each relation.
    a) $y = \sqrt{x}$
    b) $y = \sqrt{x + 1}$
    c) $y = 2x - 3$
    d) $y = \dfrac{1}{x}$
    e) $y = \dfrac{1}{x - 2}$
    f) $y = (x + 4)^2$

11. Select the graph which best illustrates each given relation.
    a) how a person's height above ground varies as time passes during a Ferris wheel ride
    b) the wages of a person who is paid hourly
    c) how the visibility of a lighthouse beam depends on the height of the lighthouse
    d) how the masses of a brother and sister vary with their ages
    e) how the amount of light penetrating the ocean depends on the depth below the surface
    f) the numbers of boys and girls in different classes in a school

    i)

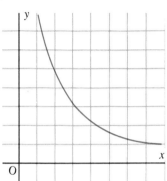

    ii)

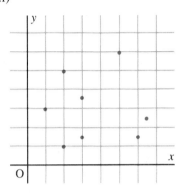

    iii)

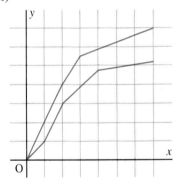

    iv)

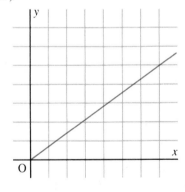

    v)

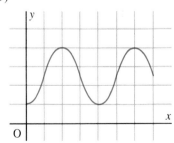

    vi)

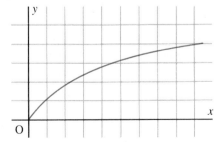

12. State the domain and range of each relation.

a)

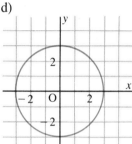

b)

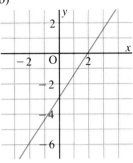

c)

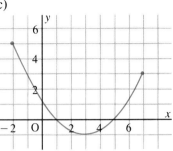

d)

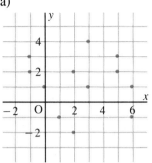

e)

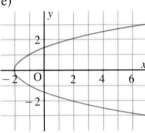

f)

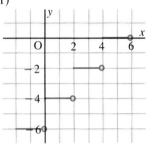

13. Graph each relation and state its domain and range.

   a) $y = 3x + 5$

   b) $y = 2 - x$

   c) $x + 2y - 6 = 0$

   d) $y = x^2$

   e) $x^2 + y^2 = 25$

   f) $x^2 + y^2 = 1$

14. Long distance track records for men are given in the table.

Distance (km)	5	10	20	25	30
Record time (min : s)	13:08	27:23	57:24	74:17	91:30

   a) Graph the relation between time and distance.

   b) State the domain and range.

15. The speed v metres per second of a freely falling object after it has fallen through a distance of h metres from the point of release is given by the formula $v \doteq 4.4\sqrt{h}$.

   a) Graph the relation.

   b) State the domain and range.

   c) Find v when h is 6.5 m.

16. Dominic fills a kettle, boils the water, makes a cup of coffee, and allows it to cool before drinking it.

   a) Sketch a graph showing how the temperature of the water is related to the time since the kettle was filled.

   b) State the domain and range of the relation.

5-2 FUNCTIONS

In mathematics, the word "function" is used to express the idea that one quantity depends on another. For each illustration below, try to express the accompanying statement without using "function".

The distance to the horizon is a function of the observer's height above the ground.

Stopping distance is a function of speed.

The length of a tree's shadow is a function of the time of day. It was measured at 2 h intervals on a summer day. The results are shown in the table and graph.

Time of day	Shadow length (m)
08:00	12.0
10:00	7.7
12:00	5.7
14:00	6.0
16:00	7.7
18:00	10.3
20:00	14.2

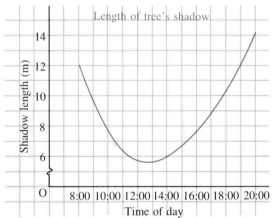

The relation between time of day and shadow length can be expressed as a set of ordered pairs.
$R = \{(8, 12.0), (10, 7.7), (12, 5.7), (14, 6.0), (16, 7.7), (18, 10.3), (20, 14.2)\}$
Since the tree's shadow cannot have two different lengths at the same time, this relation has a special property. No two ordered pairs have the same first coordinate. For this reason, this relation is called a function.

> A *function* is a relation in which no two ordered pairs have the same first coordinate.

Example 1. Is each relation a function?
  a) $\{(2, 1), (3, 5), (3, 6), (4, -2), (5, -1)\}$
  b) $\{(3, -2), (4, 1), (5, 1), (6, 0), (7, -2)\}$

Solution. a) Two ordered pairs, $(3, 5)$ and $(3, 6)$, have the same first coordinate. Therefore, the relation is not a function.
  b) Since every ordered pair has a different first coordinate, the relation is a function.

From the graphs of the relations in *Example 1*, we can find a simple way to determine if a relation is a function.

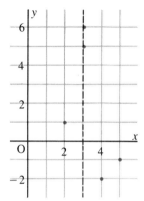

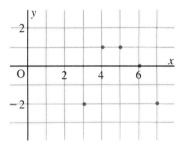

Since the points $(3, 5)$ and $(3, 6)$ have the same first coordinate, they can be joined by a vertical line. The relation is not a function.

No two points can be joined by a vertical line. The relation is a function.

Vertical-line test for a function
If no two points on a graph can be joined by a vertical line, the graph represents a function.

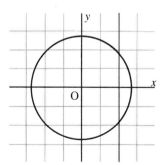

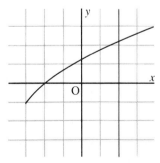

Since there is a vertical line which intersects the graph more than once, the relation is *not* a function.

Since there is no vertical line which intersects the graph more than once, the relation *is* a function.

Example 2. Given the relation $y = x^2 - 5$

    a) Graph the relation for $-3 \leqslant x \leqslant 3$, and determine if it is a function.

    b) State its domain and range.

Solution.   a)

x	y
-3	4
-2	-1
-1	-4
0	-5
1	-4
2	-1
3	4

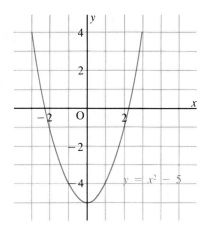

       The vertical-line test shows that the relation is a function.

    b) The domain is the set of x-values represented by the graph. Since the graph extends beyond the last points plotted, the domain is the set of all real numbers.

        The range is the set of y-values represented by the graph. This is the set of all real numbers greater than or equal to -5.

    It is not necessary to graph a relation to tell if it is a function. This can be determined from the equation of the relation.

Equation test for a function

If a value of x can be found which produces more than one value of y when substituted in the equation, the equation *does not* represent a function. If there is no such value of x, the equation *does* represent a function.

Example 3. Is each relation a function?

    a) $x^2 + y^2 = 25$ b) $y = \sqrt{x}$ c) $y = \dfrac{1}{x - 2}$

Solution.   a) Is there any value of x which produces more than one value of y when substituted into $x^2 + y^2 = 25$?

        If $x = 0$, $y^2 = 25$

$$y = \pm 5$$

        When $x = 0$, there are two values of y.

        The relation is not a function.

    b) The relation $y = \sqrt{x}$ is only defined when $x \geqslant 0$. For any value of $x \geqslant 0$ there is only one value of y. Therefore, the relation is a function.

c) The relation $y = \dfrac{1}{x - 2}$ is undefined when $x = 2$. For any other value of x, there is only one value of y. Therefore, the relation is a function.

Example 4. To deliver parcels in a metropolitan area, Rapidsend Courier Service charges $5 for the first kilogram plus $2 for each additional kilogram or part thereof, up to a maximum of 6 kg.
a) Draw a graph showing how the delivery charge depends on the mass of the parcel.
b) For the relation in part a), state the domain and range.
c) Is the relation a function? Why?

Solution.   a)

Mass (kg)	Delivery charge ($)
$0 < m \leqslant 1$	5
$1 < m \leqslant 2$	7
$2 < m \leqslant 3$	9
$3 < m \leqslant 4$	11
$4 < m \leqslant 5$	13
$5 < m \leqslant 6$	15

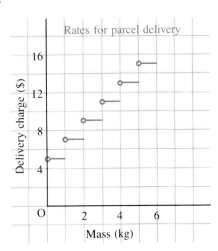

The small circles on the graph indicate points that are not part of the graph. For example, the delivery charge for a 1 kg parcel is $5, and $7 for one only slightly heavier. This is shown on the graph by the circle at (1, 7).
b) The domain of the relation is the set of all possible masses of parcels. Since the heaviest parcel accepted is 6 kg, the domain would be the set of all positive numbers less than or equal to 6. For this domain, the range is the set of delivery charges (5, 7, 9, 11, 13, 15).
c) The vertical-line test shows that the relation is a function.

Example 4 shows that a function can consist of two or more distinct parts, and these parts need not be connected on the graph.
The function in *Example 4* is an example of a *step function*.

EXERCISES 5-2

Ⓐ

1. Does each graph represent a function?

   a)

   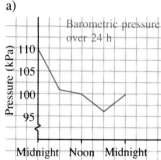

   b)

   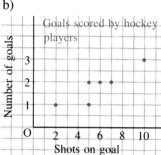

   c)

   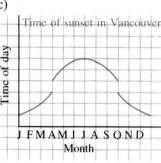

2. For each graph, if it represents a function, state its domain and range.

   a)

   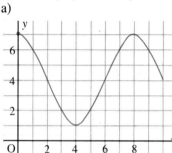

   b)

   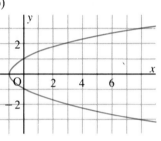

   c)

   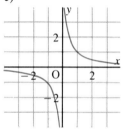

3. Does each set of ordered pairs represent a function?
   a) $\{(2, 5), (3, 10), (5, 26), (7, 50)\}$
   b) $\{(9, 2), (6, 5), (3, 1), (6, 8), (7, 11)\}$
   c) $\{(0, 4), (1, 5), (2, 8), (3, 13), (-1, 5), (-2, 8), (-3, 13)\}$

4. Determine if each relation is a function.

   a) $y = 3x - 7$ b) $y = 1 - \frac{1}{2}x$ c) $y = x^2 + 1$

   d) $x^2 + y^2 = 16$ e) $x = y^2$ f) $y = \frac{1}{x}$

   g) $x - y^2 = 4$ h) $x^2 - y^2 = 9$ i) $y = \sqrt{2x}$

Ⓑ

5. Graph each relation, and state its domain and range. Is each relation a function?
   a) $y = 3x - 1$ b) $y = x^2 - 1$ c) $x = y^2 + 1$

6. A ball bounces to a height h when dropped from a height x, where h is given by
   the formula $h = \frac{3}{4}x$.

   a) Graph the relation. Is it a function?
   b) State the domain and range.
   c) If the ball bounces to a height of 3.6 m, from what height was it dropped?

7. Select the graph which best illustrates each given function.
   a) how a person's mass changes with age
   b) how the temperature of a cup of coffee changes as time passes
   c) how the number of cars in the school parking lot changes during the day
   d) how the braking distance of a car depends on its speed
   e) how the cost of parking depends on the time a car is parked
   f) how the height of a kicked football changes as time passes

   i)

   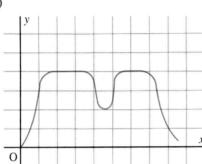

   ii)

   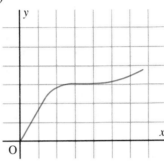

   iii)

   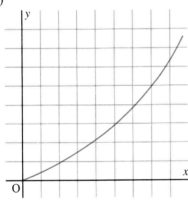

   iv)

   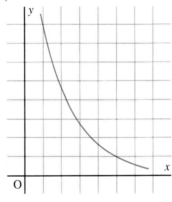

   v)

   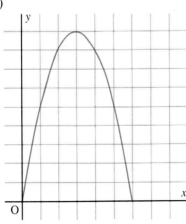

   vi)

   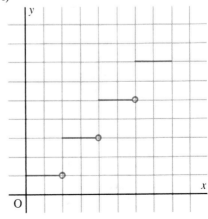

8. If the perimeter of a rectangle is 24 cm and its length is x centimetres, express each measurement as a function of x.
   a) the width
   b) the area
   c) the length of a diagonal

9. If the area of a rectangle is 24 cm² and its length is x centimetres, express each measurement as a function of x.
   a) the width
   b) the perimeter
   c) the length of a diagonal

10. Graph each function, and state its domain and range.
    a) $y = 2^x$
    b) $y = \sqrt{x}$
    c) $y = \sqrt{x^2}$

11. Long-distance telephone charges between two cities are \$3 for the first 3 min plus 50¢ for each additional minute or part of a minute.
    a) Draw a graph showing how the charge for a call depends on the length of the call.
    b) State the domain and range.
    c) Is the relation a function? Why?

12. A taxi company charges \$2.50 for distances up to 1 km plus \$1 for each additional half-kilometre or part thereof.
    a) Graph this relation. Is it a function?
    b) State the domain and range.

13. State the domain and range of each function.
    a) $y = \sqrt{x - 3}$
    b) $y = 5x$
    c) $x + y = 6$
    d) $y = \dfrac{1}{x + 2}$
    e) $y = x^2 + 1$
    f) $y = 3^x$

Ⓒ

14. a) Express as a function of x.
    i) The volume of water that must be added to 5 L of antifreeze to make a solution that is $x\%$ antifreeze.
    ii) The volume of antifreeze that must be added to 5 L of water to make a solution that is $x\%$ antifreeze.
    b) What are the domain and range of each function in part a)?
    c) Graph the functions in part a), and compare them. Account for the similarities and differences.

15. Some geography textbooks contain a graph like the one shown which illustrates how the temperature of the atmosphere varies with increasing altitude.
    a) Is the relation a function; that is, is altitude a function of temperature?
    b) Is temperature a function of altitude? How might the graph be drawn to show this? Give reasons why the graph is not drawn this way in geography textbooks.

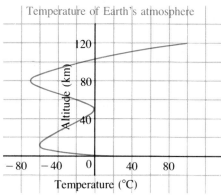

Temperature of Earth's atmosphere

MATHEMATICS AROUND US

Recording Instruments

Doctors use electrocardiograms to study the electrical activity of the heart. The data are displayed as a graph on a computer screen or on a roll of graph paper.

Similar instruments are used to record other kinds of data in medicine, industry, geography, seismography (the scientific study of earthquakes), meteorology, and so on.

The graphs shown are:
- an electrocardiogram — measuring heart activity
- a recording thermometer — showing temperature over a week
- a barograph — measuring air pressure
- an electroencephalogram — recording the electrical activity of the brain.

QUESTIONS

1. a) Can you identify each graph?
   b) Explain how each graph illustrates the concept of a function.

i)

ii)

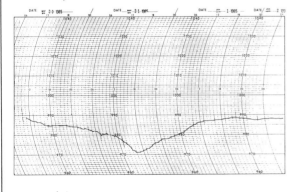

iii)

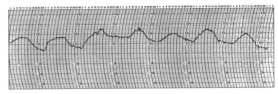

iv)

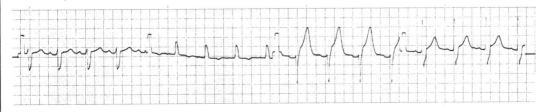

THE MATHEMATICAL MIND

The Origin of the Function Concept

The concept of a function originated in the seventeenth century, when scientists and mathematicians became interested in the study of motion.

● Galileo showed that the path of a projectile fired into the air is a parabola.

● The moon's motion was studied because knowledge of its position was used to determine longitude at sea.

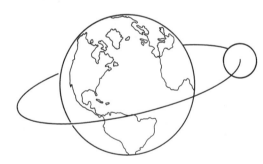

Since moving objects follow a single line or a curve, mathematicians thought that a function was defined by a single equation. For example, this definition was given by James Gregory in 1667.

> A function is a quantity obtained from other quantities by a succession of algebraic operations, or any other operation imaginable.

Leonhard Euler 1707–1783

As late as 1734, Leonhard Euler defined a function as any expression formed in any manner from a variable quantity and constants. He also introduced the $f(x)$ notation.

By 1750, scientists studying vibrating strings had encountered an example of a function that could not be defined by a single equation. This caused a controversy over the question of what a function was. Euler extended the definition to include cases where there were different expressions in different intervals of the domain. For example, Euler would have considered the following expression to be a single function.

$$f(x) = \begin{cases} x + 6, & \text{if } x \leq -2 \\ x^2, & \text{if } -2 \leq x \leq 2 \\ x + 2, & \text{if } x \geq 2 \end{cases}$$

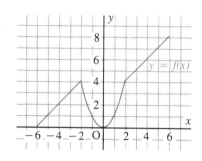

Most mathematicians found this new idea difficult to accept, and the concept of a function given by a single equation dominated mathematics until about 1800.

Joseph Fourier
1768-1830

But the definition of a function was soon to be extended even further. In 1807, Joseph Fourier published a paper about the flow of heat. He used functions whose component parts were not connected. Here is an example of such a function.

$$f(x) = \begin{cases} x + 4, & \text{if } x < -2 \\ x, & \text{if } -2 \le x < 2 \\ x - 4, & \text{if } x \ge 2 \end{cases}$$

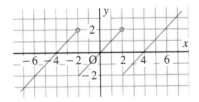

Moreover, Fourier's work implied that a function did not even have to be defined by equations. This led Lejeune Dirichlet to give a new definition of a function in 1837.

> y is a function of x when to each value of x in a given interval there corresponds a unique value of y.

Dirichlet's definition is equivalent to the one given on page 150 of this book. It is a very broad definition because it does not matter whether y depends on x according to one law or more, or whether the dependence can be expressed by equations.

QUESTIONS

1. Graph each function.
   a) $$f(x) = \begin{cases} 2 - x, & x \le -2 \\ x^2, & -2 \le x \le 2 \\ 6 - x, & x \ge 2 \end{cases}$$
   b) $$f(x) = \begin{cases} x + 2, & x < -2 \\ -x, & -2 \le x \le 2 \\ x - 2, & x > 2 \end{cases}$$
   c) $$f(x) = \begin{cases} (x + 4)^2, & x \le -2 \\ x^2, & -2 \le x \le 2 \\ (x - 4)^2, & x \ge 2 \end{cases}$$

2. Write the equations which define this function.

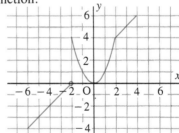

3. Refer to the functions in the examples and exercises of this chapter. Find an example of a function which does not satisfy any of the definitions given above, except the one given by Dirichlet.

4. In 1829 Dirichlet gave an example of a function of x that has one value for all rational values of x and a different value for all irrational values of x. Give an example of such a function.

5-3 FUNCTION NOTATION

In algebra, symbols such as x and y are used to represent numbers. To represent functions, we often use symbols such as $f(x)$ and $g(x)$. For example, we may write: $f(x) = x^2 - 3x - 4$.

The symbol $f(x)$ is read "f of x", and simply means that the expression which follows contains x as a variable. This notation is useful because it simplifies recording the values of the function for several values of x. For example, $f(6)$ means substitute 6 for x everywhere x occurs in the expression.

$$f(x) = x^2 - 3x - 4$$

$$f(6) = 6^2 - 3(6) - 4$$
$$= 36 - 18 - 4$$
$$= 14$$

Example 1. If $f(x) = 3x^2 - x - 6$, find:

    a) $f(2)$ b) $f(-1)$ c) $f(0.5)$.

Solution.   a) Substitute 2 for x in $f(x) = 3x^2 - x - 6$
$$f(2) = 3(2)^2 - 2 - 6$$
$$= 12 - 2 - 6$$
$$= 4$$

     b) Substitute -1 for x: $f(-1) = 3(-1)^2 - (-1) - 6$
$$= 3 + 1 - 6$$
$$= -2$$

     c) Substitute 0.5 for x: $f(0.5) = 3(0.5)^2 - (0.5) - 6$
$$= 0.75 - 0.5 - 6$$
$$= -5.75$$

Example 2. Given the function $g(x) = \sqrt{x + 2}$

    a) Graph the function for $-2 \leqslant x \leqslant 7$.   b) State the domain and range.

Solution.   a)

x	$g(x)$
-2	0.00
-1	1.00
0	1.41
1	1.73
2	2.00
3	2.24
4	2.45
5	2.65
6	2.83
7	3.00

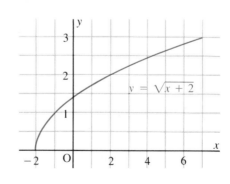

b) Since only non-negative numbers have real square roots, the function $g(x)$ is defined only when $x + 2 \geq 0$, or $x \geq -2$. The domain is the set of all real numbers greater than or equal to -2. The range is the set of non-negative real numbers.

Function notation can be used even when there is no known equation relating the variables.

Example 3.   From the graph of $y = f(x)$, find:
a) $f(5)$
b) $f(0)$
c) $f(-4)$.

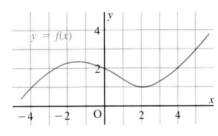

Solution.   a) When $x = 5$, $y = 3$;
that is, $f(5) = 3$
b) $f(0) = 2$
c) $f(-4) = 1$

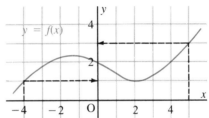

Other algebraic expressions may be substituted for the variable in the equation of a function.

Example 4.   Given $f(x) = 3x - 1$, find:

a) $f(c)$ b) $f(2x)$ c) $f\left(\dfrac{1}{x}\right)$, $x \neq 0$ d) $f(x - 2)$.

Solution.   a) Substitute c for x.
$$f(x) = 3x - 1$$
$$f(c) = 3c - 1$$

b) Substitute $2x$ for x.
$$f(x) = 3x - 1$$
$$f(2x) = 3(2x) - 1$$
$$= 6x - 1$$

c) Substitute $\dfrac{1}{x}$ for x.
$$f(x) = 3x - 1$$
$$f\left(\frac{1}{x}\right) = 3\left(\frac{1}{x}\right) - 1$$
$$= \frac{3}{x} - 1$$
$$= \frac{3 - x}{x} \quad (x \neq 0)$$

d) Substitute $x - 2$ for x.
$$f(x) = 3x - 1$$
$$f(x - 2) = 3(x - 2) - 1$$
$$= 3x - 6 - 1$$
$$= 3x - 7$$

EXERCISES 5-3

Ⓐ

1. If $f(x) = 1 - x^2$, evaluate:
   a) $f(2)$ b) $f(3)$ c) $f(0.5)$.

2. If $g(x) = 3x - 1$, evaluate:
   a) $g(1)$ b) $g(5)$ c) $g\left(\dfrac{1}{2}\right)$.

3. Find $f(-1)$, $f(2)$, and $f(0.5)$.
   a) $f(x) = 3x^2 - 2x + 1$ b) $f(x) = 2x^3 + 5x^2 + 3x - 4$

4. a) Graph.   i) $f(x) = \dfrac{1}{2}x - 1$ ii) $f(x) = \sqrt{x - 1}$
   b) State the domain and range of each function in part a).

5. For each graph of $y = f(x)$, find $f(-2)$, $f(1)$, and $f(3)$.
   a)   b)   c)

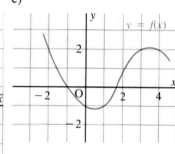

6. If $f(x) = 3x - 5$, find:
   a) $f(m)$ b) $f(4x)$ c) $2f(x)$ d) $f\left(\dfrac{2}{x}\right)$ e) $f(2x + 1)$.

7. If $g(x) = 5x + 1$, find:
   a) $g(k)$ b) $g(x - 1)$ c) $g(2x + 1)$ d) $g(4 - 3x)$.

8. Find $f(2)$, $f(-5)$, and $f(0.5)$.
   a) $f(x) = 4x - 7$ b) $f(x) = 8x^2 + x - 9$ c) $f(x) = \sqrt{6x - 1}$
   d) $f(x) = x^2 + \dfrac{1}{x}$ e) $f(x) = x^3 - x^2$ f) $f(x) = \dfrac{4x}{2x + 1}$

Ⓑ

9. Graph each function and state its domain and range.
   a) $f(x) = \dfrac{1}{2}x + 3$ b) $f(x) = x^2 + 1$ c) $f(x) = x(x - 3)$

10. Graph each function for $-3 \leqslant x \leqslant 3$.

a) $f(x) = x^3$ b) $f(x) = x^3 - 4x$ c) $f(x) = 2^x$ d) $f(x) = \dfrac{6}{x^2 + 1}$

11. State the domain and range of each function.

a) $f(x) = \sqrt{x + 5}$ b) $f(x) = \dfrac{5}{x + 2}$ c) $g(x) = 2x + 1$

d) $g(x) = x^2 + 3$ e) $f(x) = x^3$ f) $g(x) = 1 + \sqrt{x}$

12. If $f(x) = 2x^2 + 3x - 5$, find:
 a) $f(x + 1)$ b) $f(x + 2)$ c) $f(x + 3)$
 d) $f(2x)$ e) $f(3x)$ f) $f(-x)$.

13. If $f(x) = 3x - 2$ and $g(x) = 5x + 7$, find:
 a) $f(x) - g(x)$ b) $2f(x) + g(x)$ c) $f(x) \times g(x)$
 d) $4f(x) - 2g(x)$ e) $f(2x) - g(2x)$ f) $3f(2x) + 2g(3x)$.

14. The *greatest integer function* $y = int(x)$ is defined to be the greatest integer less than or equal to x.
 a) Evaluate.   i) $int(2.4)$ ii) $int(4.9)$ iii) $int(6.0)$
          iv) $int(-1.5)$ v) $int(-3.1)$ vi) $int(-5.9)$
 b) Graph the function $y = int(x)$.

15. The area A of an equilateral triangle is a function of its side length x, and is given by the formula $A = \dfrac{\sqrt{3}}{4}x^2$.

 a) Graph the function and state its domain and range.
 b) If the side length is doubled, how is the area affected?
 c) If the length of each side is increased by 3 units, by how much does the area increase?
 d) If the length of each side is decreased by h units, by how much does the area decrease?

16. If $f(x) = 5 - 3x$ and $g(x) = 4x + 1$, find a value of x such that:
 a) $f(x) = g(x)$ b) $f(x + 2) = g(x - 1)$
 c) $f(2 - 5x) = g(4x + 1)$ d) $f(2x + 2) = g(x^2)$.

17. Given $g(x) = 2x + 3$, find x when:
 a) $g(x) = 5$ b) $g(x) = -9$ c) $g(x) = 0$.

18. If $f(x) = x^2 + 3x - 10$, what values of x make:
 a) $f(x) = 0$ b) $f(x) = 8$ c) $f(x) = -6$?

Ⓒ

19. For $-5 \leqslant x \leqslant 5$, $x \neq 0$, graph: a) $f(x) = \dfrac{1}{x}$ b) $f(x) = \dfrac{1}{x^2}$.

20. Given $f(x) = \dfrac{x}{1 + x}$

    a) Find.   i) $f(2) + f\left(\dfrac{1}{2}\right)$ ii) $f(3) + f\left(\dfrac{1}{3}\right)$

    b) Predict the value of $f(n) + f\left(\dfrac{1}{n}\right)$, and prove that your prediction is correct.

    c) For what values of n does the result in part b) hold?

21. Given $g(x) = 3^x$
    a) Show that: i) $g(2x) = [g(x)]^2$ ii) $g(3x) = [g(x)]^3$.
    b) What is $g(nx)$ equal to?

22. a) If $f(x) = 3x + 2$, show that $f(a + b) \neq f(a) + f(b)$.
    b) Give an example of a function $f(x)$ such that the identity
       $f(a + b) = f(a) + f(b)$ is true for all values of a and b.

23. Let n be a positive integer and let $f(n)$ represent the number of factors of n.
    a) Graph the function $f(n)$.
    b) Describe the numbers for which:
       i) $f(n) = 2$ ii) $f(n) = 3$ iii) $f(n) = 4$ iv) $f(n) = 5$.

 **INVESTIGATE**

Dependent and Independent Variables

In Section 5-2 *Example 4* we considered a function representing the charges for delivering parcels. The charge C dollars is a function of the mass of the parcel m kilograms. That is, the value of C depends on the value of m. For this reason, C is called a *dependent variable*. Since m can represent the mass of any parcel, m is called an *independent variable*.

    These terms can be used with any function. The independent variable represents the members of the domain, and the dependent variable represents the members of the range. That is, for any function $y = f(x)$, x is the independent variable and y is the dependent variable.

1. Refer to the functions in the examples and exercises of Sections 5-2 and 5-3. Identify the dependent and independent variables in these functions.

5-4 DIRECT VARIATION

Marcie earns $6/h working as a lifeguard. Her total pay is a function of the number of hours she works. Since its graph is a straight line, we say that it is a linear function.

Hours worked, h	Pay in dollars, p
0	0
2	12
4	24
6	36
8	48
10	60

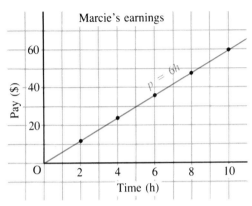

The table and graph show that when h is doubled, p is doubled; when h is tripled, p is tripled, and so on.

We say that p *varies directly as* h, and we write:

$p = kh$, where k is a constant called the *constant of proportionality*. From the table, we can verify that, for all values of p and h, $p = 6h$. The constant of proportionality is 6, and it represents Marcie's hourly rate of pay. It is also the slope of the line on the graph.

Direct Variation

If y varies directly as x, then y can be expressed as a function of x.

- The equation of the function has the form

   $y = mx$

   where m is the constant of proportionality.
- The graph of the function is a straight line with slope m through $(0, 0)$.

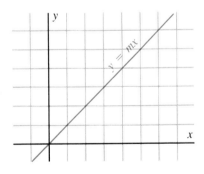

Example 1.   *y* varies directly as *x* and when *x* = 12, *y* = 16.
   a) Write *y* as a function of *x*.
   b) Find *y* when *x* = 5.
   c) Find *x* when *y* = 30.

Solution.   a) Since *y* varies directly as *x*, *y* = *kx*, where *k* is the constant of proportionality. Substitute 12 for *x* and 16 for *y* in the equation.

$$y = kx$$
$$16 = k(12)$$
$$k = \frac{4}{3}$$

Hence, the equation expressing *y* as a function of *x* is $y = \frac{4}{3}x$.

   b) When *x* = 5: $y = \frac{4}{3}(5)$
   $$= \frac{20}{3}$$

   c) When *y* = 30: $30 = \frac{4}{3}x$
   $$4x = 90$$
   $$x = 22.5$$

Example 2.   The height to which a ball bounces varies directly as the distance from which it was dropped. If it is dropped from a height of 2.4 m, it bounces to a height of 1.6 m.
   a) Express the height that the ball bounces as a function of the height from which it was dropped.
   b) If it is dropped from a height of 3.0 m, how high will it bounce?
   c) If it bounces 80 cm, from what height was it dropped?
   d) Sketch a graph of the function.

Solution.   a) Let *b* metres represent the height the ball bounces from a height of *d* metres. Since *b* varies directly as *d*:
   b = *kd*, where *k* is the constant of proportionality.
   Substitute 2.4 for *d* and 1.6 for *b*.

$$b = kd$$
$$1.6 = k(2.4)$$
$$k = \frac{1.6}{2.4}$$
$$= \frac{2}{3}$$

The equation relating *b* and *d* is $b = \frac{2}{3}d$.

b) Substitute 3.0 for d.

$$b = \frac{2}{3}(3.0)$$
$$= 2.0$$

From a height of 3.0 m, the ball will bounce 2.0 m.

c) Substitute 0.8 for b.

$$0.8 = \frac{2}{3}d$$
$$2d = 2.4$$
$$d = 1.2$$

For an 80 cm bounce, the ball was dropped from 120 cm.

d) The graph is a straight line with slope $\frac{2}{3}$ through $(0, 0)$.

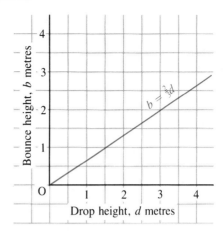

In *Example 2*, the equation relating the bounce height b metres with the height from which the ball was dropped d metres is $b = \frac{2}{3}d$. It is sometimes convenient to write such an equation using function notation. Since b is a function of d, we write $b(d) = \frac{2}{3}d$.

EXERCISES 5-4

(A)

1. In each table, y varies directly as x.
   a) State the missing numbers.   b) Express y as a function of x.

i)
x	y
0	■
1	■
2	■
3	21
4	■

ii)
x	y
1	■
2	−6
3	■
4	■
5	■

iii)
x	y
4	■
8	■
12	■
16	■
20	5

iv)
x	y
3	■
6	■
9	6
12	■
15	■

2. If y varies directly as x, what happens to y if:
   a) x is doubled   b) x is halved?

(B)

3. y varies directly as x and when $x = 12$, $y = 8$.
   a) Write y as a function of x.   b) Find y when $x = 21$.
   c) Find x when $y = 15$.

4. $f(x)$ varies directly as x. Find the missing numbers.

a)

x	■	3	5	7	13
$f(x)$	-4	■	-10	■	■

b)

x	2	■	15	45	■
$f(x)$	■	8	■	18	22

5. It is estimated that the volume of blood in the human body varies directly as the body mass. An 80 kg person has a blood volume of about 6 L.
   a) Express the blood volume as a function of the body mass.
   b) Find the blood volume of a 60 kg person.
   c) Sketch a graph of the function.
   d) Write the equation of the function using function notation.

6. A supertanker travelling at 25 km/h needs 5 km to come to a complete stop.
   a) If stopping distance varies directly as speed, express the stopping distance as a function of the speed.
   b) What distance will the supertanker need to stop from a speed of 15 km/h?
   c) Sketch a graph of the function.
   d) Write the equation of the function using function notation.

Ⓒ

7. In chemistry, Charles' Law states that if the pressure is kept constant, the volume of a gas varies directly as the absolute temperature in degrees Kelvin (°K). The relation between k degrees Kelvin and c degrees Celsius is $k = c + 273°$. A balloon contains 2 L of helium at 10°C.
   a) What is its volume when the temperature is: i) 30°C   ii) 0°C?
   b) What is its temperature if its volume is: i) 4 L   ii) 1 L?

8. If the pressure of a gas is kept constant, what happens to its volume if the absolute temperature is:
   a) doubled   b) tripled   c) divided by 2?

9. For any planet, its year is the time that it takes to circle the sun once. Kepler's Third Law in astronomy states that, for any planet, the square of the number of earth-days in its year varies directly as the cube of its mean distance from the sun. Find the number of earth-days in the year for each planet.

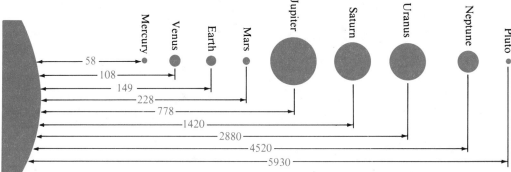

Distance in millions of kilometres

5-5 LINEAR FUNCTIONS

Sales personnel at a computer store are paid a monthly salary of $300
plus a 4% commission on monthly sales. The table and the graph show
the income for monthly sales up to $30 000.

Monthly sales, s dollars	Monthly income, I dollars
0	300
10 000	700
20 000	1100
30 000	1500

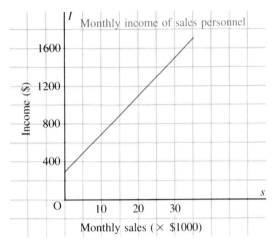

Although the graph is a straight line, it does not represent direct
variation. If the sales are doubled, the monthly income is *not* doubled.
However, from the given information we can express I as a function
of s. It is a linear function because its graph is a straight line.

$$I = 300 + 0.04s$$

Base salary   Commission, 4¢ on every dollar of sales

We say that I *varies partially as* s.

Partial Variation
If y varies partially as x, then y can be
expressed as a function of x.
- The graph of the function is a straight
  line that does not pass through $(0, 0)$.
- The equation of the function has the form
  $$y = mx + b,$$
  where m and b are constants.

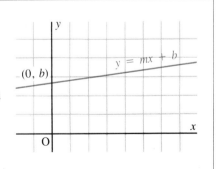

Example 1. A graduation dance costs $5000 plus $20 for each person attending.
    a) Write an equation expressing the cost as a function of the number of
       people attending.
    b) Find the cost for 400 people.
    c) Graph the function.

Solution.   a) Let C dollars represent the total cost for n people attending. Since
there is a fixed cost of $5000, and a variable cost of $20 per person,
the equation relating C and n is $C = 20n + 5000$.

b) Substitute 400 for n in the equation.

$$C = 20n + 5000$$
$$= 20(400) + 5000$$
$$= 13\ 000$$

The cost for 400 people is $13 000.

c) The cost for 0 people is
$5000; this is represented
by the point (0, 5000)
on the graph. Similarly, the
cost for 400 people is
$13 000, which is repre-
sented by (400, 13 000).
The graph of the function is
the straight line through
these two points.

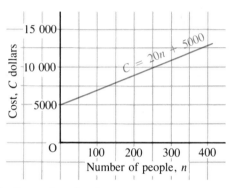

The function in *Example 1* is an example of a linear function because
its graph is a straight line. Its equation has the same form as the equation
of a line with slope m and y-intercept b. When x and y are not used,
the y-intercept is called the *vertical intercept*.

Compare $y = mx + b$
   with $C = 20n + 5000$

The slope represents   The vertical intercept
the cost per person.   represents the fixed cost.

A *linear function* has a defining equation which can be written in
the form:
$y = mx + b$ or $f(x) = mx + b$, where m and b are constants.
The graph of a linear function is a straight line with slope m and
vertical intercept b.

We will use both forms, $y = mx + b$ and $f(x) = mx + b$, in
subsequent work. The equation form is familiar from your work in
analytic geometry. The function notation, of course, denotes a function.

These are linear functions because they can be expressed in either
of the above forms.

$y = 6x$; $f(x) = 4 - 3x$; $2x - 3y + 6 = 0$

These are not linear functions because they cannot be expressed in
the above forms.

$$f(x) = \frac{1}{x + 3}; \quad f(x) = x^2 + 1; \quad y = 2^x$$

Example 2. Graph $f(x) = -\frac{1}{2}x + 3$.

Solution. The graph is the line $y = -\frac{1}{2}x + 3$ which

has slope $-\frac{1}{2}$ and y-intercept 3.

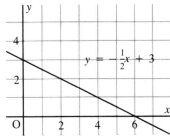

Frequently, the defining equation of a linear function can only be approximated from a graph.

Example 3. The boiling point of water is a function of altitude. The table shows the boiling points at various altitudes.

Location	Altitude, h metres	Boiling point of water, $t°C$
Halifax, N.S.	0	100
Banff, Alberta	1383	95
Quito, Ecuador	2850	90
Mount Logan	5951	80

a) Graph the relation between the altitude and the boiling point.
b) Use the graph to estimate the boiling point of water at:
  i) Lhasa, Tibet, altitude 3680 m
  ii) the summit of the Earth's highest mountain, Mount Everest 8848 m.
c) Find an equation which expresses the boiling point as a function of the altitude, and use it to check your answers in part b).
d) What are the domain and range of the function?

Solution. a) Plot the points and draw the best straight line through them.
b) i) From the graph, we see that $t = 87$ when $h = 3680$. Hence, the boiling point at Lhasa is approximately 87°C.
  ii) Similarly, $t = 70$ when $h = 8848$
    Hence, the boiling point at Mount Everest is approximately 70°C.
c) The vertical intercept is 100. Choose any two points on the line (they need not be the plotted points), say (5951, 80) and (0, 100). The slope of the line through these points is $\dfrac{100 - 80}{0 - 5951}$, or about -0.0034.

Hence, the equation of the line is $t = -0.0034h + 100$.

Check the answers in part a).
Substitute 3680 for h.
$t = -0.0034(3680) + 100$
$\doteq 87$
Substitute 8848 for h.
$t = -0.0034(8848) + 100$
$\doteq 70$
The estimates in part b) were
reasonable.

d) The domain is the set of all
possible altitudes h. Since
Mount Everest is the highest
point on the Earth, it is
reasonable to assume that
$0 \leqslant h \leqslant 8848$.
The range is the set of all
possible boiling points t.
It is reasonable to assume
that $70 \leqslant t \leqslant 100$.

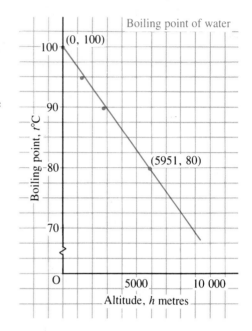

In *Example 3*, when we estimated the boiling point at Lhasa, we
were estimating the value of a variable *between* values that are known.
This is called *interpolating*. Also, when we estimated the boiling point
at Mount Everest, we were estimating the value of a variable *beyond*
values that are known. This is called *extrapolating*. We can use either
the graph or the equation to interpolate and extrapolate.

EXERCISES 5-5

1. State which functions are linear.
   a) $f(x) = 4x$ b) $f(x) = 2 - x$ c) $y = x^2$
   d) $f(x) = \dfrac{2x + 5}{10}$ e) $y = \dfrac{1}{x}$ f) $f(x) = (x - 2)(x + 1)$

2. Graph each function.
   a) $f(x) = \dfrac{3}{4}x + 2$ b) $g(x) = 2x + 3$ c) $f(x) = 4 - x$ d) $g(x) = -\dfrac{3}{2}x$

3. An airplane at an altitude of 10 000 m begins to descend at 300 m/min.
   a) Draw a graph showing the altitude of the airplane as a function of time for the
      first 10 min of descent.
   b) Find the equation giving the altitude h metres as a function of time t minutes.

4. The temperature of the Earth's crust T degrees Celsius is a function of the depth d kilometres below the surface, where $T = 10d + 20$.
   a) Graph the function for values of d up to 5 km.
   b) The deepest mine is in South Africa, and reaches 3.8 km below the surface. Use the equation or the graph to find the approximate temperature at the bottom.

5. Sales personnel are offered three choices of salary payment.
   Plan A: $1000 per month $+$ 5% of sales
   Plan B: $1000 per month $+$ 10% of sales over $20 000
   Plan C: 30% of all sales over $20 000
   Which graph represents which plan?

   a)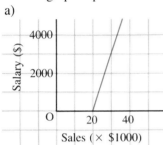

   b)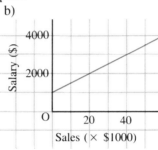

   c)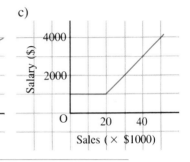

(B)

6. The approximate temperature of the Earth's atmosphere at different altitudes up to 10 km is given in the table.
   a) Draw a graph showing temperature as a function of altitude.
   b) Find the equation relating temperature and altitude.
   c) Determine approximately:
      i) the temperature at an altitude of 7 km
      ii) the altitude at which the temperature is 0°C.
   d) Above 11 km, the temperature remains fairly constant at -56°C. Show this on the graph for part a).

Altitude (km)	Temperature (°C)
0	15
2	2
4	-11
6	-24
8	-37
10	-50

7. A projector throws an image on a screen. To determine how the width of the image is related to the distance of the screen from the projector, the following measurements were made.

Distance from screen to projector, x metres	1.4	2.7	3.9	5.0
Width of image, y metres	0.9	1.8	2.6	3.4

   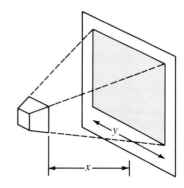

a) Graph the data and find the equation relating x and y.
b) Find the width of the image when the projector is 3.0 m from the screen.
c) Find the distance from the projector to the screen when the image is 3.0 m wide.
d) What is the domain of the relation?

8. A rectangle has a perimeter of 24 cm.
   a) Express its length as a function of its width.
   b) What is the domain of the function in part a)?

9. Express y as a function of x, and state the domain of each function
   a)   b)   c)

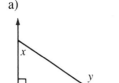
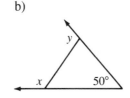

10. Michael works as a lifeguard and earns \$4.50/h for a 32 h week. He is paid time-and-a-half for any additional hours. Draw a graph showing Michael's weekly earnings for up to 50 h work.

11. Using the rates given in the table, draw a graph showing the cost of water for consumptions up to 300 kL.

Municipal Water Rates	
First 100 kL	\$0.55/kL
Next 100 kL	\$0.35/kL
Additional	\$0.15/kL

12. The graph shows how the volume of fuel in a car's fuel tank varies with time during a trip. The graph consists of six line segments.
   a) Describe what each line segment tells about the trip.
   b) Is the relation between the amount of fuel in the tank and the elapsed time a function? Explain.
   c) If the car was driven at an average speed of 100 km/h, find its rate of fuel consumption in litres per 100 km.

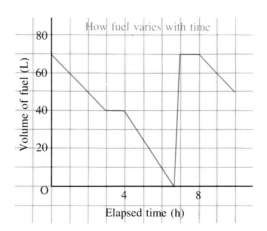

13. If $f(x) = mx + b$, find m and b if the graph of the function:

    a) has slope $\frac{2}{5}$ and y-intercept 7

    b) has slope $-\frac{4}{3}$ and $f(6) = 2$

    c) has y-intercept 4 and passes through $(-3, 10)$

    d) passes through $(5, 9)$ and $(0, -6)$

    e) has $f(-2) = 8$ and $f(3) = -12$

    f) has $f(4) = 3$ and $f(-3) = 7$.

Ⓒ

14. Archaeologists can estimate a person's height from the skeletal remains. One method uses the fact that height is a linear function of the length of the humerus, the bone of the upper arm. It is known that the humerus of a 160 cm adult is about 30 cm long, while that of a 190 cm adult is about 40 cm long.

    a) Express the height h as a function of the humerus length l.

    b) What is the approximate height of an adult whose humerus measures 38.2 cm?

15. An arena manager asks for 25% of the gate receipts for a boxing match. The match promoter wants him to accept \$10 000 plus 50% of the gate receipts over \$150 000.

    a) Draw graphs to show how the arena manager's income depends on the gate receipts for each plan.

    b) For what gate receipts does the arena manager's plan provide the greater income?

16. ABCD is a trapezoid with AB = 10 cm and DC = 6 cm. P is a point on AB such that AP = x centimetres, and Q is a point on DC such that DQ = y centimetres.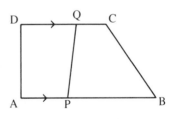

    a) If trapezoids APQD and PBCQ have equal areas, find the relation between x and y.

    b) For what positions of P on AB is it possible to find a point Q on DC such that the trapezoids APQD and PBCQ have equal areas?

17. If all the circles have a radius R, express the perimeter of each figure as a function of R.

    a)

    b)

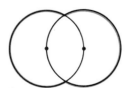

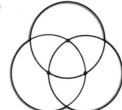

MATHEMATICS AROUND US

The Line of Best Fit

In *Example 3* and *Exercises 6* and *7* of the preceding section we graphed linear functions from given data. In those examples, the plotted points appeared to lie on a straight line. One reason for this is the fact that in each case there is an underlying physical law relating the variables.

We often encounter situations in which the plotted points only approximate a straight line. In these cases there may not be a physical law relating the variables, but nevertheless a noticeable trend may still be evident.

The Mile Record

Although the mile is not a metric distance the one-mile race has always been an important track event. The four-minute mile, once considered impossible to achieve, was accomplished in 1954 by two runners in the same race. Since then, the record for the mile has dropped steadily.

The Mile Record

Record holder	Year	Record time minutes:seconds	Record time seconds
Jules Ladoumègue	1931	4:09.2	249.2
Glenn Cunningham	1934	4:06.8	246.8
Gunder Hagg	1945	4:01.3	241.3
Roger Bannister	1954	3:59.4	239.4
John Landy	1954	3:57.9	237.9
Jim Ryun	1967	3:51.1	231.1
Sebastian Coe	1981	3:47.3	227.3
Steve Cram	1985	3:46.3	226.3

To graph the data, we converted the times to seconds by multiplying the number of minutes by 60 and adding the number of seconds.

The graph shows that the record has fallen at a fairly constant rate. An approximate relationship, between the time t seconds and y the number of years since 1930, can be found by drawing a *line of best fit* which passes near the plotted points. We can then interpolate or extrapolate using this line.

Note that extrapolation must be done with caution. For example, we might attempt to predict the mile record for some year in the distant future by extending the line far to the right. But we cannot be certain that the trend will continue indefinitely. It has been suggested that, for physiological reasons, the record may never become much lower than 3:30.

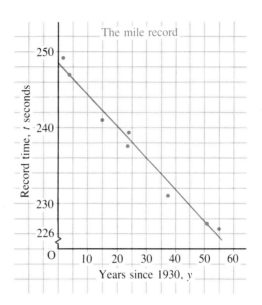

QUESTIONS

1. a) Plot the points from the table, and draw the line of best fit.
   b) Use your line of best fit to estimate what the record might be in the year 2000.
   c) Estimate when the record might be as low as 3:30.

2. Use the vertical intercept and one other point on the line to obtain an approximate equation of the line of best fit. Then use the equation to check your predictions in *Question 1*.

3. Your calculator may have the capability of determining the slope and the vertical intercept of the line of best fit when you enter the known data. For the above data, such a calculator gives the slope as -0.4397 and the vertical intercept as 248.8. Hence, the equation of the line of best fit is $t = -0.4397y + 248.8$.
   a) Use this equation to check the predictions in *Question 1*.
   b) If your calculator has this capability, use it to determine the slope and the vertical intercept for the data. Consult your manual.

The Irish Elk

A magnificent animal known as the Irish elk was once the world's largest deer. It inhabited the open tundra in northern Europe. But during the last Ice Age, about 12 000 years ago, it became extinct.

The Irish elk was noted for its extremely large antlers, which seemed out of proportion with the size of the animal. Skeletal remains show that its antlers spread as wide as 4 m. Stephen Gould, of Harvard University, wondered if the antlers grew at the same rate as the rest of the animal. He compared measures of antler size and skull length of dozens of specimens. Some results are shown in the table.

From data like this, Stephen Gould concluded that the animal's antlers grew about 2.5 times as fast as the rest of its body. Investigations of other species of deer, including those living today, have yielded similar results.

The Irish Elk					
Skull length (cm)	46.0	47.1	48.1	49.0	50.1
Antler size (cm)	31.5	34.1	36.2	39.1	41.4

QUESTIONS

1. Graph the data, and then determine the equation of the line of best fit.

2. Use the equation to find:
   a) the approximate antler size for a skull length of 47.5 cm
   b) the skull length for an antler size of 40 cm.

3. How did Stephen Gould reach his conclusion about the comparative rates of growth of the antlers and the rest of the animal from the equation of the line of best fit?

4. Suggest why the Irish elk may have become extinct.

Continental Drift

Geographers have studied sediments found near islands in the Atlantic Ocean and related the age of the sediment to the distance from the Mid-Atlantic Ridge. The table shows the results for a few islands.

Islands	Age of sediment (millions of years)	Distance to Mid-Atlantic Ridge (km)
Azores	25	350
Bahamas	135	2800
Bermuda	95	1900
Faroes	20	250
St. Helena	35	700

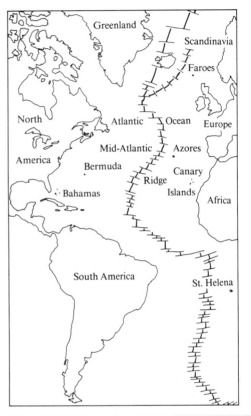

In 1961, a Canadian, J. Tuzo Wilson, theorized that this data provides evidence for the *continental drift*. He reasoned that volcanic activity at the Mid-Atlantic Ridge forms new parts of the Earth's crust. These tend to push aside the older crust. Over millions of years, this spreading of the sea floor has caused the continents to move to their present positions.

QUESTIONS

1. Find the equation of the line of best fit. What does the slope represent?

2. Use the equation of the line of best fit:
   a) to predict the age of sediment near the Canary Islands, which are about 1500 km from the Mid-Atlantic Ridge
   b) to find the approximate yearly increase in distance between Europe and North America.

5-6 INVERSE VARIATION

Police often identify speeders on a highway by measuring, from the air, the time it takes a car to cover a marked portion of the road. The table shows how the speed of a car is related to the time it takes to travel 0.5 km.

Time t (s)	Speed v (km/h)
20	90
40	45
60	30
80	22.5
100	18

The table shows that when t is doubled, v is divided by 2; when t is tripled, v is divided by 3, and so on. That is, the product of v and t is constant. We say that v *varies inversely* as t, and write $vt = k$, or $v = \dfrac{k}{t}$, where k is a constant. From the table, we can verify that $vt = 1800$ for all values of v and t.

If we plot the data, the resulting curve is part of a *rectangular hyperbola*. The equation of this hyperbola is $vt = 1800$.

The graph shows only one branch of the hyperbola. Another branch, corresponding to negative values of v and t, could be plotted in the third quadrant, but this would not be appropriate for distances and speeds, which are positive.

We can use the equation or the graph to find the speeds of the car for times other than those given in the table. For example, if the time is measured as 23 s, then the speed of the car is found by substituting 23 for v in $vt = 1800$. Solving for v, we find $v \doteq 78$. Hence, a car which takes 23 s to complete the marked portion of the road is travelling at about 78 km/h.

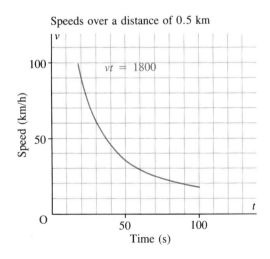

Speeds over a distance of 0.5 km

Inverse Variation

If y varies inversely as x, then y can be expressed as a function of x.

● The equation of the function has the form

$$y = \frac{k}{x},$$

where k is a constant.

● The graph of the function is a rectangular hyperbola.

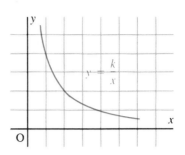

Example 1. y varies inversely as x and when $x = 3$, $y = 8$.

    a) Write y as a function of x.

    b) Find y when $x = 12$.

    c) Find x when $y = 4$.

Solution.   a) Since y varies inversely as x, $y = \frac{k}{x}$, where k is a constant. Substitute 3 for x and 8 for y in the equation.

$$y = \frac{k}{x}$$

$$8 = \frac{k}{3}$$

$$k = 24$$

Hence, the equation expressing y as a function of x is $y = \frac{24}{x}$.

    b) When $x = 12$: $y = \frac{24}{12}$, or 2

    c) When $y = 4$: $4 = \frac{24}{x}$

$$x = 6$$

Example 2. After the first year, the value of a car varies inversely as its age. After 2 years its value is $8000.

    a) Express the value of the car as a function of its age.

    b) What is its value after 5 years?

    c) Sketch a graph of the function relating value and age.

Solution.   a) Let v dollars represent the value of the car after y years. Since v varies inversely as y:

$$v = \frac{k}{y}, \text{ where } k \text{ is a constant.}$$

Substitute 2 for y and 8000 for v. $v = \dfrac{k}{y}$

$$8000 = \dfrac{k}{2}$$

$$k = 16\ 000$$

The equation relating v and y is $v = \dfrac{16\ 000}{y}$.

b) Substitute 5 for y. $v = \dfrac{16\ 000}{5}$

$$= 3200$$

At the end of 5 years, the car is worth $3200.

c) We use a table of values to draw the graph.

y	v
2	8000
3	5333
4	4000
5	3200
6	2667
7	2286

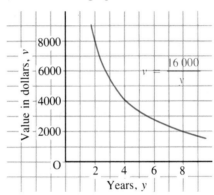

EXERCISES 5-6

(A)

1. In each table, y varies inversely as x.
   a) State the missing numbers.   b) Express y as a function of x.

i)

x	y
0	■
1	■
2	■
3	20
4	■

ii)

x	y
1	■
2	−6
3	■
4	■
5	■

iii)

x	y
4	■
8	■
12	■
16	■
20	4

iv)

x	y
3	■
6	■
9	5
12	■
15	■

2. If y varies inversely as x, what happens to y if
   a) x is doubled   b) x is halved?

(B)

3. y varies inversely as x, and when $x = 8$, $y = 5$.
   a) Write y as a function of x.   b) Find y when $x = 4$.
   c) Find x when $y = 20$.

4. y varies inversely as x, and when $x = 10$, $y = 6$.
   a) Write y as a function of x.   b) Find y when $x = 30$.
   c) Find x when $y = 12$.

5. y varies inversely as x. Find the missing numbers.

   a)

x	2	■	6	12	15
y	■	20	■	5	■

   b)

x	-3	■	2	4	■
y	■	24	-6	■	-60

6. The time it takes to complete a bike-a-thon course varies inversely as the cyclist's average speed. At an average speed of 15 km/h, it takes 3.2 h to complete the course.
   a) Express the time to complete the course as a function of the average speed.
   b) How long does it take to complete the course at: i) 12 km/h   ii) 20 km/h?
   c) If the course is completed in 2 h, what is the average speed?
   d) Graph the relation between the time to complete the course and the average speed.

7. The rotational speed of a gear varies inversely as the number of teeth on the gear. A gear with 24 teeth rotates at 40 r/min (revolutions per minute).
   a) What is the rotational speed of a gear with: i) 32 teeth   ii) 40 teeth?
   b) If a gear rotates at 60 r/min, how many teeth does it have?
   c) Graph the relation between rotational speed and number of teeth.

8. In a system of two pulleys turned by a single belt, the number of revolutions per minute of each pulley varies inversely as its radius. If one pulley has a radius of 50 cm, and rotates at 120 r/min, what is the rotational speed of the other pulley if its radius is 80 cm?

9. The time required to fly from Quebec City to Vancouver varies inversely as the average speed. When the average speed is 700 km/h, the flying time is 5.5 h.
   a) How long would the trip take at an average speed of 550 km/h?
   b) What is the average speed if the time taken is 4.25 h?

10. Boyle's Law states that if the temperature is kept constant, the volume of a gas varies inversely as the pressure. A tank contains 10 L of hydrogen at a pressure of 550 kPa. If the hydrogen is released into the atmosphere where the pressure is 100 kPa, what volume would it occupy?

11. If the temperature of a gas is kept constant, what happens to the volume when the pressure is: a) doubled   b) tripled   c) divided by 2?

Ⓒ

12. Each rectangle in a set of rectangles has an area of 360 cm².
    a) Graph the relation between the length and the width of the rectangles.
    b) Graph the relation between the length and the perimeter.
    c) Does the length vary inversely as: i) the width   ii) the perimeter?

13. If y varies inversely as x, how is y affected if:
    a) x is increased by 25%   b) x is decreased by 20%?

 PROBLEM SOLVING

Write an Expression in Two Different Ways

"Mathematics is the queen of sciences and number theory the queen of mathematics."

Carl Friedrich Gauss

What is the sum of the natural numbers from 1 to 20?

Understand the problem
- We could merely add the numbers, but that would be of little use for related problems involving, say, the sum of the natural numbers from 1 to 1000.
- Hence, the problem is really asking for a method of adding the natural numbers from 1 to n.

Think of a strategy
- Let S represent the required sum. Then:
$$S = 1 + 2 + 3 + \ldots + 18 + 19 + 20 \ldots \textcircled{1}$$
and also, $\quad S = 20 + 19 + 18 + \ldots + 3 + 2 + 1 \ldots \textcircled{2}$

Carry out the strategy
- Notice that the sums of the numbers occurring above each other on the right sides are all the same.
- Hence, we might try adding both sides of equations $\textcircled{1}$ and $\textcircled{2}$.
- What is the sum of the expressions on the left side?
- When you add the pairs of numbers on the right side, the sum is always 21. How many 21s are there in all?
- What is the sum of all the numbers on the right side in both $\textcircled{1}$ and $\textcircled{2}$?
- What does S equal?

Look back
- The strategy of writing two expressions for S led to a simpler problem of adding $21 + 21 + 21 + \ldots + 21 + 21 + 21$. Since there were 20 terms, the sum could be found.
- Use the same method to find the sum of the first 50 natural numbers.
- Generalize to prove this formula for the sum of the first n natural numbers.

$$1 + 2 + 3 + \ldots + n = \frac{n(n + 1)}{2}$$

PROBLEMS

Ⓑ

1. A right triangle has sides 3 cm, 4 cm, and 5 cm. Determine the length of the altitude to the hypotenuse.

2. Three cylindrical logs with radius 10 cm are strapped together at each end. Determine the length of strapping required if 5 cm is needed for overlapping.

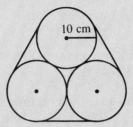

10 cm

3. The numbers 23 and 5678 are two examples of numbers with consecutive digits. How many numbers are there in all with consecutive digits?

4. Carry out calculations to determine the length of time it takes the sun to drop out of sight once it reaches the horizon during a sunset. The diameter of the sun is 1.38×10^6 km and its distance from the Earth 1.49×10^8 km. List some of the assumptions you are making.

Ⓒ

5. An isosceles triangle has sides of length 6 cm, 6 cm, and 4 cm. Determine the lengths of the three altitudes.

6. Write the numbers from 1 to 64 on an 8 by 8 grid. Then circle eight numbers as follows:
   - Select any number and draw a circle around it.
   - Strike out the row and column containing the number.
   - Repeat until 8 numbers have been circled.

   Find the sum of the 8 circled numbers.

1	2	3	4	5	6	7	8
9	10	11	12	13	14	15	16
17	18	19	20	21	22	23	24
25	26	27	28	29	30	31	32
33	34	35	36	37	38	39	40
41	42	43	44	45	46	47	48
49	50	51	52	53	54	55	56
57	58	59	60	61	62	63	64

7. The natural numbers are written in a triangle as shown. Show that the sum of the numbers in the nth row is
$$\frac{n(n^2 + 1)}{2}.$$

```
            1
          2   3
        4   5   6
      7   8   9   10
   11  12  13  14   15
```

Ⓓ

8. Solve the inequality $\left(\dfrac{x}{1 - \sqrt{x + 1}} \right)^2 > x + 5$.

5-7 EXTENDING DIRECT AND INVERSE VARIATION

In the preceding sections we studied direct, inverse, and partial variation.
In each case, the equation relating the variables had a characteristic form.

Direct Variation	*Inverse Variation*	*Partial Variation*
$y = mx$	$y = \dfrac{k}{x}$	$y = mx + b$

In this section we will study other kinds of variation problems.

Variation involving powers or roots of the variables

Variation problems can involve powers or roots of the variables.

Example 1.   In a drag race, cars accelerate from a standing start towards a finish line a fixed distance away. The elapsed time and the final speed are recorded. Shirley Muldowney once dragged a record 411.2 km/h in 5.56 s.
   a) The speed at any moment varies directly as the square of the elapsed time. Express the speed as a function of time.
   b) Calculate the speed after 4.00 s.
   c) Calculate the elapsed time when the car reaches a speed of 100 km/h.
   d) Graph the function.

Solution.   a) Let v kilometres per hour represent the speed, and t seconds the elapsed time.
Since v varies directly as t^2,
$$v = kt^2$$
where k is the constant of proportionality.
Substitute 411.2 for v and 5.56 for t.
$$v = kt^2$$
$$411.2 = k(5.56)^2$$
$$k = \frac{411.2}{5.56^2}$$
$$\doteq 13.30$$
The equation relating v and t is $v \doteq 13.30t^2$.

b) Substitute 4.00 for t.
$$v \doteq 13.30(4.00)^2$$
$$= 212.8$$
The speed after 4.00 s is about 212.8 km/h.

c) Substitute 100 for v.
$$100 \doteq 13.3t^2$$
$$t^2 \doteq \frac{100}{13.3}$$
$$\doteq 7.52$$
$$t \doteq \sqrt{7.52}$$
$$\doteq 2.74$$
The speed is 100 km/h after approximately 2.74 s.

d) Since t is squared in the equation $v = 13.30t^2$, the function is not linear. Hence, to graph the function a table of values is required.

Time t s	Speed v km/h
0	0
1	13.3
2	53.2
3	119.7
4	212.8
5	332.5

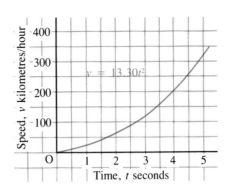

Variation involving more than two variables

When one variable varies as two or more other variables, the variation
is called *joint variation*.

Example 2. The stopping distance of a vehicle on an icy road varies as its speed and
the square of its mass. A 2 t car travelling at 50 km/h stops in a distance
of 150 m. What is the stopping distance of a 3 t truck travelling at 60 km/h?

Solution. Let d metres be the stopping distance for a vehicle of mass m tonnes
travelling at a speed of s kilometres per hour. Since d varies jointly with
s and m^2, $d = ksm^2$, where k is the constant of proportionality.
Substitute 2 for m, 50 for s, and 150 for d.

$$d = ksm^2$$
$$150 = k(50)(2)^2$$
$$k = \frac{3}{4}$$

The equation relating d, s, and m is $d = \frac{3}{4}sm^2$.

Substitute 60 for s and 3 for m.

$$d = \frac{3}{4}(60)(3)^2$$
$$= 405$$

A 3 t truck travelling at 60 km/h needs 405 m to stop.

Joint variation may involve both direct and inverse variation.

Example 3. The pressure exerted on the floor by the heel of a shoe varies directly as
the wearer's mass and inversely as the square of the width of the heel.
A 75 kg man wearing shoes with heels 6 cm wide exerts a pressure of
200 kPa. Find the pressure exerted by a 50 kg woman wearing shoes
with heels 2 cm wide.

Solution.   Let the pressure be p kilopascals for a person of mass m kilograms wearing shoes with heels w centimetres wide. Since p varies directly as m and inversely as w^2, the equation has the form $p = \dfrac{km}{w^2}$, where k is a constant.

Substitute 200 for p, 75 for m, and 6 for w.

$$200 = \frac{75k}{6^2}$$

$$k = \frac{(200)(36)}{75}$$

$$= 96$$

The equation relating p, m, and w is $p = \dfrac{96m}{w^2}$.

Substitute 50 for m and 2 for w.

$$p = \frac{(96)(50)}{4}$$

$$= 1200$$

A 50 kg woman wearing shoes with heels 2 cm wide exerts a pressure of 1200 kPa.

In *Examples 2* and *3* the corresponding functions are examples of functions of two variables.

Stopping distance is a function of the speed and the mass of the vehicle.

$$d(s, m) = \frac{3}{4}sm^2$$

Heel pressure is a function of the wearer's mass and the width of the heel.

$$P(m, w) = \frac{96m}{w^2}$$

These functions are sets of ordered triples; their graphs are surfaces in three dimensions. Functions of two or more variables are studied in higher mathematics.

EXERCISES 5-7

1. Write an equation for s if s varies:
   a) directly as the square of m
   b) inversely as the square root of m
   c) directly as m and n
   d) directly as m^2 and inversely as n.

2. Describe each variation.

   a) $A = \frac{1}{2}bh$
   b) $A = \pi r^2$
   c) $I = prt$

   d) $v = \frac{1}{3}\pi r^2 h$
   e) $d = \dfrac{m}{v}$
   f) $F = \dfrac{mn}{d^2}$

B

3. y varies directly as x^2 and when $x = 3$, $y = 45$.
   a) Write y as a function of x.
   b) Find y when $x = 6$.
   c) Find x when $y = 80$.

4. y varies inversely as x^2 and when $x = 4$, $y = 0.15$.
   a) Write y as a function of x.   b) Find y when $x = 5$.
   c) Find x when $y = 0.6$.

5. The mass of a diamond varies directly as the cube of its diameter. A diamond with a mass of 1 carat has a diameter of 5 mm.
   a) Express the mass of a diamond as a function of its diameter.
   b) What is the mass of a diamond with a diameter of 10 mm?
   c) What is the diameter of a 2-carat diamond?
   d) Graph the function.

6. The surface area of a sphere varies directly as the square of its diameter. A baseball with a diameter of 7.4 cm has a surface area of 172 cm^2.
   a) Express the surface area as a function of the diameter.
   b) Find the surface area of a soccer ball, which has a diameter of 22.2 cm.

7. The volume of a sphere varies directly as the cube of its diameter. A tennis ball with a diameter of 6.6 cm has a volume of 150 cm^3.
   a) Express the volume as a function of the diameter.
   b) Find the volume of a basketball, which has a diameter of 24.4 cm.

8. The number of trees that can be planted at a Christmas-tree farm varies inversely as the square of the average distance between the trees. When this distance is 3 m, about 1000 trees can be planted. How many trees can be planted if the average distance between the trees is 2.5 m?

9. The intensity of illumination of a screen varies inversely as the square of its distance from a projector. When the distance is 80 m, the intensity is 9 units.
   a) Find the intensity when the distance is: i) 60 m   ii) 100 m.
   b) What distance results in an intensity of: i) 12 units   ii) 36 units?

10. At a constant oven temperature, the time to cook a turkey varies directly as the square root of its mass. If it takes 4.25 h to cook a 5 kg turkey, how long would it take to cook one with a mass of 8 kg?

11. On level ground, the distance to the horizon varies directly as the square root of the observer's height above the ground. The distance to the horizon from a height of 100 m is 36 km.
    a) How far can you see from the observation deck of the Calgary Tower, 158 m?
    b) From what height would the distance to the horizon be 400 km?

12. If g varies directly as v^2, what happens to g if:
    a) v is doubled   b) v is halved?

13. If p varies directly as $\sqrt{x}$, what happens to p if:
    a) x is doubled   b) x is halved?

14. *w* varies jointly as *s* and *t*; when *s* = 4 and *t* = 5, *w* = 150.
    a) Find an equation relating *w*, *s*, and *t*.   b) Find *w* when *s* = 3 and *t* = 8.
    c) Find *s* when *w* = 60 and *t* = 4.   d) Find *t* when *w* = 15 and *s* = 3.

15. *r* varies directly as p^2 and inversely as *t*; when *p* = 5 and *t* = 6, *r* = 2.5.
    a) Find an equation relating *r*, *p*, and *t*.   b) Find *r* when *p* = 8 and *t* = 12.
    c) Find *p* when *r* = 4 and *t* = 3.   d) Find *t* when *r* = 1.5 and *p* = 5.

16. The mass of a cylindrical rod varies jointly as its length, the square of its radius, and the density of the material. A 3.00-m cylindrical rod with radius 2.00 cm and density 7.90 g/cm³ has a mass of 29.8 kg.
    a) Find the mass of a 4.50-m rod with radius 3.25 cm and density:
       i) 7.93 g/cm³   ii) 2.71 g/cm³.
    b) Find the density of the material of a 4.00-m rod with radius 3.10 cm and mass 9.64 kg.

17. If *h* varies directly as *s* and inversely as t^2, what happens to *h* if:
    a) *s* is doubled and *t* is halved   b) *s* is halved and *t* is doubled?

18. If *m* varies directly as $\sqrt{c}$ and inversely as *d*, what happens to *m* if:
    a) *c* is doubled and *d* is halved   b) *c* is halved and *d* is doubled?

---

19. The speed of a satellite varies inversely as the square root of its distance from the centre of the Earth. When the space shuttle is in orbit at an altitude of 200 km, its speed is 28 000 km/h. The radius of the Earth is 6370 km.
    a) What is the speed of the shuttle at an altitude of 500 km?
    b) What is the speed of the moon, which is about 385 000 km from the Earth?

20. The volume of a gas varies directly as the absolute temperature and inversely as the pressure. Twenty-five litres of oxygen at 10 000 kPa pressure and 5°C is released into the atmosphere where the pressure and temperature are 100 kPa and 25°C. What volume does it occupy?

21. The front sprockets of a 10-speed bicycle have 39 and 52 teeth. The rear sprockets have 14, 17, 20, 24, and 28 teeth. The speed of the bicycle varies directly as the number of teeth on the front sprocket, inversely as the number of teeth on the rear sprocket, and directly as the rate of pedalling in revolutions per minute (r/min). With the 39-tooth front sprocket engaged with the 20-tooth rear sprocket and a pedalling rate of 45 r/min, the bicycle's speed is about 10 km/h.
    a) At a constant rate of pedalling, what gear selection gives the highest speed? the lowest speed?
    b) If the maximum rate of pedalling is 120 r/min, what is the highest speed?

22. The intensity of illumination of a screen varies inversely as the square of its distance from a projector. When the distance is 4 m, the intensity is 10 units.
    a) Find an equation relating the intensity *I* units to the distance *d* metres.
    b) If a graph of the relation between *I* and *d* were drawn, explain why the curve would not be a rectangular hyperbola.
    c) Explain how a graph of the relation could be drawn such that the curve would be a rectangular hyperbola.

1. State the domain and range of each function.
   a) $y = 3x - 2$ b) $y = \sqrt{2x - 1}$ c) $y = x^2 - 4x + 4$

2. State the domain and range of each relation.
   a) b) c)

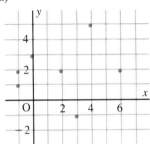
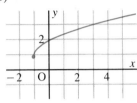
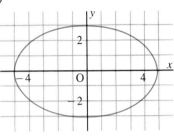

3. The area A of an equilateral triangle of side length d is given by $A \doteq 0.433d^2$.
   a) Graph the relation. Is it a function?
   b) State the domain and range.
   c) If the area is 173.2 cm², what is the side length?

4. State the domain and range of each function.
   a) $y = \sqrt{x + 2}$ b) $y = \dfrac{x}{3}$ c) $x - y = 5$
   d) $y = \dfrac{1}{1 - x}$ e) $y = 1 - x^2$ f) $y = (1.2)^x$

5. If $f(x) = 3x^2 - 4x + 5$, find:
   a) $f(x + 1)$ b) $f(2x - 1)$ c) $f(3x - 1)$.

6. If $f(x) = 2 - 5x$ and $g(x) = 3x - 2$, find a value of x such that:
   a) $f(x) = g(x)$ b) $f(x - 3) = g(x + 7)$
   c) $f(4x + 1) = g(3 - x)$ d) $f(x^2) = g\left(\dfrac{5}{3}x - 2\right)$.

7. If $f(x) = x^2 + 5x - 14$, what values of x make:
   a) $f(x) = 0$ b) $f(x) = -20$ c) $f(x) = 10$?

8. Nancy works as a lifeguard and earns \$6.80/h for a 35 h week. She is paid time-and-a-half for any additional hours. Draw a graph showing Nancy's weekly earnings for up to a 50 h week.

9. If $g(x) = mx + b$, find m and b if the graph of the function:
   a) has slope $\dfrac{3}{5}$ and $g(10) = 17$ b) has y-intercept 3 and passes through $(-4, 7)$
   c) passes through $(-2, 2)$ and $(4, 6)$ d) has $g(2) = -7$ and $g(-1) = 11$.

10. y varies directly as x and when $x = 15$, $y = 24$.
    a) Write y as a function of x. b) Find y when $x = 4$.
    c) Find x when $y = 18$.

11. Graph each function, and state its domain and range.
    a) $f(x) = 3x^2 - 14x - 5$ b) $g(t) = 2 + t - 10t^2$

12. The wavelength, or distance between crests of waves in the ocean varies directly as the height of the waves. For a height of 2.5 m, the wavelength is 17.5 m.
    a) Express the wavelength as a function of the height.
    b) Find the wavelength for waves that are 4 m high.

13. The volume of fuel n litres in a car's fuel tank is given by the formula $n = 72.5 - 0.082d$, where d kilometres is the distance the car has been driven since the tank was filled.
    a) Graph the function for reasonable values of d.
    b) i) About how much fuel would be left after 175 km?
       ii) If 10 L of fuel are left, about how far was the car driven?
    c) i) What is the car's rate of fuel consumption in litres per 100 km?
       ii) How far can the car be driven on one tank of fuel?
    d) What are the domain and range of the function?

14. The number of days required to construct a motion-picture set varies inversely as the number of workers. The set can be constructed in 3 days by 20 workers.
    a) Express the number of days as a function of the number of workers.
    b) How many days would 12 workers require?

15. The number of years required for an investment to double varies inversely as the interest rate. At 8% per annum compound interest, an investment will double in about 9 years. Find an equation expressing the time n years for an investment to double as a function of the interest rate r percent.

16. The time required to empty a tank varies inversely as the rate of pumping. It takes 10 min to empty the tank at a rate of 4 L/min.
    a) Express the time to empty the tank as a function of the rate of pumping.
    b) How long does it take to empty the tank at a rate of 5 L/min?
    c) What is the rate of pumping if the tank is emptied in 2 min?

17. The volume of wood in a tree varies jointly as the product of its height and the square of the average diameter of its trunk. A 15-m tree with an average trunk diameter of 50 cm contains about 3 m³ of wood. How much wood is in a 25-m tree with an average trunk diameter of 75 cm?

18. In house construction, the safe load that can be supported by a horizontal joist varies directly as its thickness, the square of its height, and inversely as its length. The safe load of a 4-m joist 5 cm thick and 20 cm high is 2000 kg. What is the safe load of the joist if it is turned so that it is 20 cm thick and 5 cm high?

19. The electrical resistance of a wire varies directly as its length and inversely as the square of its diameter. If 500 m of 3-mm diameter wire has a resistance of 35 Ω, what is the resistance of 12 km of 5-mm wire of the same material?

6 Quadratic Functions

Supermarket cashiers try to memorize current sale prices while they work. If the percent they memorize is a known function of time, what is the greatest percent they can memorize and how long does it take them? (See Section 6-7 *Example 2.*)

6-1 QUADRATIC FUNCTIONS

In case of a forced landing, private and military aircraft often carry a flare pistol which can be used to attract the attention of those looking for them. The height of the flare above the ground is a function of the elapsed time since firing. A typical expression for the height might be $h = -5t^2 + 100t$.

The table of values and the graph show how h depends on t.

Time, t (s)	Height, h (m)
0	0
2	180
5	375
10	500
15	375
18	180
20	0

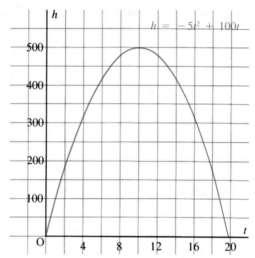

Since there is only one value of h for each value of t, the relation between h and t is a function. It is called a quadratic function because the equation contains a term $-5t^2$ in which the variable is squared.

The graph of every quadratic function is a *parabola*. Parabolic curves arise in many areas of science, and they are used in art and architecture.

> A *quadratic function* has a defining equation which can be written in the form:
> $$y = ax^2 + bx + c \quad \text{or} \quad f(x) = ax^2 + bx + c$$
> where a, b, and c are constants and $a \neq 0$. The graph of a quadratic function is a parabola.

These are quadratic functions because they can be expressed in the form $f(x) = ax^2 + bx + c$.

$$f(x) = x^2 - 6$$
$$f(x) = 3x - 0.5x^2$$
$$f(t) = 2(t - 1)^2 + 5$$

These are not quadratic functions because they cannot be expressed in the form $f(x) = ax^2 + bx + c$.

$$f(x) = \frac{1}{x^2 - 4}$$
$$f(z) = \sqrt{z}$$

Example 1. a) Graph the quadratic function $y = 2x^2 - 4x - 11$ for $-3 \leqslant x \leqslant 5$.
  b) What are the domain and range of the function?

Solution. a)

x	y
-3	19
-2	5
-1	-5
0	-11
1	-13
2	-11
3	-5
4	5
5	19

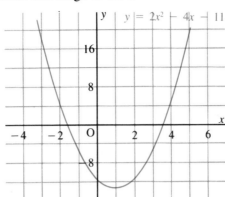

b) The domain of the function, the set of all possible values of x, is the set of all real numbers. The range is the set of all possible values of y. The table and the graph suggest that this is the set of all numbers greater than or equal to -13.

In many applications of quadratic functions, the graph shows only that part of a parabola which is in the first quadrant. This happens when the variables are restricted to positive numbers.

Example 2. In the open sea, the approximate height h metres of the waves is given by the formula $h = 0.008v^2$, where v is the speed of the wind in knots.
  a) Graph h as a function of v for $0 \leqslant v \leqslant 80$.
  b) The highest wave ever measured at sea was 34 m. Use the graph to estimate the wind speed at the time.

Solution. a)

Wind speed, v (knots)	Wave height, h (m)
0	0
20	3.2
40	12.8
60	28.8
80	51.2

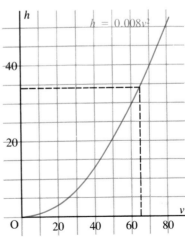

b) From the graph, a wave height of 34 m corresponds to a wind speed of about 65 knots.

EXERCISES 6-1

(A)

1. Is each function a quadratic function?
   a) $y = 3x^2 + 7x - 2$ b) $f(x) = x^2 + \sqrt{x}$ c) $f(x) = 25 - 9x^2$

   d) $y = 7 - 5x^2$ e) $y = 2x^2 + 11 - 4x$ f) $f(x) = \dfrac{1}{4x^2 - 9x + 12}$

(B)

2. a) Graph the function $y = 2x^2 + 5$.
   b) What are the domain and range of the function?

3. a) Graph the function $y = x^2 - 6x + 2$.
   b) What are the domain and range of the function?

4. A pebble is dropped from a bridge into a river. Its height h metres above the river
   t seconds after the moment of release is given by $h = 82 - 4.9t^2$.
   a) Graph the function for reasonable values of t.
   b) State the domain and range.
   c) How high is the pebble after 2.5 s?

5. The shape of a parabolic mirror in a
   certain reflecting telescope is defined by
   the equation $y = 0.1x^2 - 20$, where
   x and y are measured in centimetres.
   a) Graph the function for $0 \leqslant x \leqslant 25$.
   b) How deep is the mirror if the dia-
   meter AB is 50 cm?

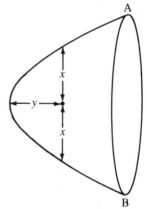

6. Graph each function and state its domain and range.
   a) $f(x) = 2x^2 - 6x + 5$ b) $g(t) = 3 + 2t - 0.5t^2$

7. The Viking 1 spacecraft made a soft landing on Mars on July 20, 1976. Its speed
   v metres per second t seconds before touchdown was given by $v = 1.2 + 3.2t$.
   Its height h metres t seconds before touchdown was given by $h = 1.2t + 1.6t^2$.
   a) Draw graphs of the speed and the height as functions of time.
   b) Determine the speed and the height of the spacecraft 90 s before touchdown.

8. When a flare is fired vertically, its height h metres after t seconds is given by
   $h = -4.9t^2 + 143.2t$.
   a) How high is the flare after 5 s?
   b) How long does it take the flare to reach a height of 1 km?

9. In *Example 2*, what is the effect on the height of the waves if the windspeed is:
   a) doubled
   b) tripled?

10. A landscape architect plans a circular flowerbed with a bordering pathway. The total diameter of the flowerbed and pathway is 20 m.
    a) If the width of the pathway is x metres, express the area A of the flowerbed as a function of x.
    b) Graph the function.
    c) What is the domain of the function?

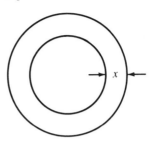

11. If each small circle has radius r, express the area of the shaded region as a function of r.
    a)

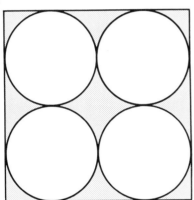

    b)

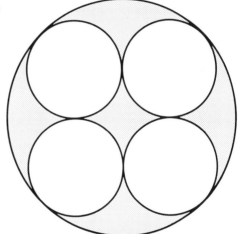

12. The velocity v millimetres per second of a particle falling through water is a function of its diameter d millimetres. The formula is $v = 655d^2$. How long will it take each particle listed to reach the seafloor where the ocean is 5000 m deep?

Particle	Diameter (mm)
Pebble	8.0
Coarse sand	0.5
Fine sand	0.1
Clay	0.004

13. The wavelength L metres of an ocean wave is a quadratic function of the form $L = kT^2$, where T is the period in seconds and k is a constant.
    a) Find the value of k if a wave with wavelength 25 m has a period of 4.0 s.
    b) What is the wavelength of a wave if its period is 6.5 s?

6-2 COMPARING THE GRAPHS OF $y = x^2$ AND $y = x^2 + q$

In this and the following sections, we shall develop a technique for graphing quadratic functions without making a table of values. The first step is to investigate the effect on the graph of $y = x^2$ of adding some number q to get $y = x^2 + q$. We do this by substituting different values for q and graphing the resulting parabolas.

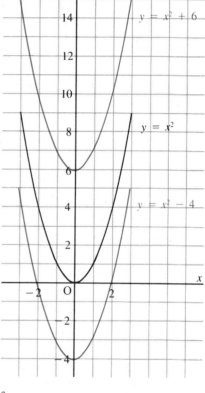

When $q = 0$, the equation becomes $y = x^2$.

x	-3	-2	-1	0	1	2	3
y	9	4	1	0	1	4	9

When $q = 6$, the equation becomes $y = x^2 + 6$.

x	-3	-2	-1	0	1	2	3
y	15	10	7	6	7	10	15

Since the y-coordinates are all 6 greater than those of $y = x^2$, the curve is *translated*, or moved, 6 units up. The y-intercept is 6. The vertex is (0, 6) and the y-axis is still the axis of symmetry.

When $q = -4$, the equation becomes $y = x^2 - 4$.

x	-3	-2	-1	0	1	2	3
y	5	0	-3	-4	-3	0	5

The curve is translated 4 units down. The y-intercept is -4, which is the minimum value of y. There are also two x-intercepts, 2 and -2.

Similar results will be found using other values of q.

$y = x^2 + q$ represents a parabola with these properties.
Vertex: (0, q)
Axis of symmetry: y-axis
Direction of opening: up
y-intercept: q
x-intercepts: There are two if $q < 0$.

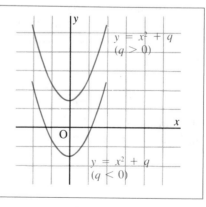

Knowing that $y = x^2 + q$ represents a parabola with the above properties, we can sketch graphs of equations in this form without making tables of values.

Example. Sketch the parabola $y = x^2 - 9$ for $-4 \leqslant x \leqslant 4$.

Solution. The parabola $y = x^2 - 9$ has vertex $(0, -9)$, opens up, and has the y-axis as the axis of symmetry.
When $x = 4$, $y = 4^2 - 9$, or 7
$(4, 7)$ is on the curve and so is $(-4, 7)$.
Knowing the vertex and these two points, we can now sketch the parabola.

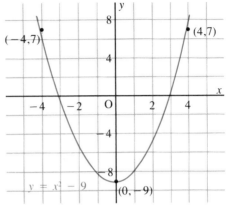

When they exist and if they are integers, the x-intercepts are useful in sketching a parabola. In the *Example*, the x-intercepts can be found by substituting 0 for y.
$0 = x^2 - 9$
$x^2 = 9$
$x = \pm 3$
$(3, 0)$ and $(-3, 0)$ are two additional points on the curve.

EXERCISES 6-2

(A)

1. a) Make a table of values and graph each parabola on the same grid for $-5 \leqslant x \leqslant 5$.
   $y = x^2$ $y = x^2 + 4$ $y = x^2 + 7$
   $y = x^2 - 2$ $y = x^2 - 5$ $y = x^2 + 1$
   b) Describe the effect of various values of q on the graph of $y = x^2 + q$.

2. Which graph best represents each equation?
   a) $y = x^2 + 1$ b) $y = x^2 - 4$ c) $y = x^2 - 1$ d) $y = x^2 + 2$
   i)   ii)   iii)   iv)

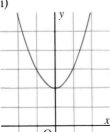
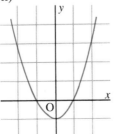
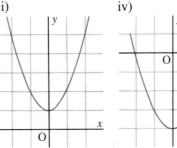

3. Write an equation that could correspond to each graph.
a) b) c) d)

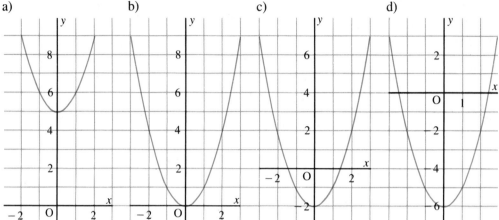

4. For each parabola state:
   i)   the direction of opening
   iii) the *y*-intercept
   ii) the coordinates of the vertex
   iv) the *x*-intercepts (if any).
a) b) c) d)

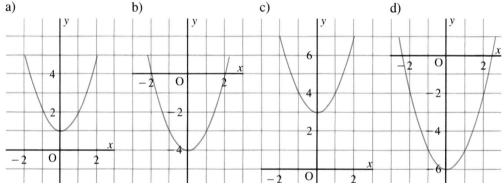

Ⓑ

5. For each parabola state:
   i)   the direction of opening
   iii) the *y*-intercept
   ii) the coordinates of the vertex
   iv) the *x*-intercepts (if any).
   a) $y = x^2 + 5$ b) $y = x^2 - 3$ c) $y = x^2 + 2$ d) $y = x^2 + 4$

6. Sketch each set of graphs on the same grid.
   a) $y = x^2 - 2$ $y = x^2 + 1$ $y = x^2 + 4$
   b) $y = x^2 - 1$ $y = x^2 - 3$ $y = x^2 + 2$

7. Find the equation of each parabola.
   a) with vertex $(0, 2)$ through $(-3, 11)$
   b) with vertex $(0, -9)$ and *x*-intercepts ± 3
   c) with vertex $(0, 5)$ through $(2, 9)$

6-3 COMPARING THE GRAPHS OF $y = x^2$ AND $y = (x - p)^2$

In $y = x^2$, if x is replaced by $(x - p)$ we obtain $y = (x - p)^2$. To investigate the effect of this on the graph of the parabola $y = x^2$, we give different values to p and graph the resulting parabolas.
When $p = 0$, the equation becomes $y = x^2$ . . . ①

x	-3	-2	-1	0	1	2	3
y	9	4	1	0	1	4	9

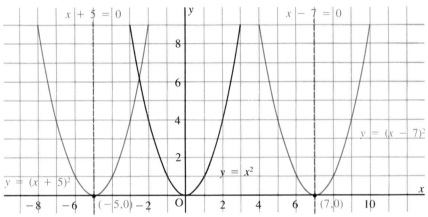

Negative values of p in $y = (x - p)^2$

When $p = -5$, the equation becomes $y = (x + 5)^2$.
For convenience, we choose x-cordinates which give the same y-coordinates as those above. All are 5 *less* than the x-coordinates in ①.

x	-8	-7	-6	-5	-4	-3	-2
y	9	4	1	0	1	4	9

The graph of $y = x^2$ is translated 5 units to the *left*. The vertex is $(-5, 0)$ and the line $x + 5 = 0$ is the axis of symmetry.

Positive values of p in $y = (x - p)^2$

When $p = +7$, the equation becomes $y = (x - 7)^2$.
For convenience, we choose x-coordinates which give the same y-coordinates as those above. All are 7 *greater* than the x-coordinates in ①.

x	4	5	6	7	8	9	10
y	9	4	1	0	1	4	9

The graph of $y = x^2$ is translated 7 units to the *right*. The vertex is $(7, 0)$ and the line $x - 7 = 0$ is the axis of symmetry.

Similar results will be found using other values of p.

$y = (x - p)^2$ represents a parabola with these properties.
Vertex: $(p, 0)$
Axis of symmetry: line $x - p = 0$
Direction of opening: up

For any equation in this form, the sign inside the brackets tells whether the parabola is moved to the left or to the right of the *y*-axis.

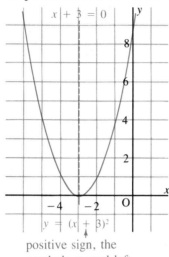

positive sign, the
parabola moved left

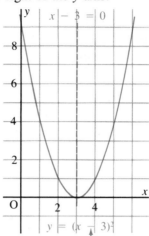

negative sign, the
parabola moved right

We can sketch graphs of equations in this form without using tables of values.

Example. Graph these parabolas on the same grid.

a) $y = (x - 5)^2$ b) $y = (x + 7)^2$

Solution. a) The parabola $y = (x - 5)^2$ has vertex (5, 0) and axis of symmetry $x - 5 = 0$. When $x = 0$, $y = 25$
Thus, one other point on the graph is (0, 25). Another point (10, 25) is its reflection in the axis of symmetry.

b) The parabola $y = (x + 7)^2$ has vertex (−7, 0) and axis of symmetry $x + 7 = 0$. When $x = 0$, $y = 49$
Thus, two other points on the graph are (0, 49) and (−14, 49).

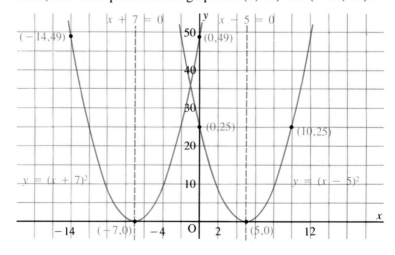

EXERCISES 6-3

(A)

1. Sketch each set of graphs on the same grid.
   a) $y = x^2$ $y = (x - 2)^2$ $y = (x + 4)^2$
   b) $y = x^2$ $y = (x + 3)^2$ $y = (x - 6)^2$
   c) $y = x^2$ $y = (x - 4)^2$ $y = (x + 6)^2$

2. Compare the graphs of $y = x^2$ and $y = (x - p)^2$ when:
   a) $p < 0$ b) $p > 0$.

3. Which graph best represents each equation?
   a) $y = (x - 1)^2$ b) $y = (x + 2)^2$ c) $y = (x + 4)^2$ d) $y = (x - 4)^2$

   i) 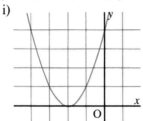   ii)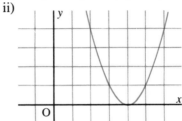

   iii) 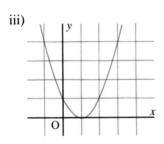   iv)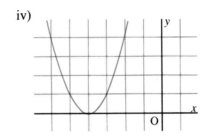

4. Write an equation that could correspond to each graph.

   a) 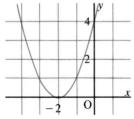   b)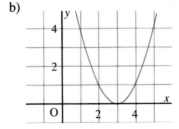

   c) 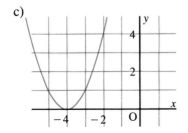   d)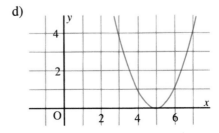

5. For each graph state:
   i)   the coordinates of the vertex   ii)   the equation of the axis of symmetry
   iii) the direction of opening   iv)   the y-intercept

a)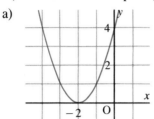

b)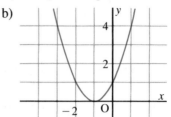

c)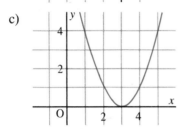

d)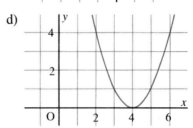

6. State the equation of each parabola in *Exercise 5*.

7. For each parabola state:
   i)   the coordinates of the vertex   ii)   the equation of the axis of symmetry
   iii) the direction of opening   iv)   the y-intercept
   a) $y = (x + 3)^2$ b) $y = (x - 8)^2$ c) $y = (x - 2)^2$ d) $y = (x + 4)^2$

8. Sketch the graphs of the parabolas in *Exercise 7*.

9. Sketch the graph of each parabola.
   a) $y = (x - 2)^2$ b) $y = (x + 5)^2$ c) $y = (x - 6)^2$ d) $y = (x + 2)^2$

10. Find the equation of each parabola.
    a) with vertex $(4, 0)$, y-intercept 16
    b) with vertex $(-3, 0)$, y-intercept 9
    c) with x-intercept 7, y-intercept 49, axis of symmetry $x - 7 = 0$

11. Sketch each set of graphs on the same grid.
    a) $y = (x + 4)^2 + 1$ and $y = (x + 4)^2 - 3$
    b) $y = (x - 1)^2 + 2$ and $y = (x - 1)^2 - 2$
    c) $y = x^2 + 6x + 9$ and $y = x^2 + 6x$
    d) $y = (x - 10)^2$ and $y = (10 - x)^2$

INVESTIGATE

What conditions must be satisfied by a and c for the parabola $y = ax^2 + c$ to have x-intercepts?

COMPUTER POWER

Turtles Which Can Draw Parabolas

Some computer languages, such as LOGO, feature turtle graphics. The computer can be programmed so that a small figure on the screen, called a turtle, is moved around leaving a trail behind it. LOGO also permits a programmer to add new commands to the language to have the turtle carry out specialized tasks, such as drawing parabolas.

When this command is entered:

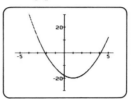

the turtle will draw this curve
on the screen.

The turtle draws a parabola congruent to $y = 2x^2$, with vertex $(1, -20)$; that is, the parabola $y = 2(x - 1)^2 - 20$.

1. Sketch the graph the turtle would draw for each command.
   a) `PARABOLA  1   1  -10`   b) `PARABOLA  -2   1  -10`
   c) `PARABOLA  1  -1   0`   d) `PARABOLA  -3  -2  25`
   e) `PARABOLA 0·5   0  -15`   f) `PARABOLA 0·01  0  10`

2. Predict the command that would make the turtle draw each parabola.
   a)   b)   c)

   d)   e) 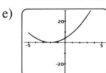   f)

3. By giving more than one command, the turtle will draw several parabolas on the same grid.
   a) Sketch the screen for these commands.

   ```
   PARABOLA      3   0   0
   PARABOLA      1   0   0
   PARABOLA    0·2   0   0
   PARABOLA   -0·2   0   0
   PARABOLA     -1   0   0
   PARABOLA     -3   0   0
   ```

   b) What commands would you give the turtle for the screen to show this?

6-4 COMPARING THE GRAPHS OF $y = x^2$ AND $y = ax^2$

In this section, we investigate the effect on the graph of $y = x^2$ of multiplying x^2 by a constant a to get $y = ax^2$.

Positive values of a

When $a = 1$, the equation becomes $y = x^2$.

x	y
-3	9
-2	4
-1	1
0	0
1	1
2	4
3	9

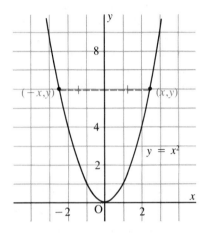

The curve is a parabola with the following properties.

Axis of symmetry: The y-axis is the axis of symmetry of the curve. If (x, y) is any point on the curve, then $(-x, y)$ is also on the curve.

Vertex: The point where the axis of symmetry intersects the curve is called the vertex. For this curve the vertex is $(0, 0)$.

Direction of opening: The curve opens up.

Using the same x-coordinates as above, graph a curve of the form $y = ax^2$ for $a > 1$ and another for $a < 1$. Compare the tables of values and graphs with those for $y = x^2$.

When $a = 2$, the equation becomes $y = 2x^2$.

x	-3	-2	-1	0	1	2	3
y	18	8	2	0	2	8	18

Since the y-coordinates are all twice those of $y = x^2$, the curve is expanded vertically.

When $a = \frac{1}{2}$, the equation becomes $y = \frac{1}{2}x^2$.

x	-3	-2	-1	0	1	2	3
y	4.5	2	0.5	0	0.5	2	4.5

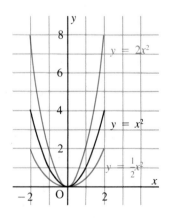

Since the y-coordinates are half those of $y = x^2$, the curve is compressed vertically.

Negative values of *a*

Using the same x-coordinates as before, we graph curves of the form $y = ax^2$ for $a < 0$, and compare the tables of values and graphs with those for $y = x^2$.

When $a = -1$, the equation becomes $y = -x^2$.

x	-3	-2	-1	0	1	2	3
y	-9	-4	-1	0	-1	-4	-9

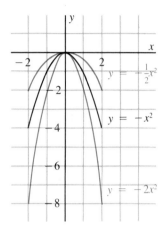

Since the y-coordinates are the opposites of those of $y = x^2$, the curve is reflected in the x-axis. It opens down.

When $a = -2$, the equation becomes $y = -2x^2$.

x	-3	-2	-1	0	1	2	3
y	-18	-8	-2	0	-2	-8	-18

The curve $y = x^2$ is reflected in the x-axis and expanded vertically.

When $a = -\frac{1}{2}$, the equation becomes $y = -\frac{1}{2}x^2$.

x	-3	-2	-1	0	1	2	3
y	-4.5	-2	-0.5	0	-0.5	-2	-4.5

The curve $y = x^2$ is reflected in the x-axis and compressed vertically.

Similar results will be found using other values of a, $a \neq 0$.

$y = ax^2$ $(a \neq 0)$ represents a parabola with these properties:

Vertex: $(0, 0)$

Axis of symmetry: y-axis

Direction of opening: up if $a > 0$
                                   down if $a < 0$

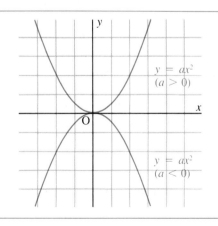

Knowing that $y = ax^2$ represents a parabola with the above properties, we can sketch graphs of equations in this form without making a table of values.

Example 1. Graph these parabolas on the same grid.
  a) $y = 5x^2$ b) $y = -2.5x^2$

Solution.   a) The parabola $y = 5x^2$ opens up.
      It has vertex (0, 0) and axis of
      symmetry the positive y-axis.
      A reasonable graph may be drawn by
      finding one other point on the curve.
      Substitute 4 for x in the equation.
      $y = 5(4)^2$, or 80
      The point (4, 80) is on the curve
      as is the point $(-4, 80)$ since the
      y-axis is the axis of symmetry.
      The parabola with vertex (0, 0) and
      passing through (4, 80) and $(-4, 80)$
      can now be sketched.
   b) The parabola $y = -2.5x^2$ opens
      down. It has vertex (0, 0) and axis of
      symmetry the negative y-axis.
      To find another point on the curve,
      substitute 4 for x in the equation.
      $y = -2.5(4)^2$, or -40
      The parabola passes through $(4, -40)$
      and $(-4, -40)$.

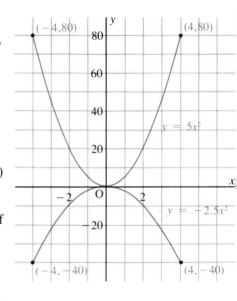

In *Example 1*, the scales on the axes were different. This is often necessary due to space requirements. While the choice of vertical scale affects the appearance of the curve, it does not change the vertex, the axis of symmetry, or the direction of opening.

Example 2. Find the equation of the parabola through (6, 27) which has the y-axis as its axis of symmetry and (0, 0) as its vertex. Sketch the graph.

Solution.   Let the equation of the parabola be
      $y = ax^2$. Since (6, 27) lies on the curve,
      its coordinates satisfy the equation.
      That is,
      $27 = a(6)^2$

      $a = \dfrac{3}{4}$

      The equation of the parabola is $y = \dfrac{3}{4}x^2$.

      The parabola is sketched using the
      fact that it passes through (0, 0),
      (6, 27), and $(-6, 27)$ since the y-axis
      is the axis of symmetry.

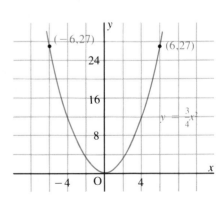

EXERCISES 6-4

1. a) Make a table of values and graph the equations on the same grid for
$-5 \leqslant x \leqslant 5$.

$$y = x^2 \qquad y = 3x^2 \qquad y = \frac{1}{2}x^2 \qquad y = -x^2 \qquad y = -\frac{1}{3}x^2 \qquad y = -4x^2$$

   b) Describe the effect on the graph of $y = ax^2$ as the value of a varies.

2. Which graph best represents each equation?
   a) $y = 5x^2$ b) $y = 0.2x^2$ c) $y = -1.5x^2$ d) $y = -3x^2$
      i)   ii)   iii)   iv)

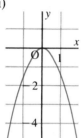
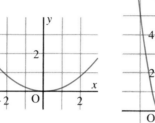
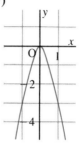

3. Sketch each set of parabolas on the same grid.
   a) $y = x^2 \qquad y = 3x^2 \qquad y = \frac{1}{2}x^2$

   b) $y = x^2 \qquad y = -x^2 \qquad y = 5x^2 \qquad y = -3x^2$

   c) $y = 2x^2 \qquad y = \frac{3}{4}x^2 \qquad y = -1.5x^2 \qquad y = -4x^2$

   d) $y = -2x^2 \qquad y = \frac{1}{4}x^2 \qquad y = 2.5x^2 \qquad y = -\frac{1}{2}x^2$

4. Find the equation of the parabola with vertex $(0, 0)$ which passes through each point.
   a) $(3, 18)$ b) $(4, -16)$ c) $(6, -9)$ d) $(2, 24)$

5. Find the equation of the parabola with vertex $(0, 0)$ which passes through each point.
   a) $(2, -10)$ b) $(3, 5)$ c) $\left(\frac{3}{2}, \frac{1}{3}\right)$ d) $(-\sqrt{2}, -6)$

6. The line $3x - y - 3 = 0$ is tangent to a parabola which has vertex $(0, 0)$ and axis of symmetry the y-axis. Find the equation of the parabola.

🕵 INVESTIGATE

If the coordinates of any point are given, is it always possible to find the equation of a parabola through the point with vertex $(0, 0)$ and axis of symmetry the y-axis?

6-5 GRAPHING $y = a(x - p)^2 + q$

In the last three sections we investigated the effect on the graph of
$y = x^2$ of the constants a, p, and q in the equations $y = ax^2$,
$y = x^2 + q$, and $y = (x - p)^2$. We now investigate the effect on the
graph when these three constants are combined in the same equation
$y = a(x - p)^2 + q$.

Example 1. Graph.   a) $y = (x - 4)^2 + 3$ b) $y = 2(x - 4)^2 + 3$

Solution.   a) $y = (x - 4)^2 + 3$ represents a parabola congruent
to $y = x^2$ which has been
translated 4 units to the
right and 3 units up from
the position of
$y = x^2$. The vertex is (4, 3)
and the line $x - 4 = 0$
is the axis of symmetry.

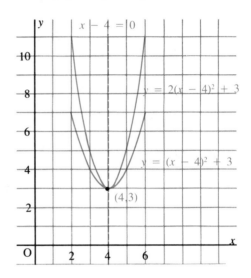

b) $y = 2(x - 4)^2 + 3$ is
similar to the equation in
part a). The vertex is (4, 3)
and the axis of symmetry
is the line $x - 4 = 0$.
The only difference is that
this parabola is expanded
vertically. It is congruent to
$y = 2x^2$.

Example 2. Sketch the graph of $y = -\frac{1}{2}(x + 3)^2 + 2$. Show on the graph the
coordinates of the vertex, the equation of the axis of symmetry, and the
coordinates of two points other than the vertex.

Solution.   The coordinates of the vertex are $(-3, 2)$.
The equation of the axis of symmetry
is $x + 3 = 0$.
The parabola opens down and is compressed vertically.

It is congruent to $y = -\frac{1}{2}x^2$.

When $x = 0$, $y = -\frac{1}{2}(0 - 3)^2 + 2$,

or -2.5.
$(0, -2.5)$ is a point on the graph.
Since $x + 3 = 0$ is the axis of symmetry,
$(-6, -2.5)$ is also on the graph.

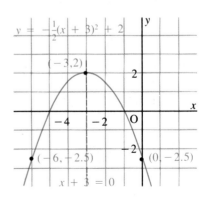

The above examples suggest that in the equation $y = a(x - p)^2 + q$, the constants a, p, and q have the following geometric meaning:

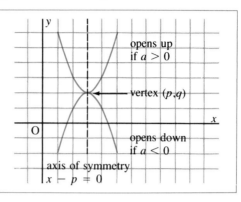

$x - p = 0$ is the axis of symmetry.

$$y = a(x - p)^2 + q$$

Congruent to the parabola $y = ax^2$

Coordinates of the vertex are (p, q)

opens up if $a > 0$

vertex (p, q)

opens down if $a < 0$

axis of symmetry $x - p = 0$

EXERCISES 6-5

(A)

1. Which graph best represents each equation?
   a) $y = (x + 3)^2 + 1$
   b) $y = -2(x + 4)^2 + 3$
   c) $y = \frac{1}{2}(x - 2)^2 - 5$
   d) $y = -(x - 3)^2 + 2$

   i)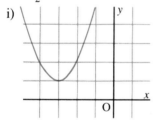

   ii)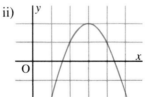

   iii)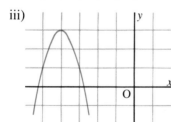

   iv)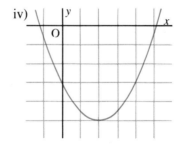

2. Sketch each set of graphs on the same grid.
   a) $y = (x - 5)^2 + 4$ $y = (x - 5)^2 + 2$ $y = (x - 5)^2$
      $y = (x - 5)^2 - 2$ $y = (x - 5)^2 - 4$
   b) $y = (x - 5)^2 + 4$ $y = (x - 3)^2 + 4$ $y = (x - 1)^2 + 4$
      $y = (x + 1)^2 + 4$ $y = (x + 3)^2 + 4$ $y = (x + 5)^2 + 4$
   c) $y = (x - 5)^2 + 4$ $y = 3(x - 5)^2 + 4$ $y = \frac{1}{2}(x - 5)^2 + 4$

   $y = -\frac{1}{2}(x - 5)^2 + 4$ $y = -(x - 5)^2 + 4$ $y = -3(x - 5)^2 + 4$

Ⓑ

3. For each parabola state:
    i)   the coordinates of the vertex   ii)   the equation of the axis of symmetry
    iii) the y-intercept   iv)   the x-intercepts, if any.
        a) $y = (x - 5)^2 + 2$ b) $y = 2(x + 3)^2 - 8$
        c) $y = -4(x + 1)^2 + 4$ d) $y = \frac{1}{2}(x - 2)^2 - 8$

4. Sketch the graphs of the functions in *Exercise 3*.

5. On a sketch of the graph of each parabola, show:
    i)   the coordinates of the vertex
    ii) the equation of the axis of symmetry
    iii) the coordinates of two points on the graph.
        a) $y = (x + 2)^2 - 5$ b) $y = -(x - 3)^2 + 2$
        c) $y = -\frac{1}{2}(x - 4)^2 - 1$ d) $y = 2(x + 1)^2 + 4$
        e) $y = -2(x - 1)^2 + 3$ f) $y = 4(x - 5)^2 - 10$

6. Sketch the graph of each parabola.
    a) $k = 2(l - 3)^2 - 1$ b) $r = -2(t + 3)^2 + 5$
    c) $m = \frac{1}{2}(n - 4)^2 - 3$ d) $p = 3(q - 5)^2 + 1$
    e) $f = -(g + 2.5)^2 + 3$ f) $u = -0.2(v + 2)^2 - 1.5$

7. Write the equation of each parabola.
    a) with vertex $(4, -1)$, that opens up, and is congruent to $y = 2x^2$
    b) with vertex $(-2, 3)$, that opens down, and is congruent to $y = \frac{1}{3}x^2$
    c) with vertex $(-3, 2)$, that opens down, and is congruent to $y = \frac{1}{2}x^2$
    d) with vertex $(3, -4)$, x-intercepts 1 and 5

8. Write the equation of each parabola.
    a) with vertex $(3, -1)$, x-intercepts 2 and 4
    b) with vertex $(-1, 4)$, y-intercept 2
    c) with vertex $(2, -27)$, y-intercept -15

Ⓒ

9. Describe what happens to each graph.
    a) $y = a(x - 4)^2 + 3$ as a varies
    b) $y = 2(x - p)^2 + 3$ as p varies
    c) $y = 2(x - 4)^2 + q$ as q varies

10. Find the equation of the parabola, with axis of symmetry the y-axis, which passes
    through each pair of points.
    a) $(2, 9)$ and $(3, 14)$ b) $(-2, 1)$ and $(4, -5)$

INVESTIGATE

Using Differences to Graph Parabolas

There is a pattern in the table of values for $y = x^2$ which is useful when graphing parabolas.

x	y	Differences
0	0	
1	1	1
2	4	3
3	9	5
4	16	7

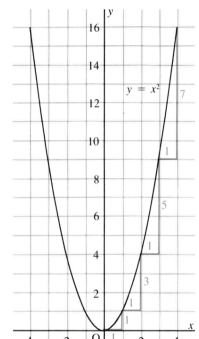

The differences in the y-coordinates are consecutive odd numbers.

Starting at the vertex, points on the parabola can be found by moving: 1 right and 1 up; then 1 right and 3 up; then 1 right and 5 up; and so on.

Other points are obtained by reflecting, in the axis of symmetry, those already found, or by repeating the above steps but moving 1 left each time.

This method can be used for any parabola which is congruent to $y = x^2$, and it can be modified to apply to parabolas congruent to $y = 2x^2$, $y = 3x^2$, $y = \frac{1}{2}x^2$, and so on.

1. Use the above method to graph each parabola.
   a) $y = (x - 3)^2 + 5$ b) $y = (x + 1)^2 - 7$ c) $y = -(x - 2)^2 + 3$

2. Modify the above method to graph each parabola.
   a) $y = 2x^2$ b) $y = 3x^2$
   c) $y = \frac{1}{2}x^2$ d) $y = 2(x - 4)^2 - 6$
   e) $y = 3(x + 2)^2 - 10$ f) $y = -\frac{1}{2}(x + 2)^2 + 5$

6-6 GRAPHING $y = ax^2 + bx + c$

In the previous section, we developed a method of sketching the graph of an equation such as $y = 2(x - 3)^2 - 7$ using the geometric meaning of the three constants in the equation. In applications of quadratic functions, however, an equation is more likely to be encountered in the form $y = 2x^2 - 12x + 11$. In this form, the constants used in drawing the graph are not obvious. To obtain these constants, we use the method of *completing the square*.

Example.   Write $y = 2x^2 - 12x + 11$ in the form $y = a(x - p)^2 + q$, then sketch the graph.

Solution.   *Step 1.* Remove 2 as a common factor from the first two terms.
$$y = 2(x^2 - 6x) + 11$$

Step 2. Add and subtract the square of $\frac{1}{2}(-6)$ inside the brackets.
$$y = 2(x^2 - 6x + 9 - 9) + 11$$

Step 3. Remove the last term from the brackets and combine with the constant term.
$$y = 2(x^2 - 6x + 9) - 18 + 11$$
$$= 2(x^2 - 6x + 9) - 7$$

Step 4. Factor the expression in the brackets as a complete square.
$$y = 2(x - 3)^2 - 7$$

By inspection of this equation
The coordinates of the vertex are $(3, -7)$.
The equation of the axis of symmetry
is $x - 3 = 0$.
When $x = 0$, $y = 2(0)^2 - 12(0) + 11$,
or 11
The y-intercept is 11.
Since $x - 3 = 0$ is the axis of symmetry,
$(6, 11)$ is also on the graph.
Knowing the coordinates of the vertex,
the point corresponding to the y-intercept
and its reflection in the axis of symmetry,
we can now sketch the curve.

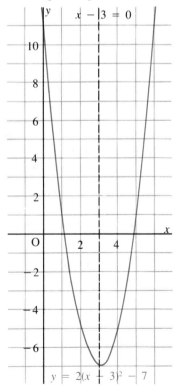

To graph $y = ax^2 + bx + c$
- Complete the square and write the equation in the form
  $y = a(x - p)^2 + q$.
- Draw the axis of symmetry $x - p = 0$.
- Draw a curve through these three points.
  — the vertex (p, q)
  — the point $(0, c)$ corresponding to the y-intercept
  — the reflection of $(0, c)$ in the axis of symmetry

EXERCISES 6-6

1. Write each equation in the form $y = a(x - p)^2 + q$.
   a) $y = x^2 - 6x + 8$ b) $y = x^2 + 10x + 14$ c) $y = 2x^2 + 4x + 7$
   d) $y = -2x^2 + 4x + 5$ e) $y = 3x^2 - 24x + 40$ f) $y = -5x^2 - 20x - 30$

2. Sketch the graphs of the parabolas in *Exercise 1*.

3. Sketch each parabola showing:
   i) the coordinates of the vertex
   ii) the equation of the axis of symmetry
   iii) the coordinates of two other points on the graph.
       a) $y = x^2 - 6x + 10$ b) $y = 2x^2 + 8x + 7$
       c) $y = -x^2 + 10x - 13$ d) $r = 3t^2 - 6t + 8$
       e) $m = -4n^2 - 24n - 20$ f) $u = -2v^2 - 16v - 35$

B

4. Sketch each parabola showing:
   i) the coordinates of the vertex
   ii) the equation of the axis of symmetry
   iii) the coordinates of two other points on the graph.

       a) $y = \frac{1}{2}x^2 - 2x + 7$ b) $r = 4t^2 + 12t - 5$

       c) $k = -2j^2 + 14j - 12$ d) $y = 3x^2 - 4x - 6$
       e) $u = -4v^2 + 10v - 7$ f) $y = -2x^2 - 12x - 14$

5. Sketch each parabola showing:
   i) the y-intercept
   ii) the coordinates of the vertex
   iii) the coordinates of two other points on the graph.
       a) $y = 2x^2 - 5x - 3$ b) $y = 2x^2 - 9x - 18$
       c) $y = 0.4x^2 + 2x + 2.5$ d) $y = -2x^2 + 5x$

C

6. a) Write $y = ax^2 + bx + c$ in the form $y = a(x - p)^2 + q$.
   b) State the coordinates of the vertex, the equation of the axis of symmetry, and
   the y-intercept.

INVESTIGATE

Compare the method of completing the square for the quadratic function
$y = 2x^2 + 8x - 9$ with the method of completing the square for the
quadratic equation $2x^2 + 8x - 9 = 0$.
In what ways are they the same? In what ways are they different?
Is it possible to use the same method for both?

INVESTIGATE

b in $y = ax^2 + bx + c$

In a quadratic function such as $y = x^2 + 4x + 3$, each constant has a geometric
meaning. You already know two of them.

$$y = x^2 + 4x + 3$$

The parabola is   The *y*-intercept
congruent to $y = x^2$.   is 3.

We will now investigate the meaning of the coefficient of the linear term.

1. Make tables of values and then graph these parabolas on the same axes.
   a) $y = x^2 + 6x + 3$ b) $y = x^2 + 4x + 3$
   c) $y = x^2 + 2x + 3$ d) $y = x^2 + 3$
   e) $y = x^2 - 2x + 3$ f) $y = x^2 - 4x + 3$
   g) $y = x^2 - 6x + 3$

2. Use the results to describe the effect of varying the value of *b* in
   $y = x^2 + bx + 3$.

3. On the graph drawn for *Question 1*, what pattern is formed by the vertices of
   the parabolas?

4. Would the pattern be true for the general parabola $y = ax^2 + bx + c$, where
   a and *c* are constant and *b* varies?

5. Write a report of your findings.

6-7 MAXIMUM AND MINIMUM VALUES OF A QUADRATIC FUNCTION

When a quadratic function is graphed, the vertex is important because it is either the highest or lowest point on the curve. Consider these examples.

The parabola $y = 2(x - 3)^2 + 4$ has vertex (3, 4) and opens up.

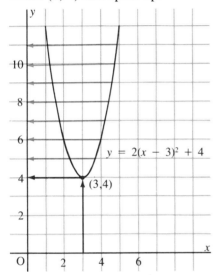

The parabola $y = -2(x - 3)^2 + 4$ has vertex (3, 4) and opens down.

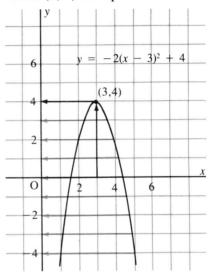

The graph shows that the values of y for points on the curve are never less than 4. That is, the function
$f(x) = 2(x - 3)^2 + 4$
has a *minimum* value of 4 which occurs when $x = 3$.

The graph shows that the values of y for points on the curve are never greater than 4. That is, the function
$f(x) = -2(x - 3)^2 + 4$
has a *maximum* value of 4 which occurs when $x = 3$.

These characteristics of a quadratic function can be obtained from its equation without drawing its graph.

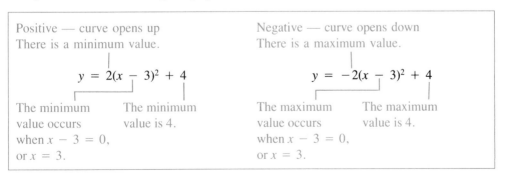

Positive — curve opens up
There is a minimum value.

$$y = 2(x - 3)^2 + 4$$

The minimum value occurs when $x - 3 = 0$, or $x = 3$.

The minimum value is 4.

Negative — curve opens down
There is a maximum value.

$$y = -2(x - 3)^2 + 4$$

The maximum value occurs when $x - 3 = 0$, or $x = 3$.

The maximum value is 4.

Example 1.   Given $y = -4x^2 - 12x + 5$

a) Find the maximum or minimum value of y and state which it is.

b) For what value of x does the maximum or minimum occur?

Solution.   a) Rearrange the expression by completing the square.

$$y = -4x^2 - 12x + 5$$
$$= -4(x^2 + 3x) + 5$$
$$= -4\left(x^2 + 3x + \frac{9}{4} - \frac{9}{4}\right) + 5$$
$$= -4\left(x^2 + 3x + \frac{9}{4}\right) + 9 + 5$$
$$= -4\left(x + \frac{3}{2}\right)^2 + 14$$

The maximum value of y is 14.

b) The maximum value occurs when $x + \frac{3}{2} = 0$, or $x = -\frac{3}{2}$.

Many applications of quadratic functions involve finding the maximum or minimum value.

Example 2.   Supermarket cashiers try to memorize current sale prices while they work. A survey showed that, on average, the percent P of prices memorized after t hours is given approximately by the formula $P = -40t^2 + 120t$.

a) What is the greatest percent of prices memorized?

b) How long does it take to memorize them?

Solution.   a) Since the coefficient of t^2 is negative, there is a maximum percent. To find this percent, rearrange the expression for P by completing the square.

$$P = -40t^2 + 120t$$
$$= -40(t^2 - 3t)$$
$$= -40\left(t^2 - 3t + \frac{9}{4} - \frac{9}{4}\right)$$
$$= -40\left(t^2 - 3t + \frac{9}{4}\right) + 90$$
$$= -40\left(t - \frac{3}{2}\right)^2 + 90$$

The greatest percent of prices memorized is 90%.

b) It takes $\frac{3}{2}$ h, or 1.5 h to memorize 90% of the prices.

EXERCISES 6-7

Ⓐ

1. Using the word maximum or minimum, and data from each graph, complete this sentence: "The . . .value of y is . . . when $x = $ . . ."

a)
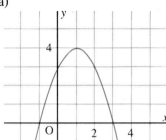

b)
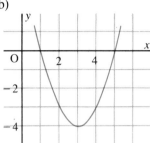

c)
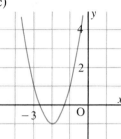

d)
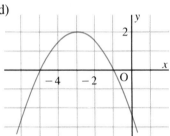

e)
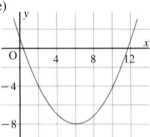

f)
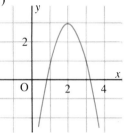

2. For each parabola, state:
   i) the maximum or minimum value of y
   ii) whether it is a maximum or minimum
   iii) the value of x when it occurs.
   a) $y = (x - 3)^2 + 5$
   b) $y = 2(x + 1)^2 - 3$
   c) $y = -2(x - 1)^2 + 4$
   d) $y = -(x + 2)^2 - 6$
   e) $y = 0.5x^2 - 9$
   f) $y = 7 - 2x^2$

3. Does each function have a maximum value? If it has, for what value of x does it occur?

   a) $y = -2(x + 5)^2 - 8$
   b) $f(x) = \frac{1}{4}(x - 2)^2 - 9$
   c) $y = -0.5(x - 3)^2 + 7.5$
   d) $y = 5 - 3x^2$
   e) $f(x) = 3\left(x - \frac{5}{2}\right)^2 + \frac{17}{2}$
   f) $f(x) = -(x + 4)^2 - 19$

4. a) Write each equation in the form $y = a(x - p)^2 + q$.
      i) $y = 2x^2 - 8x + 15$
      ii) $y = 3x^2 + 12x - 7$
      iii) $y = x^2 - 6x + 7$
      iv) $y = -2x^2 + 6x + 11$
      v) $y = -x^2 - 3x - 3$
      vi) $y = 1.5x^2 - 9x + 10$
   b) For each function in part a), state:
      i) its maximum or minimum value
      ii) the value of x for which the maximum or minimum occurs.

Ⓑ

5. On a forward somersault dive, Greg's height h metres above the water is given approximately by $h = -5t^2 + 6t + 3$, where t is the time in seconds after he leaves the board.
   a) Find Greg's maximum height above the water.
   b) How long does it take him to reach the maximum height?
   c) How long is it before he enters the water?
   d) How high is the board above the water?

6. The power P watts supplied to a circuit by a 9 V (volt) battery is given by the formula $P = 9I - 0.5I^2$, where I is the current in amperes.
   a) For what value of the current will the power be a maximum?
   b) What is the maximum power?

7. A ball thrown vertically with a velocity of 18 m/s is h metres above the ground after t seconds, where $h = -5t^2 + 18t$. What is the maximum height of the ball, and when does it reach that height?

8. A ball is thrown into the air from the balcony of an apartment building and falls to the ground. The height h metres of the ball relative to the ground t seconds after being thrown is given by $h = -5t^2 + 10t + 35$.
   a) Find the maximum height of the ball above the ground.
   b) How long does it take the ball to reach the maximum height?
   c) After how many seconds does the ball hit the ground?
   d) How high is the balcony above the ground?
   e) What would be the equation if heights were measured relative to the balcony rather than to the ground?

Ⓒ

9. A projectile is launched from a platform, and its height h metres is given as a function of the elapsed time t seconds by $h = -4.9t^2 + 180t + 2$. Draw a graph showing h as a function of t, and use it to estimate:
   a) the maximum height of the projectile
   b) the time required for the projectile to reach its maximum height
   c) the time required for the projectile to reach the ground.

10. If $f(x) = ax^2 + bx + c$ has a minimum value 0, what conditions must be satisfied by a, b, and c?

 INVESTIGATE

Graph the parabola and the line on the same grid.
$y = x^2 - 4x + 3$ $y = -4x + 3$
Compare the graphs. Is there any geometric relation between the parabola and the line?
Determine if the relation holds for other parabolas.
Write a report of your findings.

INVESTIGATE

An Analysis of Quadratic Functions

An analysis of a quadratic function, such as $y = -\frac{1}{2}x^2 + 4x - 5$, involves a combination of many algebraic and geometric skills.

$y = -\frac{1}{2}x^2 + 4x - 5$ common factors

$= -\frac{1}{2}(x^2 - 8x) - 5$ completing the square

$= -\frac{1}{2}(x^2 - 8x + 16 - 16) - 5$

$= -\frac{1}{2}(x - 4)^2 + 3$

The parabola opens down and is congruent to $y = \frac{1}{2}x^2$.   congruence

The maximum value of y is 3 and occurs when $x = 4$.   maximum and minimum values

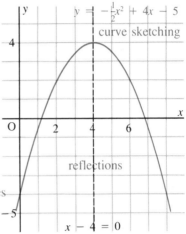

curve sketching

reflections

$x - 4 = 0$

Intercepts   finding intercepts

Let $x = 0$.

$y = -\frac{1}{2}(0)^2 + 4(0) - 5$

$= -5$

The y-intercept is -5.

Let $y = 0$.

$0 = -\frac{1}{2}x^2 + 4x - 5$

$x^2 - 8x + 10 = 0$

$x = \dfrac{-b \pm \sqrt{b^2 - 4ac}}{2a}$

$x = \dfrac{8 \pm \sqrt{24}}{2}$

$= 4 \pm \sqrt{6}$

equation of a vertical line

solving quadratic equations

working with radicals

To analyze a quadratic function in the above manner means to determine all the following information about the function.

- the coordinates of the vertex
- the equation of the axis of symmetry
- the direction of opening
- a congruent parabola
- a sketch of the function
- the y-intercept
- the x-intercepts, if any
- the maximum or minimum value of y
- the value of x for which the maximum or minimum value occurs.

1. Analyze each parabola.

a) $y = x^2 - 6x + 5$ b) $y = -\frac{1}{2}x^2 + 5x - 9$ c) $f(x) = 2x^2 - 5x - 12$

6-8 MAXIMUM AND MINIMUM PROBLEMS

In many problems involving the maximum or minimum of a function, the function is not given; it has to be found from the data. Note the steps involved in the solutions of the following examples.

Example 1.   Two numbers have a difference of 10. What are the numbers if their product is a minimum?

Solution.   *Step 1.* Identify the quantity to be maximized or minimized.
The quantity to be minimized is the product P of two numbers.

Step 2. Write the algebraic expression for this quantity.
Let the two numbers be x and y. Then, $P = xy$

Step 3. The expression must contain only one variable. If it contains more, use other information to write it in terms of one variable.
Since the numbers have a difference of 10, $x - y = 10$, where x is the greater number.
Solve for y. $y = x - 10$
Substitute $x - 10$ for y in $P = xy$.
$P = x(x - 10)$
$ = x^2 - 10x$

Step 4. The expression in Step 3 is a quadratic function. Rearrange it by completing the square.
$P = x^2 - 10x$
$ = x^2 - 10x + 25 - 25$
$ = (x - 5)^2 - 25$

Step 5. Determine the maximum or minimum value of the function and the value of the variable for which it occurs.
The minimum value of P is -25 which occurs when $x = 5$.

Step 6. Answer the question in the statement of the problem.
Since $x = 5$ and $x - y = 10$, $y = -5$
The two numbers are 5 and -5.

Example 2.   A rectangular lot is bounded on one side by a river and on the other three sides by a total of 80 m of fencing. Find the dimensions of the largest possible lot.

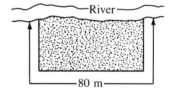

Solution.   *Step 1.* The quantity to be maximized is the area of the lot.
Step 2. Let x metres be the width of the lot and y metres the length.
Then, if A is the area, $A = xy$.

Step 3. Since the total length of fencing is 80 m,

$2x + y = 80$

or, $y = 80 - 2x$

Substitute $80 - 2x$ for y in $A = xy$.

$A = x(80 - 2x)$

$= -2x^2 + 80x$

Step 4. $A = -2(x^2 - 40x)$

$= -2(x^2 - 40x + 400 - 400)$

$= -2(x^2 - 40x + 400) + 800$

$= -2(x - 20)^2 + 800$

Step 5. The maximum value of A is 800 and occurs when $x = 20$.

Step 6. Since $x = 20$ and $2x + y = 80$, $y = 40$

The dimensions of the largest possible rectangular lot are 40 m by 20 m.

Example 3. The cost of a ticket to a hockey arena seating 800 people is \$3. At this price every ticket is sold. A survey indicates that if the price is increased, attendance will fall by 100 for every dollar of increase. What ticket price results in the greatest revenue? What is the greatest revenue?

Solution. *Step 1.* The quantity to be maximized is the total revenue R dollars from the tickets to be sold.

Step 2. Let x dollars be the increase in ticket price. Then,

$R =$ (cost per ticket)(number of tickets sold)

$= (3 + x)(800 - 100x)$

$= -100x^2 + 500x + 2400$

Step 3. The expression already contains only one variable.

Step 4. $R = -100(x^2 - 5x) + 2400$

$= -100\left(x^2 - 5x + \dfrac{25}{4} - \dfrac{25}{4}\right) + 2400$

$= -100\left(x^2 - 5x + \dfrac{25}{4}\right) + 625 + 2400$

$= -100\left(x - \dfrac{5}{2}\right)^2 + 3025$

Step 5. The maximum value of R is 3025 and occurs when $x = \dfrac{5}{2}$, or 2.5.

Step 6. Since an increase in price of \$2.50 per ticket results in the greatest revenue, the ticket price should become \$5.50. The greatest revenue is \$3025.00.

EXERCISES 6-8

Ⓑ

1. Two numbers have a difference of 8. Find the numbers if their product is a minimum.

2. The sum of two natural numbers is 12. If their product is a maximum, find the numbers.

3. The sum of two numbers is 60. Find the numbers if their product is a maximum.

4. Two numbers have a difference of 20. Find the numbers if the sum of their squares is a minimum.

5. The sum of two numbers is 16. Find the numbers if the sum of their squares is a minimum.

6. The sum of two numbers is 28. Find the numbers if the sum of their squares is a minimum.

7. The sum of a number and three times another number is 18. Find the numbers if their product is a maximum.

8. Two numbers have a difference of 16. Find the numbers if the result of adding their sum and their product is a minimum.

9. A rectangular lot is bordered on one side by a stream and on the other three sides by 600 m of fencing. Find the dimensions of the lot if its area is a maximum.

10. A lifeguard marks off a rectangular swimming area at a beach with 200 m of rope. What is the greatest area of water she can enclose?

11. Eighty metres of fencing are available to enclose a rectangular play area.
    a) What is the maximum area that can be enclosed?
    b) What dimensions produce the maximum area?

12. A rectangular area is enclosed by a fence and divided by another section of fence parallel to two of its sides. If the 600 m of fence used encloses a maximum area, what are the dimensions of the enclosure?

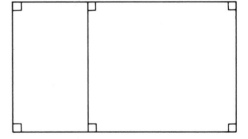

13. A theatre seats 2000 people and charges $10 for a ticket. At this price, all the tickets can be sold. A survey indicates that if the ticket price is increased, the number sold will decrease by 100 for every dollar of increase. What ticket price would result in the greatest revenue?

14. A bus company carries about 20 000 riders per day for a fare of 90¢. A survey indicates that if the fare is decreased, the number of riders will increase by 2000 for every 5¢ of decrease. What ticket price would result in the greatest revenue?

15. A trough is made from a rectangular strip of sheet metal, 50 cm wide, by bending up at right angles a strip x centimetres high, along two sides. For what value of x is the cross-sectional area a maximum?

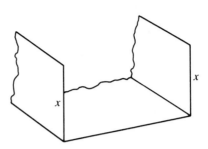

16. What is the maximum area of a triangle having 15 cm as the sum of its base and height?

17. A straight section of railroad track crosses two highways 400 m and 600 m from an intersection. Find the dimensions of the largest rectangular lot that can be laid out in the triangle formed by the railroad and highways.

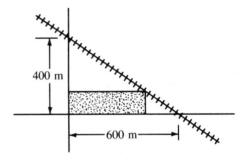

18. A 30 cm piece of wire is cut in two. One piece is bent into the shape of a square, the other piece into the shape of a rectangle with a length-to-width ratio of 2 : 1. What are the lengths of the two pieces if the sum of the areas of the square and rectangle is a minimum?

Ⓒ

19. Find the number which exceeds its square by the greatest possible amount.

20. Find the maximum possible area of a rectangle with a given perimeter.

21. In $\triangle ABC$, $\angle B = 90°$ and AC has a constant length. Prove that the area of $\triangle ABC$ is a maximum when AB $=$ BC.

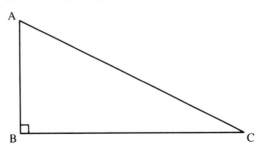

22. Find the minimum distance from $(0, 0)$ to the line $3x + 2y - 12 = 0$.

Creative Problem Posing

''Activities . . . should include open-ended investigations and the opportunity to make and test conjectures about relationships among quantities.''

M. Kathleen Heid

What happens if two angles of a triangle are the coordinates of a point?

If you know two angles of a triangle, you can find the third angle, since the sum of the three angles is 180°. Therefore, if the angles of a triangle are listed in order from smallest to largest, the first two angles form an ordered pair (x, y) which can be plotted as a point on a grid.

For example, in △ABC, the smallest angle is 40°, and the next larger angle is 55°. Hence, the point (40, 55) on the grid below represents △ABC. In a similar manner, you can plot a point to represent any given triangle.

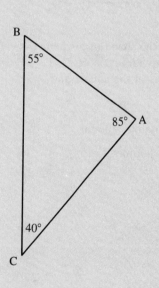

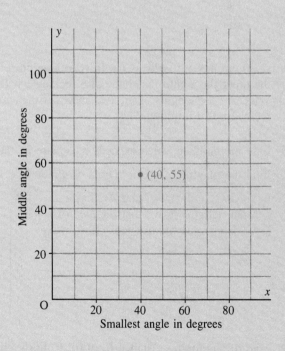

Where are all the points which represent right triangles?

Understand the problem

- If you know the angles of a triangle, how do you determine the ordered pair (x, y)? Can you do this for any triangle?
- Try drawing a few triangles and plotting the points to represent them.

Think of a strategy and carry it out

- Draw several right triangles, and plot the points to represent them.

Look back

- Do the points lie on a line segment? What are the endpoints of this segment? What is the equation of the segment?
- Is y a function of x? What are the domain and the range of the function?
- Where are the points which represent equilateral triangles? isosceles triangles? acute triangles? obtuse triangles?
- Write a report of your discoveries.

Up to now in your study of mathematics, most or all of the problems you solved have probably been in your textbook or provided by your teacher. In other words, somebody else created the problem for you. But mathematicians do not always solve problems that have been created by others. They also create their own problems.

How does a mathematician create problems? One way has been suggested in the *Look back* sections of the *PROBLEM SOLVING* pages in this book. In these sections, problems related to the problem on the page are often suggested. Perhaps you did this after solving other problems. Did you ever "look back" and think of another related problem? If you did, you created a problem.

Another way of creating problems is suggested by the problem on the facing page. How did the person who created the problem happen to think of it? This problem involves two different topics in mathematics — angles of a triangle and the coordinates of a point. Suppose we write these down, like this:

Angles of a triangle: A B C
                              ↓ ↓
Coordinates of a point: x y

The arrows suggest that the person who created the problem thought about linking the two topics together, and asking questions like this: What happens if two angles of a triangle are the coordinates of a point? What points correspond to the different kinds of triangles?

You can create your own problems if you think about other topics in this way.

1. Think of these topics.

   Quadratic equation: $x^2 + px + q = 0$

   Coordinates of a point: x y

   Create a problem based on these topics and then solve the problem. To create your problem, it may help to think, "What happens if . . . ?"

2. Create a problem based on these topics, and then solve the problem.
   a) consecutive numbers and coordinates of a point
   b) the parabola $y = ax^2 + bx + c$ and the line $y = mx + b$

   As an aid to creating problems, some of the topics you have studied in mathematics are listed in the table below. Each cell in the table links two topics — one by reading down to the right, and the other by reading up to the right. For example, cell A links the topics *angles of a triangle* and *coordinates of a point*. Hence, this cell suggests the problem on page 226. Similarly, cells B, C, and D suggest the problems on this page.

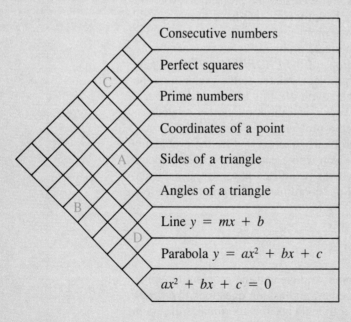

3. Choose one of the colored cells. Create a problem based on the two topics linked by the cell, and then solve the problem.

PROBLEMS

Ⓑ

1. Divide a clock face into three parts such that the sum of the numbers in each part is the same.

2. What is the second smallest number with 6 prime factors?

3. Two numbers have a difference of 2 and a product of 10. Find the difference of their squares.

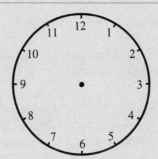

4. The first names of King, Laird, and Port are Ken, Louise, and Max, but not necessarily in that order. Port's first name is not Max. Laird is Max's uncle. What are the first and last names of each person?

Ⓒ

5. Divide the numbers 1, 2, 3, 4, 5, 6, 8, 9, and 10 into two sets such that the product of all the numbers in one set is equal to the product of all the numbers in the other set.

6. Consider the square and the cube of a 2-digit number such as 43. $43^2 = 1849$ and $43^3 = 79\,507$. The answers contain the digits 1, 4, 5, 7, 8, 9, and 0. What is the only 2-digit number whose square and cube contain all the digits from 0 to 9 with no digits repeated?

7. Prove that the sum of the squares of five consecutive integers can never be a perfect square.

Ⓓ

8. There are three different ways to draw two overlapping congruent right triangles standing on a common side.
   a) Prove that it is impossible for the areas of the shaded triangles to be all equal.
   b) Which of the three shaded triangles has the greatest area?

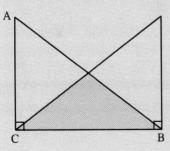

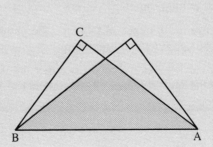

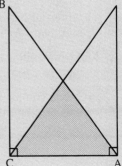

Review Exercises

1. Graph each function, and state its domain and range.

   a) $f(x) = -\frac{1}{2}x^2 - 2x + 7$ b) $f(x) = -2x^2 - 12x - 9$

2. In a Test-Your-Strength booth at a fair you strike a pad with a hammer. This projects a weight up a vertical slide. A bell rings if you have hit the pad hard enough. When the pad is struck with just sufficient force to ring the bell, the height h metres of the weight t seconds after the pad is struck is given by $h = 8t - 4.9t^2$.
   a) How high is the weight 0.5 s after the pad is struck?
   b) How high is the bell?

3. Find the equation of each parabola.
   a) with vertex $(-2, 0)$, y-intercept 4
   b) with vertex $(5, 0)$, y-intercept 25
   c) with x-intercept -6, y-intercept 36, and axis of symmetry $x + 6 = 0$

4. Find the equation of the parabola with vertex $(0, 0)$ which passes through each point.

   a) $(2, 16)$ b) $(3, -18)$ c) $(2, 6)$ d) $(-3, 15)$

   e) $\left(\frac{2}{3}, -\frac{2}{3}\right)$ f) $(4, 12)$ g) $\left(-\frac{5}{2}, 5\right)$ h) $\left(\frac{1}{2}, -\frac{1}{2}\right)$

5. Find the equation of each parabola.
   a) with vertex $(-3, 4)$, y-intercept -5
   b) with vertex $(2, -2)$, x-intercepts 1 and 3

   c) with vertex $(4, -4)$, that opens up, and is congruent to $y = \frac{1}{2}x^2$

6. Sketch each parabola showing:
   i) the coordinates of the vertex
   ii) the equation of the axis of symmetry
   iii) the coordinates of two other points on the graph.

   a) $y = x^2 - 6x + 5$ b) $w = 2z^2 - 8z - 5$

   c) $v = \frac{1}{2}t^2 + 10t + 21$ d) $p = -3q^2 + 18q - 20$

7. A producer of synfuel from coal estimates that the cost C dollars per barrel for a production run of x thousand barrels is given by $C = 9x^2 - 180x + 940$. How many thousand barrels should be produced each run to keep the cost per barrel at a minimum? What is the minimum cost per barrel of synfuel?

8. Two numbers have a difference of 24. Find the numbers if the result of adding their sum and their product is a minimum.

9. A bus company carries about 40 000 riders per day for a fare of $1.00. A survey indicates that if the fare is decreased, the number of riders will increase by 2500 for every 5¢ decrease. What fare will result in the greatest revenue?

1. Solve.
   a) $6b^2 - 5 = 7$
   b) $3(2c^2 - 1) - 2 = 4(2c^2 - 3)$
   c) $(a - 3)(a - 7) = (a - 2)(3a - 4)$

2. Solve graphically.
   a) $2x^2 - 11x - 40 = 0$ b) $4x^2 + 12x + 9 = 0$

3. Solve.
   a) $a^2 - 2a - 15 = 0$ b) $4y^2 + 20y - 24 = 0$
   c) $5x^2 - 42x + 16 = 0$ d) $4x^2 + 25x - 21 = 0$
   e) $16b^2 - 25 = 0$ f) $2(b + 3)(b + 1) = b(2b - 1)$

4. Solve.
   a) $4c^2 - 2c - 5 = 0$ b) $4x^2 + 7x - 6 = 0$
   c) $3x^2 + 7x + 2 = 0$ d) $3x^2 + 2x = 11$
   e) $\dfrac{5}{x} + \dfrac{6}{x + 2} = 5$ f) $(x + 6)(x - 1) = 5x(x - 2) + 6$

5. Determine the nature of the roots of each equation.
   a) $4a^2 - 3a - 7 = 0$ b) $2x^2 - 7x + 3 = 0$
   c) $-4a^2 + 4a = 1$ d) $3b^2 = 2b - 9$

6. For what values of k does each equation have two different real roots?
   a) $x^2 + kx - 4 = 0$ b) $kx^2 + 3x - 3 = 0$

7. For what values of p does each equation have no real roots?
   a) $x^2 + px + 9 = 0$ b) $px^2 - 3x + 3 = 0$

8. A framed picture has a border the same area as the picture. If the picture is 12 cm by 17 cm, find the width of the border.

9. A metal strip, 40 cm long, is cut in two and each piece bent to form a square. If the sum of the areas of the squares is 58 cm², how long is each piece of strip?

10. State the domain and range of each function.
    a)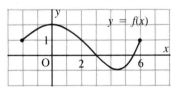
    b) $y = 2x^2 + 4$
    c) $y = \sqrt{3x - 4}$
    d) $y = \dfrac{1}{x + 3}$

11. Which relations represent functions?
    a)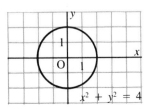
    b) $\{(3, 6), (4, 5), (-2, 5), (-1, 5)\}$
    c) $y = 6x - 2$
    d) $y^2 - x - 4 = 0$

12. If $g(x) = x^2 + 2x - 24$, for what values of x is:
    a) $g(x) = 0$ b) $g(x) = -9$ c) $g(x) = 11$?

13. The table shows the amount of batter a cook prepares for a Pancake Special.
    a) Draw a graph showing the amount of batter as a function of the number of customers.
    b) Find the equation relating the amount of batter to the number of customers.
    c) How much batter is required for:
       i) 15 customers
       ii) 35 customers
       iii) 84 customers?
    d) The cook prepared 48 cups of batter. How many customers were expected?

Number of customers expected, n	Amount of batter, c cups
10	7
30	21
50	35

14. Find the missing numbers.
    a) m varies directly as c^2.

m	2	8	12		
c	5			15	22

    b) y varies inversely as $\sqrt{t}$.

t	9	16			400
y		18	12	10	

15. The free end of a diving board dips a distance which varies directly with the mass of a person standing on it. The board dips 15 cm under Ben's mass of 67 kg. How far will it dip under Phil's mass of 74 kg?

16. Sketch each set of graphs on the same axes.
    a) $y = x^2$ $y = x^2 + 4$ $y = x^2 - 3$
    b) $y = x^2$ $y = 3x^2$ $y = \frac{1}{2}x^2$ $y = -x^2$
    c) $y = x^2$ $y = (x - 1)^2$ $y = (x + 3)^2$
    d) $y = x^2$ $y = 2(x + 1)^2 + 3$ $y = \frac{1}{2}(x - 2)^2 - 4$ $y = -(x - 3)^2 + 5$

17. For each parabola, state:
    i) the coordinates of the vertex
    iii) the direction of opening
    ii) the equation of the axis of symmetry
    iv) the y-intercept.
       a) $y = 3(x + 7)^2$
       b) $y = -2(x - 3)^2 + 4$
       c) $y = -\left(x - \frac{1}{2}\right)^2 - \frac{3}{4}$
       d) $y = \frac{1}{2}(x + 6)^2 - 3$

18. Find the equation of each parabola.
    a) with vertex $(0, 0)$, through $(2, 7)$
    b) with vertex $(-1, 4)$, and y-intercept 16
    c) with vertex $(-3, -2)$, that opens down, and is congruent to $y = 3x^2$
    d) with y-intercept 10, x-intercept 2, and axis of symmetry $x - 3 = 0$

19. A rectangular piece of land, bounded on one side by a hedge, is to be fenced on its other three sides. What is the maximum area that can be enclosed by 200 m of fencing?

The speed of a vehicle v kilometres per hour can be estimated from the length d metres of its skid marks. If $v = 12.6\sqrt{d} + 8$, sketch a graph of v as a function of d without making a table of values. (See Section 7-6 *Example 2*.)

7-1 SOME FUNCTIONS AND THEIR GRAPHS

In previous chapters the linear and quadratic functions were studied. The graphs of these functions have characteristic shapes — the graph of a linear function is a straight line and that of a quadratic function is a parabola. Here are two examples.

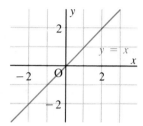 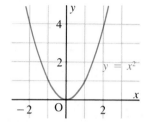

In this chapter, we investigate some other functions having graphs with characteristic shapes. The results will allow the graphs to be sketched *without* a table of values. Some of these functions are illustrated in this section.

Square-Root Functions

The problem of finding a ship's longitude at sea was so important to exploration and trade in the sixteenth and seventeenth centuries that several countries offered substantial prizes for its solution. The solution that was eventually found required the accurate recording of time using pendulum clocks.

The period T seconds of a pendulum of length l metres is given approximately by the formula $T = 2\sqrt{l}$. This function is an example of a *square-root function*.

l	T
0	0
1	2
2	2.8
3	3.5
4	4.0
5	4.5

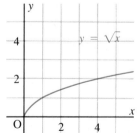

A simple square-root function is $f(x) = \sqrt{x}$. Since there are real values for $\sqrt{x}$ only when $x \geqslant 0$, the graph has an unusual property: it starts at a fixed point $(0,0)$ and extends in one direction only.

x	$f(x)$
0	0
1	1
2	1.4
3	1.7
4	2.0
5	2.2

The graphs of the two square-root functions shown are drawn to the same scale. If they were drawn on the same grid, how would they be related?

Other examples of square-root functions are:

$$f(x) = 3\sqrt{x} + 2 \qquad f(x) = -\sqrt{x} + 5 \qquad f(x) = 0.6\sqrt{x - 1} + 3.$$

Reciprocal Functions

When money is invested at an interest rate of $r\%$, the approximate number of years n it takes to double is given by $n = \dfrac{72}{r}$.

This is an example of a *reciprocal function*.

r	n
5	14.4
7.5	9.6
10	7.2
12.5	5.8
15	4.8

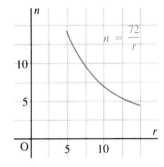

A simple reciprocal function is $f(x) = \dfrac{1}{x}$. There is no point on the graph for $x = 0$, because $\dfrac{1}{x}$ is not defined when $x = 0$. Therefore, the curve, called a *hyperbola*, has two separate branches corresponding to positive and negative values of x. In most applications, the variables are positive and the graph consists of only one branch of the hyperbola.

x	y
-4	-0.25
-2	-0.5
-1	-1
-0.5	-2
-0.25	-4
0.25	4
0.5	2
1	1
2	0.5
4	0.25

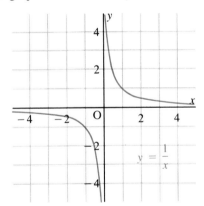

Other examples of reciprocal functions are:

$$f(x) = \frac{1}{x - 3} \qquad f(x) = \frac{1}{x + 4} - 1 \qquad V = \frac{100}{1 + i}.$$

Exponential Functions

The graph shows estimates of the world's
population over the last one thousand years.
This curve is called an *exponential curve*.

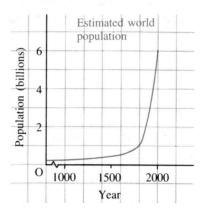

In equations of exponential functions,
the variable occurs in an exponent.
A simple example is the function $f(x) = 2^x$.
In this example the base is 2, but
exponential functions can have any
positive constant as a base.

x	$f(x)$
-3	0.125
-2	0.25
-1	0.5
0	1
1	2
2	4
3	8

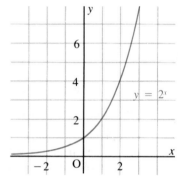

Other examples of exponential functions are $f(x) = 2.5(4^x)$ and
$f(x) = 3^{x-1}$.

Cubic Functions

An example of a cubic function is $f(x) = x^3$.

x	$f(x)$
-3	-27
-2	-8
-1	-1
0	0
1	1
2	8
3	27

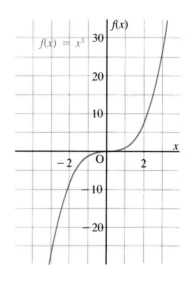

Cubic functions are examples of a large group of
functions called *polynomial functions*. Other
examples of polynomial functions are
$f(x) = x^4 + 2x^3 - x$ and $y = 3x^2 - 2x + 5$.

Absolute-Value Functions

On the number line, the numbers -3 and 3 are each located 3 units from 0. Each number is said to have an absolute value of 3. We write $|-3| = 3$ and $|3| = 3$.

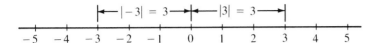

Similarly, we write $|+8| = 8$ to indicate that the number 8 is 8 units from 0, and we write $|-5| = 5$ to indicate that the number -5 is 5 units from 0. Hence, the definition of the absolute value of a number depends on whether the number is positive or negative.

Definition of Absolute Value

If a number is positive or zero, its *absolute value* is the number itself.

If $x \geq 0$, then $|x| = x$

If a number is negative, its *absolute value* is the opposite number.

If $x < 0$, then $|x| = -x$

An example of an absolute-value function is $g(x) = |x|$.

x	$g(x)$
-3	3
-2	2
-1	1
0	0
1	1
2	2
3	3

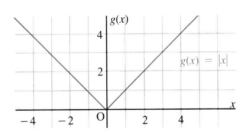

There are two parts to the graph, depending on whether x is positive or negative. If $x \geq 0$, the graph is the same as the graph of $y = x$. If $x < 0$, the graph is the same as the graph of $y = -x$.

In Chapter 6, we found that when certain changes were made in the equation of the quadratic function $f(x) = x^2$, there were corresponding changes in the appearance and position of the parabola. Similarly, when certain changes are made in equations of other functions, the appearance and position of the graphs change but their characteristic shapes do not change. In the following sections, we investigate how the changes in the equations are related to the changes in the graphs.

EXERCISES 7-1

Ⓐ

1. Classify each function as square root, reciprocal, exponential, absolute value, or cubic.

a)

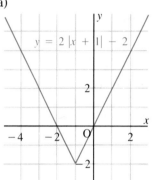

b)

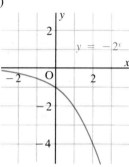

c)

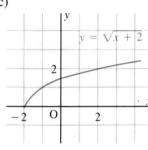

d)

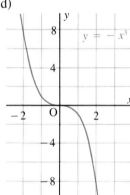

e)

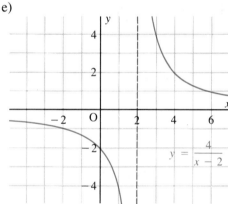

Ⓑ

2. Classify each function.
   a) The height h metres reached by a ball after n bounces is given by $h = 2(0.7)^n$.
   b) A car begins to coast down a hill. The distance d metres it rolls in t seconds is $d = 0.6t^2$.
   c) The length L metres of a steel girder is $L = 8.5 + 0.000\,012(t - 20)$ where t is the temperature in degrees Celsius.
   d) The free end of a diving board dips d centimetres when under a load of x kilograms. The relation is $d = 0.000\,01x^3 + 0.0005x^2$.
   e) The value A dollars of $100 when invested for n years at 10% compounded annually is $A = 100(1.1)^n$.

f) At an interest rate i, the amount P dollars that must be invested now to have $100 in 1 year is $P = \dfrac{100}{1 + i}$.

g) The value V dollars of a car is given by $V = \dfrac{12\ 000}{n + 1} + 400$, where n is its age in years.

h) The number of bacteria N in a culture t hours after midnight is given by $N = 1000(2^t)$.

i) In some rivers near an ocean, the incoming tide creates a single wave called a tidal bore. The speed of the bore v kilometres per hour is given by $v = 11.27\sqrt{d}$, where d is the depth in metres.

j) The percent p of surface light present in an ocean at a depth of d metres is given by $p = 100e^{-0.023d}$, where e is a constant with the approximate value of 2.718.

3. The *identity function* $i(x)$, defined by $i(x) = x$, is a special case of a linear function.
   a) Evaluate. i) $i(3)$ ii) $i(4.5)$ iii) $i(-2.7)$
   b) Graph the identity function. What is the slope of the graph? What is its y-intercept?
   c) Suggest why the name "identity function" is appropriate.

4. A *constant function* is another special case of a linear function.
   a) Given $f(x) = 5$, evaluate: i) $f(2)$ ii) $f(3.4)$ iii) $f(-1.5)$.
   b) Graph the function in part a). What is the slope of the graph? What is its y-intercept?
   c) Suggest why the name "constant function" is appropriate.

5. Exponential Functions
   a) Using a table of values, graph each function.
      i) $f(x) = (1.05)^x$ ii) $f(x) = 2^x$ iii) $f(x) = 3^x$
   b) State the domain and range of each function in part a).
   c) Describe how the graph of $f(x) = a^x$ changes as a varies, $a > 0$.

6. Power Functions
   a) Using values of x between 0 and 2, graph these functions on the same grid.
      i) $f(x) = x^{0.5}$ ii) $f(x) = x^{0.75}$ iii) $f(x) = x^{1.0}$
      iv) $f(x) = x^{1.5}$ v) $f(x) = x^{2.0}$ vi) $f(x) = x^{2.5}$
   b) State the domain and range of each function in part a).
   c) Describe how the graph of $f(x) = x^a$ changes as a varies, $a > 0$ and $x \geq 0$.

Ⓒ

7. Graph each relation and state if it is a function.
   a) $|y| = |x|$ b) $|x| + |y| = 1$ c) $|x + y| = 1$

7-2 GRAPHING $y = f(x) + q$

In the previous chapter, graphs of quadratic functions such as $y = x^2 + 4$ and $y = x^2 - 3$ were obtained from the graph of $y = x^2$ by a vertical translation. This result applies to other functions as well as quadratic functions.

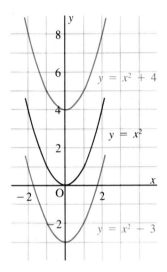

Example 1. Using a table of values, graph these functions on the same grid.
$$y = 2^x \qquad y = 2^x + 4 \qquad y = 2^x - 3$$

Solution.

x	2^x	$2^x + 4$	$2^x - 3$
-2	0.25	4.25	-2.75
-1	0.5	4.5	-2.5
0	1	5	-2
1	2	6	-1
2	4	8	1

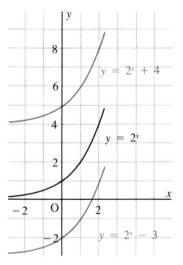

In *Example 1*, the y-coordinates of points on the curve $y = 2^x + 4$ are all 4 greater than those on $y = 2^x$. The curve has been translated 4 units up. Similarly, the y-coordinates of points on the curve $y = 2^x - 3$ are all 3 less than those on $y = 2^x$. The curve has been translated 3 units down. This result suggests how the graphs of other functions may be sketched without making tables of values.

Example 2. Sketch the graph of $y = |x| - 5$.

Solution. Sketch the graph of the absolute-value function $y = |x|$. The graph of $y = |x| - 5$ is then obtained by translating this graph 5 units down.

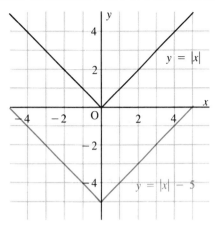

In general, adding a positive or negative constant to any function $y = f(x)$ causes a *vertical translation* of its graph.

The graph of $y = f(x) + q$ is related to that of $y = f(x)$ by a vertical translation.

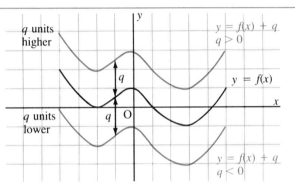

EXERCISES 7-2

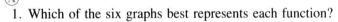

(A)

1. Which of the six graphs best represents each function?

a) $f(x) = 2^x + 1$ b) $f(x) = x^3 - 8$ c) $f(x) = \dfrac{1}{x} + 2$

i)

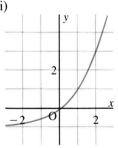

ii)

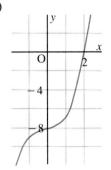

iii)

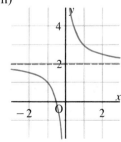

iv) 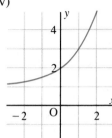 v) 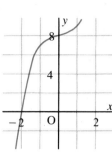 vi)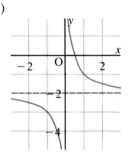

2. Without making tables of values, sketch each set of graphs on the same grid.
   a) $y = |x|$ $y = |x| + 5$ $y = |x| - 3$
   b) $y = \sqrt{x}$ $y = \sqrt{x} + 5$ $y = \sqrt{x} - 3$

(B)

3. Which of the four functions best represents each graph?
   i) $f(x) = |x| + 3$ ii) $f(x) = |x| - 3$ iii) $f(x) = \sqrt{x} + 3$ iv) $f(x) = \sqrt{x} - 3$
   a)   b)

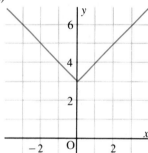   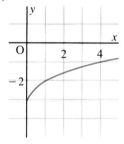

4. Sketch each set of graphs on the same grid.
   a) $y = x^3$ $y = x^3 + 5$ $y = x^3 - 3$
   b) $y = 2^x$ $y = 2^x + 5$ $y = 2^x - 3$
   c) $y = \dfrac{1}{x}$ $y = \dfrac{1}{x} + 5$ $y = \dfrac{1}{x} - 3$

5. Sketch the graph of each function.
   a) $f(x) = \sqrt{x} - 6$ b) $f(x) = |x| + 2$ c) $f(x) = 2^x - 5$
   d) $f(x) = \dfrac{1}{x} + 1$ e) $f(x) = x^3 - 4$

(C)

6. Copy the graph of $y = f(x)$. On the same grid, sketch the graphs of $y = f(x) + 5$ and $y = f(x) - 3$.

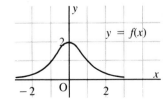

7-3 GRAPHING $y = f(x - p)$

From earlier work, we know that the graphs of quadratic functions such
as $f(x) = (x - 5)^2$ and $f(x) = (x + 2)^2$ can be obtained from the graph
of $f(x) = x^2$ by a horizontal translation. This result applies to other
functions as well as quadratic functions.

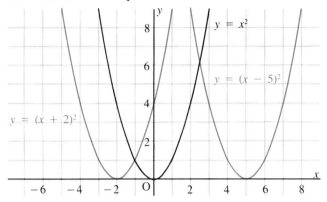

Example 1. Using tables of values, graph these functions on the same grid.
$$y = \sqrt{x} \qquad y = \sqrt{x - 5} \qquad y = \sqrt{x + 2}$$

Solution. $y = \sqrt{x}$ is defined when $x \geq 0$. Use values of x starting at 0.

x	0	1	2	3	4
y	0	1.0	1.4	1.7	2.0

$y = \sqrt{x - 5}$ is defined when $x - 5 \geq 0$, or $x \geq 5$.
Use values of x starting at 5.

x	5	6	7	8	9
y	0	1.0	1.4	1.7	2.0

$y = \sqrt{x + 2}$ is defined when $x + 2 \geq 0$, or $x \geq -2$.
Use values of x starting at -2.

x	-2	-1	0	1	2
y	0	1.0	1.4	1.7	2.0

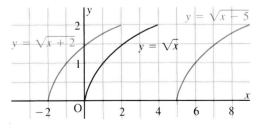

In *Example 1*, the x-coordinates of points on the curve $y = \sqrt{x} - 5$ are all 5 greater than those of the corresponding points on $y = \sqrt{x}$. The curve has been translated 5 units right. Similarly, the x-coordinates of points on $y = \sqrt{x} + 2$ are all 2 units less than those of the corresponding points on $y = \sqrt{x}$. The curve has been translated 2 units left. This result suggests how the graphs of other functions may be sketched without making tables of values.

Example 2. Sketch the graph of $y = \dfrac{1}{x - 3}$.

Solution. Sketch the graph of the reciprocal function $y = \dfrac{1}{x}$. The graph of $y = \dfrac{1}{x - 3}$ is then obtained by translating this graph 3 units right.

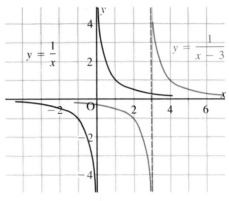

In general, adding a positive or negative constant to the variable x in any function $y = f(x)$ causes a *horizontal translation* of its graph.

The graph of $y = f(x - p)$ is related to that of $y = f(x)$ by a horizontal translation.

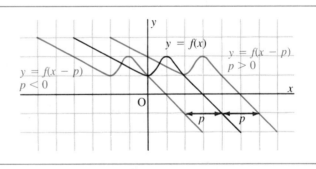

EXERCISES 7-3

Ⓐ

1. Which of the six graphs best represents each function?

   a) $f(x) = \sqrt{x + 3}$ b) $f(x) = 2^{x-3}$ c) $f(x) = \dfrac{1}{x - 2}$

   i)
   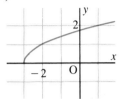

   ii)
   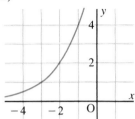

   iii)
   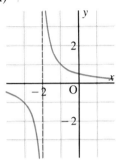

   iv)
   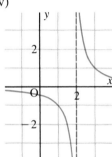

   v)
   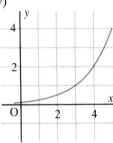

   vi)
   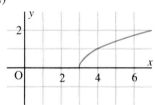

2. Without making tables of values, sketch each set of graphs on the same grid.
   a) $y = |x|$ $y = |x + 2|$ $y = |x - 5|$
   b) $y = x^3$ $y = (x + 2)^3$ $y = (x - 5)^3$

Ⓑ

3. Which of the four functions best represents each graph?
   i) $f(x) = |x + 3|$ ii) $f(x) = |x - 3|$ iii) $f(x) = (x + 2)^3$ iv) $f(x) = (x - 2)^3$
   a)   b)

   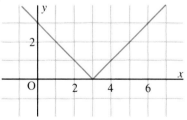

   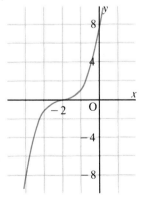

4. Sketch each set of graphs on the same grid.

   a) $y = 2^x$ $y = 2^{x+2}$ $y = 2^{x-5}$

   b) $y = \dfrac{1}{x}$ $y = \dfrac{1}{x + 2}$ $y = \dfrac{1}{x - 5}$

   c) $y = \sqrt{x}$ $y = \sqrt{x + 2}$ $y = \sqrt{x - 5}$

5. Sketch the graph of each function.

   a) $f(x) = (x - 1)^3$ b) $f(x) = |x + 7|$ c) $f(x) = \sqrt{x - 2}$

   d) $f(x) = \dfrac{1}{x - 3}$ e) $f(x) = 2^{x+3}$

6. Sketch the graph of each function.

   a) $f(x) = |x - 2| + 4$ b) $f(x) = \sqrt{x + 3} - 2$

   c) $f(x) = (x + 5)^3 + 3$ d) $f(x) = \dfrac{1}{x - 4} - 1$

Ⓒ

7. Copy the graph of $y = f(x)$. On the same grid, sketch the graphs of $y = f(x + 2)$ and $y = f(x - 5)$.

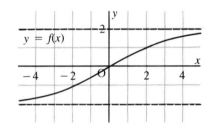

8. a) Using a table of values, graph $f(x) = \dfrac{1}{x^2 + 1}$.

   b) Without using a table of values, sketch the graph of each function.

   i) $f(x) = \dfrac{1}{(x - 3)^2 + 1}$ ii) $f(x) = \dfrac{1}{(x + 2)^2 + 1}$ iii) $f(x) = \dfrac{1}{x^2 + 10x + 26}$

9. The *rounding function*, $y = rnd(x)$ is defined to be the integer closest to x. If there are two integers closest to x, then y is the greater of these integers.

   a) Evaluate.

        i) $rnd(3.2)$ ii) $rnd(5.7)$ iii) $rnd(7.5)$

        iv) $rnd(-2.5)$ v) $rnd(-4.1)$ vi) $rnd(-6.9)$

   b) Graph the function $y = rnd(x)$.

   c) Find the value of k such that $rnd(x) = int(x + k)$, where *int* is the greatest integer function defined in Section 5-3, *Exercise 14*.

7-4 GRAPHING $y = af(x)$

We know that the graphs of quadratic functions such as $y = 2x^2$ and $y = \frac{1}{2}x^2$ can be obtained from the graph of $y = x^2$ by a vertical expansion or compression. Functions such as $y = -x^2$ involve a reflection in the x-axis. Similar results are obtained with functions other than quadratic functions.

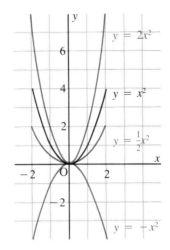

Example 1. Using a table of values, graph $y = x^3$ and $y = 2x^3$ on the same grid.

Solution.

x	x^3	$2x^3$
-2	-8	-16
-1	-1	-2
0	0	0
1	1	2
2	8	16

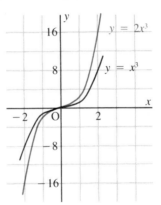

In *Example 1*, the y-coordinates of points on the curve $y = 2x^3$ are all twice as great as those on $y = x^3$. The curve has been expanded vertically.

Similarly, a curve such as $y = \frac{1}{2}x^3$ is compressed vertically.

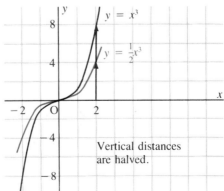

Vertical distances are halved.

A curve such as $y = -x^3$ is a reflection in the x-axis of $y = x^3$.

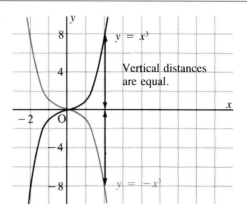

These results suggest how the graphs of other functions may be sketched without making tables of values.

Example 2. Sketch the graph of $y = -\dfrac{2}{x}, x > 0$.

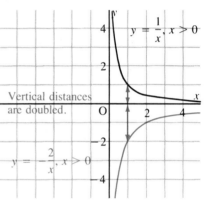

Solution. Sketch the graph of $y = \dfrac{1}{x}$. Since

$-\dfrac{2}{x} = -2\left(\dfrac{1}{x}\right)$, the graph of

$y = -\dfrac{2}{x}$ is obtained by a vertical

expansion with a factor of 2 followed by a reflection in the x-axis.

In *Example 2*, since x was restricted to positive values, only one branch of the hyperbola is shown. This restriction is reasonable because in most applications of reciprocal functions the variables represent positive quantities.

The graph of $y = af(x)$ is related to that of $y = f(x)$ by a vertical expansion or compression and/or a reflection in the x-axis if a is negative.

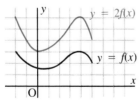

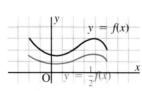

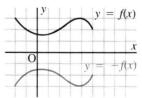

All vertical distances are doubled.

All vertical distances are halved.

The graph is reflected in the x-axis.

EXERCISES 7-4

Ⓐ

1. Which graph best represents each function?

   a) $f(x) = -\dfrac{1}{2}\sqrt{x}$ b) $f(x) = 0.25x^3$ c) $f(x) = -2^x$

   i) 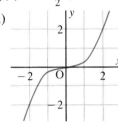   ii) 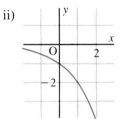   iii)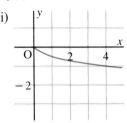

2. Without making tables of values, sketch each set of graphs on the same grid.

   a) $y = |x|$ $y = 3|x|$ $y = -\dfrac{1}{2}|x|$ b) $y = \dfrac{1}{x}$ $y = 3\left(\dfrac{1}{x}\right)$ $y = -\dfrac{1}{2}\left(\dfrac{1}{x}\right)$

Ⓑ

3. Which of the four functions best represents each graph?

   i) $f(x) = 2|x|$ ii) $f(x) = -2|x|$ iii) $f(x) = \dfrac{2}{x}$ iv) $f(x) = -\dfrac{2}{x}$

   a) 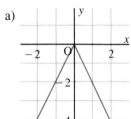   b)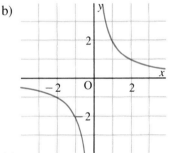

4. Sketch each set of graphs on the same grid.

   a) $y = x^3$ $y = 2x^3$ $y = -0.5x^3$ b) $y = \sqrt{x}$ $y = \dfrac{1}{3}\sqrt{x}$ $y = -2\sqrt{x}$

   c) $y = 2^x$ $y = 0.5(2^x)$ $y = -2^x$

5. Sketch the graph of each function.

   a) $f(x) = \dfrac{3}{x}$ b) $f(x) = -2|x|$ c) $f(x) = 5\sqrt{x}$ d) $f(x) = 1.5(2^x)$

6. Sketch the graph of each function.

   a) $f(x) = 2|x| + 3$ b) $f(x) = 2|x + 3|$ c) $f(x) = \dfrac{2}{x} + 3$ d) $f(x) = \dfrac{2}{x + 3}$

Ⓒ

7. Copy the graph of $y = f(x)$. On the same grid sketch the graphs of $y = 2f(x)$, $y = 0.5f(x)$, and $y = -f(x)$.

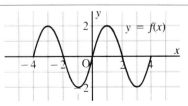

7-5 GRAPHING $y = f(x)$, $y = -f(x)$, AND $y = f(-x)$

We can use the methods of the preceding
sections to compare the graphs of $y = f(x)$
with those of $y = -f(x)$ and $y = f(-x)$.
As an example, consider the graph of
$y = 2^x$ shown at the right.

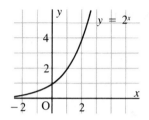

x	-3	-2	-1	0	1	2	3
y	0.125	0.25	0.5	1	2	4	8

Comparing the graphs of $y = f(x)$ and $y = -f(x)$

If we were to graph $y = -2^x$ with a table
of values using the same values of x as in the
table above, we would find that the values
of y are the opposites of those in the table.
Hence, the graph of $y = -2^x$ is reflected in
the x-axis relative to the graph of $y = 2^x$.

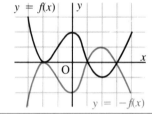

In general, changing the sign of the expression $f(x)$ in the equation of any function
$y = f(x)$ causes its graph to be reflected in
the x-axis.
   The graph of $y = -f(x)$ is a reflection of
the graph of $y = f(x)$ in the x-axis.

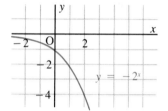

Comparing the graphs of $y = f(x)$ and $y = f(-x)$

If we were to graph $y = 2^{-x}$ with a table of
values we would start with values of x,
change their signs, and then determine the
corresponding powers of 2. To give the same
values of y, the values of x would be the
opposites of those in the table above. Hence,
the graph of $y = 2^{-x}$ is reflected in the
y-axis relative to the graph of $y = 2^x$.

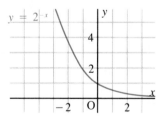

In general, changing the sign of the variable
x in the equation of any function $y = f(x)$
causes its graph to be reflected in the y-axis.
   The graph of $y = f(-x)$ is a reflection of
the graph of $y = f(x)$ in the y-axis.

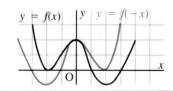

Example. Each graph is the reflection of
the other in the y-axis. Write
the equation of the graph in color.

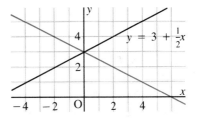

Solution. The equation of the graph is

$$y = 3 - \frac{1}{2}x.$$

EXERCISES 7-5

1. Each graph is a reflection of the other in the x-axis. Find the equation of each
graph in color.

a) 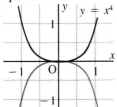   b) 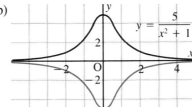   c)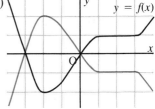

2. Each graph is a reflection of the other in the y-axis. Find the equation of each
graph in color.

a) 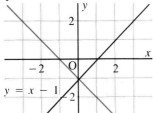   b) 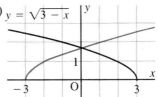   c)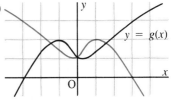

3. Copy each graph and sketch its reflection in the x-axis and the y-axis. Then write
the equation of each reflected graph.

a) 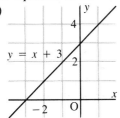   b) 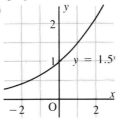   c)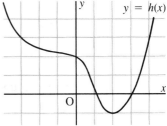

4. Without making tables of values, sketch each set of graphs on the same grid.
   a) $y = |x|$ $y = -|x|$ $y = |-x|$ b) $y = \sqrt{x}$ $y = -\sqrt{x}$ $y = \sqrt{-x}$

5. Find an example of a function that gives the same result when its graph is reflected
in the y-axis as it does when its graph is reflected in the x-axis. Use the equation
of the function to show that the two reflected graphs are the same.

INVESTIGATE

Graphing $y = f(kx)$

In Chapter 6 we did not compare the graphs of $y = x^2$ and $y = (kx)^2$ because the latter equation can be written as $y = k^2x^2$, and its graph is expanded vertically relative to the graph of $y = x^2$. However, suppose we consider the effect on the graph of replacing x with kx in the equation of a more complicated function, such as $y = \dfrac{5\sqrt{x}}{x^2 + 1}$. The graph of this function is shown below.

x	y
0	0
0.5	2.83
1	2.50
1.5	1.88
2	1.41
2.5	1.09
3	0.87
3.5	0.71
4	0.59

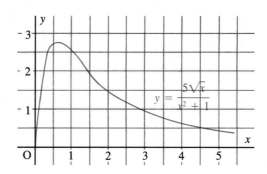

1. **Investigating the graph of $y = \dfrac{5\sqrt{kx}}{(kx)^2 + 1}$**

   a) *Positive values of k*

      i) Substitute $k = \dfrac{1}{2}$ into the equation, and make a table of values for the new equation. If you choose x-coordinates which give the same y-coordinates as those in the table above, you will not need to do any calculations. Then graph the corresponding function. How does the graph compare with the graph above?

      ii) Repeat part i) for $k = 2$.

   b) *Negative values of k*

      i) Substitute $k = -1$ into the equation, and make a table of values for the new equation. Again, use x-coordinates which give the same y-coordinates as those in the table above. Then graph the corresponding function. How does the graph compare with the graph above?

      ii) Repeat part i) for $k = -\dfrac{1}{2}$ and for $k = -2$.

2. Using the results of *Question 1* as a guide, make a summary of the effect on the graph of $y = f(x)$ of multiplying x by a constant k to get $y = f(kx)$.

3. Copy the graph of $y = f(x)$ given in Section 7-2, *Exercise 6*. On the same grid, sketch the graphs of $y = f\left(\frac{1}{2}x\right)$ and $y = f(2x)$.

4. a) Copy the graph of $y = f(x)$ given in Section 7-3, *Exercise 7*. On the same grid, sketch the graphs of $y = f\left(\frac{1}{2}x\right)$, and $y = f(2x)$.

   b) On another grid, sketch the graphs of $y = f(-x)$, $y = f\left(-\frac{1}{2}x\right)$, and $y = f(-2x)$.

5. a) Copy the graph of $y = f(x)$ given in Section 7-4, *Exercise 7*. On the same grid, sketch the graphs of $y = f\left(\frac{1}{2}x\right)$ and $y = f(2x)$.

   b) On another grid, sketch the graphs of $y = f(-x)$, $y = f\left(-\frac{1}{2}x\right)$, and $y = f(-2x)$.

6. a) Copy the graph of $y = f(x)$. On the same grid, sketch the graphs of $y = f\left(\frac{1}{2}x\right)$ and $y = f(2x)$.

   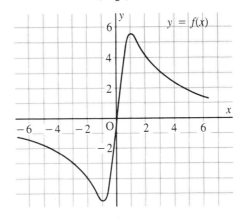

   b) On another grid, sketch the graphs of $y = f(-x)$, $y = f\left(-\frac{1}{2}x\right)$, and $y = f(-2x)$.

   c) The equation of the function $y = f(x)$ is $y = \dfrac{10x}{x^2 + 1}$. Write the equations of the images.

7. a) Graph the function $y = x^2$.

   b) Graph the image of $y = x^2$ when it is compressed horizontally by a factor of $\frac{1}{2}$. What is the equation of the image?

   c) Graph the image of $y = x^2$ when it is expanded vertically by a factor of 4. What is the equation of the image?

   d) Compare the results of parts b) and c). Explain how it is possible that the same image graph can be obtained by two different transformations.

8. *Question 7* shows that a horizontal compression of $y = x^2$ is equivalent to a vertical expansion. Similarly, a horizontal expansion of $y = x^2$ is equivalent to a vertical compression. Hence, it is not necessary to consider horizontal expansions and compressions of $y = x^2$ since these are equivalent to vertical compressions and expansions, which were studied earlier. Investigate whether this is true for the other functions studied previously in this chapter.

   - the square root function $y = \sqrt{x}$
   - the reciprocal function $y = \dfrac{1}{x}$
   - exponential functions such as $y = 2^x$
   - the cubic function $y = x^3$
   - the absolute value function $y = |x|$.

7-6 GRAPHING $y = af(x - p) + q$

In previous sections we investigated the effects of the constants a, p, and q on the graphs of such functions as $y = ax^3$, $y = 2^x + q$, and $y = \sqrt{x - p}$. We now consider the combined effects of these constants on the graph of a function such as $y = 2|x - 4| + 3$. The numbers in the equation indicate how to obtain its graph from the graph of $y = |x|$.

$$y = 2|x - 4| + 3$$

Vertical expansion   Translate   . . .and
by a factor of 2   4 units right. . .   3 units up

To graph the function, follow these steps.

Step 1. Graph $y = |x|$.

Step 2. Graph $y = 2|x|$.

Step 3. Translate all points on the graph in Step 2, 4 units to the right and 3 units up.

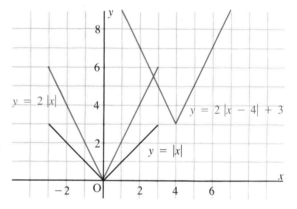

The first two steps are useful because they aid in visualizing the appearance of the graph. They can often be omitted, as Example 1 shows.

Example 1. Graph. $y = -\dfrac{1}{2}(x + 1)^3 + 2$

Solution. The numbers in the equation indicate how the graph is obtained from the graph of the cubic function $y = x^3$.

$$y = -\frac{1}{2}(x + 1)^3 + 2$$

Reflect in x-axis.   Translate   . . .and
Vertical   1 unit left. . .   2 units up
compression

by a factor of $\dfrac{1}{2}$

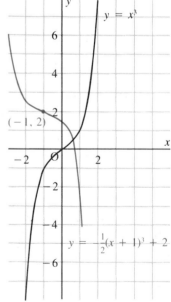
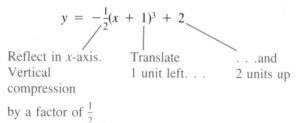

Example 2.   The speed of a vehicle v kilometres per hour can be estimated from the length d metres of its skid marks. If $v = 12.6\sqrt{d} + 8$, where $5 \leq d \leq 60$, sketch a graph of v as a function of d without making a table of values.

Solution.   The numbers in the equation indicate how the graph is obtained from the graph of the square-root function $v = \sqrt{d}$.

$$v = 12.6\sqrt{d} + 8$$

Vertical expansion   Translate
by a factor of 12.6   8 units up

The v-coordinates of the endpoints of the graph can be found with a calculator and serve to determine the scales for the axes. A third point $(0,8)$, the maximum speed at which the vehicle leaves no skid marks, enables an approximation of the graph to be drawn.

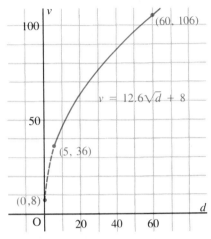

The diagram below illustrates how the graph of the function defined by $y = af(x - p) + q$ is determined by the graph of $y = f(x)$ and the values of the constants a, p, and q.

Transformations of Functions

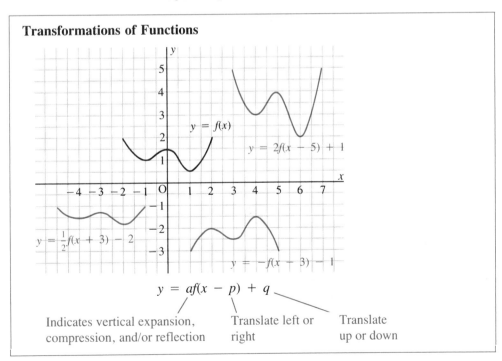

$$y = af(x - p) + q$$

Indicates vertical expansion,   Translate left or   Translate
compression, and/or reflection   right   up or down

EXERCISES 7-6

Ⓐ

1. Which graph best represents each function?

   a) $f(x) = 2\sqrt{x - 2} + 2$

   b) $f(x) = \dfrac{1}{x + 3} - 1$

   c) $f(x) = 0.5(x + 2)^3 + 1$

   i) 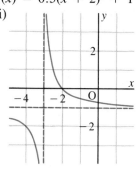 ii) 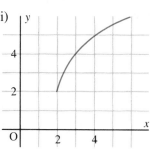 iii)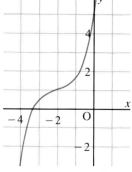

2. Sketch each pair of graphs on the same grid without making a table of values.

   a) $y = 2|x + 4| - 3$ $y = \frac{1}{2}|x + 4| - 3$

   b) $y = 2(2^x) + 4$ $y = \frac{1}{2}(2^x) + 4$

Ⓑ

3. Which of the four functions best represents each graph?

   i) $f(x) = 2|x + 3| - 1$ ii) $f(x) = -|x - 2| + 4$
   iii) $f(x) = 0.5(2^{x-1}) + 1$ iv) $f(x) = -2^{x+1} - 1$

   a) 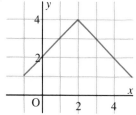   b)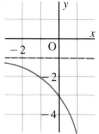

4. Sketch each pair of graphs on the same grid without making a table of values.

   a) $y = 3\sqrt{x + 5} - 1$ $y = -\sqrt{x - 2} + 3$

   b) $y = \frac{1}{2}(x + 2)^3 - 4$ $y = -x^3 + 2$

5. Sketch the graph of each function.

   a) $f(x) = \frac{1}{2}|x - 6| + 1$ $f(x) = -|x + 3| - 2$

   b) $f(x) = \dfrac{3}{x - 2} + 1$ $f(x) = \dfrac{-1}{x + 4} - 2$

6. The cost per hour C dollars of operating a power boat is given by the formula $C = 40 + 0.005v^3$, where v is the average speed in kilometres per hour. Which graph best represents this function?

a)

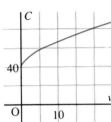

b)

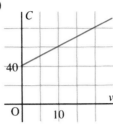

c)

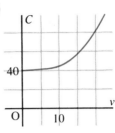

7. The value of a gravel pit V millions of dollars is given by the formula $V = \dfrac{24}{n + 1} + 1$, where n is the number of tonnes of gravel that have been removed from the pit. Which graph best represents this function?

a)

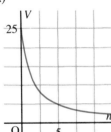

b)

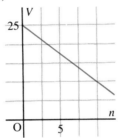

c)

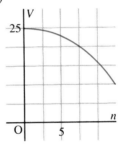

8. The amount of money A dollars that must be invested now at an interest rate i, to have \$100 after 1 year is given by $A = \dfrac{100}{1 + i}$. Without making a table of values, sketch a graph showing A as a function of i.

9. The value V hundreds of dollars of a home computer system is given by $V = \dfrac{8}{n + 1} + 1$, where n is its age in years. Without making a table of values, sketch a graph showing V as a function of n.

Ⓒ

10. The graph of $y = \dfrac{1}{x^2 + 1}$ is shown.

Sketch the graph of each function, showing the coordinates of the maximum or minimum point.

a) $y = \dfrac{3}{x^2 + 1}$

b) $y = \dfrac{-1}{(x - 2)^2 + 1}$

c) $y = \dfrac{2}{(x + 1)^2 + 1} + 3$

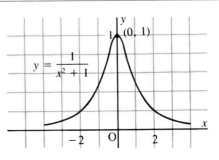

11. The graph of a function $y = f(x)$ is shown. Sketch each pair of graphs on the same grid.

a) $y = f(x)$ and $y = f(x - 2) + 4$
b) $y = f(x)$ and $y = 3f(x + 1)$
c) $y = f(x)$ and $y = \frac{1}{2}f(x + 3) - 2$
d) $y = f(x)$ and $y = -f(x - 2) - 1$

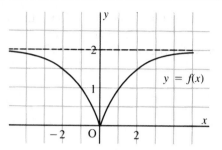

◉ INVESTIGATE

Classifying Functions

In earlier work, certain functions were classified as linear and others as quadratic. There are other ways that functions can be classified.

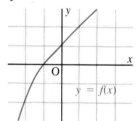

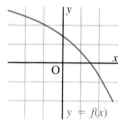

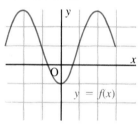

Increasing

As x increases $f(x)$ increases

Decreasing

As x increases $f(x)$ decreases

Periodic

There is a repeating pattern in the graph.

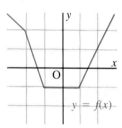

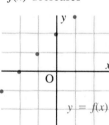

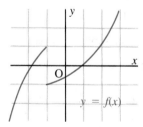

Piecewise Linear

The graph has parts all of which are linear.

Discrete

The graph consists of separate points.

Discontinuous

The graph cannot be drawn without lifting the pencil.

Refer to the functions in the examples and exercises of Chapters 5, 6, and 7.

1. Find at least two functions of each kind illustrated above.

2. Find an example of a function which has none of the above properties.

7-7 THE INVERSE OF A LINEAR FUNCTION

In previous sections we saw that when certain changes were made in the equation of a function, there was a corresponding change in its graph. We shall now investigate the effect of interchanging x and y in the equation of a function.

Consider the linear function $y = 3x + 2$. If x and y are interchanged, we get $x = 3y + 2$.

Solve for y.

$$3y = x - 2$$

$$y = \frac{x - 2}{3}$$

$$y = \frac{1}{3}x - \frac{2}{3}$$

This is also a linear function.

Graphical Comparison of $y = 3x + 2$ and $y = \dfrac{x - 2}{3}$

To compare the graphs of $y = 3x + 2$ and $y = \dfrac{x - 2}{3}$, consider first their tables of values.

$y = 3x + 2$

x	y
0	2
1	5
2	8

$y = \dfrac{x - 2}{3}$

x	y
2	0
5	1
8	2

The tables show that when x and y are interchanged in the equation $y = 3x + 2$, the coordinates of the points which satisfy the equation are interchanged as well.

The graph suggests that the line $y = \dfrac{x - 2}{3}$ is the reflection of the line $y = 3x + 2$ in the line $y = x$. To verify this, consider the line segment AB joining corresponding points A(1,5) and B(5,1).

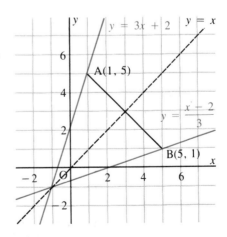

The midpoint of AB is $\left(\dfrac{1 + 5}{2}, \dfrac{5 + 1}{2}\right)$, or (3,3).

The slope of AB is $\dfrac{1 - 5}{5 - 1} = \dfrac{-4}{4}$, or -1.

(3,3) is on the line $y = x$, and -1 is the negative reciprocal of the slope of the line. Therefore, the line $y = x$ is the perpendicular bisector of AB. Other pairs of corresponding points give similar results.

When x and y are interchanged in the equation of a function:
- the coordinates of the points which satisfy the equation of the function are interchanged.
- the graph of the function is reflected in the line $y = x$.

Algebraic Comparison of $y = 3x + 2$ and $y = \dfrac{x - 2}{3}$

Let x be any number; for example, 4.
When $x = 4$, $y = 3x + 2$ becomes:

$y = 3(4) + 2$, or 14 $\quad\rightarrow\quad$ When $x = 14$, $y = \dfrac{x - 2}{3}$ becomes:

$$y = (14 - 2) \div 3, \text{ or } 4$$

Multiply by 3. Add 2.   Subtract 2.   Divide by 3.

Inverse operations

The function $y = \dfrac{x - 2}{3}$ is called the *inverse* of the function $y = 3x + 2$.

To find the inverse of a function:
- interchange x and y in the equation of the function
- solve the resulting equation for y

Example 1. Find the inverse of $y = 3 - 7x$.

Solution. Interchange x and y: $\quad x = 3 - 7y$
Solve for y: $\quad\quad\quad\quad 7y = 3 - x$

$$y = \frac{3 - x}{7}$$

The equation of the inverse function is $y = \dfrac{3 - x}{7}$.

To express the inverse of a function $f(x)$ in function notation, we use the symbol $f^{-1}(x)$. We say, "f inverse of x". In *Example 1*, the result could be written $f^{-1}(x) = \dfrac{3 - x}{7}$.

When the graph of a function is given, its inverse can be graphed as a reflection in the line $y = x$.

Example 2. Given the graph of $y = f(x)$, graph $y = f^{-1}(x)$ and $y = x$ on the same grid.

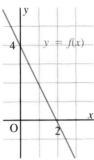

Solution.   Since $y = f(x)$ is linear, only two points are needed to graph $y = f^{-1}(x)$. The simplest ones to use are the intercepts: $(0,4) \rightarrow (4,0)$, and $(2,0) \rightarrow (0,2)$. The graph of the inverse function is the straight line through $(4,0)$ and $(0,2)$. This is the reflection of the given line in the line $y = x$.

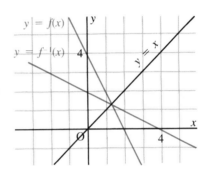

EXERCISES 7-7

(A)

1. On each grid, is one function the inverse of the other function?

a)

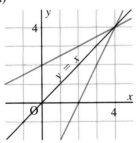

b)

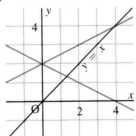

c)

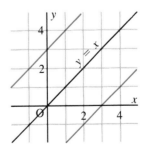

2. Find the inverse of each function.

a) $y = x + 3$

b) $y = 4x - 1$

c) $y = 2x$

d) $y = 3x - 4$

e) $y = \frac{1}{2}x + 6$

f) $y = \frac{2}{3}x - 1$

3. Graph each function, its inverse, and $y = x$ on the same grid.

   a) $y = -\frac{1}{2}x + 3$ b) $y = 3x - 3$ c) $y = -x + 2$

   d) $y = 2x + 4$ e) $y = x + 5$ f) $y = 2x$

4. Two linear functions are described in words. Is each function the inverse of the other?

   a) i) Multiply by 2, then add 5.   ii) Subtract 5, then divide by 2.

   b) i) Multiply by 2, then add 5.   ii) Divide by 2, then subtract 5.

   c) i) Add 1, then multiply by 6.   ii) Subtract 1, then divide by 6.

   d) i) Add 1, then multiply by 6.   ii) Divide by 6, then subtract 1.

Ⓑ

5. Find the inverse of each function.

   a) $f(x) = x + 6$ b) $f(x) = 2x$ c) $f(x) = 3 - x$

   d) $f(x) = \frac{1}{2}x - 3$ e) $f(x) = 5x + 1$ f) $f(x) = 2(1 + x)$

6. Determine if one function is the inverse of the other function.

   a) $y = 2x + 3$ $y = 3x + 2$ b) $y = \frac{1}{2}x - 4$ $y = 2x - \frac{1}{4}$

   c) $y = 4x - 1$ $y = \frac{x + 1}{4}$ d) $y = 3x - 6$ $y = \frac{1}{3}x + 2$

7. Which of the five functions given below is the inverse of each function?

   a) $y = \frac{1}{2}x - 5$ b) $y = 2x + 5$ c) $y = 5(x - 2)$

   i) $y = \frac{1}{2}x + 5$ ii) $y = -\frac{1}{5}x + 2$ iii) $y = 2x + 10$

   iv) $y = \frac{1}{5}x + 2$ v) $y = \frac{1}{2}(x - 5)$

Ⓒ

8. Show that the inverse of the linear function $y = mx + b$ is a function, provided that $m \neq 0$.

9. Since the inverse of a linear function is a linear function it, too, has an inverse. Find the inverse of the inverse of $f(x) = 2x + 5$.

 INVESTIGATE

Find a linear function which is its own inverse.
How many such functions are there? What properties do they have?
Write a report of your findings.

7-8 THE INVERSE OF A QUADRATIC FUNCTION

The inverse of a quadratic function can be found using the same steps
as for a linear function.

Example 1. Given $f(x) = x^2 + 4$

a) Find the inverse of $f(x)$, and graph it and $y = f(x)$ on the same grid.

b) Is the inverse of $f(x)$ a function?

Solution.

a) To find the inverse of $f(x)$,
interchange x and y in
$y = x^2 + 4$:
$x = y^2 + 4$
Solve for y: $y^2 = x - 4$
$y = \pm\sqrt{x - 4}$
$f(x) = x^2 + 4$ is a parabola
with vertex $(0,4)$, opening up,
with axis of symmetry the y-axis.
The inverse, $y = \pm\sqrt{x - 4}$,
can be graphed by reflecting
$y = f(x)$ in $y = x$.

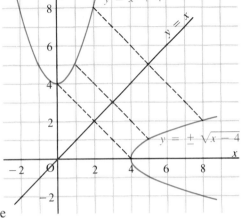

b) The inverse is not a function because
it fails the vertical-line test.

As *Example 1* indicates, the graph of the inverse of a quadratic
function is a parabola with a horizontal axis of symmetry. The example
also shows that the inverse of a quadratic function is not necessarily a
function.

It is sometimes convenient to restrict the domain of a quadratic
function so that its inverse is a function. Since the graph is a parabola,
the restriction requires limiting the values of x to those on one side
or the other of the axis of symmetry.

Example 2. Show two different ways of restricting the domain of $f(x) = x^2 + 4$ so
that its inverse is a function. Illustrate with graphs.

Solution. The domain of $y = x^2 + 4$ is
restricted to non-negative real
numbers.
That is, $y = x^2 + 4$, $x \geq 0$
Then the inverse is
$y = \sqrt{x - 4}$.

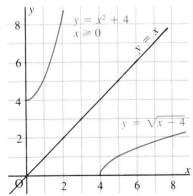

The domain of $y = x^2 + 4$ is restricted to non-positive real numbers.

That is, $y = x^2 + 4$, $x \leqslant 0$

Then the inverse is

$y = -\sqrt{x - 4}$.

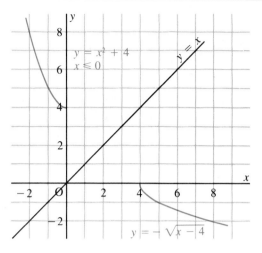

In each case, the inverse is a function because it passes the vertical-line test.

EXERCISES 7-8

Ⓐ

1. Find the inverse of each function.

    a) $y = x^2$ b) $y = x^2 - 1$ c) $y = x^2 + 3$

    d) $y = 2x^2 + 5$ e) $y = \frac{1}{4}x^2 - 2$ f) $y = \dfrac{x^2 - 2}{4}$

2. Graph each function, its inverse, and $y = x$ on the same grid.

    a)   b)   c)

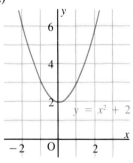 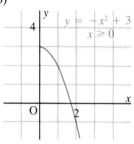 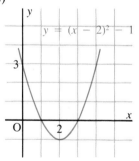

    d) $y = x^2 - 3$ e) $y = 2x^2 + 1$ f) $y = \frac{1}{3}x^2 - 2$

(B)

3. Find the inverse of each function.
   a) $f(x) = 4x^2$
   b) $f(x) = 1 - x^2$
   c) $f(x) = 2 - 3x^2$
   d) $f(x) = (x + 3)^2$
   e) $f(x) = 5(x - 2)^2$
   f) $f(x) = \frac{1}{2}(x + 1)^2 - 3$

4. Restrict the domain so that the inverse of each function is a function. Illustrate with a graph.
   a) $y = x^2 - 1$
   b) $y = x^2 + 2$
   c) $y = (x + 1)^2$
   d) $y = (x - 2)^2 + 1$
   e) $y = -2x^2 + 3$
   f) $y = \frac{1}{3}(x - 1)^2 - 2$

5. Determine if the second function is the inverse of the first function.
   a) $y = x^2 + 6,\ x \geqslant 0$ $y = \sqrt{x + 6}$

   b) $y = 2x^2 - 3,\ x \leqslant 0$ $y = -\sqrt{\dfrac{x + 3}{2}}$

   c) $y = 4(x + 1)^2,\ x \leqslant -1$ $y = \dfrac{\sqrt{x} - 2}{2}$

   d) $y = \frac{1}{3}(x - 2)^2 + 5,\ x \leqslant 2$ $y = -\sqrt{3x + 3}$

6. Which of the five functions given below is the inverse of each function?
   a) $y = x^2 - 12,\ x \geqslant 0$
   b) $y = -\frac{1}{2}x^2 + 3,\ x \geqslant 0$
   c) $y = 3(x - 1)^2 - 2,\ x \geqslant 1$

   i) $y = \frac{1}{3}\sqrt{x + 3}$ ii) $y = \sqrt{x + 12}$ iii) $y = 2\sqrt{x - 3}$

   iv) $y = \sqrt{\dfrac{x + 2}{3}} + 1$ v) $y = \sqrt{6 - 2x}$

(C)

7. Find the inverse of each function, then graph the function, its inverse, and $y = x$.
   a) $y = 1 + \sqrt{x}$
   b) $y = 3 - 2\sqrt{x}$

7-9 THE EQUATION OF A CIRCLE WITH CENTRE (0,0)

A circle is a set of points in the plane which are the same distance from a point called the *centre*. This distance is called the *radius*. An equation that is satisfied by all points P(x,y) on a circle, and only those points, is called the *equation of the circle*.

Example 1. The sun is the centre of our solar system. Of all the planets orbiting the sun, the orbit of Venus is closest to being circular. Find the equation of the path of Venus around the sun if the radius of its path is 108 Gm (1 Gm = 1 × 10⁹ m).

Solution. Let O(0,0) represent the position of the sun. At any point P(x,y) in its orbit, Venus is 108 Gm from O. That is, OP = 108
By the Pythagorean Theorem,
$x^2 + y^2 = 108^2$
The equation of the path of Venus around the sun is $x^2 + y^2 = 11\ 664$.

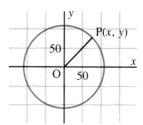

Using the method of *Example 1*, we can find the equation of any circle with centre O(0,0) and radius r. If P(x,y) is any point on the circle, OP = r and $x^2 + y^2 = r^2$. The coordinates of any point not on the circle do not satisfy this equation.

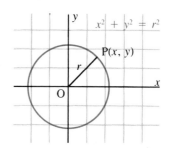

The equation of a circle with centre (0,0) and radius r is $x^2 + y^2 = r^2$.

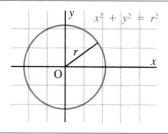

Example 2. Given the circle $x^2 + y^2 = 16$
a) State:
    i) the coordinates of the centre ii) the radius
    iii) the diameter iv) the x-intercepts
    v) the y-intercepts.
b) Graph the circle.

Solution.   a)   i) The coordinates of the centre are (0,0).

ii) $r^2 = 16$
Since $r > 0$, $r = 4$
The radius of the circle is 4.

iii) The diameter of the circle is 8.

iv) The x-intercepts are 4 and -4.

v) The y-intercepts are 4 and -4.

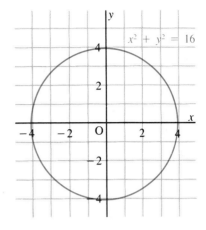

EXERCISES 7-9

Ⓐ

1. Write the equation of each circle with centre (0,0) and given radius.
   a) 5   b) 12   c) 16   d) 6.25   e) 0.3   f) 23

2. Given the circle $x^2 + y^2 = 25$
   a) State:
      i) the coordinates of the centre   ii) the radius
      iii) the diameter   iv) the x-intercepts
      v) the y-intercepts.
   b) Graph the circle.

3. a) What is the radius of each circle?
      i) $x^2 + y^2 = 81$ ii) $x^2 + y^2 = 121$ iii) $x^2 + y^2 = 64$
      iv) $x^2 + y^2 = \dfrac{49}{4}$ v) $x^2 + y^2 = 36$ vi) $x^2 + y^2 = 2.25$
   b) Graph each circle in part a).

4. An endpoint of a diameter of the circle $x^2 + y^2 = r^2$ is $(3, -4)$.
   a) What is the radius of the circle?
   b) What are the coordinates of the other endpoint of the diameter?

Ⓑ

5. Find the equation of the circle with centre (0,0) which passes through each point.
   a) (3,0)   b) (0,-4)   c) (5,2)   d) (-1,3)

6. Find the value of r if the point $(3, -7)$ lies on $x^2 + y^2 = r^2$.

7. The following points lie on $x^2 + y^2 = 32$. Find each value of k.
   a) (4,k)   b) (k,5)   c) (k,$2\sqrt{7}$)   d) ($2\sqrt{5}$,k)

8. a) Graph the circle $x^2 + y^2 = 100$.
   b) On the same graph, plot the points (6,8), $(-10,1)$, and $(-7,-7)$.
   c) Determine whether the points are on the circle, inside the circle, or outside the circle.

9. Determine whether each point is on, inside, or outside the circle $x^2 + y^2 = 64$.
   a) $(5,6)$ b) $(8,1)$ c) $(-4,7)$

10. Which of the following points are inside the circle $x^2 + y^2 = 20$?
    a) $(1,-2)$ b) $(4,2)$ c) $(-3,3)$ d) $(0,4)$ e) $(5,-1)$

11. a) A line segment has endpoints A(6,2) and B(2,-6). Show that AB is a chord of the circle $x^2 + y^2 = 100$.
    b) Find the equation of the perpendicular bisector of chord AB.
    c) Show that the perpendicular bisector is a diameter of the circle.

12. a) A line segment has endpoints M(8,6) and N(-6,8). Show that MN is a chord of the circle $x^2 + y^2 = 100$.
    b) Find the equation of the line that passes through the centre of the circle and the midpoint of chord MN.
    c) Show that the line in part b) is perpendicular to the chord MN.

13. a) A line segment has endpoints P(2,5) and Q(5,-2). Show that PQ is a chord of the circle $x^2 + y^2 = 29$.
    b) Find the equation of the line perpendicular to the chord PQ that passes through the centre of the circle.
    c) Show that the line in part b) passes through the midpoint of chord PQ.

ⓒ

14. Describe the graph of each equation.
    a) $x^2 + y^2 = 0$ b) $x^2 + y^2 = -9$
    c) $y = \sqrt{25 - x^2}$ d) $x = \sqrt{25 - y^2}$

15. Four circles, each with radius 5, touch the x- and y-axes and a smaller circle with centre (0,0). Find the equation of the smaller circle.

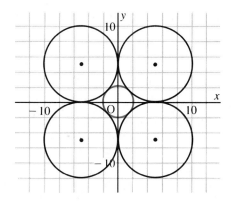

INVESTIGATE

The equation $x^2 + y^2 = r^2$ represents a circle with centre (0,0) and radius r. What do these equations represent?
$$x^2 - y^2 = 9 \qquad x^2 + 4y^2 = 4 \qquad x^4 + y^4 = 16 \qquad \sqrt{x} + \sqrt{y} = 4$$
Investigate other equations like these and write a report of your findings.

7-10 TRANSFORMING THE EQUATION OF A CIRCLE

In earlier sections of this chapter, certain changes were made in the equations of various functions. These changes resulted in translations, and expansions or compressions of their graphs. Although it does not represent a function, the equation of a circle can be transformed in a similar way. These transformations result in similar changes to the graph of the circle.

Translations

The graph of $x^2 + y^2 = 9$ is a circle, centre the origin and radius 3. Compare its equation with this equation.

$$(x - 2)^2 + (y + 5)^2 = 9 \ldots ①$$
$$x^2 + y^2 = 9 \ldots ②$$

Each equation states that the sum of the squares of two numbers is 9. In equation ①, to give the same numbers whose squares add to 9 as in equation ②, the values of x must be 2 *greater* than those in equation ②. Similarly, the values of y must be 5 *less* than those in equation ②.

Every point whose coordinates satisfy equation ① must be 2 units to the *right* of, and 5 units *below*, the corresponding point whose coordinates satisfy equation ②. Hence, the graph of $(x - 2)^2 + (y + 5)^2 = 9$ is a translation of the graph of $x^2 + y^2 = 9$. Equation ① represents a circle with centre $(2, -5)$, radius 3.

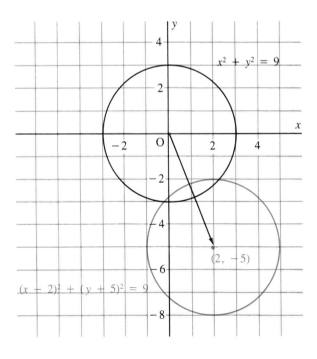

Compressions and Expansions

Compare the equation of the circle $x^2 + y^2 = 9$ with this equation.

$x^2 + (2y)^2 = 9 \ldots \text{③}$

$x^2 + y^2 = 9 \ldots \text{②}$

As before, each equation states that the sum of the squares of two numbers is 9. In equation ③, to give the same numbers whose squares add to 9 as in equation ②, the values of y must be *one-half* of those in equation ②.

Every point whose coordinates satisfy equation ③ must be one-half the distance from the x-axis as the point is whose coordinates satisfy equation ②. Hence, the graph of $x^2 + (2y)^2 = 9$ is a *vertical compression* $\left(\text{of factor } \frac{1}{2}\right)$ of the graph of $x^2 + y^2 = 9$.

Equation ③ represents an ellipse with x-intercepts 3 and -3 (the same x-intercepts as equation ②) and y-intercepts 1.5 and -1.5 (one-half the y-intercepts of equation ②).

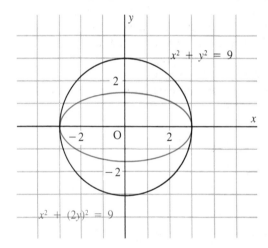

Compare these two equations.

$\left(\dfrac{x}{3}\right)^2 + y^2 = 9 \ldots \text{④}$

$x^2 + y^2 = 9 \ldots \text{②}$

In equation ④, to give the same numbers whose squares add to 9 as in equation ②, the values of x must be 3 *times* those in equation ②.

Every point whose coordinates satisfy equation ④ must be 3 times the distance from the y-axis as the point is whose coordinates satisfy equation ②. Hence, the graph of $\left(\dfrac{x}{3}\right)^2 + y^2 = 9$ is a *horizontal expansion* (of factor 3) of the graph of $x^2 + y^2 = 9$.

Equation ④ represents an ellipse with x-intercepts 9 and -9 (3 times the x-intercepts of equation ②) and y-intercepts 3 and -3 (the same y-intercepts as equation ②).

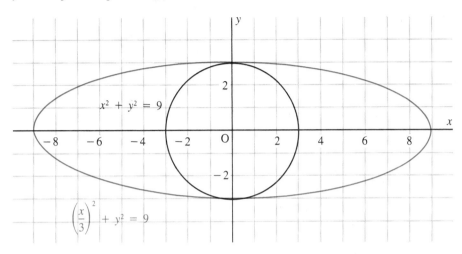

Example 1. Graph each relation.

a) $x^2 + y^2 = 4$

b) $(x + 5)^2 + (y - 1)^2 = 4$

c) $x^2 + \left(\dfrac{y}{3}\right)^2 = 4$

Solution. a) $x^2 + y^2 = 4$ represents a circle, centre $(0, 0)$ and radius 2.

b) $(x + 5)^2 + (y - 1)^2 = 4$ represents a circle, centre $(-5, 1)$ and radius 2. It is a translation of the circle $x^2 + y^2 = 4$, 5 units left and 1 unit up.

c) $x^2 + \left(\dfrac{y}{3}\right)^2 = 4$ is a vertical expansion, of factor 3, of the circle $x^2 + y^2 = 4$. Hence, the equation represents an ellipse with x-intercepts 2 and -2, and y-intercepts 6 and -6.

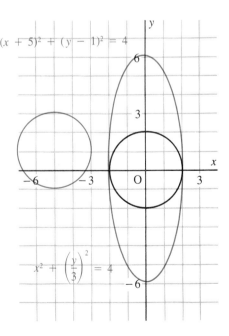

In general
- The graph of $(x - h)^2 + (y - k)^2 = r^2$ is related to the graph of $x^2 + y^2 = r^2$ by a translation of h units horizontally and k units vertically.
- The graph of $\left(\dfrac{x}{a}\right)^2 + \left(\dfrac{y}{b}\right)^2 = r^2$ is related to the graph of $x^2 + y^2 = r^2$ by:
  — a horizontal expansion of factor a if $a > 1$, or a horizontal compression if $0 < a < 1$
  — a vertical expansion of factor b if $b > 1$, or a vertical compression if $0 < b < 1$.

Example 2. Graph the relation $\left(\dfrac{x}{2}\right)^2 + (y - 2)^2 = 1$.

Solution. Compare the given equation with the circle $x^2 + y^2 = 1$, with centre $(0, 0)$ and radius 1.

$$\left(\frac{x}{2}\right)^2 + (y - 2)^2 = 1 \ldots \text{①}$$

$$x^2 + y^2 = 1 \ldots \text{②}$$

Consider the squared terms.

$\left(\dfrac{x}{2}\right)^2$ indicates a horizontal expansion of factor 2. Hence, the circle centre $(0, 0)$ becomes an ellipse with x-intercepts 2 and -2, and y-intercepts 1 and -1.

$(y - 2)^2$ indicates a vertical translation of 2 units. Hence, the ellipse is translated vertically, and its centre is $(0, 2)$.

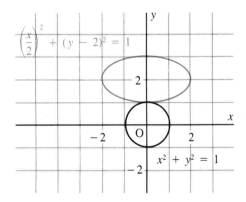

Example 3. What changes must be made to the equation $x^2 + y^2 = 1$ to produce each graph? Write the equation of each graph.

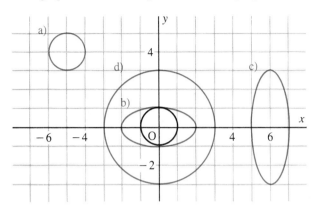

Solution. The circle $x^2 + y^2 = 1$ has centre $(0, 0)$ and radius 1.

a) To produce this graph, the circle has been translated 5 units left and 4 units up. Hence, its equation is $(x + 5)^2 + (y - 4)^2 = 1$.

b) To produce this graph, the circle has been expanded horizontally by a factor of 2. Hence, its equation is $\left(\dfrac{x}{2}\right)^2 + y^2 = 1$.

c) To produce this graph, the circle has been expanded vertically by a factor of 3, and translated 6 units right. Hence, its equation is

$$(x - 6)^2 + \left(\dfrac{y}{3}\right)^2 = 1.$$

d) To produce this graph, the circle has been expanded horizontally and vertically by a factor of 3. Its equation is $\left(\dfrac{x}{3}\right)^2 + \left(\dfrac{y}{3}\right)^2 = 1$, or $x^2 + y^2 = 9$.

EXERCISES 7-10

Ⓐ

1. State the coordinates of the centre, and the radius of each circle.
   a) $(x - 4)^2 + (y - 1)^2 = 36$
   b) $(x - 2)^2 + (y + 5)^2 = 9$
   c) $(x + 7)^2 + (y + 3)^2 = 16$
   d) $(x + 2)^2 + (y - 2)^2 = 5$
   e) $x^2 + (y - 8)^2 = 25$
   f) $(x + 3)^2 + y^2 = 13$

2. Graph each circle in *Exercise 1*.

3. Identify the translation required to transform the graph of a circle, centre $(0, 0)$ to each given graph.
   a) $(x + 4)^2 + y^2 = 49$
   b) $(x - 3)^2 + y^2 = 25$
   c) $x^2 + (y + 7)^2 = 64$
   d) $(x - 1)^2 + (y - 2)^2 = 16$
   e) $(x + 1)^2 + (y + 1)^2 = 36$
   f) $(x + 3)^2 + (y + 2)^2 = 9$

4. Graph each circle in *Exercise 3*.

5. Write the equation of each circle.

a)

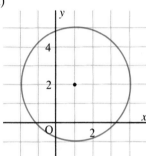

b)

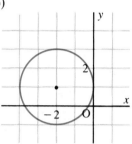

c)

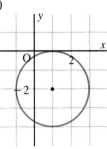

6. The graph of the circle $x^2 + y^2 = 4$ is translated so that the coordinates of its centre have the values given. Write the equation of the circle after each translation.
   a) $(3, -1)$ b) $(-2, 5)$ c) $(-1, -4)$
   d) $(0, -3)$ e) $(2, 9)$ f) $(-6, 0)$

7. State whether the expansion or compression indicated in each equation is horizontal or vertical.

   a) $x^2 + (3y)^2 = 16$ b) $x^2 + \left(\dfrac{y}{2}\right)^2 = 36$

   c) $(5x)^2 + y^2 = 81$ d) $\left(\dfrac{x}{4}\right)^2 + y^2 = 25$

   e) $(7x)^2 + y^2 = 144$ f) $\left(\dfrac{x}{3}\right)^2 + \left(\dfrac{y}{4}\right)^2 = 81$

(B)

8. A circle has centre $(3, 0)$ and radius 5.
   a) Find the equation of the circle.
   b) Find the coordinates of the points of intersection of the circle and the axes.

9. State whether each circle has:
   a) its radius less than 5
   b) its centre on the *x*-axis
   c) its centre on the line $y = x$.
     i) $(x - 3)^2 + (y - 3)^2 = 1$ ii) $(x + 2)^2 + (y - 4)^2 = 9$
     iii) $x^2 + (y + 7)^2 = 13$ iv) $(x - 5)^2 + y^2 = 20$
     v) $(x + 1)^2 + (y + 1)^2 = 25$ vi) $x^2 + y^2 = 32$

10. Graph each relation.
    a) $(x + 2)^2 + y^2 = 25$ b) $x^2 + (2y)^2 = 36$

    c) $\left(\dfrac{x}{2}\right)^2 + y^2 = 16$ d) $(x - 3)^2 + (y + 1)^2 = 9$

    e) $(3x)^2 + \left(\dfrac{y}{2}\right)^2 = 16$ f) $\left(\dfrac{x}{4}\right)^2 + \left(\dfrac{y}{2}\right)^2 = 4$

11. What changes must be made to the equation $x^2 + y^2 = 4$ to produce each graph? Write the equation of each graph.

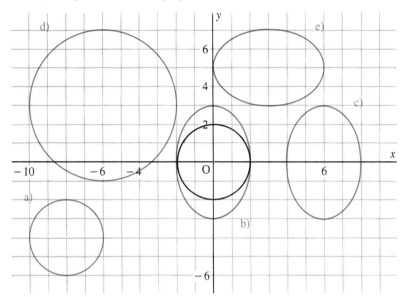

12. Graph each relation.

a) $(x + 2)^2 + (2y)^2 = 4$

b) $\left(\dfrac{x}{3}\right)^2 + (y - 2)^2 = 9$

c) $(x + 5)^2 + \left(\dfrac{4y}{3}\right)^2 = 16$

d) $(3x)^2 + (y + 1)^2 = 36$

e) $\left(\dfrac{2x}{3}\right)^2 + (y - 5)^2 = 9$

f) $(x + 1)^2 + \left(\dfrac{y}{2}\right)^2 = 4$

13. a) Graph the circle $(x - 5)^2 + (y + 3)^2 = 49$.

   b) Determine if points $A(10, 2)$, $B(-1, -6)$, and $C(5, -10)$ lie on the circle.

14. Graph $(x + 3)^2 + (y - 1)^2 = 25$ and $(x - 4)^2 + (y - 5)^2 = 9$. Do the circles intersect?

Ⓒ ───────────────────────────────────────

15. Graph each relation.

a) $\left(\dfrac{x - 1}{2}\right)^2 + \left(\dfrac{y + 1}{3}\right)^2 = 4$

b) $[3(x + 1)]^2 + [2(y - 1)]^2 = 9$

c) $[4(x - 2)]^2 + \left[\dfrac{y - 3}{2}\right]^2 = 16$

d) $\left(\dfrac{x + 3}{2}\right)^2 + [2(y + 2)]^2 = 25$

16. Graph the circle $(x + 4)^2 + (y - 2)^2 = 20$. If this circle just touches the circle $(x - 2)^2 + (y - 5)^2 = r^2$, find the value of r.

17. A circle passes through the points $A(0, 7)$ and $B(4, 3)$. If its centre lies on the line $y = 2x$, find the equation of the circle.

 PROBLEM SOLVING

Elegance in Mathematics

"Strange as it may sound, the power of mathematics rests on its evasion of all unnecessary thought and on its wonderful saving of mental operations."

Ernst Mach

In Mr. Ferguson's class there are 25 students seated in 5 rows with 5 seats each. One day he instructed his students to change seats as follows. Each student must move one seat forward or backward, *or* one seat to the left or right. Is this possible? If it is, show how it can be done; if not, prove that it is impossible.

Understand the problem
- Does every student have to change her or his seat?
- Which seats can a student move to?
- Are diagonal moves permitted?

Think of a strategy
- Draw a diagram.
- You might try labelling the seats and recording some moves. But sooner or later it will become difficult to keep track of them.
- It might help to number the seats from 1 to 25.

1	2	3	4	5
6	7	8	9	10
11	12	13	14	15
16	17	18	19	20
21	22	23	24	25

Carry out the strategy
- Some seats have even numbers, and some have odd numbers.
- Where do the students in seats with odd numbers go?
- Is it possible for every student in a seat with an odd number to move to a seat with an even number? Why?
- Can all the students change seats as Mr. Ferguson instructed?

Look back
- How many students could change seats in this way? How could they do this?
- If there were 6 rows with 6 students in each row, could they change seats as Mr. Ferguson instructed?
- Discuss how the solution of this problem illustrates the above quotation by Ernst Mach.

PROBLEMS

Ⓑ

1. If a certain natural number is doubled, the result is a perfect square. If the number is tripled, the result is a perfect cube. Find the number.

2. Two squares from opposite corners of a checkerboard are removed, as shown. Determine if it is possible to place 31 dominoes on the remaining 62 squares (a domino covers two adjacent squares). If it is possible, show how it can be done; if not, prove that it is impossible.

3. Find a rule that you could use to tell whether or not the decimal expansion of the fraction $\frac{1}{n}$ terminates or repeats. Prove that your rule is correct.

Ⓒ

4. One morning the McDougall family hiked up a trail into the mountains. They camped overnight and returned home the next day, using the same trail as the day before. Prove that there is some point on the trail where they were at the same time on both days.

5. Early yesterday morning, as I was preparing to go to a meeting, I noticed that my watch was losing time. When my watch read 7:00, I heard on the radio that it was 7:10 A.M. When my watch read 8:00, I got a transfer on the subway showing that the time was 8:15 A.M.
   a) At the meeting, we had lunch when my watch read 12:00. What time was it then?
   b) The meeting was scheduled to end at 4:00 P.M. How was I able to tell from my watch when it was 4:00 P.M.?
   c) What assumptions are you making in your solutions to parts a) and b)?

6. Prove Viviani's Theorem: In any equilateral triangle, the sum of the three distances from any point to the sides of the triangle is a constant.

Ⓓ

7. Sue went to the post office to buy twelve 38¢ stamps and one 44¢ stamp. She was surprised that the total cost was exactly $5.00. Find all the other whole dollar amounts that can be spent on 38¢ and 44¢ stamps.

7-11 QUADRATIC INEQUALITIES IN TWO VARIABLES

The graph shows the circle defined by the equation $(x - 2)^2 + (y - 3)^2 = 25$. The circle divides the plane into *three* regions.

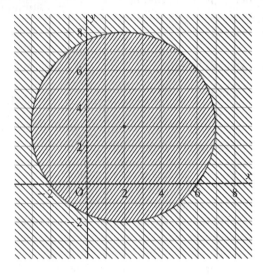

- *Region 1* contains all the points *on* the circle. These points have coordinates which satisfy the given equation. For example, the point $(-1, 7)$ is on the circle. It satisfies the equation, as shown below.

$$\text{Left side} = (x - 2)^2 + (y - 3)^2$$
$$= (-1 - 2)^2 + (7 - 3)^2$$
$$= 9 + 16$$
$$= 25$$
$$= \text{Right side}$$

For points on the circle,
$(x - 2)^2 + (y - 3)^2 = 25$

- *Region 2* contains all points *inside* the circle. If the coordinates of a point inside the circle are substituted into the left side of the equation, the result is *less than* the right side. For example, the point $(4, 2)$ is inside the circle. Substitute into the equation.

$$\text{Left side} = (x - 2)^2 + (y - 3)^2$$
$$= (4 - 2)^2 + (2 - 3)^2$$
$$= 4 + 1$$
$$= 5 \text{ which is less than 25, the right side}$$

For points inside the circle, $(x - 2)^2 + (y - 3)^2 < 25$

- *Region 3* contains all points *outside* the circle. If the coordinates of a point outside the circle are substituted into the left side of the equation, the result is *greater than* the right side. For example, the point $(8, -2)$ is outside the circle. Substitute into the equation.

$$\text{Left side} = (x - 2)^2 + (y - 3)^2$$
$$= (8 - 2)^2 + (-2 - 3)^2$$
$$= 36 + 25$$
$$= 61 \text{ which is greater than 25, the right side}$$

For points outside the circle, $(x - 2)^2 + (y - 3)^2 > 25$

To graph an inequality, follow these steps.

Step 1. Graph the corresponding equation.

Step 2. Select a point whose coordinates satisfy the inequality.

Step 3. Plot that point on the grid and shade in the region that contains it.

Example 1. Graph the inequality $(x + 2)^2 + (y + 1)^2 < 9$.

Solution. The corresponding equation is
$(x + 2)^2 + (y + 1)^2 = 9$.
This is a circle, centre $(-2, -1)$
and radius 3.
A point which satisfies the
inequality is $(0, 0)$, since
$(0 + 2)^2 + (0 + 1)^2 < 9$.
Since the point $(0, 0)$ lies
inside the circle, that region
is shaded.

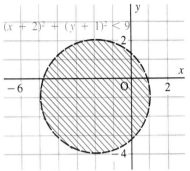

In *Example 1*, the circle is drawn as a broken curve because the
symbol $<$ indicates that the curve is not part of the inequality.

Example 2. Graph the inequality $y \geq (x + 4)^2 - 2$.

Solution. The corresponding equation is
$y = (x + 4)^2 - 2$. This is a
parabola which opens up, with
vertex $(-4, -2)$ and axis of
symmetry $x = -4$.
A point which satisfies the
inequality is $(-4, 0)$, since
$0 > (-4 + 4)^2 - 2$.
Since the point $(-4, 0)$ lies
inside the parabola, shade
this region.

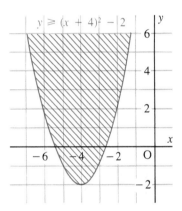

In *Example 2*, the parabola is drawn as a solid curve, because the
symbol $\geq$ indicates that the curve is part of the inequality.

EXERCISES 7-11

1. State the coordinates of a point which satisfies each inequality.
   a) $(x - 1)^2 + y^2 \leq 16$
   b) $(x + 3)^2 + (y - 7)^2 > 81$
   c) $y \leq (x + 2)^2 - 5$
   d) $(x + 4)^2 + (y + 1)^2 < 36$
   e) $y > (x - 3)^2 + 1$
   f) $(x - 2)^2 + (y + 6)^2 \geq 100$

2. State the coordinates of a point which satisfies each inequality, and whether this point is inside or outside the region enclosed by the broken curve.

a)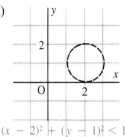

$(x - 2)^2 + (y - 1)^2 < 1$

b)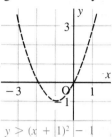

$y > (x + 1)^2 - 1$

c)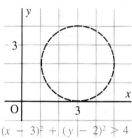

$(x - 3)^2 + (y - 2)^2 > 4$

3. Write an inequality that represents each shaded region.

a)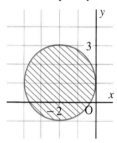

b)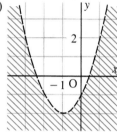

c)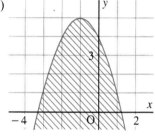

Ⓑ

4. Graph each inequality.
   a) $(x + 1)^2 + (y + 1)^2 < 16$
   b) $(x - 5)^2 + (y - 2)^2 \leq 36$
   c) $y < (x - 3)^2 + 4$
   d) $(x + 1)^2 + (y - 4)^2 \geq 25$
   e) $y \geq (x + 3)^2 - 4$
   f) $(x - 6)^2 + (y + 4)^2 \leq 64$

5. Graph each inequality.

   a) $x^2 + \left(\dfrac{y}{2}\right)^2 < 4$

   b) $\left(\dfrac{x}{3}\right)^2 + y^2 \geq 9$

   c) $(2x)^2 + y^2 > 36$

   d) $x^2 + \left(\dfrac{2y}{3}\right)^2 \leq 16$

   e) $\left(\dfrac{x}{3}\right)^2 + \left(\dfrac{y}{2}\right)^2 < 16$

   f) $(3x)^2 + \left(\dfrac{y}{2}\right)^2 \geq 36$

Ⓒ

6. Graph the region defined by each pair of inequalities.
   a) $(x - 2)^2 + (y + 4)^2 < 36$ and $(x - 2)^2 + (y + 4)^2 > 9$
   b) $(x + 3)^2 + (y - 1)^2 \geq 16$ and $(x - 1)^2 + (y - 2)^2 < 9$

   c) $(x - 1)^2 + y^2 > 25$ and $(x - 1)^2 + \left(\dfrac{y}{2}\right)^2 < 25$

   d) $(x + 4)^2 + (y - 2)^2 > 4$ and $y > (x + 4)^2 - 3$

   e) $y > (x - 1)^2 - 3$ and $\left(\dfrac{2x}{3}\right)^2 + (y - 1)^2 \geq 4$

   f) $y > (x - 3)^2 - 2$ and $y < -(x - 2)^2 + 4$

1. a) Using a table of values, graph each function.

   i) $y = \dfrac{1}{x}$
   ii) $y = \dfrac{1}{2x}$
   iii) $y = \dfrac{1}{4x} + 1$

   b) State the domain and range of each function in part a).

2. Which function best represents each graph?

   i) $y = 2^x + 2$
   ii) $y = 2^x - 2$
   iii) $y = \dfrac{1}{x} - 2$
   iv) $y = x^3 - 2$

   a)

   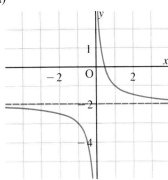

   b)

   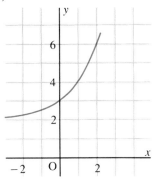

   c)

   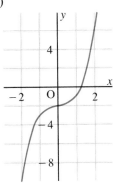

   d)

   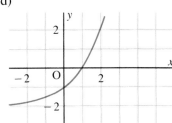

3. Without making tables of values, sketch each set of graphs on the same grid.
   a) $y = |x|$ $y = |x - 2|$ $y = |x + 2|$
   b) $y = x^3$ $y = (x - 2)^3$ $y = (x + 2)^3$

4. Without making tables of values, sketch each set of graphs on the same grid.
   a) $y = \dfrac{1}{x}$ $y = \dfrac{2}{x}$ $y = -\dfrac{2}{x}$
   b) $y = |x|$ $y = 3|x|$ $y = -3|x|$

5. Without making tables of values, sketch each set of graphs on the same grid.
   a) $y = |2x|$ $y = -|2x|$ $y = |-2x|$
   b) $y = \sqrt{\dfrac{1}{2}x}$ $y = -\sqrt{\dfrac{1}{2}x}$ $y = \sqrt{-\dfrac{1}{2}x}$

6. Which function best represents each graph?

i) $f(x) = 0.5(2^{x+1}) - 1$ ii) $f(x) = 2(2^{x-1}) + 1$

iii) $f(x) = -2|x + 1| - 2$ iv) $f(x) = -\frac{1}{2}|x - 1| - 2$

a)

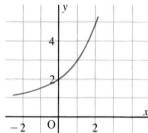

b)

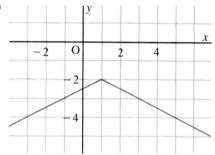

c)

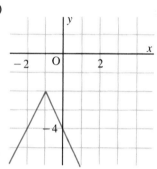

d)

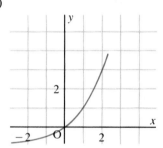

7. The value of a car V thousands of dollars is given by $V = \dfrac{12}{n + 1} + 3$, where n is its age in years. Without making a table of values, sketch a graph showing V as a function of n.

8. Find the inverse of each function.

  a) $f(x) = x + 3$ b) $f(x) = 3x$ c) $f(x) = 2 + x$

  d) $f(x) = \frac{1}{4}x + 1$ e) $f(x) = 4x + 3$ f) $f(x) = 3(2 - x)$

9. Find the inverse of each function.

  a) $f(x) = 9x^2$ b) $f(x) = 4 - x^2$ c) $f(x) = 1 - 4x^2$

  d) $f(x) = (x - 2)^2$ e) $f(x) = 3(x - 1)^2$ f) $f(x) = \frac{1}{3}(x - 2)^2 + 5$

10. Find the equation of the circle with centre $(0,0)$ which passes through each point.

  a) $(0, -2.5)$ b) $(7,3)$ c) $(5, -5)$ d) $(-1, -7)$

11. The graph of the circle $x^2 + y^2 = 9$ is translated so that the coordinates of its centre have the values given. Write the equation of the circle after each translation.

  a) $(-2, -3)$ b) $(-5,4)$ c) $(1,7)$

12. Graph each inequality.

  a) $(x - 2)^2 + (y + 3)^2 > 25$ b) $y \leq (x - 1)^2 - 3$

8 Circle Geometry

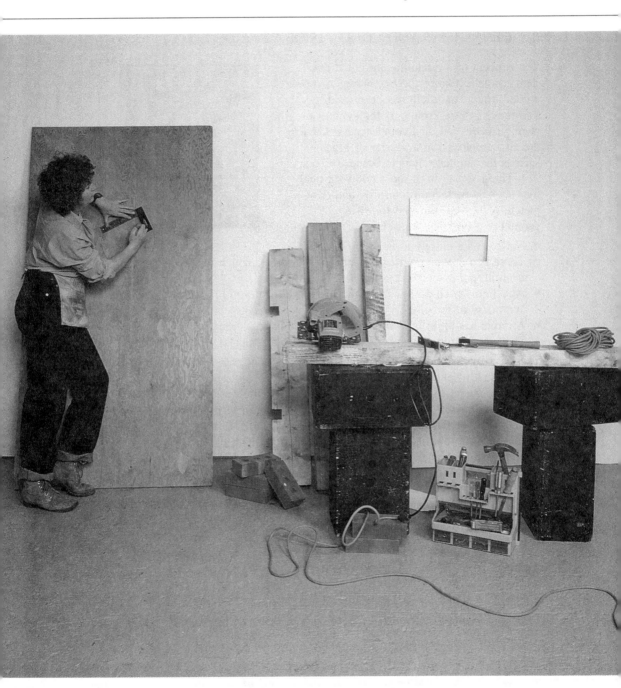

How can a carpenter find the centre of a circle drawn on a wooden panel, using only a try square? (See Section 8-3 *Example 3*.)

8-1 DEFINITIONS AND CONCEPTS OF A CIRCLE

The concept of a circle has intrigued the human intellect since the beginnings of recorded time. The circle has been used by various religious groups as the symbol of eternity, perfection, and completeness. Circles are also employed in a variety of logos, such as the familiar Olympic Games symbol.

The association of the circle with qualities such as perfection, eternity, and completeness derives from the following geometric properties of circles.

- A circle is a closed curve.
- There is a unique point, the centre of the circle, which is equidistant from all points on the circle.
- Any line which passes through the centre of a circle is a line of symmetry of the circle.
- A circle has an infinite number of lines of symmetry.
- The intersection of a sphere with a plane is a circle.

The last of these properties explains why the sun and the moon (which are essentially spherical) appear to us as disks with a circular rim.

The ancient Ptolemaic theory of planetary motion asserted that each planet moved in a circle about the sun, which in turn moved in a circle about the Earth. This theory was predominant for about 1500 years, until the publication in 1543 of the Copernican theory which asserted that all planets, including the Earth, travel in circular orbits around the sun. We know today that the planets actually travel in elliptical orbits but their orbits are in most cases almost circular. The successive theories of planetary motion are suggestive of the all-pervasive role of the circle in scientific models. This fact alone makes the study of the circle and its geometric properties of critical importance.

We begin our study of circles with some undefined terms (the point, the line, and the plane) together with terms which we defined previously.

Definition: A *circle* is the set of all points which lie a fixed distance, r (called the *radius*) from a fixed point C (called the *centre*).

Using this definition of a circle and its centre together with the terms, point, line, and line segment, we can write definitions of a chord, a diameter, a radius, and a sector of a circle (see *Exercises 3* and *4*).

The diagram below illustrates examples of other familiar terms.

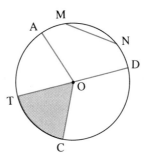

- Point O is the centre of the circle.
- Point A is any point on the circle.
- Line segment OA is a radius.
- Line segment DT (which contains O) is a diameter.
- Line segment MN is a chord.
- TC is an arc.
- The shaded region TOC is a sector, and ∠TOC is the sector angle.

We can use these basic concepts related to circles to solve problems involving circles.

Example. Calculate the perimeter of a regular octagon inscribed in a circle of diameter 15 cm. Each side of the octagon is 6.9 cm from the centre of the circle.

Solution. Draw a diagram.

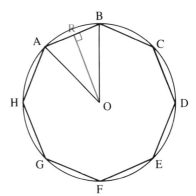

Figure ABCDEFGH is a regular octagon. Join AO and OB, which are radii of the circle.
Then, AO = OB = 7.5 cm
Drop the perpendicular from O onto AB at R.
Then, OR = 6.9 cm
Use the Pythagorean Theorem in △BOR.

$$RB^2 = OB^2 - OR^2$$
$$= 7.5^2 - 6.9^2$$
$$RB = \sqrt{7.5^2 - 6.9^2}$$
$$\doteq 2.939$$
$$AB = 2RB$$
$$\doteq 5.878$$

The perimeter of the octagon is 8(5.878) cm, or about 47 cm.

EXERCISES 8-1

1. What point is equidistant from all the points that lie on a circle?

2. What is the greatest possible distance between two points which lie on a circle with radius R?

3. Define each term as it pertains to a circle.
   a) centre   b) radius   c) diameter   d) chord

4. a) Define the term sector.   b) Can a semicircle be a sector?

5. In how many points can two circles intersect?

6. a) What is the greatest number of points in which three circles can intersect?
   b) What is the least number of points in which three circles can intersect?
   c) Draw diagrams to illustrate three circles intersecting in all possible numbers of points from the least to the greatest.

7. Give a logical argument to prove that any two diameters intersect at the centre of the circle.

8. Two intersecting circles of equal radii are drawn. How many points on each circle are equidistant from both centres?

9. How far is a chord of length 8 cm from the centre of a circle with diameter 10 cm?

10. Calculate the perimeter of each inscribed regular polygon.

   a)

   b)

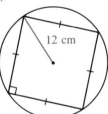

   c)

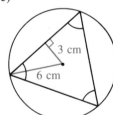

11. a) Prove that any point on the perpendicular bisector of a chord of a circle is equidistant from the ends of the chord.
    b) Write the converse of the theorem in part a) and prove it.
    c) Use part b) to deduce that the centre of a circle lies on the perpendicular bisector of every chord of that circle.
    d) Use part c) to deduce that the point of intersection of the perpendicular bisectors of two (non-parallel) chords of a circle is the centre of that circle.

12. Using the information in *Exercise 11*, describe how to locate the centre of a circular disk using only a ruler (marked in millimetres) and a set square.

8-2 PROPERTIES OF CHORDS IN A CIRCLE

In the construction of a wheel for a train, a
disk is cut from a steel cylinder. A hole
is then drilled in the centre of the circular
disk.

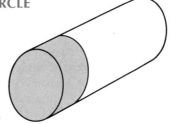

How can the centre of the disk be
located?

The following theorem suggests a method for finding the centre of a
circle using a property of its chords.

Chord Perpendicular Bisector Theorem
The perpendicular bisector of a chord of a circle passes through
the centre of the circle.

Given: A chord AB of a circle with centre O
Required to Prove: The perpendicular bisector of AB
passes through O.
Analysis: Draw the radii OA and OB.
Proof:

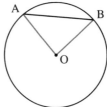

Statement	Reason
OA = OB	Radii
O is on the perpendicular bisector of AB.	Perpendicular Bisector Theorem

Therefore, the perpendicular bisector of AB passes through O.

A theorem that is closely related to another theorem and which is
a self-evident consequence of that theorem is called a *corollary* of that
theorem. The following corollaries of the Chord Perpendicular Bisector
Theorem are easily deduced from this theorem.

Corollary 1
If a radius bisects a chord, then the radius is perpendicular to
that chord.

A radius that bisects a chord passes through the midpoint of the chord
and the centre of the circle. The perpendicular bisector passes through
the same two points. Therefore, the two lines are coincident.

Corollary 2
If a radius is perpendicular to a chord, then the radius bisects
that chord.

A radius that is perpendicular to a chord must be parallel to the perpendicular bisector. Since the radius and the perpendicular bisector both pass through the centre of the circle, they must be coincident.

It follows from the Chord Perpendicular Bisector Theorem that the centre of a circle is the point of intersection of the perpendicular bisectors of any two (non-parallel) chords of the circle.

l is the perpendicular bisector of chord AB.
m is the perpendicular bisector of chord CD.
O is the centre of the circle.

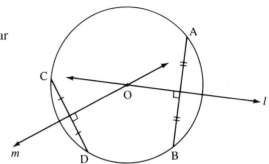

We can use the Pythagorean Theorem and the Chord Perpendicular Bisector Theorem to prove the following important property of chords in a circle.

Theorem

If two chords are equidistant from the centre of a circle, then the chords are congruent.

Given: Chords AB and DE which are equidistant from
    O. That is, OF = OG; OF ⊥ AB; OG ⊥ ED
Required to Prove: AB = DE
Analysis: Draw radii OB and OE.
    Use the Pythagorean Theorem.

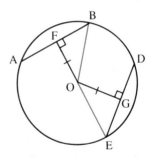

Proof:

Statement	Reason
In △OFB and △OGE	
OF = OG	Given
OB = OE	Radii
∠OFB = ∠OGE = 90°	Given
FB = $\sqrt{OB^2 - OF^2}$	Pythagorean Theorem
GE = $\sqrt{OE^2 - OG^2}$	Pythagorean Theorem
Therefore, FB = GE	OB = OE and OF = OG
FB = $\frac{1}{2}$AB and GE = $\frac{1}{2}$DE	Chord Perpendicular Bisector Theorem
Therefore, AB = DE	

The Pythagorean Theorem can also be used to prove the following converse of the theorem above. (See *Exercise 10*.)

> **Theorem**
> If chords in a circle are equal, then the chords are equidistant from the centre of the circle.

The two theorems above can be combined into a single statement using the "iff" notation. This biconditional statement is called the Equal Chords Theorem.

> **Equal Chords Theorem**
> Chords of a circle are equal iff they are equidistant from the centre.

EXERCISES 8-2

Ⓐ

1. Find each value of *x* to 1 decimal place where necessary.

   a)
   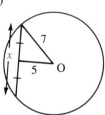
   b)
   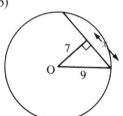
   c)
   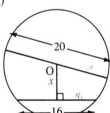

2. Find each value of *x* to 1 decimal place where necessary.

   a)
   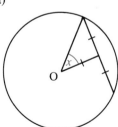
   b)
   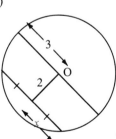
   c)
   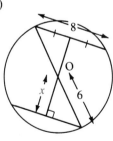

3. A circle has a diameter of 14 cm. How far from the centre of the circle is a chord of length 7 cm?

   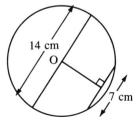

4. Find each value of z to 1 decimal place where necessary.

a) 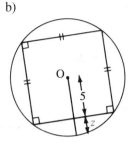   b) 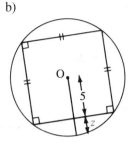   c)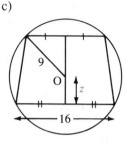

Ⓑ

5. Describe how you would find the centre of a circle which passes through three non-collinear points.

6. Describe how you would find the centre and the radius of a circle which circumscribes (passes through the vertices of) a given triangle.

7. What is the diameter of a circle in which a chord 16 cm long is 15 cm from the centre?

8. The base of a large hemispherical dome (below left) is a circle of diameter 80 m. How far apart are two 20 m parallel support beams which form "chords" of the circular base?

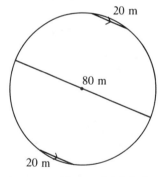

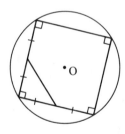

9. A square (above right) is inscribed in a circle of diameter 20 cm. What is the distance between the midpoints of adjacent sides of the square?

10. Copy the statements in this proof and write the reasons.
    Given: Chords AB and DE such that AB = DE
    OF and OG are perpendiculars from
    O to AB and DE respectively.
    Required to Prove: OF = OG
    Analysis: Draw radii OA, OB, OE, and OD to
    produce △OAB and △ODE.

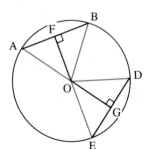

Proof:

Statement	Reason
AB = DE	_____
F and G are the midpoints of AB and DE respectively	_____
Therefore, AF = FB = DG = GE	_____
OB = OE	_____
$\angle OFB = \angle OGE = 90°$	_____
$OF = \sqrt{OB^2 - FB^2}$	_____
$\quad = \sqrt{OE^2 - GE^2}$	_____
$\quad = OG$	_____

11. Copy this proof and fill in the missing statements and reasons.
    Given: PQ and RS are equal chords of a circle centre
    O. PQ and RS intersect at T.
    Required to Prove: PT = ST and QT = RT
    Analysis: Draw perpendiculars OA and OB from O to
    PQ and RS respectively. Draw OT.

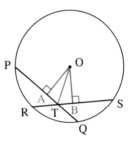

Proof:

Statement	Reason
In △OAT and △OBT	
$\quad \angle OAT = \angle OBT$	_____
$\quad AO = OB$	_____
$\quad$ OT is common.	
Therefore, _____	Hypotenuse-Side Theorem
AT = BT	_____
$PA = \frac{1}{2}PQ$ and $SB = \frac{1}{2}RS$	_____
PQ = RS	_____
Therefore, PA = SB	_____
PA + AT = SB + BT	_____
Therefore, _____	PT = PA + AT and ST = SB + BT
Also, _____	QT = PQ − PT and RT = RS − ST

8-3 PROPERTIES OF ANGLES IN A CIRCLE

When the balls on a billiard table are positioned as shown, the ⑦ ball is easier to sink than the ⑥ ball even though both balls are the same distance from the pocket.

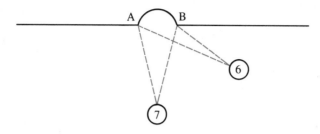

The diagram shows why. The dotted lines show the boundary of the paths for each ball. The permissible paths for the ⑥ ball lie within a small angle. The permissible paths for the ⑦ ball lie within a larger angle. We say that the angle subtended by line segment AB at the ⑦ ball is greater than the angle subtended by AB at the ⑥ ball.

Definition: If AB is a chord of a circle with centre O, then $\angle AOB$ is called the angle *subtended at the centre of the circle* by the chord AB.

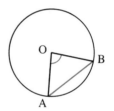

Definition: If C is a point on the circumference of a circle and AB is any chord, then $\angle ACB$ is called an angle *subtended at the circumference of the circle* by chord AB.

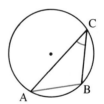

From investigations in previous grades, you may have discovered that the angle subtended at the centre of a circle by a chord is twice the measure of any angle subtended at the circumference of that circle by that same chord (provided both angles are located on the same side of the chord).

> **Angles in a Circle Theorem**
> If the angle at the centre of a circle and an angle at the circumference are subtended by the same chord and lie on the same side of that chord, then the angle at the centre is twice the measure of the angle at the circumference.

Several corollaries can be deduced from this theorem.

Corollary 1

If two angles are subtended by the same chord on the circumference of a circle, and lie on the same side of the chord, then the angles are congruent.

This corollary can be extended to any number of angles subtended by the same arc. In the diagram

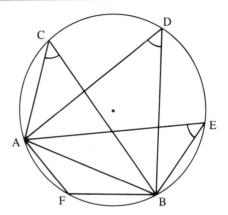

- ∠C = ∠D = ∠E because all these angles are subtended by chord AB and are on the same side of AB.
- ∠F is not equal to the other labelled angles because it is *not* on the same side of chord AB.

    However ∠F is equal to other angles subtended by AB on the same side as ∠F.

Corollary 2

If an angle on the circumference of a circle is subtended by a diameter of the circle, then that angle is a right angle.

In the diagram, AB is a diameter and
∠AOB = 180°.
AB subtends ∠ADB and ∠AEB at the circumference.

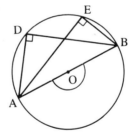

Therefore, $\angle ADB = \frac{1}{2}\angle AOB$
$$= 90°$$
Similarly, ∠AEB = 90°

Corollary 3

If a chord subtends an angle of 90° at the circumference of a circle, then that chord is a diameter of the circle.

The following examples show how the Angles in a Circle Theorem and its corollaries can be used to determine the measures of angles in a circle.

Example 1. In the diagram, the chord AB has a length equal to the radius of the circle, centre O. Find the measure of ∠APB.

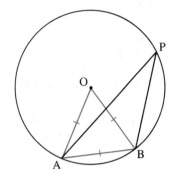

Solution. Join OA and OB.
Since AB is equal to the radius of the circle, △OAB is equilateral.
Hence, ∠AOB = 60°
Since AB subtends ∠O at the centre and ∠P at the circumference,

$$\angle APB = \frac{1}{2}\angle AOB$$

$$= \frac{1}{2}(60°), \text{ or } 30°$$

Example 2. Two lights in the roof of a spherical dome are located at points P and Q. What are the measures of the angles at P and Q subtended by RS?

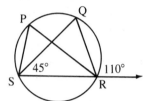

Solution. ∠SRQ = 180° − 110°   (Straight angle)
             = 70°
∠SQR = 180° − ∠SRQ − ∠QSR   (Sum of the Angles Theorem)
             = 180° − 70° − 45°
             = 65°
∠SPR = ∠SQR = 65°   (Corollary 1 of Angles in a Circle Theorem)

Example 3. Use corollary 3 of the Angles in a Circle Theorem to describe how a carpenter can find the centre of a circle using only a try square?

Solution. A try square is used by carpenters for laying out right angles.
● Place the try square so that point P lies on the circle. Trace along the sides of the try square and join XY to form right △XPY, with X and Y on the circle.
● Repeat the procedure. Start at another point Q on the circle to form right △WQZ.

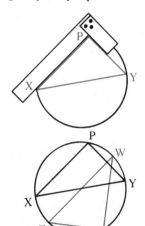

It follows from corollary 3 that XY and WZ are diameters of the circle. Therefore, their point of intersection is the centre of the circle.

EXERCISES 8-3

1. Use the diagram to name the angles in the circle, centre O.
   a) Five angles subtended by chord AB on the circumference of the circle
   b) Two angles subtended by chord AB on the circumference, and located on the same side of AB as ∠AEB
   c) Two angles subtended by chord AB on the circumference, and located on opposite sides of AB
   d) An angle subtended by chord AB on the circumference, and located on the same side as ∠AGB
   e) An angle subtended by chord AB at the centre of the circle.

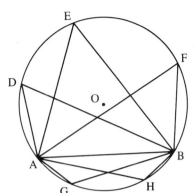

2. a) What is the measure of an angle at the circumference of a circle, subtended by a diameter?
   b) What is the measure of an angle at the centre of a circle, subtended by a diameter?

3. Find each value of x.

a)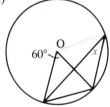

b)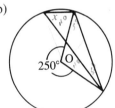

c)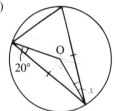

4. Find the values of x, y, and z.

a)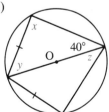

b)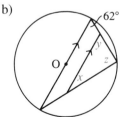

c)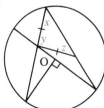

5. AB, BC, DE, and EF are equal chords of a circle with centre O, and ∠BAC = 30°. Find the measures of ∠DEF and ∠DFE.

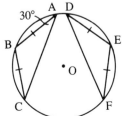

6. Trapezoid ABCD (below left) is inscribed in a circle and AD is parallel to BC. If ∠ABD = 35° and ∠DAC = 40°, find the measures of ∠DAB and ∠ADC.

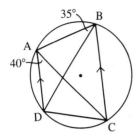
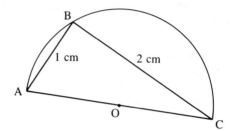

7. Calculate the radius of the semicircle (above right).

Ⓑ

8. Isosceles △ABC is inscribed in a circle of diameter 10 cm. If AB is a diameter, find the length of BC.

9. Copy the statements in this proof and write the reasons.
   Given: AB and AD are equal chords in a circle centre O.
   Required to Prove: ∠OAD = ∠OBA
   Analysis: Join OD.

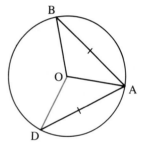

Proof:

Statement	Reason
In △OAD and △OAB	
OD = OB	_____
OA is common.	
DA = AB	_____
Therefore, △OAD ≅ △OAB	_____
But OB = OA = OD	_____
Therefore, △OAD and △AOB are isosceles.	_____
Hence, ∠OAD = ∠OBA	_____

10. Copy the statements in this proof and write the reasons.
   Given: AB and AD are equal chords in a circle
       with diameter AE.
   Required to Prove: ∠BAE = ∠DAE
   Analysis: Join BE and ED.

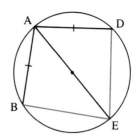

Proof:

Statement	Reason
In △BAE and △DAE	
∠B = ∠D = 90°	_____
AB = AD	_____
BE² = AE² − AB²	_____
= AE² − AD²	_____
= DE²	_____
Hence, BE = DE	
Therefore, △BAE ≅ △DAE	_____
∠BAE = ∠DAE	_____

11. Copy this proof and fill in the missing statements and reasons.
   Given: AB and CD are equal chords of a circle
       centre O.
   Required to Prove: ∠AOB = ∠COD

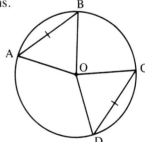

Proof:

Statement	Reason
In △AOB and △COD	
_____	Radii
_____	Radii
_____	Given
Therefore, △AOB ≅ △COD	_____
∠AOB = ∠COD	_____

12. Copy this proof and fill in the missing statement and reasons.
    Given: OD and OE bisect respectively chords AB
    and AC of a circle centre O and diameter
    BC.
    Required to Prove: OD is perpendicular to OE.
    Analysis: Prove that OD is parallel to CA, and CA
    is perpendicular to OE.

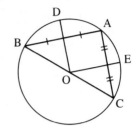

Proof:

Statement	Reason
OD ⊥ AB	_____
∠BAC = 90°	_____
OD ∥ CA	_____
CA ⊥ OE	_____
_____	OD ∥ CA and CA ⊥ OE

13. Copy this proof and fill in the missing statements and reasons.
    Given: Trapezoid PQRS inscribed in a circle so
    that PQ is parallel to SR, and diagonals
    PR and SQ intersect at T
    Required to Prove: TS = TR and PS = QR
    Analysis: To prove TS = TR, we try to prove
    ∠TSR = ∠TRS.
    To prove PS = QR, we try to prove
    △PTS ≅ △QTR.

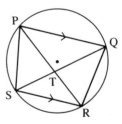

Proof:

Statement	Reason
∠PQS = ∠SRP	_____
∠PQS = ∠QSR	_____
Therefore, ∠SRP = ∠QSR	
_____	Isosceles Triangle Theorem
In △PTS and △QTR	
_____	Opposite Angles Theorem
∠PST = ∠QRT	_____
_____	Proved above
Therefore, _____	ASA
_____	Congruent triangles

14. In the diagram, A, B, C, and D are points on the circumference of a circle with centre O. Explain why:

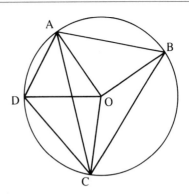

a) $\angle DAC = \frac{1}{2}\angle DOC$

b) $\angle BAC = \frac{1}{2}\angle BOC$

c) $\angle DAB = \frac{1}{2}(\angle DOC + \angle BOC)$

d) $\angle BCD = \frac{1}{2}(\angle BOA + \angle DOA)$

e) $\angle DAB + \angle BCD = 180°$

© —

15. ABCD is a quadrilateral inscribed in a circle with centre O (below left). Prove that $\angle A + \angle C = 180°$ and $\angle B + \angle D = 180°$.

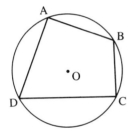

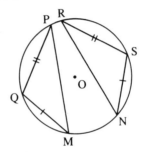

16. PQ and RS are equal chords of a circle with centre O (above right). If M and N are points on the circumference of the circle such that QM = SN, prove that $\angle QMP = \angle RNS$.

17. AB is a chord of a circle, centre O and radius 12 cm. C and D are points on the circle such that $\angle ACB$ and $\angle ADB$ are on opposite sides of chord AB. What is the length of chord AB if $\angle ACB = \angle ADB$?

18. Prove the Angles in a Circle Theorem.

 INVESTIGATE

In the diagram, major arc AOB subtends $\angle APB$ and $\angle AQB$ at the circumference of the circle.

   Does the Angles in a Circle Theorem apply in this situation? If so, do its corollaries also apply?

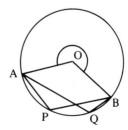

8-4 CONCYCLIC POINTS

Some of the most important theorems in mathematics have grown out of attempts to answer simple questions. Three such questions are posed below.

Question 1: Is there a circle which passes through any two given points?

The diagram suggests that infinitely many circles can be drawn through the two given points A and B.

We can deduce this by observing that any point on the perpendicular bisector of AB is equidistant from A and B (Perpendicular Bisector Theorem) and is therefore the centre of a circle through points A and B.

Since there are infinitely many points on the perpendicular bisector of AB, there are infinitely many circles through A and B.

Question 2: Is there a circle which passes through any three given points?

If the three given points are collinear, then there is no circle which passes through them.

Since A, B, and C are non-collinear, the perpendicular bisectors of AB and BC intersect in a single point O. That is, there is only one point that is equidistant from A, B, and C and therefore only one circle which contains them all.

Since any three non-collinear points form the vertices of a triangle, we can say that for any given triangle there is a unique circle which passes through its vertices. This is called the *circumcircle* of the triangle.

Question 3: Is there a circle which passes through any four given points?

Given any four points (no three of which are collinear) we can find a unique circle which passes through any 3 of them. However, if the points are chosen arbitrarily, the fourth point will not necessarily lie on that circle. The following definition will be helpful in expressing conditions under which four points lie on a circle.

Definition: Any set of points which lie on a circle are said to be *concyclic*.

The search for conditions under which points lie on a circle may now be expressed as the search for conditions under which points are concyclic. The following theorem is the converse of corollary 1 of the Angles in a Circle Theorem.

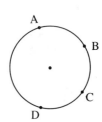

A, B, C, and D are concyclic

> **Theorem**
> If a line segment subtends equal angles at two points on the
> same side of the segment, then the two points and the ends of
> the line segment are concyclic.

The following example illustrates the use of this theorem.

Example. Prove that the midpoint of the hypotenuse of a right triangle
is equidistant from the vertices of that triangle.

Solution. *Given:* △PQR is a right triangle with ∠Q = 90°.
O is the midpoint of hypotenuse PR.
Required to Prove: OP = OQ = OR
Analysis: Construct a circle centre O and diameter PR.
Let S be any point on the circle on the same
side of PR as point Q.

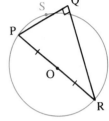

Proof:

Statement	Reason
∠PQR = 90°	Given
∠PSR = 90°	Angles in a Circle Theorem, Corollary 2
Therefore, ∠PQR = ∠PSR	
P, Q, R, and S are concyclic.	Angles in a Circle Theorem, converse of Corollary 1
Therefore, P, Q, R, and S lie on the constructed circle.	
OP = OQ = OR	Radii

EXERCISES 8-4

Ⓐ

1. What property is shared by points A, B, and C if there is no circle on which all
   three points lie?

2. In the diagram, AD, BE, and CF are
   the altitudes of △ABC and they intersect
   at G.
   a) Explain how we know that points
      B, F, E, and C are concyclic.
   b) Use part a) to deduce that
      ∠GCE = ∠FBG.
   c) Name two other pairs of acute angles
      which are equal.

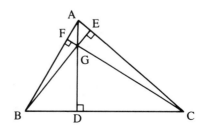

3. In the diagram, PQRS is a quadrilateral with vertices that are concyclic. Diagonals PR and QS intersect at T. Name five pairs of equal angles.

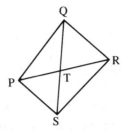

4. A television camera moves in a horizontal plane so that a rectangular billboard subtends a fixed angle at the lens of the camera. What is the shape of the camera's path?

Ⓑ

5. For each diagram, indicate whether or not points A, B, C, and D are concyclic. Give reasons for your answers.

a)

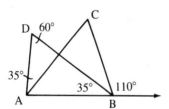

b)

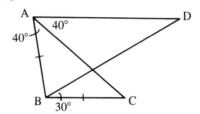

6. In the diagram (below left), PQRS is a quadrilateral with concyclic vertices.
   a) Explain why ∠QRS = ∠PQS + ∠PSQ.
   b) Use part a) to explain why ∠SPQ + ∠QRS = 180°.

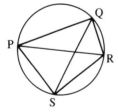

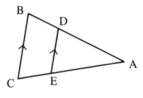

7. In the diagram (above right), isosceles △ABC has AB = AC. Points D and E are located on sides AB and AC respectively so that DE is parallel to BC. Explain why:
   a) ∠ABC = ∠ACB   b) ∠ADE = ∠AED   c) AD = AE
   d) △ABE ≅ △ACD   e) ∠ABE = ∠ACD
   f) Points D, E, C, and B are concyclic.

Ⓒ

8. Prove that there is a circle which passes through two vertices of a triangle and also passes through the base of each altitude drawn from those vertices.

8-5 CYCLIC QUADRILATERALS

In the previous section we proved that any three non-collinear points are concyclic. We can express this alternatively as follows.

> The vertices of a triangle are concyclic.

We also observed in the previous section that four points chosen arbitrarily are not necessarily concyclic. We might express this as follows.

> The vertices of a quadrilateral are not necessarily concyclic.

To investigate the conditions under which four points are concyclic, it is convenient to introduce the concept of a cyclic quadrilateral.

Definition: A quadrilateral with concyclic vertices is said to be a *cyclic quadrilateral*.

The statement that A, B, C, and D are concyclic	is equivalent to	The statement that ABCD is a cyclic quadrilateral
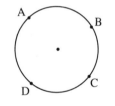		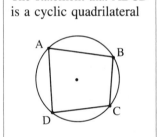

The converse of the Angles in a Circle Theorem can be expressed in terms of a cyclic quadrilateral.

> **Theorem**
> If one side of a quadrilateral subtends equal angles at its other two vertices, then the quadrilateral is cyclic.

The following theorem provides another set of conditions which are sufficient to establish that a quadrilateral is cyclic.

> **Theorem**
> If a quadrilateral is cyclic, then its opposite angles are supplementary.

Given: Cyclic quadrilateral ABCD inscribed in a circle
Required to Prove: ∠A + ∠C = 180°
∠B + ∠D = 180°
Analysis: Join AC and BD.

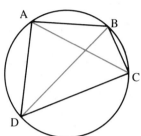

Proof:

Statement	Reason
∠ABD = ∠ACD	Corollary 1 of Angles in a Circle Theorem
∠BDA = ∠BCA	Corollary 1 of Angles in a Circle Theorem
∠ABD + ∠BDA = ∠ACD + ∠BCA	Adding the two equations
= ∠C	
∠ABD + ∠BDA + ∠A = 180°	Sum of the Angles Theorem

Therefore, ∠C + ∠A = 180°
Similarly, ∠B + ∠D = 180°

The theorem proved above enables us to relate angles subtended by the same chord but located on opposite sides of that chord. In the diagram, ∠C and ∠D are both on the circumference of the circle and subtended by the chord AB. Since they are opposite angles of a cyclic quadrilateral, they are supplementary.

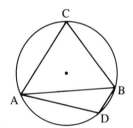

The converse of this theorem is stated below.

Theorem
If the opposite angles of a quadrilateral are supplementary, then the quadrilateral is cyclic.

The foregoing theorem and its converse can be combined into a biconditional statement called the Cyclic Quadrilateral Theorem.

Cyclic Quadrilateral Theorem
A quadrilateral is cyclic iff its opposite angles are supplementary.

> **Corollary of the Cyclic Quadrilateral Theorem**
> A quadrilateral is cyclic iff any of its exterior angles is equal
> to the interior and opposite angle.

In the diagram, ∠BCE is an exterior angle
of cyclic quadrilateral ABCD.
Since ABCD is a cyclic quadrilateral
∠BAD + ∠BCD = 180°
Since DCE is a straight line
∠BCE + ∠BCD = 180°
Therefore, ∠BAD = ∠BCE

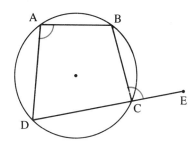

The Cyclic Quadrilateral Theorem is very useful in determining
the interior angles of cyclic quadrilaterals.

Example. Find the values of x, y, and z in each diagram. O is the centre of the
circle.

a)

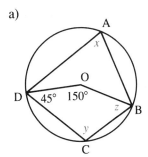

b)

Solution.

a) From the Angles in a Circle
Theorem,
$$x = \tfrac{1}{2}(150°)$$
$$= 75°$$
From the Cyclic Quadrilateral
Theorem,
$$x + y = 180°$$
$$75° + y = 180°$$
$$y = 105°$$
Since the angle sum of quadrila-
teral OBCD is 360°,
$$z + 150° + 45° + 105° = 360°$$
$$z = 60°$$

b) From the Angles in a Circle
Theorem,
$$x = \tfrac{1}{2}(100°)$$
$$= 50°$$
Since OC and OD are radii,
∠OCD = ∠ODC = y.
Since the angle sum of △ODC is
180°,
$$100° + 2y = 180°$$
$$y = 40°$$
From the Cyclic Quadrilateral
Theorem,
$$∠ABC + ∠ADC = 180°$$
$$z + 30° + y = 180°$$
$$z = 110°$$

EXERCISES 8-5

Ⓐ

1. Find each value of *x*.

a)

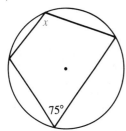

b)

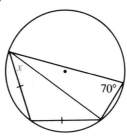

c)

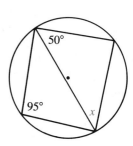

2. Find the values of *x* and *y*.

a)

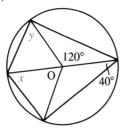

b)

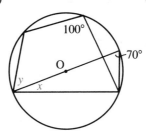

c)

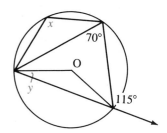

3. Name three different conditions, each of which is sufficient to prove that a quadrilateral is cyclic.

Ⓑ

4. A circle with centre O intersects parallelogram ABOD at points D, E, and F.
   Explain why:
   a) ∠B = ∠D
   b) ∠B = ∠OED
   c) ∠B + ∠OEA = 180°
   d) ∠A + ∠BOE = 180°
   e) BOEA is a cyclic quadrilateral.

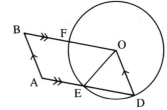

5. Copy this proof and fill in the missing statements and reasons.
   Given: Cyclic quadrilateral PQRS with PQ = PS
          and RQ = RS
   Required to Prove: △PQR and △PSR are right
                triangles.

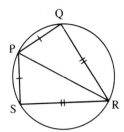

Proof:

Statement	Reason
In △PQR and △PSR	
_____	Given
_____	Given
PR is common.	
Therefore, _____	SSS
∠PQR = ∠PSR	_____
∠PQR + ∠PSR = 180°	_____
Therefore, _____	
Therefore, △PQR and △PSR are right triangles.	_____

6. Copy this proof and fill in the missing statements and reasons.
   Given: Trapezoid PQRS with PQ parallel to SR,
          and PS = QR
          PS is not parallel to QR.
   Required to Prove: Trapezoid PQRS is a cyclic
                quadrilateral.
   Analysis: Since we know more about the properties
          of parallelograms than trapezoids, extend
          SR to T so that QT is parallel to PS.
          Then PQTS is a parallelogram. Hence,
          QT = PS and so QT = QR

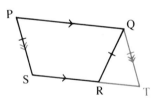

Proof:

Statement	Reason
∠SPQ = ∠QTR	_____
QT = QR	_____
_____	Isosceles Triangle Theorem
Therefore, _____	
_____	Corollary of Cyclic Quadrilateral Theorem

7. Copy this proof and fill in the missing statements and reasons.
   Given: AC is a line of symmetry of cyclic quadrilateral ABCD. E is the midpoint of AC.
   Required to Prove: E is the centre of the circle
   which passes through A, B, C,
   and D.

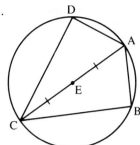

Proof:

Statement	Reason
∠ADC = ∠ABC	AC is a line of symmetry.
∠ADC + ∠ABC = 180°	_____
∠ADC = 90°	_____
_____	Corollary 3, Angles in a Circle Theorem
_____	Given AE = EC

8. Copy this proof and fill in the missing statements and reasons.
   Given: AB and AC are two equal chords with
   midpoints D and E respectively.
   Required to Prove: B, C, E, and D are concyclic
   points.
   Analysis: Draw BE and CD.
   Proof:

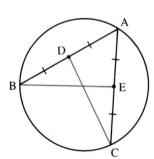

Statement	Reason
In △ACD and △ABE	
AC = AB	_____
AD = AE	_____
_____	
Therefore, _____	SAS
∠ACD = ∠ABE	_____
Therefore, B, C, E, and D are concyclic points.	_____

8-6 PROPERTIES OF TANGENTS

In *Section 8-4* we investigated, for any given number of points, the number of circles which pass through all of those points. That is, we asked, "How many circles have a given set of points in common?" We discovered that any two given points are common to an infinite family of circles, while any three given points are common to only one circle.

Our investigation of concyclic points in *Sections 8-4* and *8-5* was a study of conditions under which four points lie on only one circle.

Our answer to the question posed above reduced to several cases, depending upon the number of points in the given set.

The answers to many questions in mathematics in general, and in geometry in particular, reduce to particular cases. For example, we might ask, "How many points are common to a given circle and a given line?"

The diagrams below show the three possible cases for the intersection of a line with a circle.

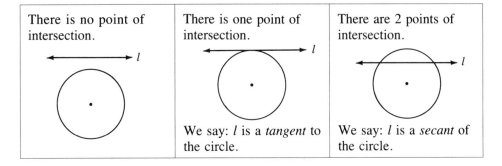

There is no point of intersection.	There is one point of intersection.	There are 2 points of intersection.
	We say: *l* is a *tangent* to the circle.	We say: *l* is a *secant* of the circle.

The diagrams illustrate the definitions of a tangent and a secant. In this section and the next, we shall discover some interesting properties of tangents to circles.

We may define a tangent to a circle as a line which intersects that circle in exactly one point. (The word tangent is derived from the Latin verb "tangere", which means to touch.)

The following theorems, which concern tangents to circles, are intuitively obvious. A rigorous proof would require careful arguments.

Theorem

If a line is perpendicular to a radius of a circle at a point of intersection with the circle, then the line is a tangent to the circle at that point.

If line *l* is perpendicular to radius OQ at Q, then *l* is a tangent to the circle at Q.

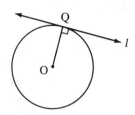

Here is the converse of that theorem.

Theorem

A tangent to a circle is perpendicular to the radius of the circle at the point of tangency.

Since there is only one line perpendicular to a tangent and passing through the point of tangency, it follows from this theorem that the radius of the circle at the point of tangency must lie along that line. This fact is contained in the following corollary.

Corollary

Any line perpendicular to a tangent to a circle at the point of tangency passes through the centre of the circle.

The two theorems above which illustrate the perpendicularity of a tangent to the radius at the point of tangency can be combined into a biconditional statement called the Tangent-Radius Theorem.

Tangent-Radius Theorem

A line is a tangent to a circle iff it is perpendicular to the radius of the circle at a point of intersection.

The Tangent-Radius Theorem shows that tangents drawn to a circle, centre O, from an external point P must be perpendicular to the radii drawn to their points of contact, Q and R.

Hence, two right triangles can be drawn with OP as their hypotenuse.

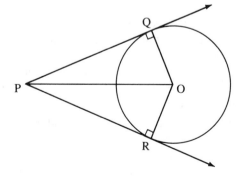

We discovered earlier in this chapter that if a circle is drawn with diameter OP, then $\angle OQP = \angle ORP = 90°$ only if Q and R lie on the circumference of the circle.

This diagram illustrates that the only points of tangency from P to the circle, centre O, are the points of intersection of the two circles. Since these circles intersect in exactly two points, then exactly two points of tangency exist.

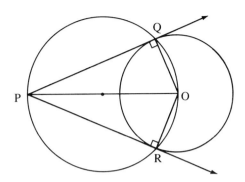

The foregoing discussion can be formalized and extended to establish the Equal Tangents Theorem.

Equal Tangents Theorem
From a point P outside a circle there are exactly two tangents which can be drawn. Furthermore, PQ = PR where Q and R are the points of tangency.

The theorems above identify properties of tangents, which are useful in solving many different types of problems involving circles, disks or spheres.

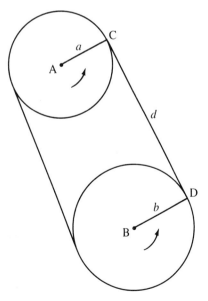

Example. A small wheel, centre A, is driven by a larger wheel, centre B, by means of a tight rubber belt.
  a) If C and D are the points of tangency of the belt with the wheels, prove that AC is parallel to BD.
  b) Write expressions for the lengths of AD and BC in terms of the radii a and b of the wheels, and the distance d between C and D.

Solution. a) From the Tangent-Radius Theorem,
$\angle ACD = \angle BDC = 90°$
Therefore, $\angle ACD + \angle BDC = 180°$
From the Parallel Lines Theorem, interior angles, AC is parallel to BD.
  b) Since $\triangle ACD$ is a right triangle,
$$AD = \sqrt{AC^2 + CD^2}$$
$$= \sqrt{a^2 + d^2}$$
Similarly, $BC = \sqrt{b^2 + d^2}$

EXERCISES 8-6

(A)

1. Find each value of *y* if AB and AC are tangents.

a)
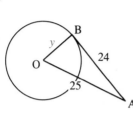

b)
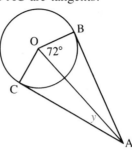

c)
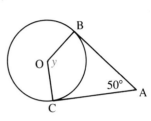

2. Find the values of *x* and *y* if AB, AC, PQ, QR, and RP are tangents.

a)
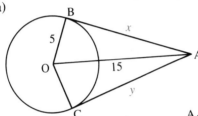

b)
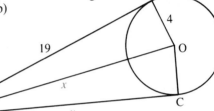

c)
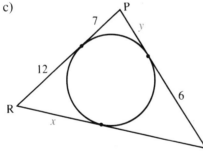

d)
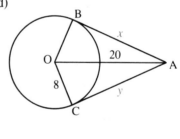

3. Find the values of *x* and *y*. O and M mark the centres of the circles.

a)
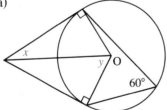

b)
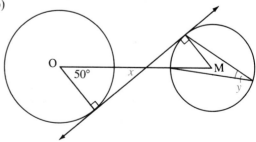

(B)

4. A circle is inscribed in a square of side 15 cm. How far is the centre of the circle from a vertex of the square?

5. Copy this proof and fill in the missing statements and reasons.
   Given: PQ is a tangent at Q to a circle centre O.
        PO intersects the circle at R. QO = QR
   Required to Prove: OR = RP

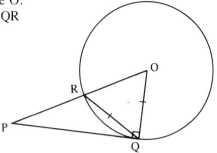

Proof:

Statement	Reason
_____	Radii
OQ = QR	_____
Therefore, _____	All sides equal
∠ROQ = 60°	_____
∠OQP = 90°	_____
∠OPQ = 30°	_____
_____	Angle in equilateral triangle
∠RQP = 30°	_____
RP = RQ	_____
OR = RP	_____

6. Copy this proof and fill in the missing statements and reasons.
   Given: PQ and RS are tangents at P and R to a
        circle centre O. QS is a tangent to the circle.
        PQ is parallel to RS.
   Required to Prove: △QOS is a right triangle.
   Analysis: Let T be the point of tangency of QS.
        Draw OP, OT, and OR.

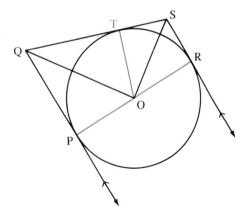

Proof:

Statement	Reason
In △TSO and △RSO ST = SR	
_____	Radii
OS is common.	
Therefore, _____	SSS
Similarly, △TQO ≅ △PQO	_____
∠TSO = ∠RSO	_____
∠TSO = $\frac{1}{2}$∠TSR	_____
∠TQO = ∠PQO	_____
∠TQO = $\frac{1}{2}$∠TQP	_____
PQ ∥ RS	_____
_____	Parallel Lines Theorem, interior angles
∠TQO + ∠TSO = 90°	_____
_____	Sum of the Angles Theorem
△QOS is a right triangle.	_____

7. Copy this proof and fill in the reasons.
   Given: Tangents PA and PB are drawn at A and B
        to a circle centre O.
   Required to Prove: P, A, O, and B are concyclic
             points.
   Analysis: Draw OA and OB.

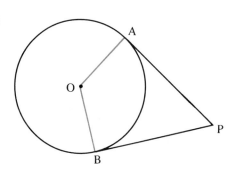

Proof:

Statement	Reason
∠PAO = 90°	_____
∠PBO = 90°	_____
Therefore, ∠PAO + ∠PBO = 180°	
∠APB + ∠AOB = 180°	_____
PAOB is a cyclic quadrilateral.	_____
P, A, O, and B are concyclic points.	_____

8. A circle is inscribed in an equilateral triangle. If XY is 3.2 cm, what is the perimeter of the triangle?

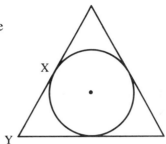

9. Copy this proof and fill in the missing statements and reason.
   Given: PQ and RS are chords of a circle centre O, and tangents to a smaller concentric circle.
   Required to Prove: PQ = RS
   Analysis: Join O to A and B, the points of tangency of PQ and RS respectively with the smaller circle.

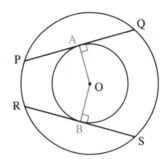

Proof:

Statement	Reason
∠OAP = 90°	
_____	Tangent-Radius Theorem
_____	Radii
_____	Equal Chords Theorem

10. Copy this proof and fill in the missing statement and reasons.
    Given: PS, PT, and QR are tangents to a circle at S, T, and X respectively.
    Required to Prove: The perimeter of △PQR is equal to 2PS.

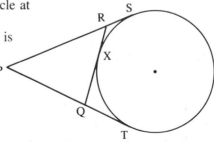

Proof:

Statement	Reason
RX = RS	_____
QX = QT	_____
Perimeter △PQR = PR + RQ + PQ	
RQ = RX + XQ	
RQ = RS + QT	_____
Perimeter △PQR = PR + RS + QT + PQ	
= PS + PT	
_____	Equal Tangents Theorem
Therefore, perimeter △PQR = 2PS	

11. Copy this proof and fill in the missing statements and reasons.
    Given: AB and CD are tangents to a circle at B
    and D, such that BD is a diameter.
    Required to Prove: AB is parallel to CD.

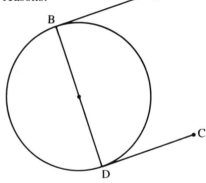

Proof:

Statement	Reason
BD passes through the centre of the circle.	_____
∠ABD = 90°	_____
_____	Tangent-Radius Theorem
Therefore, ∠ABD + ∠CDB = 180°	
_____	Parallel Lines Theorem, interior angles

12. A key fob is made by suspending a silver
    coin in the middle of a square piece
    of acrylic material. A circular hole is
    drilled along a diagonal of the square, in
    the acrylic. What is the maximum pos-
    sible diameter of the hole?

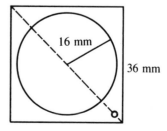

13. Copy this proof and fill in the missing reasons.

    Given: L and M are the points of intersection of two circles centres A and B. N is the midpoint of LM.

    Required to Prove: A, B, and N are collinear points.

    Analysis: We shall prove that the line AN which contains the points A and N also contains the point B.

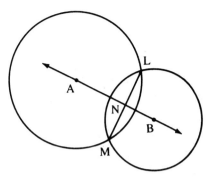

Proof:

Statement	Reason
AN is the perpendicular bisector of LM.	_____
B lies on the perpendicular bisector of LM.	_____
A, B, and N are collinear.	_____

14. Two circles of radii 10 cm and 17 cm share a common chord of length 16 cm. What is the distance between their centres?

15. The distances between the centre O of the inscribed circle and the vertices of △ABC are respectively 14 cm, 33 cm, and 16 cm. If the circle has a diameter of 18 cm, what is the perimeter of △ABC?

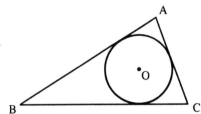

Ⓒ

16. A spherical glass globe just fits inside a cubical box of side 42 cm. Find the distance from the centre of the globe to a corner of the box.

17. AB is any diameter of a circle and PQ is a tangent to that circle. Prove that the sum of the distances of A and B from PQ is a constant.

The Nine-Point Circle

''Mathematics, rightly viewed, possesses not only truth but supreme beauty.''

Bertrand Russell

△ABC is any triangle. Prove that these *nine* points lie on a circle.
- the midpoints of the sides: D, E, F
- the feet of the altitudes: P, Q, R
- the midpoints of the segments joining the orthocentre, H, to the vertices: X, Y, Z

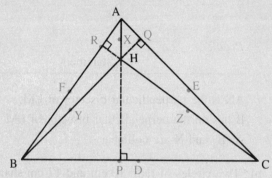

Understand the problem
- What is the orthocentre?

Think of a strategy
- Since altitudes are involved, we can see some right angles on the diagram.
- This suggests that to prove certain points lie on a circle, we may need to use the property of angles in a semicircle.

Carry out the strategy
- Can you prove that the quadrilaterals FEZY and FXZD are rectangles?
- Does this prove that the points F, E, Z, Y, X, and D lie on the same circle?
- Why do the points P, Q, and R also lie on this circle?
- Complete a proof that the points D, E, F, P, Q, R, X, Y, and Z lie on the same circle.

Look back
- For what kind of triangle do the three altitudes intersect outside the triangle? Would the result still be true for this kind of triangle?
- What happens if the triangle is a right triangle?
- What happens if the triangle is isosceles? equilateral?
- Discuss why Bertrand Russell might have felt that the nine-point circle is a good example to illustrate the quotation above.

PROBLEMS

Ⓑ

1. A triangle has sides of length 6 cm, 8 cm, and 10 cm. If a circle is drawn through its vertices, what is the diameter of the circle?

2. Two numbers have a sum of 6 and a product of 7.
   a) Find the sum of their squares.
   b) Find the difference of their squares.
   c) Find the sum of the squares of their reciprocals.

3. Write the numbers from 1 to 9 in a 3 by 3 grid such that the sums of the three numbers along any row, any column, or any diagonal are all different.

4. The Great Pyramid of Cheops has a base 230 m square. Its faces are congruent isosceles triangles, making an angle of 51.87° with the ground.
   a) Calculate the height of the pyramid, to the nearest metre.
   b) Discuss how close the faces are to being equilateral triangles.

Ⓒ

5. A cylindrical fuel tank has a diameter of 1.6 m and a length of 3.0 m. It is installed underground at a gasoline station, lying on its side. By measuring, it is found that the maximum depth of the fuel in the tank is 0.5 m. Calculate the number of litres of fuel in the tank.

6. How many real roots does this equation have?
   $(x - 1)^2 + (x - 2)^2 + (x - 3)^2 + (x - 4)^2 = 0$

7. a) If $p \neq q$, explain why this equation has no real roots:
   $(x + p)^2 + (x + q)^2 = 0$.
   b) Prove that every quadratic equation $ax^2 + bx + c = 0$ $(a \neq 0)$ which has no real roots can be written in the form $(x + p)^2 + (y + q)^2 = 0$, where p and q are real numbers.

Ⓓ

8. Prove that the centre of the nine-point circle of any triangle is the midpoint of the line segment joining the orthocentre and the circumcentre.

THE MATHEMATICAL MIND

The Mystic Hexagram

The great French mathematician, Blaise Pascal, was a child prodigy. His father realized that he was bright, and taught him languages with great care. Since Blaise was of frail health, his father did not permit him to study mathematics. He thought that Blaise needed to conserve his energy, and that the strain would be too great if he studied mathematics as well.

But the ban on mathematics naturally aroused the boy's curiosity, and when he was 12 years old he asked what geometry was. His father told him, and Blaise immediately became very interested. Without assistance from anyone, he soon discovered many theorems of elementary geometry. By age 16 he had discovered and proved many original results. His work astonished some of the leading mathematicians of the time, who could not believe that it had been done by a teenager.

One of these results concerns a pattern formed when any six points on a circle are joined in a certain way.

Step 1. Draw a circle and mark any six points on it. Make an X using the four points on the left. This locates point P.

Step 2. Make an X using the two points on the left and the two on the right. This locates point Q.

Step 3. Make an X using the four points on the right. This locates point R. Join P, Q, and R.

When he was only 15 years old, Blaise discovered and proved the remarkable fact that no matter where the six points are marked on the circle, P, Q, and R will always lie on a straight line. For this reason, he called the figure formed by joining the six points the *mystic hexagram*. Blaise also proved that the same result occurs when six points are marked on certain figures other than circles.

QUESTIONS

1. Construct a circle and follow the steps described above. Do P, Q, and R lie on the same line?

2. Construct a circle and locate any three points P, Q, and R inside it which lie on a straight line. Can you find the six points on the circle which form the mystic hexagram?

8-7 THE TANGENT-CHORD THEOREM

In the previous section we discovered that the angle between a tangent and the diameter (or radius) at the point of tangency is always 90°. In this section we extend our investigation to the angle between a tangent and *any* chord at the point of tangency. The following Tangent-Chord Theorem may be regarded as a generalization of the Tangent-Radius Theorem.

> **Tangent-Chord Theorem**
> The angle between a tangent to a circle and a chord of the circle is equal to one-half the angle subtended by the chord at the centre of the circle.

Given: A circle with centre O, a line AC which is
   tangent to the circle at point A, and a chord AB

Required to Prove: $\angle BAC = \frac{1}{2}\angle BOA$

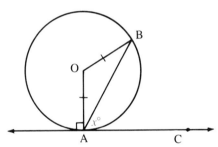

Proof:

Statement	Reason
Let $\angle BAC = x°$	
$\angle OAC = 90°$	Tangent-Radius Theorem
$\angle OAB = \angle OAC - \angle BAC$	Complementary angles
Therefore, $\angle OAB = (90 - x)°$	
$OA = OB$	Radii
$\angle OBA = \angle OAB$	Isosceles Triangle Theorem
Therefore, $\angle OBA = (90 - x)°$	
$\angle BOA = 180° - \angle OAB - \angle OBA$	Sum of the Angles Theorem
$\qquad = 180° - (90 - x)° - (90 - x)°$	
$\qquad = 2x°$	
$\qquad = 2\angle BAC$	
Therefore, $\angle BAC = \frac{1}{2}\angle BOA$	

Corollary of the Tangent-Chord Theorem
The angle between a tangent to a circle and a chord is equal
to the angle subtended on the opposite side of the chord.

In the diagram

DC is a tangent to the circle at A, with
chords AE and AB.
∠EAD = ∠EBA
∠BAC = ∠BEA

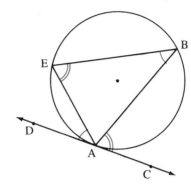

Example.   Find the values of *a*, *b*, *c*, *d*, and *e*.

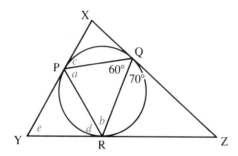

Solution.   From the Tangent-Chord Theorem,
  ∠QPR = ∠ZQR
    a = 70°
  From the Tangent-Chord Theorem,
  ∠QRP = ∠XQP
  But ∠XQP = 50°   (straight angle)
      So, *b* = 50°
  From the Tangent-Chord Theorem,
  ∠XPQ = ∠QRP
    c = 50°
  From the Tangent-Chord Theorem,
  ∠PRY = ∠PQR
      d = 60°
  In △PRY,
  ∠P = 180° − 70° − 50°   (straight angle)
    = 60°
  ∠Y = 180° − 60° − 60°   (Sum of the Angles Theorem)
    e = 60°

EXERCISES 8-7

Ⓐ

1. Find each value of *x*. AB is a tangent.

a)

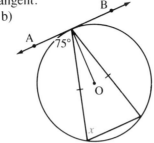

b)

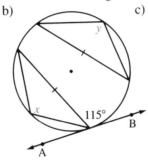

c)

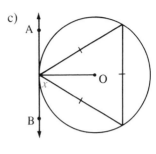

2. Find the values of *x* and *y*. AB and CD are tangents.

a)

b)

c)

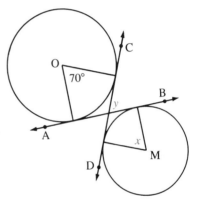

Ⓑ

3. Tangents are drawn from an external
   point P to points A and B on a circle.
   AD is a chord parallel to tangent PB. If
   ∠PAB = 60° and AP = 7 cm, find:
   a) the measure of ∠ADB
   b) the measure of ∠BAD
   c) the length of AD.

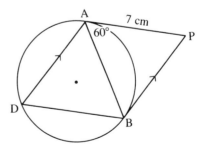

4. Copy this proof and fill in the missing statements and reasons.
   Given: AB and AC are chords which are equidistant
   from the centre O of a circle. PA and PB
   are tangents to the circle at A and B.
   Required to Prove: ∠APB = ∠BAC
   Analysis: Draw BC.

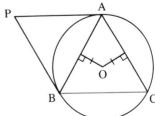

Proof:

Statement	Reason
_____	Equal Chords Theorem
∠ABC = ∠ACB	_____
∠PAB = ∠ACB	_____
∠PBA = ∠ACB	_____
_____	Sum of the Angles Theorem

5. Copy this proof and fill in the missing statements and reasons.
   Given: PA and PB are tangents to a circle at A
   and B. PQC is a secant such that
   ∠APC = ∠BPC.
   Required to Prove: ∠QAC = 90°
   Analysis: Draw BQ and CB.

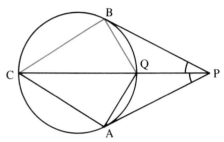

Proof:

Statement	Reason
In △PAC and △PBC	
_____	Equal Tangents Theorem
_____	Given
PC is common.	
Therefore, _____	SAS
In △QAC and △QBC	
∠ACQ = ∠BCQ	_____
_____	Congruent triangles
QC is common.	
Therefore, _____	SAS
∠QAC = ∠QBC	_____
∠QAC + ∠QBC = 180°	_____
Therefore, ∠QAC = 90°	

6. One leg of a right triangle is the diameter of a circle. Prove that the tangent drawn from the point of intersection of the circle with the hypotenuse bisects the other leg of the triangle.

7. State and prove the converse of the Tangent-Chord Theorem.

1. Calculate each value of x.

a)

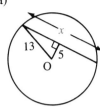

b)

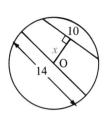

c)

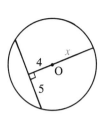

2. PQRS is a cyclic quadrilateral and $\angle P$ is an acute angle. Is $\angle R$ acute or obtuse? Explain your answer.

3. Copy this proof and fill in the reasons.
   Given: Cyclic quadrilateral ABCD, with diagonals intersecting at O, the centre of the circle
   Required to Prove: ABCD is a rectangle.
   Analysis: We need to show that
   $$\angle A = \angle B = \angle C = \angle D = 90°$$

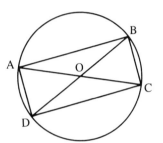

Proof:

Statement	Reason
$\angle A = \angle DAC + \angle BAC$	
$\angle DAC = \frac{1}{2}\angle DOC$	_____
$\angle BAC = \frac{1}{2}\angle BOC$	_____
$\angle DAC + \angle BAC = \frac{1}{2}(\angle DOC + \angle BOC)$	
$\qquad\qquad = \frac{1}{2}(180°)$	_____
$\qquad\qquad = 90°$	
$\angle A = 90°$	

Similarly, $\angle B = \angle C = \angle D = 90°$
Therefore, ABCD is a rectangle.

4. Copy this proof and fill in the missing statements and reasons.
   Given: $\triangle ABC$ with altitudes BE and CD
   Required to Prove: DAEF is a cyclic quadrilateral.

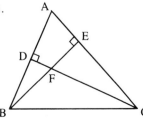

Proof:

Statement	Reason
In quadrilateral DAEF	
∠D + ∠A + ∠E + ∠F = 360°	_____
∠D + ∠E = 180°	_____
_____	Subtracting
_____	Cyclic Quadrilateral Theorem

5. Copy this proof and fill in the missing statement and reasons.

   Given: Two circles with a common tangent QPR
   Chord AC on one circle and chord DB
   on the other circle are such that APB and
   CPD are straight lines.

   Required to Prove: AC is parallel to DB.

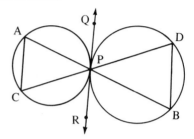

Proof:

Statement	Reason
∠ACP = ∠APQ	_____
∠APQ = ∠BPR	_____
∠BPR = ∠PDB	_____
Therefore, ∠ACP = ∠PDB	
_____	Parallel Lines Theorem, alternate angles

6. In the diagram (below left), D, E, and F are the points at which the sides of △PQR are tangent to its inscribed circle. Use the Tangent-Chord Theorem to deduce that the two tangents from each vertex of △PQR are equal in length.

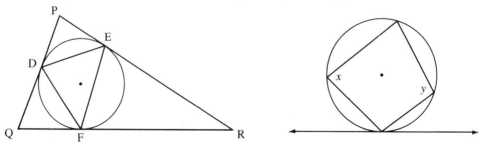

7. a) For x and y defined as in the diagram (above right), use the Tangent-Chord Theorem to deduce that $x + y = 180°$.

   b) Use the Tangent-Chord Theorem to deduce that opposite angles of a cyclic quadrilateral are supplementary.

9 Analysing Survey Data

John Chan runs a successful restaurant, which is open for lunch and dinner. He has noticed that more people seem to be going out for breakfast and wonders if it would be profitable to open his restaurant for breakfast. He asks his son Ken to help him find out how many people in the town eat breakfast out at least once a week. (See Section 9-7 *Example 1* and Exercises 9-8 *Exercise 10*.)

9-1 OPINION SURVEYS

Hardly a day goes by without someone using data collected from a survey. Every time you listen to the "Top 20" Hit Parade, you are using survey data. The Government relies heavily on survey data for the information needed in the day-to-day running of the country. Whenever you ask someone if he or she liked a particular movie, you are conducting an informal survey. If enough of your friends say that they enjoyed the movie, you might decide to see it yourself.

All over the country, people use survey data to help them make better decisions. The cost of making a bad decision is often great. So decision makers try to gather as much information as possible before deciding on a course of action. It is rarely possible to ask an opinion of the entire population, so they ask a sample of the population. It is surprising that with a sample of about 1000 people we can usually estimate, to within 3 or 4 percent, the information we would have got if we had asked everyone.

We use survey sampling in many areas that affect us all. When you read consumer reports on the latest cars, you are looking at information compiled from the opinions of several reviewers. When looking for a job in another part of the country, you might look at the unemployment figures for different provinces. Statistics Canada uses survey methods to collect this data.

The most visible of all opinion surveys are those published before an election. Professional survey companies charge large amounts to conduct a national survey for political parties. We read and listen to their reports in the press and on radio and television.

Many surveys are conducted to find out what Canadians think about environmental problems. On the next page is part of a report on one survey, published in the Toronto Star in August 1988.

Notice the statement describing the accuracy of this survey. Until 4 or 5 years ago, it was unusual to find such a statement in a survey report. Even now, not many people who read such a statement would understand what it means. By the end of this chapter you will have a better understanding of this statement, and other parts of the report. You will learn much more about the background of opinion surveys:

- How it is possible to achieve errors as low as 4% in a sample of 100 people
- The importance of finding a correct method of selecting the sample
- The ways in which data from surveys can be misinterpreted
- The difficulties that pollsters meet when conducting a survey

Most willing to pay for safe environment

Seventy-seven per cent of Canadians would pay 10 per cent more for a product if it were labelled environmentally safe, according to a poll released today.

And 56 per cent would pay a two-cent tax on a litre of milk or gasoline to help improve the environment, the poll says.

The Angus Reid poll, done exclusively for The Star and Southam News, shows the majority of Canadians are willing to pay to protect the environment because they don't think governments are doing enough.

Eighty-four per cent said they think "governments here in Canada should be doing more," compared with 14 per cent who felt governments are doing enough.

The poll said results suggest significant public despair over attention to the environment.

Sixty-five per cent said the environment "will have to become a bigger problem before enough attention is paid to improve it."

Atlantic Canadians were the strongest advocates of a special tax for the environment, with 66 per cent in favor. Quebec residents were 59 per cent in favor, while support in Ontario was 53 per cent.

A total of 1,501 Canadians were interviewed by telephone between July 25-30.

A sample this size is considered accurate to within 2.5 percentage points 19 times out of 20.

First, it is important to look at reports of survey data. When you work through the Exercises that follow, you will compile a collection of newspaper articles that report survey data. In this way you will see the wide range of subjects that appear in opinion polls.

EXERCISES 9-1

1. Read several magazines and newspapers to find at least 5 articles describing surveys. Look for surveys in which the answers to the questions are YES or NO. Cut out each article, and if possible, paste it on a single piece of paper. Leave room to write your own comments. You will need these cuttings to answer more questions in the Exercises later in the chapter.

2. Make a list of 5 common examples of the use of survey information.

3. Obtain information from Statistics Canada on the monthly unemployment data; in particular, how the data are collected and what the accuracy is.

4. The majority of workers in North America work in what is loosely called the "information industry". Thirty years ago, most workers worked in manufacturing or resource industries. The Neilsen TV ratings is one example of a branch of the information industry which uses survey data on a regular basis. Give 9 more examples of branches of the information industry which routinely use survey data.

9-2 ANSWERING YES AND NO

In this chapter we shall look at survey data collected from YES-NO populations. In a YES-NO population, every member of that population answers a question with a YES or a NO. For example, the answer to the question, "Have you bought a Led Zeppelin record this month?" is either YES or NO. The question, "How many Led Zeppelin records have you bought this year?" is not a YES-NO question.

Sometimes we have to reword a question to make it into a YES-NO question. Here is a question from a survey conducted by a student at A.Y. Jackson Secondary School.

Which of the following best describes your reaction to the statement "I prefer to be taught rather than work independently"?
Strongly Agree ☐   Agree ☐   Don't know ☐   Disagree ☐
Strongly Disagree ☐

We could turn this into a YES-NO question by asking, "Did you respond by answering Agree or Strongly Agree?"

If we could ask every member of a YES-NO population, we would be able to discover the percentage of the population who answered YES to the question. If we found that 70% of the population answered YES, we would call this a 70% YES population.

The main idea of this chapter is that by examining data from samples, it is possible to estimate the percentage of yesses that we would have got by taking a census of the population.

The word *census* indicates the process of asking questions of every member of a population.

EXERCISES 9-2

Ⓐ

1. Explain in your own words the meaning of each term.
   a) sample   b) population   c) census   d) YES-NO population

2. In a survey, students in schools in Nanaimo, North Vancouver, and Chicago answered the following questions. If the students answered a YES-NO question, they are a sample of a YES-NO population. Which questions are YES-NO questions?
   a) What is your sex?   MALE/FEMALE
   b) How much do you spend on a date?
   c) Do you play a sport at least once a week?
   d) Do you have a driver's licence?
   e) How many cigarettes do you smoke per day?
   f) How many classes did you miss last week?

(B)

3. Some questions in *Exercise 2* did not give YES-NO answers. Rewrite these questions so the answer is either YES or NO.

4. For each question that you constructed in *Exercise 3*, complete this sentence. "Using sampling methods, we would be able to estimate the percentage of . . ."

5. You want to survey students in your school to compare the drinking and smoking habits of males and females. Make a list of at least ten YES-NO questions that you might use in such a survey. Include questions on other factors related to students' smoking and drinking habits.

6. a) You have been asked to conduct a survey of residents of your school district concerning their opinions of the public and the private school systems. Make a list of 5 YES-NO questions which might be included in that survey.
   b) Do you think that YES-NO questions are the most appropriate to use in this kind of survey? Give reasons.

9-3 SAMPLES FROM YES-NO POPULATIONS

Our first task is to examine the data we get when we take samples from different populations. We will first look at samples from a 30% YES population.

There are many methods of collecting data on samples from a YES-NO population. We will use a method called *simulation*. To use simulation you will need a table of random digits. In the table on the next page the digits are in groups of 10. Each set of 20 digits represents a sample (size 20) from the population. In the experiment that follows, we will examine 40 samples.

Experiment. Collect 40 samples from a 30% YES population and analyse the results.

Step 1. Make a simulation model.
   Each digit in a set of 20 represents a YES or a NO response. For a 30% YES population of digits, we need to choose 3 out of the 10 digits to represent the YES responses. In this case we will choose 1, 2, and 3 to represent the YES responses.

Step 2. Examine the samples.
   We obtain the first sample from the first 20 digits in the table.
   0659301470   7606649757
   This set of 20 digits has two digits, 3 and 1, that represent YES responses. Hence, there are 2 YES responses in this sample.
   The second sample 4029900091   5932309464 has 5 YES responses.
   We repeat this for the remaining 38 samples.

Random-Digits Table

0659301470	7606649757	0349412385	1580473432
4029900091	5932309464	5955365408	1956618065
0539182950	4961840104	0194593086	2424236952
2215677723	9111180265	3934125583	9082929291
8195811617	6882605939	5927541175	5304794871
8319152521	0595533326	4948984027	1986989903
6111653546	7318169616	1980660628	1201486415
2303088164	2591251198	6082088660	8202845547
6021492141	1346436374	4650446649	2154994865
4974066112	7545165189	6710437842	9217985540
0001932034	8935386532	1902625141	6760258469
5723443903	7940084443	6053474525	8331891205
9637255305	1391403573	6149597660	7281714750
4006907454	0232381400	9231691541	3073046926
4803956090	3584948088	0130667625	4017492891
8854547729	7644801864	2827640643	1544473800
4450033269	1406588780	7014203762	9585762244
8151052159	6091785491	7791529740	4476766259
9637374112	8827867727	5799998684	9064825570
3953699445	0172177846	2345891590	3634248640

Step 3. Make a table to collect the data.

We record the data from each sample using tally marks. Then we can add the tally marks to get the frequency of each kind of sample.

Number of yesses in the sample	Tally	Frequency	Total number of yesses
0		0	0
1	|	1	1
2	||||	4	8
3	||||	4	12
4	||	2	8
5	⊬⊬ ||||	9	45
6	⊬⊬ ||	7	42
7	|||	3	21
8	⊬⊬	5	40
9	|||	3	27
10	||	2	20
11		0	0
•		•	•
•		•	•
•		•	•
20		0	0
	Total		224

Step 4. Analyse the results.

The samples cluster around 5 or 6 YES responses. This means that these samples occurred most often and that the rest of the samples occur on both sides of these samples. Notice, however, that even though the population had 30% YES responses, $\frac{6}{20}$ was not the sample that occurred most frequently.

We examined a total of 800 digits. Of these digits, 224 represented yesses. Hence, $\frac{224}{800}$, or 28% of the 800 digits represented yesses. This is quite close to the percentage (30%) of yesses in this population.

EXERCISES 9-3

Ⓑ

1. The table of random digits has 40 columns with 20 digits in each column. Use each column of digits to represent a sample of size 20 from a 30% YES population. Follow the steps above to make a frequency table showing the distribution of samples from a 30% YES population. Comment on the results.

2. Work in groups of 3 or 4. Use the random digits table on page 364 to collect data on 100 samples (size 20) for YES-NO populations. Each group should work with one of these YES percentages: 10%, 20%, 30%, ..., 80%, 90%. Repeat the experiment preceding this exercise, using 100 samples. Make a frequency table for each population. Keep these data for use in Exercises 3 and 4.

3. In constructing the frequency tables in *Exercise 2*, you examined 100 samples each of which contained 20 responses. Calculate the total number of YES responses in the 100 samples, and find the percentage of YES responses in the 2000 responses.

4. In *Exercise 3*, would you expect the percentage of yesses in the sample to be exactly the same as the percentage of yesses in your population? If not, why not?

COMPUTER POWER

Generating Data from a YES-NO Population

In the previous section, you used simulation to collect data from different YES-NO populations. The power of the computer makes this an ideal computer application. The following program provides data for samples from a YES-NO population.

You will be asked to enter the size of the sample (maximum 100), the percentage of yesses in the population and the number of samples. The program will display a frequency table of the sample data. The table also shows the likely and unlikely samples (see Section 9-4).

```
VAR
            F : ARRAY[0..101] OF REAL;
            LF : ARRAY[0..101] OF REAL;
            UF : ARRAY[0..101] OF REAL;
            I,SAM,NS,N,S,YE : INTEGER;
            WH,P,R: REAL;
            CH : CHAR;
BEGIN          { GENERATE 100 SAMPLES FROM YES-NO POPULATION }
            CLRSCR;
            WRITE("WHAT IS THE PERCENTAGE OF YESSES IN THE
            POPULATION?");
            READ(P);
            WRITE("WHAT IS THE SIZE OF THE SAMPLE?");
            READ(S);
            WRITE("HOW MANY SAMPLES DO YOU WANT?");
            READ(NS);
            RANDOMIZE;
            FOR I:=0 TO 101 DO BEGIN
                F[I] := 0; LF[I] := 0; UF[I] : = 0;
            END;
            IF(P < 0) THEN P : = 1;
            IF(P > 100) THEN P := 99;
            P := P / 100;
            IF(S < 10) THEN S := 10;
            IF(S > 100) THEN S := 100;
            { GENERATE SAMPLES AND COUNT YESSES }
            FOR SAM := 1 TO NS DO BEGIN
                YE := 0;
                FOR N := 1 TO S DO BEGIN
                    R := RANDOM;
                    IF(R <= P) THEN YE := SUCC(YE);
                END;
                GOTOXY(1,6);
                WRITE("EXAMINING SAMPLE",SAM);
                F[YE] := F[YE]+1;
```

```
END;
WRITELN;
{ GET CUMULATIVE FREQUENCIES TO DETERMINE LIKELY
SAMPLES }
LF[O] := UF[O];
FOR I := 1 TO S DO LF[I] := LF[I-1]+F[I];
UF[S] := F[S]; I := S;
REPEAT
     UF[I-1] := UF[I]+F[I-1];
     I := I - 1;
UNTIL I = 1;
{ DISPLAY THE DATA }
WRITELN;
WRITELN("NUMBER OF            LIKELY");
WRITELN("YESSES IN THE        FREQUENCY OR");
WRITELN("SAMPLE               UNLIKELY");
WRITELN("_____");
WH := 0.05 * NS;
FOR I := 0 TO S DO BEGIN
     IF (UF[I] <> 0) AND (LF[I] <> 0) THEN BEGIN
          WRITE(I,"          ",F[I]:3:3,"     ");
          IF(LF[I] <= WH) OR (UF[I] <= WH) THEN
          WRITELN("UNLIKELY")
          ELSE WRITELN("LIKELY");
     END;
END;
CH := READKEY;
END;
```

QUESTIONS

1. Use this program to answer the questions in *Exercises 9-3*.

2. Compare the frequency table for 1000 samples with the frequency table for 100 samples, when the sample sizes and percentage of yesses in the population remain the same. What differences do you notice?

3. Use this program to help you answer the questions in *Exercises 9-4*.

 **PROBLEM SOLVING**

The Pigeonhole Principle

"Society is not static, and the basics are not eternal."

Shirley Hill

The population of Canada is about 25 million. Prove that at least two people in Canada have the same number of hairs on their heads.

Understand the problem
- Can we do this without counting the hairs on everybody's head?
- Do we have to determine which people have the same number of hairs on their heads?

Think of a strategy
- Is it possible for someone to have 25 million hairs on her or his head?

Carry out the strategy
- Estimate the greatest number of hairs that could be on somebody's head.
- Is it possible for every person in Canada to have a different number of hairs on her or his head?

Look back
- Since there are more people than possible numbers of hairs, it follows that at least two people have the same number of hairs on the head. This kind of reasoning makes use of a principle called the pigeonhole principle.

> **The Pigeonhole Principle**
> If n objects are to be placed in $k < n$ boxes, then some box contains at least two objects.

- In the above problem, $n > 25\,000\,000$ (the number of Canadians), and $k < 25\,000\,000$ (the possible number of hairs on the head). Since $n > k$, there must be at least two people with the same number of hairs on the head.
- Of course, we have no idea who the people are with the same number of hairs on the head!

The pigeonhole principle is a very useful problem solving strategy. It can be used to solve a surprisingly wide variety of problems.

PROBLEMS

 (B)

1. How many cards must you draw from a deck of playing cards to be certain that you will have:
   a) at least two red cards or two black cards
   b) at least two cards from the same suit?

2. Given any 5 different natural numbers, prove that at least two of them leave the same remainder when divided by 4.

3. In square PQRS, A and B are points on the sides PQ and QR such that PA = QB. Prove that RA = SB and RA is perpendicular to SB.

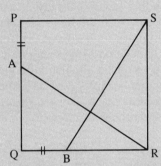

4. PQRS is any parallelogram. Prove that $PQ^2 + QR^2 + RS^2 + SP^2 = PR^2 + QS^2$.

5. Prove that for every acute angle θ, $\sin \theta + \dfrac{1}{\sin \theta} \geq 2$.

6. The arithmetic mean of a set of 30 numbers is 65. If 10 numbers having a mean of 60 are discarded, what is the mean of the remaining numbers?

(C)

7. Five points are randomly located in a square with sides 1 unit long. Prove that at least two of the points are no more than $\dfrac{\sqrt{2}}{2}$ units apart.

8. A circle has radius r. Three arcs of circles with radius r are drawn to intersect at the centre and on the circumference of the given circle as shown. Determine the shaded area as a function of r.

(D)

9. Here are ten different numbers less than 100:
   18, 33, 38, 50, 59, 64, 68, 75, 81, 97.
   Notice that there are two sets of numbers with the same sum:
   18 + 50 + 68 + 75 = 211 and 33 + 81 + 97 = 211.
   Prove that this always occurs. That is, prove that for any selection of ten different numbers less than 100 it is always possible to find two sets of numbers with the same sum.

9-4 MAKING A SAMPLE CHART

In *Exercises 9-3* you examined the distribution of 100 samples from different YES-NO populations. You may have noticed that frequencies do not always increase towards the mode (the most frequent sample) and then decrease after this. There were probably "hills and valleys". For example, in the frequency table in Step 3 of *Section 9-3*, there were 4 samples with 2 yesses but only 2 samples with 4 yesses. Variations like these occur when the frequency distribution is based on a small number of samples. In the work that follows, the data are obtained from a computer simulation using many more samples.

Using a computer simulation, a group of students collected data from 100 million samples (size 20) from a 30% YES population. The following frequency table shows their data. The frequencies have been rounded to the nearest million.

Number of yesses in the sample	Frequency (millions)
0	0
1	1
2	3
3	7
4	13
5	17
6	20
7	16
8	12
9	7
10	3
11	1
12	1
13	0
14	0
15	0
16	0
17	0
18	0
19	0
20	0

Some of the samples occur frequently. These are the samples that contain between 3 and 9 yesses. Other samples — more than 12 yesses — did not occur at all. The *likely samples* occur in the middle of the distribution. In this chapter we will use the middle 90% of the distribution for the likely samples. The first 5% and last 5% of the distribution are the *unlikely samples*. The frequency table is repeated below showing how to determine the likely and unlikely samples.

Number of yesses in the sample	Proportion of yesses in the sample	Frequency (millions)	
0	0	0	Total
Unlikely 1	0.05	1	not more
2	0.10	3	than 5
3	0.15	7	
4	0.20	13	
5	0.25	17	
6	0.30	20	
7	0.35	16	
8	0.40	12	
9	0.45	7	
10	0.50	3	
11	0.55	1	Total
Unlikely 12	0.60	1	not more
13	0.65	0	than 5
14	0.70	0	

Starting at the top of the table, count the frequencies. Stop when the count would go over 5. This occurs at 3 yesses. The 7 samples in this category would put the count above 5. Since this category is 3 yesses out of 20 we express the fraction $\frac{3}{20}$ as a decimal, 0.15. We say that the *proportion* of yesses in the sample is 0.15, and 0.15 is the first of the likely sample proportions.

Repeat the process, starting at the bottom of the table. Stop when you reach the category with 9 yesses (proportion 0.45), since the 7 samples here would put the count over 5.

The likely sample proportions begin at 3 yesses (proportion 0.15) and extend to 9 yesses (proportion 0.45).

We use a *90% boxplot* to summarize this information.

	90% boxplot for samples size 20 from a 30% YES population									
	Proportion of yesses in the sample									
0	0.10	0.20	0.30	0.40	0.50	0.60	0.70	0.80	0.90	1.00

The proportions in the box are the likely proportions. They occur 90% of the time. That is why we call the plot a 90% boxplot. The proportions outside the box are the unlikely proportions. They occur 10% of the time. The whiskers show some of the unlikely proportions. The whiskers stop at the last non-zero frequency, so they extend to 0.05 and to 0.60. Since we rounded the frequencies to the nearest million, the box and the whiskers cover 99% of the sample proportions, because frequencies less than 500 000 would be ignored. Proportions outside the range 0.05 to 0.60 occurred less than 1% of the time, and are ignored.

Here is a summary of the rules for constructing 90% boxplots, starting from a frequency table of the sampling distribution, where the frequencies total 100.
- Examine the frequencies starting from the lower end. Stop at the first proportion for which the frequency is not 0. This proportion marks the beginning of the whisker.
- Count the frequencies. Stop at the proportion in which the number would put the count greater than 5. This proportion marks the beginning of the box.
- Examine the frequencies from the upper end. Stop at the proportion for which the frequency is not 0. This proportion marks the end of the whisker.
- Count the frequencies. Stop at the proportion in which the number would put the count above 5. This proportion marks the end of the box.

On the chart on the next page, you will see the 90% boxplot for a 30% YES population. This is the beginning of our sample chart for samples of size 20. You will complete this chart in Exercise 3.

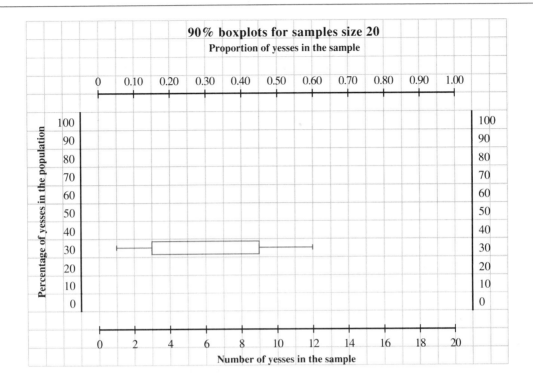

90% boxplots for samples size 20
Proportion of yesses in the sample

EXERCISES 9-4

1. Explain in your own words the meaning of each term.
   a) likely sample
   b) unlikely sample
   c) 90% boxplot
   d) 60% YES population
   e) proportion of yesses in the sample
   f) percentage of yesses in the population

Ⓑ

A computer program was used to calculate the expected frequencies for 100 million samples (size 20) from 9 YES-NO populations. Note that the tables do not include categories for which the frequency is 0. The frequencies have been rounded to the nearest million.

90% YES population

Proportion of yesses	0.70	0.75	0.80	0.85	0.90	0.95	1.0
Frequency	1	3	9	19	29	27	12

80% YES population

Proportion of yesses	0.55	0.60	0.65	0.70	0.75	0.80	0.85	0.90	0.95	1.0
Frequency	1	2	5	11	17	22	21	14	6	1

70% YES population

Proportion of yesses	0.45	0.50	0.55	0.60	0.65	0.70	0.75	0.80	0.85	0.90	0.95
Frequency	1	3	7	12	17	19	18	13	7	3	1

60% YES population

Proportion of yesses	0.30	0.35	0.40	0.45	0.50	0.55	0.60	0.65	0.70	0.75	0.80	0.85
Frequency	1	2	4	7	12	16	18	17	12	7	3	1

50% YES population

Proportion of yesses	0.25	0.30	0.35	0.40	0.45	0.50	0.55	0.60	0.65	0.70	0.75
Frequency	1	4	8	12	16	18	16	12	8	4	1

40% YES population

Proportion of yesses	0.15	0.20	0.25	0.30	0.35	0.40	0.45	0.50	0.55	0.60	0.65	0.70
Frequency	1	3	7	12	17	18	16	12	7	4	2	1

30% YES population

Proportion of yesses	0.05	0.10	0.15	0.20	0.25	0.30	0.35	0.40	0.45	0.50	0.55
Frequency	1	3	7	13	18	19	17	11	7	3	1

20% YES population

Proportion of yesses	0	0.05	0.10	0.15	0.20	0.25	0.30	0.35	0.40	0.45
Frequency	1	6	14	21	22	17	11	5	2	1

10% YES population

Proportion of yesses	0	0.05	0.10	0.15	0.20	0.25	0.30
Frequency	12	27	29	19	9	3	1

2. Use the information on the previous 2 pages. Copy and complete this table showing the likely sample proportions for each population.

Percentage of yesses in the population	Lowest likely proportion	Greatest likely proportion
90		
80		
70		
60		
50		
40		
30	0.15	0.45
20		
10		

3. Work in groups of 3 or 4. Using graph paper, make a copy of the sample chart. Construct 90% boxplots for samples of size 20 for each population listed above. Draw the boxplot on the appropriate line of the sample chart. Make one chart per group.

4. Use the computer program in *COMPUTER POWER* to construct a sample chart for a sample of size 43. Compare your chart with the chart for samples of size 40. Make a list of the differences between the two charts.

9-5 USING A SAMPLE CHART

In *Section 9-4* you learned how to construct sample charts. To construct a more complete sample chart requires a lot of time. So, in the sample chart on page 344 extra boxplots have been added to the one you constructed. This chart shows boxplots for 0% to 100% YES populations at 5% intervals. The charts on pages 365 to 368 allow even greater accuracy. They show the boxplots for the YES percentage of the population every 2%. These charts will be used in the next section.

You can use these charts to solve two kinds of problems.

From population information to sample information

The first kind of problem starts with information about the percentage of yesses in the population. Then you use the chart to obtain information about the samples you might expect to get.

Example 1. In the June 14th, 1988 issue of *PC WEEK*, there was a news item about a computer program called "LOTTO LOGIC!" The following sentence appeared in the article, which described a system for predicting winning numbers in lotteries like LOTTO 649.

> "The system is based on statistical analysis that shows that 85% of the winning numbers in any lottery have been picked in the last 10 draws."

That statement seems suspicious. So Janice decides to check out the claim. Is it true that all winning lottery numbers are an 85% YES population?

Solution. The YES-NO question for each winning number is,
"Was this also a winning number in any of the 10 previous draws?"
Janice looks at data from the LOTTO 649 lottery. There are 7 winning numbers (including the bonus number) in each draw. Janice needed 20 numbers for her sample so she looked at the 21 winning numbers in the previous 3 draws. One number was chosen at random and ignored. For each of the 20 winning numbers, Janice looked to see if it was also a winning number in any of the previous 10 draws. She found that 13 of the 20 numbers had also been winning numbers in at least one of the previous 10 draws.

Now she looks at the 90% boxplot (sample size 20) for an 85% YES population.

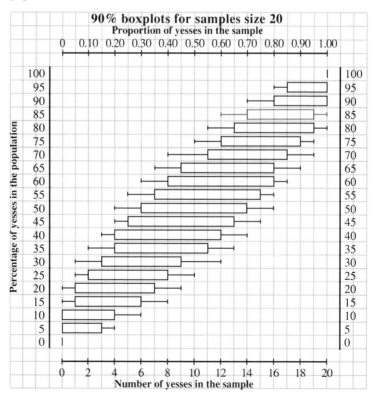

The box extends from 0.70 to 0.95. These are the proportions between which the likely samples occur. But Janice's sample had $\frac{13}{20}$, or 0.65 proportion of yesses. The proportion 0.65 does not lie in this box. So she comes to the conclusion that, based on that particular sample, she cannot agree that 85% of winning lottery numbers have occurred in the previous 10 draws.

Janice realizes that she might, in fact, be wrong in her disagreement. The likely samples make up only 90% of all samples that occur. So she is prepared to be wrong 10% of the time. This is the number of times she would get an unlikely sample from an 85% YES population. Her sample with a 0.65 YES proportion might be one of the unlikely samples from an 85% YES population.

In the situation in *Example 1*, it is not a serious matter to make a wrong decision. However, in a statistical experiment to determine the effectiveness of a new vaccine (like the Salk polio vaccine) it is very important to decide if the vaccine is truly effective. To minimise the risk of making errors, researchers use very large samples. Over 1 million children were involved in the Salk vaccine experiment.

From sample information to population information

The second kind of problem is found in opinion surveys. In this case, you start with some information about the proportion of yesses in a sample. Then you use the chart to deduce information about the YES percentage in the population from which the sample was collected.

This is the most common application of sample charts. The power of the survey technique lies in its ability to use data from a sample to deduce information about the population from which it was taken.

Example 2. A biologist was using survey methods to estimate the size of the squirrel population in a town. He set traps to catch squirrels, which he then released after marking them with a dye. After several days he had marked 40 squirrels. The next day he caught 20 squirrels, 8 of them marked. What is the percentage of marked squirrels in the population at that time?

Solution. The sample has $\frac{8}{20}$, or a 0.40 proportion of yesses, where YES represents a marked squirrel. Put a ruler down the chart on page 346 through a proportion of 0.40. You will see that the edge of the ruler lies in a box if the percentage of yesses in the population is 25%, 30%, 35%, 40%, 45%, 50%, 55% or 60%. The proportion 0.40 is a likely proportion if the percentage of marked squirrels is between 25% and 60%. This means that the percentage of marked squirrels is somewhere between 25% and 60%.

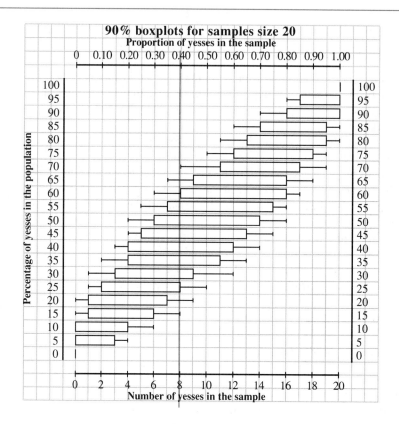

90% boxplots for samples size 20
Proportion of yesses in the sample

In *Example 2*, we call the range between 25% and 60% a *confidence interval*. The sample that the biologist caught gave him a confidence interval (25% to 60%) for the percentage of marked squirrels in the population. If he repeated this experiment, he would get a different confidence interval for each sample he caught. The sample chart used here was made up from 90% boxplots, hence 9 times out of 10, the confidence interval will contain the correct percentage of marked squirrels. So the confidence intervals that we obtain from charts of 90% boxplots are called 90% *confidence intervals*.

Because the biologist used a sample chart with 90% boxplots, he cannot be certain that every one of the confidence intervals contains the actual percentage of marked squirrels. He can only say that 9 out of 10 confidence intervals will contain the percentage of marked squirrels. In fact, a professional biologist would not be comfortable with a 90% confidence interval. He or she would use 95% boxplots, since this is the usual practice among statisticians. These charts would give wider confidence intervals because the boxes are wider. He would now be able to say that 19 out of 20 confidence intervals will contain the correct percentage of marked squirrels. We would call these *95% confidence intervals*.

EXERCISES 9-5

Ⓐ

1. Use your ruler and the chart on page 346. For the population percentages given below, say if each sample proportion is likely or unlikely. The sample size is 20.

	Percentage of yesses in the population	Proportion (number) of yesses in the sample
a)	80%	0.65 (13)
b)	20%	0.35 (7)
c)	65%	0.80 (16)
d)	65%	0.40 (8)
e)	35%	0.55 (11)
f)	35%	0.70 (14)
g)	15%	0.35 (7)

2. For each sample proportion (sample size 20), give the range of percentage of yesses in the population for which the sample proportion is likely.
   a) 0.20   b) 0.35   c) 0.60   d) 0.70   e) 0.85

3. Copy and complete the table to show the likely sample proportion of yesses for each given percentage of yesses in the population.

	Percentage of yesses in the population	Likely proportion of yesses in the sample (size 20)
	20%	0.05 to 0.35
a)	45%	
b)	60%	
c)	80%	
d)	95%	

4. Copy and complete the table to show the 90% confidence interval for each percentage of yesses in the population from which the sample came.

	Proportion of yesses in the sample	90% confidence interval
	0.15	5% to 30%
a)	0.30	
b)	0.55	
c)	0.60	
d)	0.75	

5. If you had a chart made from 95% boxplots:
   a) would the boxes be longer or shorter than those for 90% boxplots?
   b) would the confidence intervals be longer or shorter than those from charts of 90% boxplots?

Ⓑ

6. A newspaper article said that 40% of the cars on the ferries to Vancouver Island were Japanese cars. If you took samples (size 20) of the cars on a ferry, what are the likely proportions of Japanese cars? (Use the chart of 90% boxplots on page 346.)

7. On a ferry from Nanaimo to Horseshoe Bay in July 1988, a sample of 20 cars included 8 Japanese cars. Find the 90% confidence interval for the percentage of Japanese cars on the ferry.

8. A computer generated 10 samples from a 60% YES population. An x shows a YES response and an o shows a NO response. For each sample, find the corresponding 90% confidence interval. Check to see if the percentage of yesses in the population lies in 9 out of 10 confidence intervals on average.

	Sample	**Confidence interval**	**Contains 60%**
a)	X X O X X O X X X O O X X O X X X X X O	50%–85%	Yes
b)	O X X X X O X O X X X X O O O O X X O		
c)	O X O O O X X X O O X X X X X X X X O X		
d)	O O O X X O X X X O X X X X X O O O X X		
e)	O O X X O O O O X X X O X X X O O X X O		
f)	O X X X X X X O X X X X X X X X X X O X		
g)	O X X O O X X X O X X O X O X O X X X O		
h)	O O O X X X O X O X O X O X O X O X X X O X		
i)	X O X X X X O X X X X X X X O O X X O X		
j)	X X X X X O X X O X X O O O O O X X X O		

9. Repeat *Exercise 8* for the 10 samples from each of the 75% and 35% YES populations.

a) From a 75% YES population

```
X X X O X X O X X O X X O X X X X X X
X X O X X X X X X X X O O X X X X X O
X X X X X O X O X X O O X X O X O X X X
X O X X X X O X X X X O X X X X X O X
X X X O X X X X X X X X O X X X X O
O O X X X X X O O X X X O X X X O X X X
O X X X X X O O X X X O X X O X X X X O
X X X X X X O O X X O O X X O X X X X O
O X O X X X X X O X X X O X X O X X X X
X X X X O X X O X X X X O X X O O X X O
```

b) From a 35% YES population

```
X O X O O O X O O O X X O O O O X O O X
X X O O O X O O O O O X O O O X X O X O
O O X O X O O O O X O X X O O O O O O O
O O O O O O O O O O O X O O X O O X O O
X X X O X O O O O O O O X O X O O O X O
X O O O X O O X O O O O X O X O O X X O
O O O O O O X X O X O X O X O O X X O O
O O O O O O O X X O X X X O O O O O O O
X O O X X O O O O O X O X O O O X O X O
O O O O O X O X O O O O X X X O O O X O
```

9-6 USING SAMPLE CHARTS FOR DIFFERENT SIZE SAMPLES

You may have noticed that the confidence intervals for samples of size 20 are quite wide. That is, for any given sample, there is a wide range of the percentage of yesses in the population for which the sample is likely. If we increase the size of a sample, then we can obtain more precise information about the percentage of yesses in the population. Look at the two sample charts on pages 365 and 368. These are the charts for samples of size 20 and samples of size 100.

The boxes for samples of size 100 are shorter than those for samples of size 20. There is an inverse relation between the length of the box and the size of the sample (see Exercise 13). Also, the confidence intervals for samples of size 100 are shorter than the confidence intervals for samples of size 20. This is because the boxes themselves are shorter. So, the larger the sample size, the shorter the confidence interval.

One application of larger sample surveys is the capture-recapture method of estimating the size of a wildlife population. Biologists use the confidence interval for the marked percentage in the population to calculate a confidence interval for the number of animals in the population.

Example.   In *Example 2*, Section 9-5, we looked at survey data collected by a biologist. After the biologist had marked and released 60 squirrels, he continued to capture squirrels, but released them without marking. He found 25 marked squirrels in a sample of 100 squirrels. Find a 90% confidence interval for the number of squirrels in the town.

Solution.   The proportion of marked squirrels in the sample is 0.25. From the chart of 90% boxplots for samples size 100 on page 368, we see that the 90% confidence interval for the percentage of marked squirrels in the town is 18% to 32%.

The biologist knows there are 60 marked squirrels, but he does not know the total number N of the squirrels in the town.

Using the lower estimate 18%:

If 18% of N is 60

then $0.18N = 60$

$$N = \frac{60}{0.18}$$

$$\doteq 333$$

Similarly, using the upper estimate of 32%:

If 32% of N is 60, then $0.32N = 60$

$$N = \frac{60}{0.32}$$

$$\doteq 188$$

The biologist assumes that there are between 188 and 333 squirrels in the town. This is a 90% confidence interval for the number of squirrels in the town.

EXERCISES 9-6

Ⓐ

1. Explain how the size of a sample affects the size of the confidence interval obtained from the sample.

2. Explain the meaning of the term "capture-recapture method".

Ⓑ

In these exercises, use the sample charts of 90% boxplots on pages 365–368.

3. Referring to the *Example*, using a sample size 20, the biologist found that it contained 8 marked squirrels. Assuming there were 40 marked squirrels in the population, calculate a 90% confidence interval for the number of squirrels in the population.

4. Repeat *Exercise 3* for a sample size 80 which contained 32 marked squirrels. Assume that there are 40 marked squirrels in the population.

5. Explain why the confidence interval you obtained in *Exercise 4* is shorter than the one you calculated in *Exercise 3*.

6. Janice investigated 100 numbers from a published list of winning numbers in the LOTTO 649 draw. She found that, out of 100 winning numbers, 72 were also winning numbers in some of the 10 previous draws. Find a 90% confidence interval for the percentage of winning numbers that also occurred in at least one of the 10 previous draws.

7. Copy and complete the table which compares confidence intervals for samples of size 20, 40, and 100. What conclusions can you draw?

	Proportion of yesses in the sample	Confidence interval sample size 20	Confidence interval sample size 40	Confidence interval sample size 100
	0.20	8% to 40%	12% to 32%	14% to 26%
a)	0.35			
b)	0.63			
c)	0.37			
d)	0.88			
e)	0.07			
f)	0.93			

8. One hundred boys and 100 girls answered questions in two surveys. Some of the data are listed below. For each piece of sample data, calculate a 90% confidence interval. Write your answer as a complete sentence; for example, "I am 90% confident that between 15% and 25% of grade 11 and 12 boys missed at least 2 classes last week".
   a) 68 grade 11 and 12 boys said that they spend more than $20 on a date
   b) 44 grade 11 and 12 girls said that they spend more than $20 on a date
   c) 6 grade 11 and 12 boys said that they smoked 10 or more cigarettes per day
   d) 14 grade 11 and 12 girls said that they smoked 10 or more cigarettes per day

9. Look at your answers to *Exercise 8 a)* and *b)*.
   a) Do the confidence intervals overlap?
   b) When the confidence intervals from two samples do not overlap, there are no
      populations for which both samples are likely samples. Then we say there is a
      significant difference between the two samples. Complete the following sentence
      for the two samples in *Exercise 8 a)* and *b)*.
      "It seems there is a significant difference in the percentage of grade 11 and
      12 boys and girls who ..."

10. Is there a significant difference in the percentage of girls and boys who smoke 10
    or more cigarettes per day? (See *Exercise 8 c)* and *d)*.)

11. Thirty students from a grade 12 statistics class went to a shopping mall on a Friday
    afternoon. They walked around the mall individually. At 2:30, each student counted
    the number of people he or she could see, recording results until the sample
    size was 40, 80 or 100. The students also counted the number of students from
    their class in their samples. Here are the data from three students.

Sample size	40	80	100
Number of students	4	7	8

    a) For each sample, find a 90% confidence interval for the percentage of people in
       the mall who are students in the class.
    b) Knowing that there are 30 students in the mall, find three 90% confidence intervals
       for the number of people in the mall.

12. In this question there are one hundred letters. Count the e's in this question and
    estimate the percentage of e's in English.

13. a) For a sample with a 0.50 proportion of yesses, find the confidence interval for
       the percentage of yesses in the population for sample sizes $N = 20, 40, 60,$
       80, and 100. (The confidence interval for $N = 60$ is 40% to 60%.)
    b) Draw a graph, plotting the width W of the confidence interval against the sample
       size N.
    c) Is the relation between W and N inverse or direct?
    d) Investigate the graphs of W against $\frac{1}{N}$, W against $\frac{1}{N^2}$, and W against $\frac{1}{\sqrt{N}}$ to
       determine which graph is linear.
    e) Find an equation relating W and N.

14. In an experiment to test for ability in Extra Sensory Perception, a girl was shown
    20 photographs of people, none of whom she knew. Below each photograph were
    5 telephone numbers, one of which was the phone number of the person in the
    photograph. The girl had to identify the correct phone number.
    a) What is the likely number of correct phone numbers she would get if she guessed?
    b) If she correctly identified 9 phone numbers, would you think that she had ESP
       ability?

9-7 LARGE SAMPLE SIZES

If we need more precise information about the percentage of yesses in a population, we must select a larger sample. People who commission opinion surveys would not be satisfied with confidence intervals that are 10 percentage points wide. They need much more precision than that; that is, much narrower confidence intervals.

In a survey of 100 grade 11 and 12 students, 50% of them said that they spent more than $16 on a date. From the chart of 90% boxplots for samples size 100 on page 368, the confidence interval for this sample is 58% to 42%. The percentage of yesses in the population differs from the percentage of yesses in the sample by up to 8 percentage points. We say that the *sampling error* is 8%. The sampling error measures the accuracy of the survey and it depends on the size of the sample. Newspaper reports sometimes call this the *margin of error*. The sample charts that we are using in this chapter are not suitable for obtaining the greater accuracy available from samples of one thousand or more. Instead, we will use a formula for the sampling error. This formula provides the sampling error from which we can obtain 95% confidence intervals. Note that we use 95% confidence intervals with larger samples.

If the size of a sample is N, then the sampling error of the percentage of yesses in the population is approximately $\frac{100}{\sqrt{N}}$. This is quite accurate for sample sizes greater than 100, if the percentage of yesses in the population is between 30% and 70%. Outside that range, the sampling error is less than $\frac{100}{\sqrt{N}}$. So, for a sample of size N, where $N > 100$, the sampling error of the percentage of yesses in the population is no greater than $\frac{100}{\sqrt{N}}$.

Example 1.   The students in Ken Chan's class conducted a telephone survey of their town. They asked 760 people if they had eaten breakfast at a restaurant or fast food outlet at least once in the past week. One hundred forty-five people said YES. Find a 95% confidence interval for the percentage of people in that town who eat breakfast out at least once a week.

Solution.   The proportion of yesses in the sample is $\frac{145}{760}$, or approximately 0.19. So, the percentages of yesses is 19%. Hence, the sampling error for a sample size 760 is $\frac{100}{\sqrt{760}}$, or about 3.6%.

The 95% confidence interval is $19\% - 3.6\%$ to $19\% + 3.6\%$, or about 15% to 23%, rounding to the nearest percent.

Example 2. Angus Reid conducted a survey in January 1988, of 1500 Canadians. Of those surveyed, 36% said that they felt the New Democratic Party was most likely to provide honest and open government. What is the 95% confidence interval for this survey?

Solution. For a sample of 1500, the sampling error is $\frac{100}{\sqrt{1500}}$, which is about 2.6%.

So the confidence interval is from 36% − 2.6% to 36% + 2.6%, or 33.4% to 38.6%. In a report, the writer would usually round this to 33% to 39%.

Information about the percentage of yesses in a population comes in the form of a confidence interval. In *Example 2*, we have no way of knowing where the percentage of yesses lies in the interval. Just because 36% is in the middle of the interval it does not mean that the percentage of yesses is likely to be near 36%. It could be *any* number in the interval.

Two opinion polls were conducted in June 1988. The Gallup Poll (June 9) reported that 39% of those surveyed supported the Liberal Party. The Angus Reid Poll (June 21) reported that 34% supported the Liberals. Each poll sampled about 1500 people. We have just calculated the sampling error as about 3%. So, all we can say about these two surveys is that in early June, somewhere between 36% and 42% supported the Liberals. Later, somewhere between 31% and 37% supported the Liberals. We have no way of knowing if the Liberal support went up by 1% or down by 11%.

When you read a statement such as ''the survey found that 34% . . .'', do not assume that the figure of 34% is exact. It isn't. It is a ''fuzzy'' number. It really represents any number you like between 31% and 37%. When you report on a survey, use a sentence like this.

''From our survey of 1500 people, we learned that somewhere between 31% and 37% of the population would support the Liberal Party if an election were held tomorrow. We are 95% confident of this, realizing that such statements are only correct 19 times out of 20.''

Gallup regularly conducts polls across all 10 provinces. When a sample of 1500 people is taken, the number taken from each province is proportional to the population of that province. So there may be only 150 people from Atlantic Canada, which means that the sampling error for opinions from this region might be as high as 9% (see Exercise 10).

EXERCISES 9-7

Ⓑ

1. Examine the survey reports that you assembled in *Exercises 9-1*. For each report, find the size of the sample and calculate the sampling error. Write your answer on the paper on which you pasted the report. The reported sampling error may differ from yours because different sampling methods produce different sizes of the sampling error. The report may use the term margin of error instead of sampling error.

For each survey reported in *Exercises 2* to *6*, calculate the 95% confidence interval using the $\frac{100}{\sqrt{N}}$ approximation. Write each answer as a sentence.

2. Angus Reid conducted a survey in British Columbia, where 33% of the 250 people questioned approved of the performance of the leader of the Federal Progressive Conservative Party.

3. A Gallup poll reported that 27% of Canadians say that unemployment is the country's key problem. The results were based on interviews with 1022 people.

4. In the same poll as *Exercise 3*, 57% of those surveyed in Atlantic Canada said that unemployment is the country's key problem. Ninety people from Atlantic Canada took part in the survey.

5. Fifteen hundred six Canadians were asked if they approved of the decision to grant the CBC a licence for an all-news television channel; 43% of them said YES.

6. Seven hundred twelve secondary school students in Nanaimo, North Vancouver, and Chicago took part in a survey in 1982. They provided the following data.
   a) 30% of the students spent more than $15 on a date
   b) 45% of the students had a part-time job
   c) 11% of the students worked 20 or more hours per week
   d) 16% of the students watched television for more than 20 h per week
   e) 50% of the students spent more hours on school assignments than watching TV
   f) 37% of the students spent more than 10 h a week on school assignments
   g) 17% of the students smoked
   h) 52% of the students had a driver's licence

7. In an experiment to determine the number of salmon in an area, 1000 salmon were tagged by removing their adipose fins. Later in a catch of 800 salmon, 45 were found to have had their adipose fins removed.
   a) Calculate the 95% confidence interval for the number of salmon in that area.
   b) Suggest two reasons, other than statistical uncertainty, why the figures you obtained might be inaccurate.

8. In a poll conducted in February 1989, 1002 Canadians were asked if they supported an elected Senate. Five hundred two said YES and 390 said NO, while the rest did not know. Find a 95% confidence interval for the number of Canadians who agree with the Prime Minister who does not support plans for an elected Senate.

9. At the time that the Canadian Parliament was debating whether to reinstate capital punishment for first-degree murder, a poll showed that 780 in a survey of 1050 Canadians thought that capital punishment should be reinstated.

a) Find a 95% confidence interval for the percentage of Canadians who think that the Government should reinstate the death penalty for first-degree murder.

b) Members of Parliament, in a free vote, voted not to reinstate the death penalty at this time. Do you think that Members of Parliament should vote based on the results of opinion surveys? Give reasons.

Ⓒ

10. The following paragraph was written in an article titled "The Pollstergeists" in the April 1988 issue of Saturday Night magazine.

"... the tiny margins of error (*sampling error*) reported for national samples may be more significant than they look. Sub-samples ("How do Liberals feel about John Turner?", "What do Westerners feel about free trade?") are subject to bigger probabilities of error. A good example was provided by a June 1987 Macleans-Angus Reid poll. Readers were told that Brian Mulroney's approval rating was 50% in Atlantic Canada and only 36% in Ontario. But the small number of Easterners in the sample meant a big error in the comparison. If that margin of error had been reckoned in, there might not have been any difference at all between the two groups — in fact, the approval rating in Ontario could have been 41% and the Atlantic figure only 1 point lower."

Explain how the author arrived at the figure of 41% and the implied figure of 40% in the last sentence.

9-8 COLLECTING SURVEY DATA — HOW TO CHOOSE A SAMPLING METHOD

Most of the work in this chapter is based on the use of the sample charts of 90% boxplots. A computer program produced these charts based on the laws of probability. One of the assumptions made in these calculations is that every sample of that size that could be drawn from the population has the same chance of being drawn.

It is not always convenient or possible to meet this requirement. So there are now many different ways of collecting samples. Some of the methods used by professional polling organizations are complicated and costly.

It is important to use a method that reduces the risk of getting a *biased sample*. This occurs when non-random methods affect the choice of individuals for the sample. A political organization which mails a large number of replies to a newspaper poll is biasing the sample in favor of the responses it would like to see. Data collected from a "mail-in" survey are biased in favor of those who feel strongly about the subject matter of the poll.

If your sample is biased, then you may get false information about the population. If you conducted a survey on women's rights and your sample of 20 students contained 2 boys, then your results might not reflect the opinions of all students.

Sampling methods are designed to prevent the bias that occurs when a particular group of people is overrepresented in a sample. We will look at some of the more common methods.

Simple random sample

A simple random sample is a sample obtained by a method that fits the requirement stated above; that is, every sample of that size that could be drawn from the population has the same chance of being drawn. The simple random sample is the foundation for all sampling methods. Here is an alternative definition.

> Every member of a population has an equal chance of being selected for the sample, *and* every member is selected independently from each other member.

This leads to the most common method of making sure that a sampling method produces a simple random sample — using a table of random digits.

Suppose you want a sample of 30 students enrolled in a Physical Education course. First you make a list of all the students in that course (the population) and number them. Assume there are 254 students on the list. Using the table of random digits (page 364), collect 30 three-digit numbers, each less than 255. The first three columns of the first ten lines are reproduced here.

98299	62016	63936
83032	90329	**111**13
46245	**208**25	**082**75
82755	**230**37	83622
94943	57301	**005**47
52348	25591	**042**33
19537	58635	32489
66214	31057	80911
06415	66362	98910
99596	88661	**215**96

An easy way to do this is to work down the columns, picking the first 3 digits in each group of 5 that form a number less than 255. The first such number is 195 (on the 7th line), then comes 064, 208, 230, 111, 082, 005, 042, 215, and so on. The students identified by these numbers would make up the sample.

You can see that this procedure is convenient only where the population is relatively small. It would be difficult to use this method to obtain a random sample of the voters in your town, even though there is a list of voters that is readily available. In this situation, you would use a process called multi-stage sampling.

Multi-stage sampling

Suppose you wanted to obtain a sample of 100 of the voters in your town. The voters' list is 200 pages long and there are 50 names on each page. You decide that you will pick 5 names off 20 pages. First you would use a table of random digits to pick a simple random sample of 20 pages using random numbers between 1 and 200. We call this Stage 1. Then for each page, you would pick a simple random sample of 5 names, using random numbers between 1 and 50. We call this Stage 2.

This is, perhaps, the best method of picking a sample of students at your school. Students are usually grouped into divisions (or home rooms) for administration purposes. These division lists could be used as the voters' list was used.

Probability sample

If there is a large variation in the number of students in each division, then it would not be true that each student has the same chance of being chosen. Suppose that each grade 8 division had 20 students and each grade 12 division had 30 students. Then, the probability that a particular grade 8 student is chosen is greater than that for a particular grade 12 student. This is the normal situation in Gallup and other polls. If we know the probability of selecting someone for each group in a multi-stage sampling method, then it is possible to compensate for this error after collecting the data. We call this *probability sampling*. Polling organisations use this method. The details of the compensation calculations are beyond the level of this book.

Stratified random sample

You may want to be sure that a sample is representative of all parts of the population. A simple random sample can sometimes produce samples that do not represent all groups in a population. Suppose that in your school you have the following numbers of students in each grade.

Grade	Number of students
8	300
9	300
10	250
11	200
12	200
Total	1250

If you wanted a sample of 125 students, then you could collect simple random samples from each grade; 30 students from each of grades 8 and 9, 25 students from grade 11, and 20 students from each of grades 11 and 12. We call this a *stratified random sample*.

Cluster sample

You would use this method if you wanted to conduct a survey of your town using door-to-door interviews. First you get a street map of your town. This usually has a street index. You use a table of random digits to pick a simple random sample of streets; one street for each student in the project. Then each student would pick a simple random sample of houses in that street. It makes it easier to collect the information, if all the houses for a particular student are close together.

Systematic sampling

One way of making sure that a sample is representative of the population is to use systematic sampling. In this method, you put the population in some order then select a random number, say 10, and choose every 10th person for the sample.

You could use this method to sample cars leaving the school parking lot. Post a student at each exit (there may be more than one) of the parking lot and then select every 10th car. This method is also useful in selecting a sample of shoppers in a shopping mall. Select an area that is neutral; that is, not near a particular store. Decide on a time interval long enough to conduct the interview, say 10 min. Then every 10 min, select the next person who crosses the area you have selected.

The main point of any method is that you must set the rules for yourself before you start sampling and then keep to the rules. Otherwise, you may find yourself selecting people who look ''easy to talk to''. If you are a girl, you may find yourself selecting more females than males, which may introduce bias into the survey.

Bias occurs in a sampling method when factors other than random selection affect the choice of a person for the sample. One method of sampling that often gives very biased samples is convenience sampling.

Convenience sample

We give this name to any sampling method that does not meet the requirements of a simple random sample. An inspector who inspects crates of apples from the Okanagan valley will usually select her sample from the top of the crate. She takes a sample from those members of the population that are conveniently available.

If you sample the students at your school by talking to students in the cafeteria during a particular class, that would be a convenience sample. Similarly, a survey conducted by asking your friends would be using a convenience sample. Such samples are easy to collect, but they will often give biased data.

Self-selected sample
This is the least reliable method of sampling. The data are almost always biased. A well-known example of self-selected sampling involved Ann Landers. She asked her readers to write and tell her if they would have children if they could live their lives over again. Seventy percent of the 10 000 responses said, "No, they would not have children again." This caused consternation in some places. Newsweek commissioned a professional survey, asking the same question. Of the 1200 people questioned, 91% said that they would have children again. One reason that the Ann Landers data were so biased against having children may be connected with the kind of people who read and write to Ann Landers. Often these are people with personal problems, some of which concern parents or children (see Exercise 7).

Another example occurred in the 1972 American presidential election campaign. A local TV station asked viewers if they approved of President Nixon's decision to mine Haiphong Harbour in Vietnam. About 5000 said YES and 1000 said NO. Later, the station found that workers from the Nixon campaign had mailed over 2000 postcards agreeing with the decision. The bias occurred in this example because a large number of pro-Nixon responses had self-selected themselves for the sample. This was a non-random factor that strongly affected the results.

There seems to be very little value in the information obtained from self-selected samples, yet they are a very common part of media activity.

EXERCISES 9-8

1. Describe how you would obtain the following samples of 30 grade 11 students from your school.
   a) Simple random sample
   b) Stratified random sample
   c) Cluster sample
   d) Self-selected sample
   e) Convenience sample

2. The owner of a sporting goods store in a shopping mall wanted to conduct a market research survey. He thought that he would do this as soon as the mall opened on a Monday morning because he was not very busy then. So he asked the first 100 people who passed his store to answer a brief questionnaire.
   a) What kind of a sample would you call this?
   b) What kind of people would not be represented in this sample?
   c) Would the owner get a sample representative of those who used his store?
   d) How would the data be biased?
   e) What sampling method would you propose to the store owner that might avoid this bias?

3. A student surveyed grade 12 students about some of the factors involved with teenage suicide. She gave the questionnaire to all the students in the four grade 12 courses in which she was a student.
   a) What kind of a sample would you call this?
   b) What students would not be represented in this sample?
   c) What kind of bias might occur with this method?
   d) What sampling method would you propose that might avoid this bias?

4. Which of the following methods would give a simple random sample?
   a) The first 10 students who entered your classroom
   b) The students who were selected by your teacher to answer a question in class
   c) Students whose locker number ends in a randomly-selected digit
   d) The students in your class who walked to school that day
   e) Number the desks 1 to 30. Use a table of random digits to select 10 students.

5. Examine the survey reports that you collected in *Exercises 9-1*. Describe the sampling method used in each survey. Write your answer on the paper on which you pasted the report.

6. In the following examples, decide which groups might be underrepresented using the sampling methods described.
   a) The largest survey ever was conducted in 1936. The Literary Digest conducted a survey of voting preferences in the Roosevelt/Landon American presidential election campaign, using a sample of 2.4 million voters. It used a list of names from telephone directories, automobile owners, club memberships and its own subscription list. The poll predicted Landon would win 53% to 47%. In fact, Roosevelt won 62% to 38%.
   b) Ann Landers asked her readers to write in to say whether they would have children again if they had the opportunity to live their lives over again.
   c) In a survey to discover students' attitudes towards the new Star Trek series, a student asked the teachers of the grade 12 mathematics course to give the questionnaire to every third student on the class lists.
   d) In a survey to discover whether Toronto residents support a bid to hold the 1996 Summer Olympic Games in Toronto, a student surveyed 100 spectators at a Blue Jays baseball game.
   e) A Vancouver sports fan wanted to know how many people regularly watched the Vancouver Canucks on television. She asked 200 spectators at a B.C. Lions football game.
   f) A student conducted an opinion survey about the school's sports activities. He asked students at the end of afternoon school. Seven of the 20 people he asked said that they did not have time to answer his questions. Instead, he asked 7 others who were waiting for a ride home.

7. Give your reasons why the Ann Landers poll (*Exercise 6b*) might give biased results.

8. Describe how you would collect a sample of 100 people from the following populations to participate in a survey of opinions on the public and private school systems.
   a) The parents of students at your school
   b) The parents of all students in your school district
   c) Members of the public who do not have any children in school
   d) All secondary school students in the school district
   e) Members of the legal, medical, architectural and engineering professions working in your school district
   f) Listeners to an open-line radio show
   g) Shoppers at a local shopping mall

9. In *Exercise* 8, which of the samples would not be representative of the entire population in your school district?

10. Assume that you are Ken Chan who has the task of sampling the residents of his town (say 20 000 adults) to determine what percentage of the residents eat breakfast out at least once a week. Write a description of the procedure you would use to obtain a sample of about 700 people. Assume that you have the cooperation of the 25 students in your mathematics class.

9-9 CONDUCTING A SURVEY

One of the most interesting aspects of studying surveys is conducting your own survey. As a final activity in this chapter you should design, conduct, and write a brief report on an opinion survey. The work involved in doing this is reduced if you work with a team of 4 or 5 students. Each student should make up a YES-NO question. Preferably, all the questions on the questionnaire should be on the same theme. Here are some suggestions of ways to avoid some of the problems you may incur.

Wording the questions
It is sometimes very surprising to see how the results differ when you make even small changes to the wording of a question. Your group might like to use the same questionnaire as another group in the class and make *slight* changes to the wording of the questions. Then you could compare the results obtained by the two groups.

A very common problem occurs when you use vague wording. Consider the question, "Do you smoke?" A YES could include students who smoke less than 1 cigarette per month as well as heavy smokers. A more precise question would be, "Did you smoke more than 10 cigarettes last week?"

Try to word each question in such a way that there is a clear YES or NO reply. Then try out the questionnaire on some of your friends. You are not trying to get a simple random sample here. You are just testing the questions to observe any difficulties that may arise that you had not thought about.

Choosing the sampling method

You should take some time planning this phase of the survey. The most important thing to remember is that you must avoid a sample that could give a biased answer. Remember that you are using the sampling method to try to obtain information about a population. You should try to get a simple random sample which is representative of the population in which you are interested. At the same time, the method should not be so complicated that you will spend many hours collecting the data. The aim of this project is that you should learn some of the problems involved in conducting surveys. In this way you will read survey reports with some scepticism and learn to question the validity of survey reports.

You may find that a telephone survey is more comfortable than conducting personal interviews. It is not difficult to collect a simple random sample using telephone numbers. You can either generate random telephone numbers (last 4 digits) or use systematic sampling from the telephone directory. There are problems with each method. The difficulty with the first method is that you may get many "number not in service" messages. Using the second method will prevent you from sampling those people with unlisted telephone numbers.

Administering the questionnaire

If you are working with several other students, you should decide on the exact words you will use when you approach someone for data. If you have ever been interviewed by a professional pollster, you should have noticed that the person read every word from the printed question- naire, including the introductory remarks. When you compile your questionnaire, you should include *all* the words that you will use. Try to make sure each member of the group uses the same wording.

Writing the report

The report need not be lengthy, but should contain all the relevant information. There is an organization called the American Association for Public Opinion Research. It has a code of ethics which specifies some of the items that should be in a report. These include the answers to the following questions.

- Whose opinions were being surveyed? What was the population in which you were interested?
- What sampling method did you use? You should name the method as well as giving a brief description. It should be clear that you understand elementary survey methods.
- How large was the sample? What was the margin of error for this size of sample? It is better to use a sentence like the one given as an example earlier on page 353. Not many readers will understand a sentence like, ''This figure is accurate to 2.8% 19 times out of 20.''
- What was the *exact* wording of the questions?
- When and how was the survey administered? Did you use personal interviews, or telephone or mail-in surveys?

Make the report interesting to read. Use a word processor or simple desk-top publishing software. You should try to make people want to read your report. After all, you will have put some effort into compiling this information.

Making it interesting

For the survey, try to find a subject in which you have a strong personal interest. It does not really matter what the subject is as long as *you* find it interesting. Most students have, at some time or other, asked the question, ''I wonder how many people . . .''. Perhaps now is your opportunity to find out. The more interest you have in the survey, the more enjoyable it will be. Have fun!

Table of Random Digits

98299	62016	63936	42696	79412	33464	71626	91585	60512	45640	91504	14845	12356
83032	90329	11113	05030	72392	43564	24524	16443	36221	54893	26696	34281	82327
46245	20825	08275	88425	93739	77577	55718	00139	94440	89650	00680	29357	26169
87255	23037	83622	37490	51432	00083	73365	29632	79251	28412	25570	23097	50924
94943	57301	00547	04263	20935	85062	68603	22225	00080	48185	33139	25929	52365
52348	25591	04233	49508	86629	75577	52033	26456	17744	69916	31212	81012	70161
19537	58635	32489	79669	22784	13984	89615	94563	80549	88900	23192	93300	33493
66214	31057	80911	66007	42808	51823	75535	68873	37082	82744	75279	57057	63554
06415	66362	98910	39960	20965	11177	09433	23013	17323	78169	88913	30061	08361
99596	88661	21596	17513	69241	06641	09689	14563	29364	61651	67431	43471	29622
86558	31875	62192	23105	75275	58219	92246	53591	88908	73287	84285	63717	97433
90867	91666	35703	37257	30915	34229	25276	22933	54664	46204	33299	89129	40748
85068	17481	29329	53598	71516	49554	08753	14697	40096	87862	98301	16453	58627
02019	06674	70505	05516	79450	73774	42109	14206	13459	15851	92143	93455	49132
95122	23288	61670	64127	67185	75648	43277	42771	30663	90033	17542	24737	34300
02996	32054	98680	86553	25829	80882	43614	50183	18783	74654	63453	33855	28926
44234	48229	02558	94375	28724	74621	24345	85393	27376	27644	95517	19474	78433
80565	34758	36903	49513	25699	86653	30049	49562	19420	91420	52455	63980	03159
42989	31477	95475	24134	75397	69272	61904	94867	65333	72819	81794	93813	99743
92589	46721	27515	54218	08632	84504	79120	89415	61201	06450	63606	66274	46331
02240	81310	33497	01527	40858	87432	34188	83233	95127	91802	59499	53488	85799
20559	04464	57017	88591	40628	55186	43742	32273	67707	87911	07268	67230	63421
52874	41406	63374	41177	52216	27449	69470	88660	88081	69409	34617	01409	41270
82576	61832	35422	31330	84594	93327	89555	71439	75225	25619	69794	41035	28062
94713	97139	44270	21271	69439	66009	35865	95403	50113	65683	24451	43244	83159
84275	08194	45171	26506	21629	31029	01232	21545	84595	82470	98995	11079	15121
38341	88829	85103	61685	84981	08660	77671	73521	00304	16942	99491	16744	28304
00755	14648	83899	74765	51164	75375	76336	69073	59391	58938	17171	64942	88432
90575	90437	04719	28597	77252	77595	89877	26074	56756	12767	97203	04674	40438
69233	57412	94995	24667	98627	34108	31918	71374	05922	38404	01519	88149	57264
62825	12099	64288	33836	19246	63962	77023	54186	50249	92586	34410	75926	34129
11076	69454	78625	65783	41060	53270	35340	56453	04130	58385	88768	91546	81119
96145	29069	77788	57184	24303	49355	79212	62632	39065	59954	15997	88301	25120
58084	60014	30152	78117	70892	03738	54847	77704	89057	00508	65819	91880	85745
15452	64240	59950	99098	92683	08628	17308	28641	14340	17549	97771	45409	87344
27103	81698	58223	06951	52844	39332	34522	43644	51488	91803	52201	11900	76717
94809	29832	22884	56830	35332	04551	88725	37115	80527	51566	59491	01644	22299
48756	27521	76857	64597	67302	87677	48915	11504	84115	04166	34320	37382	63488
32658	26792	62341	60390	85585	95824	54161	68833	20440	21411	86863	04533	84508
05380	54390	98936	52443	68213	90935	12609	53768	28777	05975	79677	80074	50395

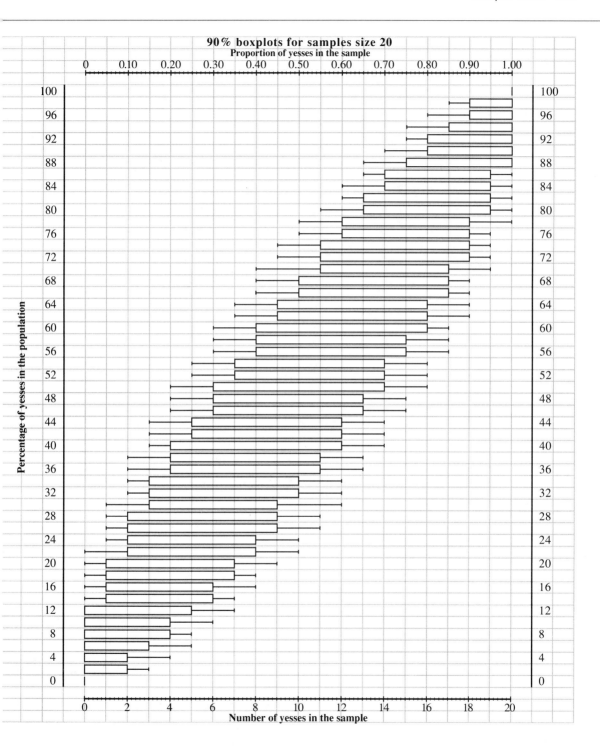

90% boxplots for samples size 20
Proportion of yesses in the sample

Percentage of yesses in the population

Number of yesses in the sample

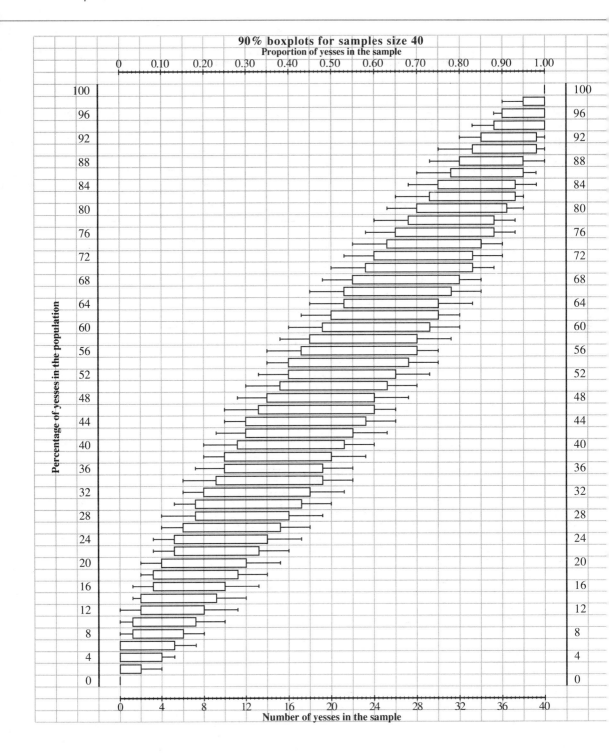

90% boxplots for samples size 40

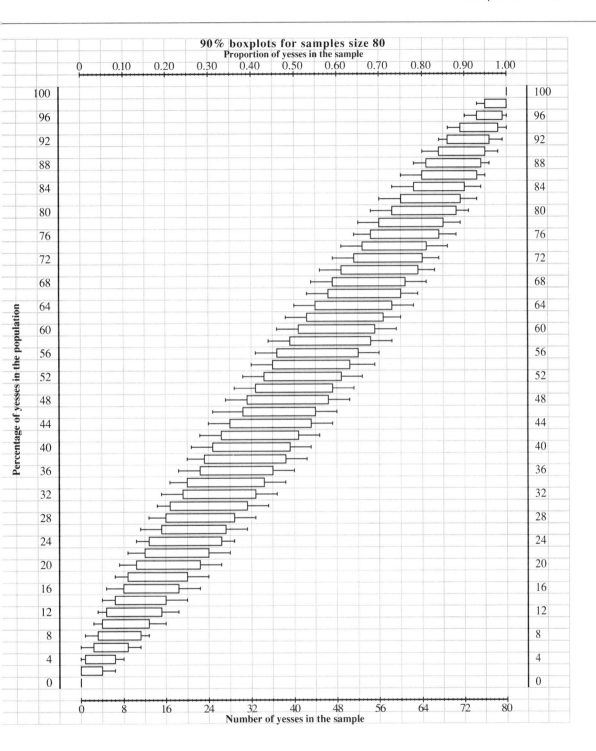

90% boxplots for samples size 80
Proportion of yesses in the sample

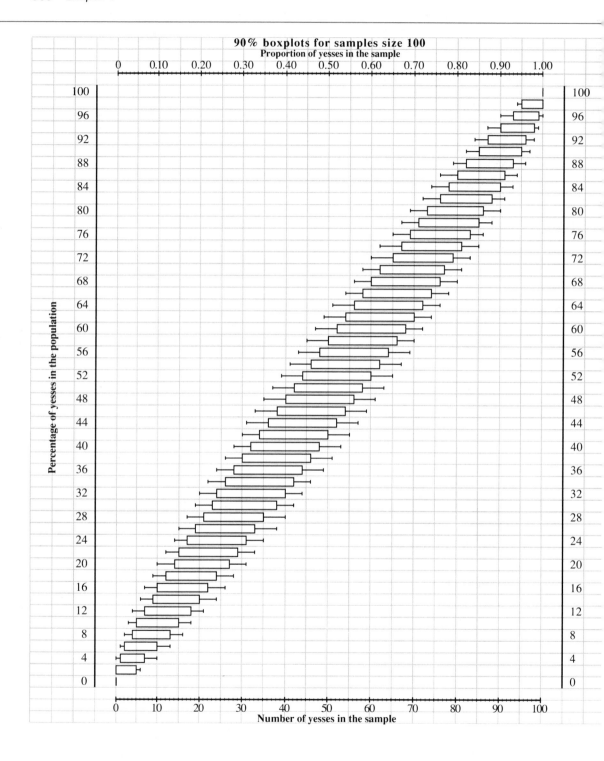

90% boxplots for samples size 100
Proportion of yesses in the sample

10 Trigonometry

The Simplon tunnel joining Italy and Switzerland was
constructed by boring from both ends. When they
met, in 1906, the engineers found that the two parts of
the tunnel were exactly in line. How was this done?
(See Section 10-11, *Example 4.*)

10-1 REVIEW: THE TANGENT RATIO

We often talk about the steepness of a roof, a hill, or a cable car ride.
This steepness can be measured in at least two ways.

The *slope* of an incline is the ratio of the
rise to the *run*.

The *angle of inclination* of a line is the angle
between the line and the horizontal line
which it intersects.

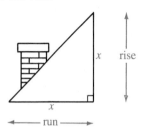

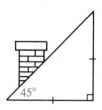

Slope = $\dfrac{\text{rise}}{\text{run}}$

$= \dfrac{x}{x}$, or 1

The angle of inclination is 45°.

All roofs inclined at 45° have a slope of 1 no matter how high or how
wide they are. This suggests that for any angle of inclination θ there
is a unique slope, which we call the *tangent of* θ. We use the symbol
tan θ to denote this slope. The relationship between θ and tan θ is
shown in the diagram below.

$\tan \theta = \dfrac{y}{x}$

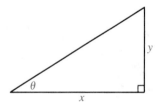

   If we know the value of θ, then tan θ can be found by drawing
and measuring.

Example 1. Construct an angle of 20° and determine tan 20° by measuring.

Solution.   Construct an angle of 20° using a protractor.

Since tan 20° is the ratio $\dfrac{BC}{AB}$, we measure these segments.

We find BC $\doteq$ 1.8 cm and
AB $\doteq$ 5.0 cm.

$\tan 20° \doteq \dfrac{1.8}{5}$

$= 0.36$

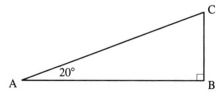

To determine tan 20° we drew a right triangle. This right triangle can be any size so long as the hypotenuse is inclined at 20°. The slope (or tangent ratio) will be the same for all such triangles since all such triangles are similar.

If we know tan θ, we can find θ by drawing and measuring.

Example 2. Given tan $\theta = 3$, find θ by measuring.

Solution. Construct a line of slope 3 by constructing a right triangle with a vertical side 6 cm and a horizontal side 2 cm.

Then, tan $\theta = \dfrac{6}{2}$

$= 3$

Measure the angle θ with a protractor.

$\theta \doteq 72°$

An angle of 72° has a tangent of about 3.

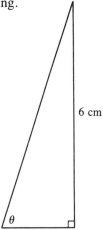

6 cm

θ

2 cm

Precise values of tan θ for various angles θ have been generated by computer and are recorded in published trigonometric tables.

A scientific calculator has a ⎡tan⎤ key, which can be used to find the tangent of an angle.

Example 3. A ski tow is inclined at an angle of 24°. What is the slope of the ski tow, to 3 decimal places?

Solution. The slope of the ski tow is tan 24°.

Use your calculator.   tan 24° $\doteq$ 0.445

The slope of the tow is about 0.445.

Example 4. A guy wire is to be connected to the top of a rocket to hold it in place. What angle of inclination must the wire have if the slope of the wire is to be 3.5?

Solution. If θ is the angle of inclination, then

tan $\theta = 3.5$.

Use your calculator. $\theta \doteq 74°$

The wire should be inclined at an angle of 74°.

3.5

θ

1

The angle of inclination is sometimes described as the *angle of elevation*.

EXERCISES 10-1

Ⓐ

1. Construct each angle and determine its tangent to 2 decimal places by measuring.
   a) 15°   b) 35°   c) 60°   d) 75°

2. For each value of tan θ, find θ to the nearest degree by drawing and measuring.

   a) tan $\theta = \dfrac{1}{2}$ b) tan $\theta = 1$ c) tan $\theta = 1.6$ d) tan $\theta = 2.5$

3. Find tan θ to 3 decimal places for each value of θ.
   a) 23°   b) 47°   c) 62°   d) 7°   e) 38°
   f) 82°   g) 51°   h) 17°   i) 70°   j) 88°

4. Find θ to the nearest degree for each value of tan θ.
   a) 0.839   b) 2.145   c) 0.532   d) 1.540   e) 5.145
   f) 0.087   g) 0.344   h) 0.649   i) 11.430   j) 2.356

Ⓑ

5. Large shopping malls make use of ramps, steps, and escalators to move people from one level to another. Find the angle of inclination to the nearest degree and the slope to 1 decimal place of each conveyor.
   a) ramp   b) steps   c) escalator

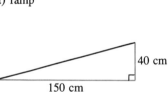
150 cm, 40 cm

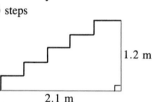
2.1 m, 1.2 m

4.5 m
5.0 m

6. The back of a chaise lounge is adjustable. Find the slope of the back for each angle of inclination. Give the answers to 3 decimal places.
   a) 5°   b) 35°   c) 60°   d) 80°

7. A TV tower is supported by guy wires (below left). Find the angle of inclination to 1 decimal place and the slope to 3 decimal places of each wire.

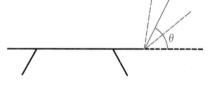
15 m, 15 m, 22 m

2.5 m, 2.65 m

8. The distance between floors in a new home is 2.5 m (above right). If the stairs require 2.65 m measured along the floor, find their slope to 3 decimal places, and the angle of inclination to 1 decimal place.

9. In a large ship the stairs between decks are much steeper than in your home. If the decks are 2.5 m apart and 0.9 m of floor space are required, find the slope of the stairs to 3 decimal places and the angle of inclination to 1 decimal place.

10. When trees are used as a windbreak the approximate path of the wind is as shown in the diagram below. Find the measures of the angles at A and at B to the nearest degree.

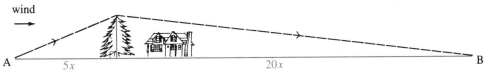

11. The seats in the balcony of a theatre are as shown in the diagram. Each seat is 40 cm above the one in front. There are 90 cm for each seat and the accompanying leg room. Find the angle of inclination of the balcony to the nearest degree.

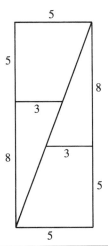

Ⓒ

12. A conveyor belt rises 2.40 m. What is the horizontal distance between the ends of the belt for each angle of inclination?
    a) 32°   b) 55°

🐟 INVESTIGATE

An 8 cm by 8 cm square is cut into 4 pieces, as shown. The pieces are then rearranged to form a 5 cm by 13 cm rectangle.
a) Are the areas of the figures equal?   b) Explain where the error is.

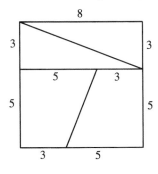

10-2 REVIEW: THE PRIMARY TRIGONOMETRIC RATIOS

In the previous section we learned that the slope of a line can be expressed as a ratio of two sides of a right triangle, or in terms of an angle of inclination. When the angle of inclination is θ, the slope is tan θ.

The next example shows how we can use the relationship between tan θ and θ to find the height of an inaccessible cliff.

Example 1. The top of a cliff has an angle of elevation of 36° when measured from a point 175 m away from its base. How high is the cliff?

Solution.　Let h metres represent the height of the cliff.

Then, $\tan 36° = \dfrac{h}{175}$

$h = 175 \tan 36°$

Use your calculator.

$h \doteq 127.144\ 94$

The cliff is about 127 m high.

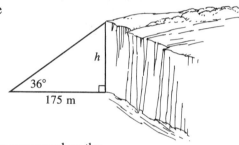

The tangent of an angle in a right triangle can be expressed as the ratio of the side *opposite* the angle to the side *adjacent* to the angle.

We write $\tan \theta = \dfrac{\text{opposite}}{\text{adjacent}}$

Example 1 demonstrated how we use the tangent ratio to calculate the length of the side opposite a given angle, given the length of the adjacent side. We could not use this ratio if we were given instead the length of the hypotenuse.

To remove this limitation we define two additional ratios called the sine and cosine ratios. The *sine ratio* for an angle θ is written *sin* θ and the *cosine ratio* is written *cos* θ. We define the sine and cosine ratios as follows.

$\sin \theta = \dfrac{\text{opposite}}{\text{hypotenuse}}$

$\cos \theta = \dfrac{\text{adjacent}}{\text{hypotenuse}}$

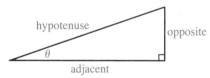

The ratios sin θ, cos θ, and tan θ are called the *primary trigonometric ratios*.

Example 2. a) Find to 4 decimal places.
   i) sin 68°   ii) cos 47°
   b) Find to the nearest degree.
   i) the angle θ for which sin θ = 0.47
   ii) the angle ϕ for which cos ϕ = 0.39

Solution. a) i) For sin 68°, use your calculator.
   sin 68° $\doteq$ 0.9272
   ii) For cos 47°, use your calculator.
   cos 47° $\doteq$ 0.6820
   b) i) If sin θ = 0.47, to find θ use your calculator.
   θ $\doteq$ 28°
   ii) If cos ϕ = 0.39, to find ϕ use your calculator.
   ϕ $\doteq$ 67°

We could have determined sin 68° and cos 47° by drawing each angle with a protractor and forming the corresponding right triangle. By measuring the sides of the triangles we could calculate the sine and cosine ratios, but these results would not be precise.

Example 3. Given $\triangle ABC$ with sides of lengths 3, 4, and 5 units
   a) Write the ratios sin A, cos A, and tan A, where $\angle A$ is opposite the side of length 3 units.
   b) Find the measures of the two acute angles to the nearest degree.

Solution. From the converse of the Pythagorean Theorem, $\triangle ABC$ is a right triangle. Draw $\triangle ABC$ with $\angle C$ = 90°.
   a) From the definitions of the trigonometric ratios

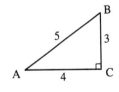

$$\sin A = \frac{3}{5} \quad \cos A = \frac{4}{5} \quad \tan A = \frac{3}{4}$$

   b) Since $\sin A = \frac{3}{5}$ or 0.6, we can use a calculator to find $\angle A$.

   $\angle A$ $\doteq$ 37°
   Since $\angle A + \angle B$ = 90°, then $\angle B$ $\doteq$ 53°.

Example 4. A 35 m cable is attached to a TV tower at a height of 30 m. What is the angle of elevation of the cable?

Solution. Let θ be the angle of elevation.
   Then, $\sin \theta = \dfrac{30}{35}$

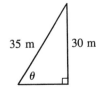

   Use your calculator.
   θ $\doteq$ 58.997 281
   The angle of elevation is about 59°.

EXERCISES 10-2

Ⓐ

1. Find each ratio to 4 decimal places.
   a) sin 30° b) cos 78° c) cos 52° d) sin 16° e) cos 28°
   f) sin 40° g) sin 82° h) cos 9° i) sin 59° j) cos 37°

2. Find θ to the nearest degree if each given value is: a) sin θ b) cos θ.
   i) 0.2079 ii) 0.4384 iii) 0.7431 iv) 0.9063 v) 0.9945

3. Write the ratios sin θ, cos θ, and tan θ for each triangle.
   a)

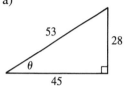

   b)

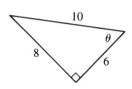

   c)

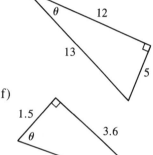

   d)

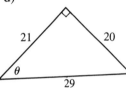

   e)

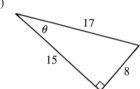

   f)

4. The lengths of the sides of △PQR are 9, 40, and 41 units. If ∠Q = 90°, find:
   a) the primary trigonometric ratios for the smallest angle
   b) the measures of the two smaller angles to 1 decimal place.

Ⓑ

5. A wheelchair ramp (below left) is 4.2 m long and rises 0.7 m. What is its angle of inclination to 1 decimal place?

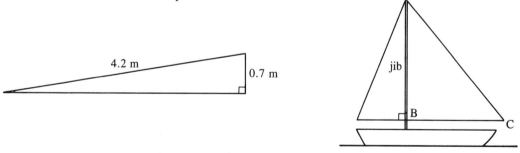

6. The guy wire for a jib sail (above right) is 3.7 m in length. It is attached at point A. The foot of the guy wire is 1.1 m from the mast AB. What is the angle of elevation of the guy wire to 1 decimal place?

7. In *Exercise 6*, the mast AB is 3.53 m long and the boom BC is 3.20 m. Find the measure of ∠C to 1 decimal place.

8. The Cinesphere at Ontario Place shows world class films on a huge curved screen. To gain access to the theatre, people walk up a series of five ramps, with the dimensions shown (below left).
   a) Find the angle of inclination of each ramp.
   b) Find the slope and the angle of inclination if only one set of steps had been built instead.
   Give the answers to 1 decimal place.

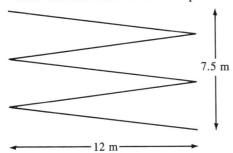

7.5 m

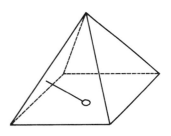

— 12 m —

9. In the Great Pyramid at Giza (above right) there is a 115 m long passage that leads from the northern face to an interior chamber. If the chamber is 50 m below the opening of the passage, find the angle of inclination of the passage to 1 decimal place.

10. The largest slide in the world drops 220 m in a horizontal distance of 1203 m.
    a) How long is the slide to the nearest metre?
    b) What is its angle of inclination to the nearest degree?

11. If AB is a diameter of a circle of radius 2 units (below left), determine these values.
    a) $\sin \theta$　　　　　　b) $\cos \theta$　　　　　　c) $\tan \theta$

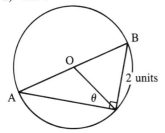

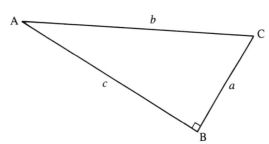

12. For the diagram (above right)
    a) State the primary trigonometric ratios for $\angle A$.
    b) State the primary trigonometric ratios for $\angle C$. What can you conclude?

13. Find the measures of the acute angles to 1 decimal place in a right triangle if its sides have lengths a, $a + d$, $a + 2d$.

14. The volume V of a right square-based pyramid is given by the formula $V = \frac{1}{3} Bh$, where B is the area of the base and h is the height. Express V in terms of the length l along an inclined edge and the angle of inclination θ of the edge.

10-3 REVIEW: SOLVING RIGHT TRIANGLES

We have learned how to find the height of a cliff given the angle of inclination of the cliff at a given distance. This amounted to finding the length of one side of a right triangle given the length of another side and the measure of an angle. Finding all the unknown sides and angles of a triangle is called *solving the triangle*. We can solve a right triangle if we know either:

● the lengths of any two sides, or
● the length of one side and the measure of an acute angle.

The following example shows how we solve a right triangle given the lengths of two sides.

Example 1. Solve $\triangle ABC$ given $AB = 25$, $AC = 18$, and $\angle C = 90°$. Give the answers to 1 decimal place.

Solution. From the Pythagorean Theorem

$$BC^2 = AB^2 - AC^2$$
$$= 25^2 - 18^2$$
$$= 301$$
$$BC = \sqrt{301}$$
$$\doteq 17.349$$

To find $\angle A$, we write $\cos A = \dfrac{18}{25}$ Use a calculator.

$$\angle A \doteq 43.9°$$

Since $\angle A + \angle B = 90°$, then $\angle B \doteq 46.1°$

We summarize these results in a table.

AB	AC	BC	$\angle A$	$\angle B$	$\angle C$
25	18	17.3	43.9°	46.1°	90°

In *Example 1*, we used the Pythagorean Theorem to calculate the unknown side, and then the ratio of any two sides to determine an unknown angle. The next example shows how we can solve a right triangle given only the length of one side and the measure of an acute angle.

Example 2. Solve $\triangle DEF$ given that $\angle E = 90°$, $\angle D = 37°$, and $EF = 12$. Give the answers to the nearest whole number.

Solution. By definition of the tangent and sine ratios

$$\tan 37° = \frac{12}{DE}$$

$$DE = \frac{12}{\tan 37°}$$ Use a calculator.

$$\doteq 15.92$$

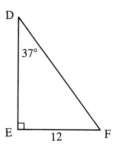

$$\sin 37° = \frac{12}{DF}$$

$$DF = \frac{12}{\sin 37°}$$

$$\doteq 19.94$$

Since $\angle D = 37°$, then $\angle F = 90° - 37°$, or $53°$

We summarize these results in a table.

EF	DE	DF	$\angle D$	$\angle E$	$\angle F$
12	16	20	37°	90°	53°

In *Example 2*, once we found DE we could have used the fact that EF = 12 and applied the Pythagorean Theorem to calculate DF.

The next examples show how we can find all the primary trigonometric ratios, given only one of them.

Example 3. If $\tan \theta = \dfrac{5}{12}$, find $\cos \theta$ and $\sin \theta$.

Solution. Sketch a right triangle with shorter sides 5 and 12, and hypotenuse h. Label the angle θ.
Using the Pythagorean Theorem
$$h = \sqrt{5^2 + 12^2}$$
$$= \sqrt{169}$$
$$= 13$$
Then, $\cos \theta = \frac{12}{13}$ and $\sin \theta = \frac{5}{13}$

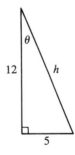

Example 4. If $\sin \theta = \dfrac{a}{b}$, find expressions for $\cos \theta$ and $\tan \theta$.

Solution. Sketch a right triangle with side a opposite θ, and hypotenuse b.
It follows from the Pythagorean Theorem that the third side has length $\sqrt{b^2 - a^2}$.
So, $\cos \theta = \dfrac{\sqrt{b^2 - a^2}}{b}$ and

$$\tan \theta = \frac{a}{\sqrt{b^2 - a^2}}$$

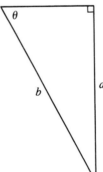

EXERCISES 10-3

Ⓐ

1. Solve each triangle. Give the answers to 1 decimal place.

a)

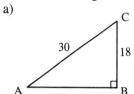

b)

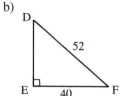

c)

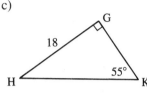

d)

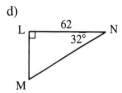

e)

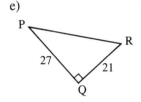

f)

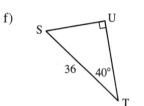

2. Solve △XYZ if ∠Y = 90° and:
   a) XY = 24, XZ = 35   b) XY = 16, ∠X = 27°
   c) XZ = 51, YZ = 13   d) XZ = 72, ∠Z = 52°
   e) YZ = 32, ∠X = 64°   f) XY = 45, YZ = 20.
   Give the answers to 1 decimal place.

3. Find the other two primary trigonometric ratios for each value of θ.

   a) $\sin \theta = \dfrac{8}{17}$ b) $\cos \theta = \dfrac{7}{25}$ c) $\tan \theta = \dfrac{20}{21}$

   d) $\sin \theta = \dfrac{15}{32}$ e) $\cos \theta = \dfrac{19}{23}$ f) $\tan \theta = \dfrac{43}{112}$

Ⓑ

4. Find expressions for the other primary trigonometric ratios for each value of θ.

   a) $\sin \theta = \dfrac{p}{q}$ b) $\cos \theta = \dfrac{a}{a + 2}$ c) $\tan \theta = \dfrac{x - y}{x + y}$

5. At a point 28 m away, the angle of elevation of a building is 65° (below left).
   a) How tall is the building?
   b) How far is the observer's eye from the top of the building?

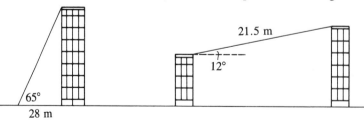

6. A tightrope walker attaches a cable to the roofs of two adjacent buildings (above right). The cable is 21.5 m long and the angle of inclination is 12°.
   a) How far apart are the buildings?   b) What is the difference in their heights?

7. A rectangle has length 10 cm and width 6 cm. Find the acute angle to the nearest degree between the diagonals.

8. The length of rectangle ABCD is three times its width. Points M and N are the midpoints of the longer sides AB and DC.
   a) Find ∠MAN.
   b) If P is the midpoint of AD, find ∠MPN.
   Give the answers to the nearest degree.

9. A funnel is placed in a glass, as shown. If the glass is 14.5 cm tall and 7.6 cm in diameter, how high is the vertex of the funnel above the bottom of the glass?

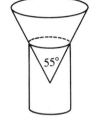

10. Prior to 1982, visitors to the observation deck of the Peace Tower in Ottawa had to ride two elevators. The Memorial Chamber at the base of the tower made a vertical assent impossible. A new elevator system carries visitors up the first 24.2 m by travelling a path inclined at 10° to the vertical. It then rises vertically for the balance of the trip.
    a) How long is the elevator shaft that runs on the incline?
    b) By how far is the elevator displaced horizontally by the incline?
    c) What is the slope of the incline to 2 decimal places?

11. Two office towers are 31.7 m apart. From the shorter one, the angle of elevation to the top of the other is 27.5°, while the angle of depression to the base is 78.2°. Find the height of each tower.

Ⓒ

12. The diagram (below left) shows how the ancient Greeks constructed line segments of lengths $\sqrt{2}, \sqrt{3}, \sqrt{4}, \sqrt{5}, \ldots$ As the process continues, the triangles turn about point A, as shown.
    a) Find these angles to 1 decimal place.
       i) ∠CAB   ii) ∠DAB   iii) ∠EAB   iv) ∠FAB
    b) How many triangles can be drawn without overlapping?

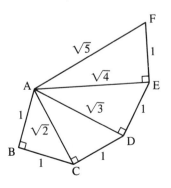

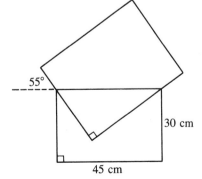

13. A box is resting inside a second box (above right). How high is the lowest corner of the first box above the bottom of the second box?

10-4 APPLICATIONS OF THE TRIGONOMETRIC RATIOS

In *Section 10-3* we learned how to solve a right triangle given either:
- the lengths of any two sides; or
- the length of one side and the measure of an acute angle.

In this section we apply these techniques to the solutions of various problems. In each case we solve for an unknown side or an unknown angle rather than solving for all sides and angles.

Example 1.   The Great Pyramid in Egypt has a square base of side length 230 m. If the angle of elevation of the sides is 52°, what is the height of the pyramid?

Solution.   Let h metres represent the height.
Then, in $\triangle ABC$

$$\frac{h}{115} = \tan 52°$$
$$h = 115 \tan 52°$$
$$\doteq 147.193\ 29$$

The pyramid is about 147 m high.

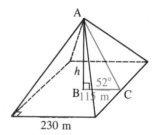

Example 2.   A fireman's ladder is inclined at an angle of 58°. The ladder is 10 m long measured from the foot to the top rung, where a fireman is standing. How high is the fireman above the ground?

Solution.   Let h metres represent the height of the top rung.

$$\text{Then, } \frac{h}{10} = \sin 58°$$
$$h = 10 \sin 58°$$
$$\doteq 8.48$$

The fireman is about 8.5 m above the ground.

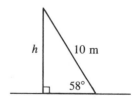

Example 3. The world's longest suspension bridge is across the Humber Estuary in England. The towers of this bridge reach about 135 m above the level of the bridge. The angles of elevation of the towers seen from the centre of the bridge and either end are 10.80° and 18.65° respectively. How long is the Humber Estuary Bridge?

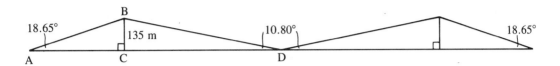

Solution. The length of the bridge is double the length of AD.

$$\frac{135}{AC} = \tan 18.65° \qquad \text{and} \qquad \frac{135}{CD} = \tan 10.8°$$

$$AC = \frac{135}{\tan 18.65°} \qquad\qquad CD = \frac{135}{\tan 10.8°}$$

$$AD = AC + CD$$

$$= \frac{135}{\tan 18.65°} + \frac{135}{\tan 10.8°}$$

$$= 135\left(\frac{1}{\tan 18.65°} + \frac{1}{\tan 10.8°}\right)$$

$$\doteq 1107.68$$

The length of the bridge is about 2(1107.68 m), or about 2215 m.

EXERCISES 10-4

Ⓑ

1. When spraying a crop with pesticides, a farmer uses a boom sprayer pulled by a tractor. The nozzles are 50 cm apart and spray at an angle of 70°. How high should the sprayer be set above the top of the crop to provide an even distribution of the pesticide?

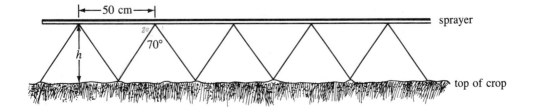

2. A hemispherical bowl of diameter 20 cm contains some liquid with a depth of 4 cm. Through what angle with the horizontal may the bowl be tipped before the liquid begins to spill out?

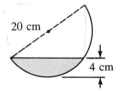

3. The Calgary Tower is 190 m high and casts a shadow 84 m long. Find the angle to the nearest degree which the sun's rays make with the ground.

4. A television antenna is supported by a guy wire connected to the mast. The angle of elevation of the guy wire is 39°, and the angle of elevation of the top of the antenna is 53°. If the guy wire is fixed to the ground 7 m from the base of the mast, find to the nearest tenth of a metre:
   a) the height of the antenna
   b) the distance from the top of the antenna to where the guy wire is connected.

5. The picture tube in a color television set is 50 cm wide, and has a deflection angle of 90° (below left).
   a) Calculate the least possible depth of a cabinet that could hold the tube.
   b) The manufacturer advertises that by increasing the deflection angle to 100°, the cabinet can be made smaller. Find the decrease in depth of the cabinet allowed by the larger deflection angle.

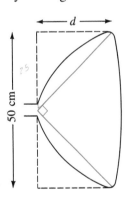

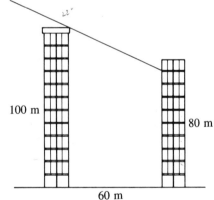

6. Two apartment buildings 100 m and 80 m high are 60 m apart (above right). The sun casts a shadow of the 100 m building on the 80 m building.
   a) If the angle of elevation of the sun is 22°, calculate the height of the shadow on the 80 m building to the nearest metre.
   b) If the angle of elevation of the sun changes at a constant rate of 15°/h, calculate the total time that the 80 m building is partly in the shadow of the 100 m building.

7. Donna measured the angle of elevation of a church steeple and found it to be 10°. Then she walked 100 m towards the steeple and measured the angle of elevation again; this time it was 20°. Find the height of the steeple, assuming that the ground is level.

8. Trigonometry can be used to find the circumference of the Earth. From the top of a mountain 5 km high the angle between the horizon and the true vertical is 87.73°. Use the diagram to calculate:

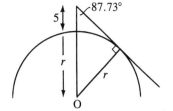

   a) the radius
   b) the circumference of the Earth.

9. Assume that the method of *Exercise 8* is used with measurements taken from a satellite at an altitude of 200 km. If the Earth's radius is 6370 km, find the angle between the horizon and the true vertical to 2 decimal places.

10. Angle parking allows more cars to park along a given street than does parallel parking. However, the cars use more of the street width when angle parked.

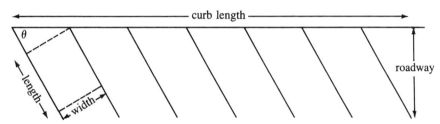

   a) If each car requires a space 2.7 m wide, how much curb length would be required to park 20 cars if θ is: i) 30° ii) 50° iii) 60°?
   b) If 20 cars had to be parked in 60 m of curb length, what would be the value of θ?
   c) If each car requires a space 6.5 m long, how much of the roadway is given up for parking if θ is: i) 30° ii) 50° iii) 60°?

11. The measure of angle θ in *Exercise 10* depends upon the amount of roadway K that can be used for parking. The relationship between θ and K is given by $\dfrac{2.7 \cos \theta}{K - 6.5 \sin \theta} = 1$. If $K = 6.9$ m, find the value of θ to the nearest degree.

12. On a sunny day, the shadows of stationary objects move slowly across the ground. This is caused by the apparent motion of the sun across the sky, due to the rotation of the Earth. Assume that the sun rises due east at 6 A.M., and sets due west at 6 P.M.
   a) Find the length of the shadow of a 150 m building at:
      i) 8 A.M.   ii) 10:30 A.M.   iii) 2 P.M.   iv) 5:30 P.M.
   b) At what times during the day is the shadow of a 150-m building 90 m long?
   c) Directly to the west of a 400-m building there is a 300-m building a distance of 200 m away. Calculate the total time during the day that the space between the buildings is entirely in shadow.

13. The top of a cylindrical oil storage tank, 55.3 m high and 28.4 m in diameter, is reached by a spiral stairway that circles the tank exactly once. Calculate the angle of inclination of the stairway to the nearest degree.

10-5 TRIGONOMETRIC RATIOS OF SPECIAL ANGLES

For angles such as 45°, 30°, and 60°, the trigonometric ratios can be calculated using an isosceles right triangle and an equilateral triangle.

Trigonometric Ratios of 45°
If the equal sides of an isosceles right triangle are 1 unit long, then from the Pythagorean Theorem, the length of the hypotenuse is $\sqrt{1^2 + 1^2}$, or $\sqrt{2}$.
Furthermore, the two acute angles are equal and since they total 90°, each angle is 45°. Therefore,

$$\sin 45° = \frac{1}{\sqrt{2}} \qquad \cos 45° = \frac{1}{\sqrt{2}} \qquad \tan 45° = \frac{1}{1}, \text{ or } 1$$

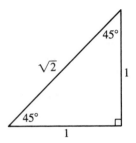

Trigonometric Ratios of 30° and 60°
If the sides of an equilateral $\triangle ABC$ are 2 units long, then from the Pythagorean Theorem, the length of the altitude AD is $\sqrt{2^2 - 1^2}$, or $\sqrt{3}$.
Furthermore, $\angle A = \angle B = \angle C = 60°$
Therefore,

$$\sin 60° = \frac{\sqrt{3}}{2} \qquad \cos 60° = \frac{1}{2} \qquad \tan 60° = \frac{\sqrt{3}}{1}, \text{ or } \sqrt{3}$$

Also, $\angle BAD = 180° - 90° - 60°$, or 30°
Therefore,

$$\sin 30° = \frac{1}{2} \qquad \cos 30° = \frac{\sqrt{3}}{2} \qquad \tan 30° = \frac{1}{\sqrt{3}}$$

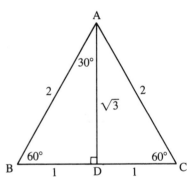

We summarize these trigonometric ratios for angles of 30°, 45° and 60° in a table.

	sin	cos	tan
30°	$\dfrac{1}{2}$	$\dfrac{\sqrt{3}}{2}$	$\dfrac{1}{\sqrt{3}}$
45°	$\dfrac{1}{\sqrt{2}}$	$\dfrac{1}{\sqrt{2}}$	1
60°	$\dfrac{\sqrt{3}}{2}$	$\dfrac{1}{2}$	$\sqrt{3}$

To determine the trigonometric ratios of 0° and 90°, we consider the ratios as θ decreases to 0° and as θ increases to 90°.

Trigonometric Ratios of 0°

Consider $\triangle ABC$ as AB rotates to AC, and $\angle BAC$ decreases to 0°. AB approaches AC in length and BC approaches 0 in length. So, as θ approaches 0°

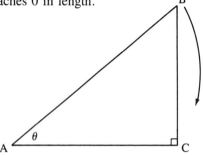

$\sin \theta = \dfrac{BC}{AB}$, which approaches $\dfrac{0}{AC}$, or 0

Hence, $\sin 0° = 0$

$\cos \theta = \dfrac{AC}{AB}$, which approaches $\dfrac{AC}{AC}$, or 1

Hence, $\cos 0° = 1$

$\tan \theta = \dfrac{BC}{AC}$, which approaches $\dfrac{0}{AC}$, or 0

Hence, $\tan 0° = 0$

Trigonometric Ratios of 90°

Consider $\triangle ABC$ as C moves along CA to A, and $\angle CAB$ increases to 90°.
AC approaches 0 in length, and BC approaches BA in length. So, as θ approaches 90°

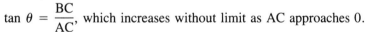

$\sin \theta = \dfrac{BC}{BA}$, which approaches $\dfrac{BA}{BA}$, or 1

Hence, $\sin 90° = 1$

$\cos \theta = \dfrac{AC}{AB}$, which approaches $\dfrac{0}{AB}$, or 0

Hence, $\cos 90° = 0$

$\tan \theta = \dfrac{BC}{AC}$, which increases without limit as AC approaches 0.

$\tan 90°$ is undefined and we use the symbol ∞ to represent a quantity which is not finite.

The trigonometric ratios for 0° and 90° are summarized in the following table.

	sin	**cos**	**tan**
0°	0	1	0
90°	1	0	∞

We can use the values of the trigonometric ratios of these special angles to calculate exact answers to problems.

Example 1. A ladder is inclined at an angle of 60° against a wall. If the foot of the ladder is 6 m from the wall, how long is the ladder?

Solution. Let the length of the ladder be x metres.

Then, $\dfrac{6}{x} = \cos 60°$

$$x = \dfrac{6}{\cos 60°}$$

$$= \dfrac{6}{0.5}, \text{ or } 12$$

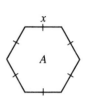

The ladder is 12 m long.

Example 2. A tiling company wants to develop a hexagonal tile with area A square centimetres. Find a formula for the edge length x centimetres of the hexagonal tile.

Solution. Divide the regular hexagon into 6 congruent triangles. Since 6 equal angles at the centre of the hexagon have total measure 360°, each angle at the centre is 60°. Furthermore the triangles are isosceles (by symmetry). So, the other two angles in each triangle are 60°. That is, the 6 triangles are equilateral with sides x centimetres long.

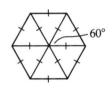

To relate x and A, we need to find the area in terms of x. To find the area of an equilateral triangle with sides of length x, let h denote the height. Then

$$\dfrac{h}{x} = \cos 30°$$

$$h = x \cos 30°$$

$$= \dfrac{\sqrt{3}}{2}x$$

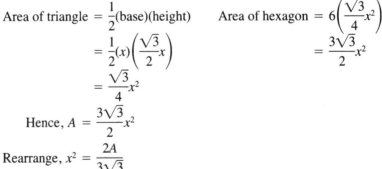

Area of triangle $= \dfrac{1}{2}(\text{base})(\text{height})$ Area of hexagon $= 6\left(\dfrac{\sqrt{3}}{4}x^2\right)$

$$= \dfrac{1}{2}(x)\left(\dfrac{\sqrt{3}}{2}x\right) \qquad\qquad\qquad = \dfrac{3\sqrt{3}}{2}x^2$$

$$= \dfrac{\sqrt{3}}{4}x^2$$

Hence, $A = \dfrac{3\sqrt{3}}{2}x^2$

Rearrange, $x^2 = \dfrac{2A}{3\sqrt{3}}$

$$x = \sqrt{\dfrac{2A}{3\sqrt{3}}}$$

Example 3.   H.M.S. Napier observes a second ship 24 km due east. The first ship sights a lighthouse at E 30° S. For the second ship the lighthouse is at W 60° S. How far is each ship from the lighthouse?

Solution.   Draw a diagram, with A, B, and L representing the positions of the ships and the lighthouse.
We need to find AL and BL.
In △ABL
Since ∠A = 30° and ∠B = 60°, then ∠L = 90°

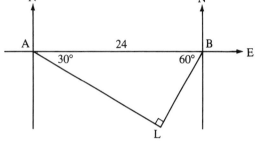

Hence, $\dfrac{BL}{24} = \sin 30°$

$BL = 24\left(\dfrac{1}{2}\right)$

$= 12$

$\dfrac{AL}{24} = \cos 30°$

$AL = 24\left(\dfrac{\sqrt{3}}{2}\right)$

$= 12\sqrt{3}$

The ships are 12 km and $12\sqrt{3}$ km from the lighthouse.

EXERCISES 10-5

(A)

1. State the value of each ratio.
   a) sin 30°   b) cos 60°   c) tan 45°   d) sin 45°
   e) cos 45°   f) tan 30°   g) sin 60°   h) cos 30°

2. State the value of each ratio.
   a) tan 60°   b) sin 0°   c) cos 90°
   d) tan 90°   e) cos 0°   f) sin 90°

3. Find each value of θ.

   a) $\tan \theta = 1$ b) $\sin \theta = 0$ c) $\cos \theta = \dfrac{1}{2}$

   d) $\cos \theta = \dfrac{1}{\sqrt{2}}$ e) $\tan \theta = 0$ f) $\sin \theta = \dfrac{\sqrt{3}}{2}$

4. Find each value of θ.

   a) $\sin \theta = \dfrac{1}{\sqrt{2}}$ b) $\cos \theta = 0$ c) $\tan \theta = \infty$

   d) $\sin \theta = \dfrac{1}{2}$ e) $\tan \theta = \sqrt{3}$ f) $\cos \theta = 1$

   g) $\sin \theta = 1$ h) $\tan \theta = \dfrac{1}{\sqrt{3}}$ i) $\cos \theta = \dfrac{\sqrt{3}}{2}$

5. One ship observes a second ship 6 km away and in the north-east direction. The first ship sights a flare due east. For the second ship the flare is due south. How far is each ship from the distress signal?

6. In a baseball diamond, each baseline is 27.4 m long. If the pitcher stands at the centre of the diamond how far is she from each base?

7. A guy wire is fastened 6.2 m from the base of a hydro pole. Find the length of the guy wire and how far up the pole it is fastened for each angle of elevation.
   a) 45°   b) 30°   c) 60°

8. A steel bridge is constructed, as shown. If the supporting towers are 12.6 m tall, how long is the bridge?

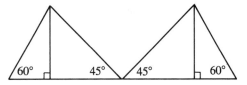

9. Rhombus ABCD has sides of length 10 cm. If the length of the diagonal AC is also 10 cm, find the length of the diagonal BD.

10. Triangle ABC is equilateral with sides of length s units.
    a) A segment of length x units is drawn parallel to BC so that $\triangle$ABC is divided into two equal areas. Find an expression for x in terms of s.
    b) Two segments of lengths y and z units ($y < z$) are drawn parallel to BC so that $\triangle$ABC is divided into 3 equal areas. Find expressions for y and z in terms of s.

11. The length of one diagonal of a rhombus is equal to the length of one of its sides. Find the length of the other diagonal in terms of the length l of its sides.

12. Right $\triangle$ABC has $\angle$B $= 60°$ and $\angle$C $= 90°$. The bisector of $\angle$B meets AC at D. Find the ratio AD : DC.

13. An equilateral triangle (below left) of side s is divided into three triangles of equal area by two line segments of length x passing through a vertex. Find x in terms of s.

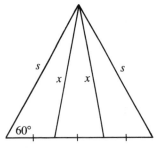

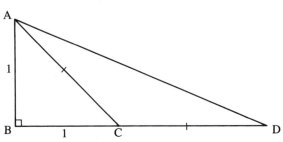

14. Right isosceles $\triangle$ABC (above right) has AB $=$ BC $= 1$ unit, and $\angle$B $= 90°$. Side BC is extended to D such that CD $=$ CA. Use the diagram to find an expression for each trigonometric ratio.
    a) tan 22.5°   b) sin 22.5°   c) cos 22.5°

15. a) Derive a formula for the area A of a regular polygon of n sides in terms of its side length x.
    b) By using the trigonometric ratios of the special angles, show how the result of part a) reduces to a formula for the area of each regular polygon.
    i) square ii) hexagon iii) equilateral triangle

16. The perpendicular bisectors of the sides of an equilateral triangle meet at the centroid. If each side is 20 cm, how far is the centroid from each side?

17. An equilateral triangle is inscribed in a circle. Find the ratio of the area of the circle to the area of the triangle.

18. The vertical angle of a cone (below left) is 60°. A sphere of radius 5 cm is dropped into the cone. How far is the centre of the sphere from the vertex of the cone?

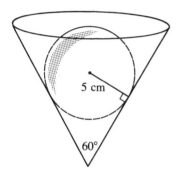
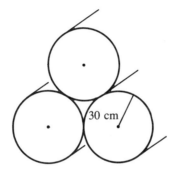

19. Three cylindrical logs of radius 30 cm are piled as shown (above right). How far is the top of the upper log from the ground?

20. From a position 10 m above the ground, the angle of elevation of the top of a tower is 45°. From a position 20 m higher up, the angle of elevation is 30°. How tall is the tower?

21. The angle of elevation of a church steeple is 45°. If the observer moves 10 m closer (on level ground) the angle of elevation is 60°. How tall is the steeple?

22. In rectangle ABCD, points E and F are located on AB and BC so that $\triangle$EBF and $\triangle$FCD are congruent 30°-60°-90° triangles. EB = FC = 1 unit
    a) Find the lengths of the unmarked sides.
    b) Use the diagram to obtain an expression for each trigonometric ratio.
     i) sin 15° ii) cos 15°
     iii) tan 15° iv) sin 75°
     v) cos 75° vi) tan 75°

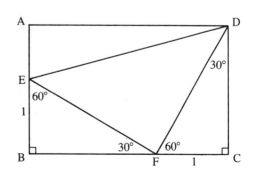

10-6 ANGLES IN STANDARD POSITION

In the next section, we shall extend the definitions of trigonometric ratios to all angles. To do this, we need to define the standard position of an angle.

Let P(x,y) represent a point which moves around a circle with radius r and centre (0,0). P starts at the point A(r,0) on the x-axis. For any position of P, an angle θ is defined, which represents the amount of rotation about the origin. When the vertex of the angle is (0,0), the *initial arm* is OA, the *terminal arm* is OP, and we say that the angle θ is in *standard position*.

If $\theta > 0$, the rotation is counterclockwise.　　If $\theta < 0$, the rotation is clockwise.

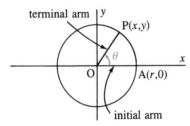　　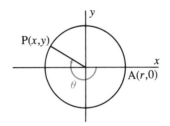

When P moves around the circle, the motion is repeated after P has rotated 360°. If any angle θ is given, we can always determine other angles for which the position of P is the same. All these angles are in standard position.

Given an angle of 60°　　Add 360°　　　　　　　　Add 360° again
　　　　　　　　　　　　60° + 360° = 420°　　　　420° + 360° = 780°

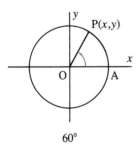　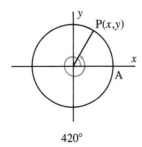　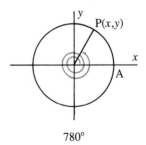

　　　60°　　　　　　　　　420°　　　　　　　　　780°

The angles shown above are in standard position, and have the same terminal arm. For this reason, they are called coterminal angles. If θ is any angle in standard position, other angles which are coterminal with θ can be found by adding or subtracting multiples of 360°.

Coterminal Angles
- Two or more angles in standard position are *coterminal angles* if the position of P is the same for each angle.
- If θ represents any angle, then any angle coterminal with θ is represented by this expression, where n is an integer.
$\theta + n(360°)$

Example 1. Given $\theta = 150°$
    a) Draw the angle θ in standard position.
    b) Find two other angles which are coterminal with θ and illustrate them on diagrams.
    c) Write an expression to represent any angle coterminal with θ.

Solution.
    a)   b) $150° + 360° = 510°$ $150° - 360° = -210°$

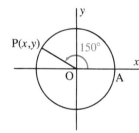 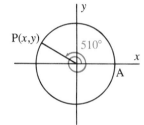 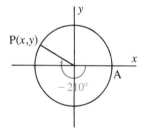

    c) Any angle coterminal with θ is represented by the expression $150° + n(360°)$, where n is an integer.

For any angle in standard position, we can find its corresponding reference angle.

For any angle θ in standard position, its *reference angle* is the acute angle between its terminal arm and the x-axis.

Example 2. Find the reference angle for each angle in standard position.
    a) 150°   b) $-280°$ c) 472°

Solution.   a) 150° lies in the second quadrant.
               Its reference angle is
               $180° - 150° = 30°$.

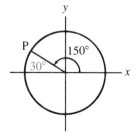

b) $-280°$ lies in the first quadrant.
Its reference angle is
$360° - 280° = 80°$.

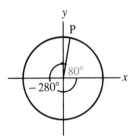

c) $472°$ lies in the second quadrant.
Its reference angle is
$360° + 180° - 472° = 68°$.

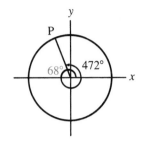

Example 3. Suppose P has rotated $830°$ about $(0,0)$ from A.
a) How many complete rotations have been made?
b) In which quadrant is P located now?
c) Draw a diagram to show the position of P.

Solution.
a) Since a complete rotation is $360°$, divide 830 by 360.
$830 ÷ 360 ≐ 2.3056$
Since the result is between 2 and 3, P has made 2
complete rotations around the circle, and part of a third
rotation.

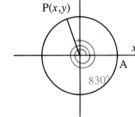

b) Two complete rotations amount to $2(360°)$, or $720°$.
The additional rotation beyond $720°$ is $830° - 720°$,
or $110°$. Since $90° < 110° < 180°$, P is now in the
second quadrant.

EXERCISES 10-6

Ⓐ

1. An angle in standard position is shown. What is the value of θ?

a)

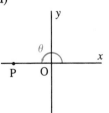

b)

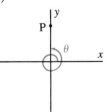

c)

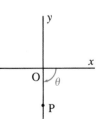

d)

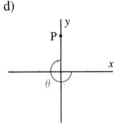

2. Draw each angle in standard position and find its reference angle.
   a) $\theta = 50°$ b) $\theta = 120°$ c) $\theta = 165°$ d) $\theta = 240°$
   e) $\theta = 90°$ f) $\theta = 45°$ g) $\theta = 60°$ h) $\theta = 270°$

3. In *Exercise 2*, find two angles which are coterminal with θ.

4. An angle θ in standard position is shown. Find two other angles which are coterminal with θ.

a)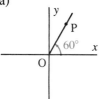

b)

c)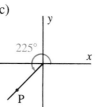

d)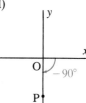

5. Find two angles which are coterminal with θ.
   a) $\theta = 180°$ b) $\theta = 90°$ c) $\theta = -60°$ d) $\theta = -360°$

(B)

6. P is a point on the terminal arm of an angle θ in standard position. Suppose P has rotated 420°.
   a) How many complete rotations have been made?
   b) In which quadrant is P located now?
   c) Draw a diagram to show the position of P.

7. Repeat *Exercise 6* if P has rotated:
   a) 480°   b) 660°   c) 870°   d) 1000°.

8. Draw each angle in standard position and find its reference angle.
   a) $\theta = 400°$ b) $\theta = 750°$ c) $\theta = -270°$ d) $\theta = -60°$

9. Repeat *Exercise 6* if P has rotated $-420°$.

10. Repeat *Exercise 6* if P has rotated:
    a) 180°   b) 270°   c) 360°   d) 450°.

11. Draw each angle in standard position.
    a) $\theta = 810°$ b) $\theta = 600°$ c) $\theta = -225°$ d) $\theta = -1260°$

12. Write an expression to represent any angle coterminal with θ.
    a) $\theta = 45°$ b) $\theta = 150°$ c) $\theta = 240°$ d) $\theta = -30°$
    e) $\theta = 180°$ f) $\theta = -45°$ g) $\theta = 450°$ h) $\theta = 120°$

(C)

13. P is a point on the terminal arm of an angle θ in standard position. Explain how you can determine the quadrant in which P is located, if you know the value of θ.

14. Let θ represent any angle. Let α represent the angle which is coterminal with θ, where $0° \leq \alpha < 360°$.
    a) Draw a graph to represent α as a function of θ.
    b) What are the domain and range of the function?

10-7 TRIGONOMETRIC FUNCTIONS OF ANGLES IN STANDARD POSITION: PART ONE

In a previous section we defined the trigonometric ratios of an angle in a right triangle. We can extend these definitions further to any angle in standard position.

Let P(x,y) represent any point in the first quadrant on a circle with radius r. Then P is on the terminal arm of an angle θ in standard position, as shown. Draw a right triangle $\triangle$PON by dropping a perpendicular from P to the x-axis. We can use $\triangle$PON to write trigonometric ratios in terms of the sides of $\triangle$PON.

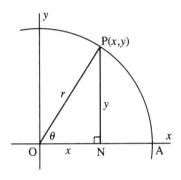

$$\sin \angle\text{PON} = \frac{\text{PN}}{\text{OP}} \qquad \cos \angle\text{PON} = \frac{\text{ON}}{\text{OP}}$$

$$\tan \angle\text{PON} = \frac{\text{PN}}{\text{ON}}$$

Since the coordinates of P correspond to two sides of $\triangle$PON, and the radius of the circle corresponds to the third side, we can write the trigonometric ratios of θ in terms of x, y, and r, where $r = \sqrt{x^2 + y^2}$.

Let P(x,y) be any point on a circle of radius r. If θ represents the angle of rotation, then the *primary trigonometric functions* of θ are defined as follows.

$$\sin \theta = \frac{y}{r} \qquad \cos \theta = \frac{x}{r} \qquad \tan \theta = \frac{y}{x}, \quad x \neq 0 \quad \text{where } r = \sqrt{x^2 + y^2}$$

First Quadrant   Second Quadrant   Third Quadrant   Fourth Quadrant

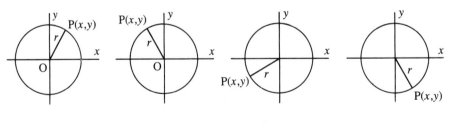

The definitions above are more general definitions of the sine, cosine and tangents of an angle than those given in *Section 10-2*. Since these definitions are given in terms of the coordinates of P and the radius of the circle, they can be applied to any angle in standard position, and not just angles between 0° and 180°. However, when applied to angles in a right triangle, they reduce to the earlier definitions.

We can use these definitions to determine the sine, cosine, or tangent of any angle θ in standard position.

Example 1. The point P(4,3) is on the terminal arm of an angle θ.
a) Draw a diagram showing θ in standard position.
b) Calculate sin θ, cos θ, and tan θ.

Solution a)

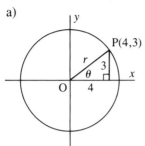

b) From the diagram,
$$r = \sqrt{4^2 + 3^2}$$
$$= 5$$
Therefore,

$$\sin \theta = \frac{y}{r} \qquad \cos \theta = \frac{x}{r} \qquad \tan \theta = \frac{y}{x}$$

$$= \frac{3}{5} \qquad\qquad = \frac{4}{5} \qquad\qquad = \frac{3}{4}$$

$$= 0.6 \qquad\qquad = 0.8 \qquad\qquad = 0.75$$

Example 2. The point P(−2,3) is on the terminal arm of an angle θ.
a) Draw a diagram showing θ in standard position.
b) Find expressions for sin θ, cos θ, and tan θ.
c) Calculate the values of sin θ, cos θ, and tan θ to five decimal places.

Solution. a)

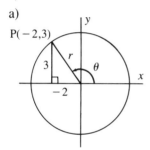

b) From the diagram,
$$r = \sqrt{(-2)^2 + 3^2}$$
$$= \sqrt{13}$$
Therefore,

$$\sin \theta = \frac{y}{r} \qquad \cos \theta = \frac{x}{r} \qquad \tan \theta = \frac{y}{x}$$

$$= \frac{3}{\sqrt{13}} \qquad = \frac{2}{\sqrt{13}} \qquad = -\frac{3}{2}$$

c) Use a calculator. $\sin \theta = \dfrac{3}{\sqrt{13}}$
$$\doteq 0.832\ 05$$
Similarly, cos $\theta = -0.554\ 70$ and tan $\theta = -1.500\ 00$

A scientific calculator can be used to find the sine, cosine or tangent of any angle.

Example 3. Find each value to five decimal places.
a) cos 152° b) sin 410°

Solution. Be sure your calculator is in *degree mode*.
a) To five decimal places, cos 152° = −0.882 95
b) To five decimal places, sin 410° = 0.766 04

There are infinitely many angles which have the same cosine as 152°, or the same sine as 410°. For example, use your calculator to verify that the following expressions are also equal to $-0.882\,95$.

cos (152° + 360°), or cos 512°   cos (152° − 360°), or cos (−208°)
cos (152° + 720°), or cos 872°   cos (152° − 720°), or cos (−568°)

Use your calculator to verify that the following expressions are also equal to 0.766 04.

sin (410° + 360°), or sin 770°   sin (410° − 360°), or sin 50°
sin (410° + 720°), or sin 1130°   sin (410° − 720°), or sin (−310°)

Example 4.   The angle θ is in the third quadrant, and $\sin \theta = -\dfrac{2}{3}$. Find $\tan \theta$.

Solution.   Draw a diagram showing θ in standard position in the third quadrant. Since

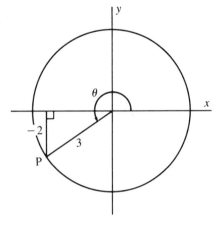

$\sin \theta = -\dfrac{2}{3}$, and $\sin \theta = \dfrac{y}{r}$, there is a

point P(x, y) on the terminal arm of the angle with $y = -2$ and $r = 3$. We can find the x-coordinate of P using the relation $r^2 = x^2 + y^2$.

From the diagram, $r^2 = x^2 + y^2$
$$9 = x^2 + 4$$
$$x^2 = 5$$
$$x = \pm\sqrt{5}$$

Since θ is in the third quadrant, $x < 0$.
Hence, $x = -\sqrt{5}$

Therefore, $\tan \theta = \dfrac{y}{x}$

$$= \dfrac{-2}{-\sqrt{5}}$$

$$= \dfrac{2}{\sqrt{5}}$$

Example 4 shows that if we know the value of the sine, cosine, or tangent of an angle in standard position, we can determine the other function values of the angle, provided that we also know the quadrant in which the angle is located.

EXERCISES 10-7

(A)

1. Determine sin θ, cos θ, and tan θ. Express your answers in decimal form, to 4 decimal places.

a)　　　　　　　　b)　　　　　　　　c)　　　　　　　　d)

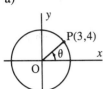
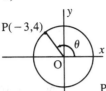
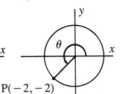
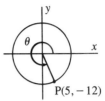

2. Determine sin θ, cos θ, and tan θ to 4 decimal places.

a)　　　　　　　　b)　　　　　　　　c)　　　　　　　　d)

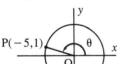
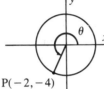
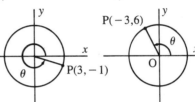

3. Use a scientific calculator in degree mode. Find each value to 3 decimal places.
   a) sin 130°   b) cos 145°   c) tan 130°   d) sin 200°
   e) cos 260°   f) sin 325°   g) tan 347°   h) cos 534°

4. Use a scientific calculator in degree mode. Find each value to 3 decimal places.
   a) sin 23°   b) cos 34°   c) tan 72°   d) sin 103°
   e) cos 172°   f) tan 238°   g) sin 309°   h) cos 501°

5. The point P(4, −3) is on the terminal arm of an angle θ.
   a) Draw a diagram showing θ in standard position.
   b) Calculate sin θ, cos θ, and tan θ.

6. The point P(−1,2) is on the terminal arm of an angle θ.
   a) Draw a diagram showing θ in standard position.
   b) Calculate sin θ, cos θ, and tan θ to 3 decimal places.

Ⓑ

7. Each point P is on the terminal arm of an angle θ. Use a diagram to calculate $\sin \theta$, $\cos \theta$, and $\tan \theta$.
   a) P(12, −5) b) P(−4, −2) c) P(−3,1) d) P(−3, −4)
   e) P(6, −2)   f) P(2,9)   g) P(0,4)   h) P(−5,0)

8. a) Find $\sin 125°$ to 5 decimal places.
   b) Find three other angles which have the same sine as 125°, and verify with a calculator.

9. a) Find $\cos 220°$ to 5 decimal places.
   b) Find three other angles which have the same cosine as 220°, and verify with a calculator.

10. a) Find $\sin 72°$ to 5 decimal places.
    b) Find three other angles which have the same sine as 72°, and verify with a calculator.

11. a) Find $\tan 269°$ to 5 decimal places.
    b) Find three other angles which have the same tangent as 269°, and verify with a calculator.

12. The angle θ is in the first quadrant, and $\tan \theta = \frac{2}{3}$.
    a) Draw a diagram showing the angle in standard position and a point P on its terminal arm.
    b) Determine possible coordinates for P.
    c) Find the other two primary trigonometric functions of θ.

13. Repeat *Exercise 12* if θ is in the second quadrant, and $\tan \theta = -\frac{5}{2}$.

14. Repeat *Exercise 12* if θ is in the second quadrant, and $\sin \theta = \frac{2}{\sqrt{5}}$.

Ⓒ

15. For each angle θ, find the other two primary trigonometric functions of θ.

	Quadrant	Given function		Quadrant	Given function
a)	Second	$\cos \theta = -\frac{5}{13}$	b)	Third	$\sin \theta = -\frac{1}{4}$
c)	Third	$\tan \theta = \frac{3}{2}$	d)	Fourth	$\sin \theta = -\frac{3}{4}$

16. Given the equation $\sin \theta = 0.5$
    a) Find three different roots for θ.
    b) How many different roots are there?

17. You can use a scientific calculator to find the sine, cosine or tangent of any angle in standard position. Determine the *largest* angle your calculator will accept.

10-8 TRIGONOMETRIC FUNCTIONS OF ANGLES IN STANDARD POSITION: PART TWO

In the preceding section we found how to determine the sine, cosine, or tangent of any angle in standard position. We now consider how to determine the angle if its sine, cosine, or tangent is given. For example, we can solve equations such as these, for θ.

$$\sin \theta = 0.548 \qquad \cos \theta = -0.255 \qquad \tan \theta = 0.65$$

Since the trigonometric functions are periodic, equations such as these have infinitely many roots. Each root is an angle in standard position with its terminal arm in one of the four quadrants. To help us determine the quadrants in which the roots occur for any given equation, the table below summarizes the possible combinations of signs for each function (the sign of r is always taken to be positive).

	Quadrant I	Quadrant II	Quadrant III	Quadrant IV
Sign of $\sin \theta = \dfrac{y}{r}$	+	+	−	−
Sign of $\cos \theta = \dfrac{x}{r}$	+	−	−	+
Sign of $\tan \theta = \dfrac{y}{x}$	+	−	+	−

Example 1. Solve the equation $\sin \theta = 0.65$ for θ to the nearest degree, where $0° \leqslant \theta \leqslant 360°$.

Solution. Since $\sin \theta$ is positive, and $\sin \theta = \frac{y}{r}$, θ lies in the quadrants in which $y > 0$, namely, Quadrants I and II.
Be sure your calculator is in degree mode.
$\sin \theta = 0.65$ gives $\theta \doteq 41°$
Hence, one value of θ is $41°$, which is in Quadrant I.

To find the root in Quadrant II, consider the diagram. $P'(-x,y)$ is the image of $P(x,y)$ under a reflection in the y-axis.
If $\angle POA = 41°$, then by the properties of a reflection,
$\angle P'OB = 41°$
Hence, $\angle P'OA = 180° - 41°$
$= 139°$

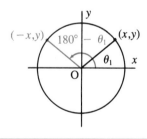

To the nearest degree, the equation $\sin \theta = 0.65$ has two roots between $0°$ and $360°$: $\theta_1 = 41°$, and $\theta_2 = 139°$.

Example 1 illustrates the following general result.

Property of sine functions
If θ_1 is any value of θ such that $\sin \theta = k$, then another value of θ which satisfies this equation is:
$\theta_2 = 180° - \theta_1$
All other values of θ can be found by adding multiples of $360°$ to θ_1 and θ_2.

Example 2. Solve the equation $\sin \theta = -0.8974$ to the nearest degree, where $0° \leqslant \theta \leqslant 360°$.

Solution. Since $\sin \theta$ is negative, and $\sin \theta = \frac{y}{r}$, θ lies in the quadrants in which $y < 0$, namely, Quadrants III and IV.
Use your calculator. $\sin \theta = -0.8974$ gives $\theta \doteq -64°$
Hence, one value of θ which satisfies the equation is $-64°$. Although this root is not between $0°$ and $360°$, we can use it to obtain two roots which are between $0°$ and $360°$.
To obtain one root, add $360°$: $-64° + 360°$, or $296°$. This is the root in Quadrant IV.
To obtain the other root, use the property of sine functions. Another angle that satisfies the equation is:
$180° - (-64°)$, or $244°$. This is the root in Quadrant III.
To the nearest degree, the equation $\sin \theta = -0.8974$ has two roots between $0°$ and $360°$: $\theta_1 = 296°$ and $\theta_2 = 244°$.
Check these results with your calculator.

Example 3. Solve the equation $\cos \theta = 0.4138$ to the nearest degree, where $0° \leqslant \theta \leqslant 360°$.

Solution. Since $\cos \theta$ is positive, and $\cos \theta = \frac{x}{r}$, θ lies in the quadrants in which $x > 0$, namely, Quadrants I and IV.
Use your calculator. $\cos \theta = 0.4138$ gives $\theta \doteq 66°$
Hence, one value of θ is $66°$, which is in Quadrant I.
To find the root in Quadrant IV,
consider the diagram.
$P'(x, -y)$ is the image of $P(x,y)$
under a reflection in the x-axis.
By the properties of a reflection,
$\angle P'OA = \angle POA$
Hence, as an angle in standard
position,
$\angle P'OA = 360° - 66°$, or $294°$
To the nearest degree, the equation
$\cos \theta = 0.4138$ has two roots
between $0°$ and $360°$:
$\theta_1 = 66°$ and $\theta_2 = 294°$.
Check these results with your
calculator.

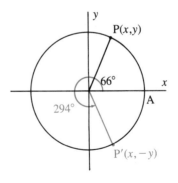

Example 3 illustrates the following general result.

Property of cosine functions
If θ_1 is any value of θ such that $\cos \theta = k$,
then another value of θ which satisfies this
equation is:
$$\theta_2 = 360° - \theta_1$$
All other values of θ can be found by adding
multiples of $360°$ to θ_1 and θ_2.

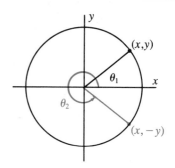

Remember, when working with trigonometric functions using a
scientific calculator, your calculator must be in degree mode.

Example 4. Solve the equation $5 \cos \theta = 2 \cos \theta + 2$ for θ to the nearest tenth of
a degree, where $0° \leqslant \theta \leqslant 360°$.

Solution. $5 \cos \theta = 2 \cos \theta + 2$ is a linear equation in $\cos \theta$.
Collect like terms.

$$5 \cos \theta - 2 \cos \theta = 2$$
$$3 \cos \theta = 2$$
$$\cos \theta = \frac{2}{3}$$

Since $\cos \theta$ is positive, θ lies in Quadrants I and IV.
Use your calculator.

$\cos \theta = \frac{2}{3}$ gives $\theta \doteq 48.189\,685°$, which is
one root of the equation.
Another root is $360° - 48.189\,685°$, or $311.810\,315°$.
To the nearest tenth of a degree, the roots are $48.2°$ and $311.8°$.

EXERCISES 10-8

(A)

1. Solve for θ to the nearest degree, $0° \leqslant \theta \leqslant 90°$.
   a) $\sin \theta = 0.35$ b) $\cos \theta = 0.112$ c) $\tan \theta = 0.485$
   d) $5 \cos \theta - 4 = 0$ e) $10 \sin \theta - 9 = 0$ f) $4 \tan \theta - 8 = 0$

2. Solve for θ to the nearest degree, $0° \leqslant \theta \leqslant 90°$.
   a) $\sin \theta = 0.82$ b) $\cos \theta = 0.75$ c) $\tan \theta = 0.685$
   d) $9 \cos \theta - 1 = 0$ e) $4 \sin \theta - 1 = 0$ f) $10 \tan \theta - 32 = 0$

(B)

3. Solve for θ to the nearest degree, $0° \leqslant \theta \leqslant 360°$.
   a) $\sin \theta = 0.75$ b) $\cos \theta = 0.0965$ c) $\sin \theta = 0.1392$
   d) $\cos \theta = 0.3558$ e) $\sin \theta = 0.6666$ f) $\cos \theta = 0.9876$

4. Solve for θ to the nearest degree, $0° \leqslant \theta \leqslant 360°$.
   a) $\cos \theta = 0.44$ b) $\sin \theta = 0.6805$ c) $\cos \theta = 0.8923$
   d) $\sin \theta = 0.2671$ e) $\tan \theta = 2.671$ f) $\cos \theta = 0.3498$

5. Solve for θ to the nearest degree, $0° \leqslant \theta \leqslant 360°$.
   a) $\sin \theta = -0.6855$ b) $\cos \theta = -0.1881$ c) $\sin \theta = -0.2550$
   d) $\cos \theta = 0.8245$ e) $\cos \theta = -0.1067$ f) $\sin \theta = -0.8040$

6. The point $P(-2, -6)$ is on the terminal arm of an angle θ in standard position. Find a value of θ to the nearest degree.

7. The point given is on the terminal arm of an angle θ in standard position. Find a value of θ to the nearest degree.
   a) $P(-1, -4)$ b) $Q(3, -4)$ c) $R(2, -3)$ d) $S(-1, 2)$

8. Solve for θ to the nearest degree, $0° \leqslant \theta \leqslant 360°$.
   a) $4 \sin \theta - 1 = 0$ b) $3 \cos \theta + 2 = 0$
   c) $3 \cos \theta = \cos \theta + 1$ d) $2 \sin \theta - 4 = 7 \sin \theta$
   e) $6 \sin^2\theta - 5 \sin \theta + 1 = 0$ f) $3 \cos^2\theta + 5 \cos \theta - 2 = 0$

9. Solve for θ to the nearest degree, $0° \leqslant \theta \leqslant 360°$.
   a) $6 \cos \theta + 1 = 0$ b) $3 \sin \theta + 1 = 2$
   c) $4 \cos \theta - 2 = -\cos \theta$ d) $-1 - 5 \sin \theta = 2 \sin \theta$
   e) $5 \cos^2\theta - 2 = 0$ f) $4 \cos^2\theta + 5 \cos \theta - 6 = 0$

Ⓒ

10. Solve for θ to the nearest tenth of a degree, $0° \leqslant \theta \leqslant 90°$.
    a) $\sin 2\theta = 0.75$ b) $4 \cos 2\theta - 3 = 0$
    c) $3 \sin^2 2\theta - 10 \sin 2\theta + 3 = 0$ d) $8 \cos^2 2\theta + 2 \cos 2\theta - 1 = 0$

11. Write a property of the tangent function which is similar to the properties of sine and cosine functions which were developed in this section.

12. Solve for θ to the nearest degree, $0° \leqslant \theta \leqslant 360°$.
    a) $3 \tan \theta - 2 = 0$ b) $2 \tan \theta + 7 = 0$
    c) $2 \tan^2\theta - 3 \tan \theta + 1 = 0$ d) $3 \tan^2\theta - 2 \tan \theta - 4 = 0$

13. Solve for θ to the nearest tenth of a degree, $0° \leqslant \theta \leqslant 90°$.
    a) $\tan 3\theta = 0.5$ b) $5 \tan 2\theta + 2 = 0$
    c) $3 \tan 2\theta - 1 = 4$ d) $4 \tan \theta - 1 = 5$
    e) $2 \tan^2 2\theta + \tan 2\theta - 1 = 0$ f) $\tan^2 2\theta - 5 \tan 2\theta + 6 = 0$

14. a) Find the smallest angle greater than $1000°$ whose cosine is 0.5.
    b) Find the greatest angle less than $2000°$ whose tangent is 2.5.

10-9 THE AREA OF A TRIANGLE

The area A of a triangle can be found using the formula $A = \frac{1}{2}bh$ where b is the base and h is the height, or altitude. If the height of the triangle is not known, the sine ratio can be used to find the area.

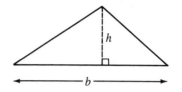

Example 1. Find the area of $\triangle XYZ$ if $\angle Y = 55°$, $YZ = 23$ cm, and $XY = 18$ cm.

Solution. Draw the altitude XW, perpendicular to YZ.
To find the length of XW, use right $\triangle XYW$.

$$\sin 55° = \frac{XW}{XY}$$
$$XW = XY \sin 55°$$

Area of $\triangle XYZ = \frac{1}{2}(\text{base})(\text{height})$

$$= \frac{1}{2}(YZ)(XW)$$
$$= \frac{1}{2}(YZ)(XY \sin 55°)$$
$$= \frac{1}{2}(23)(18 \sin 55°)$$
$$\doteq 169.6$$

The area of $\triangle XYZ$ is approximately 170 cm².

In an obtuse triangle, this same method can be used to find the area.

Example 2. Find the area of $\triangle PQR$ if $\angle Q = 125°$, $QR = 23$ cm, and $PQ = 18$ cm.

Solution. Draw the altitude PS, perpendicular to RQ extended.
To find the length of PS, use right $\triangle PSQ$, where $\angle PQS = 180° - 125°$.

$$\sin (180° - 125°) = \frac{PS}{PQ}$$
$$PS = PQ \sin (180° - 125°)$$
$$= PQ \sin 125°$$

Area $\triangle PQR = \frac{1}{2}(\text{base})(\text{height})$

$$= \frac{1}{2}(QR)(PS)$$
$$= \frac{1}{2}(QR)(PQ \sin 125°)$$
$$= \frac{1}{2}(23)(18 \sin 125°)$$
$$\doteq 169.6$$

The area of $\triangle PQR$ is approximately 170 cm².

We can extend the method of *Examples 1* and *2*, to find the area of any triangle.
In each △ABC,

Area $= \frac{1}{2}bh$

$= \frac{1}{2}b(a \sin C)$

$= \frac{1}{2}ab \sin C$

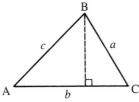
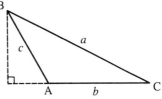

If two sides b and c, and the contained angle A of △ABC are known, then

$$\text{Area } \triangle ABC = \frac{1}{2}bc \sin A$$

EXERCISES 10-9

Ⓐ

1. Use the sine ratio to find an expression for the length of the altitude of each triangle.

a)   b)   c)   d)

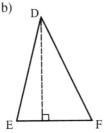
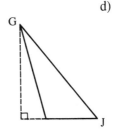
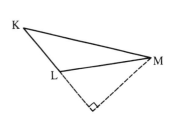

Ⓑ

2. Find the area of each triangle.

a)   b)   c)

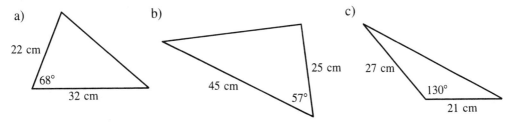

3. Find the area of each △ABC.
   a) ∠B = 28°, AB = 12, BC = 15
   b) ∠C = 52°, BC = 48, AC = 18
   c) ∠A = 110°, AB = 35, AC = 20
   d) ∠B = 140°, BC = 65, AB = 25
   e) ∠C = 81°, BC = 14.5, AC = 6.5

4. Find the area of each triangle.

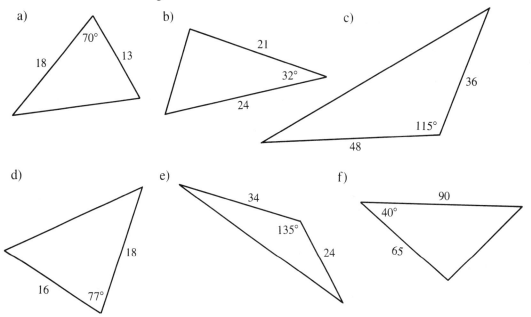

a) 70° 18 13

b) 21 32° 24

c) 36 115° 48

d) 18 16 77°

e) 34 135° 24

f) 90 40° 65

5. Two sides of a triangular field have lengths 85 m and 63 m. The angle between these sides is 62.3°. Find the area of the field.

6. Find the area of an equilateral triangle with side length 21.6 cm.

7. A triangular sail is made to fit along the full length of the 4.20 m mast and the 2.85 m boom. The angle between the boom and the mast is 86.5°. How much material is used in the sail?

8. Find the area of a parallelogram with sides of length 23.7 cm and 15.2 cm, and one angle of 105.4°.

9. The sail on a windsurfer has the dimensions shown (below left). If the "window" is made of clear plastic, how much nylon is required to make the sail?

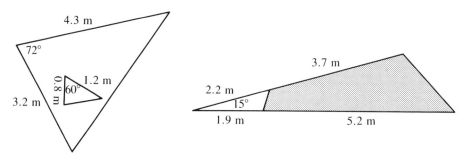

4.3 m
72°
0.8 m
1.2 m
60°
3.2 m

3.7 m
2.2 m
15°
1.9 m
5.2 m

10. Find the area of the shaded part of the triangle (above right).

11. A triangular section of a lawn in a park is to be covered with sod. Two sides of the triangle measure 28.3 m and 19.6 m. The angle between these sides is 115°.
    a) Find the area to be covered in sod.
    b) If sod costs $2.75/m², how much will it cost to buy sufficient sod?

12. A piece of carpet has the shape of a parallelogram with sides 3.2 m and 2.1 m. The angle between these sides is 81°. If carpet remnants are priced at $7.50/m², how much does this piece cost?

13. The base of a tetrahedron is an equilateral triangle with sides 12 cm. The faces of the tetrahedron are isosceles triangles with equal sides 18 cm and vertical angle 39°. Find the surface area of the tetrahedron.

14. a) Find the area of the cedar deck shown in the diagram (below left).
    b) If the cedar costs $52.50/m², how much did the deck cost?

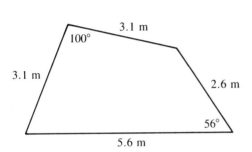

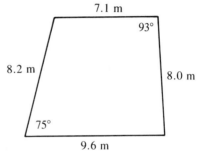

15. The foundation of a condominium unit is shown in the diagram (above right). Find its area.

16. The end wall of a hotel lobby is to be covered with wallpaper costing $8.25/m². Find the cost of the wallpaper.

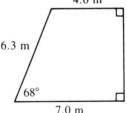

17. Two sides of a triangle have lengths 28.2 cm and 18.8 cm. The angle between them is 41.5°. Find the lengths of the sides of an isosceles right triangle with the same area.

Ⓒ

18. The edges of a pyramid with a square base are 15 cm long. Find:
    a) the surface area
    b) the volume
    c) the angle that each edge makes with the base
    d) the angle that each face makes with the base.

19. The diagonals of a quadrilateral are a and b units in length, with angle θ between them. Prove that the area of the quadrilateral is $\frac{1}{2}ab \sin \theta$.

10-10 THE COSINE LAW

Previously in this chapter we solved right triangles given the lengths of any two sides, or the length of one side and the measure of an acute angle. In this section, we will study the Cosine Law which will enable us to solve certain oblique triangles; that is, triangles which contain no right angles.

A triangle is uniquely determined by two sides and the contained angle. The following example shows how to calculate the remaining side.

Example 1. In $\triangle ABC$, $AB = 8$, $AC = 5$, and $\angle A = 35°$; find the length of BC to 1 decimal place.

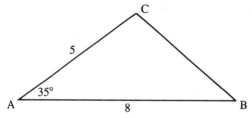

Solution. Construct CN perpendicular to AB and let $BC = a$, $CN = h$, and $AN = x$.

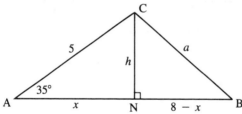

Apply the Pythagorean Theorem to $\triangle CNB$ and $\triangle CNA$.

$a^2 = h^2 + (8 - x)^2 \ldots ①$
$5^2 = h^2 + x^2 \ldots ②$
Subtract ② from ①.
$a^2 - 5^2 = 64 - 16x$
$\quad a^2 = 89 - 16x$
$\quad\quad = 89 - 16(5 \cos 35°)$ Since $\dfrac{x}{5} = \cos 35°$
$\quad a^2 \doteq 23.4678$
$\quad\quad a \doteq 4.844$

The length of BC is approximately 4.8.

Now we consider the general cases of $\triangle ABC$ where $\angle A$ is acute and where $\angle A$ is obtuse.

In both cases, construct CN perpendicular to AB or AB extended; let CN = h, and AN = x. Apply the Pythagorean Theorem to $\triangle$CNB and $\triangle$CNA.

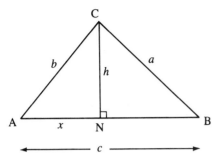

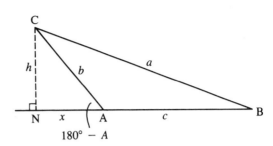

For the acute triangle
$$a^2 = h^2 + (c - x)^2$$
$$b^2 = h^2 + x^2$$
Subtract.
$$a^2 - b^2 = c^2 - 2cx$$
$$\begin{aligned} a^2 &= b^2 + c^2 - 2cx \\ &= b^2 + c^2 - 2c(b \cos A) \\ &= b^2 + c^2 - 2bc \cos A \end{aligned}$$

For the obtuse triangle
$$a^2 = h^2 + (c + x)^2$$
$$b^2 = h^2 + x^2$$
Subtract.
$$a^2 - b^2 = c^2 + 2cx$$
$$\begin{aligned} a^2 &= b^2 + c^2 + 2cx \\ &= b^2 + c^2 + 2c(b \cos (180° - A)) \\ &= b^2 + c^2 - 2bc \cos A \end{aligned}$$

In both cases, $a^2 = b^2 + c^2 - 2bc \cos A$

Similarly, by letting BN = x we can prove that $b^2 = a^2 + c^2 - 2ac \cos B$, and by constructing a perpendicular from A to BC we can prove that $c^2 = a^2 + b^2 - 2ab \cos C$.

The Cosine Law
In any $\triangle$ABC
$$a^2 = b^2 + c^2 - 2bc \cos A$$
$$b^2 = a^2 + c^2 - 2ac \cos B$$
$$c^2 = a^2 + b^2 - 2ab \cos C$$

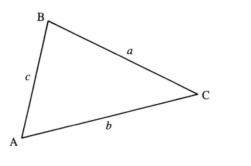

We can use the Cosine Law to find the third side of a triangle when two sides and the contained angle are given.

Example 2. In $\triangle$ABC, AB = 10 and AC = 8; find the length of BC to 1 decimal place for each value of $\angle$A.
a) $\angle A = 50°$
b) $\angle A = 130°$

Solution.   In each case we use the Cosine Law in the form
$a^2 = b^2 + c^2 - 2bc \cos A$.

a)   b)

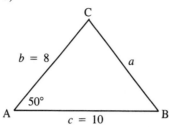

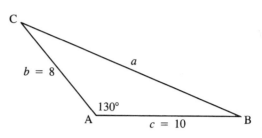

For the acute triangle   For the obtuse triangle
$a^2 = 8^2 + 10^2 - 2(8)(10)(\cos 50°)$ $a^2 = 8^2 + 10^2 - 2(8)(10)(\cos 130°)$
$\doteq 61.153\,982$ $\doteq 266.846\,02$
$a \doteq 7.8201$ $a \doteq 16.3354$
The length of BC is about 7.8.   The length of BC is about 16.3.

Example 2 and the diagrams below suggest that the Pythagorean
Theorem is a special case of the Cosine Law.

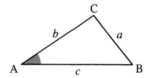

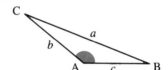

If $\angle A < 90°$, $\cos A > 0$ If $\angle A = 90°$, $\cos A = 0$ If $\angle A > 90°$, $\cos A < 0$
and $a^2 < b^2 + c^2$ and $a^2 = b^2 + c^2$ and $a^2 > b^2 + c^2$

The Cosine Law can also be used to find any angle of a triangle
when its three sides are given.

Example 3.   In $\triangle PQR$, PQ = 7, QR = 8, and RP = 10; find the measure of $\angle R$ to
the nearest degree.

Solution.   To find $\angle R$, use the Cosine Law in this form.
$$r^2 = p^2 + q^2 - 2pq \cos R$$
$$7^2 = 8^2 + 10^2 - 2(8)(10) \cos R$$
$$49 = 164 - 160 \cos R$$
$$160 \cos R = 115$$
$$\cos R = \frac{115}{160}$$
$$\angle R \doteq 44.0486$$
To the nearest degree, $\angle R = 44°$

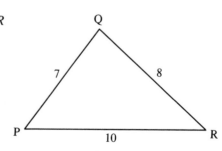

Example 4. A tunnel is to be built through a hill to connect points A and B in a straight line. Point C is chosen so that it is visible from both A and B, and measurement shows that $\angle C = 63°$, CA = 2 km, and CB = 5 km.
Find the length of AB to 2 decimal places and the measure of $\angle A$ to 1 decimal place.

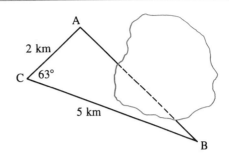

Solution. By the Cosine Law
$$c^2 = a^2 + b^2 - 2ab \cos C$$
$$= 5^2 + 2^2 - 2(5)(2)(\cos 63°)$$
$$\doteq 19.920\ 19$$
$$c \doteq 4.4632$$
The distance from A to B, through the hill, is approximately 4.46 km.
To find $\angle A$, we use the Cosine Law in this form.
$$a^2 = b^2 + c^2 - 2bc \cos A$$
Substitute the given values of a and b, and the (non-rounded) values of c and c^2.
$$5^2 \doteq 2^2 + 19.920\ 19 - 2(2)(4.463\ 204) \cos A$$
Solve for cos A.
$$\cos A \doteq -\frac{1.079\ 81}{17.853\ 216}$$
Since cos A is negative, $\angle A$ is obtuse.
$$\angle A \doteq 93.5°$$

EXERCISES 10-10

Ⓐ

1. Find the third side of each triangle to 1 decimal place.

a)

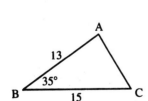

b)

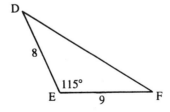

c)

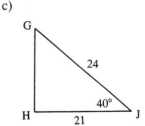

2. Use the given information to find the third side of $\triangle ABC$ to 1 decimal place.
   a) $\angle B = 42°$, $a = 6$, $c = 4$
   b) $\angle A = 130°$, $b = 15$, $c = 11$
   c) $\angle C = 95°$, $a = 18$, $b = 27$
   d) $\angle B = 28°$, $a = 17$, $c = 15$
   e) $\angle A = 105°$, $b = 7.4$, $c = 10.2$

3. Find θ to 1 decimal place.

a)

b)

c)

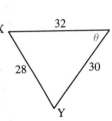

4. For a triangle with sides of the given lengths, find to 1 decimal place the measure of: i) the smallest angle   ii) the largest angle.
   a) 7, 9, 14   b) 6, 11, 15   c) 23, 31, 52
   d) 28, 45, 53   e) 8.3, 9.7, 12.5   f) 14, 55, 61

(B)

5. Use the given information to find the third side of $\triangle PQR$.
   a) $\angle Q = 72°, p = 4.3, r = 2.9$
   b) $\angle P = 112°, PQ = 25, PR = 33$
   c) $\angle R = 98°, PR = 17.4, QR = 21.3$

6. A roof truss (below left) is to span 8.2 m. One piece of the truss is 6.8 m in length and set at an angle of 35°. How long is the other piece of the truss?

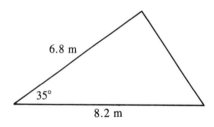

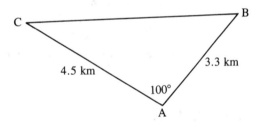

7. A radar station at A (above right) is tracking ships at B and C. How far apart are the two ships?

8. To find the distance across a marsh, a surveyor locates point C as shown in the diagram (below left). If $\angle C$ is 65°, how far is it across the marsh?

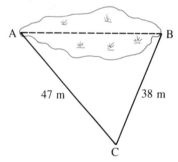

9. Find the size of each angle in $\triangle ABC$ (above right).

10. In parallelogram ABCD, AB = 4 cm and BC = 7 cm. If ∠B = 65°, how long is each diagonal to 1 decimal place?

11. Given the points P(5,8), Q(3,2), and R(7,5), calculate ∠PQR to the nearest degree.

12. The sides of a parallelogram measure 18.0 cm and 10.0 cm. The diagonals measure 14.7 cm and 25.1 cm. Find the size of each angle in the parallelogram.

13. A radar tracking station locates a fishing trawler at a distance of 5.4 km, and a passenger ferry at a distance of 7.2 km. At the station, the angle between the two boats is 118°. How far apart are they?

14. In a circle with diameter 12 cm, the chord AB subtends an angle of 140° at the centre. How long is the chord?

15. In a circle with diameter 21.4 cm, the chord AB subtends an angle of 42° at a point C on the circumference. How long is the chord?

16. Calculate, to the nearest degree, the smallest angle in the triangle formed by the points O(0,0), A(4,3), and B(3,4).

17. In a circle of radius 10 cm, AB is an arc of length 10 cm. How long is the chord AB to 1 decimal place?

18. Calculate, to 1 decimal place, the largest angle in the triangle formed by the points P(2,7), Q(8, − 3), and R(− 5,1).

19. Find the area of each △ABC with the given lengths of sides.
    a) 17 cm, 29 cm, 23 cm
    b) 32 cm, 19 cm, 15 cm
    c) 12 cm, 35 cm, 37 cm

20. The triangle formed by the points J(5,7), K(− 7, − 1), and L(8, − 4) is inscribed in a circle. Find the size of the angle at the centre of the circle subtended by KL.

21. Twelve points are equally spaced around a circle of radius *r*. Express these lengths in terms of *r*.
    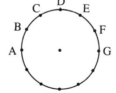
    a) AB b) AC c) AD
    d) AE e) AF f) AG

22. Two ships leave a port, sailing at 17 km/h and 21 km/h. The angle between their directions of travel from the port is 38°. How far apart are the ships after 2 h?

23. The goal posts of a hockey net are 1.8 m apart. The puck is shot from a point which is 9.2 m from one post and 10.8 m from the other post. Within what angle must the puck travel to score a goal?

24. In the diagrams below, ABCD is a square with side length 3 cm and △PBC is equilateral. Find the length of AP.

a)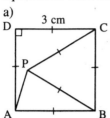

b)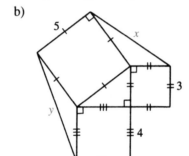

25. ABCD is a square of side 1 unit. Equilateral triangles are constructed on the sides of the square.
    a) Find the length of EH.
    b) Find the area of △EDH.

26. Find the values of *x* and *y*.

a)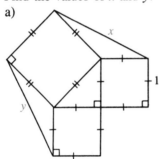

b)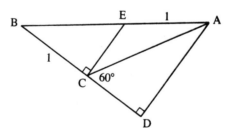

27. For the diagram (below left), show that $x^2 + y^2 = 5c^2$.

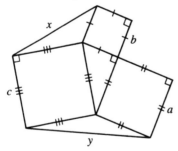

28. In the diagram (above right), EC is perpendicular to BD, ∠ACD = 60°, and AE = BC = 1 unit. Find the lengths of BE and CA.

10-11 THE SINE LAW

There are some triangles which cannot be solved using the Cosine Law; that is, triangles for which only one side is known.

A triangle is uniquely determined by two angles and a particular side. The following example shows how to find the other sides of such a triangle.

Example 1. In △ABC, ∠A = 30°, BC = 5, and ∠B = 65°; find the length of AC to 1 decimal place.

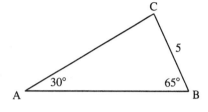

Solution. Construct CN perpendicular to AB, and let CN = h and AC = b.

In right △ANC

$$\frac{h}{b} = \sin 30°, \text{ or } h = b \sin 30°$$

In right △BNC

$$\frac{h}{5} = \sin 65°, \text{ or } h = 5 \sin 65°$$

That is, $b \sin 30° = 5 \sin 65°$

$$b = \frac{5 \sin 65°}{\sin 30°}$$

$$\doteq 9.063$$

The length of AC is approximately 9.1.

Now we consider the general cases of △ABC where ∠A is acute and ∠A is obtuse. In both cases, construct CN perpendicular to AB or AB extended, and let CN = h.

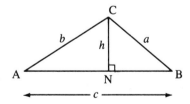

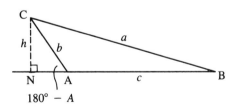

For the acute triangle

$h = b \sin A$

and $h = a \sin B$

For the obtuse triangle

$h = b \sin (180° - A)$

$= b \sin A$

and $h = a \sin B$

In both cases, $b \sin A = a \sin B$

$$\frac{\sin A}{a} = \frac{\sin B}{b}$$

Similarly, by constructing a perpendicular from A to BC, we can show that $\dfrac{\sin B}{b} = \dfrac{\sin C}{c}$.

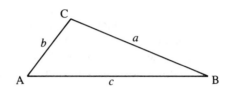

The Sine Law
In any △ABC
$$\frac{\sin A}{a} = \frac{\sin B}{b} = \frac{\sin C}{c}$$

We can use the Sine Law to find the remaining sides of a triangle when two angles and one side are given.

Example 2. Solve △PQR, given that ∠P = 57°, ∠Q = 73°, and QR = 24. Give the answers to 1 decimal place.

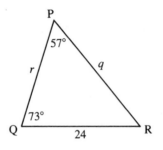

Solution. ∠R = 180° − (73° + 57°)
= 50°
By the Sine Law
$$\frac{\sin P}{p} = \frac{\sin Q}{q} = \frac{\sin R}{r}$$
$$\frac{\sin 57°}{24} = \frac{\sin 73°}{q} = \frac{\sin 50°}{r}$$

To find q
$$\frac{\sin 57°}{24} = \frac{\sin 73°}{q}$$
$$q = \frac{24 \sin 73°}{\sin 57°}$$
$$\doteq 27.366\ 304$$
$$\doteq 27.4$$

To find r
$$\frac{\sin 57°}{24} = \frac{\sin 50°}{r}$$
$$r = \frac{24 \sin 50°}{\sin 57°}$$
$$\doteq 21.921\ 679$$
$$\doteq 21.9$$

We summarize these results in a table.

∠P	∠Q	∠R	p	q	r
57°	73°	50°	24	27.4	21.9

The Sine Law actually represent three equations. Each equation relates four variables.
$$\frac{\sin A}{a} = \frac{\sin B}{b} \qquad \frac{\sin B}{b} = \frac{\sin C}{c} \qquad \frac{\sin A}{a} = \frac{\sin C}{c}$$
To use the Sine Law, we must know the values of three of the four variables in any equation. Then, we select the equation relating these three variables and solve for the unknown variable.

Since no single equation above contains the three variables a, b, and C we cannot use the Sine Law to solve a triangle given only that information. As explained in *Section 10-10*, the Cosine Law is used in this situation.

To apply the Sine Law to solve a triangle we must know the measure of one angle and the length of the opposite side, plus one other angle or side.

Example 3. Solve $\triangle ABC$ given $\angle B = 48°$, $b = 9$, and $c = 11$. Give the answers to 1 decimal place.

Solution. Use the Sine Law to find $\angle C$.

$$\frac{\sin C}{c} = \frac{\sin B}{b}$$

$$\sin C = \frac{11 \sin 48°}{9}$$

$$\doteq 0.908\ 288\ 1$$

$$\angle C \doteq 65.3°$$

Since $\sin C = \sin (180° - C)$, $\angle C$ could be 114.7°.

That is, there are two different triangles which satisfy the given conditions.

We proceed to solve the triangle for both values of $\angle C$.

If $\angle C = 65.3°$
Then $\angle A = 180° - 48° - 65.3°$
$= 66.7°$

To find a

$$\frac{a}{\sin A} = \frac{c}{\sin C}$$

$$a = \frac{11 \sin 66.7°}{\sin 65.3°}$$

$$\doteq 11.120\ 329$$

$$\doteq 11.1$$

If $\angle C = 114.7°$
Then $\angle A = 180° - 48° - 114.7°$
$= 17.3°$

To find a

$$\frac{a}{\sin A} = \frac{c}{\sin C}$$

$$a = \frac{11 \sin 17.3°}{\sin 65.3°}$$

$$\doteq 3.600\ 544$$

$$\doteq 3.6$$

We summarize these results in tables and draw a triangle to illustrate each case.

$\angle A$	$\angle B$	$\angle C$	a	b	c
66.7°	48°	65.3°	11.1	9	11

$\angle A$	$\angle B$	$\angle C$	a	b	c
17.3°	48°	114.7°	3.6	9	11

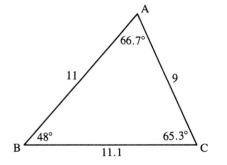

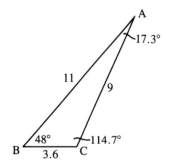

The Ambiguous Case

If we superimpose the two triangles obtained in *Example 3*, we discover why, given two sides and an angle other than the contained angle, there are two solutions.

The vertex C of △ABC can be placed in position C′ or its mirror image in AD, C″ without affecting the given values; that is, ∠B and the lengths *b* and *c*.

The case in which two triangles are possible is called the *ambiguous case*.

How can we tell when we have an ambiguous case; that is, two solutions?

Consider △ABC where ∠B, *b*, and *c* are given. The length of AD, the perpendicular from A to BC, is *c* sin *B*.

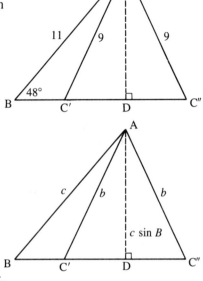

Case I   If *b* < *c* sin *B*, then there is no triangle possible because AD is the shortest distance from A to BC″.

Case II If *b* = *c* sin *B*, then *b* is the length of AD; that is, △ABC is the right triangle △ABD.

Case III If *b* > *c* sin *B*, then there are two triangles provided *b* < *c*. If b > *c*, then C can be only in position C″ and not C′.

These cases are summarized in the following statement.

> If △ABC is known to exist; and the measure of ∠B, the length *b*, and the length *c* are given, then there are exactly two different triangles which satisfy these conditions provided *c* sin *B* < *b* < *c*. Otherwise, there is exactly one triangle.

Example 4. A tunnel through the mountains is to be constructed to join A and B. Point C is 12.6 km from B. A cannot be seen from B or from C. Point D is 10.3 km from C and 6.7 km from A; ∠ADC = 125° and ∠DCB = 142°.

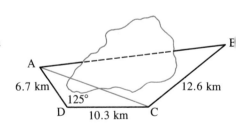

a) Find the length of the tunnel AB.
b) Find the angle between:
   i) AB and AD   ii) AB and CB.

Solution.   a) First, use the Cosine Law in △ACD to find AC.

$$d^2 = a^2 + c^2 - 2ac \cos D$$
$$= 10.3^2 + 6.7^2 - 2(6.7)(10.3)(\cos 125°)$$
$$\doteq 230.145\ 02$$
$$d \doteq 15.1705$$

Then, use the Sine Law in △ACD to find ∠C.

$$\frac{\sin C}{c} = \frac{\sin D}{d}$$

$$\sin C = \frac{6.7 \sin 125°}{15.1705}$$

$$\doteq 0.361\ 775\ 7$$

$$\angle C \doteq 21.2°$$

Subtract to find $\angle ACB$.

$$\angle ACB = 142° - 21.2°$$
$$= 120.8°$$

Use the Cosine Law in $\triangle ABC$ to find AB.

$$c^2 = a^2 + b^2 - 2ab \cos C$$
$$= 12.6^2 + 15.1705^2 - 2(15.1705)(12.6)(\cos 120.8°)$$
$$\doteq 584.6563$$

$$c \doteq 24.180$$

The tunnel is approximately 24.2 km in length.

b) Use the Sine Law in $\triangle ABC$ to find $\angle A$.

$$\frac{\sin A}{a} = \frac{\sin C}{c}$$

$$\sin A = \frac{12.6 \sin 120.8°}{24.180}$$

$$\doteq 0.447\ 597$$

$$\angle A \doteq 26.6°$$

i) The angle between AB and AD is $\angle DAB$.

$$\angle DAB = \angle BAC + \angle DAC$$
$$\angle BAC = 26.6°$$

In $\triangle ADC$

$$\angle DAC = 180° - 125° - 21.2°$$
$$= 33.8°$$
$$\angle DAB = 26.6° + 33.8°$$
$$= 60.4°$$

ii) The angle between AB and CB is $\angle ABC$.

In $\triangle ABC$, $\angle ABC = 180° - 120.8° - 26.6°$
$$= 32.6°$$

These examples show that we can solve any triangle using the Sine and/or Cosine Laws given:
- the length of one side and the measures of any two angles; or
- the lengths of two sides and the measure of any one angle; or
- the lengths of three sides.

If we are given only the measures of 3 angles, then there is an infinite number of similar triangles with this shape; the lengths of the sides of the triangles can be expressed only in terms of one of the sides of the triangle. That is, the Sine and Cosine Laws enable us to solve any triangle given any three pieces of data except the measures of the three angles. In all but the ambiguous case, the solution is unique.

The fact that the sets of conditions SSS, AAS, and SAS determine unique triangles is a direct consequence of the corresponding congruence theorems. That is, if there were another triangle satisfying any of these three conditions (such as SSS) it would be congruent to any triangle satisfying these conditions. The SSA condition is not a congruence condition and, as shown in the ambiguous case above, does not guarantee a unique solution.

These results are summarized below.

Number of Sides Given	Number of Angles Given	Method of Solution of the Triangle
1	2	Sine Law
2	1 not contained	Sine Law—ambiguous case
2	1 contained	Cosine Law
3	0	Cosine Law

EXERCISES 10-11

Ⓐ

1. Find the length of AB to 1 decimal place.

a)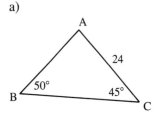

b)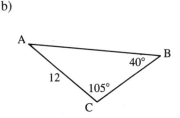

c)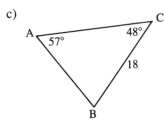

2. Find θ to 1 decimal place.

a)   b)   c)

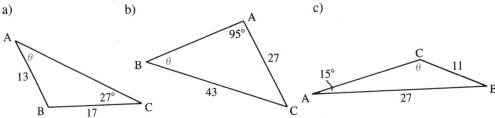

3. a) In $\triangle ABC$, $\angle A = 65°$, $\angle B = 40°$, and $a = 15$; find b.
   b) In $\triangle PQR$, $\angle P = 52°$, $\angle Q = 73°$, and $q = 27$; find p.
   c) In $\triangle ABC$, $\angle B = 27°$, $\angle C = 64°$, and $b = 14$; find c.
   d) In $\triangle ABC$, $\angle A = 38°$, $\angle B = 77°$, and $b = 16.5$; find c.
   e) In $\triangle XYZ$, $\angle Y = 84°$, $\angle Z = 33°$, and $z = 9.2$; find x.
   Give the answers to 1 decimal place.

Ⓑ

4. Solve each △PQR. Give the answers to 1 decimal place.
   a) ∠P = 105°, *p* = 12, *q* = 9   b) ∠Q = 63°, *q* = 20, *r* = 17
   c) ∠P = 112°, *p* = 32, *r* = 25   d) ∠R = 78°, *r* = 42, *p* = 28

5. Solve each △ABC. Give the answers to 1 decimal place.
   a) ∠A = 35°, *a* = 12, *b* = 15   b) ∠B = 55°, *b* = 11, *c* = 13
   c) ∠C = 78°, *b* = 19, *a* = 24   d) ∠B = 42°, *b* = 22, *c* = 27
   e) ∠A = 39°, *c* = 32, *b* = 45   f) ∠B = 124°, *b* = 27, *a* = 13

6. Solve each △XYZ. Give the answers to 1 decimal place.
   a) ∠X = 72°, ∠Z = 50°, *x* = 34   b) ∠X = 46.4°, *y* = 21, *z* = 29
   c) ∠Y = 54°, *x* = 22, *y* = 19   d) ∠Z = 61°, *y* = 6.3, *x* = 7.8

7. A bridge AB (below left) is to be built across a river. The point C is located 62.0 m from B, and ∠ABC = 74° while ∠ACB = 48°. How long will the bridge be?

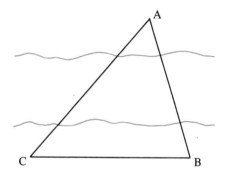
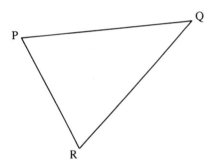

8. Two ships at P and Q (above right) are 32.0 km apart. How far is each ship from a lighthouse at R if ∠P = 68° and ∠Q = 42°?

9. A triangular park measures 251 m along one side (below left). Find the lengths of the other two sides if they form angles of 32° and 56° with the first side.

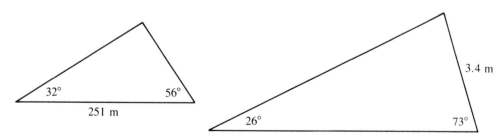

10. The roof lines of a ski chalet make angles of 26° and 73° with the horizontal (above right). The shorter roof line is 3.4 m long. Find the length of the other roof line.

11. Two girls intend to swim from a dock at D, to the island at I, and back to a dock at K (below left). The docks are 168 m apart. The angles between the line joining each dock to the island, and the line joining the docks are 64° and 70°. How far must the girls swim?

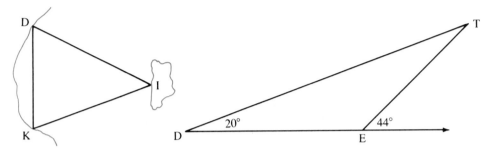

12. From points D and E (above right) the lines of sight to a tree at T make angles of 20° and 44° respectively, with DE. If DE is 62 m, how far is the tree from D, and from E?

13. Two guy wires 17.0 m and 10.0 m in length are fastened to the top of a TV tower from two points M and N on level ground. The angle of elevation of the longer wire is 28.1°.

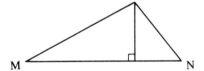

   a) How far apart are M and N?
   b) How tall is the tower?

14. In the diagram (below left)
   a) Find the length of BC.
   b) Find the length of the altitude from A.

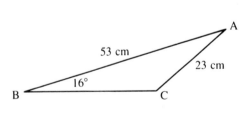

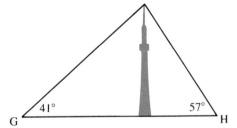

15. From points G and H, the angles of elevation of the top of the CN tower are 41° and 57° respectively (above right). If the distance between G and H is 995 m, find the height of the tower.

16. Bijan observes the angle of elevation of an ultra-light airplane to be 52°. At the same instant the angle of elevation for Therese is 36°. Bijan and Therese are 325 m apart on level ground and in the same vertical plane as the ultra-light.
   a) How far is each person from the ultra-light?
   b) How high is the ultra-light?

17. In the diagram (below left), ABCD is a square of side 1 unit. Point P is such that ∠PAD = 30° = ∠PCD. Find the length to 1 decimal place of: a) PD   b) PC.

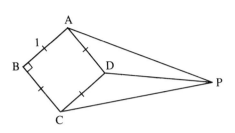

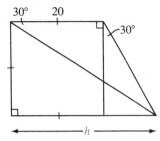

18. In the diagram (above right), find the value of *h*.

19. In a molecule of water (below left), the two hydrogen atoms and one oxygen atom are bonded in the shape of a triangle. The nuclei of the atoms are separated by the distances shown. Calculate the bond angles.

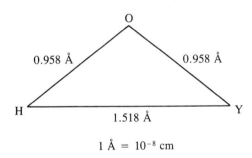

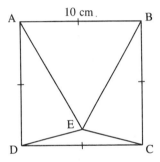

20. Square ABCD (above right) has sides of length 10 cm. Point E is inside the square so that ∠CDE = ∠DCE = 15°. Find the length of AE.

Ⓒ

21. In △ABC, AC = 2, AB = 3, and BC = 4. Prove that:

a) $\sin B = \frac{1}{2} \sin A$ b) $\sin C = \frac{3}{4} \sin A$.

22. Prove that in any △ABC the constant of proportionality for the Sine Law is the diameter of the circumscribing circle.

23. An isosceles △ABC has vertical ∠C = 20°. Points M and N are taken on AC and BC so that ∠ABM = 60° and ∠BAN = 50°. Prove that ∠BMN = 30°.

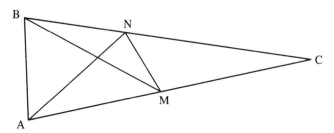

PROBLEM SOLVING

Coordinate Proofs in Geometry

"Algebra is generous; she often gives more than is asked of her."

D'Alembert

One of the most useful problem-solving strategies in mathematics is credited to the great French mathematicians of the seventeenth century, Rene Descartes and Pierre de Fermat. Their idea was to use arithmetic and algebra to solve problems in geometry.

In quadrilateral ABCD, $AB = DC$ and $AB \parallel DC$. Prove that $AD = BC$ and $AD \parallel BC$.

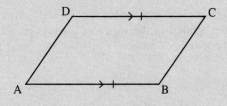

Think of a strategy
- Draw coordinate axes on the figure, assign coordinates to the vertices, and solve the problems using the coordinates.

Carry out the strategy
- Introduce a system of coordinates in which A is the origin, and AB lies along the *x*-axis. The *y*-axis is the line through A, perpendicular to AB.
- Let the coordinates of B be $(k, 0)$, where k is the length of AB. Let the coordinates of D be (a, b). Then, since $AB = DC$ and $AB \parallel DC$, the coordinates of C are $(a+k, b)$.
- Calculate the lengths of AD and BC. Are they equal?
- Calculate the slopes of AD and BC. Are they equal?

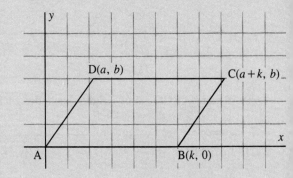

Look back
- Notice that the axes were placed to coincide as much as possible with parts of the given figure. Why was this done?
- What other positions might be good choices for the axes?
- Could we also choose a unit of length to coincide with the given figure? For example, could we let the coordinates of B be $(1, 0)$, or could we let the coordinates of D be $(a, 1)$? Could we do both?

PROGRAMS

Ⓑ

1. P is any point on the perpendicular bisector of a line segment AB (below left). Prove that PA = PB.

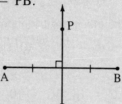

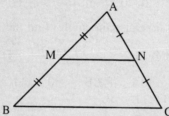

2. In △ABC (above right), M and N are the midpoints of AB and AC. Prove that MN = $\frac{1}{2}$BC and MN ∥ BC.

3. Prove that the diagonals of a parallelogram bisect each other.

4. M and N are the midpoints of the equal sides of an isosceles triangle. Prove that the medians to M and N are equal in length.

5. Prove that the angle in a semicircle is a right angle.

Ⓒ

6. AM, BN, and CP are the medians of △ABC. Prove that 4(AM² + BN² + CP²) = 3(AB² + BC² + CA²).

7. Prove that the medians of a triangle are concurrent.

8. Squares are drawn outwards on the sides of any quadrilateral ABCD. Points P, Q, R, and S are the centres of the squares. Prove that the line segments RP and SQ are perpendicular, and equal in length.

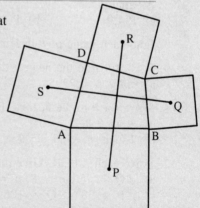

Ⓓ

9. In △ABC, ∠B = 90°, and side AB is three times as long as side BC. Square ACDE is drawn on the hypotenuse, as shown. If M is the midpoint of CD, prove that ∠MAB = 45°.

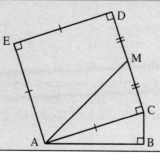

Review Exercises

1. Evaluate each trigonometric ratio to 3 decimal places.
   a) sin 55°   b) tan 27°   c) cos 81°   d) tan 37°   e) cos 65°   f) sin 22°

2. Find each value of θ to the nearest degree if $0° < \theta < 180°$.
   a) cos $\theta = 0.274$ b) tan $\theta = 0.523$ c) sin $\theta = 0.469$

3. State the exact values of the three trigonometric ratios of each angle.
   a) 0°   ·b) 30°   c) 45°   d) 60°   e) 90°   f) 120°   g) 135°   h) 150°

4. Given θ is an acute angle, find the values of the other two trigonometric ratios.

   a) cos $\theta = \dfrac{8}{17}$ b) tan $\theta = \dfrac{12}{5}$ c) cos $\theta = \dfrac{11}{21}$ d) sin $\theta = \dfrac{5}{9}$

5. Solve $\triangle$ABC, if $\angle$B $= 90°$, and:
   a) AB $= 15$, BC $= 27$ b) AC $= 18$, BC $= 10$
   c) AB $= 42$, $\angle$C $= 72°$ d) AC $= 12$, $\angle$A $= 35°$.
   Give the answers to 1 decimal place where necessary.

6. Draw each angle in standard position, then find two angles which are coterminal
   with it.
   a) 65°   b) 135°   c) 200°   d) $-450°$ e) 60°   f) 225°   g) $-30°$

7. Determine the sine, the cosine, and the tangent to 3 decimal places of each angle
   in *Exercise 6*.

8. Each point P is on the terminal arm of angle θ. Find sin θ, cos θ, and tan θ to 3
   decimal places.
   a) P(4,9)   b) P(8, -15)   c) P($-4,7$)   d) P($-6,-5$)

9. Find each value of θ in *Exercise 8* to 1 decimal place.

10. Solve for θ to the nearest degree, $0° \leqslant \theta \leqslant 360°$.
    a) sin $\theta = 0.7295$ b) cos $\theta = -0.3862$ c) tan $\theta = -5.1730$

11. Solve for θ to the nearest degree, $0° \leqslant \theta \leqslant 360°$.
    a) $3 \sin \theta + 2 = 0$ b) $2 \tan \theta - 5 = 2$
    c) $12 \sin^2 \theta - 11 \sin \theta + 2 = 0$ d) $3 \cos^2 \theta + 4 \cos \theta - 2 = 0$

12. Solve each $\triangle$PQR. Give the answers to 1 decimal place.
    a) $\angle$Q $= 75°$, $r = 8$, $p = 11$ b) $\angle$R $= 52°$, $r = 28$, $q = 25$
    c) $\angle$P $= 38°$, $\angle$Q $= 105°$, $p = 32$ d) $r = 17$, $p = 14$, $q = 26$

13. A wheelchair ramp 8.2 m long rises 94 cm. Find its angle of inclination to 1 decimal
    place.

14. The angle of elevation of the sun is 68° when a tree casts a shadow 14.3 m long.
    How tall is the tree?

15. Two identical apartment buildings are 41.3 m apart. From her balcony, Kudo notices
    that the angle of elevation to the top of the adjacent building is 57°. The angle
    of depression to the base of the building is 28°. Find the height of the buildings.

1. Classify each function as square root, reciprocal, exponential, absolute value, or cubic.

   a) $y = \dfrac{2}{x + 6}$ b) $y = 3x^3 + 6x^2 + 4$ c) $y = 10^x + 2$

2. Sketch each set of graphs on the same grid.

   a) $y = 3^x$ $y = 3^x - 1$ $y = 3^x + 4$

   b) $y = x^3$ $y = (x - 2)^3$ $y = (x + 3)^3$

3. Sketch each graph.

   a) $y = \dfrac{4}{x + 1} + 3$ b) $y = -3\,|\,x - 2\,| + 4$

4. Graph each function, its inverse, and $y = x$ on the same grid.

   a) $y = -x + 3$ b) $f(x) = 2x - 1$

5. Find the inverse of each function.

   a) $y = 4x^2 - 9$ b) $y = (x - 5)^2 + 9$ c) $f(x) = \frac{1}{4}(x - 7)^2 - 2$

6. Which of these points lie inside the circle $x^2 + y^2 = 50$?

   a) A(0,7)   b) B(7, −3)   c) C(1,8)   d) D(−4,6)   e) E(−1,−7)

7. Identify the transformation required to transform the graph of a circle, centre (0,0), to each given graph.

   a) $(x - 3)^2 + y^2 = 36$ b) $(x + 1)^2 + (y - 4)^2 = 16$

   c) $x^2 + \left(\dfrac{y}{2}\right)^2 = 9$ d) $\left(\dfrac{x}{4}\right)^2 + (y - 1)^2 = 4$

8. Graph each inequality.

   a) $y > (x + 2)^2 - 1$ b) $\left(\dfrac{x}{2}\right)^2 + y^2 < 9$

9. Define each term. Draw a sketch to illustrate each definition.

   a) concyclic points   b) cyclic quadrilateral   c) secant

10. What is the diameter of a circle in which a chord 12 cm long is 10 cm from the centre?

11. Copy this proof and fill in the missing statements and reason.

    Given: PA and PB are tangents at A and B to a circle centre O.

    Required to Prove: OP bisects $\angle$BPA.

    Analysis: Draw AO and OB.

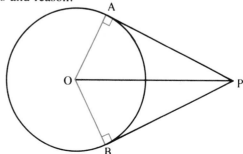

Proof:

Statement	Reason
In △PAO and △PBO	
_____	Equal Tangents Theorem
	Radii
_____	
OP is common.	
Therefore, _____	SSS
∠OPA = ∠OPB	_____
Therefore, OP bisects ∠BPA	

12. Copy the statements in this proof and write the reasons.
    Given: JK and LM are chords of a circle centre O.
    JK and LM intersect at Q so that
    ∠JQO = ∠MQO.
    Required to Prove: JK = LM
    Analysis: Draw perpendiculars OX and OY
    to JK and LM respectively.

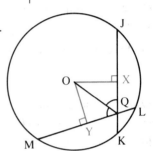

Proof:

Statement	Reason
In △OXQ and △OYQ	
∠OXQ = ∠OYQ = 90°	OX ⊥ JK, OY ⊥ LM
∠OQX = ∠OQY	_____
OQ is common.	
Therefore, △OXQ ≅ △OYQ	_____
OX = OY	_____
JK = LM	_____

13. Find each ratio to 3 decimal places.
    a) $\cos 127°$ b) $\tan 245°$ c) $\cos 74°$ d) $\sin 287°$ e) $\tan 135°$

14. Solve for θ to the nearest degree, $0° \leq \theta \leq 360°$.
    a) $\tan \theta = 2.574$ b) $\sin \theta = -0.583$ c) $\cos \theta = 0.492$

15. Solve △PQR, if ∠Q = 90° and:
    a) PQ = 11, QR = 8   b) QR = 26, ∠P = 28°.

16. Solve △XYZ if:
    a) XY = 7, YZ = 5, and ∠Y = 110°   b) $x = 3.7$, $y = 4.1$, and ∠X = 58°.

17. In △ABC, AD is the altitude from A to BC. If ∠B = 48°, ∠C = 32°, and
    BC = 12.8 m, find the length of AD.

18. Solve for θ to the nearest degree, $0° \leq \theta \leq 360°$.
    a) $4 \tan \theta - 5 = 0$ b) $6 \sin^2 \theta - \sin \theta - 2 = 0$

Answers

Chapter 1

Exercises 1-1, page 3

1. b, c, e, f, h, i

2. a) 3^3 **b)** $2 \times 3 \times 7$ **c)** $2^2 \times 17$
d) 5×19 **e)** $2 \times 3 \times 17$ **f)** 5×29
g) $5 \times 2^2 \times 3^2$ **h)** $3^2 \times 5^2$
i) $2^2 \times 3 \times 19$ **j)** $3^2 \times 43$

3. a) $15 + 10 = 25, 21 + 15 = 36,$
$28 + 21 = 49$
b) The sum is a square number.

4. a) 13, 16, 19 **b)** 162, 486, 1458
c) 25, 36, 49 **d)** 31, 43, 57
e) 91, 140, 204 **f)** 56, 84, 120

5. a) $1 + 2 + 3 + 4 + 3 + 2 + 1 = 4^2$
$1 + 2 + 3 + 4 + 5 + 4 + 3 + 2 + 1 = 5^2$
$1 + 2 + 3 + 4 + 5 + 6 + 5 + 4 + 3 + 2 + 1 = 6^2$ **6.** 59

7. Three—169, 196, 961

8. Eight—13, 17, 31, 37, 71, 73, 79, 97

9. a) 65, 71, 77, 83, 89 **b)** 53, 65, 77, 89, 101
c) 31, 41, 53, 67, 83 No

10. $33 \times 3367, 39 \times 2849, 231 \times 481$

12. a) 5, 13, 17, 29, 37, 41
b) $4 + 1, 4 + 9, 16 + 1, 25 + 4, 36 + 1,$
$16 + 25$

13. a) 3, 7, 11, 19, 23, 31, 43, 47

14. a) $1 + 10$ **b)** $1 + 3 + 15$ **c)** $1 + 28$
d) $3 + 6 + 21$ **e)** $6 + 6 + 21$
f) $1 + 21 + 28$

15. Yes

18. a) i) 82 to 100 **ii)** $(n - 1)^2 + 1$ to n^2

19. b) 36

Investigate, page 5

1. 25, 36; 81, 100 **2.** 4, 16; 4, 36
3. 9, 16; 16, 25

Computer Power, page 6

1. b, d
2. a) $2^2 \times 17 \times 53$ **b)** $41 \times 71 \times 139$
c) $3^2 \times 29 \times 47 \times 83$ **d)** $503 \times 13\ 049$

Mathematics Around Us, page 7

1. 4.5% **2.** 6.9 km
3. a) About 90 **b)** About 20 m
c) About 3 min
4. About 130 m; answers to Questions 3 and 4 depend
on the assumptions made.

Exercises 1-2, page 9

1. a) 2.25 **b)** 0.4375 **c)** $0.41\overline{6}$ **d)** $0.\overline{407}$
e) $0.\overline{2}$ **f)** $1.571\ 428$ **g)** $1.8\overline{1}$ **h)** $0.2\overline{5}$

2. a) $\dfrac{28}{11}$ **b)** $\dfrac{415}{999}$ **c)** $\dfrac{1619}{990}$ **d)** $\dfrac{322}{75}$
e) $\dfrac{3122}{999}$ **f)** $\dfrac{283}{45}$

6. a) $\dfrac{488}{333}$ **b)** $\dfrac{333}{110}$ **c)** $\dfrac{536}{99}$ **d)** $\dfrac{221}{300}$
e) $\dfrac{14\ 141}{9999}$ **f)** $\dfrac{3626}{4995}$ **7. a)** $\dfrac{9}{9}$

8. a) $0.\overline{4}$ **b)** $0.\overline{57}$ **c)** $0.\overline{31}$ **d)** $0.\overline{3}$
e) $0.\overline{074}$ **f)** $0.\overline{15}$

9. a) $\dfrac{1}{5} + \dfrac{1}{5 \times 4} = \dfrac{1}{4}; \dfrac{1}{6} + \dfrac{1}{6 \times 5} = \dfrac{1}{5};$
$\dfrac{1}{7} + \dfrac{1}{7 \times 6} = \dfrac{1}{6}; \dfrac{1}{8} + \dfrac{1}{8 \times 7} = \dfrac{1}{7};$
$\dfrac{1}{9} + \dfrac{1}{9 \times 8} = \dfrac{1}{8}$

b) i) $\dfrac{1}{9} = \dfrac{1}{10} + \dfrac{1}{10 \times 9}$
ii) $\dfrac{1}{12} = \dfrac{1}{13} + \dfrac{1}{13 \times 12}$
iii) $\dfrac{1}{20} = \dfrac{1}{21} + \dfrac{1}{21 \times 20}$

10. a) i) $\dfrac{1}{2 \times 1} + \dfrac{1}{3 \times 2} + \dfrac{1}{4 \times 3} + \dfrac{1}{5 \times 4} = \dfrac{4}{5};$
$\dfrac{1}{2 \times 1} + \dfrac{1}{3 \times 2} + \dfrac{1}{4 \times 3} + \dfrac{1}{5 \times 4} +$
$\dfrac{1}{6 \times 5} = \dfrac{5}{6};$ etc.
ii) $\dfrac{1}{3 \times 1} + \dfrac{1}{5 \times 3} + \dfrac{1}{7 \times 5} + \dfrac{1}{9 \times 7} = \dfrac{4}{9};$
$\dfrac{1}{3 \times 1} + \dfrac{1}{5 \times 3} + \dfrac{1}{7 \times 5} + \dfrac{1}{9 \times 7} +$
$\dfrac{1}{11 \times 9} = \dfrac{5}{11}$

b) i) $\dfrac{8}{9} = \dfrac{1}{2 \times 1} + \dfrac{1}{3 \times 2} + \dfrac{1}{4 \times 3} + \dfrac{1}{5 \times 4} +$
$\dfrac{1}{6 \times 5} + \dfrac{1}{7 \times 6} + \dfrac{1}{8 \times 7} + \dfrac{1}{9 \times 8}$
ii) $\dfrac{8}{17} = \dfrac{1}{3 \times 1} + \dfrac{1}{5 \times 3} + \dfrac{1}{7 \times 5} + \dfrac{1}{9 \times 7} +$
$\dfrac{1}{11 \times 9} + \dfrac{1}{13 \times 11} + \dfrac{1}{15 \times 13} + \dfrac{1}{17 \times 15}$

11. Answers may vary.
a) $0.45 = \dfrac{1}{3} + \dfrac{1}{15} + \dfrac{1}{20}$ or $\dfrac{1}{4} + \dfrac{1}{5}$ or $\dfrac{1}{4} + \dfrac{1}{6} + \dfrac{1}{30}$

b) $\dfrac{1}{2} + \dfrac{1}{20}$ **c)** $\dfrac{1}{2} + \dfrac{1}{10} + \dfrac{1}{20}$

12. The amounts of water and wine are equal.

Exercises 1-3, page 14

1. a) -29 **b)** -3 **c)** 120 **d)** -50

2. a) -18 **b)** 53 **c)** -33 **d)** 60 **e)** -3
f) -42

3. a) -36 **b)** -25 **c)** -15 **d)** -59 **e)** $\dfrac{13}{3}$

4. a) $-\dfrac{39}{2}$ **b)** $\dfrac{77}{8}$ **c)** $\dfrac{9}{40}$ **d)** $\dfrac{1}{20}$ **e)** $-\dfrac{2}{3}$ **f)** $\dfrac{11}{5}$

5. a) $\dfrac{3}{8}$ **b)** $-\dfrac{7}{12}$ **c)** $\dfrac{17}{6}$ **d)** $-\dfrac{13}{12}$ **e)** $-\dfrac{91}{12}$ **f)** $-\dfrac{61}{30}$

6. a) $\dfrac{21}{5}$ **b)** 0 **c)** $-\dfrac{4}{5}$ **d)** 1 **e)** $\dfrac{5}{12}$ **f)** $-\dfrac{137}{100}$

7. a) $-\dfrac{7}{6}$ **b)** $\dfrac{23}{72}$ **c)** $-\dfrac{1}{3}$

8. a) 3 **b)** -7 **c)** 12 **d)** -5 **e)** 4 **f)** $\dfrac{5}{14}$

9. a) $-\dfrac{15}{112}$ **b)** -1 **c)** $-\dfrac{28}{27}$

10. $3846.67; $3190

11. a) $-\dfrac{9}{2}$ **b)** 2 **c)** 8 **d)** -2

12. 50 **13. a)** 12 **b)** 14 **c)** 4 **d)** -1
14. a) 14 **b)** No solution   **c)** 20
   d) No solution

Exercises 1-4, page 18

1. a, c, d

2. a) 10 **b)** 1.6 **c)** 0.3 **d)** $\dfrac{7}{9}$ **e)** $\dfrac{11}{6}$

3. a) $\sqrt{30}$ **b)** $\sqrt{21}$ **c)** $56\sqrt{6}$ **d)** $15\sqrt{42}$
   e) $-96\sqrt{77}$ **f)** $75\sqrt{70}$

4. a) $3\sqrt{2}$ **b)** $2\sqrt{3}$ **c)** $5\sqrt{2}$ **d)** $4\sqrt{5}$
   e) $4\sqrt{7}$ **f)** $2\sqrt{33}$

5. a) $30\sqrt{2}$ **b)** $140\sqrt{2}$ **c)** $48\sqrt{15}$
   d) $-108\sqrt{10}$ **e)** $-108\sqrt{2}$ **f)** $140\sqrt{5}$

6. Mixed radicals: b, d, f
   Entire radicals: a, c, e
   a) $4\sqrt{2}$ **b)** $\sqrt{24}$ **c)** $7\sqrt{2}$ **d)** $\sqrt{45}$
   e) $8\sqrt{5}$ **f)** $\sqrt{405}$

7. a) 180 **b)** $720\sqrt{3}$ **c)** $108\sqrt{5}$
   d) $-360\sqrt{5}$

8. Estimates may vary.   **a)** 5.5 **b)** 14.1
   c) 11.2 **d)** 0.95 **e)** 12.2 **f)** 1.6

9. a) $2\sqrt{10}, 4\sqrt{3}, 5\sqrt{2}, 3\sqrt{6}, 2\sqrt{14}$
   b) $-4\sqrt{6}, -4\sqrt{5}, -5\sqrt{3}, -6\sqrt{2}, -2\sqrt{17}$
   c) $6\sqrt{3}, 4\sqrt{7}, 5\sqrt{5}, 3\sqrt{14}, 8\sqrt{2}$

11. 16 cm²

12. a) $5\sqrt{3}$ **b)** $7\sqrt{2}$ **c)** $4\sqrt{3}$ **d)** $-8\sqrt{3}$
   e) $2\sqrt[3]{7}$ **f)** $\dfrac{3}{4}\sqrt{12}$

Exercises 1-5, page 22

1. a) $3\sqrt{5}$ **b)** $3\sqrt{3}$ **c)** $5\sqrt{2}$ **d)** $13\sqrt{7}$
   e) $8\sqrt{10}$ **f)** $9\sqrt{3}$

2. a) $2\sqrt{2}$ **b)** $7\sqrt{3}$ **c)** $5\sqrt{6}$ **d)** $-2\sqrt{2}$
   e) $8\sqrt{7}$ **f)** $\sqrt{5}$

3. a) $2\sqrt{3}$ **b)** $26\sqrt{6}$ **c)** $9\sqrt{7}$ **d)** 0
   e) $63\sqrt{6}$ **f)** $-4\sqrt{5}$

4. a) $\sqrt{15} + \sqrt{21}$ **b)** $28\sqrt{6} - 12\sqrt{15}$
   c) $10\sqrt{6a} + 20\sqrt{6b}$ **d)** $90\sqrt{3} - 63\sqrt{15}$
   e) $8\sqrt{2y} - 6y$ **f)** 154

5. a) $1 + \sqrt{15}$ **b)** $-32 + \sqrt{35}$
   c) $15x - \sqrt{xy} - 6y$ **d)** $30 - 14\sqrt{6}$
   e) $192 + 90\sqrt{2}$ **f)** $16m - 46\sqrt{mn} + 15n$

6. a) $3\sqrt{7}$ **b)** $-\tfrac{1}{3}\sqrt{5}$ **c)** $-3\sqrt{13}$
   d) $6\sqrt{14}$ **e)** $-\tfrac{2}{5}\sqrt{11}$ **f)** $-15\sqrt{17}$
   g) $8\sqrt{5}$ **h)** $\tfrac{2}{3}\sqrt{5}$

7. a) $2\sqrt{5}$ **b)** $27\sqrt{2}$ **c)** $-11\sqrt{6}$ **d)** $19\sqrt{2}$
   e) $-17\sqrt{10}$ **f)** $10\sqrt{5}$

8. a) $12\sqrt{14} - 30$ **b)** -72
   c) $30(\sqrt{3} - \sqrt{2})$ **d)** $36\sqrt{2} + 8\sqrt{21} - 60$
   e) $35a - 35\sqrt{2a}$ **f)** $32\sqrt{2b} - 16\sqrt{3b} - 24b$

9. a) 3 **b)** $9m - 4n$ **c)** -32
   d) $104 - 60\sqrt{3}$ **e)** $49x + 56\sqrt{xy} + 16y$
   f) $404\sqrt{2} + 60\sqrt{42}$

10. a) 8 **b)** $-6\sqrt{3}$ **c)** $-\tfrac{1}{2}$ **d)** $4\sqrt{5}$
   e) $\tfrac{15}{4}\sqrt{2}$ **f)** $-\tfrac{20}{3}\sqrt{2}$ **g)** $\sqrt{2}$ **h)** $\sqrt{3}$

11. a) i) $\sqrt{2}$ **ii)** $\sqrt{3}$ **b)** 4

12. a) i) 2 **ii)** $\sqrt{5}$ **b) i)** 9 **ii)** 8 **13.** $\dfrac{2\sqrt{3}}{3}$

Problem Solving, page 27

1. $12.50

2. Answers may vary. Typical answers are
   $2^1 + 5^2 = 3^3$; $4^1 + 11^2 = 5^3$

3. $\dfrac{1}{2}$ **4.** $0.25x^2$

5. There are four possibilities: 192, 384, 576; 219, 438, 657; 327, 654, 981; 273, 546, 819

6. 7, 3   **7. a)** 11   **b)** 2, 4, 6

9. ± 2, -1, -5 **10.** $a + b + c + d$

Exercises 1-6, page 29

1. a) $\dfrac{2\sqrt{5}}{5}$ **b)** $\dfrac{7\sqrt{11}}{11}$ **c)** $-\dfrac{4\sqrt{3}}{3}$ **d)** $\dfrac{5\sqrt{14}}{7}$

e) $-2\sqrt{30}$ **f)** $\dfrac{12\sqrt{35}}{35}$ **g)** $3\sqrt{10}$ **h)** $-\dfrac{5\sqrt{21}}{3}$

2. a) $\dfrac{3\sqrt{30}}{10}$ **b)** $\sqrt{10}$ **c)** $-3\sqrt{6}$ **d)** $\dfrac{5\sqrt{6}}{4}$

e) $\dfrac{4\sqrt{21}}{3}$ **f)** $\dfrac{\sqrt{21}}{2}$ **g)** $\dfrac{4\sqrt{30}}{3}$ **h)** $\dfrac{27}{4}$

3. a) $\dfrac{6 + 4\sqrt{3}}{3}$ **b)** $\dfrac{35 - 3\sqrt{7}}{7}$ **c)** $\dfrac{20 - 2\sqrt{5}}{5}$

d) $2\sqrt{6} - 1$ **e)** $\dfrac{8\sqrt{30} + 5}{5}$ **f)** $3\sqrt{5} - 1$

g) $\dfrac{10\sqrt{3} + 3\sqrt{2}}{3}$ **h)** $\dfrac{\sqrt{6}}{2}$

4. a) $\dfrac{\sqrt{15} + \sqrt{6}}{3}$ **b)** $\dfrac{\sqrt{35} - \sqrt{15}}{4}$

c) $\dfrac{8\sqrt{11} + \sqrt{55}}{59}$ **d)** $\dfrac{2\sqrt{30} - 2\sqrt{15}}{3}$

e) $\dfrac{-30\sqrt{2} - 25\sqrt{6}}{13}$ **f)** $\dfrac{4\sqrt{105} + 4\sqrt{70}}{5}$

g) $\dfrac{30\sqrt{3} - 6\sqrt{6}}{23}$ **h)** $\dfrac{3\sqrt{55} + 15}{2}$

5. a) $\dfrac{\sqrt{6}}{2}$ **b)** $\dfrac{32 + 7\sqrt{6}}{10}$ **c)** $\sqrt{15}$

d) $\dfrac{42 + 17\sqrt{5}}{29}$ **e)** $\dfrac{27 - 7\sqrt{21}}{30}$

f) $\dfrac{13\sqrt{2} - 3\sqrt{7}}{25}$

6. a) $\dfrac{5x\sqrt{y}}{y}$ **b)** $\dfrac{3\sqrt{m^2 - mn}}{m - n}$ **c)** $\dfrac{3\sqrt{2a + b}}{2a + b}$

d) $\dfrac{x\sqrt{x} - x}{x - 1}$ **e)** $\dfrac{2\sqrt{6}x + 2\sqrt{3}}{2x^2 - 1}$ **f)** $\dfrac{-3 - \sqrt{x}}{9 - x}$

g) $\dfrac{2\sqrt{5}a + 2a\sqrt{a}}{5 - a}$ **h)** $\dfrac{5x(\sqrt{x} - \sqrt{3})}{x - 3}$

7. a) $\dfrac{\sqrt{2}}{2}$ **b)** $\dfrac{\sqrt{3}}{6}$ **c)** $\dfrac{\sqrt{2}}{10}$ **d)** $\sqrt{2} + 1$

e) $\sqrt{3} - \sqrt{2}$ **f)** $\dfrac{2\sqrt{5} + 3\sqrt{2}}{2}$

8. a) 4   **b)** $\dfrac{2\sqrt{5} + 4\sqrt{2}}{3}$ **c)** $5\sqrt{2} - 2$

d) $\dfrac{2\sqrt{x}}{x - y}$ **e)** $\dfrac{2m\sqrt{m}}{m - n}$ **f)** $\dfrac{3a\sqrt{2a} + 5ab}{2a - b^2}$

9. a) $\dfrac{1}{2\sqrt{2}}$ **b)** $\dfrac{5}{3\sqrt{5}}$ **c)** $\dfrac{1}{y\sqrt{x}}$ **d)** $\dfrac{x - 1}{x(\sqrt{x} - 1)}$

e) $\dfrac{a - 4b}{\sqrt{a}(\sqrt{a} - 2\sqrt{b})}$

f) $\dfrac{-m + 4n^2}{(\sqrt{m} - \sqrt{n})(\sqrt{m} + \sqrt{n})}$ **g)** $\dfrac{x - y}{(\sqrt{x} + \sqrt{y})^2}$

h) $\dfrac{4a - 9b}{(2\sqrt{a} + 3\sqrt{b})^2}$

Exercises 1-7, page 32

1. a, b, d, h   **2.** a, c, d, g, h

3. b, c—rational; a, d, e, f—irrational

4. a) Q', R **b)** Q', R **c)** N, I, Q, R
d) Q', R **e)** Q, R **f)** Q', R **g)** Q', R
h) Q', R

6. Answers may vary. Examples are:
a) 2.579 18 and 2.579 181 181 118...
b) $-6.327\ 329$ and $-6.327\ 329\ 010\ 010\ 001...$
c) 4.190 15 and 4.190 151 151 115...

7. a) $\frac{4}{9}, \frac{6}{9}$ **b)** $\sqrt{0.999\ 999\ 9}$

8. a) N, I, Q, R **b)** I, Q, R **c)** Q, R
d) N, I, Q, R and I, Q, R **e)** Q', R
f) No solution

Exercises 1-8, page 36

1. a) 16   **b)** 9   **c)** 16   **d)** 6.25   **e)** 1   **f)** 9

2. a) 23   **b)** 53   **c)** 37   **d)** 4   **e)** 4   **f)** $\frac{10}{3}$

3. a) $\frac{49}{18}$ **b)** $\frac{14}{5}$ **c)** No solution   **d)** $\frac{19}{4}$
e) 3   **f)** 4

4. a, c, e   **5.** $a = \sqrt{d^2 - b^2}$

6. a) 1   **b)** $\frac{19}{5}$ **c)** 1.5   **d)** No solution
e) $-\frac{1}{3}$ **f)** -4

7. a) 4   **b), d), e)** No solution   **c)** $\frac{27}{7}$ **f)** 1

8. a) 1   **b)** 2.5   **c), f)** No solution   **d)** -2 **e)** $-\frac{12}{7}$

9. a) 8   **b)** 32   **c)** $\frac{29}{3}$ **d)** -13 **e)** 110   **f)** $-\frac{10}{3}$

10. a) $d = \left(\dfrac{v + 7}{8.2}\right)^2$ **b) i)** 67 m   **ii)** 140 m

iii) 240 m   **c) i)** 51 km/h   **ii)** 75 km/h
iii) 93 km/h

11. a) $l = \dfrac{T^2 g}{4\pi^2}$ **b)** $a = \dfrac{v^2 - u^2}{2s}$ **c)** $W = \dfrac{2gE}{V^2}$

d) $c = \dfrac{vm}{\sqrt{m^2 - M^2}}$ **e)** $k = \dfrac{F}{m(v^2 + u^2)}$

f) $E = \dfrac{h^2 - 2ae^2 m}{2a^2 m}$

12. $h = \sqrt{\left(\dfrac{A}{\pi r} - r\right)^2 - r^2}$

13. 20 cm, 21 cm, 29 cm   **14.** 9, 16

15. $h = \dfrac{2r \pm \sqrt{4r^2 - c^2}}{2}$

16. a) $h = r$ **b)** $c \leqslant 2r$ **17.** c, d, e, f

Review Exercises, page 38

1. a) $2 \times 3 \times 5 \times 7^2$ **b)** $3 \times 5 \times 7 \times 13$
 c) $2^2 \times 7 \times 11 \times 17$

2. a) $\dfrac{191}{110}$ **b)** $\dfrac{157}{99}$ **c)** $\dfrac{707}{333}$ **d)** $\dfrac{311}{99}$

3. a) $0.\overline{3}$ **b)** $0.\overline{90}$ **c)** $0.1\overline{4}$ **d)** $0.5\overline{18}$

4. a) $\dfrac{88}{9}$ **b)** $-\dfrac{1}{3}$ **c)** $-\dfrac{51}{32}$

5. a) -55 **b)** $-\dfrac{1}{4}$ **c)** $-\dfrac{191}{43}$ **d)** $-\dfrac{1}{5}$

6. a) i) $2\sqrt{6}$ **ii)** $3\sqrt{5}$ **iii)** $4\sqrt{7}$ **iv)** $11\sqrt{5}$
 b) i) $\sqrt{63}$ **ii)** $\sqrt{50}$ **iii)** $\sqrt{80}$ **iv)** $\sqrt{294}$

7. a) 60   **b)** 120   **c)** 1200   **d)** $-60\sqrt{42}$

8. a) $3\sqrt{30} + 16 - 10\sqrt{3}$
 b) $8\sqrt{10} + 16\sqrt{6} - 12\sqrt{3}$
 c) $14\sqrt{30} - 6\sqrt{13} - 4\sqrt{7}$ **d)** $7\sqrt{6}$

9. a) $-3\sqrt{x}$ **b)** $5\sqrt{2x} - 3\sqrt{3y}$
 c) $2x + \sqrt{x} - 15$ **d)** $6\sqrt{2x} + 12\sqrt{x} + 3\sqrt{2}$

10. a) $4\sqrt{6}$ **b)** $168\sqrt{2} - 105\sqrt{6}$ **c)** 113
 d) $132 - 72\sqrt{2}$

11. a) $3\sqrt{6}$ **b)** $\dfrac{-16\sqrt{5}}{5}$ **c)** $\sqrt{10}$

 d) $3 + \sqrt{5}$
 e) $\dfrac{42 - 4\sqrt{7} + 6\sqrt{14} - 4\sqrt{2}}{5}$

 f) $\dfrac{9}{2}(\sqrt{10} - \sqrt{6})$

12. a) $\dfrac{2}{3}$ **b)** No solution   **c)** -1.25 **d)** 3.5

Chapter 2

Exercises 2-1, page 42

1. a) 2^7 **b)** a^8 **c)** $\left(-\dfrac{3}{4}\right)^5$ **d)** $(3x)^4$

2. a) 100   **b)** 196   **c)** -52 **d)** -9 **e)** 47
 f) 6

3. a) 2187   **b)** 15 625   **c)** 2.0736
 d) 31.006 277   **e)** 1.3841×10^{10}
 f) 1.0737×10^9

4. a) i) 800   **ii)** 6400   **b) i)** 2700
 ii) 72 900   **c) i)** 12.5   **ii)** 1.5625
 d) i) 2560   **ii)** 1310.72   **e) i)** 10.546 875
 ii) 4.449 45   **f) i)** 2.737 566   **ii)** 4.163 508

5. a) 100×2^5 **b) i)** 800   **ii)** 12 800

6. a) 3^3 **b)** 5^3 **c)** $(-2)^5$ **d)** $(-3)^4$
 e) $(1.2)^4$

7. a) 2^7 **b)** 3^4 **c)** $3^6 = 9^3$ **d)** 2^{10}

8. a) $7^2, 3^3, 4^2, 3^2, 2^3$
 b) $(-2)^8, 2^7, (-3)^4, (-5)^3, (-2)^9$

9. a) \$1500.73   **b)** \$2802.21   **c)** \$286.17
 d) \$1284.11

10. a) \$1340.10   **b)** \$1628.89   **c)** \$2182.87

11. \$163 988   **12.** \$161 919

13. a) \$42 100   **b)** \$67 500   **c)** \$30 000$(1.07)^n$

14. a) \$1.12   **b)** \$1.31   **c)** \$1.92

15.

M.C.	Lagos	N.Y.	Tokyo	Delhi	Calcutta
a)	28.8	9.1	16.2	17.3	11.2	17.1
b)	76.8	24.9	18.3	17.7	24.7	35.9

16. a) i) 25%   **ii)** 6.25%   **b)** $(0.5)^{\frac{n}{1600}} \times 100\%$

17. a) i) 90%   **ii)** 81%   **iii)** 12%
 b) i) 6.6 min   **ii)** 22 min   **c)** $100(0.9)^n$

18. a) i) 1.28 m   **ii)** 0.27 m   **b)** 7th

19. a) \$1700   **b)** \$10 000$(0.7)^n$

Exercises 2-2, page 46

1. a) x^{32} **b)** m^{10} **c)** y^{15} **d)** a^9 **e)** c^{27}
 f) x^{20}

2. a) $63x^{17}$ **b)** $5m^{12}$ **c)** $4n^6$ **d)** $-4a^{10}$
 e) $96y^{21}$ **f)** $-243c^{20}$

3. a) $a^{16}b^7$ **b)** $m^6 n^4$ **c)** $-42c^{20}d^{11}$ **d)** $x^3 y^6$
 e) $4a^{10}b^8$ **f)** $x^{12}y^{10}$

4. a) $9x^8$ **b)** $2000a^{18}$ **c)** $-1728m^{15}n^{33}$
 d) $6x^5 y^2$ **e)** $a^5 b^6$ **f)** $-\dfrac{5}{2}c^8 d^8$

5. a) 32 **b)** 16 **c)** -960 **d)** 48 **e)** -16
f) -1536

6. a) x^{5a+2} **b)** 3^{3m+4} **c)** c^{10a+8} **d)** $\frac{9}{2}a^{9x-4}$
e) r^{6xy} **f)** $x^{3m-1}y^{2n+3}$

7. a) 2^{3n} **b)** 2^{3n} **c)** 2^{6n+8} **d)** 2^{5n} **e)** 1
f) 2^{3n+3}

8. a) i) 1024 **ii)** 9 765 620 **iii)** 10 077 700
b) i) 8 **ii)** 10^{15} **iii)** 10^{14} **iv)** 2.5×10^8
v) 10^{21} **vi)** 3.6×10^8

9. a) $18m^7$ **b)** $729m^{24}$ **c)** $\frac{5}{3}m^8$ **d)** $\frac{225}{4}m^7$

10. a) $12a^6b^6$ **b)** $256a^8b^{18}$ **c)** $10a^4b^6$
d) $4a^{12}b^{12}$ **11. a)** x^{2a} **b)** x^{a^2} **c)** x^{5a-1}

12. a) i) 64 **ii)** 4096 **iii)** 16.8×10^6
iv) 2.8×10^{14} **b)** 2^{2n}, or 4^n

13. a) i) a^{11} **ii)** a^{14} **b) i)** bc^2 **ii)** b^2c^2

14. a) 304 **b)** $\frac{9}{5}$

16. a) 1 073 741 824 **b)** 244 140 625
c) 3 486 784 401

Exercises 2-3, page 49

1. a) 1 **b)** $\frac{1}{9}$ **c)** $\frac{1}{8}$ **d)** 1 **e)** $-\frac{1}{8}$ **f)** $\frac{1}{9}$

2. a) 1 **b)** 25 **c)** $\frac{9}{4}$ **d)** $\frac{49}{16}$ **e)** -8 **f)** $-\frac{2}{3}$

3. a) 0.1250 **b)** 0.1197 **c)** 0.0822
d) 0.8874 **e)** 97.6562 **f)** 0.2097

4. a) 147.746 **b)** 82.0348 **c)** 1197.009
d) 487.448 25

5. a) i) 1.111 **ii)** 0.004 **b) i)** 0.010 **ii)** 0
c) i) 0.444 **ii)** 0.132 **d) i)** 0.890
ii) 0.747 **e) i)** 0.718 **ii)** 0.437
f) i) 1.181 **ii)** 1.517

6. a) iii **b) i)** 2500 **ii)** 312

7. a) $\frac{64}{9}$ **b)** $-\frac{1}{72}$ **c)** 6 **d)** $-\frac{1}{16}$

8. a) $\frac{1}{8}$ **b)** $\frac{1}{9}$ **c)** $\frac{1}{36}$ **d)** 25 **e)** $\frac{1}{49}$ **f)** $\frac{9}{8}$

9. a) $\frac{9}{20}$ **b)** 4 **c)** 0 **d)** $-\frac{100}{289}$

10. a) 7^{-1} **b)** $\left(\frac{3}{5}\right)^{-2}$ **c)** $\left(-\frac{1}{5}\right)^{-3}$ **d)** 10^{-1}

12. a) x^{-5} **b)** m^{-2} **c)** $-6c^{-3}d^6$ **d)** $4m^{-9}n^8$

13. a) 144 **b)** 7 **c)** $\frac{2}{3}$

14. a) 4 **b)** $-\frac{16}{9}$ **c)** -10.5 **d)** 720 **e)** $\frac{1}{16}$
f) $\frac{7}{4}$

15. a) i) 125 g **ii)** 7.8 g **b) i)** 16 kg
ii) 512 kg **16.** $1588.80

17. a) i) a^2 **ii)** a **b) i)** b^6c^{-1} **ii)** b^7c^{-3}
iii) b^2c^{-1}

18. a) 0.003 906 25 **b)** 0.000 976 562 5
c) 0.000 002 56

Exercises 2-4, page 53

1. a) 8 **b)** 6 **c)** 2 **d)** -2 **e)** 20
f) -5

2. a) $7^{\frac{1}{2}}$ **b)** $135^{\frac{1}{2}}$ **c)** $12^{\frac{1}{3}}$ **d)** $21^{\frac{1}{4}}$ **e)** $29^{\frac{1}{2}}$
f) $19^{\frac{1}{5}}$

3. a) 4 **b)** 64 **c)** 216 **d)** 9 **e)** 10
f) 8

4. a) 32 **b)** -32 **c)** 729 **d)** 8 **e)** 0.064
f) 81

5. a) $\frac{1}{3}$ **b)** $\frac{1}{2}$ **c)** $\frac{1}{5}$ **d)** $\frac{1}{2}$ **e)** $\frac{1}{9}$ **f)** $\frac{1}{3}$

6. a) $\frac{1}{9}$ **b)** $\frac{1}{64}$ **c)** 27 **d)** $\frac{1}{4}$ **e)** 16 **f)** $\frac{1}{8}$

7. a) $\frac{3}{4}$ **b)** 27 **c)** $\frac{1}{16}$ **d)** $\frac{9}{4}$ **e)** $\frac{8}{27}$ **f)** $\frac{343}{125}$

8. a) 1.7783 **b)** 10.8140 **c)** 3.6593
d) 9.5183 **e)** 1.1017 **f)** 3.4471

9. a) i) 2074 **ii)** 2646 **b) i)** 1701 **ii)** 1311

10. a) $10^{\frac{2}{3}}$ **b)** $12^{\frac{5}{4}}$ **c)** $12^{\frac{3}{7}}$ or $6^{\frac{6}{7}}$ **d)** $94^{\frac{17}{5}}$
e) $25^{-\frac{4}{5}}$ **f)** $52^{-\frac{7}{2}}$

11. a) $2^{\frac{7}{3}}$ **b)** $6^{\frac{3}{4}}$ **c)** $2^{\frac{9}{2}}$ **d)** $5^{\frac{8}{5}}$ **e)** $7^{\frac{10}{3}}$ **f)** $3^{\frac{16}{7}}$

12. a) $V^{\frac{1}{3}}$ **b)** $V^{\frac{2}{3}}$

13. a) 6 **b)** 500 **c)** 27 **d)** 36 **e)** 80

14. a) 3 **b)** -11 **c)** $\frac{1}{4}$ **d)** -1 **e)** 3 **f)** 9

15. a) 19.95 **b)** 199.5 **c)** 0.1995
d) 0.019 95

16. a) 32 **b)** 2 **c)** 32 **d)** $\frac{1}{512}$ **e)** 16

17. a) iii **b) i)** 279 **ii)** 348 **iii)** 433
c) i) 224 **ii)** 180 **iii)** 144

18. a) i) 610 **ii)** 820 **iii)** 1346 **b) i)** 410
ii) 336 **19. a)** 1.93 m²

20. a) i) 88.4 min **ii)** 96.6 min **b) i)** 1440 min
ii) 35 849 km

21. a) i) 81% **ii)** 72.9% **iii)** $100(0.9)^n$
c) i) 92.9% **ii)** 87.2% **d) i)** About 2.73 cm
ii) About 6.58 cm

22. a) Renée **b) i)** 32.17 **ii)** 2.65

Problem Solving, page 57

1. 495   2. 3
3. 3 (right isosceles; right; equilateral)
4. $\dfrac{(3\sqrt{3} - \pi)r^2}{24}$ 5. a) 12
7. a) 2020   b) 21 200, 3 211 000, 6 210 001 000

Mathematics Around Us, page 58

1. a) i) 19   ii) 62   b) i) 58   ii) 57
   c) i) 72   ii) 85   2. 155

Exercises 2-5, page 59

1. a) $\dfrac{1}{2}$ b) 81   c) $\dfrac{1}{16}$ d) $\dfrac{1}{25}$

2. a) 36   b) 2   c) $\dfrac{1}{25}$ d) $\dfrac{1}{10}$

3. a) $\dfrac{9}{125}$ b) $5^{-\frac{3}{2}}$ c) $\dfrac{1}{3}$ d) $\dfrac{1}{2}$

4. a) x^{-3} b) m^2 c) n^{-3} d) $x^{-\frac{5}{4}}$

5. a) m^5n^{-2} b) a^2b^{-2} c) x^2y^2 d) $6a^3b^{-4}$
   e) $3x^{-\frac{3}{2}}$ f) $\dfrac{1}{2}m^3n^{-3}$

6. a) $\dfrac{1}{2}$ b) 3   c) 64   d) $\dfrac{1}{9}$

7. a) 125   b) $6^{\frac{17}{12}}$ c) $2^{-\frac{2}{5}}$ d) $5^{-\frac{1}{2}}$

8. a) $\dfrac{2}{9}a^{\frac{17}{6}}$ b) $6x^{\frac{1}{6}}$ c) $x^{-1}y^{-1}\sqrt{10y^{-1}}$
   d) $x^{-\frac{11}{2}}y^{-2}$

9. a) $a^{-6}b^9c^{-12}$ b) $3x^{-3}y^5z^{-2}$ c) $12x^{-2}y^3$
10. a) x^{6a} b) m^{n-3} c) m^5 d) c^{2a-2}
11. a) 3^{5x} b) 16   c) 5^{4a-1} d) 2^{10x+1}
    e) $6^{-3a+5b+6}$ f) $2^{5m-n} \times 3^{-m+3n}$
12. a) a^8 b) $a^{-\frac{14}{3}}$ c) $a^{-\frac{10}{9}}$ d) 1   e) $a^{\frac{13}{15}}$
    f) $a^{-\frac{7}{2}}$
13. a) $2a + a^{-1}$ b) $5x^2 - 3x$ c) $6m - 3m^2$
    d) $\dfrac{26}{5}$ e) $28x^{\frac{20}{3}} + 12x^2$ f) $\dfrac{8}{3}$
14. a) 3   b) $x^3 - x^7$
    c) $6a^4 - 2a^3 - 21a^2 + 7a$
    d) $12x^3 + 19x^2 - 18x$
15. a) $(7y^{-\frac{1}{m}})^{-\frac{1}{n}}$ b) $2\sqrt{2}x^{\frac{a}{2}}y^{\frac{3}{2a}}$ c) $\dfrac{a}{b}$

Exercises 2-6, page 62

1. a) 49   b) 64   c) 16   d) 8   e) 81
   f) 25   g) 8   h) 243
2. a) 5   b) 5   c) 4   d) 4   e) 7   f) 3
   g) 3   h) 3   i) 4
3. a) 1   b) 4   c) 7   d) -1 e) 2   f) 0
4. a) 0   b) -2 c) 1   d) -2
5. 8 years   6. 9.7 years
7. a) 1   b) 0   c) $\dfrac{4}{3}$ d) -1 e) $\dfrac{5}{2}$ f) $\dfrac{3}{2}$
   g) $-\dfrac{2}{3}$ h) $-\dfrac{1}{2}$ i) $\dfrac{5}{2}$
8. a) 2   b) 3   c) 3   d) 6   e) 3   f) 3
   g) 2   h) 0   i) $-\dfrac{1}{2}$
9. 4 months
10. a) $25 \times 2^{\frac{n}{5}}$ b) About 43 years
11. a) $\dfrac{3}{2}$ b) -2 c) 6
12. a) 1.56   b) 2.84   c) 2.51

Review Exercises, page 64

1. a) 3^4 b) 6^4 c) $(-7)^5$ d) $(-1.5)^3$
2. a) \$29 775   b) \$37 590   c) \$25 000(1.06)^n
3. a) i) 1.97 m   ii) 1.43 m   b) 11th
4. a) x^{10a+3} b) 2^{6b+4} c) w^{9xz} d) $w^{4m-1}x^{b+4}$
5. a) $108a^6b^6$ b) $243^3a^{27}b^{24}$ c) $4a^6b^2$
   d) $\dfrac{729}{8}a^9b^{12}$
6. a) x^{-5} b) w^{-2} c) $36b^{-10}$ d) $-3c^{-1}d^{10}$
7. a) $19^{\frac{2}{3}}$ b) $28^{\frac{5}{2}}$ c) $13^{\frac{2}{5}}$ d) $33^{\frac{3}{2}}$
   e) $(-7)^{\frac{11}{3}}$ f) $43^{\frac{3}{10}}$
8. a) 114.08   b) 588.032   c) 904.753 75
   d) 483.500 45
9. 1414
10. a) 81   b) $5^{\frac{1}{12}}$ c) $7^{-\frac{7}{2}}$ d) $(-6)^{\frac{21}{20}}$
11. a) 2^{6v} b) 3^8 c) 4^{2a+5}
12. a) 4   b) 3   c) -1 d) 0   e) $\dfrac{1}{2}$
13. a) 2   b) 3   c) $\dfrac{4}{3}$ d) $\dfrac{1}{2}$
14. a) 2   b) 4   c) 4
15. About 5.25 years

Chapter 3

1. a) $8x + 5$ b) $-7m - 7$ c) $-4a + 4b$
   d) $-9x + 13y$ e) $30a - 7b$
   f) $-5x - 11y$

2. a) $4a^2 + 4a - 7$ b) $5m^2 + 5m + 3$
   c) $8x^2 - 5x - 13$ d) $5s^2 + 14s - 12$
   e) $-7x^2 - 19x - 6$ f) $-6a^2 - 11a - 15$

3. a) $x^2 + 5xy + 3y^2$ b) $-6a^2 - 3ab - 7b^2$
   c) $17x^2 - 23xy + 9y^2$ d) $9x^2 + 8xy - 18y^2$
   e) $-37s^2t - 14st^2 + 28$
   f) $-22x^2y + 4xy^2 - 7$

4. a) $28a^4b^4$ b) $20x^5y^9$ c) $-24m^7n^8$
   d) $54x^5y^{10}$ e) $-36m^6n^6$ f) $42a^4b^7$

5. a) $45a^6b^5$ b) $-56x^{13}y^7$ c) $225m^8n^6$
   d) $-72x^{12}y^{13}$ e) $576a^{23}b^{13}$ f) $-288x^{22}y^{21}$

6. Sphere $V = \dfrac{\pi}{6}d^3$, cone $V = \dfrac{\pi}{12}d^2h$,

   cylinder $A = \dfrac{\pi}{2}d^2 + \pi dh$

7. a) $-4xy^6$ b) $16m^4n^6$ c) $-17a^3b^{-5}$
   d) $-4x^6y$ e) $17a^4$ f) $-29y^2$

8. a) i) $2xy$ cm ii) $\dfrac{y^2}{3x}$ cm b) $3x^2y$ cm

9. a) $\dfrac{4}{15}x^4y^{-4}$ b) $\dfrac{4}{9}x^3y^{-2}$ c) $-\dfrac{3}{28}mn$
   d) $\dfrac{32}{9}x^4y^{-4}$ e) $-\dfrac{4}{15}a^2b^3c^{-1}$ f) $-x^{-2}y^3z^{-6}$

10. a) $\pi : 2$ b) $\sqrt{2}\pi : 4$ 11. $5\pi : 8$
12. $4 : 3$ 13. a) $3 : 2$ b) $3 : 2$
14. a) $4\pi^2r^3$ b) $48\pi^2x^4y^5$ 15. $4\sqrt{2} : 3$

1. a) $-4a - 17b$ b) $x^2 - 6y^2$
   c) $-2m^2 - 14m + 11$
   d) $12a^2 - 7ab + 11b^2$
   e) $-8ab - 25bc - 12ac$ f) $7m^2 + 3$

2. a) $-7x + 34y$ b) $51a^2 - 36a$
   c) $12m^2n - 48mn^2$ d) $-6x^2 - 38xy + 14x$
   e) $31a^2 + 13ab + 20a$ f) $26x^2y - 41xy^2 + 7xy$

3. a) $25a - 3b - 41$ b) $-20x + 11y - 75$
   c) $-8x^2 - 38x - 2xy$ d) $31a^2 - 261a$
   e) $-6m^3 + 49m^2 - 8m^2n$
   f) $-4x^2 + 46x^2y - 363xy$

4. a) $15x^2 + 29x - 14$ b) $8m^2 + 46m + 45$
   c) $49x^2 - 42xy + 9y^2$
   d) $56a^2 - 123ab + 55b^2$ e) $16x^2 - 9y^2$
   f) $80x^2 - 174xy + 54y^2$

5. $2xh + h^2$
6. a) $26x^2 + 38xy + 17y^2$
   b) $2a^2 - 47ab + 32b^2$
   c) $-13m^2 - 87mn + 67n^2$
   d) $33x^2 + 4xy + 11y^2$
   e) $-40xy$ f) $-42a^4 + 49a^2b - 52b^2$

7. a) $10x^2 - 15y^2$ b) $-11x^2 - 12x + 24$
   c) $2a^2 - 12a + 19$ d) $6m^2 + 154m + 329$
   e) $12x^2 - 60x + 61$
   f) $66a^4 - 60a^3b + 75a^2b^2 + 72a^2b + 24b^2$

8. a) $10m^3 + 9m^2 + 7m + 24$
   b) $6x^2 - 26xy - 15x + 28y^2 + 35y$
   c) $6a^3 - 11a^2b - 12ab^2 + 5b^3$
   d) $15x^3 + 24x^2y - 3xy^2 + 18y^3$
   e) $2x^4 - x^3 - 5x^2 - 17x - 3$
   f) $24a^5 - 28a^4b - 16a^3b^2 + 28a^2b^3 - 8ab^4$

9. a) $x^3 + 3x^2 - 13x - 15$
   b) $4a^3 + 20a^2 - a - 5$
   c) $2x^3 - 14x^2 + 30x - 18$
   d) $8m^3 - 14m^2 - 109mn^2 - 105n^3$
   e) $54a^3 - 24ab^2 - 135a^2b + 60b^3$
   f) $160x^3 - 320x^2y - 750xy^2 - 315y^3$

10. a) $12xh + 6h^2$ b) $3x^2h + 3xh^2 + h^3$

11. a) $-11x^2 - 103x + 57$
    b) $-49a^2 + 147ab - 93b^2$
    c) $4m^3 + 18m^2 + 16m - 31$
    d) $-13x^2 - 4xy + 14x - 5y^2$
    e) $-20a^3 + 108a^2b + 193ab^2 - 53b^3$
    f) $6x^3 + 51x^2 + 22x - 24$

12. a) Volume: $(12x^3 + 26x^2 - 26x - 60)$ m^3
    Surface area: $(32x^2 + 50x - 14)$ m^2
    b) $V = 225$ m^3, $A = 311$ m^2

13. Volume: $\pi(18x^3 + 21x^2 - 52x + 20)$ cm^3
    Surface area: $2\pi(15x^2 - x - 6)$ cm^2

14. $(0.20x + 0.30vx + 0.15x^2)$ m

15. $mvx + \dfrac{1}{2}mx^2$ 16. $(38 - 4t)$ m

17. $15x^3 + 54x^2y + 17xy^2 - 4y^3$
18. $n^2 + 2n + 1$, or $(n + 1)^2$

1. a) $(x + 2)(x + 3)$ b) $(m - 5)(m - 4)$
   c) $(a + 7)(a - 2)$ d) $(m + 3)(m - 8)$
   e) $(x - 6)(x - 9)$ f) $(x - 7)(x + 12)$

2. a) $(2m + 1)(m + 3)$ b) $(5x - 2)(x - 1)$
   c) $(3a - 1)(a - 3)$ d) $(4x - 3)(x + 1)$
   e) $(3s + 2)(s - 1)$ f) $(2m + 7)(m - 1)$

3. a) $(3x + y)(x + 2y)$ b) $(2m - 3n)(m - n)$
   c) $(3a - b)(a + 2b)$ d) $(5m + 2n)(m - n)$
   e) $(7x - y)(3x - y)$ f) $(3x - y)(x - 5y)$

4. a) $(6s + 5)(s + 1)$ **b)** $(3m - 2)(2m + 1)$
c) $(2a - 3)(a - 4)$ **d)** $(3x + 1)(x - 6)$
e) $(2m + 1)(2m + 3)$ **f)** $(3m - 4)(2m - 3)$

5. a) $(2x + y)(x + 4y)$ **b)** $(3a - 5b)(a - b)$
c) $(3m - 2n)(2m - n)$ **d)** $(x + 2y)(4x + 3y)$
e) $(2p - 5q)(p + 2q)$ **f)** $(2s + 3t)(3s - 5t)$

6. a) $(3s - 2)(2s + 5)$ **b)** $(2m + 5)(3m - 8)$
c) $(5a + 3)(2a + 9)$ **d)** $(4x + 9)(2x + 5)$
e) $(6m - 5)(4m - 3)$ **f)** $(7x + 8)(3x - 2)$

7. a) $4(3x + 1)(3x - 5)$ **b)** $7(2x + 3)(x + 2)$
c) $8(3x - 5)(2x - 5)$
d) $4m(2m + 3)(3m + 4)$
e) $5ab(2a - 3)(a - 4)$ **f)** $3mn(2m - 3)(4m - 5)$

8. a) $(m^2 + 8)(m^2 - 2)$ **b)** $(3x^2 - y^2)(x^2 - 5y^2)$
c) $(a^2 - 3)(2a^2 + 5)$ **d)** $(3x^2 - 2y^2)(4x^2 + y^2)$
e) $2x(x^2 + 2)(x^2 + 5)$
f) $4s(2s^2 - 3t^2)(2s^2 - 5t^2)$

9. a) $(5p - 9q)(p + 2q)$
b) $(4m - 7n)(2m + 3n)$
c) $(5x - 3y)(3x - 5y)$ **d)** $(4s - 9t)(8s - 5t)$
e) $(6p + 5q)(4p - 3q)$ **f)** $(-3x + 2y)(2x + 7y)$

10. a) $(3x + 1)^2$ **b)** $(5x - 1)(5x - 2)$
c) $(6m + 1)(6m + 7)$ **d)** $(2a + 3)(2a + 5)$
e) $(4p - 3)(4p + 5)$ **f)** $(3x + 2)(3x - 4)$

11. a) $(a + b + 3)(a + b + 4)$
b) $(p - q - 2)(p - q - 3)$
c) $(2m + n - 2)(2m + n + 5)$
d) $(4x + y - 5)(4x + y - 3)$
e) $(x - 2y - 3)(x - 2y - 7)$
f) $(3x + 5y + 3)(3x + 5y - 6)$

12. a) $(10x + 1)(5x + 3)$ **b)** $(6m - 1)(2m + 3)$
c) $(12a - 4b + 1)(3a - b + 5)$
d) $(3x + 15y - 2)(2x + 10y - 1)$
e) $(8p + 4q - 3)(4p + 2q - 1)$
f) $(15x^2 + 10y + 3)(6x^2 + 4y - 7)$

13. a) 3 **b)** 5 **c)** 5 **d)** 7 **e)** 5 **f)** 9

Computer Power, page 75

1. a) $(2x + 1)(5x + 8)$ **b)** $(2a - 9)(4a - 3)$
c) $(3x + 5y)(4x - 15y)$ **d)** $(2 + 3t)(12 - 5t)$
e) $6(x + 5)(2x + 3)$ **f)** $5(2x - 7y)(5x + 2y)$
g) $9(3a - 8b)(6a - 5b)$ **h)** $8(4 - 7m)^2$

2. a) $17(4x - 1)(13x + 18)$
b) $23(8x + 5)(11x + 13)$

Problem Solving, page 77

1. Typical results are: **a)** $3^2 + 4^2 + 12^2 = 13^2$;
$1^2 + 2^2 + 2^2 = 3^2$
b) $3^3 + 4^3 + 5^3 = 6^3$; $1^3 + 6^3 + 8^3 = 9^3$
c) $8^2 + 1^2 = 7^2 + 4^2$; $5^2 + 5^2 = 7^2 + 1^2$
d) $12^3 + 1^3 = 10^3 + 9^3$; $9^3 + 15^3 = 2^3 + 16^3$

2. $\sqrt{33}$

4. a) i) $2(R + r)$ **ii)** $2(R - r)$ **b) i)** $\dfrac{D + d}{4}$

ii) $\dfrac{D - d}{4}$ **c)** $A = \dfrac{\pi^2(D^2 - d^2)}{4}$,

$V = \dfrac{\pi^2(D^2 - d^2)(D - d)}{32}$

5. Rotate the curve 90° inside the circle.

6. 5, 2

8. The line passes from upper left to lower right through the centre, inclined at an angle of 45° to the horizontal.

Exercises 3-4, page 79

1. a) $(2x + 5)(2x - 5)$ **b)** $(4m + 9n)(4m - 9n)$
c) $(6a + 11)(6a - 11)$ **d)** $(3s + 7t)(3s - 7t)$
e) $(8x + 13y)(8x - 13y)$
f) $(20a + 9b)(20a - 9b)$

2. a) $3(4a + 7b)(4a - 7b)$
b) $2m(5m + 3)(5m - 3)$
c) $5x(2x + 9y)(2x - 9y)$
d) $7a(3a + 4b)(3a - 4b)$
e) $4xy^2(5x + 9y)(5x - 9y)$
f) $6y(3 + 8x)(3 - 8x)$

3. a) $(x^2 + 9)(x + 3)(x - 3)$
b) $3(2m^2 + 5n^2)(2m^2 - 5n^2)$
c) $2(2a + 5b)(2a - 5b)(4a^2 + 25b^2)$
d) $t\left(3s^2 + \dfrac{1}{2}t\right)\left(3s^2 - \dfrac{1}{2}t\right)$
e) $4y^2\left(\dfrac{2}{5}x + \dfrac{3}{7}y\right)\left(\dfrac{2}{5}x - \dfrac{3}{7}y\right)$
f) $(2x + y)(2x - y)(4x^2 + y^2)(16x^4 + y^4)$

4. a) $5(5x - 9)(x + 1)$ **b)** $(-4m + 7)(8m - 7)$
c) $(12x - 13y)(12x + 5y)$
d) $5(x - y)(-x - 9y)$
e) $4(4m - 3)(m + 5)$
f) $(-8a + 21b)(20a + 9b)$

5. a) $(a + 4)(a - 2)(a^2 + 2a + 8)$
b) $4(x - 6)(x + 3)(x^2 - 3x + 18)$
c) $(2x - y)(x + 2y)(2x^2 + 3xy + 2y^2)$
d) $(3n + m)(2n - 3m)(6n^2 + 7mn + 3m^2)$
e) $(a - 10)(a - 3)(a + 2)(a - 15)$
f) $2(x - 12y)(x + 2y)(x - 6y)(x - 4y)$

6. a) $(x + 5)^2$ **b)** $(m - 7)^2$ **c)** $(2a + 3)^2$
d) $(x - 9y)^2$ **e)** $(6x + 11y)^2$ **f)** $(3x - 7y)^2$

7. a) $(7m + 5)^2$ **b)** $3(2a - 9)^2$ **c)** $(4s + 11)^2$
d) $-2(4x - 3y)^2$ **e)** $(3m - 10n)^2$
f) $5(3x - 7y)^2$

8. a) $(m + 3 - n)(m + 3 + n)$
 b) $(2x - 5 - 4y)(2x - 5 + 4y)$
 c) $(3a - 2 - 7b)(3a - 2 + 7b)$
 d) $(x + 4y - 9)(x + 4y + 9)$
 e) $(2s - 5t + 3)(2s - 5t - 3)$
 f) $(5x - 8 + 8y)(5x - 8 - 8y)$

9. a) $(a - b + 4c)(a + b - 4c)$
 b) $(x - y - 7z)(x + y + 7z)$
 c) $(5 - m - 6n)(5 + m + 6n)$
 d) $(2s + 3t + 2)(2s - 3t - 2)$
 e) $(x - a - y)(x + a + y)$
 f) $(a + b - c - 1)(a - b + c - 1)$

10. a) $(x - 3y - 5z)(x - 3y + 5z)$
 b) $(3m - 2n - 7p)(3m + 2n + 7p)$
 c) $(x + 1)^2(x - 1)$
 d) $(a - b + 4)(a + b - 2)$
 e) $(a^n + b^n)(a^n - b^n)$
 f) $2(x + 1)(x + 3)(x - 1)(x - 3)$

11. $2\pi(R + r)(R - r + h)$

12. a) $A = \pi^2(a - b)(a + b)$
 b) About 1.48×10^6 m²

13. $kx(2T + x)(2T^2 + 2Tx + x^2)$

Exercises 3-5, page 81

1. a) $(z - 3)(z^2 + 3z + 9)$
 b) $(y + 1)(y^2 - y + 1)$
 c) $8(x - 2)(x^2 + 2x + 4)$
 d) $(a - 2b)(a^2 + 2ab + 4b^2)$
 e) $(2x + 3y)(4x^2 - 6xy + 9y^2)$
 f) $(4x + 1)(16x^2 - 4x + 1)$

2. a) $x(x^2 + 3x + 3)$
 b) $(2x + 1)(4x^2 - 2x + 1)$
 c) $2(3x^2 + 6x + 4)$
 d) $(2x + 2y + 1)(4x^2 + 4y^2 - 4xy + 4x - 2y + 1)$
 e) $4b(3a^2 + 4b^2)$ **f)** $2x(x^2 + y^2)$
 g) $2x(x^2 + 27)$ **h)** $-18a(16 + 3a^2)$
 i) $2m(m^2 + 12n^2)$

3. a) $(x + y)(x - y)(x^4 + x^2y^2 + y^4)$
 b) $(x^2 + y^2)(x^4 - x^2y^2 + y^4)$
 c) $(2a - 1)(2a + 1)(16a^4 + 4a^2 + 1)$
 d) $(1 + 4y^2)(1 - 4y^2 + 16y^4)$
 e) $4xy(x^2 + 3y^2)(y^2 + 3x^2)$
 f) $2(x^2 + y^2)(x^4 + 14x^2y^2 + y^4)$

4. a) $V = \dfrac{1}{3}\pi h(a^2 + ab + b^2)$

Exercises 3-6, page 83

1. a) $3xy(2x + 5y - 9)$
 b) $7m^2n(5mn^2 - 3n + 8)$
 c) $4ab^2(3a^2 + 7ab - 11b^2)$
 d) $9st^2(4s^3 - 5st - 2t^2)$
 e) $5xy^3(4x^2 + 9xy - 7y^2)$
 f) $6ab(7ab^2 - 3a^2 + 8b)$

2. a) $6x^2y^2(2x - 3y + 4)$
 b) $4ab^2(7a^2 - 3ab - 12b^2)$
 c) $15m^2(3m^2 + 2mn - 5n^2)$
 d) $13x^3y^3(3y^2 - 5y - 2x^2)$

3. a) $(2a - 7)(3x + 5y)$
 b) $(4x + 3y)(3x - y)(3x + y)$
 c) $(2a - 5b)(4a^2 + 7b^2)$
 d) $(3m - 7n + 2)(5m^2 + 9n^2)$
 e) $(4x^2 - 7x + 9)(12x^2 - 5xy - 1)$
 f) $(7x - 2y)(4x^2 - 5xy + 1 - 11y^2)$

4. a) $(3x^2 - 11y^2)(5x^2y + 4)$
 b) $(5m^2 + 3)(2m^2 - 7n^2)$
 c) $2(4x - 7y)(3x^2 + y^2)$
 d) $(4x^2 + 5xy - 3y^2)(4x - 5y)(4x + 5y)$
 e) $(2a^2 + 9ab - 5b^2)(3a^2 + 4ab - 2b^2)$
 f) $(5m^2 - 2mn + 3n)(2m + 7mn - 13n)$

5. a) $(x + y)(m - n)$ **b)** $(2a - 3)(5x + 2y)$
 c) $(3m + 2n)(3a + b)$ **d)** $(7x - 5y)(2a - 9)$
 e) $(4x + 3)(7x - 4y)$ **f)** $(8x - 5y)(6x - 7)$

6. a) $(x - z)(x - y)$ **b)** $(x + 1)^2(x - 1)$
 c) $(7x - 2y)(3x^2 - 1)$ **d)** $(1 + a)(1 + b)$
 e) $(2x - 3)(x + 1)(x - 1)$
 f) $(x + y)(x + y - 1)$

7. a) $(x + 1)(x + 2)$ **b)** $(a - b)(2c + 3d)$
 c) $(a - 1)(a - 2)(a + 2)$
 d) $(x + y)(x + y + 4)$
 e) $a(1 + b)(1 - c)$
 f) $(a - b)[a(a - b) - 1]$

8. a) $2(3m + 1)(3m - 10)$
 b) $(6x + 3y - 2)(4x + 2y - 3)$
 c) $(2 - 4x - 5y)(2 + 16x + 5y)$
 d) $(2m - 1)(m + 8n)(m - 8n)$
 e) $(3a - 2)(2a - 1)(4a^2 + 2a + 1)$
 f) $(5x - 7y)(6x + 7y)(6x - 7y)$

9. a) $(15m - 14)(6m - 1)$
 b) $25(2m - 1)(2m + 1)(3m - 2)^2$
 c) $(2x + 6y + 1)(2x + 6y - 3)$
 d) $(5x - 7)(2x^2 - 3y^2)$
 e) $(2x + 5y)(4x - y)(x - 3y)$

10. $W = \dfrac{P - 2x}{2},\ A = \dfrac{x(P - x)}{2}$ **11.** $\dfrac{\pi}{4}(a^2 - b^2)$

12. a) $\pi(x + y)$ **b)** $\dfrac{\pi x}{4}(x + 2y)$

13. a) i) $2\pi x(h + x + 2r)$ **ii)** $\pi hx(x + 2r)$
b) i) $2\pi ry$ **ii)** $\pi r^2 y$

14. a) $a^2(a - 2)(a - b)$ **b)** $xy(x - 3)(x + y)$
c) $3m(m + 4)(m + n)$
d) $2ab^2(3a + 2)(a - b)$
e) $5m^2(2m - 3)(m - n)$
f) $4x^2y(2x - 3)(3x - y)$

15. Let $100x + 10y + z$ represent any 3-digit number.
Then $100z + 10y + x$ represents the number
formed by reversing the digits.
$100x + 10y + z - (100z + 10y + x)$
$= 99x - 99z$
This is divisible by 99.
Therefore, the difference between a 3-digit number
and the number formed by reversing the digits is
divisible by 99.

16. Let $100x + 10y + z$ represent any 3-digit number
and $x + y + z = b$.
Then $x = b - y - z$
Substitute this for x in the expression for the
number.
$100(b - y - z) + 10y + z =$
$100b - 9(10y + 11z)$
This is divisible by 9 if, and only if, b is divisible
by 9.
Therefore, a 3-digit number is divisible by 9 if, and
only if, the sum of its digits is divisible by 9.

17. Area of rectangle: lw
Area of four semicircles:

$$\pi\left(\frac{l}{2}\right)^2 + \pi\left(\frac{w}{2}\right)^2 = \frac{\pi}{4}(l^2 + w^2)$$

Total area of figure: $lw + \dfrac{\pi}{4}(l^2 + w^2)$
Diameter of circle: $\sqrt{l^2 + w^2}$
Area of circle: $\dfrac{\pi}{4}(\sqrt{l^2 + w^2})^2 = \dfrac{\pi}{4}(l^2 + w^2)$
Area of shaded portion:
$lw + \dfrac{\pi}{4}(l^2 + w^2) - \dfrac{\pi}{4}(l^2 + w^2) = lw$
The shaded area is equal to the area of the
rectangle.

Exercises 3-7, page 88

1. a) $\dfrac{8m}{5n}$ **b)** $\dfrac{-5b^2}{8ac}$ **c)** $\dfrac{t^2}{3s}$ **d)** $\dfrac{-5x}{8y}$ **e)** $\dfrac{5m^5}{2n^3}$

2. a) $\dfrac{2x - 5y}{3x + 4}$ **b)** $\dfrac{n(5m - 6)}{2m + 3}$ **c)** $\dfrac{a - 2b}{2a - b}$
d) $\dfrac{3x - 2y}{y - x}$ **e)** $\dfrac{4m^2 - 3n^2}{5m + 2n}$ **f)** $\dfrac{2x^2 - 3x + 7}{8 - 3x}$

3. a) $-\dfrac{m + 2n}{3m}$ **b)** $\dfrac{x - 3y}{2xy}$ **c)** $\dfrac{2a + 5b}{-4a}$
d) $\dfrac{5s^2t}{2s + 3t}$ **e)** $\dfrac{4y - 3x}{7xy}$ **f)** $\dfrac{-3mn}{2m - 5n}$

4. a) $\dfrac{x + 3y}{x - 2y}$ **b)** $\dfrac{5n - 2m}{m - 3n}$ **c)** $\dfrac{3a - b}{2a + 5b}$
d) $-\dfrac{4x - y}{2x + 3y}$ **e)** $\dfrac{5m + 3n}{2m + 3n}$ **f)** $\dfrac{8y - 3x}{5x + 2y}$

5. a) 0 **b)** 0, 2 **c)** 4 **d)** $-8, 1$
e) $7, -1$ **f)** 4

6. a) $\dfrac{14}{5}x$, all R except 0

b) $-\dfrac{x + 3}{3}$, all R except $\dfrac{1}{2}$

c) $\dfrac{m + 2}{m + 5}$, all R except -5

d) $-\dfrac{8ab}{a + 3}$, all R except ± 3

e) $\dfrac{x - 1}{x + 1}$, all R except 0 **f)** $\dfrac{3x^3 + 2x^2}{x^2 + 7}$, all R

7. a) $\dfrac{5(2x - y)}{2(x + 3y)}$ **b)** $-\dfrac{4m(3m - 2n)}{7n(2m - 3n)}$
c) $\dfrac{y(3x - 1)}{2x + 3}$ **d)** $-\dfrac{x(x - 7)}{2(x + 4)}$
e) $-\dfrac{5y^2(x + 2)}{3}$ **f)** $\dfrac{2b(3a + 4b)}{5(3a - 4b)}$

Exercises 3-8, page 92

1. a) $4mn$ **b)** $-\dfrac{9b^2}{8a^2}$ **c)** $\dfrac{2y^2}{5x^2}$ **d)** $\dfrac{35}{32s^3t}$
e) $-\dfrac{2y^2}{x^3}$ **f)** $\dfrac{-7ab}{8c}$

2. a) $36k^3$ **b)** $\dfrac{4k}{5}$ **c)** $128k^4$ **d)** $38\,880k^9$

3. a) $\dfrac{5a}{b^2}$ **b)** $\dfrac{375a^2}{2b^2}$ **c)** $24a^2b$ **d)** $\dfrac{a}{2b^3}$

4. a) $\dfrac{5x}{18}$ **b)** $\dfrac{3}{2}$ **c)** $\dfrac{9}{5}$ **d)** 1 **e)** -17 **f)** $-\dfrac{1}{4}$

5. a) $\dfrac{10x}{-y}$ **b)** $\dfrac{2(m - 2n)}{7m(n - 2m)}$ **c)** $\dfrac{2a^2(a - 3b)}{3b}$
d) $-\dfrac{y}{5x}$ **e)** $\dfrac{-12(2s + t)}{25s(2s - t)}$ **f)** $\dfrac{-4y}{5x}$

6. a) $\dfrac{4(3y - x)}{3}$ **b)** $-\dfrac{2(3a + 4b)}{3a^2}$ **c)** $\dfrac{-n}{9m}$
d) $-\dfrac{y}{4}$ **e)** $-\dfrac{6m(m - 2n)}{n(m + 2n)}$ **f)** $\dfrac{8a(a + b)}{-5b^2}$

7. a) $\dfrac{-x + 12}{7x - 4}$ **b)** $\dfrac{11m - 16}{10m - 8}$ **c)** $\dfrac{11x + 5}{7x - 5}$

d) $\dfrac{34x + 70}{9x - 42}$ **e)** $\dfrac{13a + 10}{11a - 14}$ **f)** $\dfrac{1}{2}$

8. a) $\dfrac{x^2 + 2x - 2}{x^2 + 2x + 3}$ **b)** $\dfrac{2m^2 - 6m + 5}{5m^2 - 15m - 2}$

c) $\dfrac{6a + 11}{10a + 22}$ **d)** 2   **e)** $\dfrac{15m^2 - 4m + 1}{5m^2 - 5m - 2}$

f) $\dfrac{15x^2 - 22x - 3}{6x^2 - 11x + 5}$

9. a) $\dfrac{x^2 - x - 8}{x^2 + 2x + 3}$ **b)** $\dfrac{2x^2 + 4x - 1}{3x^2 + 2x}$

c) $\dfrac{2 - 4m}{m^2 + m}$ **d)** $\dfrac{a^2 - 2a - 3}{6a^2 - 5a}$ **e)** $\dfrac{6}{x^2}$

f) $\dfrac{-5}{3s^2 - 2}$

10. a) $\dfrac{a + 1}{1 - a}$ **b)** $\dfrac{x - 2y}{x + 2y}$ **c)** $\dfrac{x - 4y}{x(x - 2y)}$

d) $-\dfrac{3(m + 3n)}{2(m + 8n)}$ **e)** $\dfrac{s(3s + 4t)}{2(2s + 5t)}$

11. 3 : 2   **12. a)** 28 : 25   **b)** 39 : 35

13. a) 2.25   **b)** 4

14. a) $R^2 r^2 = \dfrac{a^2 b^2 c^2}{4(a + b + c)^2};$

$R = \left(\dfrac{abc}{2(a + b + c)}\right)\left(\dfrac{1}{r}\right)$

b) $R = \dfrac{1}{2}b;\ r = \dfrac{ac}{a + b + c}$

Exercises 3-9, page 97

1. a) $\dfrac{2y + 3x}{xy}$ **b)** $\dfrac{8x - 5}{x^2}$ **c)** $\dfrac{4y + 11x}{x^2 y}$

d) $\dfrac{7x - 15y}{x^2 y^2}$ **e)** $\dfrac{12z - 9x}{xyz}$ **f)** $\dfrac{6y^2 + 19x^2}{x^2 y^2}$

2. a) $\dfrac{5m^2 - 3n^2}{mn}$ **b)** $\dfrac{17a^2 + 5b^2}{abc}$ **c)** $\dfrac{8y^3 + 13x^2}{xy^2}$

d) $\dfrac{2s - 11st}{t^2}$ **e)** $\dfrac{n(15mn + 11)}{m^2}$

f) $\dfrac{23x^2 - 16y^3}{xy^2}$

3. a) $\dfrac{3x^2 + 2xy - 5y^2}{xy^2}$ **b)** $\dfrac{2a^2 - 6ab - 11b}{ab^2}$

c) $\dfrac{7x^2 - 14xy + 5y^2}{x^2 y^2}$ **d)** $\dfrac{16a^2 + 6ab - 27b^2}{12ab}$

e) $\dfrac{45s^2 - 25st + 12t^2}{20st}$ **f)** $\dfrac{-14x^2 - 3xy - 12y^2}{28xy}$

4. a) $\dfrac{6x^2 + 40xy - 35y}{20xy}$

b) $\dfrac{-20m^2 + 15mn + 27n}{24mn}$

c) $\dfrac{-14a^2 - 4a + 6ab - 15b}{12ab}$

d) $\dfrac{9x^2 - 36xy - 22y^2}{18xy}$

e) $\dfrac{-12m^2 + 33mn - 25n^2}{30mn}$

5. a) $\dfrac{36x^2 y + 10x - 12y^2}{15x^2 y}$

b) $\dfrac{15a^2 - 28b - 35ab^2}{20ab^2}$

c) $\dfrac{57m^2 - 56n + 140mn}{28mn^2}$

d) $\dfrac{6x^2 - 92x^2 y + 9xy^2 + 8y^2}{24x^2 y}$

6. a) $\dfrac{2m + 41}{(m + 3)(m + 4)}$ **b)** $\dfrac{a(31a - 32)}{(3a - 4)(5a - 2)}$

c) $\dfrac{13m(3m - 1)}{(3m - 7)(5m - 3)}$ **d)** $\dfrac{2x^2 + 10x + 2}{(x + 5)(x + 4)}$

e) $\dfrac{x^2 - 56x - 4}{(3x - 2)(2x + 5)}$ **f)** $\dfrac{-11m^2 + 19m - 23}{(5m - 4)(2m - 3)}$

7. a) $\dfrac{29a}{6(a - 5)}$ **b)** $\dfrac{6(2x - 1)}{(2 - x)(2 + x)}$

c) $\dfrac{2x + 21}{14(2x - 5)}$ **d)** $\dfrac{35 + 22m}{3(5 - 2m)(5 + 2m)}$

e) $\dfrac{a(9a - 8)}{(a - 4)(a - 2)(a + 3)}$ **f)** $\dfrac{3x}{(x - 4)(x - 1)}$

8. a) $\dfrac{3x^2 - 17x + 14}{(x - 5)(x - 4)(x - 3)}$

b) $\dfrac{2(2x^2 - x - 14)}{(6 - x)(6 + x)(x - 2)}$

c) $\dfrac{2a^2 + 7a - 16}{(4 + a)(a + 6)(8 - a)}$

d) $\dfrac{6m^2 - 26m - 5}{(m - 5)(m - 1)(m - 4)}$ **e)** $\dfrac{2}{(x - 4)(x - 1)}$

f) $\dfrac{2(a^2 + 22a - 9)}{(a + 7)(a + 3)(5 - a)}$

9. $\dfrac{dx}{v(v + x)}$ **10.** $\dfrac{280x}{p(p + x)}$ litres

11. $-\dfrac{kx(2r + x)}{r^2(r + x)^2}$ **12.** $\dfrac{2x}{80 + x}$ hours

13. a) $15 - 28m^2$ **b)** 8   **c)** 21   **d)** $a - 3$

Exercises 3-10, page 100

1. $\dfrac{2(w^2 + w - 6000)}{w(w + 1)}$

2. **a)** $l = \dfrac{6000}{w}$ **b) i)** $\dfrac{6000x}{w(w + x)}$

   ii) $\dfrac{2x(w^2 + wx - 6000)}{w(w + x)}$

3. **a)** 40 min   **c)**

   b) $t = \dfrac{2x}{3(20 + x)}$

   d) If $x < 0$, time to overtake > 40 min If $x \leq -20$ km/h, B does not overtake A.

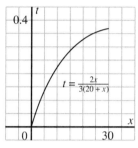

4. **a)** $t = \dfrac{5}{2(v - 30)}$ **b)** 37.5 km/h

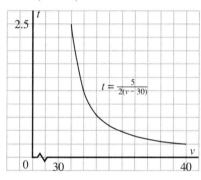

5. $\dfrac{800x}{(v - 80)(v + x - 80)}$

6. **a)** $L = \dfrac{2x^2 + 2000}{x}$ **b)** About 30 m by 67 m

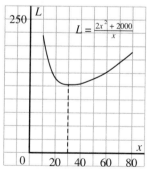

7. **a) i)** $h = \dfrac{100}{x^2}$ **ii)** $A = \dfrac{x^3 + 400}{x}$

   b) For minimum A, dimensions are: about 6 cm by 6 cm by 3 cm

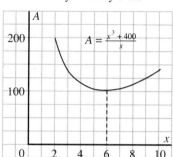

8. **a)** $h = \dfrac{20(w + 10)}{w - 10}$ **b)** $A = \dfrac{20w(w + 10)}{w - 10}$

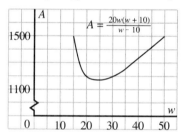

9. $\dfrac{x(s - r - x)}{r + s}$

10. **a)** 8 min

    b) $T = \dfrac{3v + 20}{v - 10}$

    c) i) 28 min

    ii) 13 min

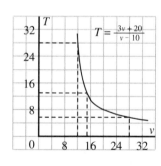

Review Exercises, page 102

1. **a)** $4m^2 - 11mn - 15n^2$ **b)** $-8s^2 + 6st + 8t^2$
   c) $-3a^2 - 5ab - 12b^2$
   d) $2mn^2(7mn + 3m - 12n)$

2. **a)** $56a^3b^4$ **b)** $-63a^4b^4$ **c)** $156x^{10}y^5$
   d) $-182m^5n^4$ **e)** $24x^5y^2$ **f)** $-102s^{11}t^7$

3. **a)** $\dfrac{39}{5}x^3$ **b)** $-10ab^{-2}$ **c)** $\dfrac{21}{64}x^{-1}$ **d)** ac

4. a) $7x^2 + 10xy + 7y^2$ **b)** $-5a^2 + 2ab - 5b^2$
c) $m^2 + 20mn + 2n^2$ **d)** $125(x - y)(x + y)$

5. a) $(2x - 5)(2x - 3)$ **b)** $(3w - 5)(w - 3)$
c) $(3x + 2)^2$ **d)** $(3m - 5)(2m + 3)$

6. a) $(3m - 2n)(2m - n)$ **b)** $(a - b)(4a + 3b)$
c) $(3a + 2b)(a - 4b)$ **d)** $(-2x + 3)(x - 5)$

7. a) $(5x + 1)(x + 7)$ **b)** $-9(6m + 1)$
c) $(2x + 5)^2$ **d)** $(3x - 4)^2$
e) $(a - b)(a - b + 1)$
f) $(3x - 5y + 1)(3x + 5y - 1)$

8. a) $(a + 2b)(2x - y)$ **b)** $(3m - 2n)(2s + 3t)$
c) $(6x - y)(3a + 4)$ **d)** $(7x - 4y)(5x - 6)$

9. a) $(5x - 3y)(25x^2 + 15xy + 9y^2)$
b) $2a(a^2 + 3)$

10. a) ± 11 **b)** -6 **c)** $t = 0, s = -\dfrac{3}{2}$

d) $a = \pm\dfrac{5b}{3}$ **e)** $c = \dfrac{3d}{2}, -\dfrac{4d}{3}$

f) $r = 0, \dfrac{4s}{3}, -\dfrac{3s}{4}$

11. a) $-\dfrac{x - 5}{2x}$ **b)** $\dfrac{3}{4}$ **c)** $\dfrac{a - 2b}{2a + b}$ **d)** $\dfrac{3x^3y^2}{x - y}$

12. a) $\dfrac{8mn - 5n + 7m}{m^2n}$ **b)** $\dfrac{9x^2 + 4x - 3y}{xy^2}$
c) $\dfrac{5s^4 - 2st + 9t}{s^2t^2}$ **d)** $\dfrac{12mn - 4n - 15m^2}{10mn}$
e) $\dfrac{35x^2 - 24xy - 6y^2}{21xy}$ **f)** $\dfrac{33n^2 + 51mn - 30m^2}{15mn}$

13. a) $\dfrac{-5x - 3y}{(x - y)(x + y)}$ **b)** $\dfrac{-x^2 + 5x + 2}{(x - 1)(x + 1)}$
c) $\dfrac{-6x^2 + 11x - 4}{(x + 2)(x - 3)}$ **d)** $\dfrac{-7(x + 3)}{(x + 4)(x - 3)}$
e) $\dfrac{x^2 + 10x + 5}{(x - 1)(x + 1)}$ **f)** $\dfrac{4 - 3a}{a - 2}$

14. a) $\dfrac{x^2 + 6x + 5}{x^2 + 4x + 2}$ **b)** $\dfrac{m^2 - 3m - 6}{m^2 + 2}$
c) $\dfrac{-2a^2 + 4a - 7}{a^2 - 14a + 8}$ **d)** $\dfrac{-x^2 - 3x - 12}{2x^2 + 2x + 2}$

15. $-\dfrac{50x}{20 - x}$ millimetres

16. a) $h = \dfrac{80}{w^2}$ **b)** $\dfrac{80(2w - 1)}{w^2(w - 1)^2}$

1. a) $13\sqrt{3}$ **b)** $-8\sqrt{2} - 4\sqrt{6}$
c) $6\sqrt{35} + 32\sqrt{15}$ **d)** 28

2. a) $\dfrac{11}{2}$ **b)** $\dfrac{12\sqrt{7}}{35}$ **c)** $8 - 3\sqrt{2}$
d) $\dfrac{30 + 2\sqrt{10}}{5}$

3. a) 9 **b)** 6 **c)** $\dfrac{6 - \sqrt{11}}{2}$

4. a) -12 **b)** 97 **c)** -409

5. a) $8a^7b^6$ **b)** $24c^4b^{-8}$ **c)** $2y^3h^2$ **d)** $3x^{-5}y^{11}$
e) $64m^{24}n^{-6}$ **f)** x^{2a-7}

6. $\$4958.98$ **7. a)** $17^{\frac{4}{3}}$ **b)** $19^{\frac{7}{2}}$ **c)** $73^{-\frac{1}{5}}$

8. a) 32 **b)** $\dfrac{2}{5}$ **c)** $\dfrac{1}{27}$ **d)** -25

9. a) 5 **b)** 3 **c)** -3 **d)** 4 **10.** 6 months

11. a) $5m^2n - 8mn^2$ **b)** $-8a^3b^4$ **c)** $x^{23}y^{21}$

12. a) $4x^2y^2(y + 3x - 5xy)$ **b)** $(x + y)(a^2 + b^2)$
c) $x^2y^2(3x - 2)(5y - 4)$ **d)** $(4a + 1)(2a + 5)$
e) $(6b - 5c)(4b - c)$ **f)** $(2a - 7)^2$
g) $9(z - 4r)(z + 4r)$
h) $(y - m + 5c)(y + m - 5c)$
i) $(y - 5)(y^2 + 5y + 25)$
j) $(3a + 2d)(9a^2 - 6ad + 4d^2)$

13. a) $\dfrac{a}{a + 6}$ **b)** $\dfrac{(x^2 + y^2)(x + 8y)}{x + y}$
c) $\dfrac{(2y + 3)(y - 5)}{2y(y - 3)}$ **d)** $\dfrac{2(x - 35)}{(x + 1)(x - 3)(x - 7)}$

Chapter 4

Exercises 4-1, page 107

1. a) ± 4 **b)** ± 1.5 **c)** ± 5 **d)** No solution
e) $4 \pm 3\sqrt{2}$ **f)** $-3 \pm 2\sqrt{2}$

2. a) 3.46 cm **b)** 5.66 m **c)** 1.22 km

3. a) 132.5 m **b)** 10.1 s

4. a) $\pm\sqrt{2}$ **b)** $\pm\sqrt{10}$ **c)** $5 \pm \sqrt{10}$
d) $\pm\sqrt{2}$ **e)** $\pm\sqrt{3}$ **f)** $\pm\sqrt{7}$

5. a) ± 2 **b)** ± 4 **c)** $\pm\sqrt{\dfrac{7}{2}}$ **d)** $\pm 3\sqrt{3}$

e) ± 7 **f)** No solution

6. a) i) 25.5 km **ii)** 36.1 km **b) i)** 69.2 m
ii) 276.9 m

7. a) $a = \sqrt{c^2 - b^2}$, $b = \sqrt{c^2 - a^2}$, $c = \sqrt{a^2 + b^2}$

b) $v = \sqrt{u^2 + 2as}$, $u = \sqrt{v^2 - 2as}$

c) $r = \sqrt{\dfrac{A}{\pi}}$ **d)** $r = \sqrt{\dfrac{V}{\pi h}}$

8. a) 5.6 cm **b)** 0.7 m **c)** 3 km

9. a) i) 201 cm^2 **ii)** 1963.5 cm^2 **b) i)** 4.9 cm
ii) 10.4 cm

10. a) 2827 m^3 **b)** $r = \sqrt{\dfrac{3V}{\pi h}}$ **c) i)** 95 m

ii) 82 m

11. a) $d = \sqrt{275C - 337.5}$ **b) i)** 25 cm
ii) 30 cm **iii)** \$7.05

12. a) i) 1.93×10^2 kJ **ii)** 7.72×10^2 kJ
b) i) 36 km/h **ii)** 113.8 km/h

13. 2.6 m square **14.** 2.5 m

15. a) 1.6 m **b)** 1.7 m

Exercises 4-2, page 112

1. a) $\frac{1}{2}x^2 + \frac{1}{2}x - 3 = 0$; -3, 2

b) $\frac{1}{4}x^2 - \frac{1}{2}x - 2 = 0$; -2, 4
c) $-x^2 + 2x - 2 = 0$; no roots
d) $x^2 + 2x - 5.25 = 0$; -3.5, 1.5

2. a) 2.5, 4 **b)** 0.5, -4.5

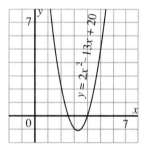

c) -0.5, -1.5 **d)** 1.5, -1.7

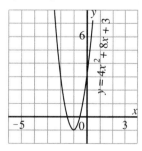
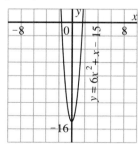

e) 2.5 **f)** No roots

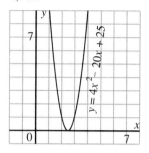
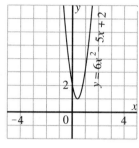

3. a) 1.5, -0.7 **b)** -2.3, 1.5

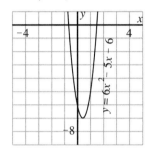
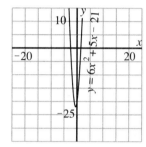

c) 2.5, -4.5 **d)** 0.6, -4.6

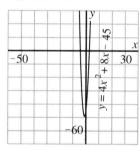
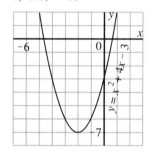

e) -0.5, -2.3 **f)** 2.3, 5.7

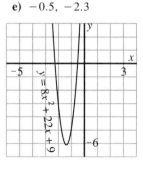
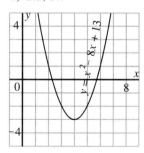

4. a) 0.5, 3

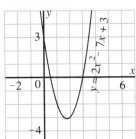

b) −2.5, 1.5

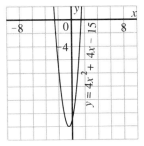

c) No roots

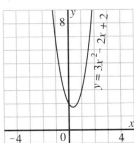

d) −3.5, −4

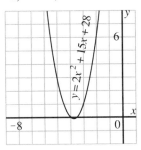

e) −3.5

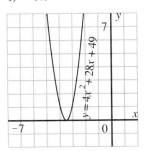

f) −0.5, 1.5

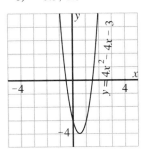

5. a) No roots
   b) Two roots

6. c

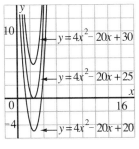

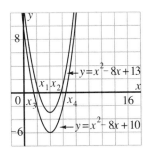

7. a) $k < 13$ **b)** $13 < k < 16$

Exercises 4-3, page 116

1. a) 3, 1   **b)** −5, −3   **c)** 8, −7
   d) $\frac{5}{2}$, −3   **e)** ± 8 **f)** $\frac{2}{3}$
2. a) −5, 2   **b)** 7, 5   **c)** 6, −1   **d)** 0, 11
   e) $\pm \frac{7}{2}$ **f)** $-\frac{3}{2}$, 5
3. a) 6   **b)** 3, −8   **c)** 4   **d)** 4, 7
   e) $-\frac{3}{2}$, 5   **f)** $-\frac{5}{2}$
4. a) $-\frac{9}{5}$, 2   **b)** $-\frac{1}{2}$, $\frac{4}{3}$ **c)** −6, 1   **d)** $-\frac{7}{2}$, $\frac{2}{3}$
   e) 6   **f)** $\pm \frac{6}{5}$
5. a) $\frac{5}{2}$, −3   **b)** −2, −4   **c)** −5, −4
   d) $\frac{2}{3}$, 4   **e)** 5, 1   **f)** 7, −4
6. a) $\frac{3}{2}$ **b)** $-\frac{1}{2}$, 2   **c)** $-\frac{2}{3}$, 3   **d)** $\frac{4}{3}$, −1
   e) 4, 6   **f)** $-\frac{2}{3}$, 5
7. a) ± 2, ± 3 **b)** ± 1 **c)** $\pm \sqrt{1.5}$, ± 1
   d) ± 1.5, ± 1 **e)** $\pm \sqrt{5}$ **f)** No solution
8. a) 2, 1   **b)** 2   **c)** 4   **d)** 5   **e)** 3, 2
   f) No solution
9. a) 7, 8   **b)** 12, 13   **10. a)** 5   **b)** 6
11. 8, 9   **12.** −8, −7, −6, or 6, 7, 8
13. 20, 21   **14.** $k = 1$
15. a) $-\frac{1}{2}$, 4   **b)** $\frac{4}{5}$, $\frac{1}{3}$ **c)** $\frac{8}{5}$, −4   **d)** $\frac{2}{3}$, −3
   e) $\frac{2}{3}$, $-\frac{7}{2}$ **f)** $\frac{3}{2}$, $\frac{9}{4}$
16. a) 3, −4   **b)** −3, −2   **c)** 3, 1
   d) −3, 2   **e)** −5, 2   **f)** −3, −5
17. a) 2 : 1 or 3 : 1   **b)** −3 : 1 or −4 : 1
   c) 1 : 2 or −5 : 1   **d)** 2 : 3 or −5 : 2
   e) 5 : 3 or −3 : 2   **f)** 5 : 4 or 7 : 2
18. a) $k = -10, x = -2$ **b)** $k = -13, x = 8$
   c) $k = -10, x = 5$ **d)** $k = 15, x = \frac{3}{2}$
19. a) $\pm \sqrt{-a}$ **b)** 0, a **c)** $\pm \sqrt{\dfrac{b}{a}}$
   d) $\pm \sqrt{-\dfrac{a}{b}}$ **e)** a, b
20. 11, 12
21. a) $-a$, b **b)** $\frac{a}{2}$, b **c)** $p + q$, $-p - q$
   d) $2a + b$, $a - b$

Computer Power, page 118

1. a) $-4.5, 3.4$ **b)** $4.137, 0.363$
c) $2.25, -0.375$ **d)** $1.618, -0.618$
2. $4.142, 5.858$ or $34.142, -24.142$

Exercises 4-4, page 121

1. a) Yes **b)** Yes **c)** No **d)** No **e)** Yes
f) Yes

2. a) 1 **b)** 1 **c)** 100 **d)** $\dfrac{49}{4}$ **e)** $\dfrac{9}{4}$

f) $\dfrac{1}{4}$ **g)** $\dfrac{121}{4}$ **h)** a **i)** $\dfrac{b^2}{4}$

3. a) $-6, 2$ **b)** $3, -11$ **c)** $3 \pm \sqrt{2}$
d) $8 \pm \sqrt{14}$ **e)** $\dfrac{3 \pm \sqrt{5}}{2}$ **f)** $\dfrac{-5 \pm \sqrt{13}}{2}$

4. a) $-6 \pm 2\sqrt{11}$ **b)** $9 \pm \sqrt{61}$
c) $\dfrac{3 \pm \sqrt{29}}{2}$ **d)** $\dfrac{1 \pm \sqrt{5}}{2}$ **e)** $\dfrac{-9 \pm \sqrt{17}}{2}$
f) $\dfrac{-5 \pm \sqrt{37}}{2}$

5. a) $-2 \pm \dfrac{\sqrt{6}}{2}$ **b)** $2 \pm \dfrac{\sqrt{21}}{3}$ **c)** $3 \pm \dfrac{\sqrt{30}}{2}$
d) $-1 \pm \dfrac{\sqrt{3}}{3}$

6. a) $3 \pm 3\sqrt{2}$ **b)** $\dfrac{-1 \pm \sqrt{41}}{4}$ **c)** $\dfrac{7 \pm \sqrt{41}}{4}$
d) $\dfrac{5 \pm \sqrt{19}}{2}$ **e)** $\dfrac{-3 \pm \sqrt{33}}{4}$ **f)** $\dfrac{1 \pm \sqrt{31}}{5}$

7. a) $2.16, -4.16$ **b)** $1.18, -10.18$
c) $2.64, -1.14$ **d)** $1.25, -2.92$
e) $-0.31, -3.19$ **f)** $3.84, 0.16$

The Mathematical Mind, page 122

1. 13 or -7 **2. a)** $\dfrac{-p \pm \sqrt{4q + p^2}}{2}$

Exercises 4-5, page 126

1. a) $3 \pm \sqrt{5}$ **b)** $\dfrac{-3 \pm \sqrt{13}}{2}$ **c)** $\dfrac{-7 \pm \sqrt{37}}{2}$
d) $\dfrac{5 \pm \sqrt{17}}{2}$ **e)** $-2 \pm \sqrt{5}$ **f)** $4 \pm \sqrt{22}$

2. a) $\dfrac{1}{2}, 2$ **b)** $-3, -\dfrac{1}{2}$ **c)** $-1, \dfrac{14}{3}$ **d)** $1, \dfrac{5}{4}$
e) $-\dfrac{2}{5}, -1$ **f)** $\dfrac{4}{3}, -\dfrac{5}{2}$

3. a) $\dfrac{2}{3}, \dfrac{1}{2}$ **b)** $7, \dfrac{11}{2}$ **c)** $\dfrac{1}{2}, -\dfrac{1}{3}$ **d)** $-\dfrac{9}{2}, 5$
e) $-\dfrac{3}{2}, 4$ **f)** $\dfrac{2}{3}, -\dfrac{1}{2}$

4. a) $5.61, 0.89$ **b)** $2.78, 0.72$
c) $1.47, -1.14$ **d)** $4.61, -0.11$
e) $0.84, -0.24$ **f)** $-0.22, -2.28$

5. a) $0.15, -1.35$ **b)** $3.16, -0.16$
c) $1.23, -1.90$ **d)** $0.65, -1.15$
e) $1.82, 0.18$ **f)** $2.82, 0.18$

6. 2.78 s

7. a) $\dfrac{4}{3}, 0$ **b)** ± 4 **c)** $-\dfrac{7}{5}$ **d)** $\dfrac{3 \pm \sqrt{19}}{10}$
e) $\dfrac{5 \pm \sqrt{89}}{2}$ **f)** $2\sqrt{2}, \dfrac{\sqrt{2}}{2}$

8. a) $4, \dfrac{1}{4}$ **b)** $\dfrac{1}{2}, \dfrac{4}{3}$ **c)** $-\dfrac{2}{3}, \dfrac{4}{3}$ **d)** $\dfrac{11}{3}, -9$
e) $3, -\dfrac{2}{5}$ **f)** $\dfrac{1}{5}, -\dfrac{2}{3}$

9. a) $\dfrac{-4 \pm \sqrt{26}}{2}$ **b)** $-4, \dfrac{2}{3}$ **c)** $\dfrac{7 \pm \sqrt{33}}{2}$
d) $1, -\dfrac{4}{3}$ **e)** $-\dfrac{3}{2}, \dfrac{1}{2}$ **f)** $-\dfrac{2}{3}$

10. a) $\dfrac{3 \pm \sqrt{321}}{4}$ **b)** $\dfrac{5 \pm \sqrt{145}}{4}$ **c)** $2, 8$
d) $10\sqrt{5}$ **e)** $2, 16$ **f)** $2, \dfrac{1}{2}$

11. a) $0.75, 1.17$ **b)** $19.75, -1.00$
c) $0.04, -0.04$ **d)** $-0.44, 1.33$
e) $1.06, 0.50$ **f)** $1.54, -0.97$

12. a) $0, 8$ **b)** $1 \pm \sqrt{14}$ **c)** $\dfrac{-9 \pm \sqrt{97}}{4}$
d) $\dfrac{1 \pm \sqrt{7}}{2}$ **e)** 0.6 **f)** $\dfrac{-15 \pm \sqrt{217}}{2}$

13. a) $0, 4$ **b)** $0, -\dfrac{2}{3}$ **c)** $\dfrac{-5 \pm \sqrt{185}}{10}$
d) $\dfrac{-1 \pm \sqrt{10}}{3}$ **e)** $\dfrac{-4 \pm \sqrt{61}}{3}$
f) No solution

14. a) i) 53.4 m **ii)** 80 m
b) i) 63 km/h **ii)** 110 km/h

15. a) i) 512.28 cm^2 **ii)** 5117.5 cm^2
b) i) 4 cm **ii)** 15 cm

16. $\dfrac{1 + \sqrt{5}}{2}$ **17. a)** $\dfrac{1 \pm \sqrt{5}}{2}$ **b)** $\dfrac{-1 \pm \sqrt{5}}{2}$

18. a) 5 **b)** 17 **c)** 0.5, 5 **d)** $\dfrac{4}{3}$
e) 3.5, 1.5 **f)** No solution

19. a) $\dfrac{-q \pm \sqrt{q^2 - 4pr}}{2q}$ **b)** $\dfrac{-n \pm \sqrt{n^2 + 60}}{6}$

c) $\dfrac{-3 \pm \sqrt{9 + 4k}}{2}$ **d)** $-2 \pm p\sqrt{5}$

e) $\dfrac{-1 \pm \sqrt{1 + 4a}}{6}$ **f)** $-3m, 2n$

20. BM = DN $\doteq$ 2.29 cm

21. a) i) $\dfrac{5 + \sqrt{-3}}{2}$ **ii)** $\dfrac{7 \pm \sqrt{-83}}{6}$

iii) $\dfrac{-5 \pm \sqrt{-23}}{4}$ **iv)** $\dfrac{7 \pm \sqrt{-71}}{6}$

b) If $b^2 - 4ac < 0$ **c)** i and ii

22. a) i) $\dfrac{1 \pm \sqrt{5}}{2}$ **ii)** 2, -1 **iii)** $\dfrac{1 \pm \sqrt{13}}{2}$

iv) $\dfrac{1 \pm \sqrt{17}}{2}$

b) When n is the product of two consecutive integers

23. a) i) $-\dfrac{4}{5}, -45$ **ii)** $-5, \dfrac{21}{4}$ **iii)** $\dfrac{29}{6}, \dfrac{35}{6}$

iv) $\dfrac{6}{5}, -\dfrac{3}{5}$ **b)** Sum $= -\dfrac{b}{a}$, product $= \dfrac{c}{a}$

24. a) $6b^2 = 25ac$ **b)** $mnb^2 = (m + n)^2 ac$

Exercises 4-6, page 131

1. a) 25 **b)** 8 **c)** 0 **d)** -39 **e)** 289
f) -24

2. a) a, b, e **b)** c **c)** d, f

3. a) 2 real **b)** 1 real **c)** 2 real **d)** 2 real
e) 0 real **f)** 1 real

4. a) i) 3, -1 **ii)** 1 **iii)** No solution
b) i) The parabola $x^2 - 2x - 3 = 0$ intersects the x-axis at $(3,0)$ and $(-1,0)$. **ii)** The parabola $x^2 - 2x + 1 = 0$ just touches the x-axis at $(1,0)$.
iii) The parabola $x^2 - 2x + 5 = 0$ does not intersect the x-axis.

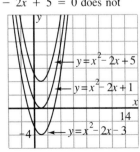

5. a) $q^2 - 4pr > 0$ **b)** $q^2 - 4pr < 0$

6. a) $|k| > 2$ **b)** $k > -\dfrac{4}{3}$ **c)** $|k| > 2\sqrt{6}$

7. a) $\pm 2\sqrt{7}$ **b)** $\dfrac{5}{6}$

8. a) No value of p **b)** $\dfrac{16}{9}$ **c)** $|p| > \dfrac{5}{2}$

9. a, c

10. a) 4, -8 **b)** $k \geqslant 4, k \leqslant -8$
c) $-8 < k < 4$ **11. a)** Yes **b)** No

12. a) i) $-24, -26$ **ii)** -25 **iii)** No solution
b) With 624 there are two different roots, -24 and -26. With 625, there are two equal roots, -25. With 626, there are no real roots.

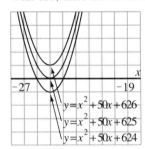

15. i) c, e **ii)** b **iii)** a, d
16. a) When k is a perfect square

b)

k	0	1	4	9	16
Roots	6, 6	8, 4	10, 2	12, 0	14, -2

c) When k is the square of a rational number

Problem Solving, page 135

2. Parallelograms **3.** $x^2 - 2px + q^2 = 0$
4. a) i) $(n - 2)^3$ **ii)** $6(n - 2)^2$ **iii)** $12(n - 2)$
iv) 8 **b)** $(n - 2)(n^2 + 2n + 4)$

Exercises 4-7, page 137

1. a) $x, x + 1$ **b)** $2x + 1, 2x - 1$
c) $x, x + 3$ **d)** $x^2 + (x + 3)^2$

e) $2x(2x + 2)$ **f)** $x^2 + \dfrac{1}{x^2}$

2. a) $\dfrac{80}{x - 12}$ **b)** $(2x + 40)(2x + 60)$

c) $\dfrac{x + 5}{x}$ **d)** $3x - 8x$ **e)** $\dfrac{16\,000}{x - 2} - \dfrac{15\,000}{x}$

f) $0.3x + 5$

3. 5 m   **4.** 16   **5.** 5 cm   **6.** 90 km/h
7. $4.00   **8.** 3 cm, 5 cm, 7 cm
9. 90 km/h   **10.** 35 km/h   **11.** 120 km/h
12. 60 km/h   **13.** 16   **14.** 75   **15.** 2 s
16. 24 min, 40 min   **17.** About 311 km

Review Exercises, page 139

1. a) $4, -7$ **b)** $3, -5$ **c)** $\dfrac{\pm \sqrt{10}}{2}$
d) $\pm 3\sqrt{3}$
2. a) 7.33 cm   **b)** 23.75 mm   **c)** 4 km
3. a) $-6, 0.5$ **b)** $4, -1.5$

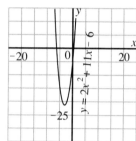

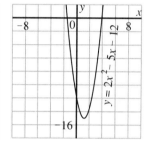

c) ± 2.5 **d)** $1.5, -2.5$

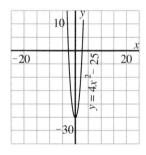

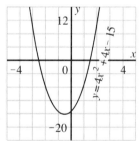

4. a) $7, -2$ **b)** $4, -8$ **c)** $1, -\dfrac{1}{3}$ **d)** $\dfrac{5}{2}, -\dfrac{2}{3}$
5. a) $9, -2$ **b)** $\dfrac{3}{2}, 2$ **c)** $2, -\dfrac{9}{2}$ **d)** $-1, 2$
6. 8 cm, 15 cm, 17 cm   **7.** 6 s
8. a) 10 cm by 15 cm   **b)** 15 cm by 20 cm
9. a) $4 \pm \sqrt{46}$ **b)** $-3 \pm 3\sqrt{11}$
c) $\dfrac{5 \pm \sqrt{17}}{2}$ **d)** $\dfrac{-15 \pm 5\sqrt{5}}{2}$
10. a) $\dfrac{-9 \pm \sqrt{57}}{4}$ **b)** $\dfrac{-1 \pm \sqrt{31}}{6}$
c) $\dfrac{8 \pm \sqrt{29}}{7}$ **d)** $\dfrac{-7 \pm \sqrt{449}}{20}$

11. a) $0.8, -3$ **b)** $2, -5.3$ **c)** 1.72, 1.28
d) $4.33, -3.67$ **e)** $1.75, -0.67$
f) $0.75, -0.8$ **12. a)** 8 cm   **b)** 11 cm
13. a) $\pm 1, \pm 2$ **b)** ± 3 **c)** $\pm \sqrt{2.5}$
d) $\pm 3\sqrt{2}, 0$
14. a) $\dfrac{5}{3}$ **b)** 6   **c)** $\dfrac{31}{3}$ **d)** 3.4   **e)** 0, 3.75
f) $\dfrac{11 \pm \sqrt{57}}{8}$ **15.** 29.2 cm, 34.2 cm
16. a) $m = 4$ or -3 **b)** $m > 4$ or $m < -3$
c) $-3 < m < 4$ **17.** a   **18.** Yes
19. $50   **20.** 90 m, 160 m   **21.** 23 mm
22. 55 m, 30 m   **23.** 50 min, 75 min

Chapter 5

Exercises 5-1, page 146

1. a) {(15, 2), (20, 10), (18, 15), (23, 30), (20, 25), (28, 40)}
b) D: {15, 18, 20, 23, 28};
R: {2, 10, 15, 25, 30, 40}
2. a) {(40, 45), (50, 55), (60, 50), (60, 65), (70, 80), (80, 70), (90, 75), (90, 80)}
b) D: {40, 50, 60, 70, 80, 90};
R: {45, 50, 55, 65, 70, 75, 80}
3. a) {Craig, Colin), (Craig, Gayle), (Colin, Craig), (Colin, Gayle)}
b) D: {Craig, Colin}, R: {Craig, Colin, Gayle}
4. a)

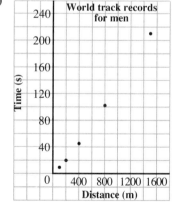

b) D (men, women): {100, 200, 400, 800, 1500}
R (men): {10, 20, 44, 102, 211},
R (women): {11, 22, 48, 113, 232}

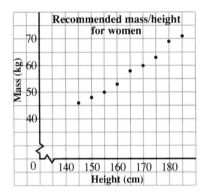

5. a)

b) D: {145, 150, 155, 160, 165, 170, 175, 180, 185}
R: {46, 48, 50, 53, 56, 60, 63, 67, 71}

6. a) D: {−2, −1, 1, 2, 3, 4}; R: {1, −1, 2, 3, −2, 0}
   b) D: {−2, −1, 0, 1, 2, 3}; R: {3, 2, 1, 0, −1, −2}
   c) −4 ≤ x ≤ 1; −1 ≤ y ≤ 3
   d) −3 ≤ x ≤ 3; −3 ≤ y ≤ 2
   e) −2 ≤ x ≤ 2; −2 ≤ y ≤ 2
   f) −4 ≤ x ≤ 2; −2 ≤ y ≤ 2

7. a)

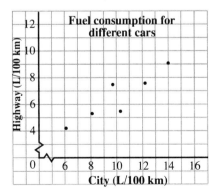

b) D: {6.1, 8.1, 9.7, 10.3, 12.2, 14.0, 18.1}
R: {4.2, 5.3, 5.5, 7.5, 7.6, 9.1, 12.7}

8. a) {(1,1), (1,2), (1,3), (1,4), (1,5), (1,6), (1,7),
(1,8), (1,9), (2,2), (2,4), (2,6), (2,8), (3,3), (3,6),
(3,9), (4,4), (4,8), (5,5), (6,6), (7,7), (8,8), (9,9)}
   b) D: {1, 2, 3, 4, 5, 6, 7, 8, 9}
   R: {1, 2, 3, 4, 5, 6, 7, 8, 9}

9. a) {(Tobie, Lise), (Tobie, Suzette), (Tobie,
Urbain), (Tobie, Claire), (Lise, Suzette), (Lise,
Urbain), (Lise, Claire), (Suzette, Urbain), (Suzette,
Claire), (Urbain, Claire)}
   b) D: (Tobie, Lise, Suzette, Urbain}
   R: {Lise, Suzette, Urbain, Claire}

10. a) x ≥ 0; y ≥ 0   **b)** x ≥ −1; y ≥ 0
   c) D, R; all real numbers   **d)** x ≠ 0; y ≠ 0
   e) x ≠ 2; y ≠ 0   **f)** D: all real numbers: y ≥ 0

11. a) v   **b)** iv   **c)** vi   **d)** iii   **e)** i   **f)** ii

12. a) D: {−1, 0, 1, 2, 3, 5, 6};
   R: {−2, −1, 1, 2, 3, 4}
   b) D, R: all real numbers
   c) −2 ≤ x ≤ 7; −1 ≤ y ≤ 5
   d) −3 ≤ x ≤ 3; −3 ≤ y ≤ 3
   e) x ≥ −2; R: all real numbers
   f) −2 ≤ x < 6; R: {−6, −4, −2, 0}

13. a) D, R: all real numbers   **b)** D, R: all real
numbers

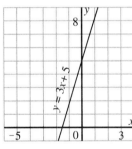
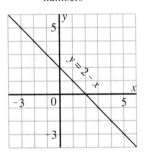

c) D, R: all real numbers   **d)** D: all real
numbers, y ≥ 0

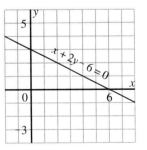
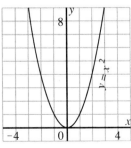

e) $-5 \le x \le 5$;
$-5 \le y \le 5$

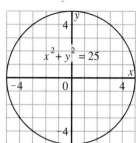

f) $-1 \le x \le 1$;
$-1 \le y \le 1$

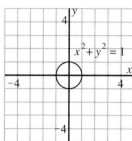

14. a)

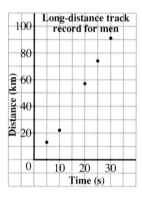

b) D: {5, 10, 20, 25, 30}
R: {13:08, 27:23, 57:24, 74:17, 91:30}

15. a)

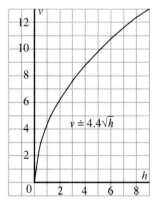

b) $h \ge 0$; $v \ge 0$ **c)** About 11.2 m/s

16. a)

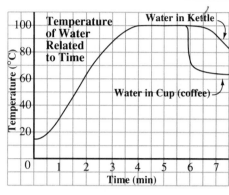

b) D: {0 min $\le t \le$ 7 min}
R: {15°C $\le T \le$ 100°C}

Exercises 5-2, page 154

1. a) Yes   **b)** No   **c)** Yes
2. a) $x \ge 0$; $1 \le y \le 7$ **b)** $x \ge -1$; R: all real
numbers   **c)** $x \ne 0$; $y \ne 0$
3. a) Yes   **b)** No   **c)** Yes
4. a) Yes   **b)** Yes   **c)** Yes   **d)** No   **e)** No
   f) Yes   **g)** No   **h)** No   **i)** Yes
5. a) Yes; D, R: **b)** Yes; D: all real
all real numbers   numbers; $y \ge -1$

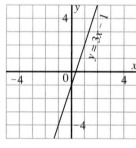 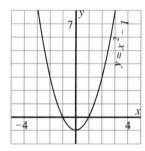

c) No; $x \ge 1$;   **6. a)** Yes
R: all real numbers

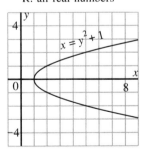 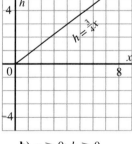

b) $x \ge 0$; $h \ge 0$
c) 4.8 m

7. a) ii   **b)** iv   **c)** i   **d)** iii   **e)** vi   **f)** v

8. a) $w = 12 - x$ **b)** $A = 12x - x^2$
   c) $l = \sqrt{2x^2 - 24x + 144}$

9. a) $w = \dfrac{24}{x}$ **b)** $P = \dfrac{2x^2 + 48}{x}$
   c) $l = \dfrac{\sqrt{x^4 + 576}}{x}$

10. a) D: all real numbers;   **b)** $x \geqslant 0$; $y \geqslant 0$
    $y > 0$

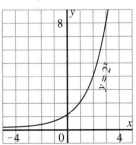

c) D: all real numbers; $y \geqslant 0$

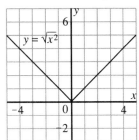

11. a)

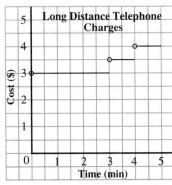

b) $t > 0$
R: $\{3, 3.50, 4, 4.50, 5, 5.50, 6, ...\}$
c) Yes. Every ordered pair has a different first coordinate.

12. a) Yes
   b) $d > 0$; R: $\{2.50, 3.50, 4.50, 5.50, 6.50, 7.50, 8.50, ...\}$

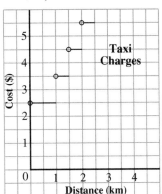

13. a) $x \geqslant 3$; $y \geqslant 0$
   b), c) D, R: all real numbers
   d) $x \neq -2$; $y \neq 0$
   e) D: all real numbers; $y \geqslant 1$
   f) D: all real numbers; $y > 0$

14. a) i) $\dfrac{5(100 - x)}{x}$ **ii)** $y = \dfrac{5x}{100 - x}$
   b) i) $0 < x \leqslant 100$; $y \geqslant 0$
   ii) $0 \leqslant x < 100$; $y \geqslant 0$
   c) i)

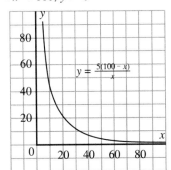

   ii)

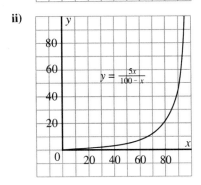

15. a) No   **b)** Yes
c)

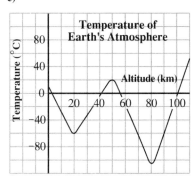

Mathematics Around Us, page 157

1. a) i) Recording thermometer   **ii)** Barograph
iii) Electroencephalogram
iv) Electrocardiogram

Exercises 5-3, page 162

1. a) -3 **b)** -8 **c)** 0.75

2. a) 2 **b)** 14 **c)** $\dfrac{1}{2}$

3. a) $6.9, 0.75$ **b)** $-4, 38, -1$

4. a) i)   **ii)**

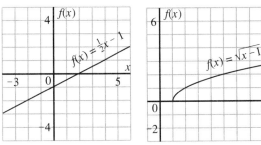

b) i) D, R: all real numbers   **ii)** $x \geqslant 1; y \geqslant 0$

5. a) $2, 4, 2$ **b)** $-1.5, 3, 1$ **c)** $2, -1, 2$

6. a) $3m - 5$ **b)** $12x - 5$ **c)** $6x - 10$
d) $\dfrac{6}{x} - 5$ **e)** $6x - 2$

7. a) $5k + 1$ **b)** $5x - 4$ **c)** $10x + 6$
d) $21 - 15x$

8. a) $1, -27, -5$ **b)** $25, 186, -6.5$
c) $\sqrt{11}, \sqrt{-31}, \sqrt{2}$ **d)** $4.5, 24.8, 2.25$
e) $4, -150, -0.125$ **f)** $\dfrac{8}{5}, \dfrac{20}{9}, 1$

9. a) D, R: all real
numbers

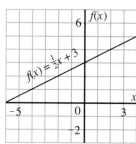

b) D: all real numbers;
$y \geqslant 1$

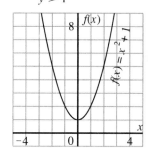

c) D: all real numbers; $y \geqslant -2.25$

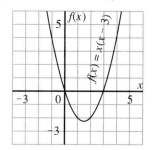

10. a)   **b)**

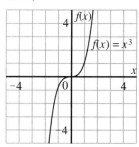

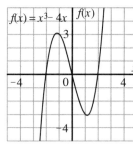

c)   **d)**

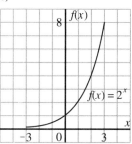

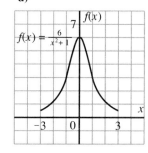

11. a) $x \geq -5; y \geq 0$ **b)** $x \neq -2; y \neq 0$
   c) D, R: all real numbers
   d) D: all real numbers; $y \geq 3$
   e) D, R: all real numbers
   f) $x \geq 0, y \geq 1$

12. a) $2x^2 + 7x$ **b)** $2x^2 + 11x + 9$
   c) $2x^2 + 15x + 22$ **d)** $8x^2 + 6x - 5$
   e) $18x^2 + 9x - 5$ **f)** $2x^2 - 3x - 5$

13. a) $-2x - 9$ **b)** $11x + 3$
   c) $15x^2 + 11x - 14$ **d)** $2x - 22$
   e) $-4x - 9$ **f)** $48x + 8$

14. a) i) 2   **ii)** 4   **iii)** 6   **iv)** -2 **v)** -4
   vi) -6
   b)

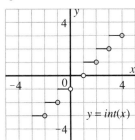

15. a) $x \geq 0; A \geq 0$
   b) It is quadrupled.
   c) $\dfrac{\sqrt{3}}{4}(6x + 9)$
   d) $\dfrac{\sqrt{3}}{4}(h^2 - 2hx)$

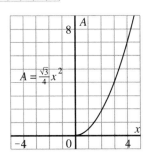

16. a) $\dfrac{4}{7}$ **b)** $\dfrac{2}{7}$ **c)** -6 **d)** $-\dfrac{1}{2}$ or -1

17. a) 1   **b)** -6 **c)** $-\dfrac{3}{2}$

18. a) $-5, 2$ **b)** $-6, 3$ **c)** $-4, 1$

19. a)   **b)**

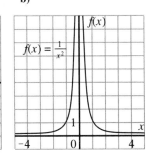

20. a) 1   **b)** 1   **c)** $n \in R, n \neq 0, -1$
21. b) $[g(x)]^n$ **22. b)** $f(x) = 3x$
23. a)

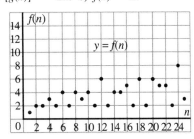

   b) i) Primes   **ii)** Squares of primes
   iii) Products of primes, or cubes of primes
   iv) 4th powers of primes

Exercises 5-4, page 167

1. a) i) 0, 7, 14, 28   **ii)** $-3, -9, -12, -15$
   iii) 1, 2, 3, 4   **iv)** 2, 4, 8, 10
2. a) y is doubled.   **b)** y is halved.
3. a) $y = \dfrac{2}{3}x$ **b)** 14   **c)** 22.5
4. a) $x : 2; y : 6, 24, 73.5$ **b)** $x: 5, 8; y : 2, 72$
5. a) $V = 0.075m$ **c)**
   b) 4.5 L
   d) $f(m) = 0.075m$

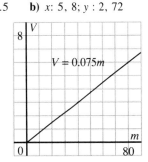

6. a) $d = 0.2v$ **c)**
   b) 3 km
   d) $f(v) = 0.2v$

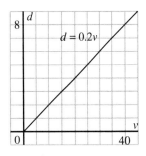

7. a) i) 2.14 L   **ii)** 1.93 L
   b) i) 293°C   **ii)** -131.5°C
8. a) Doubled   **b)** Tripled   **c)** Halved
9. Mercury 89, Venus 225, Earth 365, Mars 691,
   Jupiter 4355, Saturn 10 739, Uranus 31 017,
   Neptune 60 985, Pluto 91 642

Exercises 5-5, page 172

1. a, b, d

2. a)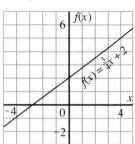
b)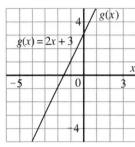

c)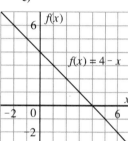
d)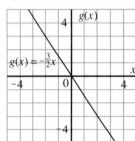

3. a)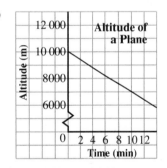

b) $h = -300t + 10\,000$

4. a)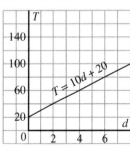
b) 58°C

5. a) C   b) A   c) B

6. a)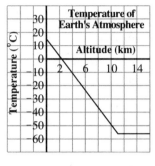
b) $t \doteq 6.5h + 15$
c) i) $-30.5°C$
   ii) 2.3 km

7. a) $y = \frac{2}{3}x$
b) 2.0 m
c) 4.5 m
d) $1.4 \leq x \leq 5.0$

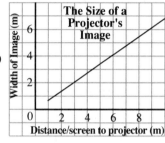

8. a) $l = 12 - w$ b) $0 < w < 12$
9. a) $y = x + 90; 0 < x < 90$
b) $y = 230 - x; 50 < x < 180$
c) $y = 180 - 2x; 0 < x < 90$

10.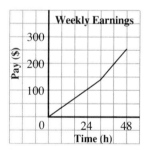

11.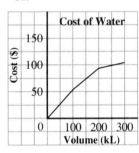

12. a) First line segment and fourth line segment: fuel decreasing at a constant rate
Second line segment: fuel stays constant as time passes — car has stopped
Third line segment: fuel increases suddenly — car is filling up with gas.
b) Yes, a vertical line cuts graph at only one point.
c) 10 L/100 km

13. a) $\frac{2}{5}, 7$ b) $-\frac{4}{3}, 10$ c) $-2, 4$ d) $3, -6$
e) $-4, 0$ f) $-\frac{4}{7}, \frac{37}{7}$

14. a) $h = 3l + 70$ b) 185 cm

15. a)

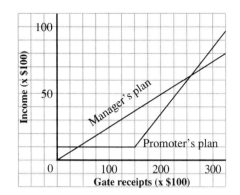

b) For gate receipts between $40 000 and $260 000

16. a) $x + y = 8$　　**b)** $2 < x < 8$

17. a) $\dfrac{8\pi}{3}R$　　**b)** $3\pi R$

Mathematics Around Us, page 177

1. b) About 3 min 38 s　　**c)** About 2008

Mathematics Around Us, page 178

1.

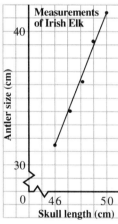

Answers may vary.
$y = 2.415x - 79.57$

2. Answers may vary.　　**a)** 35.1 cm　　**b)** 49.5 cm
3. The rate of growth is the slope of the graph.

Mathematics Around Us, page 179

1. Answers may vary. $y = 22x - 190$, where x is the age and y is the distance. The slope of the line is the average speed of the rock movement in kilometres per million years.
2. a) About 77 million years　　**b)** 2.2 cm/year

Exercises 5-6, page 182

1. a) i) Undefined, 60, 30, 15
　　ii) $-12, -4, -3, -2.4$
　　iii) 20, 10, 6.$\overline{6}$, 5　　**iv)** 15, 7.5, 3.75, 3
　　b) i) $y = \dfrac{60}{x}$　**ii)** $y = \dfrac{-12}{x}$　**iii)** $y = \dfrac{80}{x}$
　　iv) $y = \dfrac{45}{x}$

2. a) y is halved.　　**b)** y is doubled.

3. a) $y = \dfrac{40}{x}$　**b)** 10　**c)** 2

4. a) $y = \dfrac{60}{x}$　**b)** 2　**c)** 5

5. a) $x : 3, y : 30, 10, 4$
　　b) $x: -0.5, 0.2; y : 4, -3$

6. a) $t = \dfrac{48}{v}$　**d)**

b) i) 4 h
ii) 2.4 h
c) 24 km/h

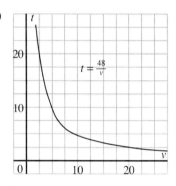

7. a) i) 30 r/min　**c)**
ii) 24 r/min
b) 16

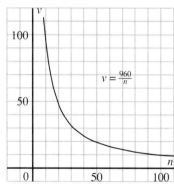

8. 75 r/min　　**9. a)** 7 h　　**b)** About 906 km/h
10. 55 L　　**11. a)** Halved　　**b)** Divided by 3
　　c) Doubled

12. a)

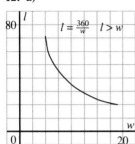

b)

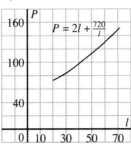

c) i) Yes   **ii)** No

13. a) y decreases by 20%.
b) y increases by 25%.

Problem Solving, page 185

1. 2.4 cm   **2.** $(65 + 20\pi)$ cm
3. 36   **4.** 2 min 7 s
5. $4\sqrt{2}, \dfrac{8\sqrt{2}}{3}, \dfrac{8\sqrt{2}}{3}$ **6.** 260
8. $-1 \leqslant x \leqslant 2.25, x \neq 0$

Exercises 5-7, page 188

1. a) $s = km^2$ **b)** $s = \dfrac{k}{\sqrt{m}}$ **c)** $s = kmn$
d) $s = k\dfrac{m^2}{n}$

2. a) A varies jointly with b and h.
b) A varies directly as r^2.
c) I varies jointly with p, r, and t.
d) v varies jointly with r^2 and h.
e) d varies directly with m and inversely with v.
f) F varies directly with m and n, and inversely with d^2.

3. a) $y = 5x^2$ **b)** 180   **c)** ± 4
4. a) $y = \dfrac{2.4}{x^2}$ **b)** 0.096   **c)** ± 2
5. a) $m = \dfrac{d^3}{125}$ **d)**

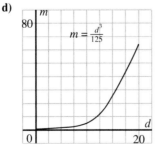

b) 8 carats
c) About 6.3 mm

6. a) $A \doteq 3.14d^2$ **b)** 1548 cm²
7. a) $V \doteq 0.52d^3$ **b)** 7579 cm³
8. 1440
9. a) i) 16 units   **ii)** 5.76 units   **b) i)** 69 m
ii) 40 m
10. 5.4 h   **11. a)** About 45 km
b) About 12.3 km
12. a) Quadrupled   **b)** Divided by 4
13. a) Multiplied by $\sqrt{2}$ **b)** Divided by $\sqrt{2}$
14. a) $w = 7.5st$ **b)** 180   **c)** 2   **d)** $0.\overline{6}$
15. a) $r = \dfrac{0.6p^2}{t}$ **b)** 3.2   **c)** $2\sqrt{5}$ **d)** 10
16. a) i) About 118 kg   **ii)** 40.5 kg
b) About 0.798 g/cm³
17. a) Multiplied by 8   **b)** Divided by 8
18. a) Multiplied by $2\sqrt{2}$ **b)** Divided by $2\sqrt{2}$
19. a) About 27 400 km/h   **b)** About 3630 km/h
20. 2680 L
21. a) 52, 14; 39, 28   **b)** About 51 km/h
22. a) $I = \dfrac{160}{d^2}$ **b)** I does not vary inversely as d.
c) Graph I against d^2.

Review Exercises, page 191

1. a) D, R: all real numbers   **b)** $x \geqslant 0.5, y \geqslant 0$
c) D: all real numbers, $y \geqslant 0$
2. a) D: $\{-1, 0, 2, 3, 4, 6\}$; R: $\{-1, 1, 2, 3, 5\}$
b) $x \geqslant -1; y \geqslant 1$
c) $-5 \leqslant x \leqslant 5; -3 \leqslant y \leqslant 3$
3. a)

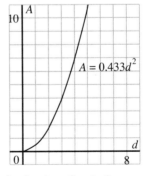

b) $d > 0; A > 0$
c) 20 cm

4. a) $x \geqslant -2; y \geqslant 0$
b), c) D, R: all real numbers
d) $x \neq 1; y \neq 0$ **e)** D: all real numbers; $y \leqslant 1$
f) D: all real numbers; $y > 0$
5. a) $3x^2 + 2x + 8$ **b)** $12x^2 - 20x + 12$
c) $27x^2 - 30x + 12$

6. a) $\dfrac{1}{2}$ **b)** $-\dfrac{1}{4}$ **c)** $-\dfrac{10}{17}$ **d)** 1 or -2

7. a) 2 or -7 **b)** -2 or -3 **c)** 3 or -8

8.

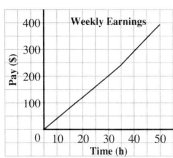

9. a) $\dfrac{3}{5}$, 11   **b)** -1, 3   **c)** $\dfrac{2}{3}$, $\dfrac{10}{3}$ **d)** -6, 5

10. a) $y = 1.6x$ **b)** 6.4   **c)** 11.25

11. a) D: all real numbers;   **b)** D: all real numbers;

$y \geqslant -\dfrac{64}{3}$ $y \leqslant \dfrac{81}{40}$

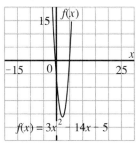 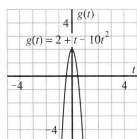

12. a) $w = 7h$ **b)** 28 m

13. a)

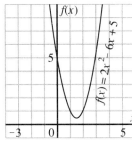

b) i) About 58 L
ii) About 760 km
c) i) 8.2 L/100 km
ii) About 885 km
d) $0 \leqslant d \leqslant 885$;
     $0 \leqslant n \leqslant 72.5$

14. a) $d = \dfrac{60}{w}$ **b)** 5 days   **15.** $n = \dfrac{72}{r}$

16. a) $t = \dfrac{40}{r}$ **b)** 8 min   **c)** 20 L/min

17. 11.25 m³   **18.** 500 kg   **19.** About 302Ω

Chapter 6

Exercises 6-1, page 196

1. a), c), d), e) Yes   **b), f)** No

2. a)   **3. a)**

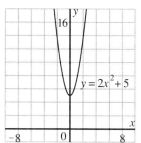 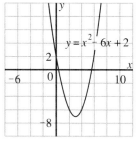

b) D; all real numbers;   **b)** D: all real numbers;
   $y \geqslant 5$ $y \geqslant -7$

4. a)   **b)** $t \geqslant 0$; $0 \leqslant h \leqslant 82$
                         c) 51.4 m

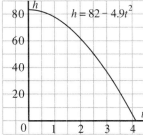

5. a)   **b)** 42.5 cm

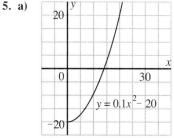

6. a) D: all real numbers;   **b)** D: all real numbers;
   $y \geqslant 0.5$ $y \leqslant 5$

7. a)

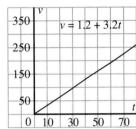

$v = 1.2 + 3.2t$

b) 289 m/s, 13 068 m

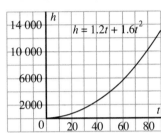

$h = 1.2t + 1.6t^2$

8. a) 593.5 m   **b)** 11.5 s
9. a) Height is quadrupled.
   b) Height is multiplied by 9.
10. a) $A = \pi x^2 - 20x\pi + 100\pi$
   b)
   $A = 3.14x^2 - 62.8x + 314.16$

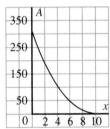

c) $0 < x < 10$

11. a) $A = (16 - 4\pi)r^2$ **b)** $A = (2\sqrt{2} - 1)\pi r^2$
12. 2 min, 8.5 h, 9 days, 15 years
13. a) $k \doteq 1.56$ m/s²   **b)** 66 m

Exercises 6-2, page 199

1. a)

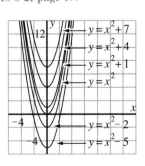

$y = x^2 + 7$
$y = x^2 + 4$
$y = x^2 + 1$
$y = x^2$
$y = x^2 - 2$
$y = x^2 - 5$

b) The vertex is on the y-axis. When q is positive, the vertex is q units above the x-axis. When q is negative, it is q units below the x-axis.
2. a) iii   **b)** iv   **c)** ii   **d)** i
3. a) $y = x^2 + 5$ **b)** $y = x^2$ **c)** $y = x^2 - 2$
   d) $y = x^2 - 6$
4. a) i) up   **ii)** (0, 1)   **iii)** 1
   b) i) up   **ii)** (0, −4)   **iii)** −4   **iv)** ±2
   c) i) up   **ii)** (0, 3)   **iii)** 3
   d) i) up   **ii)** (0, −6)   **iii)** −6   **iv)** ±2.5
5. a) i) up   **ii)** (0, 5)   **iii)** 5
   b) i) up   **ii)** (0, −3)   **iii)** −3   **iv)** ±1.7
   c) i) up   **ii)** (0, 2)   **iii)** 2
   d) i) up   **ii)** (0, 4)   **iii)** 4
6. a)   **b)**

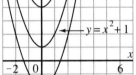
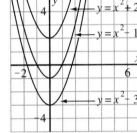

7. a) $y = x^2 + 2$ **b)** $y = x^2 - 9$
   c) $y = x^2 + 5$

Exercises 6-3, page 203

1. a)   **b)**

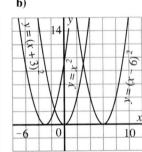
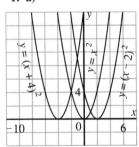

c)

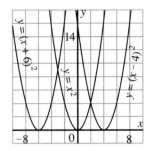

2. a) When $p < 0$, the graph of $y = (x - p)^2$ is to the left of that of $y = x^2$.
  b) When $p > 0$, the graph of $y = (x - p)^2$ is to the right of that of $y = x^2$.

3. a) iii   **b)** i   **c)** iv   **d)** ii

4. a) $y = (x + 2)^2$ **b)** $y = (x - 3)^2$
  c) $y = (x + 4)^2$ **d)** $y = (x - 5)^2$

5. a) i) $(-2,0)$ **ii)** $x + 2 = 0$ **iii)** up
  iv) 4
  b) i) $(-1,0)$ **ii)** $x + 1 = 0$ **iii)** up
  iv) 1
  c) i) $(3,0)$ **ii)** $x - 3 = 0$ **iii)** up   **iv)** 9
  d) i) $(4,0)$ **ii)** $x - 4 = 0$ **iii)** up   **iv)** 16

6. a) $y = (x + 2)^2$ **b)** $y = (x + 1)^2$
  c) $y = (x - 3)^2$ **d)** $y = (x - 4)^2$

7. a) i) $(-3,0)$ **ii)** $x + 3 = 0$ **iii)** up
  iv) 9
  b) i) $(8,0)$ **ii)** $x - 8 = 0$ **iii)** up   **iv)** 64
  c) i) $(2,0)$ **ii)** $x - 2 = 0$ **iii)** up   **iv)** 4
  d) i) $(-4,0)$ **ii)** $x + 4 = 0$ **iii)** up
  iv) 16

8. a)

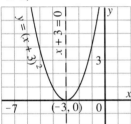

b)

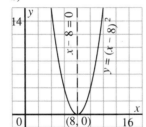

c)

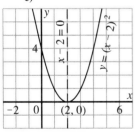

d)

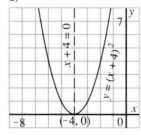

9. a)

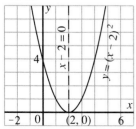

b)

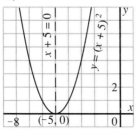

c)

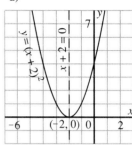

d)

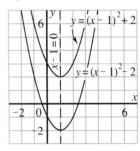

10. a) $y = (x - 4)^2$ **b)** $y = (x + 3)^2$
  c) $y = (x - 7)^2$

11. a)

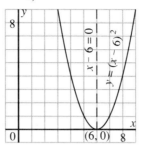

b)

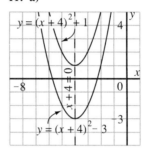

c)

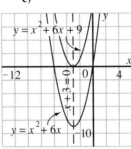

d)

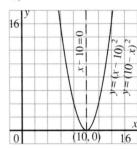

Computer Power, page 205

1. a)

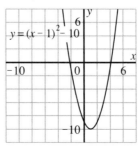

b)

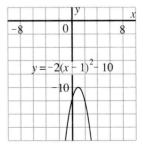

c)

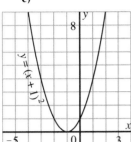

d)

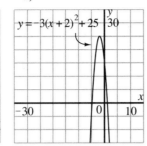

$y = -3(x + 2)^2 + 25$

e)

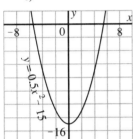

$y = 0.5x^2 - 15$

f)

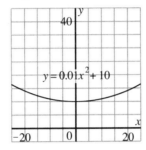

$y = 0.01x^2 + 10$

2. a) PARABOLA $\quad 2 \quad 0 \quad 0$
b) PARABOLA $\quad -1 \quad 0 \quad 0$
c) PARABOLA $\quad 1 \quad 0 \quad -16$
d) PARABOLA $\quad 3 \quad 2 \quad -20$
e) PARABOLA $\quad 1 \quad -2 \quad 0$
f) PARABOLA $\quad -4 \quad 2 \quad 20$

3. a)

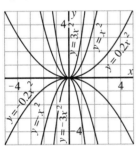

b) PARABOLA $\quad 1 \quad 0 \quad 20$
PARABOLA $\quad 1 \quad 0 \quad 10$
PARABOLA $\quad 1 \quad 0 \quad 0$
PARABOLA $\quad 1 \quad 0 \quad -10$
PARABOLA $\quad 1 \quad 0 \quad -20$

Exercises 6-4, page 209

1. a)

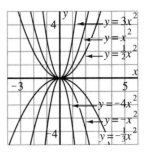

$y = 3x^2$
$y = x^2$
$y = \frac{1}{2}x^2$
$y = -4x^2$
$y = -x^2$
$y = -\frac{1}{3}x^2$

b) The parabola is expanded more: as a increases when $a > 0$; and as a decreases when $a < 0$.

2. a) iii **b)** ii **c)** i **d)** iv

3. a)

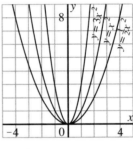

b)

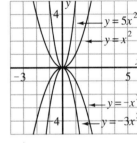

$y = 5x^2$
$y = x^2$
$y = -x^2$
$y = -3x^2$

c)

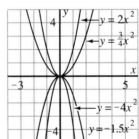

$y = 2x^2$
$y = \frac{3}{4}x^2$
$y = -4x^2$
$y = -1.5x^2$

d)

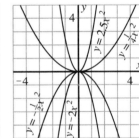

$y = 2.5x^2$
$y = \frac{1}{4}x^2$
$y = -\frac{1}{2}x^2$
$y = -2x^2$

4. a) $y = 2x^2$ **b)** $y = -x^2$ **c)** $y = -\frac{1}{4}x^2$
d) $y = 6x^2$

5. a) $y = -2.5x^2$ **b)** $y = \frac{5}{9}x^2$ **c)** $y = \frac{4}{27}x^2$
d) $y = -3x^2$

6. $y = \frac{3}{4}x^2$

Exercises 6-5, page 211

1. a) i   **b)** iii   **c)** iv   **d)** ii

2. a)

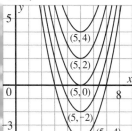

b)

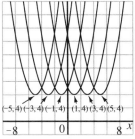

c)

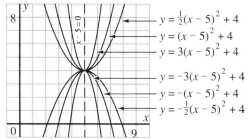

3. a) i) (5,2)   **ii)** $x - 5 = 0$ **iii)** 27
  b) i) $(-3, -8)$ **ii)** $x + 3 = 0$ **iii)** 10
  iv) $-1, -5$ **c) i)** $(-1, 4)$ **ii)** $x + 1 = 0$
  iii) 0   **iv)** $0, -2$ **d) i)** $(2, -8)$ **ii)** $x - 2 = 0$
  iii) -6 **iv)** $6, -2$

4. a)

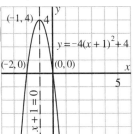

b)

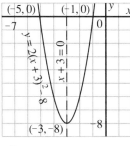

c)

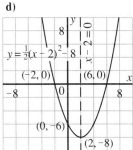

d)

5. a)

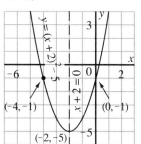

b)

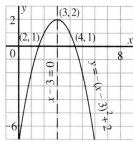

c)

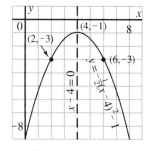

d)

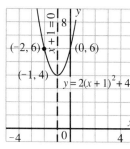

e)

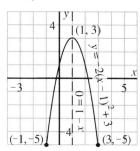

f)

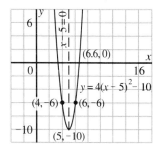

6. a)

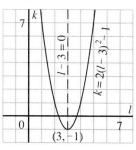

b)

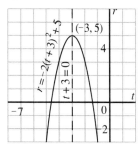

c)

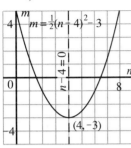

$m = \frac{1}{2}(n - 4)^2 - 3$

$n - 4 = 0$

$(4, -3)$

d)

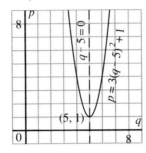

$q - 5 = 0$

$p = 3(q - 5)^2 + 1$

$(5, 1)$

e)

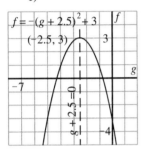

$f = -(g + 2.5)^2 + 3$

$(-2.5, 3)$

$g + 2.5 = 0$

f)

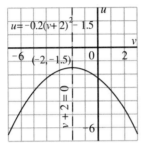

$u = -0.2(v + 2)^2 - 1.5$

$(-2, -1.5)$

$v + 2 = 0$

7. a) $y = 2(x - 4)^2 - 1$

b) $y = -\frac{1}{3}(x + 2)^2 + 3$

c) $y = -\frac{1}{2}(x + 3)^2 + 2$

d) $y = (x - 3)^2 - 4$

8. a) $y = (x - 3)^2 - 1$

b) $y = -2(x + 1)^2 + 4$

c) $y = 3(x - 2)^2 - 27$

9. a) If $a > 0$ the parabola opens upward, and if $a < 0$ it opens downward. As the magnitude $|a|$ increases, the parabola becomes narrower and "closes up"; that is, the parabola is expanded vertically with increasing $|a|$.

b) As p increases, the parabola is translated to the right along the line $y = 3$. As p decreases, the parabola is translated to the left along the line $y = 3$.

c) As q increases, the parabola is translated upward along the line $x = 4$. As q decreases, the parabola is translated downward along the line $x = 4$.

10. a) $y = x^2 + 5$ **b)** $y = -\frac{1}{2}x^2 + 3$

1. a)

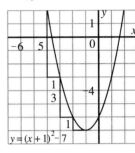

$y = (x - 3)^2 + 5$

b)

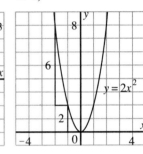

$y = (x + 1)^2 - 7$

c)

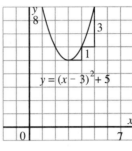

$y = -(x - 2)^2 + 3$

2. a)

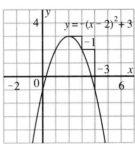

$y = 2x^2$

b)

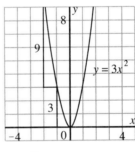

$y = 3x^2$

c)

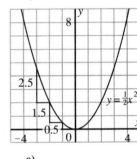

$y = \frac{1}{2}x^2$

d)

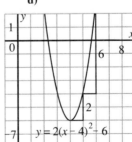

$y = 2(x - 4)^2 - 6$

e)

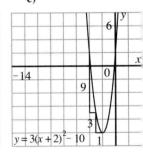

$y = 3(x + 2)^2 - 10$

f)

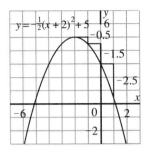

$y = -\frac{1}{2}(x + 2)^2 + 5$

Exercises 6-6, page 215

1. a) $y = (x - 3)^2 - 1$ **b)** $y = (x + 5)^2 - 11$
  c) $y = 2(x + 1)^2 + 5$ **d)** $y = -2(x - 1)^2 + 7$
  e) $y = 3(x - 4)^2 - 8$
  f) $y = -5(x + 2)^2 - 10$

2. a)

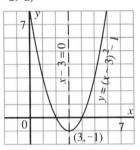

b)

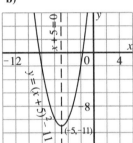

c)

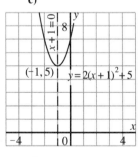

d)

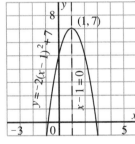

e)

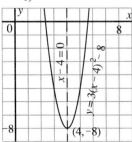

f)

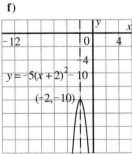

3. a)

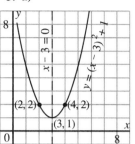

b)

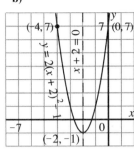

c)

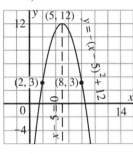

d)

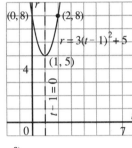

e)

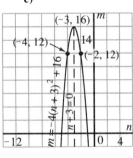

f)

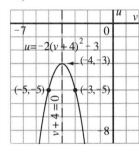

4. a)

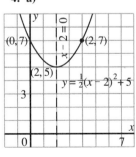

b)

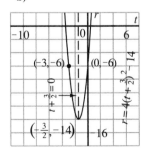

c)

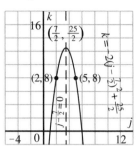

d)

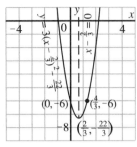

e)

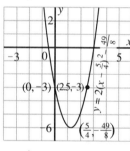

f)

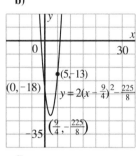

5. a)

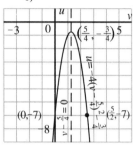

b)

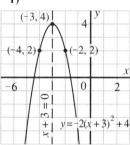

c)

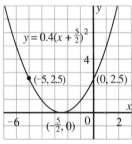

d)

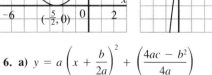

6. a) $y = a\left(x + \dfrac{b}{2a}\right)^2 + \left(\dfrac{4ac - b^2}{4a}\right)$

b) $\left(-\dfrac{b}{2a}, \dfrac{4ac - b^2}{4a}\right)$, $x + \dfrac{b}{2a} = 0$, c

Exercises 6-7, page 219

1. a) max., 4, 1   **b)** min. -4, 3
c) min. -1, -2 **d)** max., 2, -3
e) min., -8, 5   **f)** max., 3, 2

2. a) 5, min., 3   **b)** -3, min., -1
c) 4, max., 1   **d)** -6, max., -2
e) -9, min., 0   **f)** 7, max., 0

3. a) Yes, -5 **b)** No   **c)** Yes, 3   **d)** Yes, 0
e) No   **f)** Yes, -4

4. a) i) $y = 2(x - 2)^2 + 7$
ii) $y = 3(x + 2)^2 - 19$
iii) $y = (x - 3)^2 - 2$
iv) $y = -2(x - 1.5)^2 + 15.5$
v) $y = -(x + 1.5)^2 - 0.75$
vi) $y = 1.5(x - 3)^2 - 3.5$
b) i) 7, min   **ii)** 2
i) -19, min.   **ii)** -2
i) -2, min.   **ii)** 3
i) 15.5, max.   **ii)** 1.5
i) -0.75, max.   **ii)** -1.5
i) -3.5, min.   **ii)** 3

5. a) 4.8 m   **b)** 0.6 s   **c)** 1.58 s   **d)** 3 m
6. a) 9 A   **b)** 40.5 W   **7.** 16.2 m, 1.8 s
8. a) 40 m   **b)** 1 s   **c)** 3.8 s   **d)** 35 m
e) $h = -5t^2 + 10t$

9.

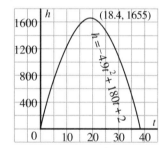

a) 1650 m   **b)** 18 s   **c)** 37 s
10. $b = \pm 2\sqrt{ac}$, $a > 0$, $c \geqslant 0$

Exercises 6-8, page 224

1. 4, -4 **2.** 6, -6 **3.** 30, 30   **4.** 10, -10
5. 8, 8   **6.** 14, 14   **7.** 9, 3
8. 7, -9 **9.** 150 m by 300 m   **10.** 5000 m²
11. a) 400 m²   **b)** 20 m by 20 m
12. 100 m by 150 m   **13.** $15
14. 70¢   **15.** 12.5 cm   **16.** 28.125 cm²
17. 300 m by 200 m   **18.** 14.1 cm, 15.9 cm
19. $\dfrac{1}{2}$ **20.** $\dfrac{p^2}{16}$ units²   **22.** 3.33

Problem Solving, page 229

1. (1, 2, 11, 12); (3, 4, 9, 10); (5, 6, 7, 8)

2. 60 060 **3.** $4\sqrt{11}$

4. Ken Laird, Louise Port, Max King

5. Many solutions are possible, for example,
{1, 2, 3, 4, 5, 6}, {8, 9, 10} and {3, 4, 6, 10},
{1, 2, 5, 8, 9}

6. 69 **7. b)** The second triangle

Review Exercises, page 230

1. a)

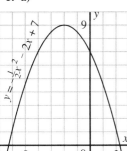

b)

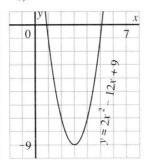

2. a) 2.78 m **b)** 3.26 m

3. a) $y = (x + 2)^2$ **b)** $y = (x - 5)^2$
   c) $y = (x + 6)^2$

4. a) $y = 4x^2$ **b)** $y = -2x^2$ **c)** $y = \frac{3}{2}x^2$

   d) $y = \frac{5}{3}x^2$ **e)** $y = -\frac{3}{2}x^2$ **f)** $y = \frac{3}{4}x^2$

   g) $y = \frac{4}{5}x^2$ **h)** $y = -2x^2$

5. a) $y = -(x + 3)^2 + 4$
   b) $y = 2(x - 2)^2 - 2$
   c) $y = \frac{1}{2}(x - 4)^2 - 4$

6. a)

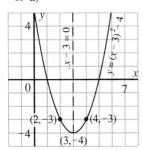

b)

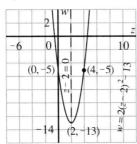

c)

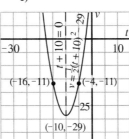

d)

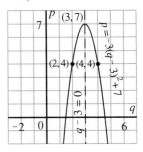

7. 10, $40 **8.** 11, -13 **9.** 90¢

Cumulative Review, Chapters 4-6, page 231

1. a) $\pm\sqrt{2}$ **b)** $\pm\sqrt{3.5}$ **c)** $\pm\sqrt{6.5}$
2. a) $-2.5, 8$ **b)** -1.5

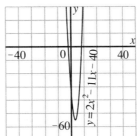

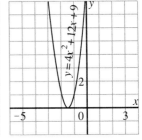

3. a) $-3, 5$ **b)** $1, -6$ **c)** 0.4, 8
   d) 0.75, -7 **e)** ± 1.25 **f)** $-\frac{2}{3}$

4. a) $\frac{1 \pm \sqrt{21}}{4}$ **b)** $\frac{-7 \pm \sqrt{145}}{8}$ **c)** $-2, -\frac{1}{3}$

   d) $\frac{-1 \pm \sqrt{34}}{3}$ **e)** $\frac{1 \pm \sqrt{201}}{10}$

   f) $\frac{15 \pm \sqrt{33}}{8}$

5. a), b) Two different real roots **c)** Two equal
   real roots **d)** No real roots

6. a) All values **b)** $k > -0.75$

7. a) $-6 < p < 6$ **b)** $p > 0.75$

8. About 2.9 cm **9.** 28 cm, 12 cm

10. a) $-2 \leqslant x \leqslant 6$; $-1 \leqslant y \leqslant 2$
   b) D: all real numbers; $y \geqslant 4$

   c) $x \geqslant \frac{4}{3}$; $y \geqslant 0$ **d)** $x \neq -3$; $y \neq 0$

11. b), c) Represent functions

12. a) $-6, 4$ **b)** $-5, 3$ **c)** $-7, 5$

13. a)

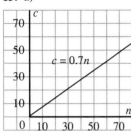

b) $c = 0.7n$
c) i) 10.5 cups
ii) 24.5 cups   **iii)** 59 cups
d) About 69 customers

14. a) m: 18, 38.72; c: 10, $5\sqrt{6}$
b) t: 36, 51.84; y: 24, 3.6

15. About 16.6 cm

16. a)

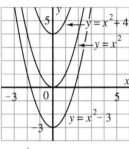

b)

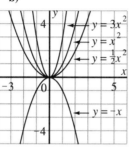

c)

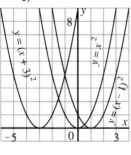

d)

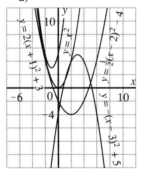

17. a) i) $(-7, 0)$ **ii)** $x + 7 = 0$ **iii)** up
iv) 147   **b) i)** $(3, 4)$ **ii)** $x - 3 = 0$
iii) down   **iv)** -14 **c) i)** $\left(\frac{1}{2}, -\frac{3}{4}\right)$

ii) $x - \frac{1}{2} = 0$ **iii)** down   **iv)** -1
d) i) $(-6, 3)$ **ii)** $x + 6 = 0$ **iii)** up
iv) 15

18. a) $y = \frac{7}{4}x^2$ **b)** $y = 12(x + 1)^2 + 4$
c) $y = -3(x + 3)^2 - 2$
d) $y = \frac{5}{4}(x - 3)^2 - \frac{5}{4}$ **19.** 500 m²

Chapter 7

Exercises 7-1, page 238

1. a) Absolute value   **b)** Exponential
c) Square root   **d)** Cubic   **e)** Reciprocal
2. a) Exponential   **b)** Quadratic   **c)** Linear
d) Cubic   **e)** Exponential   **f)** Reciprocal
g) Reciprocal   **h)** Exponential   **i)** Square root
j) Exponential
3. a) i) 3   **ii)** 4.5
iii) -2.7
b) Slope is 1,
y-intercept is 0.
c) Answers may vary.

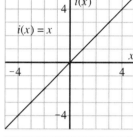

4. a) i) 5   **ii)** 5
iii) 5
b) Slope is 0,
y-intercept is 5.
c) Answers may vary.

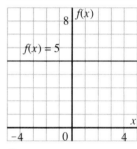

5. a) i)

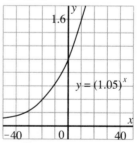

ii)

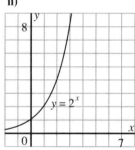

iii)

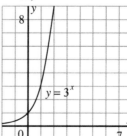

b) i), ii), iii)
D: all real numbers;
$y > 0$

6. a) i), ii), iii)   **iv), v), vi)**

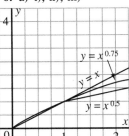   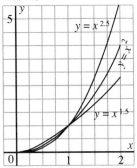

b) $0 \leq x \leq 2$ **i)** $0 \leq y \leq \sqrt{2}$
ii) $0 \leq y \leq 2^{0.75}$ **iii)** $0 \leq y \leq 2$
iv) $0 \leq y \leq 2^{1.5}$ **v)** $0 \leq y \leq 4$
vi) $0 \leq x \leq 2^{2.5}$

7. None is a function.
   a)   **b)**

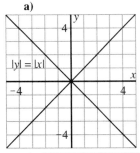   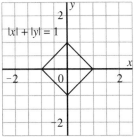

   c)

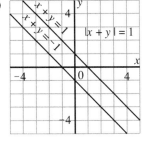

Exercises 7-2, page 241

1. a) iv   **b)** ii   **c)** iii
2. a)   **b)**

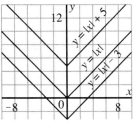   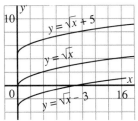

3. a) i   **b)** iv
4. a)   **b)**

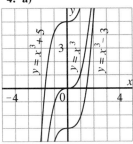   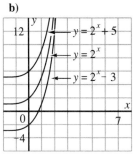

   c)

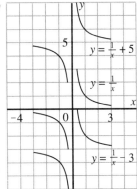

5. a)   **b)**

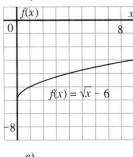   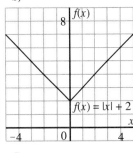

   c)   **d)**

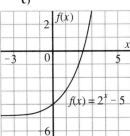   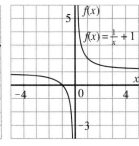

e)

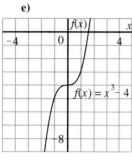

6.

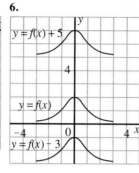

c)

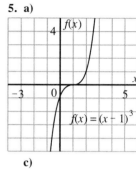

5. a)

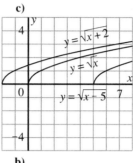

Exercises 7-3, page 245

1. a) i   **b)** v   **c)** iv

2. a)

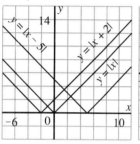

b)

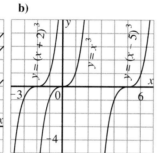

b)

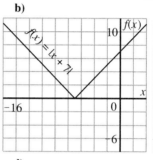

c)

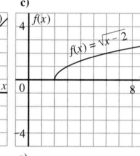

3. a) ii   **b)** iii

4. a)

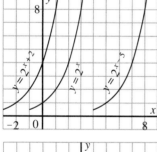

d)

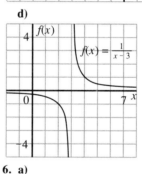

e)

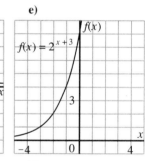

b)

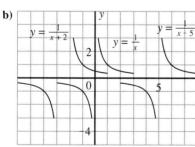

6. a)

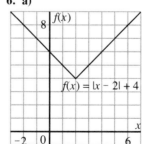

b)

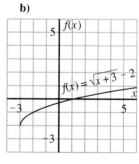

c)

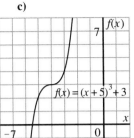

$f(x) = (x+5)^3 + 3$

d)

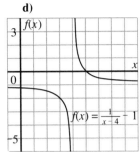

$f(x) = \frac{1}{x-4} - 1$

b)

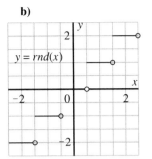

$y = rnd(x)$

Exercises 7-4, page 249

1. a) iii   **b)** i   **c)** ii

2. a)

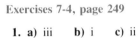

b)

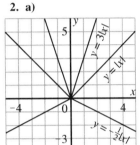

7.

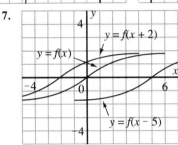

$y = f(x+2)$

$y = f(x)$

$y = f(x-5)$

3. a) ii   **b)** iii

4. a)

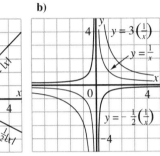

b)

8. a)

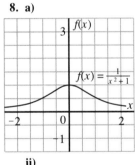

$f(x) = \frac{1}{x^2+1}$

b) i)

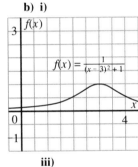

$f(x) = \frac{1}{(x-3)^2+1}$

ii)

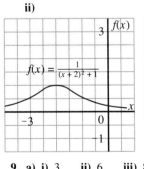

$f(x) = \frac{1}{(x+2)^2+1}$

iii)

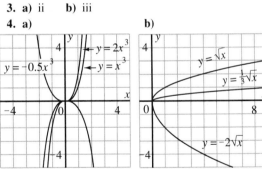

$y = \frac{1}{(x+5)^2+1}$

c)

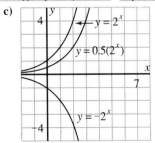

$y = 2^x$

$y = 0.5(2^x)$

$y = -2^x$

9. a) i) 3   **ii)** 6   **iii)** 8   **iv)** -2 **v)** -4
    vi) -7
    c) 0.5

5. a)

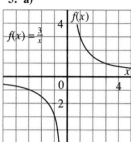

$f(x) = \frac{3}{x}$

b)

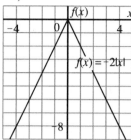

$f(x) = -2|x|$

c)

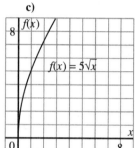

$f(x) = 5\sqrt{x}$

d)

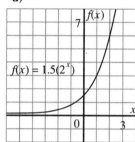

$f(x) = 1.5(2^x)$

6. a)

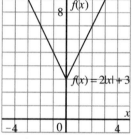

$f(x) = 2|x| + 3$

b)

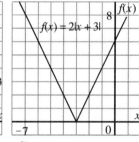

$f(x) = 2|x + 3|$

c)

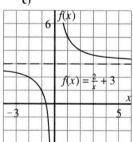

$f(x) = \frac{2}{x} + 3$

d)

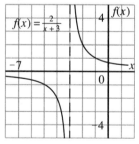

$f(x) = \frac{2}{x + 3}$

7.

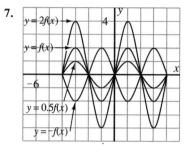

$y = 2f(x)$
$y = f(x)$
$y = 0.5f(x)$
$y = -f(x)$

Exercises 7-5, page 251

1. a) $y = -x^4$ **b)** $y = \dfrac{-5}{x^2 + 1}$ **c)** $y = f(-x)$

2. a) $y = -x - 1$ **b)** $y = \sqrt{3 + x}$
   c) $y = g(-x)$

3. a)

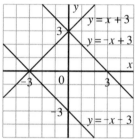

$y = x + 3$
$y = -x + 3$
$y = -x - 3$

b)

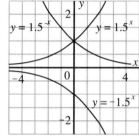

$y = 1.5^{-x}$
$y = 1.5^x$
$y = -1.5^x$

c)

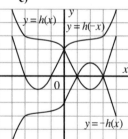

$y = h(x)$
$y = h(-x)$
$y = -h(x)$

4. a)

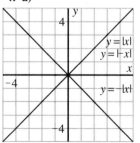

$y = |x|$
$y = |-x|$
$y = -|x|$

b)

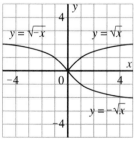

$y = \sqrt{-x}$
$y = \sqrt{x}$
$y = -\sqrt{x}$

5. Answers may vary. $y = x^3$

Investigate, page 252

1. a) i) The graph of $y = \dfrac{5\sqrt{0.5x}}{0.25x^2 + 1}$ is expanded horizontally by a factor of 2, relative to the graph of $y = \dfrac{5\sqrt{x}}{x^2 + 1}$.

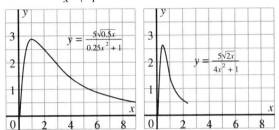

ii) The graph of $y = \dfrac{5\sqrt{2x}}{4x^2 + 1}$ is compressed horizontally by a factor of $\dfrac{1}{2}$, relative to the graph of $y = \dfrac{5\sqrt{x}}{x^2 + 1}$.

b) i) The graph of $y = \dfrac{5\sqrt{-x}}{x^2 + 1}$ is a reflection of $y = \dfrac{5\sqrt{x}}{x^2 + 1}$ in the y-axis.

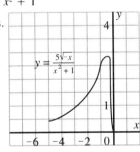

ii) The graph of $y = \dfrac{5\sqrt{-0.5x}}{0.25x^2 + 1}$ is expanded horizontally by a factor of 2, and reflected in the y-axis, relative to the graph of $y = \dfrac{5\sqrt{x}}{x^2 + 1}$; a reflection of the graph in *Question 1 a) i)*.

The graph of $y = \dfrac{5\sqrt{-2x}}{4x^2 + 1}$ is compressed horizontally by a factor of $\dfrac{1}{2}$, and reflected in the y-axis, relative to the graph of $y = \dfrac{5\sqrt{x}}{x^2 + 1}$;

a reflection of the graph in *Question 1 a) ii)*.

2. The graph of $y = f(kx)$ is related to that of $y = f(x)$ by: a horizontal compression if $|k| > 1$; a horizontal expansion if $0 < |k| < 1$; and a reflection in the y-axis if $k < 0$.

3.

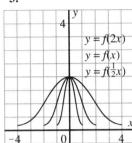

4. a)

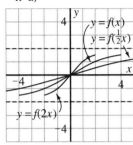

b) Each graph in *Question 4 a)* is reflected in the y-axis.

5. a)

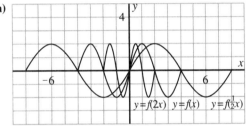

b) Each graph in *Question 5 a)* is reflected in the y-axis.

6. a)

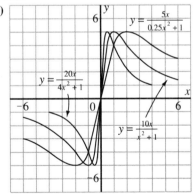

b) Each graph in *Question 6 a)* is reflected in the y-axis. The image equations are $y = \dfrac{-10x}{x^2 + 1}$, $y = \dfrac{-5x}{0.25x^2 + 1}$, $y = \dfrac{-20x}{4x^2 + 1}$.

7. a), b), c)

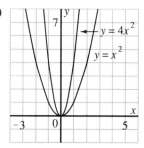

Exercises 7-6, page 256

1. a) ii   **b)** i   **c)** iii

2. a)

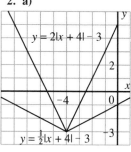

b)

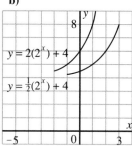

3. a) ii   **b)** iv

4. a)

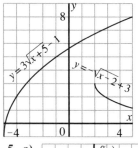

b)

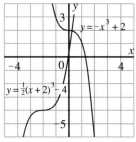

5. a)

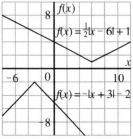

b)

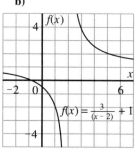

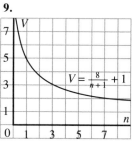 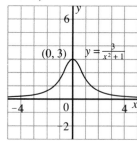

6. c   **7.** a

8.

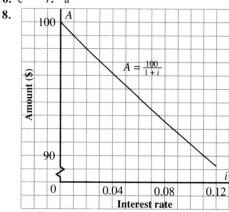

9.

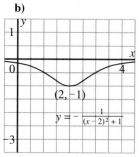

10. a)

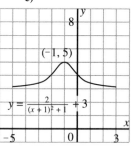

b)   **c)**

11. a)

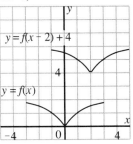

b)

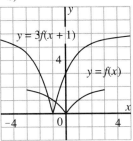

3. a)

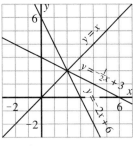

b)

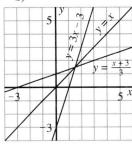

c)

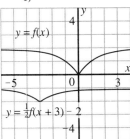

d)

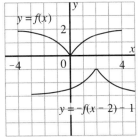

c)

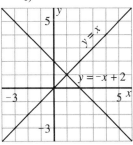

d)

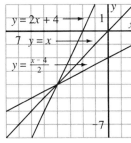

Investigate, page 258

Answers may vary.

1. Increasing: pages 160, 169
 Decreasing: pages 171, 235 (top)
 Periodic: page 154, Exercise 2 a)
 Piecewise linear: page 154, Exercise 1 a);
 page 173, Exercise 5 b)
 Discrete: pages 142, 143
 Discontinuous: pages 153; 154, Exercise 1 c)

2. Example 2, page 144

Exercises 7-7, page 261

1. a), c) Yes   **b)** No

2. a) $y = x - 3$ **b)** $y = \dfrac{x + 1}{4}$ **c)** $y = \dfrac{1}{2}x$

d) $y = \dfrac{x + 4}{3}$ **e)** $y = 2x - 12$

f) $y = \dfrac{3}{2}x + \dfrac{3}{2}$

e)

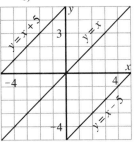

f)

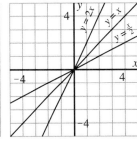

4. a) Yes   **b)** No   **c)** No   **d)** Yes

5. a) $f(x) = x - 6$ **b)** $f(x) = \dfrac{1}{2}x$

c) $f(x) = 3 - x$ **d)** $f(x) = 2(x + 3)$

e) $f(x) = \dfrac{x + 1}{5}$ **f)** $f(x) = \dfrac{x - 2}{2}$

6. a) No   **b)** No   **c)** Yes   **d)** Yes

7. a) iii   **b)** v   **c)** iv   **9.** $f(x) = 2x + 5$

Investigate, page 262

The linear function $y = -x + 3$ is its own inverse.
There is an infinite number of such functions. They all
have a slope of -1, which means they are
perpendicular to the line $y = x$.

Exercises 7-8, page 264

1. a) $y = \pm\sqrt{x}$ **b)** $y = \pm\sqrt{x+1}$

   c) $y = \pm\sqrt{x-3}$ **d)** $y = \pm\sqrt{\dfrac{x-5}{2}}$

   e) $y = \pm\sqrt{4x+8}$ **f)** $y = \pm\sqrt{4x+2}$

2. a)   **b)**

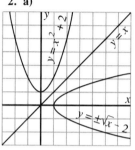   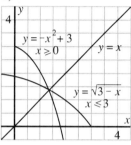

c)   **d)**

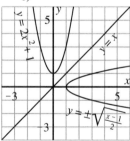   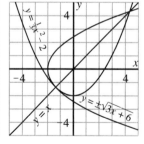

e)   **f)**

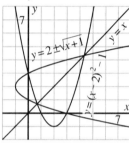   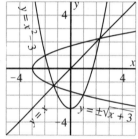

3. a) $y = \pm\dfrac{1}{2}\sqrt{x}$ **b)** $y = \pm\sqrt{1-x}$

   c) $y = \pm\sqrt{\dfrac{2-x}{3}}$ **d)** $y = \pm\sqrt{x}-3$

   e) $y = \pm\sqrt{\dfrac{x}{5}+2}$ **f)** $y = \pm\sqrt{2x+6}-1$

4. a)   **b)**

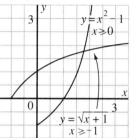   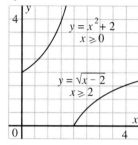

c)   **d)**

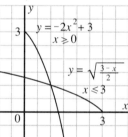   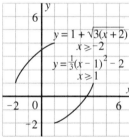

e)   **f)**

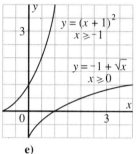   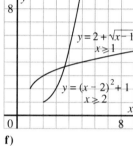

5. a), d) No   **b), c)** Yes

6. a) ii   **b)** v   **c)** iv

7. a)   **b)**

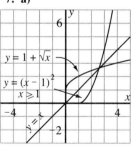   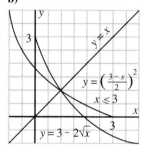

Exercises 7-9, page 267

1. a) $x^2 + y^2 = 25$ **b)** $x^2 + y^2 = 144$
    c) $x^2 + y^2 = 256$ **d)** $x^2 + y^2 = 39.0625$
    e) $x^2 + y^2 = 0.09$ **f)** $x^2 + y^2 = 529$

2. a) i) $(0,0)$ **ii)** 5   **iii)** 10   **iv)** ± 5
    v) ± 5

3. a) i) 9   **ii)** 11   **iii)** 8   **iv)** 3.5   **v)** 6
    vi) 1.5

4. a) 5   **b)** $(-3, 4)$

5. a) $x^2 + y^2 = 9$ **b)** $x^2 + y^2 = 16$
    c) $x^2 + y^2 = 29$ **d)** $x^2 + y^2 = 10$

6. $\sqrt{58}$ **7. a)** ± 4 **b)** $\pm\sqrt{7}$ **c)** ± 2
    d) $\pm 2\sqrt{3}$

8. c) $(6,8)$ on; $(-10,1)$ outside; $(-7,-7)$ inside

9. a) Inside   **b), c)** Outside

10. a, c, d   **11. b)** $y = -\dfrac{1}{2}x$ **12. b)** $y = 7x$

13. b) $y = \dfrac{3}{7}x$

14. a) A point at the origin   **b)** There is no graph.
    c) A semicircle, radius 5, $y \geqslant 0$
    d) A semicircle, radius 5, $x \geqslant 0$

15. $x^2 + y^2 = 25(3 - 2\sqrt{2})$

Investigate, page 268

$x^2 - y^2 = 9$ is a hyperbola centred at the origin with
x-intercepts ± 3.
$x^2 + 4y^2 = 4$ is an ellipse centred at the origin with
x-intercepts ± 2 and y-intercepts ± 1.
$x^4 + y^4 = 16$ resembles a square with rounded corners,
with intercepts ± 2 on both axes.
$\sqrt{x} + \sqrt{y} = 4$ represents a curve in the first quadrant
with endpoints $(0,16)$ and $(16,0)$.

Exercises 7-10, page 273

1. a) $(4,1)$; 6   **b)** $(2,-5)$; 3   **c)** $(-7,-3)$; 4
    d) $(-2,2)$; $\sqrt{5}$ **e)** $(0,8)$; 5   **f)** $(-3,0)$; $\sqrt{13}$

3. a) 4 units left   **b)** 3 units right
    c) 7 units down   **d)** 1 unit right, 2 units up
    e) 1 unit left, 1 unit down
    f) 3 units left, 2 units down

5. a) $(x - 1)^2 + (y - 2)^2 = 9$
    b) $(x + 2)^2 + (y - 1)^2 = 4$
    c) $(x - 1)^2 + (y + 2)^2 = 4$

6. a) $(x - 3)^2 + (y + 1)^2 = 4$
    b) $(x + 2)^2 + (y - 5)^2 = 4$
    c) $(x + 1)^2 + (y + 4)^2 = 4$
    d) $x^2 + (y + 3)^2 = 4$
    e) $(x - 2)^2 + (y - 9)^2 = 4$
    f) $(x + 6)^2 + y^2 = 4$

7. a) Vertical compression   **b)** Vertical expansion
    c) Horizontal compression
    d) Horizontal expansion
    e) Horizontal compression
    f) Vertical and horizontal expansion

8. a) $(x - 3)^2 + y^2 = 25$
    b) $(0,\pm 4)$, $(8,0)$, $(-2,0)$

9. a) i, ii, iii, iv   **b)** iv, vi   **c)** i, v

10. a)

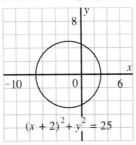

$(x + 2)^2 + y^2 = 25$

b)

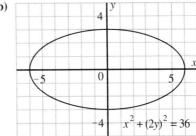

$x^2 + (2y)^2 = 36$

c)

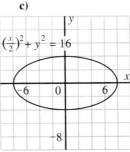

$\left(\dfrac{x}{2}\right)^2 + y^2 = 16$

d)

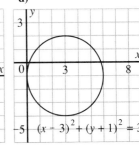

$(x - 3)^2 + (y + 1)^2 = 3$

e)

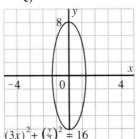

$(3x)^2 + \left(\dfrac{y}{2}\right)^2 = 16$

f)

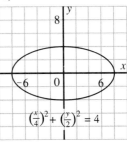

$\left(\dfrac{x}{4}\right)^2 + \left(\dfrac{y}{2}\right)^2 = 4$

11. a) A translation of 8 units left and 4 units down, $(x + 8)^2 + (y + 4)^2 = 4$

b) A vertical expansion of factor $\frac{3}{2}$, $x^2 + \left(\frac{2y}{3}\right)^2 = 4$

c) A horizontal translation of 6 units right, and a vertical expansion of factor $\frac{3}{2}$, $(x - 6)^2 + \left(\frac{2y}{3}\right)^2 = 4$

d) A horizontal translation of 6 units left; a vertical translation of 3 units up; and vertical and horizontal expansions of factor 2 $\left(\frac{x + 6}{2}\right)^2 + \left(\frac{y - 3}{2}\right)^2 = 4$,

or $(x + 6)^2 + (y - 3)^2 = 16$

e) A horizontal translation of 3 units right; a vertical translation of 5 units up; and a horizontal expansion of factor $\frac{3}{2}$ $\left(\frac{2(x - 3)}{3}\right)^2 + (y - 5)^2 = 4$

12. a)

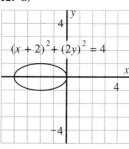

$(x + 2)^2 + (2y)^2 = 4$

b)

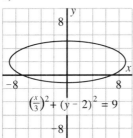

$\left(\frac{x}{3}\right)^2 + (y - 2)^2 = 9$

c)

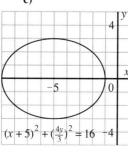

$(x + 5)^2 + \left(\frac{4y}{3}\right)^2 = 16$

d)

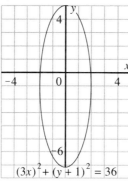

$(3x)^2 + (y + 1)^2 = 36$

e)

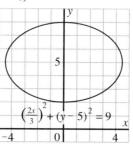

$\left(\frac{2x}{3}\right)^2 + (y - 5)^2 = 9$

f)

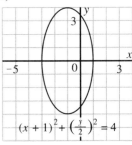

$(x + 1)^2 + \left(\frac{y}{2}\right)^2 = 4$

13. a) Circle, centre $(5, -3)$, radius 7
b) C lies on the circle.

14. Circle, centre $(-3, 1)$, radius 5 and circle, centre $(4, 5)$ radius 3; the circles do not intersect

15. a)

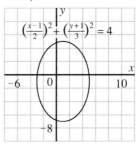

$\left(\frac{x - 1}{2}\right)^2 + \left(\frac{y + 1}{3}\right)^2 = 4$

b)

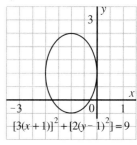

$[3(x + 1)]^2 + [2(y - 1)^2] = 9$

c)

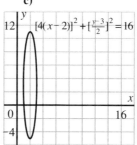

$[4(x - 2)]^2 + \left[\frac{y - 3}{2}\right]^2 = 16$

d)

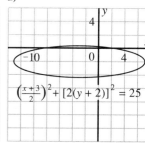

$\left(\frac{x + 3}{2}\right)^2 + [2(y + 2)]^2 = 25$

16. $\sqrt{5}$ **17.** $(x - 3)^2 + (y - 6)^2 = 10$

Problem Solving, page 277

1. Two numbers are 72 and 4608. A general formula is $72n^6$, where $n \in \mathbb{N}$.

5. a) 12:35 P.M.   **b)** 3:09:14 P.M.

7. All whole dollar amounts except $1, $2, $3, and $4.

Exercises 7-11, page 279

1. Answers may vary. **a)** (0,0) **b)** (10,10)
  c) (1,0) **d)** (0,0) **e)** (0,20) **f)** (10,10)

2. Answers may vary. **a)** (2,1) inside
  b) (0,2) inside **c)** (0,2) outside

3. **a)** $(x + 2)^2 + (y - 1)^2 \leq 4$
  b) $y < (x + 1)^2 - 2$
  c) $y < -(x + 1)^2 + 5$

4. **a)**

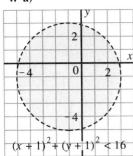

$(x + 1)^2 + (y + 1)^2 < 16$

b)

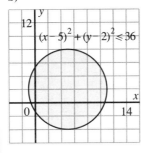

$(x - 5)^2 + (y - 2)^2 \leq 36$

c)

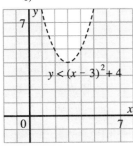

$y < (x - 3)^2 + 4$

d)

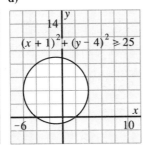

$(x + 1)^2 + (y - 4)^2 \geq 25$

e)

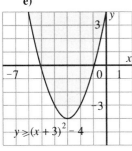

$y \geq (x + 3)^2 - 4$

f)

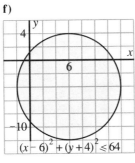

$(x - 6)^2 + (y + 4)^2 \leq 64$

5. **a)**

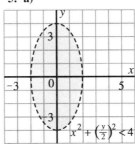

$x^2 + \left(\frac{y}{2}\right)^2 < 4$

b)

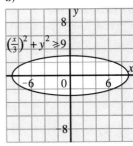

$\left(\frac{x}{3}\right)^2 + y^2 \geq 9$

c)

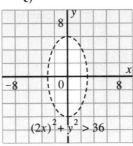

$(2x)^2 + y^2 > 36$

d)

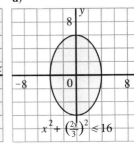

$x^2 + \left(\frac{2y}{3}\right)^2 \leq 16$

e)

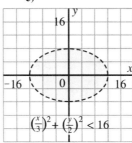

$\left(\frac{x}{3}\right)^2 + \left(\frac{y}{2}\right)^2 < 16$

f)

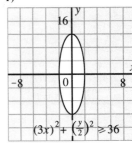

$(3x)^2 + \left(\frac{y}{2}\right)^2 \geq 36$

6. **a)**

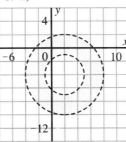

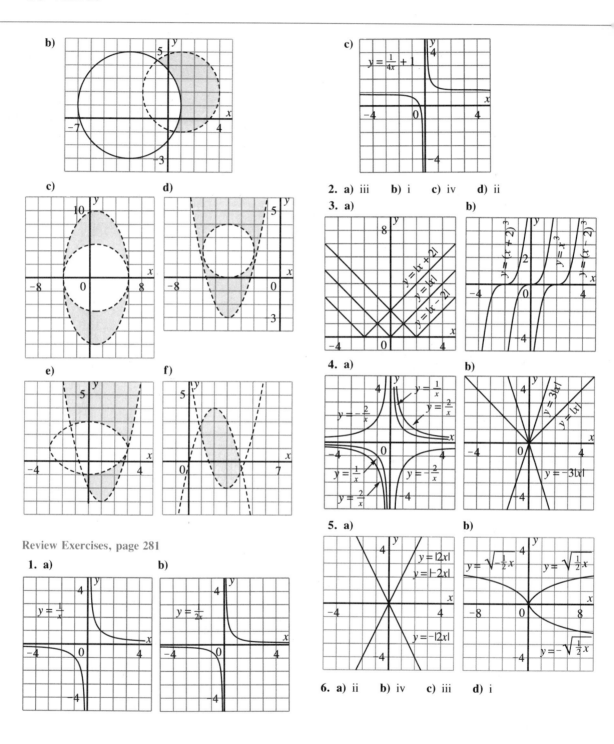

b)

c)

$y = \frac{1}{4x} + 1$

c)

d)

2. a) iii **b)** i **c)** iv **d)** ii

3. a)

b)

e)

f)

4. a)

$y = -\frac{2}{x}$ $y = \frac{1}{x}$ $y = \frac{2}{x}$

$y = \frac{1}{x}$ $y = -\frac{2}{x}$

$y = \frac{2}{x}$

b)

$y = 3|x|$ $y = |x|$

$y = -3|x|$

Review Exercises, page 281

1. a)

$y = \frac{1}{x}$

b)

$y = \frac{1}{2x}$

5. a)

$y = |2x|$

$y = |-2x|$

$y = -|2x|$

b)

$y = \sqrt{-\frac{1}{2}x}$ $y = \sqrt{\frac{1}{2}x}$

$y = -\sqrt{\frac{1}{2}x}$

6. a) ii **b)** iv **c)** iii **d)** i

7.

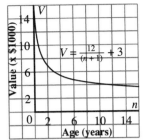

8. a) $f^{-1}(x) = x - 3$ **b)** $f^{-1}(x) = \dfrac{x}{3}$

c) $f^{-1}(x) = x - 2$ **d)** $f^{-1}(x) = 4x - 4$

e) $f^{-1}(x) = \dfrac{1}{4}(x - 3)$ **f)** $f^{-1}(x) = 2 - \dfrac{x}{3}$

9. a) $y = \pm\dfrac{1}{3}\sqrt{x}$ **b)** $y = \pm\sqrt{4 - x}$

c) $y = \pm\dfrac{1}{2}\sqrt{1 - x}$ **d)** $y = \pm\sqrt{x} + 2$

e) $y = \pm\sqrt{\dfrac{x}{3} + 1}$ **f)** $y = \pm\sqrt{3(x - 5)} + 2$

10. a) $x^2 + y^2 = 6.25$ **b)** $x^2 + y^2 = 58$
c) $x^2 + y^2 = 50$ **d)** $x^2 + y^2 = 50$

11. a) $(x + 2)^2 + (y + 3)^2 = 9$
b) $(x + 5)^2 + (y - 4)^2 = 9$
c) $(x - 1)^2 + (y - 7)^2 = 9$

12. a)   **b)**

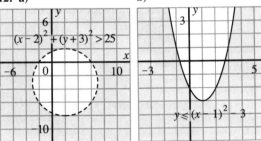

Chapter 8
Exercises 8-1, page 286

1. The centre   **2.** $2R$ **4. b)** Yes
5. 0, 1, or 2

6. a) 6   **b)** 1
c)

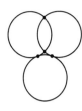

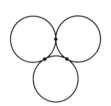

8. 2   **9.** 3 cm
10. a) 51 cm   **b)** About 68 cm   **c)** About 31 cm

Exercises 8-2, page 289

1. a) 9.8   **b)** 5.7   **c)** 6
2. a) 45°   **b)** 2.2   **c)** 4.5
3. About 6 cm   **4. a)** 8   **b)** 2.1   **c)** 4.1
7. 34 cm   **8.** About 77 m   **9.** 10 cm

Exercises 8-3, page 295

1. a) $\angle$D, $\angle$E, $\angle$F, $\angle$G, $\angle$H   **b)** $\angle$D, $\angle$F
c) Typical answers are: $\angle$D, $\angle$G   **d)** $\angle$H
e) $\angle$AOB
2. a) 90°   **b)** 180°   **3. a)** 60°   **b)** 55°
c) 20°
4. a) 90°, 50°, 40°   **b)** 28°, 62°, 90°
c) 45°, 90°, 45°
5. 120°, 30°   **6.** 100°, 100°
7. $\dfrac{\sqrt{5}}{2}$ cm   **8.** $5\sqrt{2}$ cm   **17.** 24 cm

Investigate, page 299

The Angles in a Circle Theorem and its corollaries do apply.

Exercises 8-4, page 301

1. They are collinear.
2. **c)** Answers may vary. ∠FEB = ∠FCB; ∠EFC = ∠EBC
3. Answers may vary. ∠PQS = ∠PRS; ∠SQR = ∠SPR; ∠RPQ = ∠RSQ; ∠QSP = ∠QRP; ∠QTR = ∠PTS
4. A circle 5. **a)** Yes **b)** No

Exercises 8-5, page 306

1. **a)** 105° **b)** 35° **c)** 45°
2. **a)** 50°, 60° **b)** 20°, 60° **c)** 115°, 20°

Exercises 8-6, page 312

1. **a)** 7 **b)** 18° **c)** 130°
2. **a)** $10\sqrt{2}$, $10\sqrt{2}$ **b)** $\sqrt{377}$, 19 **c)** 12, 7 **d)** $4\sqrt{21}$
3. **a)** 30°, 60° **4.** $\dfrac{15\sqrt{2}}{2}$ cm **8.** 19.2 cm
12. About 9.5 mm **14.** 21 cm
15. $(34\sqrt{7} + 2\sqrt{115})$ cm, or 111 cm
16. $21\sqrt{3}$ cm, or 36 cm

Problem Solving, page 319

1. 10 cm **2. a)** 22 **b)** $12\sqrt{2}$ **c)** $\dfrac{22}{49}$
3. There are many solutions, two of which are 184, 369, 752 and 926, 741, 358
4. **a)** 147 m **5.** 1610 L **6.** None

Exercises 8-7, page 323

1. **a)** 30° **b)** 75° **c)** 60°
2. **a)** 70°, 70° **b)** 115°, 115° **c)** 70°, 70°
3. **a)** 60° **b)** 60° **c)** 7 cm

Review Exercises, page 325

1. **a)** 24 **b)** $2\sqrt{6}$ **c)** $\sqrt{41}$
2. Obtuse

Chapter 9

Exercises 9-1, page 329

2. For example: pre-election opinion surveys; market research — new products; television ratings; monthly unemployment data; consumer price indices; Gallup, Harris, Angus Reid, Environics opinion polls; railway freight charges between rail companies; industrial quality control; traffic flow patterns in a city; environmental scientists; medical researchers

4. For example: political organizations; environmental organizations; network television; market research organizations; boards of school trustees; newspapers; Statistics Canada; sports organizations; consumer testing organizations; quality control departments

Exercises 9-2, page 330

2. c and d
3. **a)** Are you a male?
   b) Did you spend more than $20 on a date in the last 2 weeks?
   e) Did you smoke more than 5 cigarettes yesterday?
   f) Did you miss at least 1 class last week?
4. Answers may vary.
   a) . . . males in Algebra 12 classes.
   b) . . . boys and girls who spent more than $20 on a date in the past 2 weeks.
   e) . . . students in the school who smoked more than 5 cigarettes yesterday.
   f) . . . students in the school who missed at least 1 class last week.
5. For example:
   Are you over the legal drinking age?
   Are you male?
   Have you consumed alcohol at least once in the last 6 months?
   Did you smoke at least 5 cigarettes last week?
   Did you drink at least the equivalent of 8 bottles of beer on any day in the last 2 weeks?
   Did you drink at least the equivalent of 2 bottles of beer on more than 4 separate days in the last 2 weeks?
   Have you ever driven a car after drinking more than 3 bottles of beer?
   Do your parents approve of your drinking habits?
   Do either of your parents smoke at least 5 cigarettes per week?

6. a) A range of questions is possible depending on the particular emphasis of the survey; for example: Do you have children in the public school system? Do you have children in the private school system? Do you think that the private schools provide a better education than the public schools? If the fees were covered by your school tax payments, would you want your children to attend a private school of your choice? Parents whose children attend a private school are required to pay taxes to support the public school systems. Would you support a proposal to allow such parents to use their schools taxes to support the private school instead?

Exercises 9-3, page 333

1. The distribution should be similar to that in the table on page 332, but it will not be an exact copy.

2., 3. Answers may vary.

4. You would not expect the percentage of yesses in your 100 samples to be exactly the same as the percentage of yesses in the population. You have taken a sample of size 2000 from the population and not a census. But because of the size of the sample, the difference between the population percentage and the samples percentage might be small.

Problem Solving, page 337

1. a) 3   **b)** 5   **6.** 67.5   **8.** $\dfrac{3\sqrt{3}r^2}{2}$

Exercises 9-4, page 341

3. The sample chart should match that on page 365.

4. The differences between the chart for samples size 43 and the table at the end of the book may vary because of the randomise function in the computer program.

Exercises 9-5, page 347

1. a to e are likely proportions, f and g are unlikely proportions.

2. a) 10% to 40%   **b)** 20% to 55%
 c) 40% to 75%   **d)** 50% to 85%
 e) 70% to 95%

3. a) 0.25 to 0.65   **b)** 0.40 to 0.80   **c)** 0.65 to 0.95
 d) 0.85 to 1.00

4. a) 15% to 50%   **b)** 35% to 70%   **c)** 40% to 70%
 d) 55% to 85%

5. a) The boxes for 95% boxplots are longer than those for 90% boxplots.

b) The confidence intervals from charts of 95% boxplots are longer than the intervals from charts of 90% boxplots.

6. 0.20 to 0.60   **7.** 25% to 60%

8. b) 40% to 75%, yes   **c)** 45% to 80%, yes
 d) 40% to 70%, yes   **e)** 35% to 65%, yes
 f) 70% to 95%, no   **g)** 40% to 75%, yes
 h) 35% to 70%, yes   **i)** 55% to 85%, yes
 j) 40% to 75%

9. a) 60% to 90%, yes; 60% to 90%, yes; 50% to 85%, yes; 60% to 90%, yes; 70% to 95%, yes; 60% to 90%, yes; 60% to 90%, yes; 60% to 90%, yes; 55% to 85%, yes; 50% to 85%, yes
b) 20% to 55%, yes; 20% to 55%, yes; 15% to 45%, yes; 5% to 30%, no; 20% to 55%, yes; 20% to 55%, yes; 20% to 55%, yes; 15% to 45%, yes; 20% to 55%, yes; 15% to 50%, yes

Exercises 9-6, page 350

1. For a given population, the confidence interval for large sample sizes is shorter than the confidence interval for small sample sizes.

3. 22% to 60%; population between 67 and 182

4. 32% to 48%; population between 67 and 100

5. The confidence interval in *Exercise 4* is shorter because its sample size is larger than the sample size in *Exercise 3*.

6. 64% to 78%

7. a) 18% to 40%; 24% to 48%; 28% to 42%
 b) 46% to 78%; 50% to 74%; 56% to 70%
 c) 22% to 54%; 26% to 48%; 30% to 46%
 d) 72% to 94%; 76% to 94%; 82% to 92%
 e) 2% to 20%; 4% to 14%; 4% to 12%
 f) 80% to 98%; 86% to 96%; 88% to 96%

8. a) I am 90% confident that between 60% and 74% of grade 11 and 12 boys spend more than $20 on a date.
 b) I am 90% confident that between 36% and 52% of grade 11 and 12 girls spend more than $20 on a date.
 c) I am 90% confident that between 4% and 10% of grade 11 and 12 boys smoke 10 or more cigarettes a day.
 d) I am 90% confident that between 10% and 20% of grade 11 and 12 girls smoke more than 10 cigarettes a day.

9. a) No   **b)** . . . spend more than $20 on a date.

10. The confidence intervals do overlap so there does not seem to be a significant difference.

11. a) 4% to 20%; 6% to 14%; 6% to 18%
 b) 150 to 750; 220 to 500; 170 to 500

12. 19 e's in the sentence; 14% to 26%

13. a)

Sample size	Confidence interval	Width
20	32% to 68%	36%
40	38% to 62%	24%
60	40% to 60%	20%
80	42% to 58%	16%
100	42% to 58%	16%

There is some inaccuracy because the tables only give data for even population percentages.

c) The relation is an inverse relation.

d) The graph of W against $\dfrac{1}{\sqrt{N}}$ is closest to being linear. **e)** $W = \dfrac{160}{\sqrt{N}}$

14. a) The student has a 20% chance of guessing the right phone number. The experiment is like obtaining a sample of size 20 from a 20% YES population. The likely number of correct guess is between 1 and 7.

b) The 90% confidence interval for a sample of 9 yesses out of 20 is 26% to 64%. We can be 90% confident that factors other than chance have affected this experiment.

Exercises 9-7, page 354

2. I am 95% confident that between 27% and 39% of the people in British Columbia approve of the performance of the leader of the Federal Progressive Conservative Party.

3. I am 95% confident that between 24% and 30% of Canadians believe that unemployment is the country's key problem.

4. I am 95% confident that between 47% and 67% of Canadians in Atlantic Canada believe that unemployment is the country's key problem.

5. I am 95% confident that between 40% and 46% of Canadians approve of the decision to grant the CBC a licence for an all-news television channel.

6. I am 95% confident that of the students in the three schools, between:
a) 26% and 34% spent more than $15 on a date
b) 41% and 49% had a part-time job
c) 7% and 15% worked more than 20 h a week
d) 12% and 20% watched TV more than 20 h a week
e) 46% and 54% spent more hours on school assignments than watching TV
f) 33% and 41% spent more than 10 h a week on assignments
g) 13% and 21% smoked
h) 48% and 56% had a driver's licence

7. a) A 95% confidence interval is no greater than 2.1% to 9.1%. A 95% confidence interval for the population size is no greater than 11 000 to 47 600.

8. 36% to 42%

9. a) 69% to 75%

10. We need to make some reasonable assumptions to answer this question. If we base these assumptions on the data in *Exercises 3* and *4*, it is reasonable to assume that 100 are from Atlantic Canada and 400 from Ontario. This gives a sampling error of 5% for Ontario and 10% for Atlantic Canada. The reported figure of 50% for Atlantic Canada is really a figure between 40% and 60%, and the figure of 36% is a figure between 31% and 41%. So it is conceivable that 41% of Ontario voters and 40% of Atlantic voters approved of Brian Mulroney's performance.

Exercises 9-8, page 359

2. a) Convenience sample
b) People who are at work or who are late risers.
c) No; if he only asked those who passed his store then the users of his store would be underrepresented. Also he would not ask anyone of school age, since they are normally at school at that time.
d) Since many people active in sports are either working or at school at that time, the survey would be biased against those active in sports.
e) He must include people who shop at all times in the week, not just at those times when he is not busy. If he wants to survey only those people active in sports then he should question, for example, every 20th person who enters his store during a given week. But this would exclude those who do not shop at his store. If he wants to include all shoppers who use the mall then he would assign someone to ask every nth person who passes a chosen spot (or spots) in the mall. Alternatively, he could position a person at each mall exit and ask every nth person leaving the mall.

3. a) Convenience sample
b) Students who had different course selections
c) The sample would be biased towards students who took the same kinds of courses as the student who conducted the survey. If the student had a concentration of business education courses, the survey would be biased towards the attitudes of business education students; similarly for other courses.
d) Use a simple random sample of all grade 12 students. Alternatively, if there is a course that is compulsory for grade 12 students, use a cluster sample using classes of that course.

4. a) Convenience sample
b) Convenience sample
c) Systematic sample
d) Convenience sample
e) Simple random sample

6. a) People who were unable to afford an automobile or a telephone
b) People who do not feel strongly enough about the issue to write a letter
c) Students who have no interest in math/science and avoid such courses
d) People who have no interest in any kind of sport as well as other groups who never attend baseball games
e) People who would rather watch sports on television than attend such games; also many other groups who are unable to attend B.C. Lions games
f) Students who were involved with sports activities after school

7. Typically, those who have enjoyed being parents might not be inclined to write to Ann Landers about this. Write-in polls are usually biased in favor of those who have strong opinions on the issue and who want their opinions known.

8. Answers may vary, for example:
a) Select a simple random sample of the students (using a numbered list of students and random digit tables), then send the survey to their parents.
b) Use a multi-stage technique to select elementary and secondary schools and then an appropriate number of students from the selected schools. The number of students selected from each level should be in proportion to the total number of students at that level.
c) If the area is such that almost every home has a telephone, then a phone survey is probably the most convenient. A more reliable method is a face-to-face interview.
d) Use a stratified random sample choosing some students from each secondary school in proportion to the number of students in the school.
e) Make a list of members of these professions from the Yellow Pages or Business Directory. Then use random digits to obtain a simple random sample.
f) A self-selected sample of listeners is the easiest method but it is not reliable. A phone survey using simple random sampling is better, but it may be necessary to ask many people before you find enough people who are listening to the radio show.
g) Position students near the exits of the mall. Ask every nth person. You will need to cover all exits and choose a randomly selected number of time intervals during which the interviews are

conducted. Alternatively, select every nth person who crosses predetermined areas in the mall.

9. None of the samples would be representative of the entire population. Each sample is taken from a distinctive sub population.

Chapter 10

Exercises 10-1, page 372

1. a) 0.27   **b)** 0.70   **c)** 1.73   **d)** 3.73
2. a) 27°   **b)** 45°   **c)** 58°   **d)** 68°
3. a) 0.424   **b)** 1.072   **c)** 1.881   **d)** 0.123
 e) 0.781   **f)** 7.115   **g)** 1.235   **h)** 0.306
 i) 2.747   **j)** 28.6
4. a) 40°   **b)** 65°   **c)** 28°   **d)** 57°   **e)** 79°
 f) 5°   **g)** 19°   **h)** 33°   **i)** 85°   **j)** 67°
5. a) 15°, 0.3   **b)** 30°, 0.6   **c)** 42°, 0.9
6. a) 0.087   **b)** 0.700   **c)** 1.732   **d)** 5.671
7. 34.3°, 0.682; 53.7°, 1.364
8. 0.943, 43.3°
9. 2.778, 70.2°   **10.** 11°, 3°   **11.** 24°
12. a) 3.84 m   **b)** 1.68 m

Exercises 10-2, page 376

1. a) 0.5000   **b)** 0.2079   **c)** 0.6157
 d) 0.2756   **e)** 0.8829   **f)** 0.6428
 g) 0.9903   **h)** 0.9877   **i)** 0.8572
 j) 0.7986
2. a) i) 12°   **ii)** 26°   **iii)** 48°   **iv)** 65°
 v) 84°   **b) i)** 78°   **ii)** 64°   **iii)** 42°
 iv) 25°   **v)** 6°
3. a) $\dfrac{28}{53}, \dfrac{45}{53}, \dfrac{28}{45}$ **b)** $\dfrac{8}{10}, \dfrac{6}{10}, \dfrac{8}{6}$ **c)** $\dfrac{5}{13}, \dfrac{12}{13}, \dfrac{5}{12}$
 d) $\dfrac{20}{29}, \dfrac{21}{29}, \dfrac{20}{21}$ **e)** $\dfrac{8}{17}, \dfrac{15}{17}, \dfrac{8}{15}$ **f)** $\dfrac{3.6}{3.9}, \dfrac{1.5}{3.9}, \dfrac{3.6}{1.5}$
4. a) $\sin P = \dfrac{9}{41}, \cos P = \dfrac{40}{41}, \tan P = \dfrac{9}{40}$
 b) 12.7°, 77.3°
5. 9.6°   **6.** 72.7°   **7.** 47.8°
8. a) 7.1°   **b)** 0.6, 32.0°
9. 25.8°   **10. a)** 1223 m   **b)** 10°
11. a) $\dfrac{1}{2}$ **b)** $\dfrac{\sqrt{3}}{2}$ **c)** $\dfrac{1}{\sqrt{3}}$
12. a) $\sin A = \dfrac{a}{b}, \cos A = \dfrac{c}{b}, \tan A = \dfrac{a}{c}$
 b) $\sin C = \dfrac{c}{b}, \cos C = \dfrac{a}{b}, \tan C = \dfrac{c}{a};$

$\sin A = \cos C$; $\cos A = \sin C$; $\tan A = \dfrac{1}{\tan C}$

13. 36.9°, 53.1°   **14.** $\dfrac{2}{3} l^3 (\cos \theta)^2 \sin \theta$

Exercises 10-3, page 380

1. a) AB = 24, ∠A = 36.9°, ∠C = 53.1°
  b) DE = 33.2, ∠D = 50.3°, ∠F = 39.7°
  c) ∠H = 35°, GK = 12.6, HK = 22.0
  d) ∠M = 58°, LM = 38.7, MN = 73.1
  e) PR = 34.2, ∠P = 37.9°, ∠R = 52.1°
  f) ∠S = 50°, SU = 23.1, UT = 27.6
2. a) YZ = 25.5, ∠X = 46.7°, ∠Z = 43.3°
  b) ∠Z = 63°, YZ = 8.2, XZ = 18.0
  c) XY = 49.3, ∠X = 14.8°, ∠Z = 75.2°
  d) ∠X = 38°, XY = 56.7, YZ = 44.3
  e) ∠Z = 26°, XY = 15.6, XZ = 35.6
  f) XZ = 49.2, ∠Z = 66.0°, ∠X = 24.0°
3. a) $\cos \theta = \dfrac{15}{17}$, $\tan \theta = \dfrac{8}{15}$
  b) $\sin \theta = \dfrac{24}{25}$, $\tan \theta = \dfrac{24}{7}$
  c) $\sin \theta = \dfrac{20}{29}$, $\cos \theta = \dfrac{21}{29}$
  d) $\cos \theta = \dfrac{\sqrt{799}}{32}$, $\tan \theta = \dfrac{15}{\sqrt{799}}$
  e) $\sin \theta = \dfrac{\sqrt{168}}{23}$, $\tan \theta = \dfrac{\sqrt{168}}{19}$
  f) $\sin \theta = \dfrac{43}{\sqrt{14\,393}}$, $\cos \theta = \dfrac{112}{\sqrt{14\,393}}$
4. a) $\cos \theta = \dfrac{\sqrt{q^2 - p^2}}{q}$, $\tan \theta = \dfrac{p}{\sqrt{q^2 - p^2}}$
  b) $\sin \theta = \dfrac{2\sqrt{a+1}}{a+2}$, $\tan \theta = \dfrac{2\sqrt{a+1}}{a}$
  c) $\sin \theta = \dfrac{x-y}{\sqrt{2x^2 + 2y^2}}$, $\cos \theta = \dfrac{x+y}{\sqrt{2x^2 + 2y^2}}$
5. a) 60 m   **b)** 66 m
6. a) 21.0 m   **b)** 4.5 m
7. 62°   **8. a)** 34°   **b)** 37°   **9.** 7.2 cm
10. a) 24.6 m   **b)** 4.3 m   **c)** 5.67
11. 151.7 m, 168.2 m
12. a) i) 45.0°   **ii)** 80.3°   **iii)** 110.3°
  iv) 136.8°   **b)** 16
13. 8.9 cm

Exercises 10-4, page 383

1. About 36 cm   **2.** 37°   **3.** 66°
4. a) 9.3 m   **b)** 3.6 m
5. a) 25 cm   **b)** 4 cm
6. a) 76 m   **b)** 2 h 42 min
7. 34.2 m   **8. a)** 6367 km   **b)** 40 003 km
9. 75.83°
10. a) i) 108 m   **ii)** 70.5 m   **iii)** 62.4 m
  b) 64°   **c) i)** 5.6 m   **ii)** 6.7 m   **iii)** 7.0 m
11. 56°, 79°
12. a) i) 260 m   **ii)** 62 m   **iii)** 87 m
  iv) 1139 m   **b)** 9:52 A.M. and 2:08 A.M.
  c) 7 h and 59 min
13. 32°

Exercises 10-5, page 389

1. a) $\dfrac{1}{2}$ **b)** $\dfrac{1}{2}$ **c)** 1   **d)** $\dfrac{1}{\sqrt{2}}$ **e)** $\dfrac{1}{\sqrt{2}}$
  f) $\dfrac{1}{\sqrt{3}}$ **g)** $\dfrac{\sqrt{3}}{2}$ **h)** $\dfrac{\sqrt{3}}{2}$
2. a) $\sqrt{3}$ **b)** 0   **c)** 0   **d)** ∞   **e)** 1   **f)** 1
3. a) 45°   **b)** 0°   **c)** 60°   **d)** 45°   **e)** 0°
  f) 60°
4. a) 45°   **b)** 90°   **c)** 90°   **d)** 30°   **e)** 60°
  f) 0°   **g)** 90°   **h)** 30°   **i)** 30°
5. $3\sqrt{2}$ km   **6.** 19.4 m
7. a) 8.8 m, 6.2 m   **b)** 7.2 m, 3.6 m
  c) 12.4 m, 10.7 m   **8.** 39.7 m   **9.** $10\sqrt{3}$
10. a) $x = \dfrac{s}{\sqrt{2}}$ **b)** $y = \dfrac{s}{\sqrt{3}}$; $z = \sqrt{\dfrac{2}{3}}s$
11. $\sqrt{3}l$ **12.** 2 : 1   **13.** $x = \dfrac{\sqrt{7}s}{3}$
14. a) $\dfrac{1}{1 + \sqrt{2}}$ **b)** $\dfrac{1}{\sqrt{4 + 2\sqrt{2}}}$ **c)** $\dfrac{1 + \sqrt{2}}{\sqrt{4 + 2\sqrt{2}}}$

Exercises 10-6, page 394

1. a) 180°   **b)** 450°   **c)** −90°   **d)** −270°
2. a) 50°   **b)** 60°   **c)** 15°   **d)** 60°   **e)** 90°
  f) 45°   **g)** 60°   **h)** 90°
3. Typical answers:
  a) 410°, −310°   **b)** 480°, −240°
  c) 525°, −195°   **d)** 600°, −120°
  e) 450°, −270°   **f)** 405°, −315°
  g) 420°, −300°   **h)** 630°, −90°

4. Typical answers:
   a) 420°, −300°   **b)** 150°, −570°
   c) 585°, −135°   **d)** 270°, −450°

5. Typical answers:
   a) 540°, −180°   **b)** 450°, −270°
   c) 300°, −420°   **d)** 0°, −720°

6. **a)** 1   **b)** First   **c)** Reference angle 60°

7. **a)** 1; second; reference angle 60°   **b)** 1; fourth;
reference angle 60°   **c)** 2; second; reference
angle 30°   **d)** 2; fourth; reference angle 80°

8. **a)** First quadrant, reference angle 40°
   b) First quadrant, reference angle 30°
   c) Between first and second quadrants, reference
   angle 90°
   d) Fourth quadrant, reference angle 60°

9. **a)** 1   **b)** Fourth; reference angle 60°

10. **a)** 0; between second and third   **b)** 0; between
third and fourth   **c)** 1; between fourth and first
d) 1; between first and second

11. **a)** 2 rotations; between first and second quadrants
   b) 1 rotation; third quadrant; reference angle 60°
   c) 0 rotations; second quadrant; reference angle 45°
   d) 3 rotations; between second and third quadrants

12. **a)** 45° + 360°n **b)** 150° + 360°n
   c) 240° + 360°n **d)** −30° + 360°n
   e) 180° + 360°n **f)** −45° + 360°n
   g) 450° + 360°n **h)** 120° + 360°n

14. **a)**

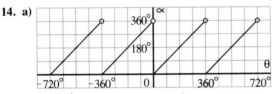

   b) R; $\{\alpha \mid 0 \leq \alpha < 360°, \alpha \in R\}$

Exercises 10-7, page 399

1. **a)** 0.8000, 0.6000, 1.3333
   b) 0.8000, −0.6000, −1.3333
   c) −0.7071, −0.7071, 1.000
   d) −0.9231, 0.3846, −2.4000

2. **a)** 0.1961, −0.9806, −0.2000
   b) −0.8944, − 0.4472, −2.0000
   c) −0.3162, 0.9487, −0.3333
   d) 0.8944, −0.4472, −2.0000

3. **a)** 0.766   **b)** −0.819   **c)** −1.192
   d) −0.342   **e)** −0.174   **f)** −0.574
   g) −0.231   **h)** −0.995

4. **a)** 0.391   **b)** 0.829   **c)** 3.078   **d)** 0.974
   e) −0.990   **f)** 1.600   **g)** −0.777
   h) −0.777

5. **a)** P is the fourth quadrant.
   b) −0.6, 0.8, −0.75

6. **a)** P is the second quadrant.
   b) 0.894, −0.447, −2.000

7. **a)** $-\dfrac{5}{13}, \dfrac{12}{13}, -\dfrac{5}{12}$ **b)** $-\dfrac{1}{\sqrt{5}}, -\dfrac{2}{\sqrt{5}}, \dfrac{1}{2}$
   c) $\dfrac{1}{\sqrt{10}}, -\dfrac{3}{\sqrt{10}}, -\dfrac{1}{3}$ **d)** $-\dfrac{4}{5}, -\dfrac{3}{5}, \dfrac{4}{3}$
   e) $-\dfrac{1}{\sqrt{10}}, \dfrac{3}{\sqrt{10}}, -\dfrac{1}{3}$ **f)** $\dfrac{9}{\sqrt{85}}, \dfrac{2}{\sqrt{85}}, 4.5$

8. **a)** 0.819 15
   b) Typical answers: 485°, 845°, −235°

9. **a)** −0.766 04
   b) Typical answers: 580°, 940°, −140°

10. **a)** 0.951 06
   b) Typical answers: 108°, 432°, −288°

11. **a)** 57.289 96
   b) Typical answers: 89°, 449°, −91°

12. **b)** P(3,2)   **c)** $\sin \theta = \dfrac{2}{\sqrt{13}}, \cos \theta = \dfrac{3}{\sqrt{13}}$

13. **b)** P(−2,5)   **c)** $\sin \theta = \dfrac{5}{\sqrt{29}}, \cos \theta = -\dfrac{2}{\sqrt{29}}$

14. **b)** P(−1,2)   **c)** $\cos \theta = -\dfrac{1}{\sqrt{5}}, \tan \theta = -2$

15. **a)** $\sin \theta = \dfrac{12}{13}, \tan \theta = -2.4$
   b) $\cos \theta = -\dfrac{\sqrt{15}}{4}, \tan \theta = \dfrac{1}{\sqrt{15}}$
   c) $\sin \theta = -\dfrac{3}{\sqrt{13}}, \cos \theta = -\dfrac{2}{\sqrt{13}}$
   d) $\cos \theta = \dfrac{\sqrt{7}}{4}, \tan \theta = -\dfrac{3}{\sqrt{7}}$

16. **a)** Typical answers: 30°, 150°, 390°
   b) An infinite number

Exercises 10-8, page 404

1. 20° **b)** 84° **c)** 26° **d)** 37° **e)** 64° **f)** 63°

2. **a)** 55° **b)** 41° **c)** 34° **d)** 84° **e)** 14° **f)** 73°

3. **a)** 49°, 131°   **b)** 84°, 276°   **c)** 8°, 172°
   d) 69°, 291°   **e)** 42°, 138°   **f)** 9°, 351°

4. **a)** 64°, 296°   **b)** 43°, 137°   **c)** 27°, 333°
   d) 15°, 165°   **e)** 69°, 249°   **f)** 70°, 290°

5. **a)** 223°, 317°   **b)** 101°, 259°   **c)** 195°, 345°
   d) 34°, 326°   **e)** 96°, 264°   **f)** 306°, 234°

6. 252° **7.** **a)** 256° **b)** 307° **c)** 304° **d)** 117°

8. **a)** 14°, 166°   **b)** 132°, 228°   **c)** 60°, 300°
   d) 233°, 307°   **e)** 19°, 30°, 150°, 161°
   f) 71°, 289°

9. a) 100°, 260°   **b)** 199°, 341°   **c)** 66°, 294°
  d) 188°, 352°   **e)** 51°, 129°, 231°, 309°
  f) 41°, 319°

10. a) 24.3°, 65.7°   **b)** 20.7°   **c)** 9.7°, 80.3°
  d) 37.8°, 60.0°

12. a) 34°, 214°   **b)** 106°, 286°   **c)** 27°, 45°,
  207°, 225°   **d)** 57°, 139°, 237°, 319°

13. a) 8.9°, 68.9°   **b)** 79.1°   **c)** 29.5°
  d) 56.3°   **e)** 13.3°, 67.5°   **f)** 31.7°, 35.8°

14. a) 1020°   **b)** 1868°

Exercises 10-9, page 407

1. a) $b \sin C$, or $c \sin B$ **b)** $e \sin F$, or $f \sin E$
  c) $h \sin J$ **d)** $l \sin K$

2. Answers to the nearest square centimetre
  a) 326 cm²   **b)** 472 cm²   **c)** 217 cm²

3. Answers to the nearest square unit   **a)** 42
  b) 340   **c)** 329   **d)** 522   **e)** 47

4. Answers to the nearest square unit   **a)** 110
  b) 134   **c)** 783   **d)** 140   **e)** 288
  f) 1880

5. 2371 m²   **6.** 202.0 cm²   **7.** 5.97 m²

8. 347 cm²   **9.** 6.2 m²   **10.** 4.9 m²

11. a) 251.4 m²   **b)** $691.35   **12.** About $50

13. 368.2 cm²   **14. a)** 10.8 m²   **b)** $565.30

15. 66.4 m²   **16.** $280

17. 18.7 cm, 18.7 cm, 26.5 cm

18. a) 615 cm²   **b)** 796 cm³   **c)** 45°   **d)** 55°

Exercises 10-10, page 413

1. a) 8.6   **b)** 14.3   **c)** 15.6

2. a) 4.0   **b)** 23.6   **c)** 33.7   **d)** 8.0
  e) 14.1

3. a) 129.1°   **b)** 26.4°   **c)** 53.6°

4. a) i) 25.2°   **ii)** 121.6°   **b) i)** 20.0°
  ii) 121.0°   **c) i)** 13.4°   **ii)** 148.4°
  d) i) 31.9°   **ii)** 90°   **e) i)** 41.6°   **ii)** 87.6°
  f) i) 12.5°   **ii)** 108.9°

5. a) 4.4   **b)** 48   **c)** 29.3   **6.** 4.7 m

7. 6.0 km

8. About 46 m   **9.** 112.0°, 15.4°, 52.6°

10. 6.4 cm, 9.4 cm   **11.** 35°

12. 55°, 55°, 125°, 125°   **13.** 10.8 km

14. 11.3 cm   **15.** 14.3 cm   **16.** 16°

17. 9.6 cm   **18.** 80.4°

19. a) 195 cm²   **b)** 91 cm²   **c)** 210 cm²

20. 143°   **21. a)** $r\sqrt{2 - \sqrt{3}}$ **b)** r **c)** $r\sqrt{2}$
  d) $r\sqrt{3}$ **e)** $r\sqrt{2 + \sqrt{3}}$ **f)** $2r$

22. About 26 km

23. 4.7°

24. a) $3\sqrt{2 - \sqrt{3}}$ cm   **b)** $3\sqrt{2 + 2\sqrt{3}}$ cm

25. a) $\sqrt{2 + \sqrt{3}}$ cm   **b)** 0.25 cm²

26. a) $\sqrt{5}$ cm, $\sqrt{5}$ cm   **b)** $2\sqrt{13}$ cm, $\sqrt{73}$ cm

28. $\sqrt[3]{2}$, $\sqrt[3]{4}$

Exercises 10-11, page 422

1. a) 22.2   **b)** 18.0   **c)** 15.9

2. a) 36.4°   **b)** 38.7°   **c)** 140.6°

3. a) 10.6   **b)** 22.2   **c)** 27.7   **d)** 15.3
  e) 15.1

4. a) $\angle Q = 46.4°$, $\angle R = 28.6°$, $r = 5.9$
  b) $\angle R = 49.2°$, $\angle P = 67.8°$, $p = 20.8$
  c) $\angle R = 46.4°$, $\angle Q = 21.6°$, $q = 12.7$
  d) $\angle P = 40.7°$, $\angle Q = 61.3°$, $q = 37.7$

5. a) $\angle B = 45.8°$, $\angle C = 99.2°$, $c = 20.7$ or
  $\angle B = 134.2°$, $\angle C = 10.8°$, $c = 3.9$
  b) $\angle C = 75.5°$, $\angle A = 49.5°$, $a = 10.2$ or
  $\angle C = 104.5°$, $\angle A = 20.5°$, $a = 4.7$
  c) $c = 27.3$, $\angle B = 42.9°$, $\angle A = 59.1°$
  d) $\angle C = 55.2°$, $\angle A = 82.8°$, $a = 32.6$ or
  $\angle C = 124.8°$, $\angle A = 13.2°$, $a = 7.5$
  e) $a = 28.5$, $\angle C = 45.0°$, $\angle B = 96.0°$
  f) $\angle A = 23.5°$, $\angle C = 32.5°$, $c = 17.5$

6. a) $\angle Y = 58°$, $y = 30.3$, $z = 27.4$
  b) $x = 21.0$, $\angle Y = 46.4°$, $\angle Z = 87.2°$
  c) $\angle X = 69.5°$, $\angle Z = 56.5°$, $z = 19.6$ or
  $\angle X = 110.5°$, $\angle Z = 15.5°$, $z = 6.3$
  d) $z = 7.3$, $\angle X = 69.2°$, $\angle Y = 49.8°$

7. 54.3 m   **8.** 31.6 km, 22.8 km

9. 133 m, 208 m   **10.** 7.4 m   **11.** About 429 m

12. 106 m, 52 m   **13. a)** 21 m   **b)** 8 m

14. a) 33 m   **b)** 15 cm   **15.** 553 m

16. a) 191 m, 256 m or 929 m, 693 m
  b) 151 m or 546 m

17. a) 1.9   **b)** 2.7   **18.** 30

19. $\angle O = 104.8°$, $\angle Y = \angle H = 37.6°$ **20.** 10 cm

Review Exercises, page 428

1. a) 0.819   **b)** 0.510   **c)** 0.156   **d)** 0.754
  e) 0.423   **f)** 0.375

2. a) 74°   **b)** 28°   **c)** 28°, 152°

3. sin: **a)** 0 **b)** $\dfrac{1}{2}$ **c)** $\dfrac{1}{\sqrt{2}}$ **d)** $\dfrac{\sqrt{3}}{2}$ **e)** 1

f) $\dfrac{\sqrt{3}}{2}$ **g)** $\dfrac{1}{\sqrt{2}}$ **h)** $\dfrac{1}{2}$

cos: **a)** 1 **b)** $\dfrac{\sqrt{3}}{2}$ **c)** $\dfrac{1}{\sqrt{2}}$ **d)** $\dfrac{1}{2}$ **e)** 0

f) $-\dfrac{1}{2}$ **g)** $-\dfrac{1}{\sqrt{2}}$ **h)** $-\dfrac{\sqrt{3}}{2}$

tan: **a)** 0 **b)** $\dfrac{1}{\sqrt{3}}$ **c)** 1 **d)** $\sqrt{3}$

e) Undefined **f)** $-\sqrt{3}$ **g)** -1 **h)** $-\dfrac{1}{\sqrt{3}}$

4. a) $\sin\theta = \dfrac{15}{17}$, $\tan\theta = \dfrac{15}{8}$ **b)** $\sin\theta = \dfrac{12}{13}$,

$\cos\theta = \dfrac{12}{13}$ **c)** $\sin\theta = \dfrac{8\sqrt{5}}{21}$, $\tan\theta = \dfrac{8\sqrt{5}}{11}$

d) $\cos\theta = \dfrac{2\sqrt{14}}{9}$, $\tan\theta = \dfrac{5}{2\sqrt{14}}$

5. a) AC = 31.0, ∠A = 61°, ∠C = 29°
b) AB = 15, ∠C = 56°, ∠A = 34°
c) BC = 13.6, AC = 44.2, ∠A = 18°
d) ∠C = 55°, AB = 9.8, BC = 6.9

6. Typical answers:
a) 425°, −295° **b)** 495°, −225° **c)** 560°,
−160° **d)** −90°, 270° **e)** 420°, −300°
f) 585°, −135° **g)** 330°, −390°

7. a) 0.906, 0.423, 2.145 **b)** 0.707, −0.707,
−1.000 **c)** −0.342, −0.940, 0.364
d) −1.000, 0, ∞ **e)** 0.866, 0.500, 1.732
f) −0.707, −0.707, 1.000 **g)** −0.500, 0.866,
−0.577

8. a) 0.914, 0.406, 2.250 **b)** −0.882, 0.471,
−1.875 **c)** 0.868, −0.496, −1.750
d) −0.640, −0.768, 0.833

9. a) 66.0° **b)** 298.1° **c)** 119.7° **d)** 219.8°

10. a) 47°, 133° **b)** 113°, 293° **c)** 101°, 281°

11. a) 222°, 318° **b)** 74°, 254° **c)** 14°, 42°,
138°, 166° **d)** 67°, 93°

12. a) $q = 11.8$, ∠P = 64.0°, ∠R = 41.0°
b) ∠Q = 44.7°, ∠P = 83.3°, $p = 35.3$
c) ∠R = 37.0°, $q = 50.3$, $r = 31.3$
d) ∠Q = 113.7°, ∠R = 36.8°, ∠P = 29.6°

13. 6.6° **14.** 35.4 m **15.** 85.6 m

Cumulative Review, Chapters 7, 8, and 10, page 429

1. a) Reciprocal **b)** Cubic **c)** Exponential

2. a)

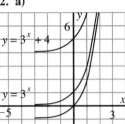

b)

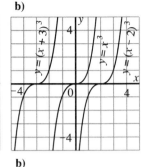

3. a)

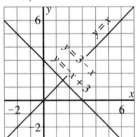

b)

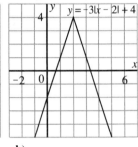

4. a)

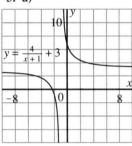

b)

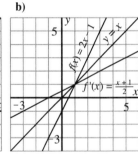

5. a) $y = \pm\dfrac{1}{2}\sqrt{x+9}$ **b)** $y = 5 \pm \sqrt{x-9}$

c) $y = 7 \pm \sqrt{x+2}$

6. a

7. a) Translated 3 units right
b) Translated 1 unit left and 4 units up
c) Expanded vertically by a factor of 2
d) Expanded horizontally by a factor of 4, and
translated 1 unit up

8. a)

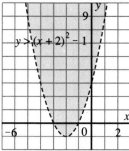

b)

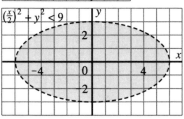

9. a) Points which lie on a circle
b) A quadrilateral with its vertices on a circle
c) A line intersecting a circle in two points

10. $4\sqrt{34}$ cm

13. a) -0.602 **b)** 2.144 **c)** 0.276
    d) -0.956 **e)** -1.000

14. a) $69°, 249°$ **b)** $216°, 324°$ **c)** $61°, 299°$

15. a) $q = 13.6$; $\angle R = 54°$, $\angle P = 36°$
    b) $\angle R = 62°$, $r = 48.9$; $q = 55.4$

16. a) $y = 9.9$, $\angle Z = 42°$; $\angle X = 28°$
    b) $\angle Y = 70°$; $\angle Z = 52°$, $z = 3.4$

17. 5.1 m

18. a) $51°, 231°$ **b)** $42°, 138°, 210°, 330°$

Index